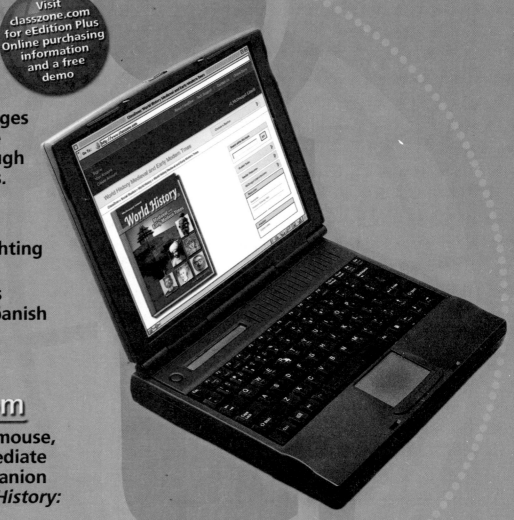

World History

Medieval and
Early Modern Times

McDougal Littell

A DIVISION OF HOUGHTON MIFFLIN COMPANY

Early Mayan figurine

Suleyman

Theodora

Charlemagne

Queen Elizabeth I

West African mask

World History

Medieval and Early Modern Times

McDougal Littell

A DIVISION OF HOUGHTON MIFFLIN COMPANY

Senior Consultants

Douglas Carnine

Douglas Carnine is Professor of Education and Director of the National Center for Improving the Tools of Educators at the University of Oregon. He is the author of seven books and more than 100 other scholarly publications, primarily in the areas of instructional design and effective instructional strategies for diverse learners. Dr. Carnine is a member of the National Institute for Literacy Advisory Board.

Carlos E. Cortés

Carlos E. Cortés is Professor Emeritus of History at the University of California, Riverside. He has edited three major book series on Latinos in the United States. He has many other books, articles, documentaries, and educational materials to his credit. Fluent in Portuguese and Spanish, he often focuses on issues of multiculturalism, diversity, and media representation. Dr. Cortés has served on the summer faculty of the Harvard Institutes for Higher Education since 1990 and on the faculty of the Summer Institute for Intercultural Communication since 1995.

Kenneth R. Curtis

Kenneth R. Curtis is Professor of History and Liberal Studies at California State University, Long Beach, where he is Faculty Advisor to the California History/Social Science Project. He has been closely involved with the College Board's course and examination in Advanced Placement World History, serving as Chief Reader and as a member of the Test Development Committee. Dr. Curtis has co-authored a number of college-level world history texts.

Anita T. Robinson

Anita T. Robinson is Program Director for a Teaching American History/Department of Education grant. She served as a Master Lead Teacher and Social Studies Specialist in the Los Angeles Unified School District. Mrs. Robinson is an expert professional development presenter. Her topics include standards-based instruction, engaging English learners, literacy support, technology, visual literacy, and "big ideas."

Acknowledgments begin on page R111.
ISBN-13: 978-0-618-53294-0   ISBN-10: 0-618-53294-3

Printed in the United States of America.
4 5 6 7 8 9–DWO–09 08 07 06   Updated California Edition

Consultants and Reviewers

Reading Consultant

MaryEllen Vogt
Professor Emeritus,
California State University,
Long Beach, California
President of International
Reading Assocation, 2004-2005

English Learner Consultants

Mary Lou McCloskey
Georgia State University,
Atlanta, Georgia
President of TESOL, 2002-2003

Lydia Stack
Administrator, San Francisco
Unified School District
San Francisco, California

Content Consultants

The content consultants reviewed the text for historical depth and accuracy and for clarity of presentation.

David G. Atwill
Department of History and
Religious Studies
Pennsylvania State University
University Park, Pennsylvania

Douglas C. Baxter
Department of History
Ohio University
Athens, Ohio

Roger Beck
Department of History
Eastern Illinois University
Charleston, Illinois

Beverly Bossler
Department of History
University of California, Davis
Davis, California

Philip Cunningham
Boston College
Chestnut Hill, Massachusetts

Susan L. Douglass
Council on Islamic Education
Fountain Valley, California

Joël DuBois
Humanities and Religious Studies
Department
California State University,
Sacramento
Sacramento, California

Vincent Farenga
Department of Comparative
Literature
University of Southern
California
Los Angeles, California

Claudio Fogu
Department of History
University of Southern
California
Los Angeles, California

Charles L. Geshekter
Department of History
California State University,
Chico
Chico, California

Erik Gilbert
Department of History
Arkansas State University
Jonesboro, Arkansas

Charles Hallisey
University of Wisconsin
Madison, Wisconsin

Dakota L. Hamilton
Department of History
Humboldt State University
Arcata, California

Charles C. Haynes
First Amendment Center
Arlington, Virginia

Lezlie Knox
Department of History
Marquette University
Milwaukee, Wisconsin

Geoffrey Koziol
Department of History
University of California,
Berkeley
Berkeley, California

John Wolte Infong Lee
Department of History
University of California,
Santa Barbara
Santa Barbara, California

Maritere Lopez
Department of History
California State University,
Fresno
Fresno, California

Shabbir Mansuri
Council on Islamic Education
Fountain Valley, California

Jacob Meskin
Shoolman Graduate School
of Jewish Education
Hebrew College
Newton, Massachusetts

Phillip Naylor
Department of History
Marquette University
Milwaukee, Wisconsin

Lawrence Okamura
Department of History
University of Missouri,
Columbia
Columbia, Missouri

Robert Patch
Department of History
University of California,
Riverside
Riverside, California

David D. Phillips
Department of History
University of California,
Los Angeles
Los Angeles, California

Swami Tyagananda
Hindu Chaplain
Harvard University
Cambridge, Massachusetts

Kenneth Baxter Wolf
Department of History
Pomona College
Claremont, California

R. Bin Wong
Department of History
University of California,
Los Angeles
Los Angeles, California

Teacher Consultants

The following educators provided ongoing review during the development of the program.

Yusuff Allahyah
Berendo Middle School
Los Angeles, California

Laura Carroll
Castillero Middle School
San Jose, California

Neal Cates
Hoover Middle School
Lakewood, California

Jeff Davis
Tioga Middle School
Fresno, California

Michele de Masi
Sinaloa Middle School
Simi Valley, California

Merrell Frankel
Berendo Middle School
Los Angeles, California
2003 CCSS Middle Level
Teacher of the Year
2004 NCSS Middle Level
Teacher of the Year

Dan Green
Goleta Valley Junior
High School
Goleta, California

Kim Maruyama
Castillero Middle School
San Jose, California

Lisa Meyers
La Paz Intermediate School
Mission Viejo, California

Randal Mitchell
Chaboya Middle School
San Jose, California

Rebecca O'Connor
Castillero Middle School
San Jose, California

Betty Parsons
Dartmouth Middle School
San Jose, California

Sally Reimers
Sinaloa Middle School
Simi Valley, California

Brenda Riddlesprigger
Kastner Intermediate School
Fresno, California

Teresa Sadler
Shirakawa School
San Jose, California

Joseph Staub
Thomas Starr King
Middle School
Los Angeles, California

Susan Tracy
Black Mountain
Middle School
San Diego, California

Chris Watson
Foothills Farms Junior High
Sacramento, California

Rhonda Weltz
Bret Harte Middle School
San Jose, California

Unit 1 Introduction to World History

▲ Astrolabe from Yemen (p. 14)

▲ Fresco Mask from Pompeii (p. 66)

Hadrian's Wall in England (p. 53) ▼

▲ The Ka'aba in Mecca
(p. 88)

▼ The Great Mosque at Córdoba (p. 133)

▲ **Lion Mask** (p. 170)

▲ **Great Mosque** (p. 160)

Great Zimbabwe ▶
(p. 188)

Unit 4 Asian Civilizations

Technology
For more on Asian civilizations . . .
ClassZone.com

▲ Han Military Watchtower (p. 212)

▲ Japanese Buddha (p. 256)

▼ Angkor Wat (p. 278)

Unit 5

Medieval Europe

▲ Women in Medieval
Europe (p. 306)

▲ Suleyman I (p. 317)

▼ Medieval Castle (p. 299)

▲ **Zapotec Jaguar Head**
(p. 377)

▲ **Emperor Pachacuti**
(p. 410)

Machu Picchu, Peru
(p. 409) ▶

European Renaissance and Reformation

Technology
For more on the Renaissance and Reformation . . .
ClassZone.com

▲ Gutenburg Bible (p. 424)

▲ King Henry VIII (p. 470)

The Duomo,
Florence, Italy (p. 439) ▼

▲ Magellan's Ship (p. 510)

▲ Voltaire, Locke, and Franklin (p. 542)

◀ Women at the Bastille (p. 540)

xiii

Reference

Reading & Writing Support

Before You Read Strategies

Reading Activities

Writing Activities

Writing About History

Reading & Writing Support

Visual Vocabulary

Visual Vocabulary

Japanese calligraphy: Numbers show the order of strokes for the character *eternal*.

Vocabulary Strategies

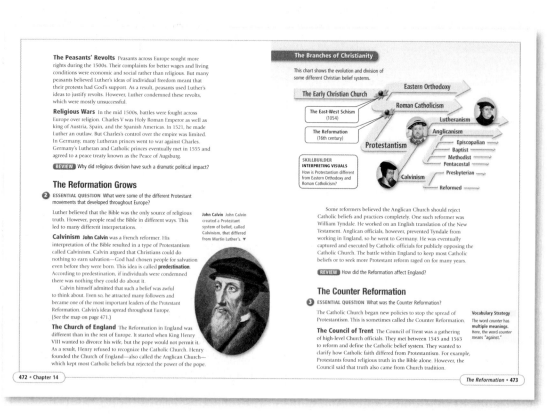

Features

Comparisons Across Cultures

Geography

Geography

Oasis

An oasis is a fertile or green spot in the midst of a desert.

- Oases occur where water in underlying rock rises to the surface to provide a source for wells and springs. The water usually seeps upward when it hits a fault, or fracture, in the rock.
- Some large oases can support an entire city. Others might simply be a small spring.

GEOGRAPHY SKILLBUILDER
INTERPRETING VISUALS
Human-Environment Interaction
Why might oases be important to people who live on the Arabian peninsula?

Spring
Sand
Fault line
Underground water
Rock

History Makers

Primary Sources

Features

Skillbuilders

Starting with a Story

Daily Life

Connect to Today

Literature Connections

Reader's Theater

Activities

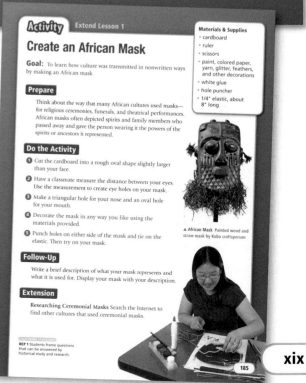

Activity Extend Lesson 1

Create an African Mask

Goal: To learn how culture was transmitted in nonwritten ways by making an African mask

Materials & Supplies
- cardboard
- ruler
- scissors
- paint, colored paper, yarn, glitter, feathers, and other decorations
- white glue
- hole puncher
- 1/4" elastic, about 8" long

Prepare

Think about the way that many African cultures used masks—for religious ceremonies, funerals, and theatrical performances. African masks often depicted spirits and family members who passed away and gave the person wearing it the powers of the spirits or ancestors it represented.

Do the Activity

1. Cut the cardboard into a rough oval shape slightly larger than your face.
2. Have a classmate measure the distance between your eyes. Use the measurement to create eye holes on your mask.
3. Make a triangular hole for your nose and an oval hole for your mouth.
4. Decorate the mask in any way you like using the materials provided.
5. Punch holes on either side of the mask and tie on the elastic. Then try on your mask.

▲ **African Mask** Painted wood and straw mask by Kuba craftsperson

Follow-Up

Write a brief description of what your mask represents and what it is used for. Display your mask with your description.

Extension

Researching Ceremonial Masks Search the Internet to find other cultures that used ceremonial masks.

CALIFORNIA STANDARDS
REP 1 Students frame questions that can be answered by historical study and research.

185

Infographics & Interactives

Infographics

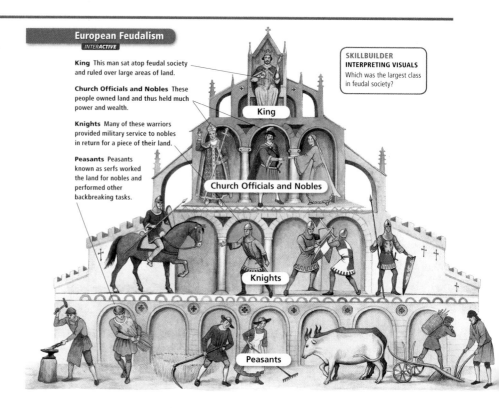

European Feudalism
INTERACTIVE

King This man sat atop feudal society and ruled over large areas of land.

Church Officials and Nobles These people owned land and thus held much power and wealth.

Knights Many of these warriors provided military service to nobles in return for a piece of their land.

Peasants Peasants known as serfs worked the land for nobles and performed other backbreaking tasks.

**SKILLBUILDER
INTERPRETING VISUALS**
Which was the largest class in feudal society?

King

Church Officials and Nobles

Knights

Peasants

INTERACTIVE Maps and Visuals

Maps

Visuals

Maps

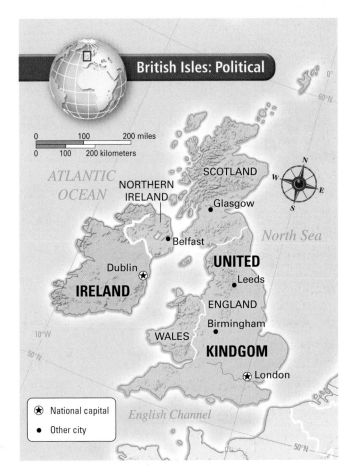

British Isles: Political

0   100   200 miles
0   100   200 kilometers

ATLANTIC OCEAN
SCOTLAND
NORTHERN IRELAND
Glasgow
North Sea
Belfast
Dublin
UNITED
Leeds
IRELAND
ENGLAND
Birmingham
WALES
KINDGOM
London

★ National capital
• Other city

English Channel

Maps

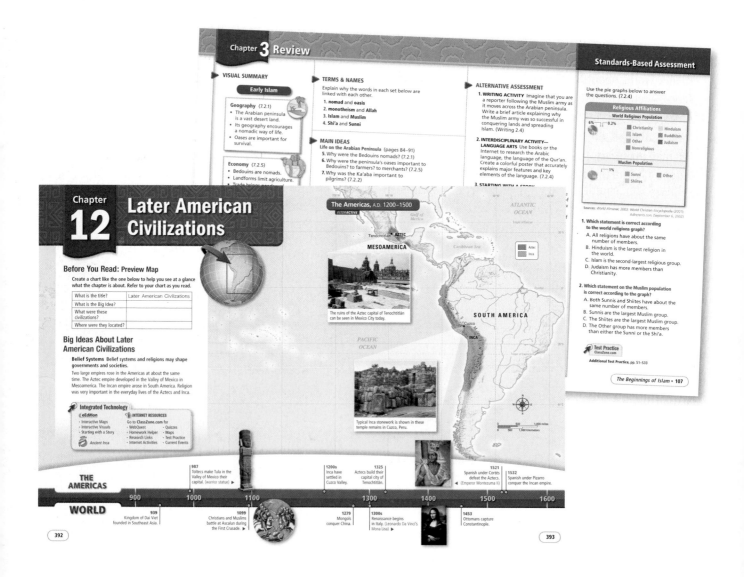

Charts, Graphs & Time Lines

Charts

Graphs

Time Lines

Five Pillars of Islam	
Faith	Believe and say, "There is no God but Allah, and Muhammad is his prophet."
Prayer	Pray in Arabic five times a day, at specific times, and facing Mecca.
Alms	Give to the poor and the needy.
Fasting	Fast during the month of Ramadan each year, avoiding all food and beverages between sunrise and sunset.
Pilgrimage	If possible, make a pilgrimage to the holy city of Mecca once during a lifetime.

Student Guide to the California State Standards for Grade 7

The state of California has developed standards that guide the content taught in its public schools. At the beginning of every lesson in this book, you will see a listing of the California content standards and skills standards that are addressed in that lesson. The standards begin with a code that combines numbers and letters (such as 7.2.3 or HI 2), followed by the statement of the standard. These standards describe the knowledge and skills you are expected to have learned by the end of specific grades.

Standards that use numbers only (such as 7.2.3) are content standards, which describe the actual historical people and events that you will study in this book. Standards that combine letters and numbers (such as HI 2 or CST 3) refer to standards that cover the Historical and Social Sciences Analysis Skills that you will apply to the content standards for Grade 7.

The following charts contain the complete wording of the content and skills standards for Grade 7. These charts will help you keep track of what you learn throughout the year.

History–Social Science Standards

Grade 7 World History and Geography: Medieval and Early Modern Times	
Standard 7.1	Students analyze the causes and effects of the vast expansion and ultimate disintegration of the Roman Empire.
7.1.1	Study the early strengths and lasting contributions of Rome (e.g., significance of Roman citizenship; rights under Roman law; Roman art, architecture, engineering, and philosophy; preservation and transmission of Christianity) and its ultimate internal weaknesses (e.g., rise of autonomous military powers within the empire, undermining of citizenship by the growth of corruption and slavery, lack of education, and distribution of news).
7.1.2	Discuss the geographic borders of the empire at its height and the factors that threatened its territorial cohesion.
7.1.3	Describe the establishment by Constantine of the new capital in Constantinople and the development of the Byzantine Empire, with an emphasis on the consequences of the development of two distinct European civilizations, Eastern Orthodox and Roman Catholic, and their two distinct views on church-state relations.

Standard 7.2 Students analyze the geographic, political, economic, religious, and social structures of the civilizations of Islam in the Middle Ages.

7.2.1 Identify the physical features and describe the climate of the Arabian peninsula, its relationship to surrounding bodies of land and water, and nomadic and sedentary ways of life.

7.2.2 Trace the origins of Islam and the life and teachings of Muhammad, including Islamic teachings on the connection with Judaism and Christianity.

7.2.3 Explain the significance of the Qur'an and the Sunnah as the primary sources of Islamic beliefs, practice, and law, and their influence in Muslims' daily life.

7.2.4 Discuss the expansion of Muslim rule through military conquests and treaties, emphasizing the cultural blending within Muslim civilization and the spread and acceptance of Islam and the Arabic language.

7.2.5 Describe the growth of cities and the establishment of trade routes among Asia, Africa, and Europe, the products and inventions that traveled along these routes (e.g., spices, textiles, paper, steel, new crops), and the role of merchants in Arab society.

7.2.6 Understand the intellectual exchanges among Muslim scholars of Eurasia and Africa and the contributions Muslim scholars made to later civilizations in the areas of science, geography, mathematics, philosophy, medicine, art, and literature.

Standard 7.3 Students analyze the geographic, political, economic, religious, and social structures of the civilizations of China in the Middle Ages.

7.3.1 Describe the reunification of China under the Tang Dynasty and reasons for the spread of Buddhism in Tang China, Korea, and Japan.

7.3.2 Describe agricultural, technological, and commercial developments during the Tang and Song periods.

7.3.3 Analyze the influences of Confucianism and changes in Confucian thought during the Song and Mongol periods.

7.3.4 Understand the importance of both overland trade and maritime expeditions between China and other civilizations in the Mongol Ascendancy and Ming Dynasty.

7.3.5 Trace the historic influence of such discoveries as tea, the manufacture of paper, wood-block printing, the compass, and gunpowder.

7.3.6 Describe the development of the imperial state and the scholar-official class.

Standard 7.4	Students analyze the geographic, political, economic, religious, and social structures of the sub-Saharan civilizations of Ghana and Mali in Medieval Africa.
7.4.1	Study the Niger River and the relationship of vegetation zones of forest, savannah, and desert to trade in gold, salt, food, and slaves; and the growth of the Ghana and Mali empires.
7.4.2	Analyze the importance of family, labor specialization, and regional commerce in the development of states and cities in West Africa.
7.4.3	Describe the role of the trans-Saharan caravan trade in the changing religious and cultural characteristics of West Africa and the influence of Islamic beliefs, ethics, and law.
7.4.4	Trace the growth of the Arabic language in government, trade, and Islamic scholarship in West Africa.
7.4.5	Describe the importance of written and oral traditions in the transmission of African history and culture.

Standard 7.5	Students analyze the geographic, political, economic, religious, and social structures of the civilizations of Medieval Japan.
7.5.1	Describe the significance of Japan's proximity to China and Korea and the intellectual, linguistic, religious, and philosophical influence of those countries on Japan.
7.5.2	Discuss the reign of Prince Shotoku of Japan and the characteristics of Japanese society and family life during his reign.
7.5.3	Describe the values, social customs, and traditions prescribed by the lord-vassal system consisting of *shogun*, *daimyo*, and *samurai* and the lasting influence of the warrior code in the twentieth century.
7.5.4	Trace the development of distinctive forms of Japanese Buddhism.
7.5.5	Study the ninth and tenth centuries' golden age of literature, art, and drama and its lasting effects on culture today, including Murasaki Shikibu's *Tale of Genji*.
7.5.6	Analyze the rise of a military society in the late twelfth century and the role of the samurai in that society.

Standard 7.6	Students analyze the geographic, political, economic, religious, and social structures of the civilizations of Medieval Europe.
7.6.1	Study the geography of the Europe and the Eurasian land mass, including its location, topography, waterways, vegetation, and climate and their relationship to ways of life in Medieval Europe.
7.6.2	Describe the spread of Christianity north of the Alps and the roles played by the early church and by monasteries in its diffusion after the fall of the western half of the Roman Empire.
7.6.3	Understand the development of feudalism, its role in the medieval European economy, the way in which it was influenced by physical geography (the role of the manor and the growth of towns), and how feudal relationships provided the foundation of political order.
7.6.4	Demonstrate an understanding of the conflict and cooperation between the Papacy and European monarchs (e.g., Charlemagne, Gregory VII, Emperor Henry IV).
7.6.5	Know the significance of developments in medieval English legal and constitutional practices and their importance in the rise of modern democratic thought and representative institutions (e.g., Magna Carta, parliament, development of habeas corpus, an independent judiciary in England).
7.6.6	Discuss the causes and course of the religious Crusades and their effects on the Christian, Muslim, and Jewish populations in Europe, with emphasis on the increasing contact by Europeans with cultures of the Eastern Mediterranean world.
7.6.7	Map the spread of the bubonic plague from Central Asia to China, the Middle East, and Europe and describe its impact on global population.
7.6.8	Understand the importance of the Catholic church as a political, intellectual, and aesthetic institution (e.g., founding of universities, political and spiritual roles of the clergy, creation of monastic and mendicant religious orders, preservation of the Latin language and religious texts, St. Thomas Aquinas's synthesis of classical philosophy with Christian theology, and the concept of "natural law").
7.6.9	Know the history of the decline of Muslim rule in the Iberian Peninsula that culminated in the Reconquista and the rise of Spanish and Portuguese kingdoms.

Standard 7.7	Students compare and contrast the geographic, political, economic, religious, and social structures of the Meso-American and Andean civilizations.
7.7.1	Study the locations, landforms, and climates of Mexico, Central America, and South America and their effects on Mayan, Aztec, and Incan economies, trade, and development of urban societies.
7.7.2	Study the roles of people in each society, including class structures, family life, warfare, religious beliefs and practices, and slavery.
7.7.3	Explain how and where each empire arose and how the Aztec and Incan empires were defeated by the Spanish.
7.7.4	Describe the artistic and oral traditions and architecture in the three civilizations.
7.7.5	Describe the Meso-American achievements in astronomy and mathematics, including the development of the calendar and the Meso-American knowledge of seasonal changes to the civilizations' agricultural systems.

Standard 7.8	Students analyze the origins, accomplishments, and geographic diffusion of the Renaissance.
7.8.1	Describe the way in which the revival of classical learning and the arts fostered a new interest in humanism (i.e., a balance between intellect and religious faith).
7.8.2	Explain the importance of Florence in the early stages of the Renaissance and the growth of independent trading cities (e.g., Venice), with emphasis on the cities' importance in the spread of Renaissance ideas.
7.8.3	Understand the effects of the reopening of the ancient "Silk Road" between Europe and China, including Marco Polo's travels and the location of his routes.
7.8.4	Describe the growth and effects of new ways of disseminating information (e.g., the ability to manufacture paper, translation of the Bible into the vernacular, printing).
7.8.5	Detail advances made in literature, the arts, science, mathematics, cartography, engineering, and the understanding of human anatomy and astronomy (e.g., by Dante Alighieri, Leonardo da Vinci, Michelangelo di Buonarroti Simoni, Johann Gutenberg, William Shakespeare).

Standard 7.9	Students analyze the historical developments of the Reformation.
7.9.1	List the causes for the internal turmoil in and weakening of the Catholic church (e.g., tax policies, selling of indulgences).
7.9.2	Describe the theological, political, and economic ideas of the major figures during the Reformation (e.g., Desiderius Erasmus, Martin Luther, John Calvin, William Tyndale).
7.9.3	Explain Protestants' new practices of church self-government and the influence of those practices on the development of democratic practices and ideas of federalism.
7.9.4	Identify and locate the European regions that remained Catholic and those that became Protestant and explain how the division affected the distribution of religions in the New World.
7.9.5	Analyze how the Counter-Reformation revitalized the Catholic church and the forces that fostered the movement (e.g., St. Ignatius of Loyola and the Jesuits, the Council of Trent).
7.9.6	Understand the institution and impact of missionaries on Christianity and the diffusion of Christianity from Europe to other parts of the world in the medieval and early modern periods; locate missions on a world map.
7.9.7	Describe the Golden Age of cooperation between Jews and Muslims in medieval Spain that promoted creativity in art, literature, and science, including how that cooperation was terminated by the religious persecution of individuals and groups (e.g., the Spanish Inquisition and the expulsion of Jews and Muslims from Spain in 1492).

Standard 7.10	Students analyze the historical developments of the Scientific Revolution and its lasting effect on religious, political, and cultural institutions.
7.10.1	Discuss the roots of the Scientific Revolution (e.g., Greek rationalism; Jewish, Christian, and Muslim science; Renaissance humanism; new knowledge from global exploration).
7.10.2	Understand the significance of the new scientific theories (e.g., those of Copernicus, Galileo, Kepler, Newton) and the significance of new inventions (e.g., the telescope, microscope, thermometer, barometer).
7.10.3	Understand the scientific method advanced by Bacon and Descartes, the influence of new scientific rationalism on the growth of democratic ideas, and the coexistence of science with traditional religious beliefs.

▶ Standard 7.11	Students analyze political and economic change in the sixteenth, seventeenth, and eighteenth centuries (the Age of Exploration, the Enlightenment, and the Age of Reason).
7.11.1	Know the great voyages of discovery, the locations of the routes, and the influence of cartography in the development of a new European worldview.
7.11.2	Discuss the exchanges of plants, animals, technology, culture, and ideas among Europe, Africa, Asia, and the Americas in the fifteenth and sixteenth centuries and the major economic and social effects on each continent.
7.11.3	Examine the origins of modern capitalism; the influence of mercantilism and cottage industry; the elements and importance of a market economy in seventeenth-century Europe; the changing international trading and marketing patterns, including their locations on a world map; and the influence of explorers and map makers.
7.11.4	Explain how the main ideas of the Enlightenment can be traced back to such movements as the Renaissance, the Reformation, and the Scientific Revolution and to the Greeks, Romans, and Christianity.
7.11.5	Describe how democratic thought and institutions were influenced by Enlightenment thinkers (e.g., John Locke, Charles-Louis Montesquieu, American founders).
7.11.6	Discuss how the principles in the Magna Carta were embodied in such documents as the English Bill of Rights and the American Declaration of Independence.

Grades 6 through 8 Historical and Social Sciences Analysis Skills

▸ Chronological and Spatial Thinking (CST)

1. Students explain how major events are related to one another in time.

2. Students construct various time lines of key events, people, and periods of the historical era they are studying.

3. Students use a variety of maps and documents to identify physical and cultural features of neighborhoods, cities, states, and countries and to explain the historical migration of people, expansion and disintegration of empires, and the growth of economic systems.

▸ Research, Evidence, and Point of View (REP)

1. Students frame questions that can be answered by historical study and research.

2. Students distinguish fact from opinion in historical narratives and stories.

3. Students distinguish relevant from irrelevant information, essential from incidental information, and verifiable from unverifiable information in historical narratives and stories.

4. Students assess the credibility of primary and secondary sources and draw sound conclusions from them.

5. Students detect the different historical points of view on historical events and determine the context in which the historical statements were made (the questions asked, sources used, author's perspectives).

▸ Historical Interpretation (HI)

1. Students explain the central issues and problems from the past, placing people and events in a matrix of time and place.

2. Students understand and distinguish cause, effect, sequence, and correlation in historical events, including the long- and short-term causal relations.

3. Students explain the sources of historical continuity and how the combination of ideas and events explains the emergence of new patterns.

4. Students recognize the role of chance, oversight, and error in history.

5. Students recognize that interpretations of history are subject to change as new information is uncovered.

6. Students interpret basic indicators of economic performance and conduct cost-benefit analyses of economic and political issues.

Historical Themes and Big Ideas

Beginning with Your Own Experience

Welcome to the study of world history. As you know, world history is the story of the most important things that ever happened to human beings. This book covers more than 2,000 years of that history.

You may be wondering how you will learn all the facts about such a long period of time. The best way is to sort the information into categories (similar groupings). The broad categories are called themes. This opening section of the book will introduce you to six major themes of history.

Let's begin with your life. Although you may not know it, you have already had many experiences that will help you to understand the themes. Consider the questions below and discuss your answers with your classmates.

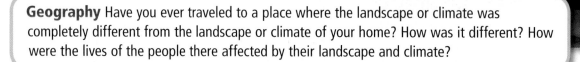

Geography Have you ever traveled to a place where the landscape or climate was completely different from the landscape or climate of your home? How was it different? How were the lives of the people there affected by their landscape and climate?

Culture Have you ever been in a situation where you had to change the way you acted because the people around you expected different behavior? How quickly did you change? How did you feel about changing?

Economics In most societies, people earn money by working in jobs that provide goods and services. The amount of money people earn depends partially on the type of work they do. What considerations will help you decide what kind of work to do?

Government Think of some rules that your family has. Who made the rules? How do those rules affect the way your family lives together? Have any of your family's rules changed as you grew older? How?

Belief Systems How do you decide what is the right or wrong thing to do? Where did you get your ideas about behaviors that are right or wrong?

Science & Technology In your opinion, what is the one invention that has most improved your life? How would your life be different without this invention?

Understanding Historical Themes

As you and your classmates shared your answers, you probably discovered you had many different experiences. But you probably also found that you had things in common too.

For example, people who live in cold climates usually build houses with steep roofs so the winter snow will slide off. They may own several coats, each one suited for a different range of temperatures. Some people in cold climates ski or ice skate. Others spend winter indoors reading books, watching movies, or playing games. Each of those activities is a different response to a cold climate. Yet, what these people have in common is that the place where they live affects their lives.

Once you understand what a group of facts has in common, you are ready to talk about themes. The six themes of this history program are described below. As you read this book, you will notice that many statements and questions are labeled by one of these themes.

Geography

Geography refers to the characteristics of a physical place, the ways that environment affects human life, and the ways that humans change the environment. It also refers to the movement of people, goods, and ideas from place to place.

Culture

Culture is the way of life that a society or group shares. It includes the way people act, the way they express themselves, and the way they are organized.

Economics

Economics includes the ways that people use their limited resources to satisfy their needs and desires. It also refers to the ways that societies produce wealth and how they organize labor.

Government

Government refers to the system of laws and authority that a society uses to guide or control its members.

Belief Systems

Belief systems are often religions, which are beliefs in a god or gods. Belief systems may also be systems of ethics, or principles of right and wrong.

Science & Technology

The theme of science and technology includes discoveries, inventions, and improved methods of doing things.

Looking for Big Ideas

As you read this book, you will begin to notice that certain patterns occur over and over in history. Different societies go through similar stages, make similar choices, or organize themselves in similar ways. We call those patterns the **Big Ideas** of history.

For example, you are going to learn about the invention of such things as the compass and the printing press. Each of these new technologies dramatically changed the way people lived, so one of the Big Ideas in this book is:

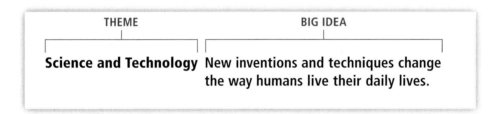

As you can see from that example, the Big Idea is a statement of the historical pattern. The first page of every chapter lists a Big Idea, which introduces a pattern that occurs in the chapter. Each Big Idea starts with a theme, as shown above. Think about the Big Idea before you start to read. It will help you to know what to focus on as you study.

This book highlights 12 different Big Ideas, two for each theme:

Big Ideas are Patterns in History		
Geography	Many geographic factors influenced history.	Migration, trade, warfare, and the action of missionaries spread ideas and beliefs.
Culture	Ways of living change as humans interact with each other.	Many societies rely on family roles and social classes to keep order.
Economics	Societies trade the surplus goods that they produce to obtain goods they lack.	Economic interests may shape a society's territorial growth.
Government	Governments create law codes and political bodies to organize a society.	New ideas and beliefs can challenge a government's authority, leading to change.
Belief Systems	People adopt new beliefs that give meaning to life.	Belief systems and religions may shape governments and societies.
Science & Technology	New scientific discoveries change human understanding of the world.	New inventions and techniques change the way humans live their daily lives.

Asking Historical Questions

You can use themes and Big Ideas to ask questions about historic periods and people. As you read this book, ask yourself questions that you will try to answer as you read. This approach will help you understand the importance of various facts and will help you remember them.

Sample Historical Questions

Geography Throughout history, how have societies adjusted to their surroundings? How have they attempted to overcome obstacles created by geography?

Culture How have cultural changes come about throughout history? Why did some changes come about by force and other changes come about through voluntary choices?

Economics Throughout history, how have societies acted in order to gain control of more resources, goods, and services? What activities have societies used to produce wealth?

Government How have societies developed laws to control the behavior of their members? How have societies enforced their laws? How and why have laws been changed?

Belief Systems Throughout history, how have humans used their belief systems to understand the relationship between themselves and the entire universe? How have humans responded to people with different belief systems?

Science & Technology How have scientific inventions and discoveries improved the lives of people throughout history? How have they caused problems?

To help guide your reading, we have included historical questions in every lesson of this book. They appear at the beginning of each section and are labeled **ESSENTIAL QUESTIONS**. By looking for the answers to these questions as you read, you will focus on the most important information in each lesson.

Be careful when you ask historical questions. Don't assume that life in the past was the same as life today. For example, consider this question: In the past, how did people get rid of a ruler they didn't like?

Because we have frequent elections in the United States, we can vote officials out of office. In the past, however, most societies were ruled by a monarch who controlled the army. It was difficult to replace such powerful rulers.

In conclusion, as you study world history, remember these three tips:

- Consider how facts and details relate to the six themes.
- Look for the patterns explained in the Big Ideas.
- Ask and answer historical questions.

STRATEGIES for TAKING TESTS

This section will help you develop and practice the skills you need to study history and to take tests.

Part 1, **Strategies for Studying History,** shows you the features of this book. It also shows you how to improve your reading and study skills.

Part 2, **Test-Taking Strategies and Practice,** gives you strategies to help you answer the different kinds of questions that appear on tests. Each strategy is followed by a set of questions you can use for practice.

CONTENTS

Part 1: Strategies for Studying History

Reading is the central skill in the effective study of history or any other subject. You can improve your reading skills by using helpful techniques and by practicing. The better your reading skills, the more you will remember what you read. The next four pages show how some of the features of *World History: Medieval and Early Modern Times* can help you learn and understand history.

Preview Chapters Before You Read

Each chapter begins with a two-page chapter opener. Study these pages to help you get ready to read.

1 Read the chapter title for clues to what will be covered in the chapter.

2 Study the **Before You Read** and **Big Ideas** sections. The activities and information in these sections will help to guide your reading.

3 Preview the time line and note the years covered in the chapter. Consider the important events that took place during this time period. Study the map to get an idea of where these events took place.

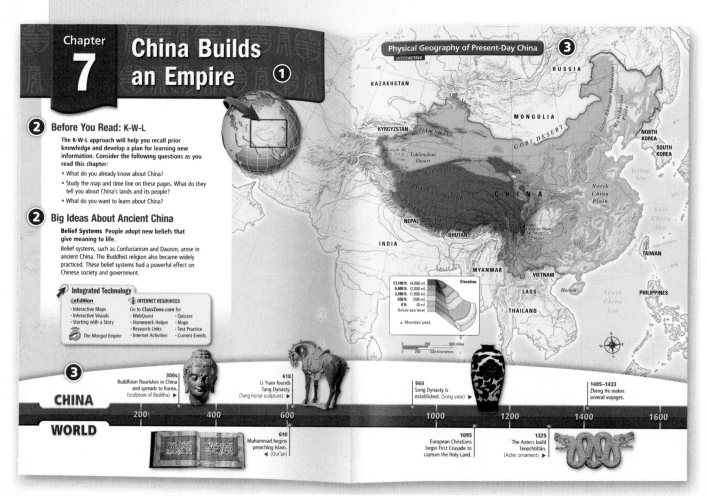

Chapter 7

China Builds an Empire ①

2 Before You Read: K-W-L

The K-W-L approach will help you recall prior knowledge and develop a plan for learning new information. Consider the following questions as you read this chapter:

- What do you already know about China?
- Study the map and time line on these pages. What do they tell you about China's lands and its people?
- What do you want to learn about China?

2 Big Ideas About Ancient China

Belief Systems People adopt new beliefs that give meaning to life.

Belief systems, such as Confucianism and Daoism, arose in ancient China. The Buddhist religion also became widely practiced. These belief systems had a powerful effect on Chinese society and government.

Integrated Technology

eEdition
- Interactive Maps
- Interactive Visuals
- Starting with a Story
- *The Mongol Empire*

INTERNET RESOURCES
Go to ClassZone.com for
- WebQuest
- Homework Helper
- Research Links
- Internet Activities
- Quizzes
- Maps
- Test Practice
- Current Events

3 Physical Geography of Present-Day China
INTERACTIVE

CHINA

300s
Buddhism flourishes in China and spreads to Korea. (sculpture of Buddha) ▶

618
Li Yuan founds Tang Dynasty. (Tang horse sculpture) ▶

960
Song Dynasty is established. (Song vase) ▶

1405–1433
Zheng He makes several voyages.

200 400 600 1000 1200 1400 1600

WORLD

610
Muhammad begins preaching Islam. ◀ (Qur'an)

1095
European Christians begin First Crusade to capture the Holy Land.

1325
The Aztecs build Tenochtitlán. (Aztec ornament) ▶

Preview Lessons Before You Read

Each chapter consists of between two and five lessons. These lessons focus on specific time periods or on particular historical themes.

1 Study the information under the heading **Main Ideas.** It tells you what is important in the lesson.

2 Preview the **Terms & Names** list. This list tells you the people, places, or issues that will be covered in the lesson.

3 Read the paragraph under the heading **Build on What You Know.** This relates the content of the lesson to your personal experience or to subjects you've already studied.

4 Notice the structure of the lesson. Red heads label the major topics; run-in heads signal smaller topics within those major topics. Together, these heads provide you with a quick outline of the lesson.

5 Each lesson opener lists the California standards covered in that lesson.

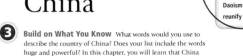

► **TERMS & NAMES**

nomad

Confucianism

Buddhism

Daoism

reunify

Lesson 1

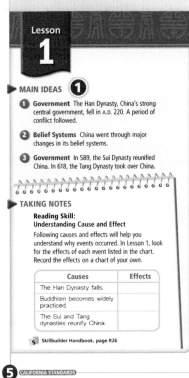

► **MAIN IDEAS** **1**

1 **Government** The Han Dynasty, China's strong central government, fell in A.D. 220. A period of conflict followed.

2 **Belief Systems** China went through major changes in its belief systems.

3 **Government** In 589, the Sui Dynasty reunified China. In 618, the Tang Dynasty took over China.

► **TAKING NOTES**

Reading Skill:
Understanding Cause and Effect
Following causes and effects will help you understand why events occurred. In Lesson 1, look for the effects of each event listed in the chart. Record the effects on a chart of your own.

Causes	Effects
The Han Dynasty falls.	
Buddhism becomes widely practiced.	
The Sui and Tang dynasties reunify China.	

S Skillbuilder Handbook, page R26

5 **CALIFORNIA STANDARDS**

7.3.1 Describe the reunification of China under the Tang Dynasty and reasons for the spread of Buddhism in Tang China, Korea, and Japan.

7.3.2 Describe agricultural, technological, and commercial developments during the Tang and Song periods.

7.3.3 Analyze the influences of Confucianism and changes in Confucian thought during the Song and Mongol periods.

HI 1 Students explain the central issues and problems from the past, placing people and events in a matrix of time and place.

▲ **Han Watchtower** The Han often placed pottery models of buildings, like the military watchtower above, in tombs. These models provided the deceased with shelter and protection in the afterlife.

Reunifying China

► **TERMS & NAMES**
nomad
Confucianism
Buddhism
Daoism
reunify
2

3 **Build on What You Know** What words would you use to describe the country of China? Does your list include the words huge and powerful? In this chapter, you will learn that China was a huge and powerful country 1,500 years ago.

4 **Fall of the Han Dynasty**

1 **ESSENTIAL QUESTION** What happened after the Han Dynasty fell in A.D. 220?

The Han Dynasty, founded in 206 B.C., was a period of progress and prosperity for China. In time, however, political struggles, social problems, and a widening gap between rich and poor weakened the Han Dynasty. It fell in A.D. 220.

Conflict and Chaos A time of great disorder followed. Various kingdoms fought among themselves. Invading nomads from the north crossed the Mongolian Plateau into northern China. (A **nomad** is a person who moves from place to place.) Floods, droughts, and food shortages also plagued the land.

Despite these troubles, Chinese culture survived. In the north, the invading nomads eventually settled down and adopted Chinese customs. In the south, good harvests and growing trade helped people to prosper. Even so, most Chinese people led difficult lives.

REVIEW What were the effects of the fall of the Han Dynasty on China?

The Himalayas This great mountain range provided a barrier to protect China from invasion from the southwest. ▼

Use Active Reading Strategies As You Read

Now you're ready to read the chapter. Read one lesson at a time, from beginning to end.

1 Ask and answer questions as you read. Look for the **Essential Question** under each main heading. Finding the answer to this question will help to guide your reading.

2 Look for the story behind the events. Study the captions and boxed features for additional information and interesting sidelights on the lesson content.

3 Try to visualize the people, places, and events you read about. Studying the pictures, maps, and other illustrations will help you do this.

4 Read to build your vocabulary. Use the **Vocabulary Strategy** in the margin to find information on unfamiliar words and word usage.

Vocabulary Strategy

The suffix *-ism* refers to an action, a process, or a practice. Confucianism is the practice of Confucius' teachings.

Changes in Belief Systems

1 2 ESSENTIAL QUESTION What changes took place in China's belief systems?

The turmoil after the fall of the Han Dynasty led to major changes in China's belief systems.

Confucianism For centuries, the Chinese had looked to Confucianism (kuhn•FYOO•shuh•nihz•uhm) for comfort and guidance. **Confucianism** is a belief system based on the ideas of Confucius (551–479 B.C.). He was a scholar who taught moral virtues and ethics—ideas of right and wrong. In his teachings, Confucius emphasized these principles.

- Use right relationships to produce social order.
- Respect family and older generations.
- Educate individuals and society.
- Act in morally correct ways.

4 Vocabulary Strategy
The suffix *-ism* refers to an action, a process, or a practice. Confucianism is the practice of Confucius' teachings.

Confucianism Influences Chinese Life Confucianism affected many aspects of Chinese government and society. For example, Confucius taught that people could advance in life through education. An emphasis on education helped to produce an efficient, well-trained set of government officials.

Confucius' ideas also influenced society. He thought society should be organized around five basic relationships. A code of conduct governed these relationships. For example, one relationship was between ruler and subject. Confucius taught that the ruler should be virtuous and kind. The subject should be loyal and obey the law. Other relationships were based on the family. Confucius wanted children to have respect for their parents and older generations. Around A.D. 200, however, Confucianism began to lose its influence as the Han Dynasty lost power.

The Spread of Buddhism As Confucianism lost influence, many Chinese turned to Buddhism. **Buddhism** is a religion that started in India and is based on the teachings of Siddhartha Gautama (sihd•DAHR•tuh GOW•tuh•muh) (c. 566–486 B.C.). Siddhartha was known as the Buddha, or "Enlightened One."

2 Buddha This huge seated Buddha, located in caves about 150 miles west of Beijing, was carved in the fifth century A.D. ▶

3

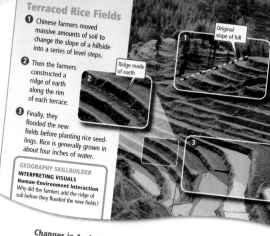

Geography

Terraced Rice Fields

1 Chinese farmers moved massive amounts of soil to change the slope of a hillside into a series of level steps.

2 Then the farmers constructed a ridge of earth along the rim of each terrace.

3 Finally, they flooded the new fields before planting rice seedlings. Rice is generally grown in about four inches of water.

Original slope of hill

Ridge made of earth

GEOGRAPHY SKILLBUILDER
INTERPRETING VISUALS
Human-Environment Interaction
Why did the farmers add the ridge of soil before they flooded the new fields?

Changes in Agriculture Around A.D. 1000, Chinese farmers began planting a new type of rice from Southeast Asia. This rice ripened faster than the type they had used before. With the new rice, farmers could raise two or even three crops a year instead of one. The food supply expanded rapidly, allowing the population to grow to about 100 million.

During Tang and Song times, the Chinese turned areas of the Chang Jiang valley into productive rice paddies, or fields. Farmers used pumps and canals to drain water from marshes. They built terraces on hillsides and used elaborate irrigation systems to water them. By changing their environment, the Chinese farmers gained additional land enabled them to grow more rice.

These changes and a mild climate allowed southern China to grow more rice than the people in that region needed. Farmers sold the extra rice to merchants, who shipped it by canal to imperial centers in northern China. Having extra food meant that fewer people needed to work as farmers. As a result, more people could work in trade.

Review and Summarize What You Have Read

When you finish reading a lesson, review and summarize what you have read. If necessary, go back and reread information that was not clear the first time through.

1 Answer the **Review** questions at the end of each section of the lesson.

2 Reread the main heads and the run-in heads for a quick summary of the major points covered in the lesson.

3 Study any charts, graphs, or maps in the lesson. These visual materials usually provide a condensed version of the information in the lesson.

4 Complete all the questions in the **Lesson Review.** This will help you think critically about what you have just read. Notice that a California standard is identified for each question.

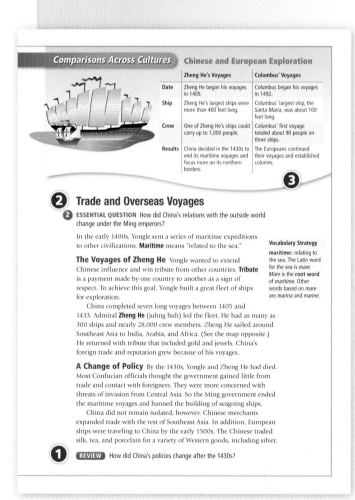

Comparisons Across Cultures — Chinese and European Exploration

	Zheng He's Voyages	Columbus' Voyages
Date	Zheng He began his voyages in 1405.	Columbus began his voyages in 1492.
Ship	Zheng He's largest ships were more than 400 feet long.	Columbus' largest ship, the *Santa Maria*, was about 100 feet long.
Crew	One of Zheng He's ships could carry up to 1,000 people.	Columbus' first voyage totaled about 90 people on three ships.
Results	China decided in the 1430s to end its maritime voyages and focus more on its northern borders.	The Europeans continued their voyages and established colonies.

3

2 Trade and Overseas Voyages

2 ESSENTIAL QUESTION How did China's relations with the outside world change under the Ming emperors?

In the early 1400s, Yongle sent a series of maritime expeditions to other civilizations. **Maritime** means "related to the sea."

The Voyages of Zheng He Yongle wanted to extend Chinese influence and win tribute from other countries. **Tribute** is a payment made by one country to another as a sign of respect. To achieve this goal, Yongle built a great fleet of ships for exploration.

China completed seven long voyages between 1405 and 1433. Admiral **Zheng He** (juhng huh) led the fleet. He had as many as 300 ships and nearly 28,000 crew members. Zheng He sailed from Southeast Asia to India, Arabia, and Africa. (See the map opposite.) He returned with tribute that included gold and jewels. China's foreign trade and reputation grew because of his voyages.

A Change of Policy By the 1430s, Yongle and Zheng He had died. Most Confucian officials thought the government gained little from trade and contact with foreigners. They were more concerned with threats of invasion from Central Asia. So the Ming government ended the maritime voyages and banned the building of seagoing ships.

China did not remain isolated, however. Chinese merchants expanded trade with the rest of Southeast Asia. In addition, European ships were traveling to China by the early 1500s. The Chinese traded silk, tea, and porcelain for a variety of Western goods, including silver.

Vocabulary Strategy
maritime: relating to the sea. The Latin word for the sea is *mare*. *Mare* is the **root word** of *maritime*. Other words based on *mare* are *marina* and *marine*.

1 REVIEW How did China's policies change after the 1430s?

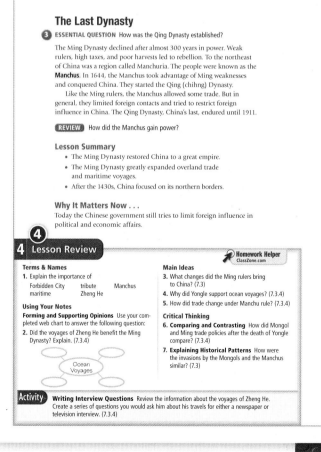

The Last Dynasty

3 ESSENTIAL QUESTION How was the Qing Dynasty established?

The Ming Dynasty declined after almost 300 years in power. Weak rulers, high taxes, and poor harvests led to rebellion. To the northeast of China was a region called Manchuria. The people were known as the **Manchus**. In 1644, the Manchus took advantage of Ming weaknesses and conquered China. They started the Qing (chihng) Dynasty.

Like the Ming rulers, the Manchus allowed some trade. But in general, they limited foreign contacts and tried to restrict foreign influence in China. The Qing Dynasty, China's last, endured until 1911.

REVIEW How did the Manchus gain power?

Lesson Summary
- The Ming Dynasty restored China to a great empire.
- The Ming Dynasty greatly expanded overland trade and maritime voyages.
- After the 1430s, China focused on its northern borders.

Why It Matters Now . . .
Today the Chinese government still tries to limit foreign influence in political and economic affairs.

4

4 Lesson Review

Homework Helper ClassZone.com

Terms & Names
1. Explain the importance of
Forbidden City   tribute   Manchus
maritime   Zheng He

Using Your Notes
Forming and Supporting Opinions Use your completed web chart to answer the following question:
2. Did the voyages of Zheng He benefit the Ming Dynasty? Explain. (7.3.4)

Ocean Voyages

Main Ideas
3. What changes did the Ming rulers bring to China? (7.3)
4. Why did Yongle support ocean voyages? (7.3.4)
5. How did trade change under Manchu rule? (7.3.4)

Critical Thinking
6. **Comparing and Contrasting** How did Mongol and Ming trade policies after the death of Yongle compare? (7.3.4)
7. **Explaining Historical Patterns** How were the invasions by the Mongols and the Manchus similar? (7.3)

Activity **Writing Interview Questions** Review the information about the voyages of Zheng He. Create a series of questions you would ask him about his travels for either a newspaper or television interview. (7.3.4)

Part 2: Test-Taking Strategies and Practice

Use the strategies in this section to improve your test-taking skills. First read the tips on the left page. Then use them to help you with the practice items on the right page.

Multiple Choice

A multiple-choice question is a question or incomplete sentence and a set of choices. One of the choices correctly answers the question or completes the sentence.

1 Read the question or incomplete sentence carefully. Try to answer it before looking at the choices.

2 Look for key words in the question. They may help you figure out the correct answer.

3 Read each choice with the question. Don't decide on your final answer until you have read all the choices.

4 Rule out any choices that you know are wrong.

5 Watch for choices with words like *all, never,* and *only.* These choices are often incorrect.

6 Sometimes the last choice is "all of the above." Make sure that the other choices are all correct if you pick this answer.

7 Be careful with questions that include the word *not.*

❶ 1. The Sahara is (mostly)

❷ Words like *mostly* or *partly* are key words in multiple-choice questions. Look for answers that are mostly true or partly true.

❸ choices
  A. sand, rocks, and gravel.
  B. boulders and sand.
  C. cliffs and gulleys.
  D. grasses and bushes.

❹ If you know that the Sahara is a desert, you know that **D** is incorrect. A desert cannot be mostly grasses and bushes.

2. Over hundreds of years, Bantu-speaking peoples migrated from West Africa to
  A. South Asia and Southwest Asia.
  B. (every) continent on Earth.
  C. eastern and southern Africa.
  D. (all) of North Africa and Arabia.

❺

3. The people of West Africa passed on their history by
  A. painting pictures.
  B. telling stories.
  C. creating dances.
  ❻ D. all of the above

4. Which of the following is (not) one of the nations in southern Africa?
  A. Zimbabwe
  B. Nigeria
  C. Mozambique
  D. Namibia

❼ First rule out all the choices that name southern African countries. The choice that remains is the correct answer.

answers: 1 (A); 2 (C); 3 (D); 4 (B)

For more test practice online . . .
TEST PRACTICE
CLASSZONE.COM

Directions: Read each question and choose the *best* answer from the four choices.

1. Which of the following was *not* a result of the Black Death?

   A. Cities worked together during the plague.
   B. Europe lost one-third of its population.
   C. The Church lost its prestige among the people.
   D. The economies of many countries were ruined.

2. Martin Luther started a reform movement when he

   A. published the New Testament in German.
   B. criticized some of the Church's practices.
   C. wrote his Ninety-Five Theses and made them public.
   D. all of the above

3. The Ottoman Empire reached its greatest size and glory under the rule of

   A. Mehmet II.
   B. Selim the Grim.
   C. Suleyman the Lawgiver.
   D. Timur the Lame.

4. During the 1700s, England controlled which of the following?

   A. the sugar trade
   B. the Atlantic slave trade
   C. the cotton trade
   D. the coconut trade

Primary Sources

Sometimes you will need to look at a document to answer a question. Some documents are primary sources. Primary sources are written or made by people who either saw an event or were actually part of the event. A primary source can be a photograph, a letter, a diary, a speech, or an autobiography.

❶ Look at the source line to learn about the document and its author. If the author is well-known and has been quoted a lot, the information is probably reliable.

❷ Skim the document to get an idea of what it is about.

❸ Note any special punctuation. For example, ellipses (. . .) indicate that words or sentences have been left out.

❹ Ask yourself questions about the document as you read.

❺ Review the questions. This will give your reading a purpose and also help you find the answers more easily. Then reread the document.

Good Government

Chap 2.20 Lord Ji Kang asked, "What should I do in order to make the people respectful, loyal, and zealous [hard-working]?" The Master said: "Approach them with dignity and they will be respectful. Be yourself a good son and kind father, and they will be loyal. Raise the good and train the incompetent, and they will be zealous."

Chap. 13.2 Ran Yong (. . .) asked about government. The Master said: "Guide the officials. Forgive small mistakes. Promote [people] of talent." "How does one recognize that a [person] has talent and deserves to be promoted?" The Master said: "Promote those you know. Those whom you do not know will hardly remain ignored."

—*The Analects of Confucius*

The *Analects* is a book of the thoughts and ideas of Confucius. He was a scholar and teacher in ancient China. **❶**

1. Confucius is giving advice on

   A. how to be a gentleman.

   B. how to be a good ruler.

   C. how to become wealthy.

   D. how to raise a good family.

2. Which sentence *best* expresses the idea of these paragraphs?

   A. The wise ruler governs people through fear.

   B. People should obey their rulers no matter what.

   C. A good ruler gives a lot of orders to people.

   D. If rulers do things well, people will follow them.

answers: 1 (B); 2 (D)

For more test practice online . . .

TEST PRACTICE
CLASSZONE.COM

Directions: Use the passage to answer the following questions.

> No constable or other bailiff [officer] . . . shall take anyone's grain or other chattels [property] without immediately paying for them in money. . . .
>
> No sheriff or bailiff, or any one else, shall take horses or wagons of any free man . . . except on the permission of that free man.
>
> Neither we nor our bailiffs will take the wood of another man for castles, or for anything else . . . except by the permission of him to whom the wood belongs.
>
> —Magna Carta (1215)

1. These paragraphs place limits on the
   A. rights of the king.
   B. powers of officials to take property.
   C. rights of nobles to tax people.
   D. power of Parliament.

2. The rights guaranteed by the Magna Carta are similar to those listed in the Bill of Rights of
   A. France.
   B. the Netherlands.
   C. the United States.
   D. Germany.

Secondary Sources

A secondary source is an account of events by a person who did not actually experience them. The author often uses information from several primary sources to write about people and events. Biographies, many newspaper articles, and history books are examples of secondary sources.

1 Read the title to get an idea of what the passage is about. (The title here indicates that the passage is about a person named Malinche about whom people have different opinions.)

2 Skim the passage to find its main idea.

3 Look for words that help you understand the order in which events happen.

4 Ask yourself questions as you read. (You might ask yourself, Why did people's opinions about Malinche change over time?)

5 Review the questions to see what information you will need to find. Then reread the passage.

❶ Malinche—Heroine or Traitor?

No one knows much about Malinche's early life. People do know that in 1519 she met Hernán Cortés. The Spanish conquistador had landed in Mexico earlier that year. Malinche was only 15 years old. Even though she was **❷** very young, Malinche helped Cortés conquer the Aztecs. She spoke the languages of the Aztecs and the Maya. Over time, she learned Spanish. She translated for Cortés and advised him on Native American politics.

The Spanish conquistadors admired Malinche, calling **❸** her Doña Marina. For many centuries, the Spanish people regarded her as a heroine. In the 1800s, however, Mexico won its independence from Spain. People rejected their Spanish rulers. Writers and artists started calling Malinche a traitor to her people. Today, however, she is seen as a heroine again. **❹**

1. Which of the following statements about Malinche is an (opinion)?

> Remember that an opinion is a statement that cannot be proved. A fact is a statement that can be proved.

  A She was very young when she met Cortés.

❺ **B.** She became a translator for Cortés.

  C. She was a traitor to her own people.

  D. She advised Cortés on Native American politics.

2. According to information in this source, which person or group might view Malinche as a heroine?

  A. a fighter for Mexican independence from Spain

  B. the soldiers and officers in Cortés' army

  C. the Aztec ruler and his court in Mexico

  D. a historian writing about Mexico in the 1800s

answers: 1 (C); 2 (B)

Directions: Use the passage to answer the following questions.

The Five Pillars of Islam

Muslims—believers in Islam—have five duties. These are called the Pillars of Islam because the faith is based on them.

The first duty is to profess faith in God. Muslims must say the sentence, "There is no God but Allah, and Muhammad is his prophet." They must say this in public at least once during their lives.

The second pillar is to pray five times a day. The prayers must be said while facing toward the holy city of Mecca in Saudi Arabia.

The third is to give support to the poor and needy. Charity to those in need has been an important part of Islam from the beginning.

The fourth duty is to fast—not eat or drink—from dawn to sunset during the holy month of *Ramadan*.

The final duty is the *hajj*, or pilgrimage to Mecca. Every Muslim who can do so is expected to travel to Mecca at least once in his or her life. People who are physically unable or too poor to do so are excused from this requirement.

1. What is the first pillar of Islam?
   A. making the *hajj*
   B. giving charity to the poor
   C. praying five times a day
   D. professing faith in God

2. What particular duty must Muslims perform during the holy month of *Ramadan?*
   A. fasting from dawn to sunset
   B. praying five times a day
   C. giving charity to the poor
   D. professing faith in God

Political Cartoons

Cartoonists who draw political cartoons use both words and art to express opinions about political issues.

1 Try to figure out what the cartoon is about. Titles and captions may give clues.

2 Study any labels that may identify the people, places, and events represented in the cartoon.

3 Note when and where the cartoon was published.

4 Look for symbols—that is, people, places, or objects that stand for other things.

5 A cartoonist often exaggerates the physical features of people and objects. This technique will give you clues as to how the cartoonist feels about the subject.

6 Try to figure out the cartoonist's message and summarize it in a phrase.

2 The letters are the initials of the colonies.

This snake has been cut into several pieces. **5**

The Granger Collection, New York

3 Benjamin Franklin (1754)

1. What do the sections of the snake in the cartoon represent?

A. army units

B. states

C. Native American groups

D. colonies

6 2. Which quotation *best* states the message of the cartoon?

A. "East is East, and West is West, and never the twain shall meet."

B. "Taxation without representation is tyranny."

C. "United we stand, divided we fall."

D. "Out of many, one."

answers: 1 (D); 2 (C)

Directions: Use the cartoon to answer the following questions.

The Barber Wants to Cut Off an Old Believer's Beard

The Granger Collection, New York

1. This cartoon shows Peter the Great of Russia as a barber. He is cutting off the beard of a Russian nobleman. The shaving of beards was a part of Peter's program of

   A. westernization.

   B. nationalization.

   C. modernization.

   D. democratization.

2. This cartoon shows Peter forcing change on his subjects. What kind of government does this represent?

   A. absolute monarchy

   B. constitutional monarchy

   C. democracy

   D. plutocracy

Charts

Charts present facts in a visual form. History textbooks contain several types of charts. The chart that is most often found on tests is the table. A table organizes information in columns and rows.

❶ Read the title of the chart to find out what information is presented.

❷ Read the heading at the top of each column. Then read the heading at the left of each row.

❸ Notice how the information in the chart is organized.

❹ Compare the information from column to column and row to row.

❺ Try to draw conclusions from the information in the chart.

❻ Read the questions and then study the chart again.

❶ Major Trade Networks

❹ Notice that there were several modes of transport.

❷

	Trading Partners	Trade Goods	Modes of Transport
Trans-Arabian	• Sassanid Empire • Arabia • Byzantine Empire	• East Asia: silk, gems, dyes, cotton cloth • Arabia: incense, spices • Southwest Asia: wool, gold, silver	• camel caravans
Silk Roads	• China • India • Persia and Central Asia • Europe	• Asia: silk, porcelain, spices, precious woods, gems • Europe: wool cloth, gold, silver	• caravans of camels and other pack animals
Mediterranean	• Europe • North Africa • Southwest Asia	• Europe: wool and linen cloth, wine, metal • North Africa: wool • Asia: spices, fruit, cloth	• by sea, galleys with numerous rowers • overland, caravans of pack animals
Trans-Saharan	• North Africa • West Africa	• North Africa: cloth, salt, horses, guns	• camel caravans
Indian Ocean	• China • India • Arabia • East Africa	• Asia: porcelain, silk, jewelry, cotton • East Africa: ivory, gold, tortoise shell, leopard skins, slaves	• Arab dhows • Chinese junks

❸ This chart lists networks. Other charts organize information by years or by numbers.

❺ Notice that some regions traded in more than one network.

❻

1. Camel caravans were used on which trade routes?

   A. Trans-Arabia and Indian Ocean
   B. Trans-Sahara and Indian Ocean
   C. Trans-Sahara and Trans-Arabia
   D. Silk Roads and Indian Ocean

2. Which was a trading partner in the Mediterranean network?

   A. West Africa
   B. North Africa
   C. China
   D. Byzantine Empire

answers: 1 (C); 2 (B)

Directions: Use the chart to answer the following questions.

Inventions of Tang and Song China		
	Description	**Impact**
Porcelain Late 700s	Bone-hard white ceramic made of a special clay and a mineral found only in China	Became a valuable export—so associated with Chinese culture that it is now called china; technology remained a Chinese secret for centuries
Mechanical clock 700s	Clock in which machinery (driven by running water) regulated the movements	Early Chinese clocks short-lived; idea for mechanical clock carried by traders to medieval Europe
Printing Block printing: 700s Movable type: 1040s	Block printing: one block on which a whole page is cut; movable type: individual characters arranged in frames, used over and over	Printing technology spread to Korea and Japan; movable type also developed later in Europe
Explosive powder 800s	Made from mixture of saltpeter, sulfur, and carbon	First used for fireworks, then weapons; technology spread west within 300 years
Paper money 1020s	Paper currency issued by Song government to replace cumbersome strings of metal cash used by merchants	Contributed to development of large-scale commercial economy in China
Magnetic compass (for navigation) 1100s	Floating magnetized needle that always points north-south; device had existed in China for centuries before it was adapted by sailors for use at sea	Helped China become a sea power; technology quickly spread west

1. Which invention helped China become a sea power?

   A. mechanical clock

   B. magnetic compass

   C. porcelain

   D. explosive powder

2. Which invention became a valuable export?

   A. paper money

   B. explosive powder

   C. porcelain

   D. mechanical clock

Line and Bar Graphs

Graphs show numbers in visual form. Line graphs are useful for showing changes over time. Bar graphs make it easy to compare numbers.

1 Read the title of the graph to find out what information is presented.

2 Study the labels on the graph.

3 Look at the source line, which tells where the information is from. Decide whether you can depend on the source to provide reliable information.

4 See if you can make any generalizations about the information in the graph. Note whether the numbers change over time.

5 Read the questions carefully and then study the graph again.

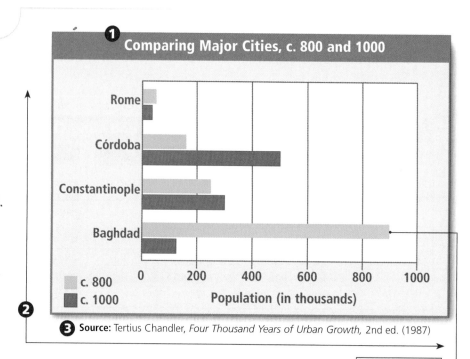

1 Comparing Major Cities, c. 800 and 1000

Rome, Córdoba, Constantinople, Baghdad

☐ c. 800 ☐ c. 1000

Population (in thousands)
0 200 400 600 800 1000

3 **Source:** Tertius Chandler, *Four Thousand Years of Urban Growth,* 2nd ed. (1987)

4 Notice that some cities lost a great deal of their population.

1. Which city showed the greatest growth between the early 800s and the early 1000s?

A. Baghdad
B. Constantinople
C. Córdoba
D. Rome

2. Which statement reflects information in the bar graph?

A. All cities grew in population between the early 800s and the early 1000s.
B. During this time period, the largest cities were located in Europe.
C. Constantinople was the largest city in the world.
D. Some cities in the Muslim world were very large.

answers: 1 (C); 2 (D)

S16

Directions: Use the graphs to answer the following questions.

Exports of English Manufactured Goods, 1699–1774

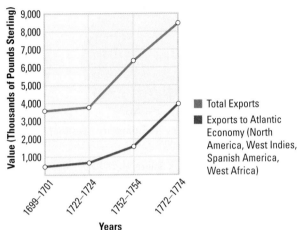

Source: R. Davis, "English Foreign Trade, 1700–1774," *Economic History Review* (1962)

1. Which of the following is a true statement?

   A. Exports to the Atlantic economy declined over time.

   B. Total exports stayed the same over time.

   C. Total exports rose sharply after 1724.

   D. Exports to the Atlantic economy fell sharply after 1754.

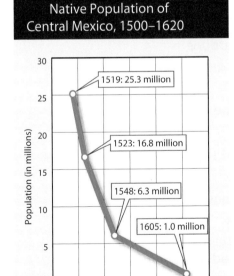

Source: *The Population of Latin America: A History*

2. Between which years did the native population of Central Mexico reach its lowest point?

   A. between 1500 and 1510

   B. between 1580 and 1620

   C. between 1540 and 1580

   D. between 1610 and 1620

Pie Graphs

A pie, or circle, graph shows relationships among parts of a whole. These parts look like slices of a pie. Each slice represents a percentage of the whole pie.

❶ Read the title of the graph to find out what information is presented.

❷ The graph may have a legend, or key, that tells you what the slices represent.

❸ The size of each slice is related to a percentage. The larger the percentage, the larger the slice.

❹ Look at the source line, which tells where the information is from. Ask yourself if you can depend on this source to provide reliable information.

❺ Read the questions carefully and study the graph again.

❸ Remember, the numbers compare the sizes of the slices of the entire pie.

❶ Types of Pottery in a Spanish Colonial Town

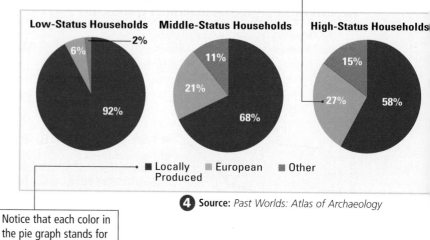

Low-Status Households 2% 6% 92%

Middle-Status Households 11% 21% 68%

High-Status Households 15% 27% 58%

■ Locally Produced ■ European ■ Other

❷ Notice that each color in the pie graph stands for a type of pottery.

❹ **Source:** *Past Worlds: Atlas of Archaeology*

❺

1. What groups of people do the three pie graphs compare?

A. English and Spanish colonists

B. Spanish colonists from different social groups

C. Native Americans and Spanish colonists

D. all of the above

2. Since European pottery had to be imported, it was probably

A. older than the locally produced pottery.

B. more durable than the locally produced pottery.

C. of poorer quality than the locally produced pottery.

D. more expensive than the locally produced pottery.

answers: 1 (B); 2 (D)

Directions: Use the graph to answer the following questions.

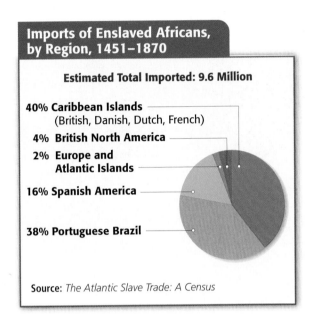

Imports of Enslaved Africans, by Region, 1451–1870

Estimated Total Imported: 9.6 Million

40% **Caribbean Islands** (British, Danish, Dutch, French)

4% **British North America**

2% **Europe and Atlantic Islands**

16% **Spanish America**

38% **Portuguese Brazil**

Source: *The Atlantic Slave Trade: A Census*

1. Which region imported the most enslaved Africans?

   A. Europe and Atlantic Islands
   B. Spanish America
   C. Caribbean Islands
   D. Portuguese Brazil

2. The fewest enslaved Africans were imported to

   A. Europe and Atlantic Islands.
   B. British North America.
   C. the Spanish America.
   D. Portuguese Brazil.

Political Maps

Political maps show the divisions between and within countries. A country may be divided into states or provinces. These maps also show where major cities are. They may also show mountains, oceans, seas, lakes, and rivers.

1 Read the title of the map. This will tell you the subject and purpose of the map.

2 Read the labels on the map. They also give information about the map's subject and purpose.

3 Study the key or legend to help you understand the symbols and/or colors on the map. (This legend shows the colors that indicate the three empires.)

4 Use the scale to estimate distances between places shown on the map. Scales usually show distances in both miles and kilometers.

5 Use the North arrow to figure out directions on the map.

6 Read the questions. Carefully study the map to find the answers.

1 **Empires in South and Southwest Asia, 1500–1660**

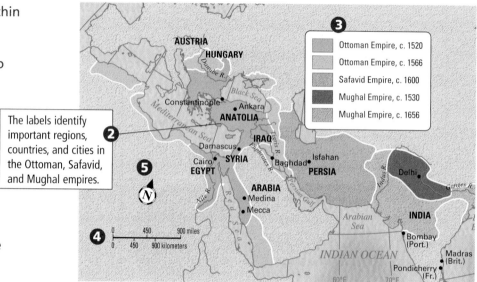

The labels identify important regions, countries, and cities in the Ottoman, Safavid, and Mughal empires.

Legend:
- Ottoman Empire, c. 1520
- Ottoman Empire, c. 1566
- Safavid Empire, c. 1600
- Mughal Empire, c. 1530
- Mughal Empire, c. 1656

1. Which city was within the Mughal Empire in 1530?

A. Bombay

B. Delhi

C. Madras

D. Pondicherry

2. Which empire controlled part of Europe?

A. Ottoman

B. Safavid

C. Mughal

D. all of the above

answers: 1 (B); 2 (A)

Directions: Use the map to answer the following questions.

The Roman Empire, A.D. 400

1. Which area was part of the Eastern Roman Empire?

   A. Spain

   B. Gaul

   C. Anatolia

   D. All of the above

2. The northernmost region in the Western Roman Empire was

   A. Syria.

   B. Gaul.

   C. Spain.

   D. Britain.

Thematic Maps

Thematic maps focus on special topics. For example, a thematic map might show a country's natural resources or major battles in a war.

1 Read the title of the map. This will give you a general idea of the subject and purpose of the map.

2 Read the labels on the map. They also give information about the map's subject and purpose.

3 Study the key or legend to help you understand the symbols on the map. (The arrows show how Buddhism spread.)

4 Ask yourself whether the symbols show a pattern.

5 Read the questions. Carefully study the map to find the answers.

1 The Spread of Buddhism

2 The labels name the major areas of southern and eastern Asia. The dates show when Buddhism first came to each area.

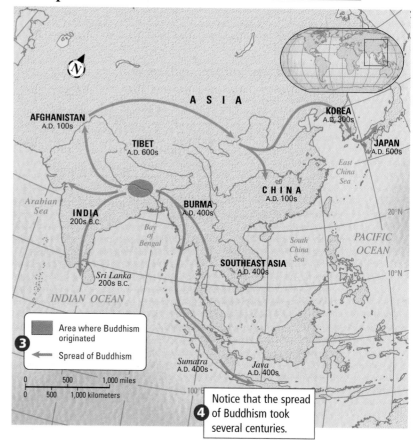

3

Area where Buddhism originated

Spread of Buddhism

0   500   1,000 miles
0 500 1,000 kilometers

4 Notice that the spread of Buddhism took several centuries.

5

1. Where did Buddhism start?

  A. Japan

  B. India

  C. Borneo

  D. Afghanistan

2. Buddhism spread from China to

  A. Japan and Tibet.

  B. Tibet and Korea.

  C. Korea and Japan.

  D. all of the above

answers: 1 (B); 2 (C)

Directions: Use the map to answer the following questions.

The Christian Reconquest of Muslim Spain

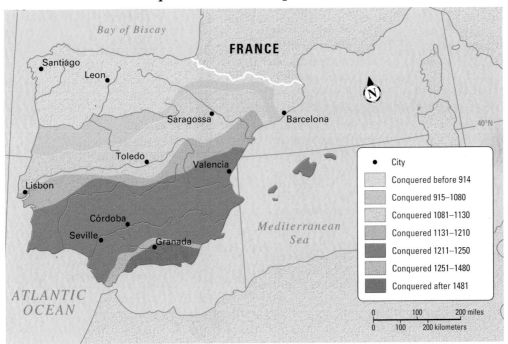

Map showing Bay of Biscay, FRANCE, cities Santiago, Leon, Saragossa, Barcelona, Toledo, Valencia, Lisbon, Córdoba, Seville, Granada; Mediterranean Sea; 40°N; ATLANTIC OCEAN.

Legend:
- City
- Conquered before 914
- Conquered 915–1080
- Conquered 1081–1130
- Conquered 1131–1210
- Conquered 1211–1250
- Conquered 1251–1480
- Conquered after 1481

Scale: 0 100 200 miles / 0 100 200 kilometers

1. By A.D. 1250, how much of Spain did Christians control?

   A. only a small portion
   B. about one third
   C. about one half
   D. almost all

2. When did Christian Spain recover Granada?

   A. 1000
   B. 1150
   C. 1450
   D. 1492

Time Lines

A time line is a chart that lists events in the order in which they occurred. Time lines can be vertical or horizontal.

1 Read the title to learn what period of time the time line covers.

2 Note the dates when the time line begins and ends.

3 Read the events in the order they occurred.

4 Think about what else was going on in the world on these dates. Try to make connections.

5 Read the questions. Then carefully study the time line to find the answers.

❶ The Byzantine Empire

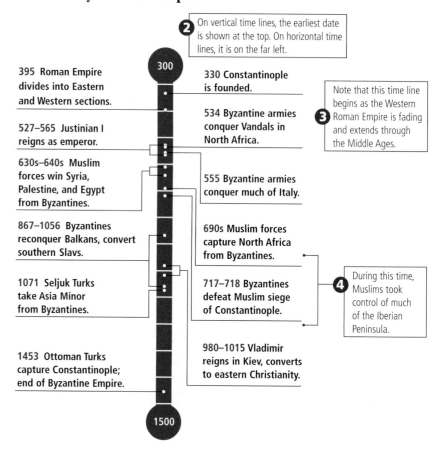

❷ On vertical time lines, the earliest date is shown at the top. On horizontal time lines, it is on the far left.

300

395 Roman Empire divides into Eastern and Western sections.

330 Constantinople is founded.

❸ Note that this time line begins as the Western Roman Empire is fading and extends through the Middle Ages.

527–565 Justinian I reigns as emperor.

534 Byzantine armies conquer Vandals in North Africa.

630s–640s Muslim forces win Syria, Palestine, and Egypt from Byzantines.

555 Byzantine armies conquer much of Italy.

867–1056 Byzantines reconquer Balkans, convert southern Slavs.

690s Muslim forces capture North Africa from Byzantines.

1071 Seljuk Turks take Asia Minor from Byzantines.

717–718 Byzantines defeat Muslim siege of Constantinople.

❹ During this time, Muslims took control of much of the Iberian Peninsula.

980–1015 Vladimir reigns in Kiev, converts to eastern Christianity.

1453 Ottoman Turks capture Constantinople; end of Byzantine Empire.

1500

1. The Byzantine Empire began to lose territory in the

A. 500s.

B. 600s.

C. 700s.

D. 800s.

❺

2. Which event marked the end of the Byzantine Empire?

A. Muslim forces capture North Africa.

B. Seljuk Turks take Asia Minor.

C. Muslim forces win Syria, Palestine, and Egypt.

D. Ottoman Turks capture Constantinople.

answers: 1 (B); 2 (D)

Directions: Use the time line to answer the following questions.

Three Worlds Meet, 1492–1700

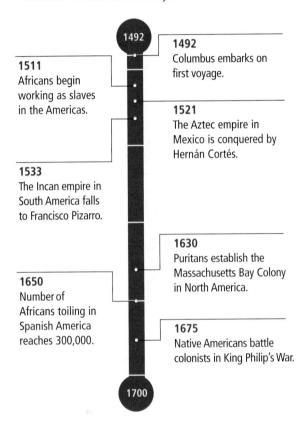

1492
Columbus embarks on first voyage.

1511
Africans begin working as slaves in the Americas.

1521
The Aztec empire in Mexico is conquered by Hernán Cortés.

1533
The Incan empire in South America falls to Francisco Pizarro.

1630
Puritans establish the Massachusetts Bay Colony in North America.

1650
Number of Africans toiling in Spanish America reaches 300,000.

1675
Native Americans battle colonists in King Philip's War.

1. What happened after Hernán Cortés conquered the Aztec empire?

   A. Africans began working as slaves in the Americas.

   B. Francisco Pizarro conquered the Incan empire.

   C. Columbus conquered the Incan empire.

   D. Africans established the Massachusetts Bay Colony.

2. In which year did the number of enslaved Africans in Spanish America reach 300,000?

   A. 1511

   B. 1150

   C. 1650

   D. 1675

Constructed Response

A constructed-response question focuses on a document, such as a photograph, cartoon, chart, graph, or time line. Instead of picking one answer from a set of choices, you write a short response. Sometimes you can find the answer in the document. At other times, you will need to use what you already know about the subject to answer the question.

1 Read the title of the document to get an idea of what it is about.

2 Study the document.

3 Read the questions carefully. Study the document again to find the answers.

4 Write your answers. You don't need to use complete sentences unless the directions say so.

> Constructed-response questions use a wide range of documents. These include short passages, cartoons, charts, graphs, maps, time lines, posters, and other visual materials. This document **2** is a drawing of a confrontation between Aztecs and Spanish soldiers.

1 **Aztecs and Spanish Clash**

The Granger Collection, New York

In this drawing, Aztec warriors and Spanish conquistadors are fighting each other. Hernán Cortés and his men conquered the Aztecs in 1521.

3 **1.** What are the Spanish soldiers standing in?

4 _some sort of stone building_

2. What are the Aztec warriors wearing?

traditional battle dress, including animal skins
and headdresses

3. How are the Spanish and Aztec weapons different?

The Spanish have crossbows and guns, while the
Aztecs have spears and shields.

Directions: Read the following passage from *The Travels of Marco Polo*. Then answer the questions that follow the passage.

On this [New Year's] day all the rulers, and all the provinces and regions and realms where men hold land or lordship under [the Great Khan's] sway, bring him costly gifts of gold and silver and pearls and precious stones and abundance of fine white cloth, so that throughout the year their lord may have no lack of treasure and may live in joy and gladness. . . . I can also assure you for a fact that on this day the Great Khan receives gifts of more than 100,000 white horses, of great beauty and price. And on this day also there is a procession of his elephants, fully 5,000 in number, all draped in fine cloths embroidered with beasts and birds. . . . Let me conclude with one more fact, a very remarkable one well worthy of mention in our book. You must know that a great lion is led into the Great Khan's presence; and as soon as it sees him it flings itself down prostrate before him with every appearance of deep humility and seems to acknowledge him as lord. There it stays without a chain, and is indeed a thing to marvel at.

—*The Travels of Marco Polo*

1. What did the lion do when it was brought before the Great Khan?

   _____

   _____

2. Why did people bring the Great Khan so many gifts?

   _____

   _____

3. What kinds of animals are mentioned in the passage?

   _____

   _____

Extended Response

An extended-response question, like a constructed-response question, focuses on a document of some kind. However, it is more complicated and requires more time to complete.

Some extended-response questions ask you to present the information in the document in a different form. You might be asked to present the information in a chart in graph form, for example. Other questions ask you to complete a document such as a chart or graph. Still others require you to apply your knowledge to information in the document to write an essay.

1 Read the title of the document to get an idea of what it is about.

2 Carefully read directions and questions.

3 Study the document.

4 Sometimes a question may give you part of the answer.

5 A question may require you to write an essay. Write down some ideas in an outline. Then use your outline to write the essay. (A good essay will contain the ideas shown in the sample response to the right.)

3 Like constructed-response questions, extended-response questions involve a wide range of documents. This document is a chart that provides information on three West African kingdoms.

1 Comparing the Kingdoms of West Africa

Kingdom	Key Facts
Ghana (7th–13th centuries)	• Active trans-Saharan trade in gold and salt • King gained wealth by controlling this trade • Rulers converted to Islam in 8th century.
Mali (13th–16th centuries)	• Rose when Ghana was weak and new sources of gold were found • Able leaders included Sundiata (founder) and Mansa Musa • Timbuktu became one of the empire's major cities
Songhai (15th–16th centuries)	• Gained control of the area by building a strong army • Strong leaders included Sunni Ali and Askia Muhammad • Defeated by Moroccans using guns

2 1. In the right-hand column of the chart, note key facts about each of the West African kingdoms listed in the left-hand column. The first entry has been completed for you.

4 This sample answer gives three key facts about the kingdom of Ghana. Your answers for the other kingdoms should provide similar information.

2. Write a short essay describing the trade that was carried on in the West African kingdoms and the ways rulers benefited from it.

5 **Sample Response** *Merchants from North Africa brought salt, textiles, and manufactured goods to the savanna areas where Ghana was located. Salt was vital to the survival of the people of the region, but the area had few deposits. At the same time, Africans from the forests brought gold to the same place. They exchanged these goods, with merchants from both sides paying taxes to the king, who was able to expand his power through the wealth he gained. The Mali and Songhai empires were also built on control of this trade.*

Directions: Use the drawing and passage below to answer question 1.

Smallpox Spreads Among the Aztecs

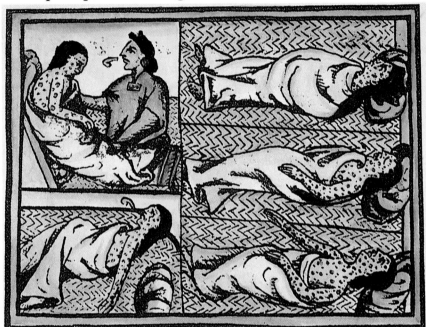

The Granger Collection, New York.

European diseases were like a second "army" of conquerors. Native people had no way to treat diseases like smallpox, typhus fever, or measles. This "army" was more deadly than swords or guns.

— Based on P. M. Ashburn, *The Ranks of Death* (1947)

1. What role did disease play in the Spanish conquest of the Aztecs and Inca?

Document-Based Questions

To answer a document-based question, you have to study more than one document. First you answer a question about each document. Then you use those answers and information from the documents as well as your own knowledge of history to write an essay.

1 Read the "Historical Context" section. It will give you an idea of the topic that will be covered in the question.

2 Read the "Task" section carefully. It tells you what you will need to write about in your essay.

3 Study each document. Think about the connection the documents have to the topic stated in the "Task" section.

4 Read and answer the question about each document. Think about how your answers connect to the "Task" topic.

Introduction

1 **Historical Context:** For hundreds of years, Mongol nomads lived in different tribes. They sometimes fought among themselves. In the late 1100s, a new leader—Genghis Khan—united these tribes. He turned the Mongols into a powerful fighting force.

2 **Task:** Discuss how the Mongols conquered Central Asia and East Asia and how their rule affected Europeans' lives.

Part 1: Short Answer

Study each document carefully. Answer the questions that follow.

3 ### Document 1: Mongol Warrior

4 **What were the characteristics of a Mongol warrior?**

The Mongols were great horsemen who could ride a long way without rest. They attacked without warning and showed no mercy. They used clever tricks to frighten their enemies. Also, they borrowed or invented new weapons of war.

Painting: Victoria & Albert Museum, London/Art Resource, New York.

Document 2: The Mongol Empire

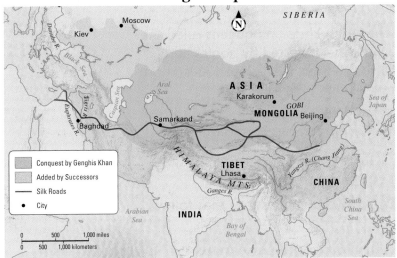

What route linked the Mongol Empire to Europe? What was the main purpose of this route?

Silk Roads; as a trade route between Asia and Europe

Document 3: The Great Khan's Wealth

All those who have gems and pearls and gold and silver must bring them to the Great Khan's mint. . . . By this means the Great Khan acquires all the gold and silver and pearls and precious stones of all his territories [lands]. . . .

The Great Khan must have, as indeed he has, more treasure than anyone else in the world. . . . All the world's great [rulers] put together have not such riches as belong to the Great Khan alone.

—The Travels of Marco Polo (c. 1300)

Why do you think Marco Polo's travels made Europeans want to see East Asia?

Europeans were interested in the treasure of the Great Khan and East Asia.

Part 2: Essay

❺ Write an essay discussing how the Mongols conquered Central Asia and East Asia and how their rule affected Europeans' lives. Use information from the documents, your short answers, and your knowledge of history. **❻**

❺ Read the essay question carefully. Then write a brief outline for your essay.

❻ Write your essay. The first paragraph should introduce your topic. The middle paragraphs should explain it. The closing paragraph should restate the topic and your conclusion. Support your ideas with quotations or details from the documents. Add other supporting facts or details from your knowledge of world history.

❼ A good essay on this topic will contain the ideas in the rubric below.

❼ Essay Rubric The best essays will describe how the Mongols' tactics, fierce will, and strong military organization enabled them to conquer Central Asia and East Asia. (Documents 1 and 2). The essays will also state that Mongol rule brought a period of peace and unity to regions that had been divided. This peace allowed trade to start again along the Silk Roads (Document 2). This trade brought new ideas and products to Europe. Stories of the immense wealth in Mongol lands made Europeans want to tap into those riches (Document 3).

Introduction

Historical Context: For many centuries, kings and queens ruled the countries of Europe. Their power was supported by nobles and armies. European society began to change. In the late 1700s, those changes produced a violent revolution in France.

Task: Discuss how social conflict and new ideas contributed to the French Revolution and why the Revolution turned radical.

Part 1: Short Answer

Study each document carefully. Answer the questions that follow.

Document 1: Social Classes in Prerevolutionary France

LE GRAND ABUS

This cartoon shows a peasant woman carrying women of the nobility and the Church. What does the cartoon say about the lives of the poor before the Revolution?

Engraving: *Le Grand Abus*. Engraving of a cartoon held in the collection of M. de baron de Vinck d'Orp of Brussels/Mary Evans Picture Library, London.

Document 2: A Declaration of Rights

> 1. Men are born and remain free and equal in rights. . . .
>
> 2. The aim of all political association is the preservation of the natural and [unlimited] rights of man. These rights are liberty, property, security, and resistance to oppression.
>
> —*Declaration of the Rights of Man and of the Citizen* (1789)

According to this document, what rights belong to all people?

Document 3: The French Revolution—Major Events

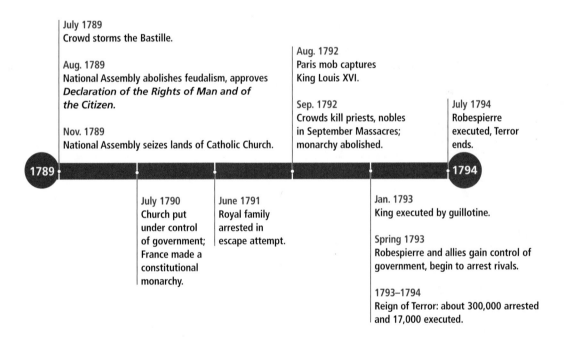

July 1789
Crowd storms the Bastille.

Aug. 1789
National Assembly abolishes feudalism, approves *Declaration of the Rights of Man and of the Citizen.*

Nov. 1789
National Assembly seizes lands of Catholic Church.

Aug. 1792
Paris mob captures King Louis XVI.

Sep. 1792
Crowds kill priests, nobles in September Massacres; monarchy abolished.

July 1794
Robespierre executed, Terror ends.

1789 — 1794

July 1790
Church put under control of government; France made a constitutional monarchy.

June 1791
Royal family arrested in escape attempt.

Jan. 1793
King executed by guillotine.

Spring 1793
Robespierre and allies gain control of government, begin to arrest rivals.

1793–1794
Reign of Terror: about 300,000 arrested and 17,000 executed.

Over time, the Revolution became more violent. How does the information in the time line show this?

Part 2: Essay

Write an essay discussing how social conflict and new ideas led to the French Revolution and why it became so violent. Use information from the documents, your short answers, and your knowledge of history to write your essay.

World Atlas

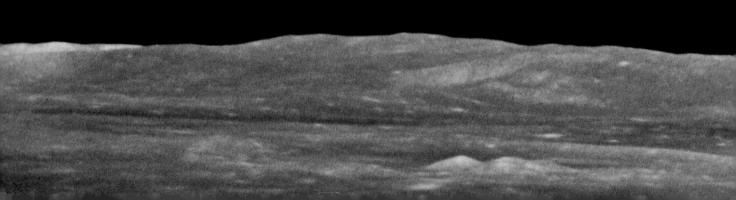

Contents

Complete Legend for Physical and Political Maps

Symbols

 Lake

 Seasonal Lake

 River

 Waterfall

 Canal

 Mountain Peak

Cities

 Los Angeles City over
1,000,000 population

⊡ Calgary City under 1,000,000
population

✪ *Paris* National Capital

Boundaries

 International
Boundary

 Secondary
Boundary

Type Styles Used to Name Features

CHINA Country

O N T A R I O State, Province,
or Territory

PUERTO
RICO (U.S.) Possession

A T L A N T I C
O C E A N Ocean or Sea

A l p s Physical Feature

Borneo Island

Land Elevation and Water Depths

Land Elevation

Meters		Feet
3,000 and over --		-- 9,840 and over
2,000 - 3,000 --		-- 6,560 - 9,840
500 - 2,000 --		-- 1,640 - 6,560
200 - 500 --		-- 656 - 1,640
0 - 200 --		-- 0 - 656

Water Depth

Less than 200 --		-- Less than 656
200 - 2,000 --		-- 656 - 6,560
Over 2,000 --		-- Over 6,560

ARCTIC OCEAN

GREENLAND
(Den.)

Arctic Circle

ICELAND

FAROE IS.
(Den.)

RUSSIA   ALASKA
Yukon (U.S.)

UNITED
KINGDOM

IRELAND

London

Baffin
Bay

Hudson
Bay

C A N A D A

Newfoundland

FRANCE

Missouri

Montréal
Ottawa

Chicago

New York
Washington D.C.

UNITED   STATES

Azores
(Port.)

PORTUGAL

SPAIN

Los Angeles

Colorado

ATLANTIC

MOROCCO

Houston

Mississippi

MIDWAY IS.
(U.S.)

Tropic of Cancer

Gulf of Mexico

BAHAMAS

Canary
Islands
(Sp.)

W. SAHARA

Hawaiian
Islands
(U.S)

MEXICO

CUBA

DOM. REP.

CAPE VERDE

MAURITANIA

MALI

Mexico City

HAITI   PUERTO RICO (U.S.)

JAMAICA

BELIZE

HOND.

SENEGAL

THE GAMBIA

NIGER

PACIFIC

GUAT.

EL. SAL.   NIC.

Caribbean
Sea

GUINEA-BISSAU

GUINEA

BURK
FASO

COSTA
RICA

Caracas

TRINIDAD AND TOBAGO

SIERRA LEONE

CÔTE
D'IVOIRE

GHANA

PANAMA

VENEZUELA

GUYANA

LIBERIA

COLOMBIA

SURINAME

FRENCH GUIANA

KIRIBATI

Equator

Galapagos Islands
(Ecuador)

ECUADOR

Amazon

OCEAN

SAMOA

PERU

BRAZIL

OCEAN

ST. HELENA
(U.K.)

AMERICAN
SAMOA

COOK
ISLANDS
(N.Z.)

TONGA

FRENCH POLYNESIA

BOLIVIA

Tropic of Capricorn

Easter Island
(Chile)

PARAGUAY

Rio de Janeiro

ARGENTINA

URUGUAY

CHILE

Buenos
Aires

N

0   1000   2000 Miles

0   1000   2000   3000 Kilometers

FALKLAND IS.
(U.K.)

South
Georgia
(U.K.)

Copyright by Rand McNally & Co.
Robinson Projection

South
Orkney Is.
(U.K.)

Antarctic Circle

South
Shetland Is.
(U.K.)

Weddell
Sea

ARCTIC OCEAN

Spitsbergen
(Nor.)

Franz Josef
Land

Novaya
Zemlya

NORWAY
FINLAND
SWEDEN
EST.
LAT.
DEN.
LITH.
orth
Sea
BEL.
GERMANY
POLAND
BELARUS
NETH.
CZ.
SWITZ.
AUS. HUNG. SLVK.
MOLD.
UKRAINE
ITALY
CRO. BOS.
SERB.
ROM.
Rome
ALB. MA.
BUL.
GREECE
TURKEY
TUNISIA
Crete
CYPRUS
LEB.
ISRAEL
SYRIA
JORDAN
IRAQ
ALGERIA
LIBYA
EGYPT
Cairo
KUWAIT
QATAR
U.A.E.
SAUDI
ARABIA
NIGER
CHAD
SUDAN
YEMEN
DJIBOUTI
NIGERIA
Lagos
CENTRAL
AFRICAN
REPUBLIC
Addis
Ababa
ETHIOPIA
CAMEROON
EQUAT. GUIN.
GABON
Congo
REP. OF
CONGO
RWANDA
DEM. REP.
OF CONGO
BURUNDI
UGANDA
KENYA
SOMALIA
TANZANIA
ANGOLA
ZAMBIA
COMOROS
MALAWI
NAMIBIA
ZIMBABWE
MOZAMBIQUE
BOTSWANA
MADAGASCAR
MAURITIUS
REUNION
(Fr.)
SWAZILAND
SOUTH
AFRICA
LESOTHO
Cape Town

Volga
Moscow
RUSSIA
Ob'
Yenisey
Lena
Sea of Okhotsk
Bering
Sea
KAZAKHSTAN
Black Sea
GEO.
ARM. AZER.
UZBEKISTAN
KYRG.
TAJIK.
TURKMENISTAN
AFGHANISTAN
IRAN
PAKISTAN
MONGOLIA
Beijing
CHINA
NORTH
KOREA
SOUTH
KOREA
Sea of Japan
JAPAN
Tokyo
Chang Jiang
(Yangtze)
Shanghai
NEPAL
BHU.
Ganges
Kolkata
(Calcutta)
BNGL.
MYANMAR
TAIWAN
Mumbai
(Bombay)
INDIA
Arabian
Sea
LAOS
Bay of
Bengal
THAILAND
VIETNAM
Bangkok
CAMBODIA
South China
Sea
PHILIPPINES
PALAU
SRI LANKA
MALDIVES
BRUNEI
MALAYSIA
SINGAPORE
Borneo
Sumatra
Java
Jakarta
INDONESIA
EAST TIMOR
PAPUA
NEW GUINEA
New Guinea
SEYCHELLES
Nile
Red Sea
ERITREA
OMAN

Mediterranean Sea

PACIFIC
Tropic of Cancer
NORTHERN
MARIANA ISLANDS
(U.S.)
WAKE ISLAND
(U.S.)
GUAM (U.S.)
OCEAN
FED. STATES OF
MICRONESIA
MARSHALL
ISLANDS
Equator
SOLOMON
ISLANDS
VANUATU
NEW CALEDONIA
(Fr.)
FIJI
Coral Sea
Tropic of Capricorn

INDIAN

OCEAN

Kerguelen
Islands
(Fr.)

AUSTRALIA
Darling
Sydney
Tasmania
NEW ZEALAND

SOUTHERN OCEAN

Antarctic Circle

ANTARCTICA

15° 30° 45° 60° 75° 90° 105° 120° 135° 150° 165° 180°

ARCTIC OCEAN

Baffin
Island

Baffin
Bay

Greenland

Jan Mayen

Arctic Circle

Iceland

Mt. McKinley
20,320 Ft.
6,194m

Yukon

Mackenzie

Canadian Shield

Hudson
Bay

Faroe Is.

British
Isles

Aleutian Islands

NORTH

Rocky Mountains

Great Plains

St. Lawrence

Newfoundland

London

AMERICA

Los Angeles

Colorado

Appalachian Mts.

Washington D.C.

Iberian
Peninsula

Azores

Atlas
Mts.

Mississippi

Cape Hatteras

ATLANTIC

Midway Is.

Baja
California

Gulf of Mexico

Canary
Islands

Tropic of Cancer

Hawaiian Islands

Yucatan
Peninsula

Cuba

Hispaniola

Jamaica

Puerto Rico

Cape
Verde
Islands

Caribbean
Sea

Cape Verde

Niger

PACIFIC

Orinoco

Trinidad

OCEAN

Palmyra

Galapagos Islands

Amazon

Amazon

Equator

SOUTH

Kiribati

Basin

Andes

AMERICA

OCEAN

Marquesas Is.

St. Helena

Samoa Islands

Mato Grosso
Plateau

Tonga
Is.

Cook
Islands

Tahiti

Rio de Janeiro

Tropic of Capricorn

Andes

Parana

Easter Island

N

Mt. Aconcagua
22,831 Ft.
6,959m

Buenos Aires

Chatham Is.

Patagonia

Falkland Is.

South
Georgia

0   1000   2000 Miles

Tierra del Fuego

South
Sandwich Is.

0   1000   2000   3000 Kilometers

Cape Horn

South
Orkney Is.

Copyright by Rand McNally & Co.
Robinson Projection

South
Shetland Is.

Antarctic Circle

Antarctic
Peninsula

Weddell
Sea

Ross
Sea

Marie
Byrd
Land

Vinson Massif
16,066 Ft.
4,897m

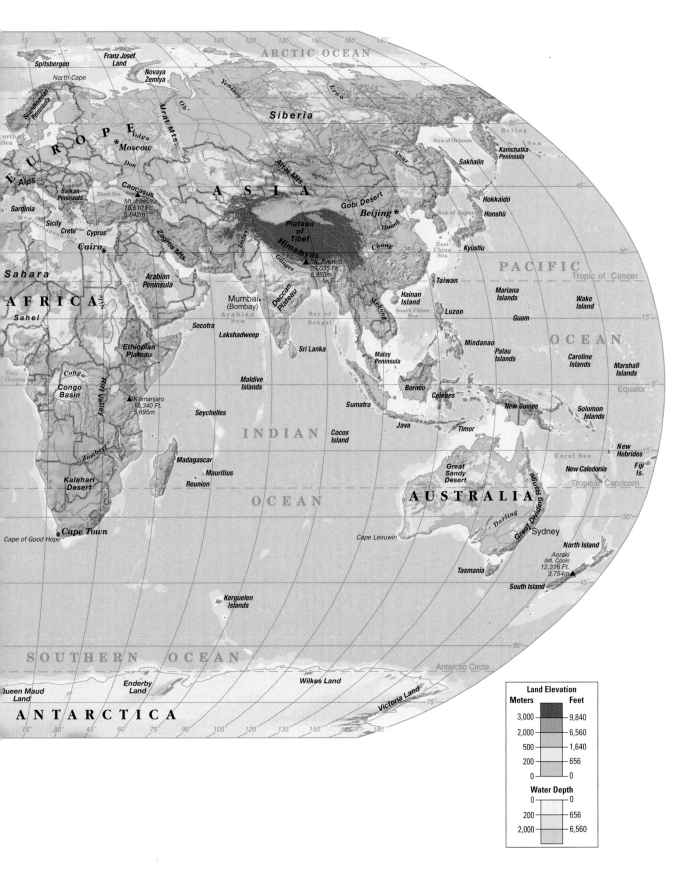

ARCTIC OCEAN

Spitsbergen
Franz Josef Land
North Cape
Novaya Zemlya

Scandinavian Peninsula

EUROPE
*Moscow
Volga
Don
Caucasus
Mt. Elbrus 18,510 Ft. 5,642m
Black Sea
Balkan Peninsula
Alps
Sardinia
Sicily
Crete
Cyprus
Mediterranean Sea

North Sea
Aral Sea
Caspian Sea

Ural Mts.
Ob'
Yenisey
Lena

SIBERIA

ASIA

Altai Mts.
Amur

Sea of Okhotsk
Bering Sea
Kamchatka Peninsula
Sakhalin

Gobi Desert
Beijing*
Huang
Chang

Hokkaidō
Honshū
Sea of Japan
Kyūshū

Plateau of Tibet
Himalayas
Mt. Everest 29,035 Ft. 8,850m
Indus
Ganges

East China Sea
Taiwan

Zagros Mts.
Cairo*
Sahara
Red Sea

Nile
Arabian Peninsula

Arabian Sea

Mumbai (Bombay)
Deccan Plateau

Bay of Bengal

Hainan Island
South China Sea
Luzon

PACIFIC

Tropic of Cancer

Mariana Islands
Guam

Wake Island

OCEAN

AFRICA
Sahel

Socotra
Lakshadweep

Sri Lanka

Malay Peninsula

Mindanao
Palau Islands

Caroline Islands

Marshall Islands

Gulf of Guinea

Ethiopian Plateau

Congo Basin
Congo

Rift Valley

▲Kilimanjaro 19,340 Ft. 5,895m

Maldive Islands

Seychelles

INDIAN

Sumatra

Java

Cocos Island

Borneo
Celebes
Timor

New Guinea
Solomon Islands

Equator

New Hebrides

Zambezi

Madagascar

Mauritius
Reunion

OCEAN

Great Sandy Desert

AUSTRALIA
Darling
Great Dividing Range
Sydney

Coral Sea
New Caledonia
Fiji Is.

Tropic of Capricorn

Kalahari Desert

Cape Town*
Cape of Good Hope

Kerguelen Islands

Cape Leeuwin

Tasmania

North Island
Aoraki (Mt. Cook) 12,316 Ft. 3,754m▲
South Island

SOUTHERN OCEAN

Antarctic Circle

Queen Maud Land
Enderby Land

Wilkes Land

Victoria Land

ANTARCTICA

Land Elevation		
Meters		**Feet**
3,000		9,840
2,000		6,560
500		1,640
200		656
0		0

Water Depth		
0		0
200		656
2,000		6,560

✿ RAND MᶜNALLY

A5

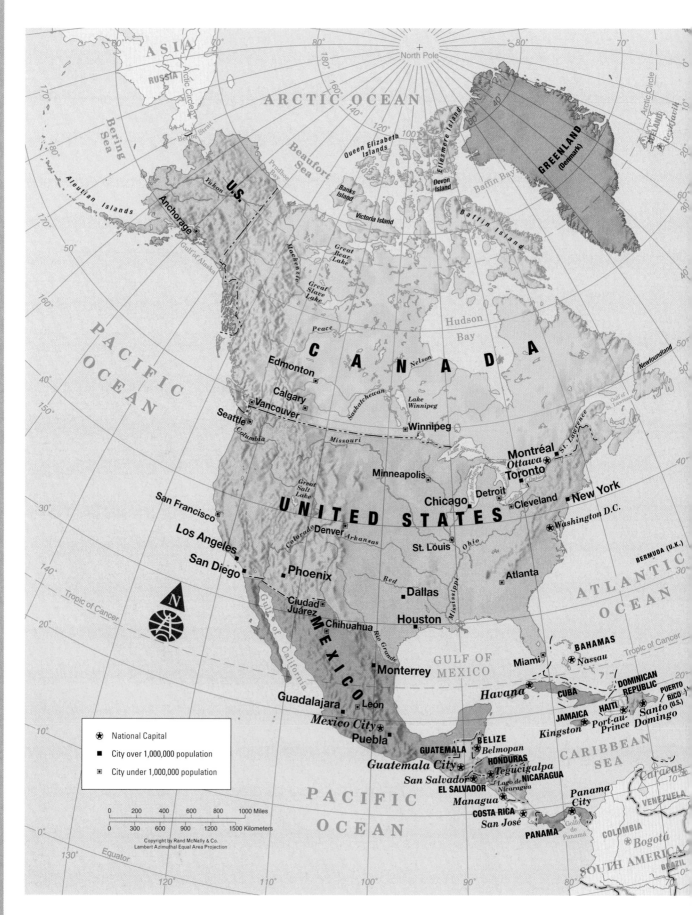

ASIA

RUSSIA

Arctic Circle

ARCTIC OCEAN

North Pole

GREENLAND
(Denmark)

ICELAND
Reykjavik

Arctic Circle

Bering
Sea

Beaufort
Sea

Queen Elizabeth
Islands

Ellesmere Island

Devon
Island

Aleutian Islands

Bering Strait

Prudhoe
Bay

U.S.

Anchorage

Gulf of Alaska

Yukon

Mackenzie

Banks
Island

Victoria Island

Baffin Bay

Baffin Island

Great
Bear
Lake

Great
Slave
Lake

Hudson
Bay

Newfoundland

PACIFIC

OCEAN

Peace

Nelson

C A N A D A

Gulf of
St. Lawrence

Edmonton

Calgary

Vancouver

Seattle

Columbia

Saskatchewan

Lake
Winnipeg

Winnipeg

Missouri

Lake Superior

St. Lawrence

Montréal
Ottawa
Toronto

Minneapolis

Lake Michigan

Lake Huron

Chicago

Detroit

Lake Ontario

Cleveland

New York

San Francisco

UNITED STATES

Great
Salt
Lake

Colorado

Denver

Arkansas

St. Louis

Ohio

Washington D.C.

BERMUDA (U.K.)

Los Angeles

San Diego

Phoenix

Red

Dallas

Mississippi

Atlanta

ATLANTIC

OCEAN

N

Ciudad
Juárez

Chihuahua

M E X I C O

Houston

Gulf of California

Rio Grande

GULF OF
MEXICO

Miami

BAHAMAS

Nassau

Tropic of Cancer

Tropic of Cancer

Monterrey

Havana

CUBA

DOMINICAN
REPUBLIC

PUERTO
RICO
(U.S.)

Guadalajara

León

JAMAICA

HAITI

Santo
Domingo

Mexico City

Puebla

Kingston

Port-au-
Prince

Caracas

Guatemala City

GUATEMALA

BELIZE

Belmopan

HONDURAS

Tegucigalpa

NICARAGUA

CARIBBEAN
SEA

VENEZUELA

San Salvador

EL SALVADOR

Lago de
Nicaragua

Managua

COSTA RICA

San José

Panama
City

PANAMA

Golfo
de
Panamá

COLOMBIA

Bogotá

PACIFIC

OCEAN

SOUTH AMERICA

BRAZIL

Equator

⊛ National Capital

■ City over 1,000,000 population

☐ City under 1,000,000 population

0   200   400   600   800   1000 Miles

0   300   600   900   1200   1500 Kilometers

Copyright by Rand McNally & Co.
Lambert Azimuthal Equal Area Projection

⊛ RAND McNALLY

A6

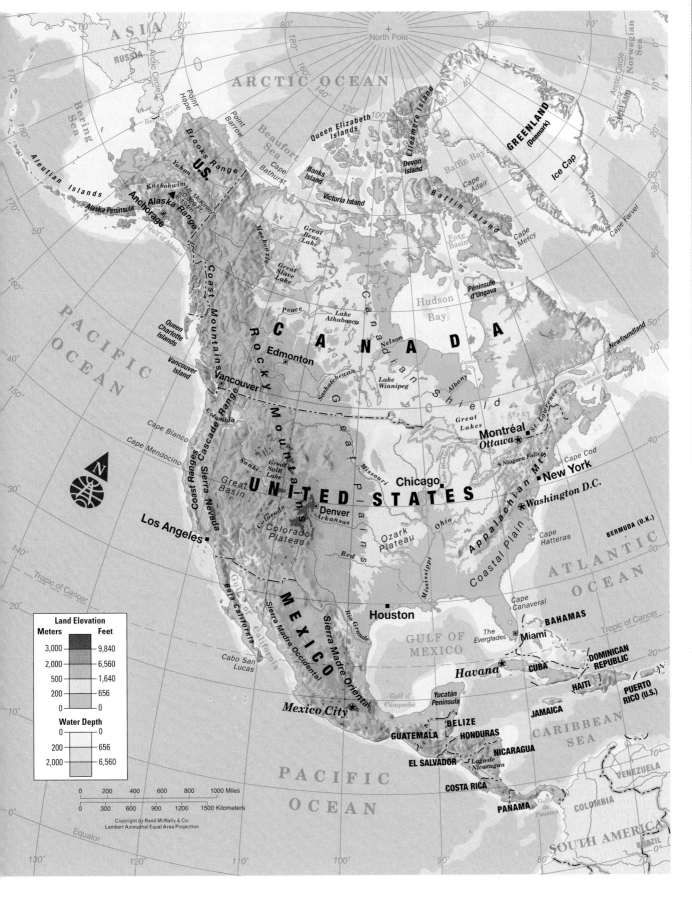

Land Elevation

Meters		Feet
3,000		9,840
2,000		6,560
500		1,640
200		656
0		0

Water Depth

0		0
200		656
2,000		6,560

0	200	400	600	800	1000 Miles

0	300	600	900	1200	1500 Kilometers

Copyright by Rand McNally & Co.
Lambert Azimuthal Equal Area Projection

RAND McNALLY

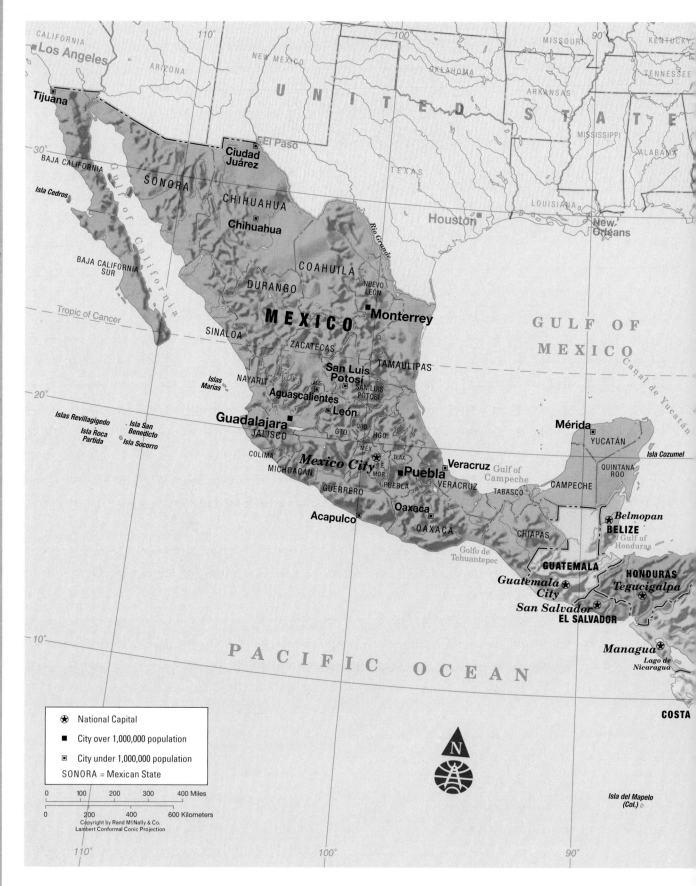

CALIFORNIA
Los Angeles
Tijuana
110°
NEW MEXICO
30°
El Paso
Ciudad
Juárez
BAJA CALIFORNIA
SONORA
CHIHUAHUA
ARIZONA
Isla Cedros
Chihuahua
TEXAS
UNITED STATES
OKLAHOMA
ARKANSAS
MISSOURI
90°
KENTUCKY
TENNESSEE
MISSISSIPPI
ALABAMA
LOUISIANA
Houston
New
Orleans
100°
Río Grande
COAHUILA
DURANGO
NUEVO
LEÓN
BAJA CALIFORNIA
SUR
Tropic of Cancer
MEXICO
Monterrey
GULF OF
MEXICO
SINALOA
ZACATECAS
TAMAULIPAS
Canal de Yucatán
20°
Islas
Marías
NAYARIT
San Luis
Potosí
SAN LUIS
POTOSÍ
Aguascalientes
Islas Revillagigedo
Isla San
Benedicto
Isla Roca
Partida
Isla Socorro
AGS
León
Guadalajara
JALISCO
GTO.
QRO.
HGO.
Mérida
YUCATÁN
Isla Cozumel
QUINTANA
ROO
COLIMA
MEX.
Mexico City
D.F.
MOR.
TLAX.
Veracruz
Gulf of
Campeche
MICHOACÁN
PUEBLA
Puebla
VERACRUZ
CAMPECHE
GUERRERO
TABASCO
Acapulco
Oaxaca
OAXACA
CHIAPAS
Belmopan
BELIZE
Gulf of
Honduras
Golfo de
Tehuantepec
GUATEMALA
HONDURAS
Tegucigalpa
Guatemala
City
San Salvador
EL SALVADOR
10°
PACIFIC OCEAN
Managua
Lago de
Nicaragua
COSTA

Gulf of California
Gulf of California

National Capital
■ City over 1,000,000 population
▣ City under 1,000,000 population
SONORA = Mexican State

0   100   200   300   400 Miles
0   200   400   600 Kilometers
Copyright by Rand McNally & Co.
Lambert Conformal Conic Projection

N

110°
100°
90°

Isla del Mapelo
(Col.)

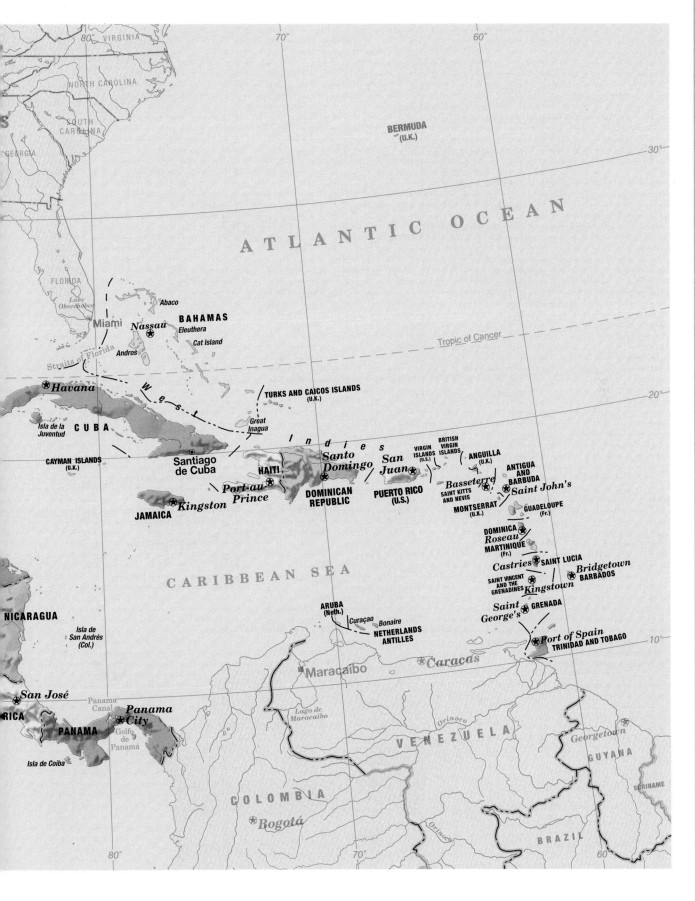

80° VIRGINIA

NORTH CAROLINA

70°

60°

SOUTH CAROLINA

GEORGIA

30°

BERMUDA
(U.K.)

A T L A N T I C   O C E A N

FLORIDA

Lake
Okeechobee

Abaco

Tropic of Cancer

Miami

Nassau

BAHAMAS

Eleuthera

Cat Island

20°

Straits of Florida

Andros

West

Havana

Isla de la
Juventud

CUBA

TURKS AND CAICOS ISLANDS
(U.K.)

Indies

CAYMAN ISLANDS
(U.K.)

Santiago
de Cuba

Great
Inagua

Santo
Domingo

San
Juan

VIRGIN
ISLANDS
(U.S.)

BRITISH
VIRGIN
ISLANDS

ANGUILLA
(U.K.)

ANTIGUA
AND
BARBUDA

HAITI

Basseterre

Saint John's

Port-au-
Prince

DOMINICAN
REPUBLIC

PUERTO RICO
(U.S.)

SAINT KITTS
AND NEVIS

Kingston

MONTSERRAT
(U.K.)

GUADELOUPE
(Fr.)

JAMAICA

DOMINICA
Roseau

MARTINIQUE
(Fr.)

C A R I B B E A N   S E A

Castries

SAINT LUCIA

Bridgetown
BARBADOS

SAINT VINCENT
AND THE
GRENADINES

Kingstown

NICARAGUA

Isla de
San Andrés
(Col.)

ARUBA
(Neth.)

Curaçao

Bonaire

NETHERLANDS
ANTILLES

Saint
George's

GRENADA

San José

Panama
Canal

Port of Spain
TRINIDAD AND TOBAGO

10°

Caracas

RICA

Maracaibo

Panama
City

PANAMA

Golfo
de
Panamá

Lago de
Maracaibo

Orinoco

V E N E Z U E L A

Georgetown

Isla de Coiba

GUYANA

SURINAME

80°

70°

COLOMBIA

Bogotá

Orinoco

60°

B R A Z I L

RAND M°NALLY

A9

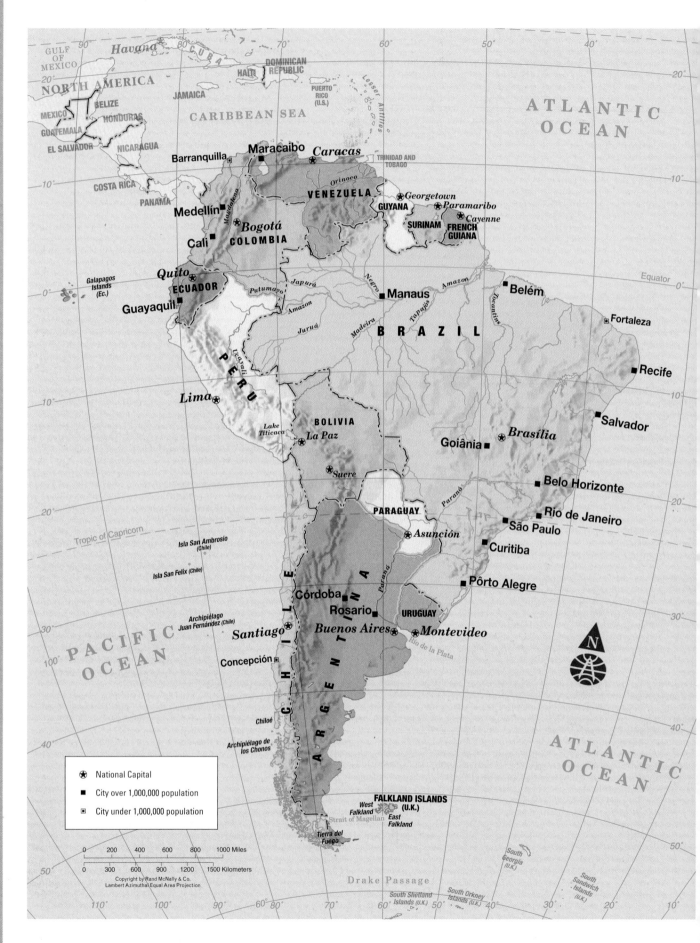

GULF OF MEXICO

Havana

CUBA

DOMINICAN REPUBLIC

HAITI

NORTH AMERICA

BELIZE

MEXICO

JAMAICA

PUERTO RICO (U.S.)

GUATEMALA

HONDURAS

EL SALVADOR

NICARAGUA

CARIBBEAN SEA

Lesser Antilles

ATLANTIC OCEAN

COSTA RICA

PANAMA

Barranquilla

Maracaibo

Caracas

TRINIDAD AND TOBAGO

Medellín

VENEZUELA

Georgetown

Paramaribo

Cayenne

Orinoco

GUYANA

SURINAM

FRENCH GUIANA

Bogotá

Cali

COLOMBIA

Magdalena

Quito

Galapagos Islands (Ec.)

ECUADOR

Guayaquil

Putumayo

Japurá

Negro

Amazon

Belém

Equator

Manaus

Fortaleza

Amazon

Juruá

Madeira

Tapajós

Tocantins

B R A Z I L

Ucayali

P E R U

Lima

Recife

Lake Titicaca

BOLIVIA

La Paz

Salvador

Goiânia

Brasília

Sucre

Belo Horizonte

Paraná

Rio de Janeiro

PARAGUAY

São Paulo

Tropic of Capricorn

Isla San Ambrosio (Chile)

Asunción

Curitiba

Paraná

Isla San Felix (Chile)

Pôrto Alegre

Archipiélago Juan Fernández (Chile)

Córdoba

Rosario

URUGUAY

PACIFIC OCEAN

Santiago

C H I L E

A R G E N T I N A

Buenos Aires

Montevideo

Río de la Plata

Concepción

N

Chiloé

ATLANTIC OCEAN

Archipiélago de los Chonos

FALKLAND ISLANDS (U.K.)

West Falkland

East Falkland

★ National Capital

■ City over 1,000,000 population

▣ City under 1,000,000 population

Strait of Magellan

Tierra del Fuego

South Georgia (U.K.)

0 200 400 600 800 1000 Miles

0 300 600 900 1200 1500 Kilometers

Copyright by Rand McNally & Co.
Lambert Azimuthal Equal Area Projection

Drake Passage

South Shetland Islands (U.K.)

South Orkney Islands (U.K.)

South Sandwich Islands (U.K.)

ne110

NORTH AMERICA

GULF OF MEXICO

MEXICO
BELIZE
GUATEMALA
Gulf of Honduras
HONDURAS
EL SALVADOR
NICARAGUA
COSTA RICA
PANAMA
Gulf of Panama

CUBA
JAMAICA
Greater Antilles
HAITI
DOMINICAN REPUBLIC
PUERTO RICO (U.S.)
CARIBBEAN SEA
Lesser Antilles
TRINIDAD AND TOBAGO

ATLANTIC OCEAN

⊛ Caracas

Orinoco
Llanos
VENEZUELA
GUYANA
SURINAM
FRENCH GUIANA
Cape Orange

Magdalena
⊛ Bogotá
COLOMBIA

Galapagos Islands (Ec.)

ECUADOR

Putumayo
Japurá
Negro
Amazon
Ilha de Marajó
Belém
Equator

Amazon
Manaus
Tapajós
Amazon Basin
Juruá
Madeira
BRAZIL

Ucayali
Selvas

A N D E S
P E R U

Lima ⊛

Lake Titicaca

Cordillera Oriental

BOLIVIA

Mato Grosso Plateau

Brasília ⊛
São Francisco
Brazilian Highlands

Recife

Gran Chaco

PARAGUAY

Paraná

São Paulo
Rio de Janeiro

Tropic of Capricorn

Isla San Ambrosio (Chile)

Isla San Felix (Chile)

A N D E S

C H I L E

A R G E N T I N A

Paraná

PACIFIC OCEAN

Archipiélago Juan Fernández (Chile)

Santiago ⊛
Mt. Aconcagua 22,831 Ft. 6,959m
Buenos Aires ⊛
Pampas
Río de la Plata

URUGUAY

Atacama Desert

Land Elevation

Meters		Feet
3,000		9,840
2,000		6,560
500		1,640
200		656
0		0

Water Depth

0		0
200		656
2,000		6,560

San Matías Gulf
Península Valdés

Patagonia

Chiloé

San Jorge Gulf

Point Medanoso

ATLANTIC OCEAN

Grand Bay
West Falkland
FALKLAND ISLANDS (U.K.)
East Falkland

Strait of Magellan

Tierra del Fuego
Cape Horn

South Georgia (U.K.)

N

0   200   400   600   800   1000 Miles
0   300   600   900   1200   1500 Kilometers

Copyright by Rand McNally & Co.
Lambert Azimuthal Equal Area Projection

Drake Passage

South Shetland Islands (U.K.)
South Orkney Islands (U.K.)
South Sandwich Islands (U.K.)

A11

ICELAND
Reykjavik

ATLANTIC
OCEAN

Arctic Circle

NORWEGIAN
SEA

FAROE ISLANDS
(Den.)

NORWAY   SWEDEN

Gulf of Bothnia

Oslo

Stockholm

SCOTLAND

Glasgow

Edinburgh

Vänern   Vättern
Göteborg

Skagerrak

NORTH
SEA

DENMARK

BALTIC SEA

Copenhagen

LITHUANIA

Kaliningrad   RUSSIA

UNITED
KINGDOM

NORTHERN
IRELAND

Belfast

Irish
Sea

Dublin
IRELAND

Liverpool   Manchester

WALES

Birmingham

ENGLAND

London

Thames

St. George's Channel

English Channel

Strait of Dover

NETHERLANDS

Amsterdam
The Hague

Hamburg

Berlin

Elbe

Oder

POLAND

Warsaw

Łódź

Wrocław

Kraków

Brussels   BELGIUM
Luxembourg   LUX.

Cologne
Rhine

GERMANY

Frankfurt

Prague

CZECH
REPUBLIC

Danube

SLOVAKIA

Paris

Seine

Loire

FRANCE

Bordeaux

Bay of Biscay

Lyon

Rhône

Toulouse

Marseille

Bern   LIECH.
SWITZERLAND

Munich

Vienna
AUSTRIA

Bratislava

Budapest
HUNGARY

Milan

SLOVENIA   Ljubljana

Zagreb

Belgrade

Genoa

Po

CROATIA

SAN
MARINO

BOSNIA AND
HERZEGOVINA

Sarajevo

SERBIA AND
MONTENEGRO

ADRIATIC SEA

Skopje

MACE-
DONIA

ALBANIA

Tirané

MONACO

Corsica
(Fr.)

Rome
VATICAN CITY

ITALY

ANDORRA

Barcelona

Lisbon
PORTUGAL

Madrid

Tagus

SPAIN

Valencia

Seville

Ebro

Strait of Gibraltar

GIBRALTAR
(U.K.)

Rabat

Algiers

AFRICA

MOROCCO

ALGERIA

TUNISIA

Tunis

Sardinia
(It.)

Naples

TYRRHENIAN
SEA

Palermo

Sicily

IONIAN
SEA

MEDITERRANEAN SEA

Valletta   MALTA

N

National Capital

City over 1,000,000 population

City under 1,000,000 population

0	100	200	300	400 Miles
0	200	400		600 Kilometers

Copyright by Rand McNally & Co.
Lambert Conformal Conic Projection

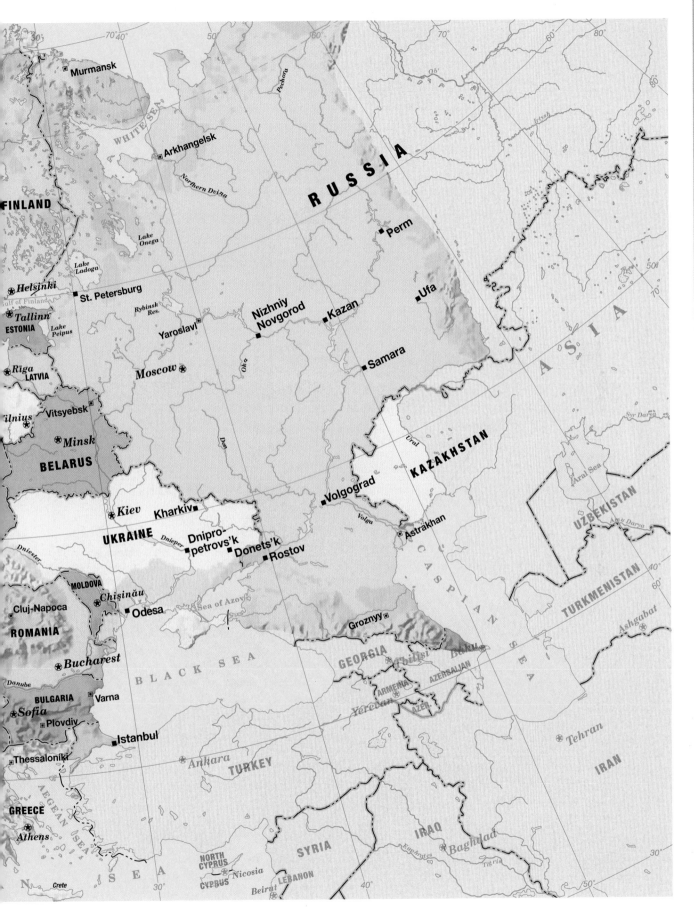

Murmansk

WHITE SEA

Arkhangelsk

Northern Dvina

Pechora

R U S S I A

FINLAND

Lake Onega

Perm

Ob'

Lake Ladoga

Helsinki

St. Petersburg

Rybinsk Res.

Nizhniy Novgorod

Kazan

Ufa

Gulf of Finland

Tallinn

ESTONIA

Lake Peipus

Yaroslavl

Oka

A S I A

Syr Darya

Riga

LATVIA

Moscow

Samara

Don

Vilnius

Vitsyebsk

Ural

Aral Sea

Minsk

KAZAKHSTAN

BELARUS

UZBEKISTAN

Kiev

Kharkiv

Volgograd

Amu Darya

Dnieper

Dnipro-petrovs'k

Volga

Astrakhan

TURKMENISTAN

UKRAINE

Donets'k

Rostov

Dniester

MOLDOVA

Chişinău

Sea of Azov

Ashgabat

Cluj-Napoca

Odesa

Groznyy

CASPIAN SEA

ROMANIA

Bucharest

B L A C K   S E A

GEORGIA

Tbilisi

Baku

Danube

AZERBAIJAN

BULGARIA

Varna

ARMENIA

AZER.

Sofia

Plovdiv

Yerevan

Tehran

Istanbul

Ankara

IRAN

Thessaloníki

TURKEY

GREECE

AEGEAN SEA

IRAQ

Baghdad

Athens

Euphrates

SYRIA

Tigris

N

Crete

NORTH CYPRUS

Nicosia

LEBANON

CYPRUS

Beirut

ICELAND

ATLANTIC
OCEAN

Arctic Circle

NORWEGIAN
SEA

Lofoten Islands

Lap

Tornedalen

Scandinavian
Peninsula

NORWAY   SWEDEN

Glama

Klarälven

Dalälven

Stockholm

Vänern   Vättern

Gulf
of
Bothnia

BALTIC   SEA

Öland

FAROE ISLANDS
(Den.)

Hebrides

Orkney
Islands

UNITED
KINGDOM

NORTH
SEA

DENMARK

Skagerrak

Bornholm
(Den.)

RUSSIA

Irish
Sea

IRELAND

St. George's Channel

Great
Britain

Thames

London

English Channel

Strait of Dover

NETHERLANDS

Elbe

Northern   Europ

Berlin

Oder

POLAND

BELGIUM

GERMANY

Rhine

LUX.

Wisla

Paris

Paris
Basin

Seine

Loire

FRANCE

Black
Forest

Bohemian
Forest

CZECH
REPUBLIC

Danube

SLOVAKIA

Saone

Jura

SWITZERLAND

LIECH.

AUSTRIA

HUNGARY

Great Hungarian
Plain

Bay of Biscay

Dordogne

Massif
Central

Rhone

A l p s

SLOVENIA

Drava

CROATIA

Po

Apennines

SAN
MARINO

Dinaric Alps

BOSNIA AND
HERZEGOVINA

Balkan

MONACO

Douro

Ebro

Duero

PORTUGAL

Pyrenees

ANDORRA

Corsica
(Fr.)

Lisbon

Iberian
Peninsula

Tagus

SPAIN

Rome

ITALY

ADRIATIC SEA

SERBIA AND
MONTENEGRO

ALBANIA

MACE-
DONIA

Pindus Mts.

Balearic Islands

Minorca

Sardinia
(It.)

Strait of Gibraltar

GIBRALTAR
(U.K.)

Ibiza   Majorca

TYRRHENIAN
SEA

MEDITERRANE

Algiers

AFRICA

MOROCCO

ALGERIA

Sicily

IONIAN
SEA

TUNISIA

MALTA

Land Elevation

Meters	Feet
3,000	9,840
2,000	6,560
500	1,640
200	656
0	0

Water Depth

0	0
200	656
2,000	6,560

N

0   100   200   300   400 Miles

0   200   400   600 Kilometers

Copyright by Rand McNally & Co.
Lambert Conformal Conic Projection

Murmansk

Kola
Peninsula
Ponoy

Mezen

Pechora

WHITE SEA

Ural Mountains

ASIA

80°
70°
60°

Irtysh

Ob

FINLAND

Northern Dvina

Onega

Sukhona

Kama

Lake
Onega

Lake
Ladoga

Helsinki

Gulf of Finland

Rybinsk
Res.

R U S S I A

ESTONIA

Lake
Peipus

Moscow

Oka

Ural

KAZAKHSTAN

50°

70°

Aral Sea

Syr Darya

UZBEKISTAN

LATVIA

Central
Russian
Upland

Khopër

Caspian Depression

LITHUANIA

ean

Plain

Neman

Don

Amu Darya

BELARUS

Volga

TURKMENISTAN

Pripyat

60°

40°

Kiev

UKRAINE

Dnieper

CASPIAN SEA

Dniester

Baku

MOLDOVA

Carpathian Mts.

Sea of Azov

Crimean
Peninsula

Caucasus

Mt. Elbrus
18,510 Ft.
5,642m

GEORGIA

ROMANIA

Transylvanian Alps

BLACK SEA

ARMENIA

AZERBAIJAN

AZER.

Tehran

Danube

Peninsula

BULGARIA

Istanbul

IRAN

Mt. Olympus
9,570 Ft.
2,917m

TURKEY

GREECE

AEGEAN SEA

30°

IRAQ

SYRIA

Euphrates

Tigris

30°

Rhodes

NORTH
CYPRUS

LEBANON

Crete

SEA

CYPRUS

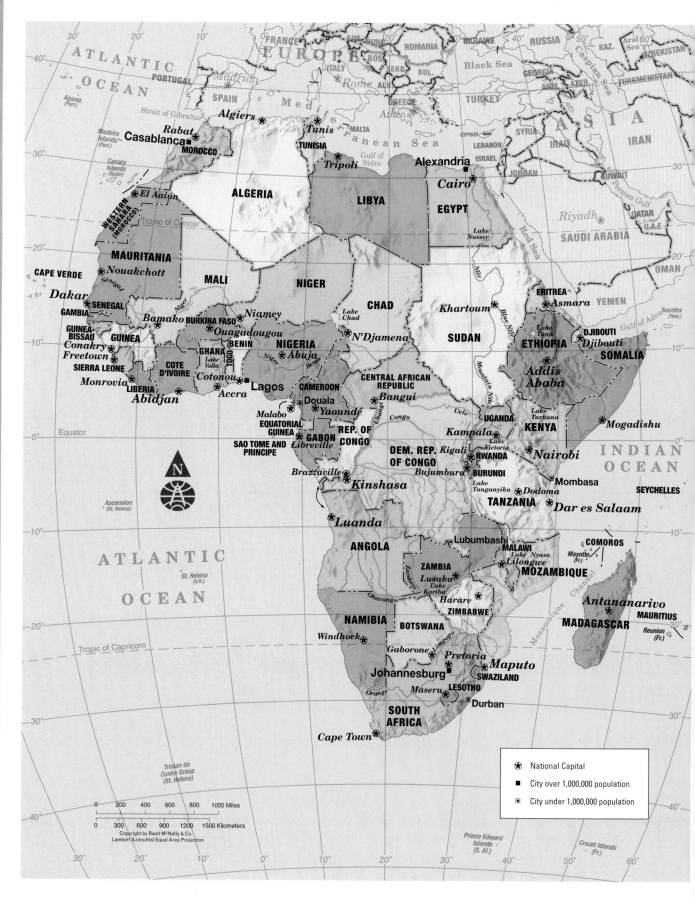

Legend:

⊛ National Capital

■ City over 1,000,000 population

▢ City under 1,000,000 population

Scale:
0 200 400 600 800 1000 Miles
0 300 600 900 1200 1500 Kilometers
Copyright by Rand McNally & Co.
Lambert Azimuthal Equal Area Projection

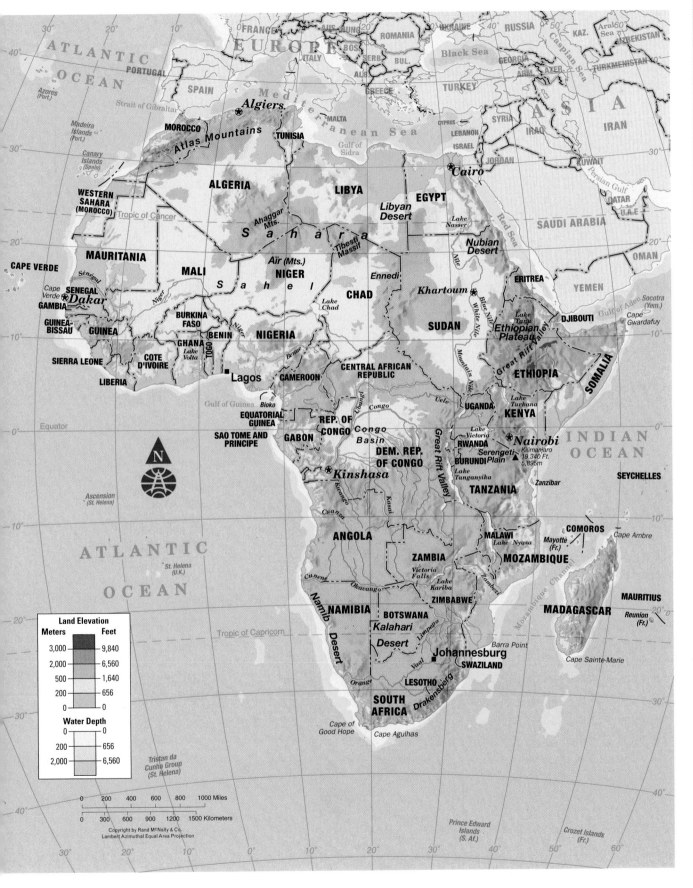

ATLANTIC OCEAN

Azores
(Port.)

Madeira
Islands
(Port.)

Canary
Islands
(Spain)

CAPE VERDE

PORTUGAL

SPAIN

Strait of Gibraltar

FRANCE

EUROPE

ITALY

Mediterranean Sea

MALTA

GREECE

ALB.

BOS.
SERB.
BUL.

ROMANIA

Black Sea

UKRAINE

RUSSIA

KAZ.

Aral 60
Sea

UZBEKISTAN

GEORGIA
ARM. AZER.

Caspian Sea

TURKMENISTAN

TURKEY

CYPRUS
LEBANON
SYRIA
ISRAEL
JORDAN

IRAQ

IRAN

ASIA

KUWAIT

Persian Gulf

QATAR
U.A.E.

Algiers

MOROCCO

Atlas Mountains

TUNISIA

Gulf of Sidra

LIBYA

EGYPT

Cairo

SAUDI ARABIA

OMAN

WESTERN SAHARA (MOROCCO)

Tropic of Cancer

ALGERIA

Libyan Desert

Lake Nasser

Red Sea

Ahaggar Mts.

Sahara

Tibesti Massif

Nubian Desert

Nile

YEMEN

Socotra (Yem.)

Cape Gwardafuy

MAURITANIA

Aïr (Mts.)

Ennedi

Gulf of Aden

MALI

NIGER

CHAD

Khartoum

Sénégal

Sahel

Niger

Lake Chad

White Nile

Blue Nile

ERITREA

DJIBOUTI

Cape Verde

SENEGAL

Dakar

GAMBIA

GUINEA-BISSAU

GUINEA

BURKINA FASO

BENIN

Niger

NIGERIA

SUDAN

Ethiopian Plateau

Lake Tana

ETHIOPIA

Great Rift Valley

SIERRA LEONE

COTE D'IVOIRE

GHANA

Lake Volta

TOGO

Benue

CENTRAL AFRICAN REPUBLIC

Mountain Nile

SOMALIA

LIBERIA

Lagos

CAMEROON

Uele

Gulf of Guinea

Bioko

EQUATORIAL GUINEA

Ubangi

Congo

UGANDA

KENYA

Lake Turkana

SAO TOME AND PRINCIPE

GABON

REP. OF CONGO

Congo Basin

DEM. REP. OF CONGO

Kinshasa

Great Rift Valley

RWANDA

BURUNDI

Lake Victoria

Nairobi

Serengeti Plain

Kilimanjaro 19,340 Ft. 5,895m

INDIAN OCEAN

Equator

Kasai

Kwango

Lake Tanganyika

TANZANIA

Zanzibar

SEYCHELLES

Cuanza

Cunene

ATLANTIC

Ascension (St. Helena)

St. Helena (U.K.)

OCEAN

ANGOLA

ZAMBIA

MALAWI

Lake Nyasa

Mayotte (Fr.)

COMOROS

Cape Ambre

MOZAMBIQUE

Victoria Falls

Lake Kariba

Zambezi

Mozambique Channel

MAURITIUS

Reunion (Fr.)

MADAGASCAR

Okavango

ZIMBABWE

Namib Desert

NAMIBIA

BOTSWANA

Kalahari Desert

Limpopo

Barra Point

Tropic of Capricorn

Cape Sainte-Marie

Johannesburg

Vaal

SWAZILAND

Orange

LESOTHO

Drakensberg

SOUTH AFRICA

Cape of Good Hope

Cape Agulhas

Tristan da Cunha Group (St. Helena)

Prince Edward Islands (S. Af.)

Crozet Islands (Fr.)

Land Elevation

Meters		Feet
3,000		9,840
2,000		6,560
500		1,640
200		656
0		0

Water Depth

0		0
200		656
2,000		6,560

0 200 400 600 800 1000 Miles

0 300 600 900 1200 1500 Kilometers

Copyright by Rand McNally & Co.
Lambert Azimuthal Equal Area Projection

N

RAND McNALLY

A17

Copyright by Rand McNally & Co.
Lambert Azimuthal Equal Area Projection

0	200	400	600	800 Miles

| 0 | 200 | 400 | 600 | 800 | 1000 Kilometers |

National Capital
City over 1,000,000 population
City under 1,000,000 population

East Siberian Sea
New Siberian Islands
Laptev Sea
Yana
Lena
Bering Sea
ALEUTIAN ISLANDS (U.S.)
Kamchatka Peninsula
Petropavlovsk-Kamchatskiy
Sea of Okhotsk
Sakhalin
Kuril Islands
Tropic of Cancer
PACIFIC OCEAN
Hokkaido
Sea of Japan
Vladivostok
Harbin
Honshu
Tokyo
Angara
Kraynoyarsk
Lake Baikal
Lena
Amur
Changchun
Ulaanbaatar
MONGOLIA
Shenyang
NORTH KOREA
Pyongyang
Seoul
SOUTH KOREA
Osaka
JAPAN
Beijing
Tianjin
Yellow Sea
Pusan
Shikoku
Kyushu
CHINA
Lanzhou
Huang
Huang
Xi'an
Nanjing
Wuhan
Shanghai
East China Sea
NORTHERN MARIANA ISLANDS (U.S.)
Chengdu
Chang (Yangtze)
Chongqing
Taipei
Guangzhou
TAIWAN
GUAM (U.S.)
FEDERATED STATES OF MICRONESIA
BHUTAN
Brahmaputra
Hong Kong
Luzon Strait
Luzon
BNGL
Dhaka
Hanoi
Hainan Island
PHILIPPINES
Chittagong
MYANMAR
LAOS
Gulf of Tonkin
South China Sea
Samar
PALAU
Vientiane
Manila
Mindanao
Equator
Yangon
THAILAND
Mekong
Bangkok
VIETNAM
CAMBODIA
Phnom Penh
Ho Chi Minh City
Sulu Sea
Celebes Sea
Andaman Islands (India)
Andaman Sea
Gulf of Thailand
Bandar Seri Begawan
BRUNEI
MALAYSIA
New Guinea
PAPUA NEW GUINEA
Nicobar Islands (India)
MALAYSIA
Medan
Kuala Lumpur
Borneo
Ceram
Arafura Sea
Coral Sea
Singapore
Celebes
INDONESIA
Banda Sea
Gulf of Carpentaria
AUSTRALIA
Sumatra
Java Sea
Dili
EAST TIMOR
Jakarta
Bandung
Java
Timor Sea

RAND McNALLY

A19

ATLANTIC OCEAN

ARCTIC OCEAN

ICELAND

Arctic Circle

Severnaya Zemlya

Novaya Zemlya

Kara Sea

Barents Sea

Yamal Pen.

Ob

FAROE ISLANDS (Den.)

IRELAND

UNITED KINGDOM

London

North Sea

NORWAY

SWEDEN

FINLAND

ESTONIA

LATVIA

LITH.

BELARUS

DENMARK

GERMANY

POLAND

UKRAINE

ROMANIA

BULGARIA

Moscow

Volga

Ural Mountains

West Siberian Lowland

Ishim

Novosibirsk

Ob

Irtysh

Yenisey

Astana

KAZAKHSTAN

Lake Balkhash

PORTUGAL

SPAIN

FRANCE

ITALY

GREECE

Black Sea

Caucasus

GEORGIA

ARM.

AZER.

Caspian Depression

Aral Sea

Syr Darya

Amu Darya

Ishim

Tian Shan

ALGERIA

TUNISIA

MOROCCO

GIBRALTAR (U.K.)

Mediterranean Sea

Ankara

TURKEY

N. CYPRUS

CYPRUS

LEBANON

SYRIA

ISRAEL

JORDAN

IRAQ

Tigris

Euphrates

Caspian Sea

Tehran

Dasht-e Kavir

Zagros Mts.

IRAN

UZBEKISTAN

TURKMENISTAN

KYRGYZSTAN

TAJIKISTAN

Pamirs

Tarim Basin

Altun Shan

Kunlun Mts.

Hindu Kush

LIBYA

Cairo

Nile

Suez Can.

EGYPT

An-Nafud

SAUDI ARABIA

KUWAIT

Persian Gulf

BAHRAIN

QATAR

U.A.E.

Gulf of Oman

AFGHANISTAN

PAKISTAN

Indus

New Delhi

Thar Desert

HIMALAYAS

NEPAL

Mt. Everest 29,035 Ft. 8,850m

Ganges

CHAD

SUDAN

Red Sea

ERITREA

ETHIOPIA

DJIBOUTI

Arabian Peninsula

Rub Al-Khali

YEMEN

OMAN

Gulf of Aden

Socotra (Yem.)

Arabian Sea

Mumbai (Bombay)

Godavari

Western Ghats

Deccan Plateau

Eastern Ghats

INDIA

Bay of Bengal

DEM. REP. OF THE CONGO (ZAIRE)

UGANDA

RWANDA

BURUNDI

KENYA

SOMALIA

TANZANIA

ZAMBIA

MALAWI

MOZAMBIQUE

Lakshadweep (India)

MALDIVES

SRI LANKA

INDIAN OCEAN

N

0 200 400 600 800 Miles

0 200 400 600 800 1000 Kilometers

Copyright by Rand McNally & Co.
Lambert Azimuthal Equal Area Projection

Land Elevation

Meters	Feet
3,000	9,840
2,000	6,560
500	1,640
200	656
0	0

Water Depth

0	0
200	656
2,000	6,560

New Siberian Islands

Taymyr Peninsula

Laptev Sea

East Siberian Sea

Indigirka

Kolyma

Central Siberian Uplands

Verkhoyansk Mts.

Lena

RUSSIA

Siberia

Angara

Stanovoy Range

Lake Baikal

Amur

Greater Khingan Range

Sayan Mountains

Altai Mts.

MONGOLIA

Gobi Desert

Qilian Shan

CHINA

Qinling Shandi

Huang

Chang (Yangtze)

BHUTAN

Brahmaputra

Irrawaddy

Salween

Red

BNGL.

MYANMAR

LAOS

Mekong

THAILAND

Bangkok

CAMBODIA

VIETNAM

Andaman Islands (India)

Andaman Sea

Gulf of Thailand

Nicobar Islands (India)

Str. of Malacca

MALAY PENINSULA

MALAYSIA

Singapore

Sumatra

Greater Sunda Islands

Jakarta

Java

Java Sea

Bering Sea

Aleutian Islands (U.S.)

Sea of Okhotsk

Kamchatka Peninsula

Sakhalin

Kuril Islands

Tatar Strait

Hokkaido

Sea of Japan

Honshu

Tokyo

JAPAN

Shikoku

Kyushu

NORTH KOREA

SOUTH KOREA

Beijing

Yellow Sea

Shanghai

East China Sea

Xi

TAIWAN

Luzon Strait

Luzon

Hainan Island

Gulf of Tonkin

South China Sea

Manila

PHILIPPINES

Mindanao

Sulu Sea

BRUNEI

MALAYSIA

Borneo

Celebes Sea

Celebes

Ceram

Moluccas

Banda Sea

INDONESIA

EAST TIMOR

Timor

Timor Sea

PACIFIC OCEAN

NORTHERN MARIANA ISLANDS (U.S.)

GUAM (U.S.)

FEDERATED STATES OF MICRONESIA

Philippine Sea

PALAU

Equator

New Guinea

PAPUA NEW GUINEA

AUSTRALIA

Gulf of Carpentaria

Arafura Sea

Coral Sea

Tropic of Cancer

Arctic Circle

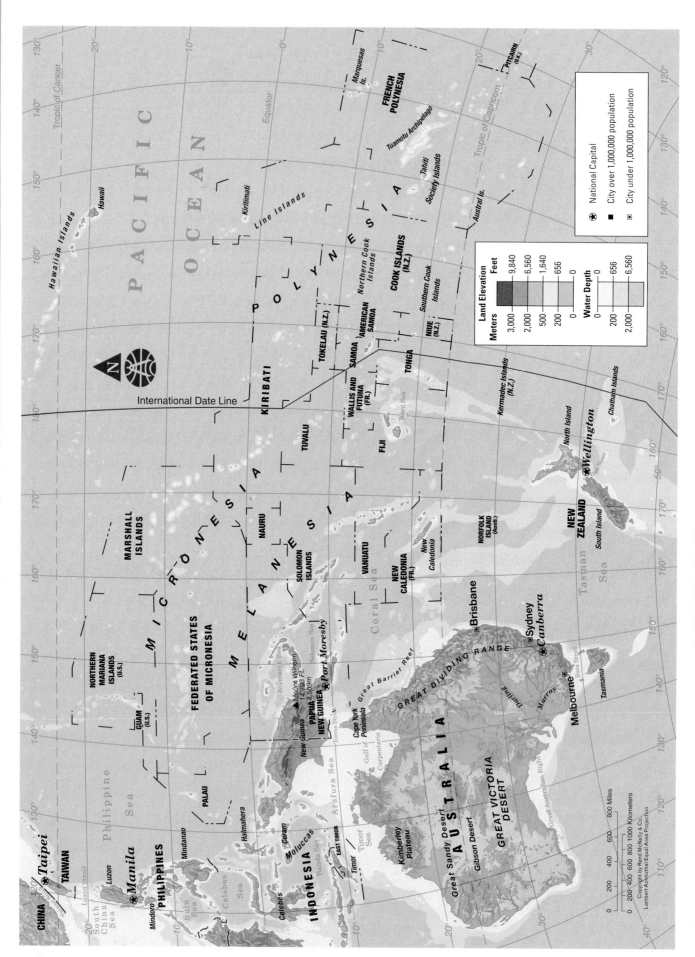

RAND McNALLY

TAIWAN

CHINA

Taipei

Manila

PHILIPPINES

Mindanao

Luzon

South China Sea

Sulu Sea

Celebes Sea

Celebes

Moluccas

Ceram

Halmahera

Mindoro

Philippine Sea

PALAU

GUAM (U.S.)

NORTHERN MARIANA ISLANDS (U.S.)

FEDERATED STATES OF MICRONESIA

M I C R O N E S I A

MARSHALL ISLANDS

NAURU

P A C I F I C

O C E A N

Hawaiian Islands

Hawaii

Kiritimati

Line Islands

Equator

Tropic of Cancer

International Date Line

N

M E L A N E S I A

SOLOMON ISLANDS

Bismarck Sea

New Guinea

Mount Wilhelm 14,793 Ft. 4,509m

PAPUA NEW GUINEA

Port Moresby

Solomon Sea

Torres Strait

Cape York Peninsula

Gulf of Carpentaria

Arafura Sea

Timor Sea

Timor

EAST TIMOR

Banda Sea

INDONESIA

VANUATU

NEW CALEDONIA (FR.)

New Caledonia

Coral Sea

Great Barrier Reel

GREAT DIVIDING RANGE

Brisbane

Sydney

Canberra

Melbourne

Tasmania

Bass Strait

NORFOLK ISLAND (Austl.)

P O L Y N E S I A

TUVALU

KIRIBATI

WALLIS AND FUTUNA (FR.)

FIJI

TOKELAU (N.Z.)

SAMOA

AMERICAN SAMOA

TONGA

NIUE (N.Z.)

Koro Sea

Northern Cook Islands

COOK ISLANDS (N.Z.)

Southern Cook Islands

Society Islands

Tahiti

Tuamotu Archipelago

FRENCH POLYNESIA

Marquesas Is.

Austral Is.

Tropic of Capricorn

PITCAIRN (U.K.)

Kermadec Islands (N.Z.)

Chatham Islands

Tasman Sea

NEW ZEALAND

North Island

Wellington

South Island

Cook Strait

A U S T R A L I A

Great Sandy Desert

Gibson Desert

GREAT VICTORIA DESERT

Kimberley Plateau

Great Australian Bight

Darling

Murray

Kosciuszko

Taiwan Strait

Luzon Strait

Legend

⊛ National Capital

■ City over 1,000,000 population

▣ City under 1,000,000 population

Land Elevation

Meters	Feet
3,000	9,840
2,000	6,560
500	1,640
200	656
0	0

Water Depth

0	0
200	656
2,000	6,560

0 200 400 600 800 Miles

0 200 400 600 800 1000 Kilometers

Copyright by Rand McNally & Co.
Lambert Azimuthal Equal Area Projection

The Maya World, A.D. 300–900

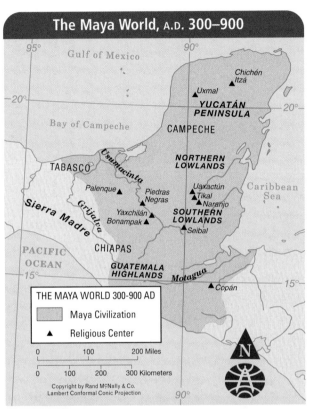

THE MAYA WORLD 300-900 AD

▨ Maya Civilization

▲ Religious Center

0   100   200 Miles
0   100   200   300 Kilometers

Copyright by Rand McNally & Co.
Lambert Conformal Conic Projection

The Inca Empire, 1463–1532

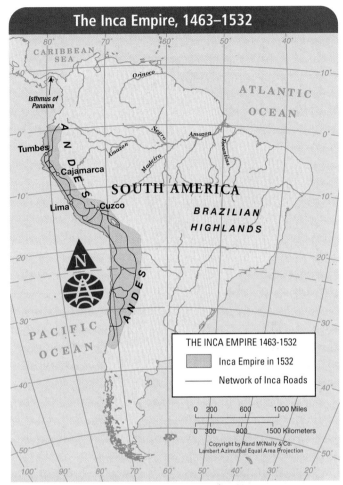

THE INCA EMPIRE 1463-1532

▨ Inca Empire in 1532

— Network of Inca Roads

0   200   600   1000 Miles
0   300   900   1500 Kilometers

Copyright by Rand McNally & Co.
Lambert Azimuthal Equal Area Projection

The Aztec Empire, 1519

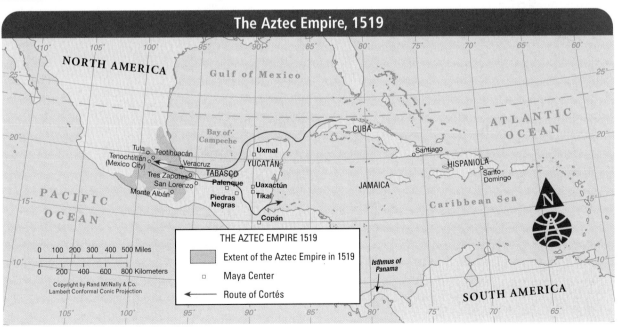

THE AZTEC EMPIRE 1519

▨ Extent of the Aztec Empire in 1519

□ Maya Center

← Route of Cortés

0 100 200 300 400 500 Miles
0   200   400   600   800 Kilometers

Copyright by Rand McNally & Co.
Lambert Conformal Conic Projection

ATLANTIC

OCEAN

IRELAND

North Sea

Baltic Sea

BRITAIN
Wall of Antoninus
Wall of Hadrian
Eburacum
BRITAIN
Londinium

English Channel

Elbe

Vistula

(Lost in 9 A.D.)

LOWER GERMANY
Colonia Agrippina

BELGICA

GERMANY

Carpathians

Seine
Lutetia
LUGDUNENSIS

Loire

GAUL

AQUITANIA

Lugdunum

Rhine

UPPER GERMANY

Rhône

RHAETIA

NORICUM

Vindobona
Danube
Aquincum

ILLYRICUM

PANNONIA

DACIA

Douro

TARRACONENSIS

Numantia

Pyrenees

Ebro

Garonne

Tolosa

Caesar Augusta

NARBONENSIS

Alps

Mediolanum

ALPINE PROVS.

Po

Patavium

Ravenna

DALMATIA

Olisipo

LUSITANIA

SPAIN

Salmantica

Tagus

Toletum

Guadiana

Corduba

BAETICA

Massilia

ITALY

Rome

Ostia

Pompeii

Adriatic Sea

MACEDONIA

Gades

Tarraco

Valentia

Balearic Islands

CORSICA AND SARDINIA

Carales

Tyrrhenian Sea

Corcyra

Ionian Sea

EPIRUS

Thessalonica

Aegean Sea

New Carthage

MEDITERRANEAN

SICILY

Syracuse

Corinth

ACHAIA

Athens

MAURETANIA

Atlas Mountains

Carthage

SEA

Crete

GAETULIA

AFRICA

NUMIDIA

Cyrene

AFRICA

CYRENAICA

Roman Empire	Parthian Empire	—— Provincial Boundary
Armenia	Temporarily held by Rome	BRITAIN Roman Province

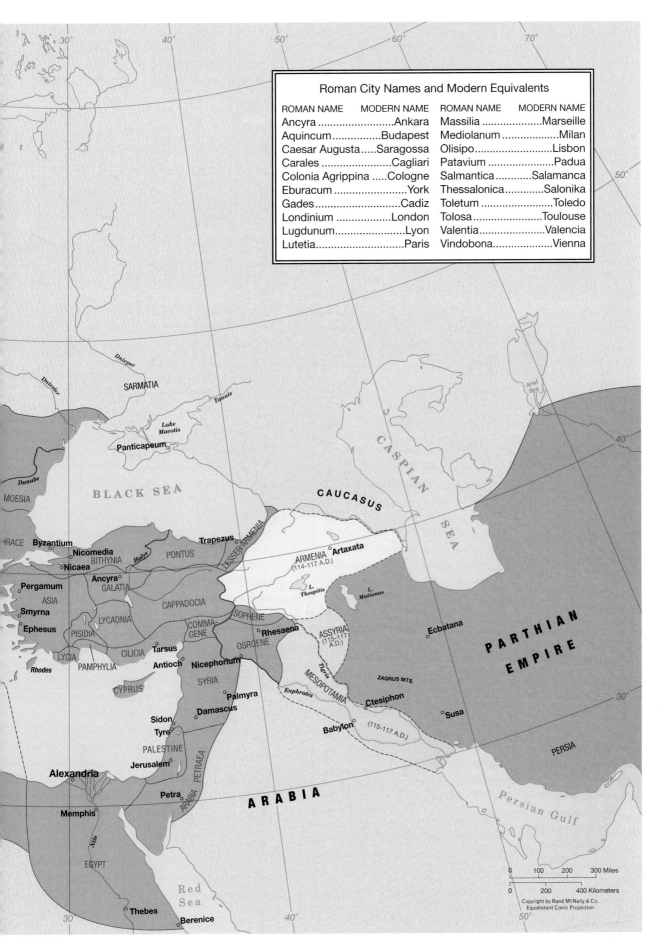

Roman City Names and Modern Equivalents

ROMAN NAME	MODERN NAME	ROMAN NAME	MODERN NAME
Ancyra	Ankara	Massilia	Marseille
Aquincum	Budapest	Mediolanum	Milan
Caesar Augusta	Saragossa	Olisipo	Lisbon
Carales	Cagliari	Patavium	Padua
Colonia Agrippina	Cologne	Salmantica	Salamanca
Eburacum	York	Thessalonica	Salonika
Gades	Cadiz	Toletum	Toledo
Londinium	London	Tolosa	Toulouse
Lugdunum	Lyon	Valentia	Valencia
Lutetia	Paris	Vindobona	Vienna

Dnieper

Dniester

SARMATIA

Tanais

Lake
Maeotis

Panticapeum

Danube

Aral
Sea

BLACK SEA

CAUCASUS

CASPIAN SEA

MOESIA

THRACE

Byzantium

Nicomedia

BITHYNIA

Halys

PONTUS

Trapezus

LESSER ARMENIA

ARMENIA
(114-117 A.D.)

Artaxata

Nicaea

Ancyra

GALATIA

L.
Thospitis

L.
Matianus

Pergamum

ASIA

CAPPADOCIA

Smyrna

LYCAONIA

SOPHENE

COMMA-
GENE

Rhesaena

ASSYRIA
(115-117
A.D.)

Ecbatana

Ephesus

PISIDIA

OSROENE

Tigris

PARTHIAN

EMPIRE

LYCIA

CILICIA

Tarsus

Rhodes

PAMPHYLIA

Antioch

Nicephorium

ZAGRUS MTS.

MESOPOTAMIA

CYPRUS

SYRIA

Euphrates

Ctesiphon

Palmyra

Susa

Sidon

Damascus

Tyre

Babylon

(115-117 A.D.)

PERSIA

PALESTINE

Jerusalem

Alexandria

ARABIA PETRAEA

Persian Gulf

Petra

A R A B I A

Memphis

Nile

EGYPT

Red
Sea

Thebes

Berenice

0   100   200   300 Miles

0   200   400 Kilometers

Copyright by Rand McNally & Co.
Equidistant Conic Projection

RAND McNALLY

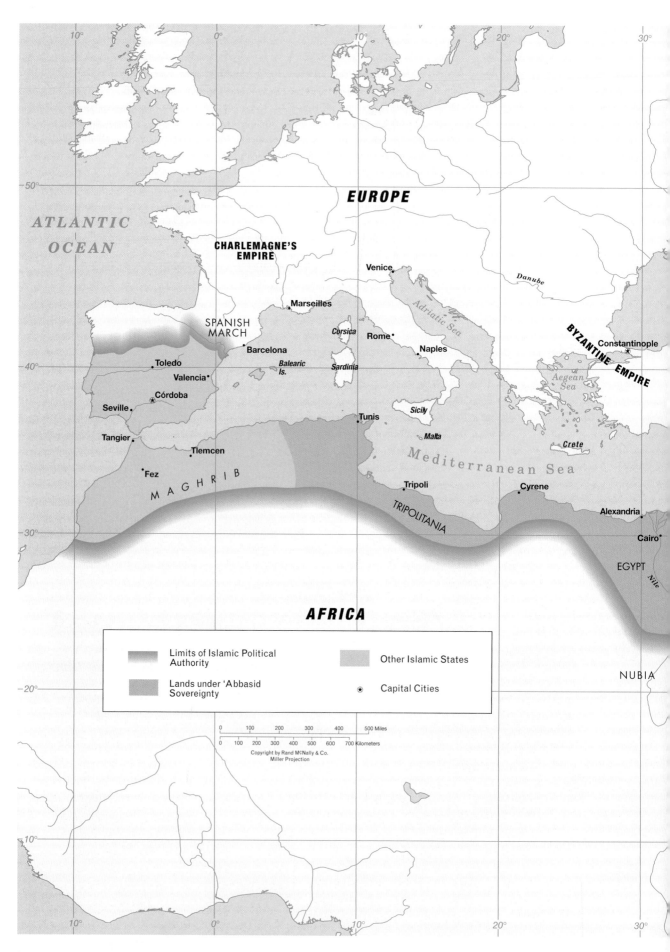

EUROPE

ATLANTIC
OCEAN

CHARLEMAGNE'S
EMPIRE

Venice

Danube

Adriatic Sea

Marseilles

BYZANTINE EMPIRE

Constantinople

SPANISH
MARCH

Corsica

Rome

Naples

Barcelona

*Balearic
Is.*

Sardinia

Toledo

*Aegean
Sea*

Valencia

Córdoba

Seville

Sicily

Tunis

Crete

Tangier

Malta

Mediterranean Sea

Tlemcen

Fez

MAGHRIB

Tripoli

Cyrene

TRIPOLITANIA

Alexandria

Cairo

EGYPT

Nile

AFRICA

NUBIA

	Limits of Islamic Political Authority			Other Islamic States
	Lands under 'Abbasid Sovereignty		✳	Capital Cities

0   100   200   300   400   500 Miles

0   100   200   300   400   500   600   700 Kilometers

Copyright by Rand M℠Nally & Co.
Miller Projection

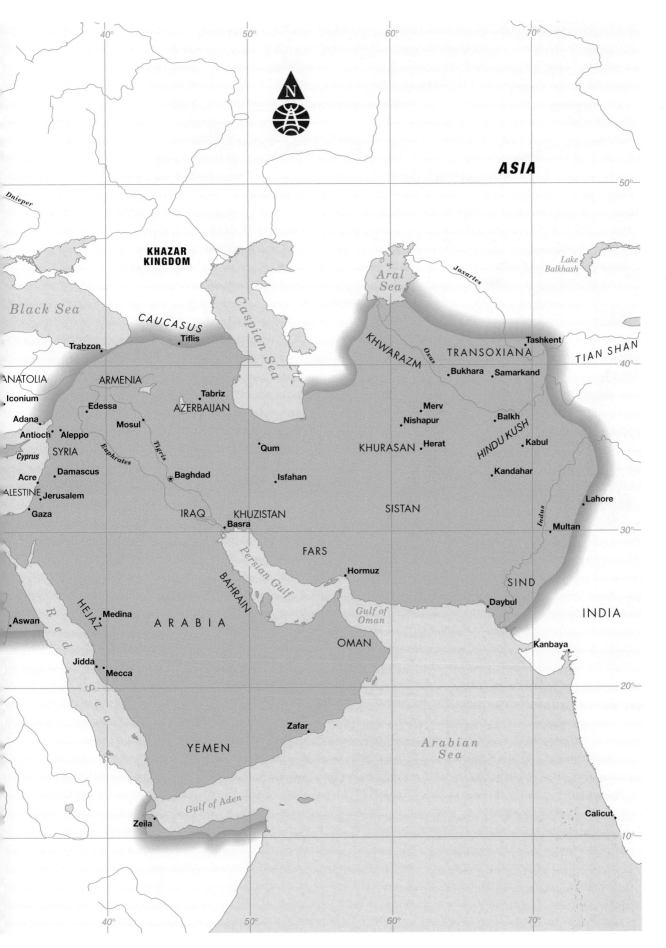

ASIA

50°

Dnieper

KHAZAR KINGDOM

Black Sea

Caspian Sea

Aral Sea

Jaxartes

Lake Balkhash

CAUCASUS

Trabzon

Tiflis

40°

KHWARAZM

Oxus

TRANSOXIANA

Tashkent

TIAN SHAN

ANATOLIA

Iconium

ARMENIA

Tabriz

AZERBAIJAN

Bukhara

Samarkand

Edessa

Mosul

Merv

Nishapur

Balkh

Adana

Antioch

Aleppo

Euphrates

Tigris

Qum

KHURASAN

Herat

HINDU KUSH

Kabul

Cyprus

SYRIA

Damascus

Baghdad

Isfahan

Kandahar

Acre

PALESTINE

Jerusalem

IRAQ

KHUZISTAN

SISTAN

Lahore

Indus

Gaza

Basra

Multan

30°

FARS

Hormuz

SIND

BAHRAIN

Persian Gulf

Daybul

INDIA

HEJAZ

Medina

ARABIA

Gulf of Oman

Aswan

Red Sea

OMAN

Kanbaya

Jidda

Mecca

20°

Zafar

Arabian Sea

YEMEN

Gulf of Aden

Calicut

Zeila

10°

40°

50°

60°

70°

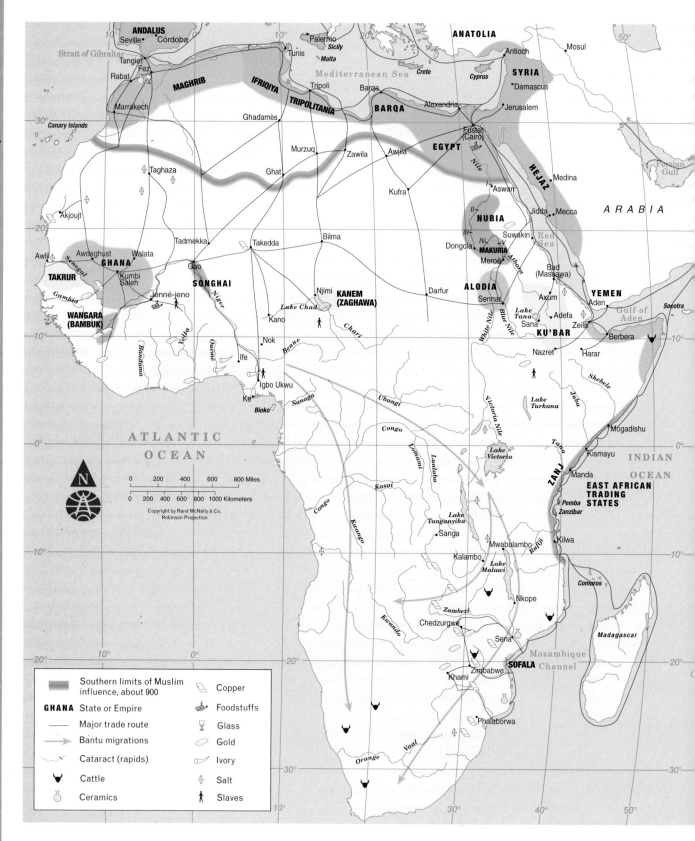

ANDALUS
Seville • Córdoba
Strait of Gibraltar
Tangier
Fez
Rabat
Marrakech
MAGHRIB
IFRIQIYA
Tunis
Palermo
Sicily
Malta
Tripoli
Mediterranean Sea
Crete
TRIPOLITANIA
Barqa
BARQA
Alexandria
ANATOLIA
Antioch
Mosul
SYRIA
Damascus
Jerusalem
Cyprus

Canary Islands
Ghadamès
Murzuq
Zawila
Awjila
EGYPT
Fustat
(Cairo)
Nile
HEJAZ
Medina
Persian
Gulf

Taghaza
Ghat
Kufra
Aswan
ARABIA
Jidda
Mecca

Akjoujt
Tadmekka
Takedda
Bilma
NUBIA
Suwakin
Dongola
MAKURIA
Meroë
Red
Sea
Bad
(Massawa)

Awlil
Awdaghust
Walata
GHANA
Kumbi
Saleh
Gao
SONGHAI
Senegal
TAKRUR
Gambia
Jenné-jeno
Niger
WANGARA
(BAMBUK)
Volta
Kano
Nok
Oueme
Ife
Bandama
Njimi
KANEM
(ZAGHAWA)
Lake Chad
Chari
Darfur
ALODIA
Sennar
Axum
Atbara
YEMEN
Aden
Gulf of
Aden
Socotra
Lake
Tana
Adefa
Sana
Zeila
KU'BAR
Nazret
Berbera
Harar
Shebele

Ke
Igbo Ukwu
Bioko
Benue
Sanaga
Ubangi
Congo
White Nile
Blue Nile
Victoria Nile

ATLANTIC
OCEAN
Kasai
Lomami
Lualaba
Lake
Turkana
Juba
Tana
Mogadishu

Congo
Kwango
Lake
Victoria
Kismayu
INDIAN
OCEAN
Lake
Tanganyika
Sanga
ZANJ
Manda
EAST AFRICAN
TRADING
STATES
Pemba
Zanzibar

Mwabulambo
Rufiji
Kilwa
Kalambo
Lake
Malawi
Nkope
Comoros

Zambezi
Chedzurgwe
Sena
Madagascar
Mozambique
Channel

Kwando
Zimbabwe
SOFALA
Khami
Phalaborwa

Orange
Vaal

N
0   200   400   600   800 Miles
0 200 400 600 800 1000 Kilometers
Copyright by Rand McNally & Co.
Robinson Projection

Legend:

- Southern limits of Muslim influence, about 900
- **GHANA** State or Empire
- —— Major trade route
- → Bantu migrations
- Cataract (rapids)
- Cattle
- Ceramics
- Copper
- Foodstuffs
- Glass
- Gold
- Ivory
- Salt
- Slaves

RAND McNALLY

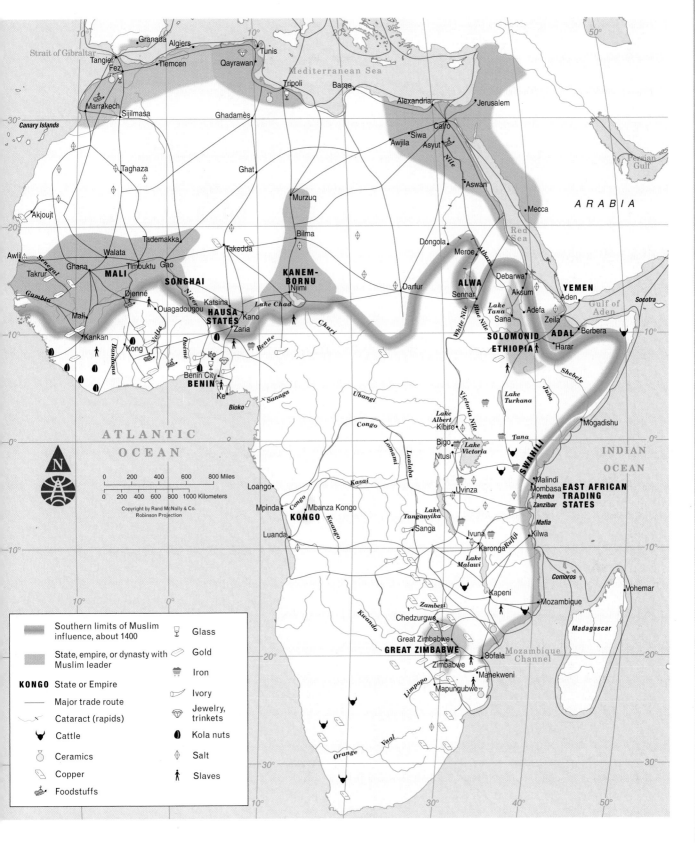

ARABIA

Mediterranean Sea

Strait of Gibraltar

Granada · Algiers
Tangier · Tlemcen · Qayrawan · Tunis
Fez
Marrakech · Sijilmasa
Ghadamès
Canary Islands

Tripoli · Barqa

Alexandria · Jerusalem
Cairo
Siwa · Asyut
Awjila
Ghat
Aswan
Taghaza
Mecca
Akjoujt
Murzuq
Bilma
Red Sea
Persian Gulf

Awlil
Tademakka
Takedda
Dongola
Walata
Meroe
Debarwa
YEMEN
Ghana · Timbuktu · Gao
Socotra
Takrur
SONGHAI
KANEM-
Aden
Djenné
BORNU
Darfur
ALWA
Gulf of Aden
MALI
Njimi
Aksum
Senegal
Katsina
Sennar
Adefa
Gambia
Ouagadougou
Kano
Lake Chad
Zeila
Berbera
Mali
HAUSA
Chari
Lake
SOLOMONID
ADAL
STATES
Zaria
Tana
Harar
Kankan
Benue
Sana
ETHIOPIA
Kong
White Nile
Blue Nile
Shebele
Bandama
Volta
Ife
Oueme
Benin City
Juba
BENIN
Ke
Sanaga
Ubangi
Lake
Turkana
Bioko
Mogadishu

ATLANTIC

OCEAN

Congo
Lake Albert
Kibiro
Victoria Nile
Tana

N

Bigo
Lake Victoria
Ntusi
SWAHILI
INDIAN
Lomami
Uvinza
OCEAN
0   200   400   600   800 Miles
Lualaba
Malindi
0   200 400 600 800 1000 Kilometers
Kasai
Mombasa
EAST AFRICAN
Copyright by Rand McNally & Co.
Pemba
TRADING
Robinson Projection
Loango
Congo
Zanzibar
STATES
Mpinda · Mbanza Kongo
Lake
Mafia
Tanganyika
KONGO
Sanga
Ivuna
Kilwa
Luanda
Kuango
Karonga
Rufiji
Lake
Malawi
Comoros
Kapeni
Vohemar
Mozambique
Zambezi
Chedzurgwe
Madagascar
Kwando
Great Zimbabwe
GREAT ZIMBABWE
Sofala
Mozambique Channel
Zimbabwe
Manekweni
Limpopo
Mapungubwe
Kavango
Orange
Vaal

Legend:

Southern limits of Muslim
influence, about 1400

State, empire, or dynasty with
Muslim leader

KONGO State or Empire

—— Major trade route

Cataract (rapids)

Cattle

Ceramics

Copper

Foodstuffs

Glass

Gold

Iron

Ivory

Jewelry,
trinkets

Kola nuts

Salt

Slaves

DENMARK — Country or Larger Political Region

AUSTRIA — Smaller Region

Boundary of Holy Roman Empire

Boundary of France

0   100   200   300 Miles
0   200   400 Kilometers

Copyright by Rand McNally & Co.
Lambert Conformal Conic Projection

Faeroes

NORWAY

Shetland Islands

Bergen

Orkney Islands

Oslo

Hebrides

SCOTLAND

N

Edinburgh

NORTH SEA

DENMARK

Calmar

Copenhagen

IRELAND

Dublin

York

S

POMERANIA

Hamburg

Bremen

BRADENBURG

WALES ENGLAND

HOLLAND

Elbe

SILESIA

Thames

London

Oder

ATLANTIC

Bruges

HOLY

Prague

OCEAN

Rouen

Rhine

Mainz

BOHEMIA

English Channel

Paris

ROMAN

BRITTANY

Seine

MORAVIA

FRANCE

Strassburg

Danube

Vienna

Loire

LORRAINE

Bay of Biscay

BURGUNDY

Basel

BAVARIA

EMPIRE

AUSTRIA

SWISS CONFED.

Bordeaux

Lyon

Milan

Trieste

AQUITAINE

Rhône

SAVOY

Garonne

DAUPHINY

Venice

Avignon

Bologna

REPUBLIC

PORTUGAL

Toulouse

PROVENCE

Po

BOS

Duero

Marseille

OF

Lisbon

NAVARRE

VENICE

ADRIATIC

Tagus

Ebro

Corsica

PAPAL STATES

CASTILE

ARAGON

Barcelona

Toledo

Rome

Córdoba

Balearic Islands

KINGDOM

Seville

(To Aragon)

Sardinia (To Aragon)

OF

Cadiz

Granada

Naples

NAPLES

GRANADA

MEDITERRAN

Palermo

Algiers

KINGDOM OF SICILY

Tunis

M O S L E M   S T A T E S

Malta

S W E D E N

Upsala
Stockholm

Wisby

Lake Ladoga

R U S S I A N   S T A T E S

Novgorod

PRINCIPALITY OF MOSCOW

Yaroslavl

Moscow

Smolensk

N. Dvina

Kama

Kazan

Bulgar

Volga

KNIGHTS

Riga

Düna

TEUTONIC

Königsberg

Danzig

Niemen

K H A N A T E   O F

T H E   G O L D E N   H O R D E

Ural

Sarai

Volga

Astrakhan

Vistula

Warsaw

L I T H U A N I A

P O L A N D

Cracow

Kiev

Dniester

U K R A I N E

Bug

Dnieper

Azov
(To Genoa)

K U B A N

CASPIAN SEA

Buda Pest

M O L D A V I A

H U N G A R Y

Drave

Save

VIA

Belgrade

W A L L A C H I A

Bucharest

Danube

B L A C K   S E A

G E O R G I A

Tiflis

S E R B I A N
P R I N C E S

B U L G A R I A

Sofia

Trebizond

EMP. OF TREBIZOND

DOMINIONS OF
MOHAMMED ARTIN

Adrianople

BYZANTINE EMPIRE

Constantinople

Tigris

PRIN. OF
ALBANIA

Thessalonica

O T T O M A N   T U R K S

SEA

AEGEAN

SEA

DUCHY OF
ATHENS

Athens

ACHAEA

Chios

KNIGHTS OF
ATHENS

S E L J U K   T U R K S

A R M E N I A

Armenia

T U R K O M E N S

Mosul

Euphrates

RHODES

Rhodes

Crete
(To Venice)

KINGDOM OF
CYPRUS

A R A B I A

Tripoli

Damascus

E A   20°N

S E A   30°

40°

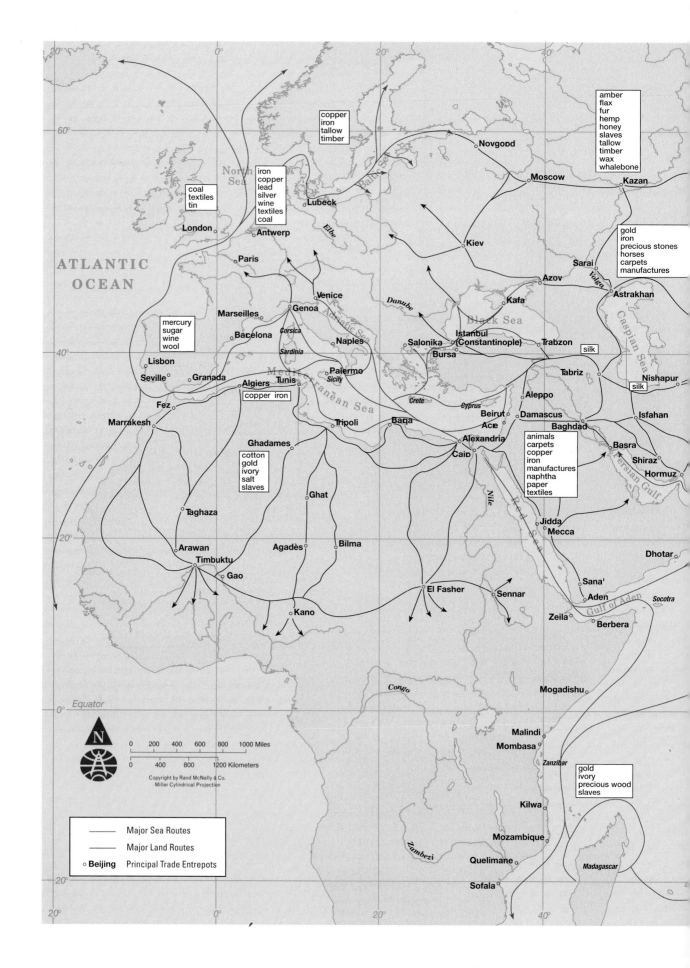

International Trade, 1350–1450

ATLANTIC OCEAN

North Sea

coal
textiles
tin

copper
iron
tallow
timber

iron
copper
lead
silver
wine
textiles
coal

amber
flax
fur
hemp
honey
slaves
tallow
timber
wax
whalebone

London

Antwerp

Lübeck

Novgorod

Moscow

Kazan

Elbe

Paris

Baltic Sea

Kiev

Venice

Genoa

Marseilles

Barcelona

Corsica

Naples

Sardinia

Danube

Kafa

Sarai

Volga

Azov

Astrakhan

gold
iron
precious stones
horses
carpets
manufactures

Salonika

Istanbul
(Constantinople)

Bursa

Trabzon

Black Sea

silk

Caspian Sea

mercury
sugar
wine
wool

Lisbon

Seville

Granada

Algiers

Tunis

Adriatic Sea

Palermo

Sicily

Mediterranean Sea

Crete

Cyprus

Tabriz

silk

Nishapur

Fez

copper iron

Marrakesh

Baña

Aleppo

Beirut

Acre

Damascus

Isfahan

Tripoli

Alexandria

Cairo

Baghdad

animals
carpets
copper
iron
manufactures
naphtha
paper
textiles

Basra

Shiraz

Hormuz

Persian Gulf

Ghadames

cotton
gold
ivory
salt
slaves

Ghat

Nile

Red Sea

Jidda

Mecca

Dhotar

Taghaza

Agadès

Bilma

Arawan

Timbuktu

Gao

Kano

El Fasher

Sennar

Sana'

Aden

Gulf of Aden

Socotra

Zeila

Berbera

Congo

Mogadishu

Equator

N

| 0 | 200 | 400 | 600 | 800 | 1000 Miles |

| 0 | 400 | 800 | 1200 Kilometers |

Copyright by Rand McNally & Co.
Miller Cylindrical Projection

Malindi

Mombasa

Zanzibar

gold
ivory
precious wood
slaves

Kilwa

Zambezi

Mozambique

Quelimane

Madagascar

Sofala

———— Major Sea Routes
———— Major Land Routes
○ Beijing   Principal Trade Entrepots

RAND McNALLY

A32

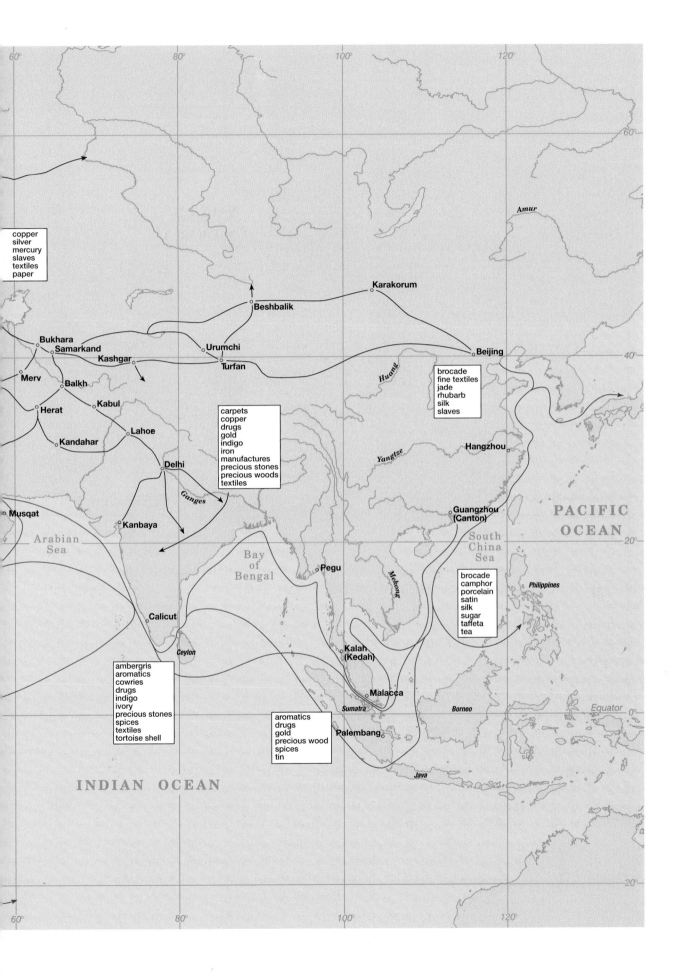

copper
silver
mercury
slaves
textiles
paper

Amur

Karakorum

Beshbalik

Bukhara
Samarkand
Kashgar
Merv
Balkh
Herat
Kabul
Kandahar
Lahoe

Urumchi
Turfan

Beijing

Huang

brocade
fine textiles
jade
rhubarb
silk
slaves

carpets
copper
drugs
gold
indigo
iron
manufactures
precious stones
precious woods
textiles

Yangtze

Hangzhou

Delhi

Ganges

Musqat

Kanbaya

Arabian
Sea

Guangzhou
(Canton)

PACIFIC
OCEAN

South
China
Sea

Bay
of
Bengal

Pegu

Mekong

brocade
camphor
porcelain
satin
silk
sugar
taffeta
tea

Philippines

Calicut

Ceylon

ambergris
aromatics
cowries
drugs
indigo
ivory
precious stones
spices
textiles
tortoise shell

Kalah
(Kedah)

Malacca

Sumatra

Borneo

Equator

aromatics
drugs
gold
precious wood
spices
tin

Palembang

Java

INDIAN OCEAN

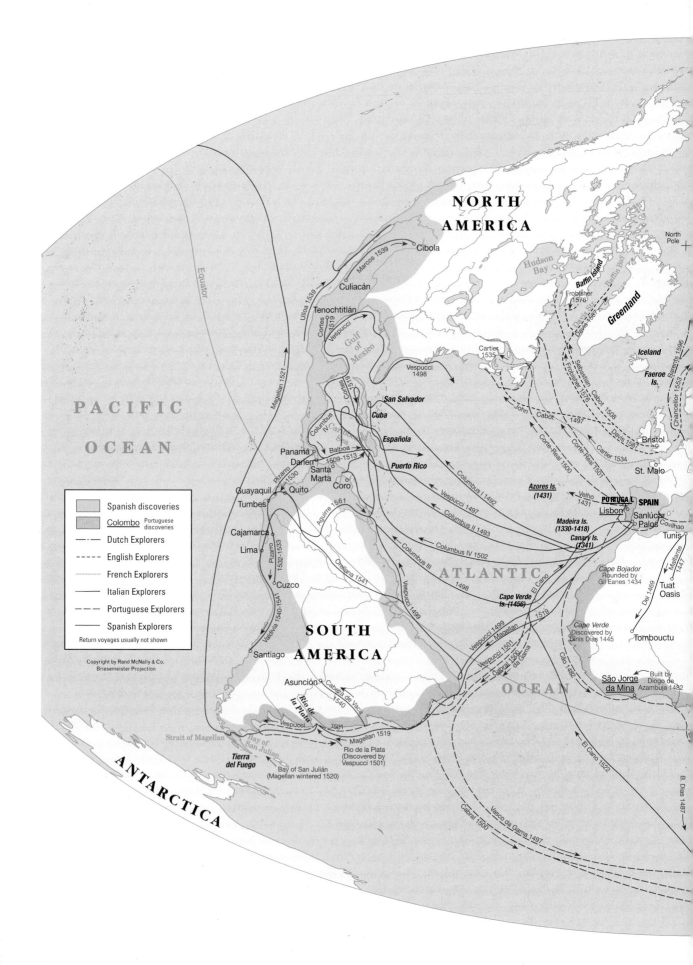

NORTH
AMERICA

North
Pole

Hudson
Bay

Baffin Island
Frobisher
1576

Greenland

Davis Str.

Baffin Bay

Davis 1587

Iceland

*Faeroe
Is.*

Cibola

Marcos 1539

Culiacán

Ulloa 1539

Tenochtitlán

Cortes
1519

Vespucci
1519

Gulf
of
Mexico

Cartier
1535

Sebastian Cabot 1508

Frobisher 1576

Barents 1596

Chancellor 1553

Cortes
1519

Vespucci
1498

PACIFIC

OCEAN

San Salvador

Cuba

Columbus
IV

Caribbean
Sea

Española

Balboa
1509–1513

Puerto Rico

John Cabot
1497

Corte-Real 1500

Corte-Real 1501

Cartier 1534

Bristol

St. Malo

Magellan 1521

Equator

Panamá
Darien
Santa
Marta
Coro

Columbus I 1492

Vespucci 1497

Columbus II 1493

Columbus IV 1502

Azores Is.
(1431)

Velho
1431

PORTUGAL

SPAIN

Lisbon

Sanlúcar
Palos

Covilhao

Pizarro
1530

Guayaquil
Tumbes

Quito

Aguirre 1561

Columbus III
1498

ATLANTIC

Madeira Is.
(1330–1418)

Canary Is.
(1341)

Tunis

Cajamarca

Lima

Orellana 1541

Vespucci 1499

Cape Bojador
Rounded by
Gil Eanes 1434

Tuat
Oasis

Maltante
1447

Pizarro
1532–1533

Cuzco

Cape Verde
Is. (1456)

El Cano

1519

Cape Verde
Discovered by
Dinis Dias 1445

Del 1469

Tombouctu

Valdivia 1540–1541

SOUTH
AMERICA

Vespucci 1499

Magellan

Vespucci 1501

Cabral 1500
da Gama

Cão 1482

OCEAN

São Jorge
da Mina

Built by
Diogo de
Azambuja 1482

Santiago

Asunción

Cabeza de Vaca
1540

*Rio de
la Plata*

Vespucci
1501

Magellan 1519

Rio de la Plata
(Discovered by
Vespucci 1501)

El Cano 1522

Strait of Magellan

Bay of
San Julian

*Tierra
del Fuego*

Bay of San Julián
(Magellan wintered 1520)

B. Dias 1487

ANTARCTICA

Cabral 1500

Vasco da Gama 1497

Legend

▨	Spanish discoveries
▨	*Colombo* Portuguese discoveries
–·–·–	Dutch Explorers
– – –	English Explorers
········	French Explorers
———	Italian Explorers
– – –	Portuguese Explorers
———	Spanish Explorers

Return voyages usually not shown

Copyright by Rand McNally & Co.
Briesemeister Projection

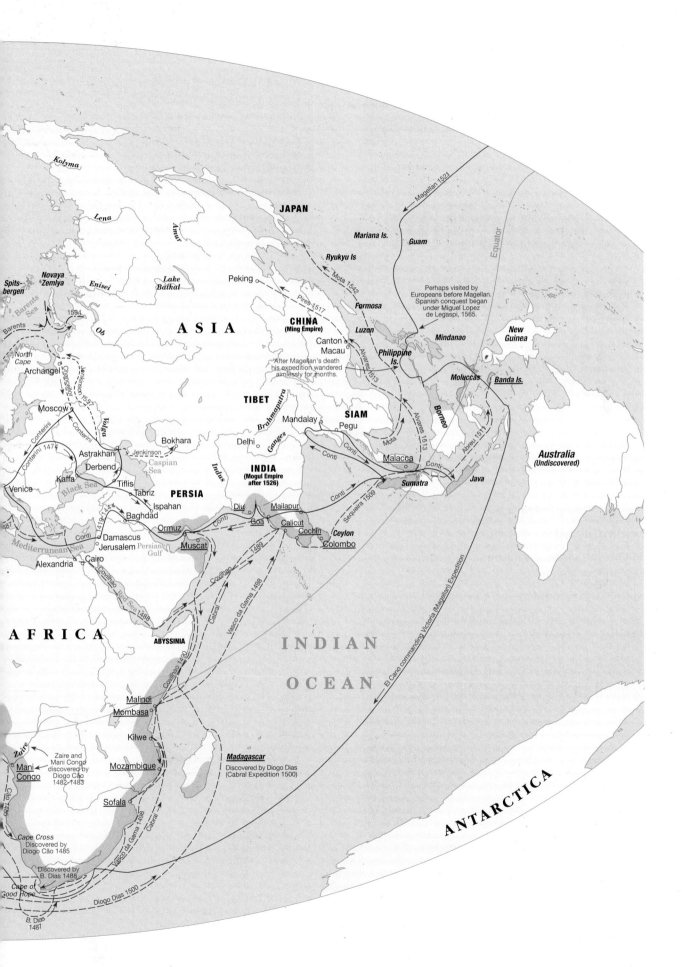

Kolyma

Lena

Amur

JAPAN

Mariana Is.

Guam

Ryukyu Is

Magellan 1521

Spits-
bergen

*Novaya
Zemlya*

Enisei

*Lake
Baikal*

Peking

Formosa

Mota 1542

Barents
Sea

1594

Barents

Ob

ASIA

Pires 1517

CHINA
(Ming Empire)

Canton
Macau

Luzon

Perhaps visited by
Europeans before Magellan.
Spanish conquest began
under Miguel Lopez
de Legaspi, 1565.

Equator

**New
Guinea**

North
Cape

Archangel

Chancellor

Jenkinson 1557

After Magellan's death
his expedition wandered
aimlessly for months.

Mindanao

Alvares 1513

**Philippine
Is.**

Moluccas

Banda Is.

Moscow

Conterini

Volga

Conterini

TIBET

Brahmaputra

Mandalay

SIAM

Pegu

Alvares 1513

Borneo

Abreu 1511

**Australia
(Undiscovered)**

Conterini 1474

Astrakhan

Derbend

Jenkinson

*Caspian
Sea*

Delhi

Ganges

Conti

Conti

Mota

Conti

Java

Venice

Kaffa

Black Sea

Tiflis

Tabriz

PERSIA

Indus

INDIA
(Mogul Empire
after 1526)

Malacca

Conti

Sumatra

1419

Ispahan

Baghdad

Diu

Mailapur

Conti

Goa

Sequeira 1509

1487

Conti

Ormuz

Muscat

Conti

Calicut

Cochin

Ceylon

Colombo

Mediterranean Sea

Damascus

Jerusalem

*Persian
Gulf*

1499

Cabral

Alexandria

Cairo

Covilhao

Covilhao

Vasco da Gama 1498

Red Sea 1488

El Cano commanding Victoria (Magellan Expedition)

AFRICA

ABYSSINIA

INDIAN

Covilhao 1490

OCEAN

Malindi

Mombasa

Vasco da Gama 1498

Cabral

Kilwe

Madagascar
Discovered by Diogo Dias
(Cabral Expedition 1500)

Zaire

**Mani
Congo**

Zaire and
Mani Congo
discovered by
Diogo Cão
1482-1483

Mozambique

Cão 1485

Sofala

Vasco da Gama 1498

Cabral

ANTARCTICA

Cape Cross
Discovered by
Diogo Cão 1485

Discovered by
B. Dias 1488

Diogo Dias 1500

*Cape of
Good Hope*

B. Dias
1487

UNIT 1

When Mount Vesuvius erupted in A.D. 79, it also buried Herculaneum, Stabiae, and other communities.

What questions about Roman culture could these buried communities answer?

Introduction to World History

Interact with History ▶

Roman City of Pompeii, about A.D. 60

The volcano in the background is Mount Vesuvius. In A.D. 79, Mount Vesuvius erupted and rapidly buried the city of Pompeii under ash. Imagine you are a historian trying to learn about Pompeii.

How would you use the ruins of Pompeii to learn about the past?

WebQuest
ClassZone.com

The city of Pompeii was similar to other Roman cities. It had temples, like this one, and shops and government offices.

What does this building tell you about Roman society?

This group of archaeologists is digging in the Temple of Apollo at Pompeii.

Plaster form of a victim from Pompeii

Before You Read: Knowledge Rating

Recognizing what you already know about each of these terms can help you study it more effectively:

excavation   cartography   artifact

In your notebook, rate how well you know each term:

3 = I know what this word means.
2 = I've seen this word, but I don't know what it means.
1 = I've never seen this word before.

Define each term when you read it in the text.

Big Ideas About History

Science and Technology New scientific discoveries change human understanding of the world.

Scientific discoveries have deepened our understanding of history. For example, the ability to take photographs from airplanes and from space has led to the making of better maps. Satellites are able to scan Earth and discover the buried ruins of lost societies. Such discoveries provide new knowledge of the past.

Integrated Technology

eEdition
- Interactive Maps
- Interactive Visuals
- Starting with a Story

INTERNET RESOURCES
Go to ClassZone.com for
- WebQuest
- Homework Helper
- Research Links
- Internet Activities
- Quizzes
- Maps
- Test Practice
- Current Events

Mayan Carving An archaeologist examines a wall carving found in the ruins of Copán, a Mayan city.

c. 3300 B.C.
The "iceman" dies in the mountains of Austria.

2700 B.C.
The Old Kingdom begins in Egypt.

WORLD   3500 B.C.   2500 B.C.

2300 B.C.
The earliest surviving map is created in Babylon.
◄ (clay tablet map)

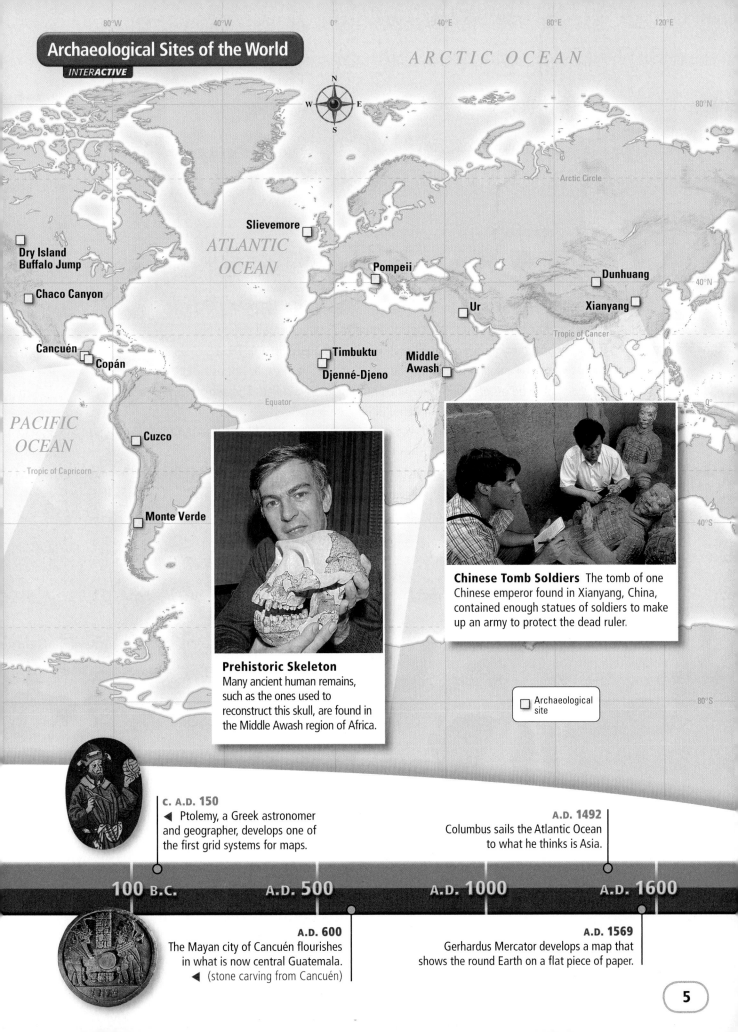

Archaeological Sites of the World
INTERACTIVE

ARCTIC OCEAN

Arctic Circle

80°N

ATLANTIC OCEAN

Dry Island Buffalo Jump

Slievemore

Pompeii

Dunhuang

40°N

Chaco Canyon

Ur

Xianyang

Tropic of Cancer

Cancuén

Copán

Timbuktu

Djenné-Djeno

Middle Awash

Equator

PACIFIC OCEAN

Cuzco

0°

Tropic of Capricorn

40°S

Monte Verde

Chinese Tomb Soldiers The tomb of one Chinese emperor found in Xianyang, China, contained enough statues of soldiers to make up an army to protect the dead ruler.

Prehistoric Skeleton
Many ancient human remains, such as the ones used to reconstruct this skull, are found in the Middle Awash region of Africa.

☐ Archaeological site

80°S

C. A.D. 150
◄ Ptolemy, a Greek astronomer and geographer, develops one of the first grid systems for maps.

A.D. 1492
Columbus sails the Atlantic Ocean to what he thinks is Asia.

100 B.C.   **A.D. 500**   **A.D. 1000**   **A.D. 1600**

A.D. 600
The Mayan city of Cancuén flourishes in what is now central Guatemala.
◄ (stone carving from Cancuén)

A.D. 1569
Gerhardus Mercator develops a map that shows the round Earth on a flat piece of paper.

THE BURIED CITY OF POMPEII

CALIFORNIA STANDARDS
Reading 3.4
Identify and analyze recurring themes across works (e.g., the value of bravery, loyalty, and friendship; the effects of loneliness).

Background: Pompeii (pahm•PAY) was a small city in ancient Italy. Many wealthy Romans lived there. In A.D. 79, a nearby volcano (Mount Vesuvius) erupted. As a result, hot ash buried Pompeii, and thousands of people were killed. The ash preserved the objects and buildings that it covered.

In the 1700s, the city was discovered, and people began to dig there. Today, about three-fourths of Pompeii has been uncovered by archaeologists (AHR•kee•AHL•uh•jihstz)—scientists who find and study physical evidence about the past. Imagine what it might be like to be one of those archaeologists.

Gold bracelet found in Pompeii ▲

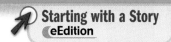
Y ou are a college student working with archaeologists at Pompeii. Most of the people digging in Pompeii are students. Universities around the world send archaeology students to Pompeii as part of their educations.

Much of Pompeii has already been uncovered. The buildings show how ancient Romans built their homes and public buildings. Artwork reveals what the people looked like and how they dressed. Household utensils give clues about their daily lives.

Although people have studied Pompeii for decades, there are still areas to dig out. For weeks, you have been searching for interesting objects. You are hoping to find jewelry or a coin, but finding such objects in Pompeii is unusual. Apparently, when the volcano erupted, many of the fleeing Pompeians took their valuable possessions with them.

Today you are inside the courtyard of a house. The courtyard is more than half filled with dirt and ash. For hours, you have been on your knees, searching. Your back aches, and flies buzz around your face. Digging in Pompeii is hot and dirty work.

You use a trowel, a tool with a triangular blade, to carefully scrape through the dirt. Suddenly, your trowel hits a hard object. This might be it! Excited, you remove the dirt from around the object with your brush and realize that you have found . . . a rock!

Moving to a new area, you notice what seems to be an oddly shaped rock. Carefully, you remove the dirt around it. The piece is curved. It resembles— yes, of course—a bracelet! Excitedly, you record your discovery, carefully lift up the bracelet, and brush off the ash. You feel that your weeks of searching have been worth the effort.

How can archaeologists help us learn about history?

Reading & Writing

1. **READING: Themes** What is one theme or main point of this story?

2. **WRITING: Summarize** Write a paragraph describing what the bracelet looks like and what you can learn from it.

CALIFORNIA STANDARDS **Writing 2.5**
Write summaries of reading materials.

Lesson 1

▶ MAIN IDEAS

1 **Geography** The geography of Earth consists of various landforms and bodies of water.

2 **Geography** Climate, weather, and vegetation influence the ways people live.

3 **Geography** Geographers use five themes to help them understand the use of space on Earth.

▶ TAKING NOTES

Reading Skill: Finding Main Ideas

Finding main ideas will help you organize the information in Lesson 1. A main idea is the major focus of a section or paragraph. Use a chart like the one below to list each main idea and details about it.

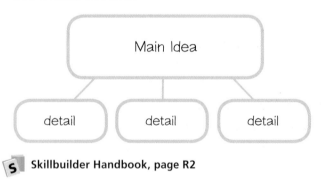

S Skillbuilder Handbook, page R2

▲ **NASA Photograph of Earth** Space travel has allowed us to see Earth in ways that humans of the past could only imagine.

CALIFORNIA STANDARDS

CST 3 Students use a variety of maps and documents to identify physical and cultural features of neighborhoods, cities, states, and countries and to explain the historical migration of people, expansion and disintegration of empires, and the growth of economic systems.

HI 1 Students explain the central issues and problems from the past, placing people and events in a matrix of time and place.

HI 2 Students understand and distinguish cause, effect, sequence, and correlation in historical events, including the long- and short-term causal relations.

Geography of the World

TERMS & NAMES

geography

continent

landform

weather

climate

Build on What You Know Think about where you live. How does where you live affect what you do? Are there mountains to snowboard on or an ocean to surf in? Can you walk to school? Do you have to stay inside because of bad weather, or are you out in the sun? In other words, how has geography affected your history?

Looking at Earth

1 ESSENTIAL QUESTION What covers the surface of Earth?

In this lesson, you will learn some of the basics of geography. You will also learn how geography can help you learn history. **Geography** is the study of Earth's features, such as rivers and deserts. Geographers study how people and other living things interact with Earth's features. That interaction is where history comes in. Geography has shaped where and how people have lived, as well as important historical events.

Continents Geographers divide the world into seven **continents**, or large landmasses. The seven continents are North America, South America, Europe, Africa, Asia, Australia, and Antarctica. You might notice that the continents differ in size. That is because geographers define continents not just by size, but by landforms and even common cultural characteristics.

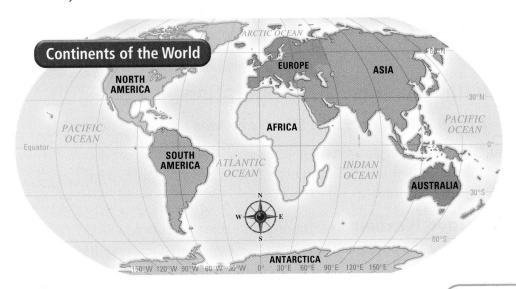

Continents of the World

ARCTIC OCEAN

EUROPE   ASIA
NORTH
AMERICA   60°N

                                      30°N

PACIFIC   PACIFIC
OCEAN   AFRICA   OCEAN

Equator   0°

SOUTH   ATLANTIC
AMERICA   OCEAN   INDIAN
                          OCEAN

                                AUSTRALIA   30°S

                                      60°S

ANTARCTICA
150°W 120°W 90°W 60°W 30°W 0° 30°E 60°E 90°E 120°E 150°E

Geography Handbook

▲ The Alps are a towering mountain range in Europe.

The Chang Jiang of China is the longest river in Asia. ▶

▲ The central part of North America is a mostly flat region that includes the Great Plains.

Landforms and Bodies of Water A **landform** is a feature of Earth's land surface. Earth has many types of landforms, including mountains, plateaus, hills, valleys, and plains. Understanding landforms is important for historians. By thinking about landforms, historians can better understand the peoples they are researching. For example, the farming methods of people living in mountainous regions will differ from those of people living in plains regions.

Nearly 75 percent of Earth is covered by water. Bodies of water include oceans, lakes, and rivers. Some water is fresh, but most is too salty to drink. Still, most bodies of water can be important sources of food by providing fish. Since ancient times, waterways have allowed people to move goods and communicate with other regions. Some landforms and bodies of water are shown in the images above.

REVIEW What are some ways in which geography might affect history?

Climate, Weather, and Vegetation

2 ESSENTIAL QUESTION What is the difference between climate and weather?

Landforms and bodies of water are not the only parts of physical geography that have affected humans. Climate and vegetation have also shaped ways of life.

Climate and Weather The condition of the atmosphere at a particular place and time is called **weather**. The typical weather conditions at a particular place over a period of time are the place's **climate**.

For a dramatic example of the relationship of climate and history, see the History Makers feature about the "iceman" on this page.

Throughout history, climate has affected the ways people live. For example, the Arabian peninsula has a very hot, dry climate with very short rainy seasons. During dry seasons, people would move with their animal herds to permanent sources of water. During rainy seasons, they would move their animals to pastures. Over time, people built a way of life that involved moving along established routes.

Vegetation Vegetation, or plant life, varies from place to place. The types of plants in a place depend on the place's temperature, rainfall, and type of soil. For example, tropical rain forests grow in areas that always have warm, wet weather. The trees grow so close together that only a little sunlight reaches the forest floor.

Vegetation also affects ways of life. For instance, a thousand years ago, Northern Europe had many large forests. People used the forests as sources of fuel and building materials and hunted the animals in them. In contrast, parts of Southwest Asia had very few trees. Southwest Asians used mud bricks for building. Also, they developed trade relations with India and East Africa to get wood and other goods.

People living in the same climate and vegetation region can have different ways of life. In ancient Greece, the climate supported farming. But Greece also borders the Mediterranean Sea, and many Greeks sailed the sea as fishermen or as traders to other countries.

REVIEW How have climate and vegetation affected people's ways of living?

Geography Handbook

History Makers

The Iceman

In 1991, a German tourist found a frozen body in the Ötztal Alps. The body, nicknamed Ötzi, is more than 5,000 years old. It is the oldest mummified human body ever found intact. A mummy is the body of a person or animal that has been preserved.

Ötzi was between 25 and 35 when he died. Recent evidence shows that Ötzi was shot in the back with an arrow. Some scholars think he was murdered. Others believe he was a human sacrifice. Whatever the cause of his death, his body can tell scientists a great deal about climate and vegetation. The fact that his body is so well preserved shows that the climate when he died was very cold—the ice kept his body from decaying. Vegetation found with Ötzi came from very far away, indicating that he had traveled a great distance.

Five Themes of Geography

3 **ESSENTIAL QUESTION** How do geographers organize the study of geography?

One way to think about geography is in terms of major themes or ideas. The five themes of geography are location, place, region, human-environment interaction, and movement. The images and descriptions below show you how these themes apply to California. Keep these themes in mind as you read this book. Understanding the geography of a region helps you understand the history of the region.

Themes of Geography

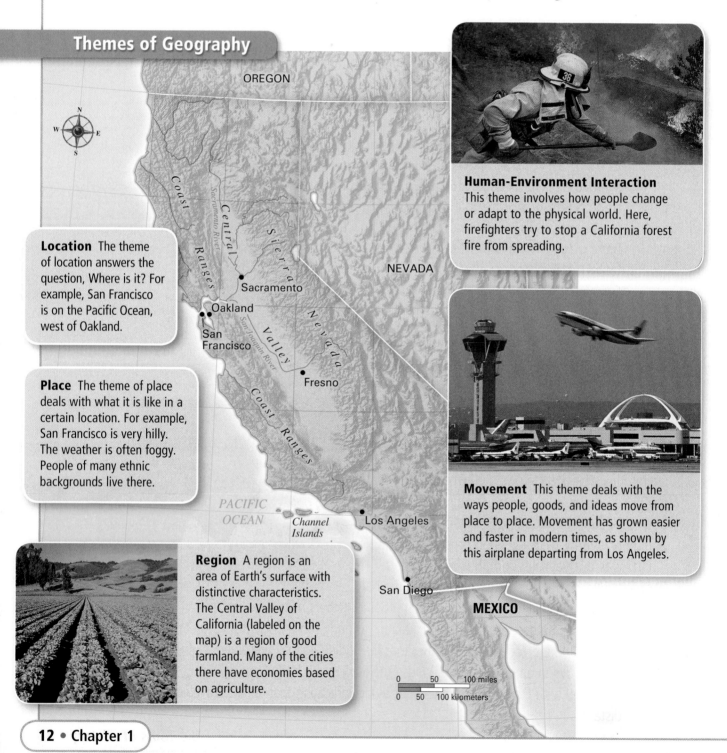

Location The theme of location answers the question, Where is it? For example, San Francisco is on the Pacific Ocean, west of Oakland.

Place The theme of place deals with what it is like in a certain location. For example, San Francisco is very hilly. The weather is often foggy. People of many ethnic backgrounds live there.

Region A region is an area of Earth's surface with distinctive characteristics. The Central Valley of California (labeled on the map) is a region of good farmland. Many of the cities there have economies based on agriculture.

Human-Environment Interaction This theme involves how people change or adapt to the physical world. Here, firefighters try to stop a California forest fire from spreading.

Movement This theme deals with the ways people, goods, and ideas move from place to place. Movement has grown easier and faster in modern times, as shown by this airplane departing from Los Angeles.

Historians and Geography In this lesson, you have read about geography and some ways in which a knowledge of geography is useful to historians. Historians study what people did in the past. One basic influence on what people did was the conditions in which they lived— their geography. For example, the "iceman" you read about on page 11 was wearing a fur robe because it was cold. But how did he get the robe? Did he kill the animal himself, or did he trade something for it? If you knew the geography of where the iceman lived, you might be able to answer these questions. Understanding geography is an important part of being a historian.

REVIEW What are the five themes of geography?

Lesson Summary

- Earth is covered with various landforms and bodies of water.
- Climate and vegetation have shaped human history.
- The five themes of geography help people describe and explain the uses of space on Earth.

Why It Matters Now . . .

Understanding the five themes of geography can make us more aware of the world we live in and our effects on it.

Geography Handbook

---

1 Lesson Review

Homework Helper
ClassZone.com

Terms & Names

1. Explain the importance of

geography	landform	climate
continent	weather	

Using Your Notes

Finding Main Ideas Use your completed chart to answer the following question:

2. List one example of how geography shapes human lives or history. (HI 2)

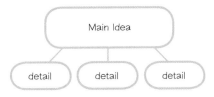

Main Ideas

3. Bodies of water can be sources of food. What else can they be used for? (HI 1)

4. How does vegetation affect people? (HI 1)

5. Use the map on page 12 to explain the difference between place and location. (CST 3)

Critical Thinking

6. **Comparing and Contrasting** How might the lives of people living in a cold climate differ from those of people living in a warm climate? How might they be similar? (HI 2)

7. **Making Inferences** Why might the theme of movement be important to a historian? (HI 2)

Activity **Internet Activity** Pick a landform or body of water to research. Use its name as a keyword to research it on the Internet. Write a paragraph about what you find. (CST 3)
INTERNET KEYWORDS: *Rocky Mountains, Pacific Ocean*

▶ MAIN IDEAS

1 **Geography** Over time, new learning and new discoveries changed maps of the world.

2 **Culture** Many elements found on maps today were developed centuries ago.

3 **Science and Technology** Modern mapmakers use ancient principles and modern technology to produce maps.

▶ TAKING NOTES

Reading Skill: Summarizing

Summarizing means to restate the important points of a passage in your own words. For Lesson 2, summarize each of the main sections, using a chart similar to this one.

Section	Summary
History of Mapmaking	
Features of Maps	
Technology Changes Mapmaking	

 Skillbuilder Handbook, page R3

▲ **Astrolabe** An astrolabe is an instrument that helped sailors to determine their distance from the equator. Astrolabes like the ones shown above helped make long voyages of exploration possible. These voyages produced knowledge that improved maps.

CALIFORNIA STANDARDS

CST 3 Students use a variety of maps and documents to identify physical and cultural features of neighborhoods, cities, states, and countries and to explain the historical migration of people, expansion and disintegration of empires, and the growth of economic systems.

HI 1 Students explain the central issues and problems from the past, placing people and events in a matrix of time and place.

HI 2 Students understand and distinguish cause, effect, sequence, and correlation in historical events, including the long- and short-term causal relations.

Mapping the World

TERMS & NAMES

cartography

projection

hemisphere

latitude

longitude

Build on What You Know Have you ever drawn a map to show a friend where something was? Drawing maps is a skill that humans have used for thousands of years. Understanding and reading maps is an important skill for historians because they need to know where events took place.

History of Mapmaking

1 ESSENTIAL QUESTION What were important advances in maps?

In Lesson 1, you learned about geography and the ways it affects history. Maps, a basic tool of geographers, allow historians to show where and how historical events occurred. The skills and methods people use to make maps are called **cartography** (kahr•TOG•ruh•fee). The oldest surviving map was drawn on a clay tablet in Babylon more than 4,000 years ago. Old maps show how ancient people saw their world.

Early Cartography Ptolemy (TAHL•uh•mee), an ancient Greek geographer, wrote about making maps more accurate. Over the years, the works of Ptolemy became lost to Europeans. However, his techniques were still known in the Muslim world. In the 800s, Muslim scholars translated the works of Ptolemy into Arabic. His ideas remained important and influenced many Islamic mapmakers. Their maps often showed their holy city of Mecca at the center. This could be very useful to Muslims traveling to Mecca.

World Map This map of the world is from a European atlas published in 1570. North America looks incorrect because Europeans at the time had little accurate knowledge of it. ▼

TYPVS ORBIS TERRARVM

Cartography Advances Around 1155, the first known printed map appeared in a Chinese encyclopedia. This development was important because printing allowed more copies of a map to be made. In the early 1400s, the Chinese explorer Zheng He (juhng huh) made detailed maps that helped China expand its trading network. Europeans were also seeking to expand their trading networks.

Thanks to Muslim scholars, Europeans rediscovered the works of Ptolemy in the 1400s. His writings helped European cartographers make more accurate maps. At the time, educated Europeans knew that the world is round. But on a flat map of the round Earth, parts of Earth look smaller or larger than they really are. This stretching or shrinking is called distortion. To control this problem, cartographers developed various types of projections. A **projection** is a way of keeping the distortion of a flat map consistent and manageable. (See the Geography feature below.)

Better maps were a great help to European sailors. Still, sailing was dangerous, and accurate navigation was very hard. Even the famous explorer Christopher Columbus had trouble figuring out his exact location. He thought he was in or near Asia when he was really near the coast of Florida.

REVIEW What technology allowed more copies of maps to be made?

Geography

Map Projections

Because Earth is round, every flat map distorts its surface to some extent. A projection is a way of controlling the distortion. Many types of projections exist. Each one distorts areas on Earth in a certain way. Three common projections are shown at right.

GEOGRAPHY SKILLBUILDER
INTERPRETING VISUALS
Location What is the most accurate way to represent the round Earth without using a projection?

Mercator Projection In a Mercator projection, the continents are more and more distorted as one moves farther from the equator. However a Mercator projection is an excellent reference for directions.

Homolosine (hoh•MAHL•uh•SYN) **Projection** In a homolosine projection, the oceans are divided. This projection accurately shows the shapes and sizes of the landmasses. But the distances on the map are not correct.

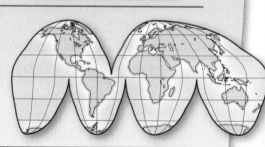

Robinson Projection A Robinson projection is often used in textbooks. It shows the entire Earth. The relative sizes of the continents and oceans are almost accurate. But regions near the poles appear flattened.

Features of Maps

2 ESSENTIAL QUESTION What are the main elements of maps?

Mapmaking has improved over the centuries. Still, the maps of today contain many elements that people developed hundreds of years ago.

Hemispheres On maps, Earth can be divided into two equal halves. Each half is called a **hemisphere**. An imaginary line is used to divide Earth into north and south halves. This line is called the equator. The half of Earth north of the equator is the Northern Hemisphere. The half south of the equator is the Southern Hemisphere.

Another imaginary line divides Earth into east and west halves. This line is called the prime meridian (muh•RIHD•ee•uhn). The prime meridian is also known as the Greenwich (GREHN•ihch) meridian because it goes through Greenwich, England. The half that is west of the prime meridian is the Western Hemisphere. The half that is east of the prime meridian is the Eastern Hemisphere.

Latitude and Longitude As you have read, Ptolemy thought of ideas that improved mapmaking. One of his ideas was to create two sets of lines to locate places on Earth. Imaginary lines that run parallel to the equator are called **latitude** lines. They are used to identify coordinates in the northern and southern hemispheres. **Longitude** lines are imaginary lines that go around Earth through the north and south poles. They are used to identify coordinates in the eastern and western hemispheres.

By using a grid of latitude and longitude lines, you can find the absolute location of a place, the point where its latitude and longitude lines cross. The grid is based on the system of dividing a circle into 360 degrees. Every place on Earth has a unique absolute location. For example, the absolute location of Istanbul, Turkey, is 48° north latitude and 28° east longitude.

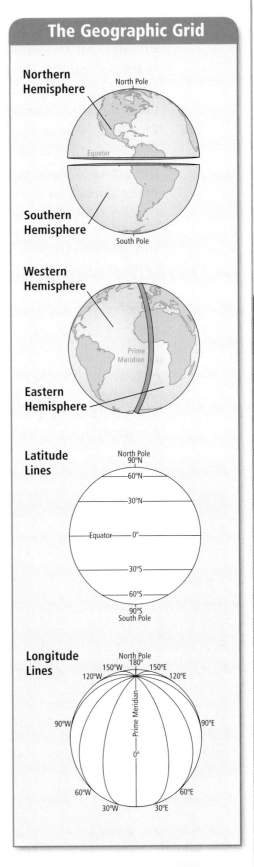

The Geographic Grid

Physical Maps Physical maps show the landforms and bodies of water that are found in particular areas. They also show the shapes of regions. The physical map on this page shows the British Isles. Physical maps have color and shading and sometimes show elevations. On this map, darker green indicates hills and mountains. Blue lines indicate rivers.

Notice that the physical map shows modern country borders, but the names of England, Ireland, Scotland, and Wales are not on the map. Physical maps do not focus on political divisions, such as countries.

Political Maps Political maps show features on Earth's surface that humans created. A political map might include such features as cities and countries. The political map on this page shows the British Isles. Notice how it is different from the physical map of the British Isles. Ireland and the United Kingdom are shown in different colors on the political map.

Political maps also often show capitals, major cities, and important landforms. This map shows the two national capitals of Dublin and London, as well as several major cities. It also shows four political regions within the United Kingdom. They are England, Northern Ireland, Scotland, and Wales.

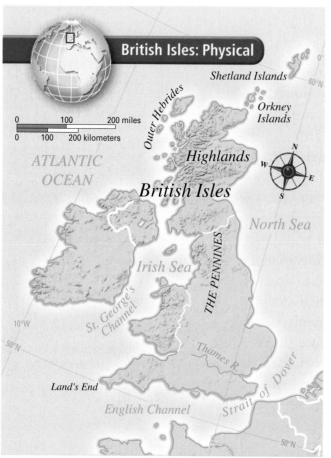

Thematic Maps Thematic maps focus on specific types of information. They might show physical and political information, but that is not their main purpose. For example, the map on this page shows where different types of Christianity were dominant in the British Isles during the Reformation. (You will learn about the Reformation in Chapter 14.)

The colors show where the different belief systems dominated. In other thematic maps, colors can be used to show climates, natural resources, population, or movements of people or ideas. Thematic maps can show a variety of information. Because of this, thematic maps are important tools for historians. You can practice your map-reading skills by using the Skillbuilder on pages 22–23.

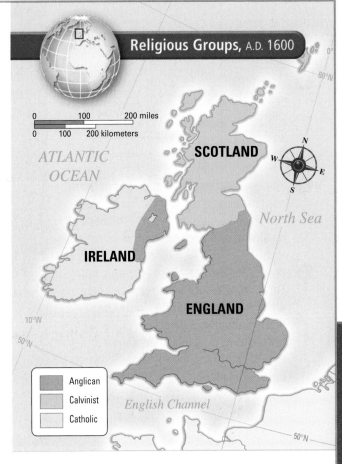

REVIEW What elements are common to physical, political, and thematic maps?

Technology Changes Mapmaking

3 ESSENTIAL QUESTION How can new technology make better maps?

Geographers and historians are always looking for better, more accurate maps—physical, political, and thematic. Today geographers use satellites to get information about Earth.

Global Positioning System The Global Positioning System (GPS) can tell a person his or her exact location on Earth. GPS uses a series of 24 satellites called Navstars that send radio signals to Earth. People can pick up these signals by using a certain type of receiver. The receiver displays latitude, longitude, altitude, and time.

This technology was originally developed by the U.S. military to provide more accurate battlefield information. Now hikers, explorers, sailors, drivers, and, of course, mapmakers use GPS to figure out locations.

How Satellites Gather Data
INTER*ACTIVE*

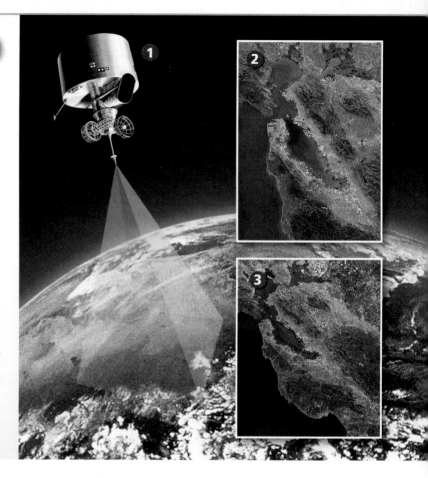

1 An artificial satellite is a device sent into space, where it orbits Earth or some other object. Many satellites gather information that helps mapmakers, historians, and archaeologists.

2 Some satellites take photographs of Earth such as the one shown here. As a result, geographers make more accurate maps of landforms and bodies of water.

3 Some satellites scan infrared waves from Earth. Images such as this one can help archaeologists locate sites for future digs. In addition, such scans can reveal to historians how past humans changed their environments and where natural disasters have taken place.

Weather Forecasting Technology has improved weather maps. The Geostationary Operational Environmental Satellite (GOES) is a weather satellite. This satellite flies in orbit at the speed of Earth's rotation. As a result, it always views the same area. GOES gathers information that is helpful in producing more accurate weather maps.

Geographic Information Systems Finally, a new high-tech tool that geographers use is geographic information systems (GIS). A GIS stores information about the world in a computer. It is able to combine information from many sources and show it in the form of a map.

Geographers often use GIS to solve problems. First, the geographers must decide what kinds of information will help them solve a problem. This information could include maps, photographs, statistical data, and pictures taken by satellites. The geographers then divide the information into layers. For example, one layer might show the physical features, such as hills and valleys, of a region.

A GIS then forms a map by combining the layers of information. The geographers can add or subtract layers to focus their research. Then they study the map. Using GIS in this way, geographers can study an area much more quickly, and in more detail, than they ever could before. The layers of information from GIS are very detailed and useful. But geographers are not the only ones who can make use of this technology.

Historians' Use of Maps By entering historical data into GIS, historians can make layered historical maps. For example, historians might put ancient trade routes on top of a modern satellite image. Then they could compare the courses of the routes with the locations of cities in the region to see whether cities developed along those routes.

REVIEW How might satellite mapping help historians?

Lesson Summary

- Over the centuries, cartographers from many cultures have developed and improved maps.
- Reading maps involves skill in understanding features developed by mapmakers over hundreds of years. There are many types of maps, including physical, political, and thematic maps.
- Geographers use satellites and GIS to get geographic information and to solve problems.

Why It Matters Now . . .

When you read a map, you interpret many features developed by cartographers over the centuries. People today also benefit from new mapping technologies. For example, GPS helps make accurate maps, but it can also guide rescuers quickly to wherever they are needed.

2 Lesson Review

Homework Helper
ClassZone.com

Terms & Names

1. Explain the importance of

cartography   hemisphere   longitude
projection   latitude

Using Your Notes

Summarizing Use your completed chart to answer the following question:

2. How has technology changed mapmaking? (HI 2)

Section	Summary
History of Mapmaking	
Features of Maps	
Technology Changes Mapmaking	

Main Ideas

3. How did Ptolemy's works affect European mapmakers during the 1400s? (HI 1)

4. What types of features are shown on a physical map? (CST 3)

5. How can historians use the same technology as geographers in their work? (CST 3)

Critical Thinking

6. **Making Inferences** Why are maps important to historians? (CST 3)

7. **Drawing Conclusions** Why might it be useful for major landforms to be shown on a political map? (CST 3)

Activity   **Making a Map** Draw a map of the area where you live. Show streets, landmarks, and physical features. Show which way is north. Then describe the relative location of where you live by using the elements in your map. (CST 3)

Reading a Map

Purpose: To learn how to read and understand basic features common to most maps

CALIFORNIA STANDARDS

CST 3 Students use a variety of maps and documents to identify physical and cultural features of neighborhoods, cities, states, and countries and to explain the historical migration of people, expansion and disintegration of empires, and the growth of economic systems.

Learn the Skill

Maps are representations of features on Earth's surface. Some maps show political features, such as national boundaries. Other maps show physical features, such as mountains and bodies of water. Historians use maps to locate historical events, to show how geography has influenced history, and to illustrate human interaction with the environment. Use the numbered points at right to help you understand this map.

See the Skillbuilder Handbook, page R9.

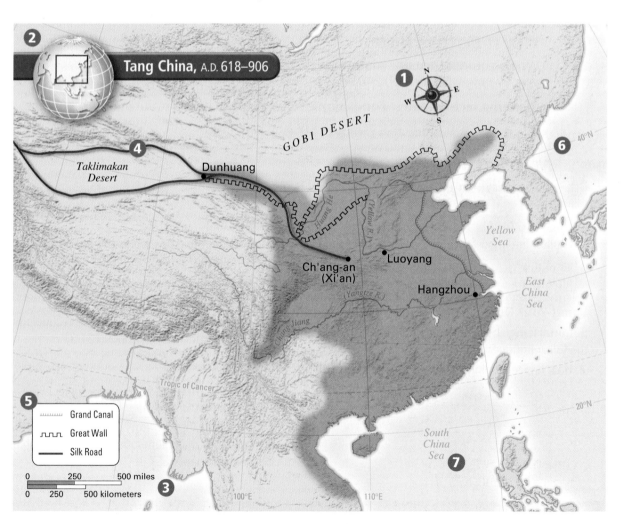

Tang China, A.D. 618–906

The numbers below refer to the numbers on the map.

① **Compass Rose** The compass rose indicates the orientation of directions on the map.

② **Locator** A locator map shows which part of the world the map covers. This locator shows that the map depicts part of eastern Asia.

③ **Scale** The scale shows the ratio between lengths on the map and distances on Earth. The scale on this map indicates that one inch on the map represents 500 miles.

④ **Lines** Lines can indicate rivers, political boundaries, roads, or many other things. The meanings of certain lines might be shown in the legend or key. Here, the red lines represent the Silk Road.

⑤ **Legend or Key** The legend or key explains the symbols, lines, and special colors that appear on the map.

⑥ **Lines of Latitude and Longitude** Lines of latitude and longitude show where places are located on Earth. Hangzhou, for example, is located at about 30° north latitude, 120° east longitude.

⑦ **Labels** Key cities, bodies of water, and landforms are labeled. One label for a body of water on this map is "South China Sea."

You can make a chart like the one below to help you understand a map.

Example:

TANG CHINA, A.D. 618–906	
Location	roughly between latitudes 15° N and 43° N and between longitudes 95° E and 125° E
Map-key information	blue comb line = Grand Canal; black square line = Great Wall; red line = Silk Road
Scale	1 inch = 500 miles
Summary	The Great Wall extended along the entire northern border of Tang China. Dunhuang was located at the western end of the Great Wall.

Apply the Skill

Turn to Chapter 14, page 457, and study the map titled "Christianity in Europe, A.D. 1600." Make a chart like the one in this Skillbuilder to identify the information on the map.

▶ **MAIN IDEAS**

1 **Culture** Archaeologists help us understand the material cultures of ancient people.

2 **Culture** Anthropologists study humans and human cultures.

3 **Culture** Archaeologists and anthropologists can change their theories about the past in light of new discoveries.

▶ **TAKING NOTES**

Reading Skill: Making Generalizations

To make generalizations is to make broad judgments based on information. For Lesson 3, use a diagram like the one below to record the details of what archaeologists do. Then write a general statement about the work of archaeologists.

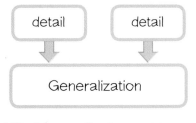

 Skillbuilder Handbook, page R8

▲ **Nazca Skull** The Nazca flourished in southern Peru between 200 B.C. and A.D. 600. Archaeologists know that the Nazca produced detailed fabrics because of pieces such as the cap shown with this mummified head.

CALIFORNIA STANDARDS

HI 1 Students explain the central issues and problems from the past, placing people and events in a matrix of time and place.

HI 2 Students understand and distinguish cause, effect, sequence, and correlation in historical events, including the long- and short-term causal relations.

HI 5 Students recognize that interpretations of history are subject to change as new information is uncovered.

Discovering the Past

TERMS & NAMES
archaeology
artifact
excavation
anthropology
culture

Build on What You Know You have learned about geographers and mapmakers and the ways their work is important for the study of history. Now you will read about archaeology and anthropology and their relationships to history.

Digging Up the Past

1 ESSENTIAL QUESTION How do we learn about ancient societies?

Archaeology is the recovery and study of physical evidence from the past. The scientists who practice archaeology are called archaeologists. They search for artifacts from particular time periods. An **artifact** is an object made by a human. Tools, pottery, and jewelry are examples of artifacts.

Archaeologists also look for other evidence of past human activity or material culture. For example, an irrigation ditch might provide an archaeologist with important clues about how people farmed. Archaeologists can even figure out what people ate by studying the animal bones they discarded.

Beginning the Search All of this information provides archaeologists with clues about the past. But how do archaeologists find these clues? First, they must select a location, or site. Next they survey the site. This involves making a map of the area. Then they collect any artifacts that lie on the surface. The place where each artifact was found is noted on the map.

Connect to Today

Tower of Ubar These archaeologists are digging out remains of the south wall and tower of the city of Ubar, on the Arabian peninsula. ▼

This photograph shows an archaeologist carefully cleaning dirt from a sculpture that was found in the Mayan city of Cancuén. Archaeologists and historians can learn a great deal from such artifacts—and from the places they were found.

1 This large sculpture was part of a building that archaeologists think was a palace. The person it represents was probably a king.

2 See how detailed the sculpture is. Great skill was required to make it. This implies that the culture had a group of people who focused on this craft.

3 This carving is of a person. Facial features, such as the nose and lips, reveal what the ancient Maya looked like.

Buried Clues Archaeologists then dig to find buried evidence. This type of digging is called **excavation**. After retrieving objects (everything from small beads to large weapons), archaeologists record what they found. They describe, photograph, and count their findings. Archaeologists then preserve artifacts. For example, they might store metal artifacts in a low-humidity environment to prevent rust.

Finally, archaeologists try to draw conclusions from evidence. To do this, they ask questions. An archaeologist might ask, When was the pottery I found made? To answer this question, he or she might use carbon dating. This is a scientific process that is used to estimate the ages of objects that contain carbon. For historians, knowing the date of an artifact is very important because it helps them know the order in which events occurred.

P Primary Source Handbook

See the excerpt from Cancuén Archaeological Project, page R35.

REVIEW What is the process archaeologists go through to learn about ancient societies?

Studying Humans

2 ESSENTIAL QUESTION What do anthropologists study?

You may also have heard of anthropology. It is different from archaeology, but related. **Anthropology** is the study of humans and human cultures. Within the study of anthropology are two major areas—physical anthropology and cultural anthropology.

Physical anthropologists study the physical traits of humans, both past and present. For example, they might study how large human brains were 50,000 years ago and compare their findings with the sizes of human brains today.

Vocabulary Strategy

In the word *anthropology*, *-logy* is a **suffix**. Most words containing the suffix *-logy* refer to sciences, theories, or studies.

Studying Culture Cultural anthropologists study human cultures. A **culture** is a way of life shared by a group of people. It includes the arts, beliefs, customs, language, and technology of a people. Cultural anthropologists study the past and present cultures of the world. Like archaeologists, they study artifacts, but they also study the religious beliefs and values of cultures. Also like archaeologists, anthropologists ask questions and test their conclusions against new evidence. In this way, anthropologists hope to better explain how and why people live the ways they do.

▲ **Margaret Mead** The U.S. anthropologist Margaret Mead studied how culture affects human behavior. She did most of her work on Pacific islands.

REVIEW What types of work do archaeologists and anthropologists do?

Changing Views of the Past

3 ESSENTIAL QUESTION Why do theories about the past change?

Archaeologists and anthropologists use their skills to interpret history. But sometimes interpretations of history can change. The ancient Mayan city of Cancuén (kahn•KWEHN) in what is now the Central American country of Guatemala provides an example of how interpretations of the past can change.

Rediscovering Cancuén More than a thousand years ago, Cancuén was a thriving Mayan city. Mayan civilization flourished between A.D. 250 and 900 in Central America. The people created huge temples and palaces. When the Mayan civilization declined, the jungle grew over and hid many of its cities.

Archaeologists discovered Cancuén in 1905. At the time, they thought it was just a small Mayan city. Then, in 2000, archaeologists discovered something amazing. In excavating the site, they found a huge palace. It had 170 rooms, 11 courtyards, and walls 6 feet thick. Smaller houses and workshops surrounded the palace, forming part of a much larger Mayan city.

Old Theory All of the Mayan cities found before Cancuén seemed to have temples. Because of this, many archaeologists and anthropologists believed that Mayan cities had a mostly religious function. Mayan kings, scientists thought, based their power on religion and warfare. They thought this until they began to explore and study the ruins of Cancuén.

New Theory However, Cancuén is a Mayan city with no temples. After studying the evidence, archaeologists concluded that Cancuén was a center of trade. This new evidence has caused archaeologists and anthropologists to rethink their ideas about the Maya. Perhaps religion played a smaller role in Mayan culture than they had thought.

Experts will continue to debate the role of religion in Mayan cities. Recent advances in historians' ability to read Mayan writing will add to the discussion. But the important lesson for us is this: new evidence can cause archaeologists, anthropologists, and historians to change their theories about the past. Studying new evidence and questioning current theories are essential tools in learning about history.

REVIEW What did archaeologists discover after excavating Cancuén?

Lesson Summary

- Archaeologists find and study artifacts.
- Anthropologists study human cultures.
- Views of the past can change in light of new evidence.

Why It Matters Now . . .

Studying the artifacts a society has left behind teaches us about that society. The more we know about the way the world was, the better can be our understanding of the way it is today.

---

3 Lesson Review

Homework Helper
ClassZone.com

Terms & Names

1. Explain the importance of

archaeology	excavation	culture
artifact	anthropology	

Using Your Notes

Making Generalizations Use your completed diagram to answer the following question:

2. What do archaeologists study? (HI 2)

```
┌─────────┐   ┌─────────┐
│  detail │   │  detail │
└────┬────┘   └────┬────┘
     ↓             ↓
   ┌─────────────────────┐
   │   Generalization    │
   └─────────────────────┘
```

Main Ideas

3. Why does an archaeologist carry out an excavation? (HI 1)

4. What is a culture and what aspects of life does it include? (HI 1)

5. Why is new evidence important to archaeologists and anthropologists? (HI 5)

Critical Thinking

6. Comparing and Contrasting What different types of information do archaeologists and anthropologists provide for historians? (HI 5)

7. Making Inferences Why is it important for people researching the past to keep an open mind? (HI 5)

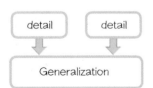
Activity

Recording Artifacts Make a display of objects that a future archaeologist might find at your house. Draw or photograph them, and write captions that describe what they are used for. (HI 5)

Prepare a Time Capsule

Goal: To make a time capsule with artifacts from our culture for future archaeologists and anthropologists to analyze

> **Materials & Supplies**
> - various items that represent U.S. culture
> - box
> - colored pens or paints
> - tape

Prepare

1. Research time capsules and the kinds of objects they contain.

2. With your classmates, discuss what kinds of artifacts you might put in your time capsule.

Do the Activity

1. Discuss with family or friends what types of artifacts they would put in a time capsule.

2. Bring in one artifact from home that you think would be a good addition to a time capsule.

3. Analyze your artifact. What makes it a good addition? What does it say about the culture you live in?

4. Present your artifact to the class and describe why you chose it.

5. With your classmates, evaluate what all the artifacts say about you as a group.

6. Decorate the box and label it as a time capsule.

Follow-Up

What questions might a future archaeologist or anthropologist have about your class on the basis of the artifacts in the time capsule?

Extension

Predicting Imagine opening your time capsule in 50 years. Write a prediction about how things will have changed. Think about your own life, the country, and the world.

CALIFORNIA STANDARDS

HI 5 Students recognize that interpretations of history are subject to change as new information is uncovered.

MAIN IDEAS

1 **Culture** Historians ask questions about the past to focus their research.

2 **Culture** Historians interpret the past on the basis of a study of evidence.

3 **Culture** New discoveries can cause historians to change their interpretations of the past.

TAKING

Reading Skill: Finding Main Ideas

Finding main ideas will help you organize the information in Lesson 4. Use a chart like the one below to list each main idea and details about it.

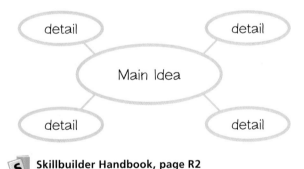

S **Skillbuilder Handbook, page R2**

▲ **Great Chronicles of France**
Historians use many types of documents in their research, such as the illuminated manuscript page shown here. It comes from the *Great Chronicles of France*, a record of French kings up to the 1300s.

Interpreting the Past

TERMS & NAMES

history

historian

primary source

oral history

secondary source

Build on What You Know You have read about how archaeology can help us learn about history. In Lesson 4, you will read about what history is and how people study history. To begin, think about your own history and the ways someone in the future might go about researching you.

The Story of the Past

1 ESSENTIAL QUESTION Why do historians ask questions about the past?

Throughout the ages, people have been interested in history. They want to know why the world is the way it is. Studying history helps them do that. Simply put, **history** is the study of past events. A **historian** is a person who studies and interprets, or explains the importance of, the past.

Why Is History Important? History is important because it can help us learn about today and our future. Studying the past is more than knowing when and where a particular battle was fought. Investigating a historical event involves investigating

- who was involved
- what the issues were
- why the event happened the way it did
- how the event affected what happened next

In other words, much of historical study is about asking questions.

Archives Many historians study documents and images stored in archives. An archive is a collection of documents and other items of historical interest. ▼

31

Historical Questions Historians begin their study of the past by asking questions—historical questions. These questions help historians investigate the past in a meaningful way. Questions can also focus a historian's research. Below is a list of some historical questions. As you read them, try to apply them to a history you are familiar with.

- In what order did events happen?
- How have belief systems developed and changed?
- How have societies dealt with differences among their people?
- How are societies similar and different?
- Why did things happen the way they did?
- How have groups or societies interacted, and what have been the results?

Asking the right questions is central to historical research. Clear historical questions are the foundation for historians' work.

REVIEW Why do people study history?

How Historians Work

2 ESSENTIAL QUESTION How do historians answer their questions?

Once a historian has a question, he or she looks for possible answers. Like detectives, historians examine evidence. Then they interpret the evidence. You have already read about how historians use evidence from archaeologists and anthropologists. Here you will read about other forms of evidence that historians use.

Primary Sources A **primary source** is a document or artifact created during a particular historical period. Primary source documents can include military records, marriage certificates, diaries, and private letters.

Not all primary sources are written, however. Artifacts, such as those discovered by archaeologists, can also be primary sources. Buildings, artworks, pottery, and tools are all examples of artifacts that can be primary sources.

Some primary sources are spoken. **Oral history** includes the stories a culture has passed from generation to generation. For example, West African storytellers

U.S. Constitution
Primary sources include government and legal documents. One example is the U.S. Constitution, which sets forth the principles on which the U.S. government was founded. ▼

Background: The text to the right is part of a letter Christopher Columbus wrote. It is an example of why primary sources need to be carefully examined. Columbus recorded what he believed to be true—that he had reached Asia. But he was mistaken.

from *Concerning the Islands Recently Discovered in the Indian Sea*

By Christopher Columbus
Translated by the Trustees of the Lenox Library

On the thirty-third day after I departed Cadiz,[1] I came to the Indian Sea,[2] where I found many islands. . . .

As soon as we had arrived at that island which I have just now said was called Juana,[3] I proceeded along its coast towards the west for some distance; I found it so large and without perceptible end, that I believed it to be not an island, but the continental country of Cathay.[4]

---

1. **Cadiz:** a city in Spain.
2. **Indian Sea:** He was actually in what is known today as the Caribbean Sea.
3. **Juana:** probably modern Cuba.
4. **Cathay:** This is what Europeans in Columbus' time called China.

DOCUMENT–BASED QUESTION
What are three things you can learn from this primary source?

---

can recite local histories going back hundreds of years. Many cultures around the world have forms of oral tradition. Primary sources of all kinds help historians answer their questions.

Secondary Sources Another type of evidence is a **secondary source**, a work produced about a historical event by someone who was not actually there. Newspapers, books, and paintings are often secondary sources. Oral histories can also sometimes be secondary sources. A secondary source might contain an insight about a historical event that the primary sources do not reflect. For example, a secondary source about Columbus might note that he had not sailed to Asia, something that Columbus himself never realized.

Examining Written Records Historians must carefully examine all of the evidence they use. Part of this examination involves learning the details of sources' creations and evaluating their points of view. This involves asking questions such as the following:

- Why was the source written or recorded?
- Whom was the source written for?
- What was the author's point of view?

By answering these types of questions, historians can learn more about sources and their usefulness as evidence.

REVIEW What do historians use evidence for?

Interpreting History

3 ESSENTIAL QUESTION What do historians do with their evidence?

Historians take evidence from their primary and secondary sources and interpret it. The interpretation can take different forms, including articles, books, and museum displays. Often, historians have conflicting interpretations, as shown below.

In Lesson 3, you learned how new archaeological finds changed theories about the Maya. The same thing can happen with historians. For example, in 1900 a sealed cave was discovered in China. It contained centuries-old documents that described everyday life in Tang China (A.D. 618–907). The documents showed that farmers, not the government, often regulated farm operations. Some documents also showed that government control of local education was limited. From the evidence, historians concluded that the Tang government did not control as much of Chinese society as they previously thought.

Different Interpretations of History

The Roman Empire was a great power that ruled the Mediterranean world and beyond. Eventually, it split into two empires. One question that historians have debated for centuries is, Why did the Western Roman Empire fall?

> This historian believes that the growing weakness of the army caused the empire to fall.

from *The Fall of the Roman Empire* (1986), Arther Ferrill

At the opening of the fifth century a massive army, perhaps more than 200,000 strong, stood at the service of the Western emperor and his generals. In 476 it was gone. The destruction of Roman military power in the fifth century was the obvious cause of the collapse of government in the west.

> This historian believes that peace and wealth made the rich stop worrying about the future. Also, the poor grew jealous of the rich. As a result, neither group could be motivated to defend the empire.

from *Rome* (1960), Michael Ivanovitch Rostovtzeff

[I]n the calm atmosphere of peace, order, and prosperity, . . . The development of . . . apathy [lack of interest] in the rich and discontent among the poor . . . was at first slow and secret. But suddenly it became acute [very serious] when the empire was forced, after nearly two centuries of peace and tranquility, to defend itself against enemies from without. The time called for a great display of enthusiasm. But the rich could not be roused from their indifference; and the poor . . . were filled with hatred and envy.

In this book, you will read about the histories of different societies around the world. As you read, remember to ask historical questions about the societies you are studying. Evaluate and think critically about the evidence you find. Look for similarities and differences between the different societies. Think about how what is happening today will be interpreted by future historians. Finally, have fun. History is full of exciting stories and interesting people that can teach us about the world as it is today.

REVIEW How can new evidence change historical interpretations?

Lesson Summary

- Historians begin their work by asking questions about the past.
- Historians find, evaluate, and interpret evidence to gain knowledge about the past.
- By studying new evidence, historians can change or expand their knowledge of the past.

Why It Matters Now . . .

Studying history teaches us how the past has influenced the present. It also teaches us that what we do today affects the future.

4 Lesson Review

Homework Helper
ClassZone.com

Terms & Names

1. Explain the importance of

history   primary source   secondary source
historian   oral history

Using Your Notes

Finding Main Ideas Use your completed chart to answer the following question:

2. What are two types of evidence that historians use? (REP 4)

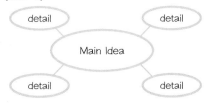

Main Ideas

3. How does asking questions help historians? (REP 1)

4. How are historians similar to detectives? (REP 4)

5. What factors can change a historical interpretation? (HI 5)

Critical Thinking

6. Comparing How might using an artifact as a primary source compare with using a written primary source? (REP 4)

7. Assessing Credibility of Sources How believable would a general's diary entry about a battle be? Explain. (REP 4)

Activity **Asking Historical Questions** Review the information about asking historical questions. Then write 3 historical questions that interest you and explain how you might research them. (REP 1)

Literature CONNECTIONS

from
Discovering the Inca Ice Maiden
My Adventures on Ampato

by Johan Reinhard

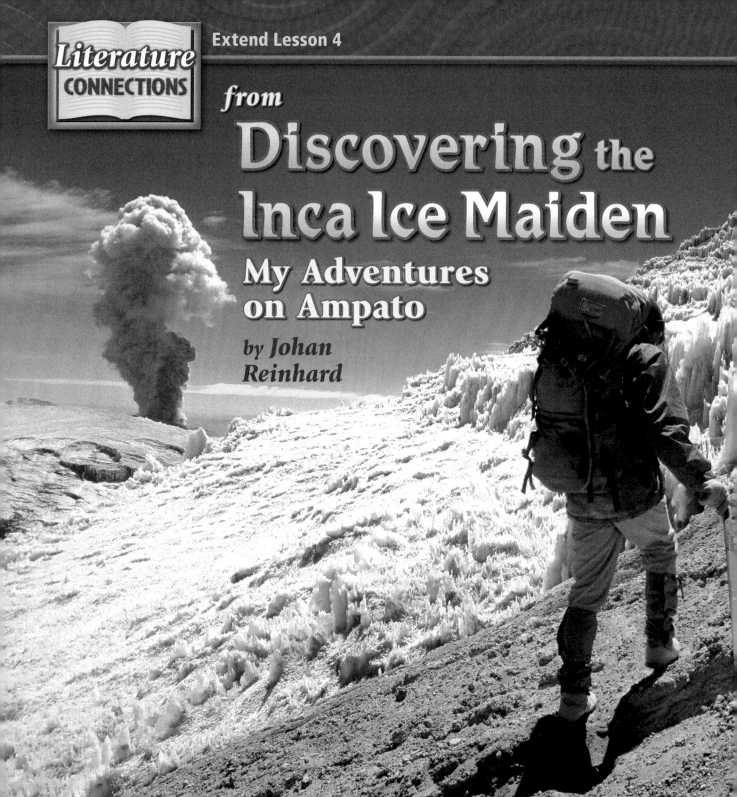

Background: The Inca were a people that lived in the Andes (AN•deez) Mountains of South America. They had elaborate religious rituals that have left behind mummies. Most Incan mummies have been preserved in dry lowlands. But some, believed to be human sacrifices, have been found frozen on high mountain peaks. This account describes a 1995 expedition to Peru by the anthropologist Johan Reinhard (shown above). He was accompanied by his climbing partner, Miguel Zárate.

CALIFORNIA STANDARDS
Reading 2.4
Identify and trace the development of an author's argument, point of view, or perspective in text.

September 6

During our first ascent of Ampato[1] on September 6, we made our way up the northern slope. We thought this would be a fairly simple route, but, as we neared the top, ice pinnacles blocked our way. They had been formed by erosion caused by the sun and wind.

We had to break through a mile of ice pinnacles to reach one of the lower summits at 20,400 feet. Much to our surprise, just as we were about to reach it, we saw a long layer of grass encased in the ice. We were puzzled. How did so much grass get here? Grass could not grow at this altitude!

We climbed the rest of the way to the summit and found that it was rounded and covered with grass, the "grass site." Pieces of Inca pottery and textiles, rope, chunks of wood, and even leather and wool sandals were scattered about. Flat slabs of rock had been carried from over a thousand feet below to make flooring. One slab still had a rope around it. The rock floor had been covered with thick layers of grass, to make a resting place. . . .

September 7

The next day, using a different route along a ridge, we moved our tent up to a small plateau at 19,200 feet. There we found the remains of several Inca ruins, including wooden poles that could have been used to make large tents. After setting up our own tent, we searched for the route the Incas had used to the top. We found grass and pieces of wood that had been placed onto the steeper sections of the slope to help make a trail to the summit.

September 8

The next morning we crossed over the "grass site" at 20,400 feet and made our way through and around ice pinnacles inside Ampato's crater until we were about 200 feet below the summit. . . .

[O]n the summit ridge, we saw stones that had formed a corner of a building. Most of the structure had fallen down one of two naturally formed gullies that dropped 200 feet to the inside of the crater. From the ridge we could not see where these led. So I wrapped two stones in yellow plastic that I had carried in case we needed to mark our way. I threw a stone down each of the gullies, thinking "It'll be a miracle if we ever see them again."

We then climbed down off the ridge and scrambled our way around beneath it. We soon spotted yellow plastic below us where the rocky slope met the ice pinnacles where we had been climbing to the summit only a few hours before.

REVIEW Why did they throw stones wrapped in yellow plastic down the gullies?

---

1. **Ampato:** an inactive volcano in Peru.

A little farther we saw what looked to us like a mummy bundle lying on the ice. It seemed so unlikely to find a mummy out in the open, we literally couldn't believe our eyes. Miguel said, "Maybe it's a climber's backpack."

Only half joking, I replied, "Maybe it's a climber."

As we drew closer, I knew from the stripes on the cloth that it was probably a mummy bundle. This would mean only one thing: The Incas had performed a human sacrifice on the ridge top. The bundle containing the victim had been buried in the structure that had collapsed when part of the summit ridge crashed into the crater.

I knew that even a partially frozen body would be invaluable for science. A frozen body is like a time capsule, which allows scientists to look back into the past and find out things difficult to know otherwise— such as what foods were eaten, what diseases and bacteria existed, who was related to the mummy, where it came from, and much more.

I grew more excited as I remembered that only three frozen mummies had been recovered in all of South America.

Descending towards it, we found fragments of a torn textile. A seashell, two cloth bags containing food offerings (maize kernels and a maize cob), llama bones, and pieces of Inca pottery were strewn about on the slope above the bundle.

After I photographed these items, Miguel used his ice ax to cut loose the bundle from the ice.

He turned it on its side for a better grip. Both of us were momentarily stunned as the body turned.

We looked straight into the face of a young girl.

She was the first *frozen* female mummy found in South America!

Her dried-out features made me fear that we had arrived too late. However, the bundle weighed about 90 pounds, which meant the body was still frozen. A dried-out mummy would have weighed much less.

REVIEW How could they tell that the mummy was not dried out?

I wondered what to do next. If we left the mummy behind in the open, the sun and volcanic ash would cause further damage. Climbers might find her and take her and the other artifacts as souvenirs or to sell. The ground was frozen rock hard, and it was impossible to bury the mummy. A

▲ **Wooden Cups**
This pair of cups was found on the mountain near the mummy, along with many other artifacts.

heavy snowfall could cover the summit and make recovery impossible. . . .

Thoughts rushed through my mind. It could take weeks, if not months, to get a government permit that would allow me to return and recover the mummy. Obtaining the funding to organize a scientific expedition could take even longer.

I decided that we should try to carry the mummy and the statues down the mountain. This would be difficult under the best of circumstances. Unfortunately, we were both feeling weak, and I had an upset stomach.

REVIEW Why did the anthropologist feel it was important to get the mummy down the mountain?

Just as I thought things couldn't be worse, it began to snow! Then, in the darkening light, Sabancaya[2] erupted. We'd seen the volcano erupt before, but now it looked threatening.

Brushing aside a feeling of dread, we wrapped the bundle in plastic and attached it to my backpack. We had to scramble for a mile around the ice pinnacles inside the crater to link up with the route back to camp.

The "Ice Maiden" ▼

This was one of the hardest things I've ever done. My backpack was so heavy that any slip meant a hard fall, and I crashed to the ground a dozen times. I could only get back on my feet by propping myself against the ground with my ice ax and lunging upward. Every fall meant precious minutes lost.

▲ **Ceramic Jar**
This jar shows evidence that lightning hit the mountain grave where it was buried. The heat burned dirt into the finish of the jar.

---

2. **Sabancaya:** an active volcano in Peru, located very close to Ampato.

Reading & Writing

1. **READING: Author's Perspective** What reasons does the author give for trying to recover the mummy?

2. **WRITING: Persuasion** This story was written by the anthropologist who made the discovery. Write a paragraph about why he is or is not a good source of information.

CALIFORNIA STANDARDS Writing 2.4
Write persuasive compositions.

VISUAL SUMMARY

The Tools of History

GEOGRAPHY (CST 3)
- Geography helps us understand the surroundings in which history happens.
- The five themes of geography are location, place, region, movement, and human-environment interaction.

CULTURE (HI 1, REP 1, REP 4)
- Learning about the past helps us understand the present.
- New learning and discoveries have led to better maps, better science, and a better understanding of history.

SCIENCE & TECHNOLOGY (HI 2, HI 3, HI 5)
- Ancient mapping standards are still useful today.
- Modern technology helps produce accurate and informative maps.

TERMS & NAMES

Explain why the words in each set below are paired with each other.

1. **climate** and **weather**
2. **longitude** and **cartography**
3. **artifact** and **excavation**
4. **historian** and **secondary sources**

MAIN IDEAS

Geography of the World (pages 8–13)
5. What are some examples of landforms? (CST 3)
6. What is absolute location? (CST 3)

Mapping the World (pages 14–23)
7. What types of information can a thematic map show? (CST 3)
8. How do satellites help modern mapmakers? (CST 3)

Discovering the Past (pages 24–29)
9. What do archaeologists study? (HI 1)
10. How can new discoveries affect interpretations of history? (HI 5)

Interpreting the Past (pages 30–39)
11. What is the first step in the historical process? (REP 1)
12. What are primary and secondary sources? (REP 4)

CRITICAL THINKING
Big Ideas: Science and Technology

13. **UNDERSTANDING CAUSES** What development in science and technology helped the knowledge of mapmaking spread from culture to culture? (HI 2)
14. **EXPLAINING HISTORICAL PATTERNS** How did advances in technology, such as the astrolabe, and the creation of better maps help lead to a new historical period? (HI 3)
15. **RECOGNIZING CHANGING INTERPRETATIONS OF HISTORY** How might the scanning ability of satellites lead to changes in interpretations of history? (HI 5)

ALTERNATIVE ASSESSMENT

1. **WRITING ACTIVITY** Use the Internet and your library to learn about the "ice maiden." On the basis of your research, write a one-page report about what scientists have learned about her so far. (Writing 2.3)

2. **INTERDISCIPLINARY ACTIVITY—ARCHITECTURE** Use books and the Internet to learn about Mayan temples. Use your research to make a drawing of a Mayan temple. Describe how archaeologists think it was built and what role temples played in Mayan culture. (HI 5)

3. **STARTING WITH A STORY**

 Using books and the Internet, find pictures of artifacts found in Pompeii. On the basis of your research, draw a picture of the bracelet you found and ask a historical question involving the artifact. (REP 1)

Technology Activity

4. **CREATING A MULTIMEDIA PRESENTATION**
Use the Internet or a library to find old maps of the world. Create a multimedia presentation on how the world has been shown over the centuries. Include

- information about how maps of the world have changed
- conclusions about the accuracy of historical maps
- text for each slide
- documentation of your sources

Research Links
ClassZone.com

Reading a Map Use your knowledge of world history and the map below to answer the questions. (CST 3)

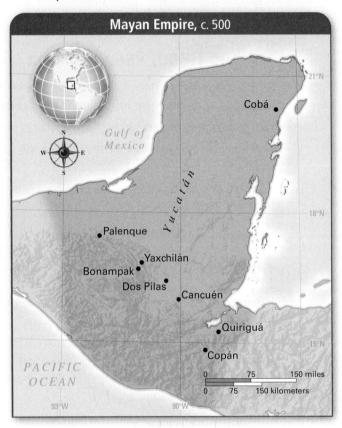

Mayan Empire, c. 500

1. **What is the relative location of Cobá with reference to the other Mayan cities?**

   A. on a plain
   B. at 20° N, 80° W
   C. in the jungle
   D. near water

2. **Which line of longitude is Cancuén closest to?**

   A. 15° N
   B. 18° N
   C. 90° W
   D. 93° W

Test Practice
ClassZone.com

Additional Test Practice, pp. S1–S33

Chapter 2

The Expansion and Fall of Rome

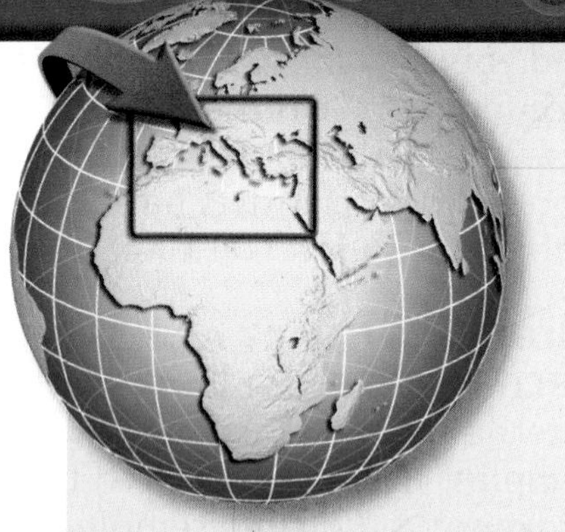

Before You Read: People Search

Use the following sentences to conduct a search for classmates who have the following information:

- Find someone to explain who Caesar Augustus was.
- Find a person who knows something about the Byzantine Empire.
- Find someone who can point to a modern-day legacy of Rome.

Record what you learn in your notebook.

Big Ideas About Ancient Rome

Government Governments create law codes and political bodies to organize a society.

The Romans built a large and powerful empire. They held their empire together with military force and a highly organized government. After Rome's fall, the Byzantines created a long-lasting empire.

Integrated Technology

eEdition
- Interactive Maps
- Interactive Visuals
- Starting with a Story

INTERNET RESOURCES
Go to **ClassZone.com** for
- WebQuest
- Homework Helper
- Research Links
- Internet Activities
- Quizzes
- Maps
- Test Practice
- Current Events

ROME

284
Diocletian becomes emperor.
◄ (gold coin showing Diocletian)

330
Emperor Constantine moves capital from Rome to Byzantium.

476
Western Roman Empire falls.

200

400

WORLD

300s
Aksum kingdom in East Africa reaches its height.
(ruin of Aksum tower) ▶

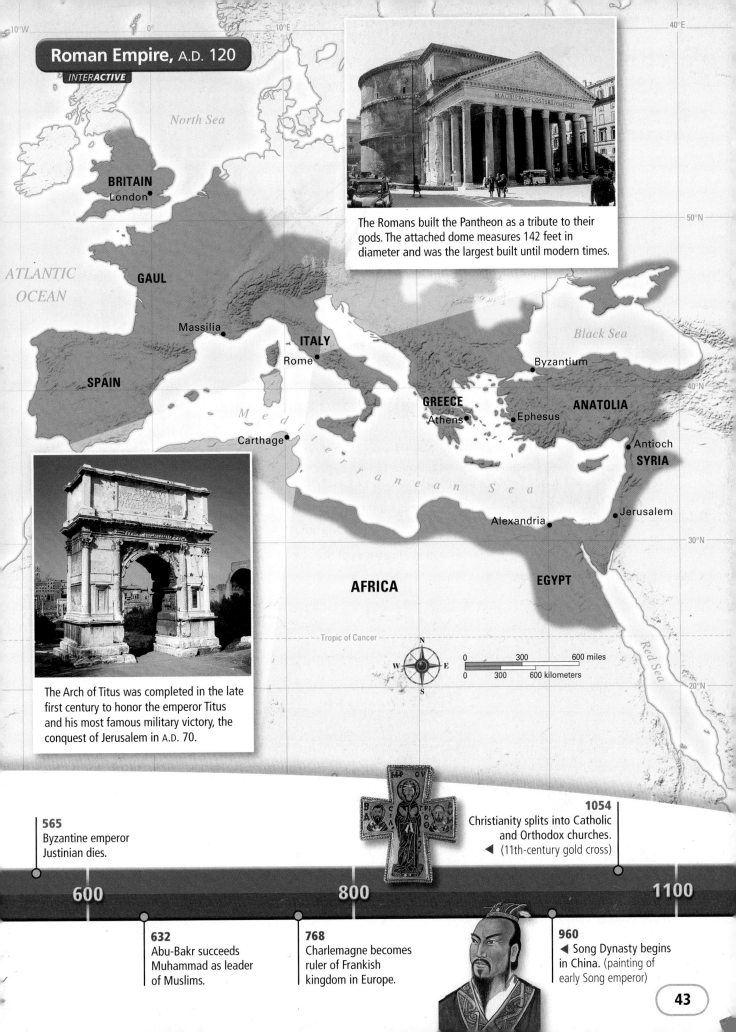

Roman Empire, A.D. 120
INTER*ACTIVE*

The Romans built the Pantheon as a tribute to their gods. The attached dome measures 142 feet in diameter and was the largest built until modern times.

The Arch of Titus was completed in the late first century to honor the emperor Titus and his most famous military victory, the conquest of Jerusalem in A.D. 70.

565
Byzantine emperor Justinian dies.

632
Abu-Bakr succeeds Muhammad as leader of Muslims.

768
Charlemagne becomes ruler of Frankish kingdom in Europe.

1054
Christianity splits into Catholic and Orthodox churches.
◀ (11th-century gold cross)

960
◀ Song Dynasty begins in China. (painting of early Song emperor)

600   800   1100

A DANGEROUS RACE

CALIFORNIA STANDARDS
Reading 3.4
Identify and analyze recurring themes across works (e.g., the value of bravery, loyalty, and friendship; the effects of loneliness).

Background: Many of you have learned about the rise of one of the most famous civilizations in history: Rome. Rome emerged on the Italian peninsula around 500 B.C. From there, it grew into a large empire that lasted nearly 1,000 years.

As mighty as it was, Rome had its share of problems. As the empire declined, Roman rulers kept citizens happy with an increasing number of games and sporting events. One of the most popular events was chariot racing in the massive arena, the Circus Maximus.

Second-century Roman relief of a chariot race ▶

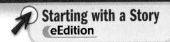

The bright sun is making you warm under your helmet and racing coat. The whip in your hand is damp with sweat. Some of that is from nerves, not from the heat. Since you were a child, you wanted to be a great chariot racer. And now your time has come. You are about to begin your first chariot race. You are excited, but also a little bit afraid.

The chariot races are the most popular entertainment in Rome. Racers can win hundreds of races and earn a great amount of money. But they can also die in one of the spectacular crashes that happen frequently.

You scan the large crowd all around you. There is no way to shut out the roar of screams and cheers. But soon your attention focuses on the man just beyond the starting line. It is he who will drop the *mappa*, the white starting flag, that signals the beginning of your race and your career.

In front of the chariot, your four stallions stamp and kick up dust. They seem as nervous as you do, and with good reason. The sharp turns and hard surfaces on the track cause many horses to suffer broken bones and concussions. You wrap the horse reins around your body for better control of the giant animals.

Then you look down to be sure your knife is still secured in your belt. If your chariot overturns, you will need the blade to cut yourself free of the reins. Otherwise, your chariot or the horses might crush you to death. Suddenly, the crowd grows quiet. You look up to see that the man beyond the starting line has raised the flag. You grip the reins tightly and suck in your breath. And then the flag drops.

What did it take to be a successful chariot racer?

Reading & Writing

1. **READING: Themes** Analyze the text to determine what characteristics you think the Romans valued based upon the popularity of the chariot races.

2. **WRITING: Response to Literature** Write a headline and brief news article based upon how you think this chariot race ended.

CALIFORNIA STANDARDS Writing 2.2
Write responses to literature.

► MAIN IDEAS

1 **Government** Early Rome grew from a small village to a thriving republic on the Italian peninsula.

2 **Culture** The Romans eventually built a large empire that spread their culture to many lands.

3 **Belief Systems** During the Roman Empire, a powerful new religion known as Christianity emerged.

► TAKING NOTES

Reading Skill: Explaining Sequence

Placing historical events in order helps you understand relationships among events.
As you read about the rise and expansion of Rome, record major events on a time line like the one shown below.

510 B.C.   A.D. 14

S Skillbuilder Handbook, page R15

▲ **Trajan's Column** Trajan's Column stands as a monument to Rome's power. Built by order of the emperor Trajan and finished in A.D. 113, it depicts scenes of the emperor's military conquests.

CALIFORNIA STANDARDS

7.1.1 Study the early strengths and lasting contributions of Rome (e.g., significance of Roman citizenship; rights under Roman law; Roman art, architecture, engineering, and philosophy; preservation and transmission of Christianity) and its ultimate internal weaknesses (e.g., rise of autonomous military powers within the empire, undermining of citizenship by the growth of corruption and slavery, lack of education, and distribution of news).

7.1.2 Discuss the geographic borders of the empire at its height and the factors that threatened its territorial cohesion.

CST 3 Students use a variety of maps and documents to identify physical and cultural features of neighborhoods, cities, states, and countries and to explain the historical migration of people, expansion and disintegration of empires, and the growth of economic systems.

The Rise and Expansion of Rome

TERMS & NAMES

republic

Augustus

empire

emperor

Christianity

Build on What You Know Consider what you know about ancient Rome. Perhaps images of gladiators and chariot races come to mind. Indeed, both were part of Roman civilization. As you will read, however, Rome is most remembered for being one of the most influential empires in all of history.

The Origins of Rome

1 ESSENTIAL QUESTION How did Rome begin?

Rome began near the center of what is now Italy. From about 700 to 500 B.C., the Italian peninsula was home to three groups—the Latins, the Greeks, and the Etruscans. The Latins built the original settlement of Rome on a series of hills along the Tiber River. These settlers are considered to be the first Romans.

The Geography of Rome

As the settlement of Rome grew, it benefited from a favorable environment. The region experienced cool, rainy winters that created acres of productive farmland. Meanwhile, Rome's location near the Apennines Mountain range protected it from harsh weather. It also kept the settlement safe from easy foreign invasion. In addition, the nearby Tiber River enabled the Romans to engage in a busy and prosperous trade network throughout Italy, and later throughout the Mediterranean Sea.

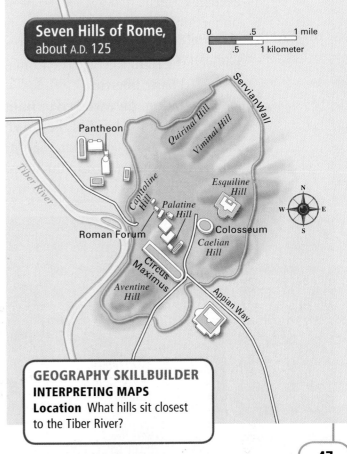

Seven Hills of Rome, about A.D. 125

Pantheon · Quirinal Hill · Viminal Hill · Servian Wall · Capitoline Hill · Palatine Hill · Esquiline Hill · Roman Forum · Colosseum · Caelian Hill · Circus Maximus · Aventine Hill · Appian Way · Tiber River

GEOGRAPHY SKILLBUILDER
INTERPRETING MAPS
Location What hills sit closest to the Tiber River?

A Kingdom Emerges Historians believe that sometime during the eighth century B.C., Rome became a kingdom. For the next several centuries, a series of kings ruled over the growing Roman civilization. Many of these kings were related to the Etruscans, a powerful group from northern Italy that had a great impact on Roman culture.

The last king to rule Rome was Tarquin the Proud. He often ruled with a harsh hand. As a result, the Romans rose up in 510 B.C. and drove Tarquin from power. They refused to live under the rule of a king again. Instead, they decided to base their government largely on the will of the people.

REVIEW What brought an end to the kingdom of Rome?

From Republic to Empire

2 **ESSENTIAL QUESTION** Why did Rome change from a republic to an empire?

The Romans established a form of government known as a **republic**. In a republic, power rests with citizens, who vote to select their leaders. For the next 500 years, the Romans operated under a political system that serves as a model for many of today's democratic nations.

The Roman Republic The Romans created a government in which average citizens had a voice. To be sure, the wealthy and members of noble families wielded great influence in the Roman Republic. What's more, Roman women had few rights. Even so, all free-born males enjoyed the right to vote. The Romans also created laws that protected basic liberties.

In addition, they worked to limit the power that one person could hold. At the head of the government were two leaders known as consuls. However, their power was limited. They could rule only for one year, and the Roman lawmaking body, the Senate, acted as a check to the consuls' power.

Connect to Today

Roman Forum The political center of Rome was known as the Forum—the ruins of which still stand. ▼

In addition to their government, the Romans prided themselves on their powerful and well-organized army. And they used that army to expand their territory. The Romans eventually conquered all of what is modern-day Italy as well as other nearby lands. During a series of wars between 264 and 146 B.C., Roman forces defeated a powerful North African civilization known as Carthage. (These wars were known as the Punic Wars.) The victory gave the Romans control over much of the Mediterranean Sea.

Decline of the Republic As the Roman Republic grew larger and more populated, the task of maintaining order and stability became increasingly difficult. In addition, tensions arose between the different classes in Roman society. Eventually, Rome fell into a civil war, which is a conflict between different groups within a country.

In 45 B.C., a powerful Roman general named Julius Caesar brought order to Rome and named himself sole ruler. This brought an end to the Roman Republic. In 44 B.C., political opponents of Caesar killed him. A bloody power struggle followed. Caesar's adopted son Octavian emerged as the winner and unchallenged ruler of Rome. He took the title **Augustus** (aw•GUHS•tuhs), or "divine one." His rule began an era of great growth for Rome as the empire reached the greatest extent of its size and influence.

Augustus Under the leadership of Augustus, Rome became a mighty empire. ▼

Rome Becomes an Empire Under Augustus, Rome became an empire. An **empire** is a group of different cultures or territories led by a single all-powerful ruler. The ruler of an empire is known as the **emperor**. Augustus was a careful and brilliant leader. He used his power to create a strong government. The Senate continued to represent citizens' interests, but it now had little power. During his rule, a long period of peace and prosperity began. It is known as the Pax Romana, or "Roman Peace."

Augustus died in A.D. 14, but the policies he began enabled Rome to grow and become stronger. By the second century A.D., the Roman Empire reached its largest size. It ruled over two million square miles. Tied together by more than 50,000 miles of roads, the empire extended from Spain in the west to Mesopotamia in the east. It took in lands from Britain in the north to the Sahara in the south. Approximately 60 million people lived under Roman rule. They included Celts, Germans, North Africans, Greeks, Syrians, Jews, and Egyptians.

REVIEW How did Rome build such a powerful empire?

The Rise of Christianity

3 **ESSENTIAL QUESTION** How did Christianity grow so powerful?

At the height of its power, Rome was indeed a strong and influential empire. But it couldn't control everything. One thing that Roman leaders could not contain was the spread of a new religion known as **Christianity**. From its emergence during the Roman Empire, Christianity would become one of the dominant religions in history and retain its great influence through today.

Jesus and His Teachings Christianity is the religion based on the teachings of Jesus, who is believed by Christians to be the son of God. Jesus was born in the Roman province of Judea sometime around 6 to 4 B.C. He was a member of a group known as the Jews. They practiced a religion known as Judaism. Many of Jesus' teachings contained ideas from Judaism, including the belief in a single god. Jesus encouraged people to love God as well as their neighbors, and even to love their enemies. He also taught that God had created a kingdom in heaven for all people who followed his teachings.

Jesus began his teachings as a young adult. He achieved a great following. This troubled many Roman leaders. They viewed him as a threat to their own power and authority. Eventually, authorities arrested Jesus and put him to death.

Jesus This 16th-century painting of Jesus healing a blind man illustrates the belief among many of his followers that Jesus had great powers. ▼

According to Christian belief, Jesus rose from the dead and went to heaven. His followers continued to spread his teachings across the Roman Empire. Those who became Christians did so at great risk. They believed in a single god, and so refused to worship Roman gods. For that reason, Roman officials imprisoned and killed many Christians. Nonetheless, Christianity continued to spread throughout the empire.

While Christianity grew stronger, the Roman Empire itself eventually grew weaker. In the next lesson, you'll read about the forces that led to the fall of Rome.

REVIEW What were some of the main teachings of Jesus?

Lesson Summary

- The Romans established an early form of a republic, in which average citizens had a strong voice in government.
- Rome eventually became a large empire that spread its influence to many lands.
- Christianity emerged during the Roman era and became one of the world's influential religions.

Why It Matters Now . . .

Christianity remains one of the most popular and significant religions today with some two billion followers worldwide.

---

1 Lesson Review

Homework Helper
ClassZone.com

Terms & Names

1. Explain the importance of

republic   empire   Christianity
Augustus   emperor

Using Your Notes

Explaining Sequence Using your completed time line, answer the following question:

2. What events marked the beginning and the end of the Roman Republic? (CST 3)

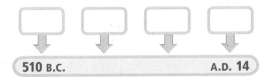

510 B.C.   A.D. **14**

Main Ideas

3. What rights did most male citizens enjoy in the Roman Republic? (7.1.1)

4. What factors led to the Roman Empire's growth? (7.1.2)

5. Why did Roman leaders treat Christians harshly? (HI 1)

Critical Thinking

6. **Drawing Conclusions** Why did the creators of the Roman Republic work to ensure that no leader became too powerful? (7.1.1)

7. **Identifying Issues and Problems** What challenges do you think came with governing an empire as large and diverse as Rome? (7.1.2)

Activity   **Internet Activity** Use the Internet to research a town or region outside Italy that Rome ruled. Determine what Roman influences still exist there and deliver your findings in a short speech.
INTERNET KEYWORD: *Roman Legacy* (7.1.2)

► MAIN IDEAS

1 **Culture** A series of internal problems weakened the Roman Empire.

2 **Government** Under the leadership of two strong emperors, the struggling empire underwent significant changes.

3 **Government** Foreign groups invaded Rome and conquered the western half of the empire.

► TAKING NOTES

Reading Skill: Categorizing

Categorizing means grouping similar things together. After reading this lesson, use a graphic organizer like the one shown here to list the internal factors that weakened the Roman Empire.

Internal Factors

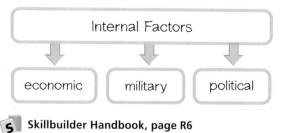

economic   military   political

S **Skillbuilder Handbook, page R6**

▲ **Germanic Invaders** Rome could not stop the waves of invaders from the outlying Germanic tribes. This sculpture belonged to a Germanic group called the Lombards.

CALIFORNIA STANDARDS

7.1.1 Study the early strengths and lasting contributions of Rome (e.g., significance of Roman citizenship; rights under Roman law; Roman art, architecture, engineering, and philosophy; preservation and transmission of Christianity) and its ultimate internal weaknesses (e.g., rise of autonomous military powers within the empire, undermining of citizenship by the growth of corruption and slavery, lack of education, and distribution of news).

7.1.2 Discuss the geographic borders of the empire at its height and the factors that threatened its territorial cohesion.

7.1.3 Describe the establishment by Constantine·of the new capital in Constantinople and the development of the Byzantine Empire, with an emphasis on the consequences of the development of two distinct European civilizations, Eastern Orthodox and Roman Catholic, and their two distinct views on church-state relations.

Decline and Fall of the Empire

► TERMS & NAMES
Constantine
Clovis

Build on What You Know Consider what problems any large empire might face, from economic difficulties to invasion by outsiders. Think about what problems might be the most serious and how they might cause an empire to collapse and cease to exist.

Internal Weaknesses Threaten Rome

1 ESSENTIAL QUESTION What internal problems weakened the Roman Empire?

Late in the second century A.D., Rome began to decline. The empire still appeared as strong as ever to most who lived under its control. Yet a series of internal problems had begun that would put mighty Rome on the road to ruin.

Economic and Social Difficulties During the second century A.D., the empire stopped expanding. The end of new conquests meant an end to new sources of wealth. Officials grew desperate to pay the empire's growing expenses, including the rising cost of maintaining its army. As a result, the government raised taxes. This caused a hardship for many citizens.

Other aspects of Roman society suffered as well. For example, many poor Romans found it harder to become educated—as the cost of education grew out of reach. In addition, distributing news across the large empire became more difficult. As a result, people grew less informed about civic matters.

Hadrian's Wall
Hadrian's Wall in Britain marked the northern reach of the Roman Empire. ▼

Decline in Agriculture A decline in agriculture also weakened the empire. Throughout Italy and western Europe the soil had become difficult to farm due to constant warfare and overuse. As a result, harvests grew increasingly weak.

The use of slave labor added to the problem. Like other societies throughout history, the Romans practiced slavery. The slaves were mainly war captives who were forced to work in the fields. The use of slave labor discouraged improvements in technology that might have improved farming. As Roman agriculture suffered, disease and hunger spread and the population declined.

Military and Political Problems Meanwhile, Rome's once powerful military began showing signs of trouble. Over time, Roman soldiers in general became less disciplined and loyal. They pledged their allegiance not to Rome, but to individual military leaders.

Feelings of loyalty eventually declined among average citizens as well. In the past, Romans eagerly engaged in civic duties and public affairs. Roman politics, however, grew increasingly corrupt. Politicians became more interested in financial gain than in public service. As a result, many citizens lost their sense of pride in the government. They no longer showed a willingness to sacrifice for the good of Rome.

REVIEW How did military and political problems weaken the empire?

Rome Divides into East and West

2 ESSENTIAL QUESTION What changes did Rome undergo?

Despite all its difficulties, the Roman Empire continued on for another 200 years. This was due in part to the strong leadership of two emperors: Diocletian (Dy•uh•KLEE•shuhn) and Constantine.

Power Shifts East Diocletian became the leader of Rome in A.D. 284. He restored order to the empire by ruling with an iron fist and tolerating little opposition. In addition, he took the bold step of dividing the empire into east and west as a way of making Rome's immense territory easier to govern.

Constantine succeeded Diocletian as emperor and took two steps of great significance. The first occurred in A.D. 313, when he declared an end to all attacks on Christians. By allowing Christians to worship freely, he played a key role in Christianity's growth.

Constantine's second significant action came in A.D. 330. He moved the capital of the empire from Rome to the Greek city of

Byzantium (bih•ZAN•tee•uhm), which then became known as Constantinople. The new capital signaled a shift in power from the western part of the empire to the east.

REVIEW What key changes did Constantine make to Rome?

Fall of the Roman Empire

3 ESSENTIAL QUESTION What brought about the fall of Rome?

In addition to internal difficulties, the Romans faced another major problem. Foreign groups were swarming all around Rome's borders. Soon they would invade, and the empire's slow decline would turn into a rapid downfall.

Invasion and Conquest A number of Germanic peoples and other groups lived beyond Rome's borders. During the late 300s, these groups began pushing into Roman lands. Their reasons for invading varied. Some came looking for better land or to join in Rome's wealth. Many others were fleeing a fierce group of invaders from Asia known as the Huns. Eventually, the Huns themselves would invade the empire. In 476, Germanic tribes conquered Rome. It was this date, according to most scholars, that marks the fall of the Western Roman Empire.

P Primary Source Handbook

See the excerpt from Letter 123, page R36.

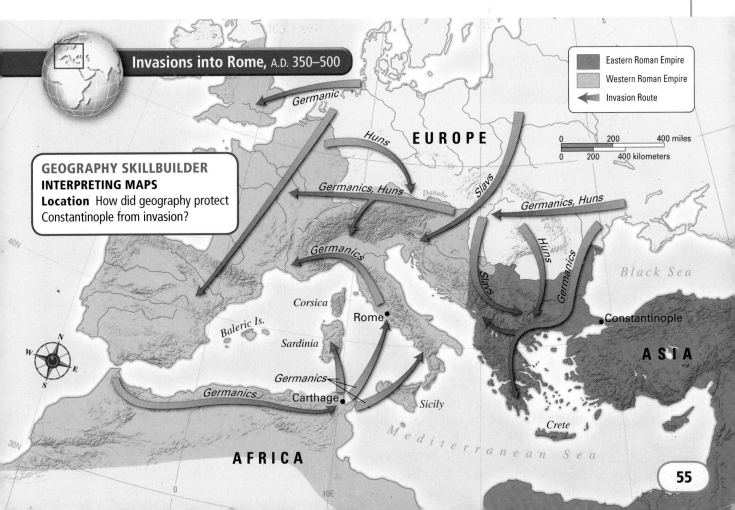

Invasions into Rome, A.D. 350–500

Germanic
Huns
EUROPE
Germanics, Huns
Danube
Slavs
Germanics, Huns
Germanics
Slavs
Huns
Germanics
Black Sea
Corsica
Rome
Baleric Is.
Sardinia
Germanics
Germanics
Carthage
Sicily
Constantinople
ASIA
Crete
Mediterranean Sea
AFRICA

Eastern Roman Empire
Western Roman Empire
Invasion Route

0   200   400 miles
0   200   400 kilometers

GEOGRAPHY SKILLBUILDER
INTERPRETING MAPS
Location How did geography protect Constantinople from invasion?

End of the Empire In the years that followed, the final holdouts of Roman power in the west fell. In 486, **Clovis**, the leader of a Germanic group known as the Franks, conquered the remaining Roman land in the province of Gaul (present-day France and Switzerland). Clovis founded a Frankish kingdom that would grow large and powerful.

Though the western part of the empire had crumbled, the eastern part survived. As you will read in the next lesson, this civilization became known as the Byzantine Empire. It remained a power in the region for another thousand years.

REVIEW What significant event occurred in 476?

Lesson Summary

- Internal problems weakened the Roman Empire.
- Two emperors brought key reforms to Rome.
- Foreign invaders conquered the Western Empire.

Why It Matters Now . . .
Lands once ruled by Rome still use many Roman institutions.

Causes of the Fall of the Western Roman Empire

- **Economic Decline:** few new sources of wealth; increased taxes; weakened agriculture

- **Disloyal Military:** less-disciplined soldiers; allegiance to generals instead of Rome

- **Political Corruption:** more interest in financial gain than public service

- **Slavery:** discourages advances in farming

- **Lack of Patriotism:** less willingness to sacrifice for Rome

- **Invasions:** Germanic tribes and others attack the empire.

---

2 Lesson Review

Terms & Names
1. Explain the importance of

Constantine   Clovis

Using Your Notes
Categorizing Using your completed graphic, answer the following question:

2. How did Rome's military problems weaken the empire? (7.1.1)

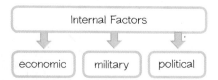

Main Ideas
3. What were the main internal problems of the Roman Empire? (7.1.1)

4. In what ways did Constantine reform the Roman Empire? (7.1.3)

5. Why were the Germanic tribes able to conquer the Roman Empire? (7.1.2)

Critical Thinking
6. Evaluating Information How did moving the capital from Rome to Constantinople weaken the western part of the empire? (7.1.2)

7. Forming and Supporting Opinions Which of Rome's internal problems hurt the empire the most? (7.1.1)

Activity **Making a Map** Use the world map on pages A6–A7 of the Atlas to sketch a world outline map. You will add to this map in later units. Use the map on page 43 to draw in the geographic borders of the Roman Empire during its height. (CST 3)

Play a Board Game

Goal: To gain a greater understanding of the fall of Rome

Prepare

Work with a partner to develop nine questions about the decline and fall of Rome. Answers may be a single word or date and should not be longer than a sentence. Have the teacher examine your work. Make any suggested revisions.

Do the Activity

1 Cut the cardboard into a large square or rectangle.

2 Create a tic-tac-toe board (two vertical lines intersecting two horizontal lines) on the front and back of the cardboard.

3 Write your questions in each of the nine tic-tac-toe spaces. Write the answers in the corresponding spaces on the back. Tape a cut-out piece of paper over each answer.

4 Pass the boards around the room.

5 Play with your partner using each board you receive. Place your game piece on each question you answer correctly or that your partner answers incorrectly.

Follow Up

Work with your partner to review any questions that either of you missed.

Extension

Making Comparisons Compare all the board games to determine the most frequently asked questions.

Materials & Supplies

- cardboard
- scissors
- paper
- tape
- marker or thick pen
- five-six similar game pieces (hand-made or otherwise)

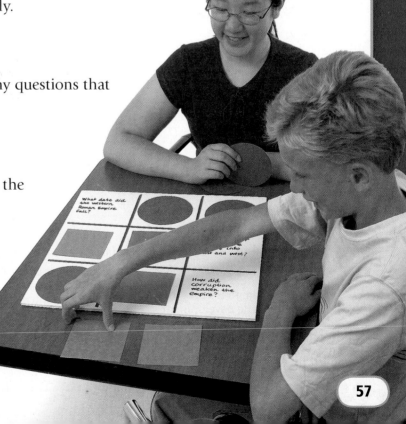

CALIFORNIA STANDARDS

7.1.1 Study the early strengths and lasting contributions of Rome (e.g., significance of Roman citizenship; rights under Roman law; Roman art, architecture, engineering, and philosophy; preservation and transmission of Christianity) and its ultimate weaknesses (e.g., rise of autonomous military powers within the empire, undermining of citizenship by the growth of corruption and slavery, lack of education, and distribution of news).

▶ **MAIN IDEAS**

① **Government** The legacy of Rome continued with the Byzantine Empire.

② **Geography** Located between the East and the West, the Byzantines created a unique society.

③ **Belief Systems** Christianity thrived in the Byzantine Empire but eventually split into two separate churches.

▶ **TAKING NOTES**

Reading Skill:
Understanding Cause and Effect

Cause and effect deals with why an event happened and what impact it had. Fill in a chart like the one below to help you recognize the causes and effects of the split in Christianity.

Causes	Effects

 Skillbuilder Handbook, page R26

▲ **Emperor Constantine** This stone bust depicts Constantine, the Roman emperor after whom the city of Constantinople was named.

CALIFORNIA STANDARDS

7.1.3 Describe the establishment by Constantine of the new capital in Constantinople and the development of the Byzantine Empire, with an emphasis on the consequences of the development of two distinct European civilizations, Eastern Orthodox and Roman Catholic, and their two distinct views on church-state relations.

HI 1 Students explain the central issues and problems from the past, placing people and events in a matrix of time and place.

CST 3 Students use a variety of maps and documents to identify physical and cultural features of neighborhoods, cities, states, and countries and to explain the historical migration of people, expansion and disintegration of empires, and the growth of economic systems.

The Early Byzantine Empire

TERMS & NAMES
Byzantine Empire
Justinian I
Justinian Code
schism
Roman Catholic
Orthodox

Build on What You Know You have learned that during the later years of Rome, the empire split into east and west. The western part fell to invaders. The eastern part survived and became known as the **Byzantine Empire**. It carried on the glory of Rome for many more centuries.

Justinian Builds a New Rome

1 ESSENTIAL QUESTION What were the main characteristics of the Byzantine Empire?

In the years after the Western Roman Empire fell, the Byzantine Empire rose to great heights. This was due in large part to the efforts of a powerful ruler named **Justinian I**.

The Rule of Justinian During his reign (527–565), Justinian expanded the Byzantine Empire and recaptured some of the land Rome had lost. Justinian also enacted key measures at home. He is best remembered for the legal code developed during his rule. The **Justinian Code** regulated much of Byzantine life and served the Byzantine Empire for 900 years.

Justinian also left his mark on Byzantine society through his many public works and building projects. He built a large and impressive palace complex, where he lived and ruled with his wife and trusted adviser, Empress Theodora.

Hagia Sophia
The Hagia Sophia is an enduring symbol of the Byzantine Empire. Justinian built the church after an earlier church was damaged during a public uprising. ▼

59

Theodora (c. 500–548) and Justinian (482–565)

Justinian met Theodora when she was an actress. An old Roman law actually forbade government officials from marrying actresses. So Justinian got rid of the law—and the couple became husband and wife.

As empress, Theodora displayed much power and influence. In 532, for example, she convinced her husband and advisers to put down a rebellion instead of fleeing the palace. Tens of thousands of protestors were killed. However, many historians believe that Theodora's actions saved Justinian's crown.

Hagia Sophia Justinian also built churches and directed the building of the famous church of Hagia Sophia (HAY•ee•uh soh•FEE•uh). Visitors hailed its beauty. "Such an abundance of light poured into this church," said one observer, "you would declare that the place is not lighted by the sun from without, but that the rays are produced within."

REVIEW What were some of Justinian's main accomplishments?

The Rise of Constantinople

2 **ESSENTIAL QUESTION** What was life like in Constantinople?

Hagia Sophia was just one of the magnificent structures that towered over the empire's impressive capital, Constantinople.

The Capital City Constantinople's location played a key role in its growth. It stood between Europe and southwest Asia. As a result, it became a thriving center of business and trade. The wealth and energy of Constantinople could be seen in its everyday activities. The main street running through the city was the Mese (MEHS•ee), or "Middle Way." Merchant stalls lined the street and sold products from distant corners of Asia, Africa, and Europe. Citizens also could enjoy free entertainment at the city's large arena, the Hippodrome.

REVIEW What were some of the main attractions of Constantinople?

Disagreements Split Christianity

③ ESSENTIAL QUESTION What two churches emerged from the split in Christianity?

The location of the Byzantine Empire on the edge of both Europe and Asia meant that the empire was influenced by ideas and goods from both regions. While the empire was built on Roman foundations, it developed its own ways. An example of this can be seen in the area of religion. Christianity was the main religion in both the Byzantine Empire and the West. Over time, however, Christianity developed differently in each place. These differences led to a split in the Christian church—and the emergence of two distinct European civilizations.

Christianity Remains Strong As you recall from your reading, Christianity emerged during the Roman Empire. By the fall of Rome, Christianity had developed a well-defined structure. At the local level, a priest led small groups of Christians. A bishop supervised several churches. The bishop of Rome was known as the pope. He was the head of the entire Christian church. After the Western Roman Empire fell, Christianity remained a strong influence in the region. Despite its fall from glory, the city of Rome remained the home of the pope—and the center of Christianity.

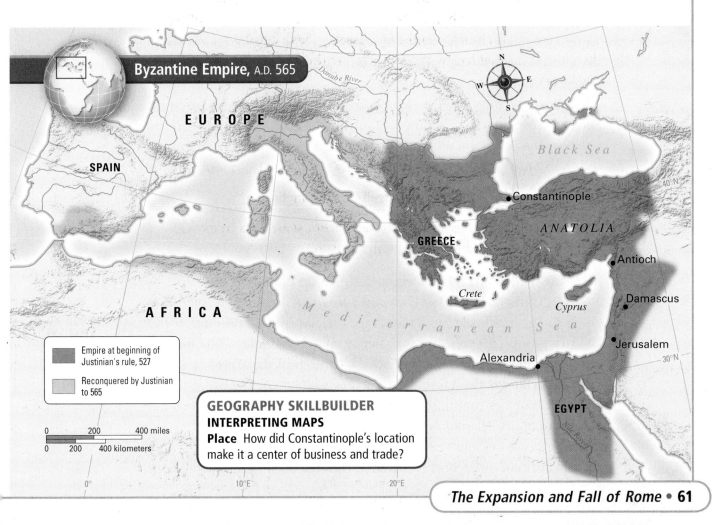

Byzantine Empire, A.D. 565

EUROPE

SPAIN

Danube River

Black Sea

40°N

•Constantinople

ANATOLIA

GREECE

•Antioch

Crete

Cyprus

•Damascus

AFRICA

M e d i t e r r a n e a n   S e a

•Jerusalem

Alexandria

30°N

Empire at beginning of Justinian's rule, 527

Reconquered by Justinian to 565

EGYPT

Nile River

0   200   400 miles
0   200   400 kilometers

GEOGRAPHY SKILLBUILDER
INTERPRETING MAPS
Place How did Constantinople's location make it a center of business and trade?

0°   10°E   20°E

Roman Catholicism and Eastern Orthodox Christianity

Patriarch Nicolas, who served in the 900s ▶

▲ Pope Gregory I, who served from 590 to 604

Roman Catholic
- Services are conducted in Latin or local languages.
- The pope has authority over all other bishops.
- The pope claims authority over all kings and emperors.
- Priests may not marry.

Similarities
- They base their faith on the gospel of Jesus and the Bible.
- They use sacraments such as baptism.
- Their religious leaders are priests and bishops.
- They seek to convert people.

Eastern Orthodox
- Services are conducted in Greek or local languages.
- The patriarch and other bishops head the church as a group.
- The emperor claims authority over all religious leaders.
- Priests may be married.

Tensions Rise As the Byzantine Empire grew, popes and Byzantine emperors often clashed. Byzantine emperors took a great interest in religious matters. They considered themselves the final authority on religious issues. The popes, however, insisted that they had the ultimate say on such matters.

One of the most intense debates over religious power occurred in the eighth century. In 730, the Byzantine emperor Leo III banned the use of icons. Icons are religious images used by Eastern Christians to aid their prayers. The emperor viewed the use of icons as idol worship, or the belief in false gods.

The pope quickly weighed in on this Eastern dispute. He supported the use of icons. He also excommunicated, or removed from the church, the Byzantine emperor.

The Church Splits Differences between the Eastern and Western Christian churches continued to grow. In 1054, these disagreements led to a **schism**, or official split, between the two groups. The result was the creation of two new Christian religions: the **Roman Catholic** Church in the West and the **Orthodox** church in the East.

Both churches continued to embrace many of the same principles of Christianity. Still, each church established different structures and beliefs that set them apart. One of the most significant differences occurred in the area of church-state relations.

Visual Vocabulary

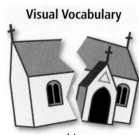

schism

As Roman Catholicism developed, the pope claimed authority over not just the church but also kings and emperors. Under Eastern Orthodoxy, the emperor ruled over the patriarch, the leader of the Orthodox church.

The schism of 1054 highlights how the Byzantine Empire gradually developed its own unique civilization. Rome's influence, however, would live on. As you will read in Lesson 4, Rome's ideas, customs, and institutions have played a key role in the development of Western civilization—and still do today.

REVIEW How did the schism of 1054 affect the Christian church?

Lesson Summary

- After the Western Roman Empire fell, the Byzantine Empire continued many Roman ways.
- Influenced by both Rome and the East, the Byzantines developed a unique culture.
- Disagreements within the Christian church caused it to split into two separate churches.

Why It Matters Now . . .

Today, millions of people still practice Roman Catholicism and Eastern Orthodoxy.

---

3 Lesson Review

Homework Helper
ClassZone.com

Terms & Names

1. Explain the importance of

Byzantine Empire	schism
Justinian I	Roman Catholic
Justinian Code	Orthodox

Using Your Notes

Understanding Cause and Effect Use your completed chart to answer the following question:

2. What event caused a strain in the Christian church in 730? (HI 1)

Causes	Effects

Main Ideas

3. What factors helped Constantinople to become a thriving city? (CST 3)

4. What two churches emerged from the schism in the Christian church? (7.1.3)

5. How did the two churches differ in their views on church-state relations? (7.1.3)

Critical Thinking

6. **Evaluating Information** How did Justinian help to strengthen the Byzantine Empire? (7.1.3)

7. **Making Inferences** Which church leader appeared to be more powerful, the pope or the patriarch? Why? (7.1.3)

Activity **Creating a Chart** Use research materials to determine the approximate number of members of the Roman Catholic and the Eastern Orthodox churches today. Then show the numbers in a chart or graphic. (7.1.3)

Research Links
ClassZone.com

Life in Constantinople

Purpose: To learn about daily life in the Byzantine capital of Constantinople

Constantinople was a bustling city where people of diverse backgrounds came to exchange goods and ideas. Most city life took place toward the eastern edge of town, where the city's palace, public stadium, and most notable church were located.

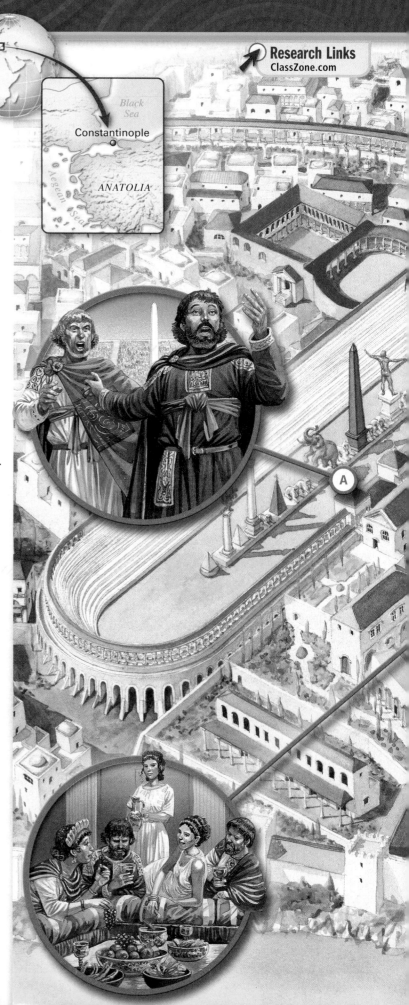

A **Hippodrome** This massive stadium played host to chariot races, imperial and military ceremonies, political demonstrations, and even public executions.

B **Mese** The city's main commercial street was filled with merchant stalls, street entertainers, and shoppers. With their favorable scents, the perfumers got the stalls closest to the imperial palace.

C **Hagia Sophia** Worshipers flocked to the city's most magnificent church, which rose 180 feet in the air and was decorated with rare stones from all parts of the empire.

D **Housing** Most dwellings in and around the city were three-story buildings made of stone, brick, or wood. Families usually occupied one floor of the building.

E **Imperial Palace** The home of the emperor and his court boasted a lavish banquet hall, as well as polo grounds, several libraries, and a swimming pool.

CALIFORNIA STANDARDS

7.1.3 Describe the establishment by Constantine of the new capital in Constantinople and the development of the Byzantine Empire, with an emphasis on the consequences of the development of two distinct European civilizations, Eastern Orthodox and Roman Catholic, and their two distinct views on church-state relations.

Activities

1. **TALK ABOUT IT** In what way did the average family live differently from the royal court in Constantinople?

2. **WRITE ABOUT IT** Imagine you are an official charged with increasing tourism to Constantinople. Using the information in this feature, write a paragraph encouraging travel to the city. (Writing 2.4)

MAIN IDEAS

① **Culture** Aspects of Roman culture influenced later societies.

② **Science and Technology** The Romans made a lasting contribution in the field of engineering.

③ **Government** A number of nations today base their political and legal systems on Roman ideals.

TAKING NOTES

Reading Skill: Finding Main Ideas
Finding the main ideas of a lesson involves identifying its key points. Create a graphic organizer like the one shown below to highlight the lasting achievements of the Roman Empire.

```
   Law              The Arts
        Lasting
      Achievements
 Building          Government
```

S Skillbuilder Handbook, page R2

▲ **Roman Mask** This Roman wall painting of a theatrical mask shows the Romans' appreciation for the theater.

CALIFORNIA STANDARDS

7.1.1 Study the early strengths and lasting contributions of Rome (e.g., significance of Roman citizenship; rights under Roman law; Roman art, architecture, engineering, and philosophy; preservation and transmission of Christianity) and its ultimate internal weaknesses (e.g., rise of autonomous military powers within the empire, undermining of citizenship by the growth of corruption and slavery, lack of education, and distribution of news).

HI 3 Students explain the sources of historical continuity and how the combination of ideas and events explains the emergence of new patterns.

REP 4 Students assess the credibility of primary and secondary sources and draw sound conclusions from them.

The Legacy of Rome

Build on What You Know Look at the buildings in your community. Do some have columns or domes? Are there bridges with arches? If so, these structures may have features that developed during the Roman Empire.

The Impact of Roman Culture

1 ESSENTIAL QUESTION What lasting contributions of Roman culture influenced later societies?

As Roman culture developed, it borrowed many aspects of Greek civilization. The Greeks, as you recall, were the dominant civilization in the Mediterranean before the Romans. The Romans conquered the Greeks but kept alive many of their ways. In addition, Roman artists, philosophers, and writers created their own styles that would influence many societies to follow.

Roman Art The Romans popularized an earlier type of floor art called mosaic. A **mosaic** is a picture made out of many small, colored tiles or pieces of glass. Examples of mosaics can still be found in churches and government buildings around the world.

Sculptural styles from the Roman era are also a regular sight in modern times. The Greeks were the first to create statues based on realistic forms. The Romans adopted this style. The Statue of Liberty in New York Harbor is one example of a modern statue whose style dates back to Greek and Roman times.

Roman Mosaic
This mosaic shows Roman fighters battling wild animals, a popular spectator sport among Romans. ▼

Background: One of the most important Stoic thinkers of the Roman era was the scholar and politician Marcus Tullius Cicero (106–43 B.C.). He stressed the importance of citizenship and believed that Romans should work for the good of each other and Rome.

from "On Duty"
By Marcus Tullius Cicero
Translated by Walter Miller

As the Stoics hold, everything that the earth produces is created for man's use; and as men, too, are born for the sake of men, that they may be able mutually to help one another . . . we ought to . . . contribute to the general good by an interchange of acts of kindness, by giving and receiving, and thus by our skill, our industry, and our talents to cement human society more closely together, man to man.

DOCUMENT–BASED QUESTION
What are ways that people can demonstrate good citizenship, according to Cicero?

Philosophy and Citizenship The Romans borrowed much of their philosophy from the Greeks. The philosophy of **Stoicism** was especially influential in Rome. It was developed by the Greek philosopher Zeno. Stoicism stressed the importance of virtue, duty, and endurance in life. These were all values that many Romans prized.

The beliefs of Stoicism helped create a strong sense of citizenship in Rome. Citizenship refers to the relationship individuals have with their country. As part of this relationship, a country provides protection and security for its citizens. In return, citizens are expected to take an active part in society in order to strengthen their country. Today, these aspects of Stoicism are viewed by many as necessary qualities for being a good citizen.

Roman Language Another lasting aspect of Roman culture was its language, known as Latin. Because the Romans conquered most of Europe, Latin is the basis for several European languages. These include Spanish, Italian, French, Portuguese, and Romanian. In addition, more than half of the words in English have a basis in Latin. What's more, Latin was the official language of the Roman Catholic Church into the 20th century.

REVIEW What influence did Latin have on the larger world?

Architectural and Engineering Feats

2 **ESSENTIAL QUESTION** What advancements did the Romans make in the field of engineering?

The Romans were talented engineers. Their styles have influenced architects and builders throughout history.

New Building Methods Roman architecture used many arches, vaults, and domes. An arch is a curved opening that holds up a structure. A vault is an arched structure that forms a ceiling or roof. A dome is a large, half-globe-shaped roof. All these structures existed before Rome emerged. However, the Romans used these forms to build higher and larger than anyone had before.

The Romans used arches to create large public buildings, like the Colosseum. This giant outdoor arena is one of the great achievements of Roman engineering and served as a model for many future public stadiums. Roman builders also utilized arches in the building of **aqueducts**. Aqueducts are bridge-like structures designed to bring fresh water into cities and towns.

Countless modern structures include these Roman forms. Highway bridges are often built on arches. The U.S. Capitol and capitols in many states—including California, Texas, and Massachusetts—have large domes, arches, and vaults just like Roman buildings.

Roman Roads To improve communications and travel across their far-reaching empire, the Romans built some 50,000 miles of roads. Workers built many roads for the specific purpose of transporting Rome's powerful army. The Appian Way was the first one of these and it is probably the most famous. Today, tourists still visit Rome to walk on it.

The Romans built roads over mountains, across rivers, and over swamps. These roads were so well built that some can still be seen today. In addition, many modern highways in Europe still follow the routes first laid out by the Romans.

REVIEW What three architectural styles did the Romans use most often?

Roman Aqueducts
The remains of this Roman aqueduct still stand over the Gard River in France. ▼

INTERACTIVE

Contributions to Religion and Law

3 **ESSENTIAL QUESTION** What contributions did the Romans make to religion and law?

Great civilizations, such as that of Rome, have passed on not only things we can touch and see. They have also given us powerful ideas.

Preserving Christianity One of Rome's key contributions was its support and encouragement of Christianity. Although they resisted Christianity early on, Roman officials later embraced its teachings and even made it the official religion of the empire. As the most powerful empire in the world at that time, Rome was able to give Christianity the strength and support it needed to thrive.

When the Western Roman Empire fell, Christianity prospered in the former imperial lands. Germanic kings and queens became Christians. In addition, the Byzantine Empire promoted Christianity in the East. All of this enabled Christianity to become the force it is today. Currently, one-third of the people in the world are Christians.

Roman Law and Rights Perhaps Rome's most lasting and widespread contribution was its system of laws. Roman judges and political leaders established laws that reflected the Stoic ideals of duty and virtue. They stressed fairness and common sense.

Roman laws promoted such principles as equal treatment under the law and the presumption of innocence for those accused of crimes. The principles of Roman law endured to form the basis of legal systems in many European countries and in the United States of America.

Connect to Today

U.S. Capitol The United States owes aspects of its representative style of government to a number of early Roman institutions. ▼

Finally, Rome established aspects of a representative government that many nations use today. As you recall, Rome began as a republic in which average citizens held great power. During this time, the Romans established various assemblies, including a senate, to make laws and represent the views of the people. Centuries later such a political structure exists in countries around the globe. In the United States, for example, the House of Representatives and the Senate are the nation's two main representative bodies. The nation's citizens elect their members. The members of each body work to create and pass laws and address the needs of the people they represent.

REVIEW What were some of the principles that Roman law promoted?

Lesson Summary

- The Romans mixed aspects of Greek culture with their own to create enduring forms of art.
- The Romans were talented engineers who made many advances in architecture and building.
- The Romans made lasting contributions to the fields of government and law.

Why It Matters Now . . .

From its architectural styles to its legal principles, Rome has had a significant influence on modern society.

4 Lesson Review

Homework Helper
ClassZone.com

Terms & Names
1. Explain the importance of

  mosaic   Stoicism   aqueduct

Using Your Notes
Finding Main Ideas Use your completed cluster diagram to answer the following questions:
2. Which of these lasting achievements do you consider most significant? Why? (7.1.1)

Main Ideas
3. What art form did the Romans enhance? (7.1.1)
4. In what ways is Roman architecture evident in the United States today? (HI 3)
5. What were some of the rights that citizens enjoyed under Roman law? (7.1.1)

Critical Thinking
6. **Making Inferences** How did Stoicism help to promote citizenship in Rome? (REP 4)
7. **Identifying Issues and Problems** What problem did Roman engineering help to overcome? (7.1.1)

Activity **Making a Speech** Use various resources to find examples of Rome's influence on modern-day public works and architecture. Compare these modern structures with those of Rome in a brief speech. (Framework)

Connect to Today
Extend Lesson 4

Rome's Enduring Influence

Purpose: To recognize Rome's effect on modern society

Numerous aspects of Roman civilization continue to influence the world today. From their ideas about government and citizenship to their feats of engineering, the Romans left an important legacy.

CALIFORNIA STANDARDS

7.1.1 Study the early strengths and lasting contributions of Rome (e.g., significance of Roman citizenship; rights under Roman law; Roman art, architecture, engineering, and philosophy; preservation and transmission of Christianity) and its ultimate internal weaknesses (e.g., rise of autonomous military powers within the empire, undermining of citizenship by the growth of corruption and slavery, lack of education, and distribution of news).

Architecture

▼ **Past** Opened in A.D. 79, the Colosseum in Rome held up to 50,000 spectators for various athletic contests. Roman builders used arches to support the massive structure. They also provided numerous staircases and entrances to ensure comfort and safety for the large crowds.

▲ **Present** The Los Angeles Coliseum can hold more than 90,000 people for football games and other events. It is also supported by a series of arches and contains many entrance and exit areas.

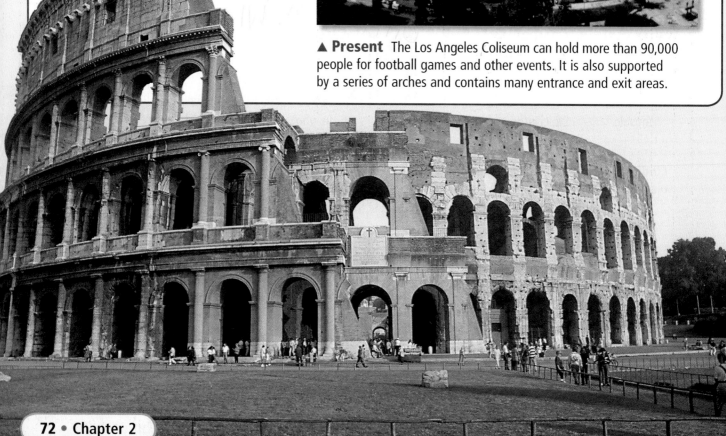

▶ **Past** Many Romans had a strong sense of citizenship, or a commitment to helping each other and society. This sense of duty was instilled by Roman Stoic philosophers such as Seneca (shown at right). Seneca and other Stoics encouraged people to take an active role in public affairs.

◀ **Present** ▶ The Stoic ideal of public duty still helps to promote citizenship. Examples of good citizenship in the United States include voting and activities that benefit all of society, such as recycling.

Law

▶ **Past** The Roman Republic promoted the democratic idea that no leader should have too much power. Under the Roman Republic, for example, the Senate (shown here) acted as a powerful check on the rule of the consuls.

▼ **Present** In the United States, the members of Congress act as a check on the power of the president.

Activities

1. **TALK ABOUT IT** Why do you think it is important to have checks on the power of leaders?

2. **WRITE ABOUT IT** Determine another example of good citizenship where you live. Write a paragraph explaining how this act benefits your community. (Writing 2.3)

► **VISUAL SUMMARY** — **The Roman World**

Government (7.1.2)
- Rome built a well-organized and far-reaching empire.
- Byzantines created a strong and long-lasting empire.

Culture (7.1.1)
- Byzantines created a society with Roman and Eastern influences.
- Romans passed on aspects of their art, philosophy, and language.

Belief Systems (7.1.3)
- Christianity continued to spread after the fall of Rome.
- Disagreements split Christianity into Roman Catholicism and Eastern Orthodoxy.

Geography (7.1.3)
- The Byzantine Empire was situated between the Eastern and Western worlds. Their location enabled the Byzantines to incorporate both cultures.

Science & Technology (7.1.1)
- Romans developed arch, dome, and vault building elements.
- Romans were master engineers who built aqueducts and the Colosseum.

► **TERMS & NAMES**

Match each numbered term or name to the correct meaning.

1. **Augustus**   a. a split

2. **schism**   b. philosophy important to Rome

3. **mosaic**   c. structure for carrying water

4. **aqueduct**   d. first Roman emperor

5. **Stoicism**   e. a type of Roman art

► **MAIN IDEAS**

The Rise and Expansion of Rome (pages 46–51)

6. What were the main characteristics of the Roman Republic? (7.1.1)

7. What factors helped make the Roman Empire so powerful? (7.1.1)

Decline and Fall of the Empire (pages 52–57)

8. What key changes did Constantine make to the Roman Empire? (7.1.1)

9. For what reasons did outside groups invade Rome? (7.1.2)

The Early Byzantine Empire (pages 58–65)

10. What was the Justinian Code? (HI 1)

11. What two churches emerged from the split in Christianity? (7.1.3)

The Legacy of Rome (pages 66–73)

12. What values did Roman Stoic philosophers promote? (7.1.1)

13. How did Rome help with the preservation and spread of Christianity? (7.1.3)

CRITICAL THINKING
Big Ideas: Government

14. **EVALUATING INFORMATION** How did Roman laws help average citizens? (7.1.1)

15. **COMPARING AND CONTRASTING** What was similar about the Roman and Byzantine empires? (7.1.3)

16. **EXPLAINING HISTORICAL PATTERNS** Why do you think aspects of Roman law and government continue to guide nations today? (7.1.1)

ALTERNATIVE ASSESSMENT

1. **WRITING ACTIVITY** Write a paragraph describing which of Rome's internal weaknesses you think was the most damaging and why. (7.1.1)

2. **INTERDISCIPLINARY ACTIVITY—MATH** The Roman numeral system, one of many lasting legacies of Rome, is used in a variety of ways today. Use books and the Internet to locate a modern-day use of Roman numerals. Then do research to determine their number in English. (7.1.1)

3. **STARTING WITH A STORY**

Based on what you have read about Roman culture, why do you think the chariot races were so popular among Romans? (7.1.1)

Technology Activity

4. **WRITING A VIDEO SCRIPT**
Use a variety of resources to research modern-day Constantinople (Istanbul). With a partner, write a script for a televised travel program on Istanbul.
- Choose historical and cultural locations to visit.
- Include notes on what the viewer will see and hear.
- Write the narration for each location. (7.1.3)

Research Links
ClassZone.com

Interpreting Charts Use the chart and your knowledge of history to answer the questions below. (7.1.2)

Size of Selected Civilizations		
Civilization	**Dates**	**Size (est.)** millions of square miles
Persia	612 –338 B.C.	2.0
Rome	27 B.C.–A.D. 476	3.4
Mongol	1206–1380	11.7
Aztec	1325–1520	0.2
United States	1776–	3.7

Source: *Encyclopaedia Britannica*

1. **Which of the following civilizations was nearly equal to Rome in size?**
   A. Persia
   B. Mongol
   C. Aztec
   D. United States

2. **How would Rome rank in order of size among the civilizations shown here?**
   A. first
   B. second
   C. third
   D. fifth

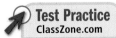
Test Practice
ClassZone.com

Additional Test Practice, pp. S1–S33

Writing About History

Autobiographical Narrative:
A Story About Your Life

CALIFORNIA STANDARDS
Writing 2.1 Write fictional or autobiographical narratives.

Purpose: To write a narrative about a turning point in your life for a classroom display

Audience: Your classmates

History is the story of the past. Like all good stories, it is kept in motion by events. In this unit, you studied some of those events—the rise of Christianity, the split of the Roman Empire, the fall of Rome. Each of these events was a turning point, something that brought change. Just as societies have histories, each person also has a history. An **autobiography** is a person's account of his or her own life. An **autobiographical narrative** is the true story of a part of a life, told by the person who experienced it.

▲ The Forum and bust of Augustus

Organization & Focus

The plot, or story line, of a narrative often follows a pattern. The **beginning** sets the scene and starts the story. Then a **conflict** occurs—either a disagreement between people or mixed feelings inside the main character. The conflict leads to the **rising action,** in which complications occur. The story reaches a turning point, or **climax.** Finally, in the **denouement,** the conflict is resolved.

Choosing a Topic Brainstorm a list of times when you changed dramatically. These might include the first time you rode a bike, the first time you were home alone, or a time you worked out a conflict with a friend. Decide which one would make the best story.

Identifying Purpose and Audience Your purpose is to write a true story about yourself that shows how you went through a turning point. You will be the main character in your story and will write from the first-person point of view, using *I.* Be sure to describe the setting, or time and place, of your story. Use vivid details to help your audience—your classmates—visualize the setting.

Finding Details Use a time line like the one below to create an organizational structure for your narrative. In the boxes, write events in the order they happened. If you want, you can label the events **beginning, conflict, rising action, climax,** and **denouement.** On the time line, record when each event took place.

In the column beneath each event, list vivid details about the event. Such details include facts and descriptions of sensations and emotions.

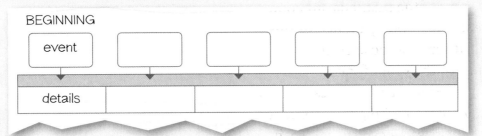

BEGINNING

event

details

Research & Technology

If you need more details for your story, you can ask other people who were involved in the events what they remember. Take notes of your conversations and add these details to your time line.

Outlining and Drafting Use the events and details in your time line as your outline. Draft a story with dialogue and lifelike actions. Use transitions between sentences.

> **Technology Tip** If your narrative is set in the past, you can use the Internet to help you recall what life was like then. Use a search engine to research the period by typing in the year or decade the story is set in and a search term such as *weather, fashions,* or *events.* Use the information that you learn to make your narrative more accurate.

Evaluation & Revision

When revising, make sure that you presented your events in chronological order and that you used transitions. Read your story again, looking just at your choice of words. Could you replace any of them with stronger, livelier words? When you are satisfied with your draft, make a clean copy.

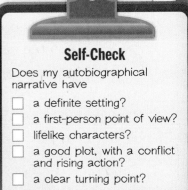

Self-Check
Does my autobiographical narrative have

- [ ] a definite setting?
- [ ] a first-person point of view?
- [ ] lifelike characters?
- [ ] a good plot, with a conflict and rising action?
- [ ] a clear turning point?

Publish & Present

With your classmates, design and title a bulletin-board display, with illustrations, for the class's compositions.

The Growth of Islam

Interact with History ▶

The Holy City of Mecca, about A.D. 660

You are a Bedouin nomad living in the Arabian Peninsula. For years, you have heard tales of the holy city of Mecca. Its fame has spread far and wide among the desert peoples. Now you have decided to travel to see Mecca for yourself.

What does your first sight of Mecca tell you about the city?

WebQuest
ClassZone.com

Mecca is an oasis. At an oasis, underground water comes close enough to the surface to form springs and to be brought up in wells.

Why might water be valuable in a desert area like Arabia?

Mecca is a religious center. People come from all over Arabia to worship at the Ka'aba, a cube-shaped religious monument in the center of the city.

Why might worshipers want to visit sites believed to be holy places?

Mecca is a trade city. Because of its location at an oasis and near the west coast of Arabia, merchants come from many lands to trade their goods.

Why might trade be important for life in a land that has few fertile areas?

Chapter 3

The Beginnings of Islam

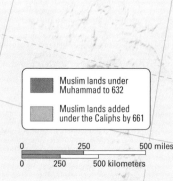

Before You Read: K-W-L

Before you read this chapter, think about what you know about Islam and what you want to learn about Islam and the Muslim peoples.

- Study the map and the time line on these pages.
- What do they tell you about Islam and the lands and the peoples of the Arabian peninsula?

Big Ideas About Early Islam

Belief Systems People adopt new beliefs that give meaning to life.

The Arabian peninsula in Southwest Asia was an important trading region in the 500s. A religious leader named Muhammad was born there in the city of Mecca. He brought the message of the religion of Islam to the Arab peoples and created an empire that would spread throughout the region during his lifetime.

	Muslim lands under Muhammad to 632
	Muslim lands added under the Caliphs by 661

0   250   500 miles
0   250   500 kilometers

Integrated Technology

eEdition
- Interactive Maps
- Interactive Visuals
- Starting with a Story

What Is Islam?

INTERNET RESOURCES
Go to **ClassZone.com** for
- WebQuest
- Homework Helper
- Research Links
- Internet Activities
- Quizzes
- Maps
- Test Practice
- Current Events

ARABIA

c. 570
◀ Muhammad is born. (Qur'an)

550

575

WORLD

565
Byzantine emperor Justinian dies.

597
◀ St. Augustine brings Christianity to Britain.

Spread of Islam, A.D. 661
INTERACTIVE

EUROPE

Rome

Danube River

Black Sea

Caucasus Mts.

Caspian Sea

Aral Sea

Merv

ASIA

BYZANTINE EMPIRE

Constantinople

Sicily

Crete

Cyprus

Mediterranean Sea

MESOPOTAMIA

Tigris River

Euphrates River

PERSIA

Jerusalem

Alexandria

EGYPT

Persian Gulf

SAHARA

Red Sea

Nile River

ARABIAN PENINSULA

Medina

Tropic of Cancer

Mecca

Arabian Sea

AFRICA

N
W   E
S

610
Muhammad starts to spread Islam.

630
Muhammad returns to Mecca after making the Hijrah to Medina.

632
Abu Bakr becomes caliph after Muhammad's death.
(Abu Bakr's name in Arabic) ▶

661
Islam splits into factions.

625

650

675

618
Tang Dynasty begins 289-year rule in China.
(Tang camel sculpture) ▶

646
The emperor becomes the sole ruler of Japan for the first time.

81

A Journey to Mecca

CALIFORNIA STANDARDS
Reading 3.2
Identify events that advance the plot and determine how each event explains past or present action(s) or foreshadows future action(s).

Background: The religion of Islam was revealed in the seventh century A.D. among the Arab peoples living on the Arabian peninsula. It was spread by the man called the Prophet Muhammad. He began preaching some time after 610.

Muhammad taught that there was only one God, called Allah in the Arabic language. At first, his message was not widely welcomed. He was forced to flee his home in the city of Mecca. Muhammad settled in Medina to the north. Soon, he had many thousands of followers, called Muslims. Imagine you are there as Muhammad spreads Islam across Arabia. (See map on page 81.)

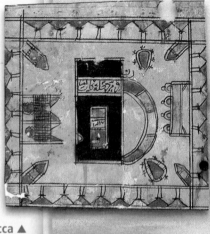

A certificate of pilgrimage to Mecca ▲

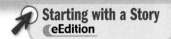

Ayesha is 13 years old. Her brother, Yazid, is 12. They are part of a Muslim family that lives in the city of Medina in Arabia. It is the year 632. Their parents have told them that the Prophet Muhammad is planning to make a journey, which he calls the *hajj*, to the holy city of Mecca. Their parents explain that the hajj will be a way for people who share Muhammad's religion to demonstrate their faith in God. Their family will follow Muhammad to Mecca and participate in the hajj.

The day of the hajj has finally come. As Ayesha and Yazid set out on the family's camels, they are amazed to see so many other people. Their parents say that nearly 100,000 have gathered for the journey. Others also join the caravan along the way. The journey to Mecca is a difficult one. For nine days, the family faces many hardships in the grueling desert heat.

Finally, they reach Mecca. There, Ayesha and Yazid join the other pilgrims in prayers and rituals. After spending time in Mecca, everyone travels to Arafat. At Arafat, the people listen to Muhammad give a sermon from atop a mountain. That afternoon, Ayesha and Yazid stand with their parents for hours, praying in the blistering sun. But that memory soon fades when the sister and brother learn that they will spend the evening camping in the desert under the stars. After more prayers and rituals, everyone eventually returns to Mecca.

Many days after the journey began, the family is on the way back to Medina. Ayesha tells Yazid that the trip has been very hard, but it was also satisfying. They agree with their parents that being near Muhammad was especially meaningful. And they are deeply saddened when, just two months later, they hear that the Prophet has died. They wonder what will happen to their religion now.

What do you think will happen to the Muslim community after the death of Muhammad?

Reading & Writing

1. **READING: Plot** The plot is a sequence of events in the story. Usually, each event is caused by an event that came before it. With a partner, identify the various events that make up the plot of this story.

2. **WRITING: Response to Literature** Write a paragraph describing what Muslims might do following the death of their leader, the Prophet Muhammad.

CALIFORNIA STANDARDS Writing 2.2
Write responses to literature.

▶ MAIN IDEAS

① **Geography** The geography of the Arabian peninsula encouraged a nomadic way of life.

② **Economics** Trade routes opened the Arabian peninsula to goods and ideas from many parts of the world.

③ **Belief Systems** Mecca was an important religious center as well as a trade city.

▶ TAKING NOTES

Reading Skill: Categorizing

As you read each part of Lesson 1, look for important information about life on the Arabian peninsula. Record this information on a cluster diagram like the one shown below.

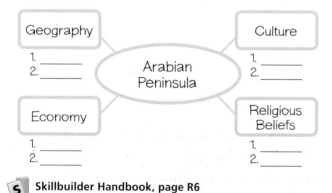

Geography		Culture
1. _____	Arabian Peninsula	1. _____
2. _____		2. _____
Economy		Religious Beliefs
1. _____		1. _____
2. _____		2. _____

S **Skillbuilder Handbook, page R6**

▲ **Ancient Water Jug** Storing water was a necessity on the arid Arabian peninsula. It was kept in clay jugs, similar to the one shown above.

CALIFORNIA STANDARDS

7.2.1 Identify the physical features and describe the climate of the Arabian peninsula, its relationship to surrounding bodies of land and water, and nomadic and sedentary ways of life.

7.2.2 Trace the origins of Islam and the life and teachings of Muhammad, including Islamic teachings on the connection with Judaism and Christianity.

7.2.5 Describe the growth of cities and the establishment of trade routes among Asia, Africa, and Europe, the products and inventions that traveled along these routes (e.g., spices, textiles, paper, steel, new crops), and the role of merchants in Arab society.

Life on the Arabian Peninsula

TERMS & NAMES

nomad

oasis

clan

Allah

monotheism

pilgrimage

Build on What You Know What movies have you watched that included a scene from a desert region? The scene probably showed a hot, sandy area with a limited supply of water. Well, this is what the Arabian peninsula in southwest Asia is like. It was there that the Muslim Empire was built.

#1 Forced to become nomads because

A Desert Culture

1 ESSENTIAL QUESTION How did the geography of the Arabian peninsula encourage a nomadic way of life?

The deserts of the Arabian peninsula cover hundreds of thousands of square miles. One desert in the south covers nearly 250,000 square miles. (See map on page 81.) It is so enormous and so desolate that Arabs call it the Rub al-Khali, which means "the empty quarter."

how much the desert covers

Physical Features and Climate The Arabian peninsula is a region of Southwest Asia. It lies between the Red Sea and the Persian Gulf. The peninsula is about 1,200 miles at its longest point from north to south and 1,300 miles at its widest point from east to west. This is about one-fourth the size of the United States. The region is very arid. It receives little rain and is covered mainly by deserts. Because of its desert climate, only a small amount of land is useful for agriculture. Farmland is found in the southern mountains and along the northern coastline.

#2

Arabian Peninsula
This peninsula in Southwest Asia is a vast area that is mainly desert. ▼

Nomads For centuries, Arab herders called Bedouins (BEHD•oo•ihnz) have adapted their lives to arid land. Bedouins are **nomads**. Because there is little farmland, nomads move from place to place instead of settling permanently. Bedouins travel within a specific area as they seek water and grazing land for their herds. The path they follow is affected by such factors as the landscape they must cross and the amount of rainfall. Another geographic factor is the location of an oasis.

An **oasis** is a desert area that contains water. (See Geography feature below.) Bedouins interacted with people who settled at oases and lived a sedentary, or settled, life. Often, this interaction meant that the settled population traded food that they grew to the nomads for animals and animal products.

Family Life Bedouins organized themselves into groups called clans. **Clans** were families of people related by blood or marriage. Each clan was its own unit of government. Clans also provided security and support in the extreme conditions of the desert.

Bedouins took pride in their ability to adapt to life in the desert. They were also proud of their fighting skills. Clans had to defend themselves against raids by other clans who wanted water, livestock, or food supplies. Because of their fighting ability, Bedouins became the core of armies that would help create the Muslim Empire.

REVIEW How did people of Arabia adapt to its landforms and climate?

Geography

Oasis

An oasis is a fertile or green spot in the midst of a desert.

- Oases occur where water in underlying rock rises to the surface to provide a source for wells and springs. The water usually seeps upward when it hits a fault, or fracture, in the rock.
- Some large oases can support an entire city. Others might simply be a small spring.

GEOGRAPHY SKILLBUILDER
INTERPRETING VISUALS
Human-Environment Interaction
Why might oases be important to people who live on the Arabian peninsula?

Spring

Sand

Fault line

Underground water

Rock

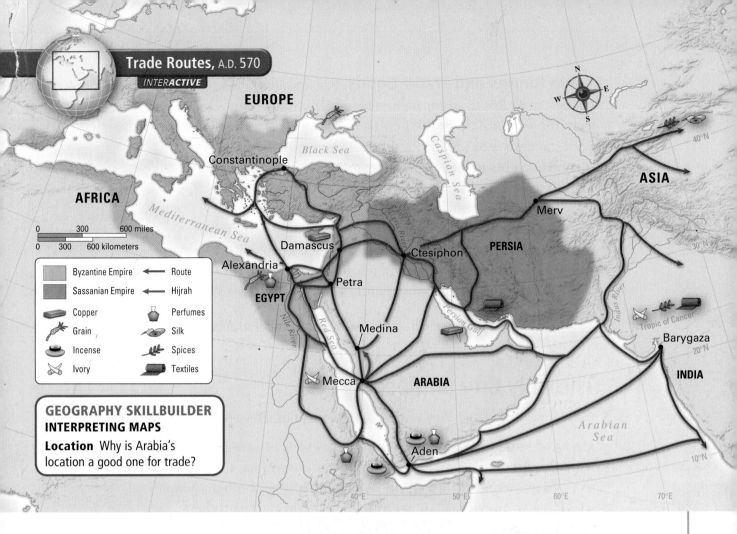

Trade Routes, A.D. 570
INTERACTIVE

EUROPE

AFRICA

Black Sea

Constantinople

Mediterranean Sea

Damascus

Alexandria

EGYPT

Petra

Medina

Mecca

ARABIA

Aden

Caspian Sea

Merv

ASIA

Ctesiphon

PERSIA

Persian Gulf

Indus River

Tropic of Cancer

Barygaza

INDIA

Red Sea

Nile River

Arabian Sea

N
W   E
S

Legend		
Byzantine Empire	←	Route
Sassanian Empire	←	Hijrah
Copper		Perfumes
Grain		Silk
Incense		Spices
Ivory		Textiles

GEOGRAPHY SKILLBUILDER
INTERPRETING MAPS
Location Why is Arabia's location a good one for trade?

Crossroads of Three Continents

2 **ESSENTIAL QUESTION** What made the Arabian peninsula important for trade?

The Arabian peninsula is well situated for trade. It is a crossroads of three continents—Asia, Africa, and Europe. Also, it is surrounded by bodies of water. These include the Mediterranean Sea, the Red Sea, the Arabian Sea, and the Persian Gulf. (See map above.)

Growth of Trade Cities By the early 600s, growing numbers of Arabs had moved to market towns or oases. Market towns grew into cities because of trade. Larger settlements near the western coast of Arabia became centers for local, regional, and long-distance trade.

In these cities, Arabs could meet travelers from near and distant lands and trade a variety of goods, including spices from India and ivory from Africa. (See feature "Life Along a Trade Route" on pages 90–91.) Some seaports, such as Aden on the southwestern coast, were important trading centers long before the 600s.

Other areas, such as larger oases, prospered because they had good soil and enough water to support farming. These oases, too, were important for trade. They became stops along the many trade routes that crossed the peninsula. Mecca and Medina were such oasis cities.

Trade Routes and Trade Goods Sea and land routes connected Arabia to major trade centers. These trade routes ran from the southern tip of the peninsula to the Byzantine and Persian empires to the north. Products and inventions from three continents moved along these routes by camel *caravans*. Merchants traded animals, textiles, metals, crops, and spices such as pepper and saffron.

Trade was also important in cultural exchange. Merchants carried information as well as products. For example, they would gain knowledge of different religions practiced in the cities they visited. Judaism and Christianity were spread this way.

REVIEW Why did so many trade routes develop on the Arabian peninsula?

A **caravan** is a company of travelers journeying together, such as these traders and their camels.

The Holy City of Mecca

3 ESSENTIAL QUESTION Why was Mecca important as a religious center?

Mecca was an important religious center as well as a trading center. It was located along the trade routes in western Arabia. Caravans stopped in Mecca during certain holy months. They brought people who came to worship at an ancient religious shrine called the Ka'aba, which was located in the middle of the city. The shrine was a cube-shaped stone building.

Abraham in Mecca Arabs associated the Ka'aba with Abraham. Abraham was an important early figure in the Jewish, Christian, and Islamic religions. Many Arabs thought themselves descendants of Abraham. They believed that Abraham and his son Ishmael built the Ka'aba as a temple to God (called **Allah** in Arabic). The belief in one God is called **monotheism**.

Connect to Today

The Holy City of Mecca Each year, Muslim pilgrims from around the world come to Mecca to worship at the Ka'aba. ▼

people in the desert believed in many gods

Many Religions Other Arabs, especially those in the desert, believed in many gods. This belief is called polytheism. Over the years, these Arabs began to worship at the Ka'aba. Each year, people flocked to Mecca from all over the peninsula. The journey to a sacred place is called a **pilgrimage**.

Many Jews and Christians lived in Arab lands, so the belief in one God continued on the Arabian peninsula. Also, some Arabs blended Christian and Jewish beliefs and rituals with their own traditions. It was into this religious environment that Muhammad, the Prophet of Islam, was born in Mecca around A.D. 570.

REVIEW What factors made Mecca a center of religious activity?

Lesson Summary

- The harsh physical features of the Arabian peninsula and its arid climate caused many people to be nomads.
- The peninsula's location at the crossroads of three continents encouraged trade and cultural exchange.
- Mecca was a trade center and a religious center.

▲ **Ka'aba Key** The key is a symbol given to those chosen to guard the holy site of the Ka'aba.

Why It Matters Now . . .

Muslims from every corner of the globe try to make a pilgrimage to Mecca once in their lives.

---

1 Lesson Review

Homework Helper
ClassZone.com

Terms & Names

1. Explain the importance of

nomad	clan	monotheism
oasis	Allah	pilgrimage

Using Your Notes

Categorizing Use your completed diagram to answer the following question:

2. What two important geographic features determined life on the Arabian peninsula? (7.2.1)

Main Ideas

3. Why did people live a nomadic life on the Arabian peninsula? (7.2.1)

4. Why did trade often lead to cultural exchange? (7.2.5)

5. Why was the Ka'aba significant for Mecca? (7.2.2)

Critical Thinking

6. Making Inferences What aspect of the life of Bedouins prepared them for their role as warriors in the spread of the Muslim Empire? (7.2.1)

7. Summarizing What were the religious beliefs on the Arabian peninsula before Muhammad? (7.2.2)

Activity **Internet Activity** Use the Internet to research the Ka'aba. Then write a paragraph summarizing your findings in your own words. (7.2.2)

INTERNET KEYWORD: *Ka'aba*

Research Links
ClassZone.com

Life Along a Trade Route

Purpose: To learn about life in a trade center on the Arabian peninsula during the early Islamic period

If you were a merchant in Arabia in the 600s, you probably often visited important trade centers such as Medina, Mecca, and Aden. In fact, most people who wished to trade came to these trading cities. Nomads, farmers, craftspeople, and merchants came to the city.

There they traded goods in a central marketplace. These products included food, livestock, textiles, leather goods, spices, and metals from Arabia and also Europe, Africa, and other parts of Asia. As shown below, many different activities took place in the markets of the trade centers.

A Textiles A variety of cloth products, including cotton from India and silk from China, were available at fabric stalls.

B Accommodations Sleeping quarters for merchants were usually found on the second level above the stalls.

C Market Inspectors In some markets, a market inspector observed the trading. The inspector's job was to make sure that merchants dealt fairly with each other and their customers. This position became official in the 700s.

D Livestock The trading of livestock, including sheep and horses, was usually done near the marketplace. Traders also sold camels to be used for transportation.

Medina
Mecca
Arabia
Red Sea
Aden *Arabian Sea*

A

CALIFORNIA STANDARDS

7.2.5 Describe the growth of cities and the establishment of trade routes among Asia, Africa, and Europe, the products and inventions that traveled along these routes (e.g., spices, textiles, paper, steel, new crops), and the role of merchants in Arab society.

Activities

1. **TALK ABOUT IT** What types of activities are taking place in this trading center? Which people are involved in the activities?

2. **WRITE ABOUT IT** Choose one of the activities shown and explain why the activity is important. (Writing 2.1)

MAIN IDEAS

1 **Belief Systems** Muhammad taught that he was a messenger of God and spread the religion of Islam.

2 **Culture** The teachings of Islam provided laws and guidelines for religious practice and everyday life.

3 **Belief Systems** Judaism, Christianity, and Islam share some beliefs, and all have sacred scriptures believed to be God's revelation.

TAKING NOTES

Reading Skill: Summarizing

When you summarize, you supply only main ideas and important details. Identify the main ideas and important details in each section of Lesson 2. Then put them in your own words and record them in a diagram like the one below.

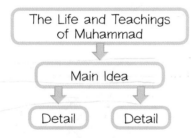

 Skillbuilder Handbook, page R3

▲ **The Angel Gabriel** According to the Muslim faith, Gabriel is the angel of revelation, having brought God's message to Muhammad. This is a detail from a 14th-century painting.

CALIFORNIA STANDARDS

7.2.2 Trace the origins of Islam and the life and teachings of Muhammad, including Islamic teachings on the connection with Judaism and Christianity.

7.2.3 Explain the significance of the Qur'an and the Sunnah as the primary sources of Islamic beliefs, practice, and law, and their influence in Muslims' daily life.

7.2.4 Discuss the expansion of Muslim rule through military conquests and treaties, emphasizing the cultural blending within Muslim civilization and the spread and acceptance of Islam and the Arabic language.

Islam and Muhammad

Build on What You Know As you learned in Lesson 1, Mecca was a busy economic and religious center. Mecca is also where the Prophet Muhammad was born and began to spread the religion of **Islam**.

The Life and Teachings of Muhammad

1 **ESSENTIAL QUESTION** Why did Muhammad spread Islam?

Muhammad was born into a powerful Meccan family around A.D. 570. But he was orphaned as a child and had to work in the caravan trade. At age 25, he married a wealthy businesswoman. Eventually, Muhammad prospered as a merchant.

he is the prophet

Muhammad the Prophet At about the age of 40, Muhammad's life abruptly changed. One day when praying, he later taught, a voice called out to him, "You are the Messenger of God." Muhammad believed that God spoke to him through the angel Gabriel. He then began preaching that there is only one God (named Allah) and that all other gods must be rejected. People who believed in this basic principle of Islam were called **Muslims.** In Arabic, *Islam* means "peace through submission to the will of God." A Muslim is one who believes in Islam.

Muhammad Begins Preaching
Muhammad had little success at first. In fact, Meccans persecuted the early Muslims. In 622, he fled with supporters to Yathrib, more than 200 miles to the north. This migration is called the **Hijrah.** Muhammad's followers renamed the town Medina. It means "city of the Prophet." In Medina, Muhammad's teachings won many converts to Islam. People found his simple message to obey the will of Allah appealing. They also were attracted to Muhammad's strength as a leader.

Muhammad's Birth
Turkish Muslim artists showed angels covering the sun to protect Muhammad at his birth. ▼

Muhammad's Leadership Meccans continued to fight against Muhammad and his followers. There were several battles. In 630, Muhammad and 10,000 Muslims returned to Mecca. They forced the city to surrender. Muhammad then forgave the Meccans and went to the Ka'aba. There, he dedicated the shrine to Allah.

Muhammad was a religious leader, but also a political and military leader. Muhammad ruled Medina and united his followers with other Arabs, Jews, and Christians. He made treaties of alliance with nomadic tribes in the peninsula, which helped Islam to find acceptance and be spread during his lifetime. He used his military skills to defend Medina against attacks. By the time of his death in 632, Muhammad had unified much of the Arabian peninsula under Islam.

REVIEW What was Muhammad's role in the development of Islam?

he spread it

Islamic Beliefs, Practices, and Law

2 **ESSENTIAL QUESTION** How do the teachings of Islam provide laws and guidelines for religious practice and everyday life?

Muslims find guidance on how to live their lives in two primary sources of authority.

The Qur'an and the Sunnah The main teaching of Islam is that there is only one God, Allah. Muslims believe God revealed his words through the angel Gabriel, who passed them on to Muhammad. While Muhammad lived, his followers listened to his teachings. They also memorized and recited the revelations, which formed the scripture called the Qur'an. After Muhammad's death, his followers collected the Qur'an into a written book in Arabic. It is the Muslim holy book.

Muslims believe that Muhammad's mission as a prophet was not only to receive the Qur'an but also to show how to apply its teachings to everyday life. To them, the **Sunnah**, or Muhammad's words and deeds, are guides for proper living.

Primary Source Handbook

See the excerpt from the Qur'an, page R37.

The Qur'an Making a beautifully decorated Qur'an is considered an act of devotion. ▼

Legal thinkers later organized the guidelines of the Qur'an and Sunnah into a system of law. This body of law is used by Muslim communities to decide legal matters. These include rules for inheritance and punishment for criminals.

Muslim Daily Life Muslims try to connect their personal and religious lives. They live their religion and serve their community by following the Five Pillars of Islam. These are the five duties all Muslims must perform to demonstrate their submission to the will of God. (See chart above.)

Other Islamic customs and laws also affect the daily lives of Muslims. Believers are forbidden to eat pork or to drink alcoholic beverages. Friday afternoons are set aside for community worship and prayer. Those who are able gather at a **mosque**, a building used for Muslim worship. All mosques face Mecca so that Muslims pray in the proper direction.

REVIEW What rules do Muslims use to guide their daily lives?

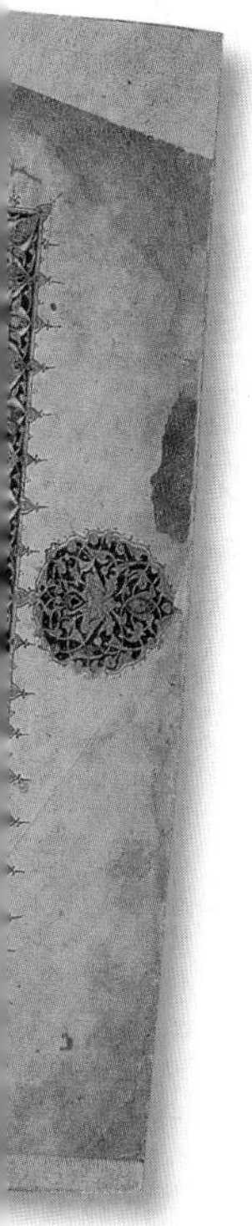

Five Pillars of Islam	
Faith	Believe and say, "There is no God but Allah, and Muhammad is his prophet."
Prayer	Pray in Arabic five times a day, at specific times, and facing Mecca.
Alms	Give to the poor and the needy.
Fasting	Fast during the month of Ramadan each year, avoiding all food and beverages between sunrise and sunset.
Pilgrimage	If possible, make a pilgrimage to the holy city of Mecca once during a lifetime.

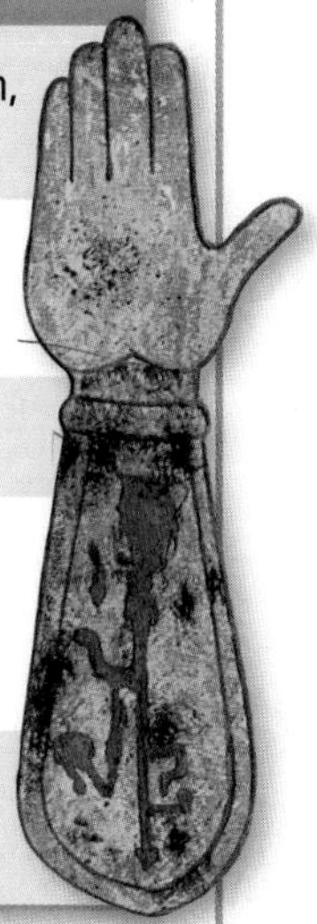

▲ **Five Pillars of Islam**
The symbol of an open hand was often used to represent the Five Pillars.

Primary Source Handbook
See the excerpt from Sunnah, page R38.

Connections to Judaism and Christianity

3 **ESSENTIAL QUESTION** What are the connections between Islam and Judaism and Christianity?

Muslims trace the beginnings of their religion to Abraham. They believe he was a prophet of God, as do Jews and Christians. To Muslims, Allah is the same God that is worshiped by Christians and Jews. However, Muslims view Jesus as a prophet, not as the son of God as Christians do.

People of the Book Muslims called both Christians and Jews "people of the book" because their religions have holy books with teachings similar to the Qur'an's. Muslims believe the Qur'an is the word of God as revealed to Muhammad. Jews and Christians also believe that God's word is revealed in their holy books. But Muslims believe that the Qur'an is the final book. They also think that Muhammad is the last prophet. Followers of all three religions believe in heaven, hell, and a final judgment day.

Religious Toleration Muslim law requires that Muslim leaders offer religious toleration to non-Muslims, though non-Muslims have restricted rights and must pay extra taxes. This policy of toleration of non-Muslims would play an important role in the expansion of the Muslim Empire under Muhammad's successors.

REVIEW What do Judaism, Christianity, and Islam have in common?

Lesson Summary

- Muhammad established the religion of Islam and spread Islamic beliefs and way of life across the Arabian peninsula.

- The Qur'an and Sunnah are the main sources of Islamic beliefs and practices, and Muslims try to live by their teachings every day.

- Muslims, Christians, and Jews have some beliefs in common.

Why It Matters Now . . .

The relationship among Muslims, Christians, and Jews continues to be an important issue for the world in the 21st century.

▲ **Islamic Tile** This Turkish ceramic tile shows the Ka'aba at the center of Mecca.

---

2 Lesson Review

🖱 **Homework Helper** ClassZone.com

Terms & Names

1. Explain the importance of

Islam	Hijrah	Sunnah
Muslim	Qur'an	mosque

Using Your Notes

Summarizing Use your completed diagram to answer the following question:

2. What is the main idea of the section "The Life and Teachings of Muhammad"? (7.2.2)

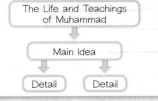

Main Ideas

3. How was Muhammad's message received in Mecca and in Medina? (7.2.2)

4. Why are the Five Pillars important in the lives of Muslims? (7.2.3)

5. What role did Muhammad play in the spread of Islam? (7.2.4)

Critical Thinking

6. **Comparing and Contrasting** How are the Qur'an and Sunnah similar? How are they different? (7.2.3)

7. **Understanding Effects** In what ways does Islam affect the personal lives of Muslims? (7.2.3)

Activity **Sketching a Web Page** Use the information in Lesson 2 to sketch a Web page for Muhammad and early Islam. Show what categories of information should be included. (7.2.2)

Create a Distribution Map

Goal: To create a distribution map showing the percentage of Muslims in the ten largest nations on Earth

Materials & Supplies
- blank world map
- world atlas
- colored pencils

Optional: graph paper

Prepare

1 Look at the information in the table at the right.

2 Make a list of the nations by population of Muslims going from the highest percentage to the lowest percentage.

Do the Activity

1 Use the atlas to locate each of the ten nations listed. Write the names of the nations in the correct location on the blank map.

2 Refer to your list of nations by percentage of Muslims. Then create a color key dividing the percentages into three or four categories.

3 Using your key, color each of the countries you have labeled on the map with the correct color for its percentage of Muslims.

4 Add a legend and a title to your map.

Muslim Population, 2005	
Nation	**Percentage of Muslims**
China	1.5
India	13.4
United States	1.0
Indonesia	88.0
Chad	51.0
Pakistan	97.0
Philippines	5.0
Bangladesh	83.0
Nigeria	50.0
Japan	0.1

Source: CIA *World Factbook 2005*

Follow-Up

1 On which continent are the nations with the greatest percentage of Muslims found? What reasons might be given for the large Muslim population found there?

2 What reasons might be given for the low percentage of Muslims in the Western Hemisphere?

Extension

Creating a Bar Graph Use the data in the table to create a bar graph showing the percentage of Muslims in the ten listed countries.

CALIFORNIA STANDARDS
CST 3 Students use a variety of maps and documents to identify physical and cultural features of neighborhoods, cities, states, and countries and to explain the historical migration of people, expansion and disintegration of empires, and the growth of economic systems.

Lesson 3

▲ **Mosque Lamp** Glass oil lamps were used to light mosques. They hung from the ceiling and were elaborately decorated with enamel.

▶ MAIN IDEAS

1 **Belief Systems** The leaders following Muhammad continued to spread the Prophet's message.

2 **Culture** The caliphs who expanded the Muslim Empire showed tolerance to those they conquered.

3 **Government** The issue of how to choose leaders divided the Muslim community.

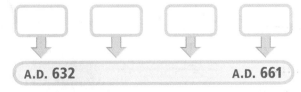

▶ TAKING NOTES

Reading Skill:
Explaining Chronological Order and Sequence

Placing events in sequence means putting them in order based on the time they happened. As you read about Islam under the early rulers, record major events on a time line, like the one shown below.

A.D. 632   A.D. 661

S Skillbuilder Handbook, page R15

CALIFORNIA STANDARDS

7.2.2 Trace the origins of Islam and the life and teachings of Muhammad, including Islamic teachings on the connection with Judaism and Christianity.

7.2.4 Discuss the expansion of Muslim rule through military conquests and treaties, emphasizing the cultural blending within Muslim civilization and the spread and acceptance of Islam and the Arabic language.

HI 2 Students understand and distinguish cause, effect, sequence, and correlation in historical events, including the long- and short-term causal relations.

Islam After Muhammad's Death

TERMS & NAMES
caliph
Shi'a
Sunni

Build on What You Know Muhammad's death in 632 brought a crisis. How would Islam survive without the leadership of the Prophet?

New Muslim Leaders Emerge

1 ESSENTIAL QUESTION Who were the leaders who spread Islam after Muhammad's death?

For more than 20 years, Muhammad had spread the word of Allah across the Arabian peninsula. He had begun to establish a Muslim Empire. In particular, Arab nomads had responded to his message. Islam brought order, justice, and hope of heaven into their lives. Then, in June 632, Muhammad died. Muslims were suddenly without a leader.

After Muhammad's Death

According to the traditions of the most numerous group of Muslims today, Muhammad had not named a successor or instructed his followers how to choose one upon his death. Panic swept through the Muslim community. Muhammad's father-in-law and trusted friend, Abu Bakr (AH•boo BAH•kuhr), spoke to reassure Muslims. He said, "If there are any among you who worshiped Muhammad, he is dead. But if it is God you worship, he lives forever."

Abu Bakr was a man respected for his devotion to Muhammad and to Islam. The leaders of the dominant group within the Muslim community selected him as Muhammad's successor.

Muhammad's Successors Muslims declared their allegiance to one of Muhammad's successors. ▶

Abu Bakr (c. 573–634)

Abu Bakr was Muhammad's closest companion and adviser. Like Muhammad, Abu Bakr was from a Mecca clan that was important in the caravan trade. He was one of the first Meccans to convert to Islam. His daughter A'ishah became Muhammad's wife. Abu Bakr's loyalty to the Prophet was an important factor to the high-ranking Muslims who selected him as Muhammad's successor.

Abu Bakr's name written in Arabic ▶

Abu Bakr Succeeds Muhammad In 632, Abu Bakr became the first **caliph** (KAY•lihf), a title that means "successor." He promised Muslims that he would closely follow Muhammad's example. Shortly after the Prophet's death, some clans on the Arabian peninsula abandoned Islam. Others refused to pay taxes, and a few individuals even declared themselves prophets. During his two-year reign, Abu Bakr used military force to reunite the Muslim community. He brought central Arabia under Muslim control and started the conquests of lands to the north that are now Iraq and Syria.

REVIEW What difficulties did Muslims face after Muhammad's death?

First Four Caliphs

2 ESSENTIAL QUESTION How did the caliphs who expanded the Muslim Empire treat those they conquered?

Abu Bakr and the next three caliphs selected from and by the top ranks of Muslim believers—Umar, Uthman, and Ali—had known Muhammad and supported his mission to spread Islam. According to the traditions of the most numerous group of Muslims today, the first four caliphs used the Qur'an and Muhammad's actions to guide them. Hence, this group of Muslims call them the "rightly guided caliphs." Their rule was called a caliphate.

Caliphs Expand the Muslim Empire Muslims controlled most of Arabia when Abu Bakr died in 634. The second elected caliph, Umar, ruled until 644. His swift and highly disciplined armies conquered Syria and lower Egypt, which were part of the Byzantine Empire. Muslim armies also took territory from the Persian Empire.

The next two caliphs continued to expand Muslim territory and completed the conquest of Persia. By 661, Muhammad's successors had increased the size of the Muslim Empire nearly four times, either through conquest or by treaty. The empire then included all of Southwest Asia and stretched into North Africa.

Reasons for Success Muslims saw the military victories as signs of Allah's support. They were energized by their faith and were willing to fight to spread Islam. In battle, Muslim armies proved to be disciplined, and their leaders were highly skilled.

The Muslims' success also resulted from weaknesses in the two empires north of Arabia. The Byzantine and Persian empires had been fighting each other for a long time. Their armies were exhausted.

Another reason for the success was the Byzantine and Persian policy of persecuting people who did not support their conquerors' religions. For this reason, persecuted people often welcomed Muslim invaders as liberators. Muslims let conquered peoples keep their own religions if they wished to do so. The Qur'an did not allow Muslims to force conversions.

Muslims Rule There was much blending of cultures under Muslim rule. Over time, many peoples in Muslim-ruled territories converted to Islam. They were attracted by Islam's message of equality and hope for salvation. There was also an economic benefit—Muslims did not have to pay certain taxes.

Jews and Christians, as "people of the book," received special treatment. They paid a poll tax each year in exchange for not having to perform military duties. Jews and Christians also held important roles in the Muslim state as officials and scholars. However, they were not allowed to convert others.

REVIEW Why were the caliphs tolerant of the people they conquered?

◄ **Muslim Army** Highly skilled Muslim troops on camels conquered much territory in the name of Allah.

Background: The Qur'an (seventh century) is the holy book of Islam. Muslims believe that the Qur'an is the word of God as revealed to the Prophet Muhammad. The Qur'an is written in Arabic, as shown below.

from the *Qur'an*
Volume I, 2:62
Translated by A. J. Arberry

Surely they that believe, and those of Jewry, and the Christians, . . . whoso [whoever] believes in God and the Last Day, and works righteousness[1]—their wage[2] awaits them with their Lord, and no fear shall be on them, neither shall they sorrow.

---

1. **works righteousness:** behaves according to divine law.
2. **wage:** reward.

> **DOCUMENT–BASED QUESTION**
> What does this verse from the Qur'an tell us about the beliefs Muslims had about Jews and Christians at this time?

A Split in Islam

3 ESSENTIAL QUESTION How did the issue of choosing leaders divide the Muslims?

Muslims found it difficult to keep a unified rule even though they were successful on the battlefield.

Umayyads Seize Power In 656, a group of rebels opposed the leadership of Uthman (uth•MAHN) and murdered him. His murder started a civil war. Various groups struggled for power. Muhammad's cousin and son-in-law, Ali, was a logical choice as the next caliph. But his leadership, too, was challenged. In 661, Ali was assassinated. The system of selecting a caliph died with him.

A family known as the Umayyads (oo•MY•adz) took power and set up a hereditary dynasty. This meant that rulers would come from one family and inherit the right to rule. The Umayyads also moved the Muslim capital from Medina to Damascus, a distant city in newly conquered Syria. Arab Muslims felt Damascus was too far away. Some Muslims after the time of the Umayyads looked back and disapproved of the Umayyads' claims of religious authority. These later critics said the Umayyads abandoned the Bedoin ways of earlier caliphs and surrounded themselves with luxury. These actions divided Muslims and raised questions about how to choose leaders.

Muslim Community Splits Because they wanted peace, most Muslims accepted the Umayyads' rule. But a minority resisted. They believed that the caliph should always be a relative of the Prophet.

This group was called **Shi'a**, meaning the "party" of Ali. Its members were known as Shiites. Those who did not resist the Umayyads and accepted the rule of the elected caliphs were called **Sunnis**. The word meant followers of the Sunnah, or followers of Muhammad's example. This split in Islam would become permanent, and opposition to the Umayyads would cause their caliphate to collapse.

REVIEW How did leadership issues divide the Muslim community?

Basic Differences Between Muslims

	Sunni Beliefs	Shi'a Beliefs
Early caliphs	The first four caliphs were rightful rulers.	Only Ali, Muhammad's son-in-law, was legitimate.
Muslim ruler	Any Muslim who follows Muhammad's example may be ruler.	Only a descendant of Muhammad and Ali may be imam, or ruler.
Sources of Islam	Qur'an and Sunnah of Muhammad	Qur'an, Sunnah, and teachings of imams

Lesson Summary

- The Muslim community faced a difficult job in choosing a successor after Muhammad died.
- The Muslim Empire rapidly expanded under the "rightly guided" caliphs.
- Conflict over the caliphate caused a split in the Muslim community in the mid-seventh century.

Why It Matters Now. . .

The division between Sunnis and Shiites continues to cause conflict in the Muslim world today.

3 Lesson Review

Homework Helper
ClassZone.com

Terms & Names

1. Explain the importance of

    caliph   Shi'a   Sunni

Using Your Notes

Explaining Chronological Order and Sequence
Use your completed time line to answer the following question:

2. When did the Umayyad dynasty begin? (7.2.4)

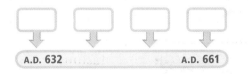

A.D. 632   A.D. 661

Main Ideas

3. Why was Abu Bakr elected the first caliph? (HI 2)

4. How did the Muslim Empire spread? (7.2.4)

5. Why were Jews and Christians given special treatment by conquering Muslim armies? (7.2.2)

Critical Thinking

6. **Drawing Conclusions** What do you think was the most important factor in the spread of Islam? Why? (7.2.4)

7. **Comparing** How did the Muslim policy of ruling conquered peoples compare with that of the Byzantines and the Persians? (7.2.4)

Activity **Creating a Brochure** Choose one of the religious groups in Lesson 3. Then create a short brochure that discusses the history and beliefs of that group. Include the writing skills you have practiced in this unit. (7.2.2)

The Beginnings of Islam • 103

Skillbuilder

Summarizing

CALIFORNIA STANDARDS
REP 3 Students distinguish relevant from irrelevant information, essential from incidental information, and verifiable from unverifiable information in historical narratives and stories.

Goal: To summarize the main ideas of a selection in order to better understand information on the Muslim world

Learn the Skill

When you summarize a passage, you restate the content in fewer words. You include only the main ideas and the most important details. It is important to use your own words when you summarize. When you write a passage in your own words, you can see how well you understand it.

 See the Skillbuilder Handbook, page R3.

Practice the Skill

1 Read the passage at right. Look for a topic sentence stating the main idea. This is often at the beginning of a section or paragraph. Briefly restate the main idea in your own words. The topic sentences can also help you find the most important details.

2 Include key facts, numbers, dates, amounts, or percentages from the text.

3 Write your summary in a paragraph. The paragraph below is a summary of the passage on the Muslim world on the opposite page.

4 After writing your summary, review it to make sure that you have included the main ideas and the most important details.

Example:

> **3** **Summary**
>
> By 661, Muhammad's successors had increased the size of the Muslim empire nearly four times. Many conquered people converted to Islam. In 656, a civil war started. During the 660s, a family known as the Umayyads took power. Soon the Muslim community split into factions. A minority called the Shi'a opposed the Umayyads. The majority, called the Sunnis, accepted the Umayyads.

In the following passage, the author describes the expansion and division of the Muslim world after the death of Muhammad. Use the strategies listed under Practice the Skill to help you follow the sequence of events.

The Muslim World After Muhammad

1 After Muhammad's death in Medina in 632, the Muslim world quickly expanded and then divided. The expansion began under the first caliph, Abu Bakr. Syria, lower Egypt, and parts of the Persian Empire were conquered by the second caliph, Umar.

▲ **The City of Medina**
Sites in Medina are illustrated on this Egyptian tile.

The next two caliphs were Uthman and Ali. They continued to expand Muslim territory and completed the conquest of Persia. **2** By 661, the Muslim Empire had been expanded to nearly four times its size by Muhammad's successors. It then included all of Southwest Asia and stretched into North Africa.

2 Many conquered people became Muslims. They found Islam's message of equality and hope attractive. There was also an economic benefit—Muslims did not have to pay a poll tax.

2 In 656, a civil war started. After rebels murdered Uthman, various groups struggled for power. Ali, a relative of Muhammad, became the next caliph. Before long, he was assassinated. **2** During the 660s, a family known as the Umayyads took power. They set up a hereditary dynasty. This meant that rulers would come from one family.

2 Soon the Muslim community split. A minority called the Shi'a opposed the Umayyads. The Shi'a believed that the caliph should be a relative of the Prophet. The majority, called the Sunnis, accepted the Umayyads.

Apply the Skill

Turn to pages 87–88 in Lesson 1 of this chapter. Read the paragraphs under "Crossroads of Three Continents." Find the main idea and write a paragraph summarizing the section.

VISUAL SUMMARY

Early Islam

Geography (7.2.1)
- The Arabian peninsula is a vast desert land.
- Its geography encourages a nomadic way of life.
- Oases are important for survival.

Economy (7.2.5)
- Bedouins are nomads.
- Landforms limit agriculture.
- Trade brings goods and ideas from many places.
- Important trade centers, including Mecca and Medina, develop.

Belief Systems (7.2.2)
- Muhammad is the Prophet of Islam.
- Mecca is Islam's holy city.
- The Qur'an and the Sunnah are sources of authority.
- The Five Pillars of Islam are Muslims' basic religious duties.

Government (7.2.4)
- Clans are a basic unit of government on the Arabian peninsula.
- Muhammad governs as the leader of all Muslims.
- Caliphs rule Muslim Empire after Muhammad.

TERMS & NAMES

Explain why the words in each set below are linked with each other.

1. **nomad** and **oasis**
2. **monotheism** and **Allah**
3. **Islam** and **Muslim**
4. **Shi'a** and **Sunni**

MAIN IDEAS

Life on the Arabian Peninsula (pages 84–91)

5. Why were the Bedouins nomads? (7.2.1)
6. Why were the peninsula's oases important to Bedouins? to farmers? to merchants? (7.2.5)
7. Why was the Ka'aba important to pilgrims? (7.2.2)

Islam and Muhammad (pages 92–97)

8. What are the Five Pillars of Islam? (7.2.3)
9. How did early Muslims treat Jews and Christians? (7.2.2)
10. How did Muslims view the relationship between their lives and their religion? (7.2.3)

Islam After Muhammad's Death (pages 98–105)

11. Why are Muhammad's elected successors called the "rightly guided" caliphs? (7.2.4)
12. Why is Abraham important to Muslims? (7.2.2)
13. What caused the split between Sunnis and Shiites? (HI 2)

CRITICAL THINKING
Big Ideas: Belief Systems

14. **UNDERSTANDING CAUSE AND EFFECT** How did Islam help spread Arabic culture? (7.2.4)
15. **EVALUATING INFORMATION** What skills did Muhammad have that allowed him to gain authority over so many people? (7.2.2)
16. **MAKING INFERENCES** To what source might Muslim leaders turn for guidance to shape their society and government? Why? (7.2.3)

ALTERNATIVE ASSESSMENT

1. **WRITING ACTIVITY** Imagine that you are a reporter following the Muslim army as it moves across the Arabian peninsula. Write a brief article explaining why the Muslim army was so successful in conquering lands and spreading Islam. (Writing 2.4)

2. **INTERDISCIPLINARY ACTIVITY— LANGUAGE ARTS** Use books or the Internet to research the Arabic language, the language of the Qur'an. Create a colorful poster that accurately explains major features and key elements of the language. (7.2.4)

3. **STARTING WITH A STORY**

 Review your response to the question about the future of the Muslim community. Now that you've read the chapter, would you answer this question differently? If so, how? (Writing 2.2)

Technology Activity

4. **ESTABLISHING E-MAIL CORRESPONDENCE**

As a class project, establish e-mail correspondence with a class in Saudi Arabia to learn more about the hajj. Ask about

- sites that Muslims visit when they make the hajj
- duties and rituals that are performed
- experiences students have had (7.2.3)

Research Links
ClassZone.com

Use the pie graphs below to answer the questions. (7.2.4)

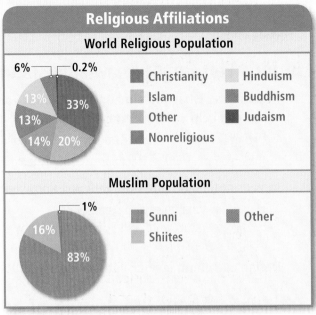

Sources: *World Almanac 2003; World Christian Encyclopedia* (2001); Adherents.com (September 6, 2002)

1. **Which statement is correct according to the world religions graph?**

   A. All religions have about the same number of members.

   B. Hinduism is the largest religion in the world.

   C. Islam is the second-largest religious group.

   D. Judaism has more members than Christianity.

2. **Which statement on the Muslim population is correct according to the graph?**

   A. Both Sunnis and Shiites have about the same number of members.

   B. Sunnis are the largest Muslim group.

   C. The Shiites are the largest Muslim group.

   D. The Other group has more members than either the Sunni or the Shi'a.

 **Test Practice**
ClassZone.com

Additional Test Practice, pp. S1–S33

Chapter 4

The Rise of Muslim States

Before You Read: Knowledge Rating

Recognizing what you already know about each of these terms can help you understand the chapter:

Iberian Peninsula	bureaucracy	standing army
golden age	factions	mercenaries

In your notebook, rate how well you know each term.

3 = I know what this word means.
2 = I've seen this word, but I don't know what it means.
1 = I've never seen this word before.

Define each term in your notebook as you read.

Big Ideas About the Spread of Islam

Geography Migration, trade, warfare, and the action of missionaries spread ideas and beliefs.

Arab armies conquered a huge empire. The Arabs introduced to the newly conquered lands the Arabic culture and the Muslim faith. In turn, they adopted features of the cultures of these lands. This cultural blending created a distinct way of life.

- Lands conquered by 661
- Lands conquered by 750
- Extent of Muslim influence, 1200

```
0        500      1000 miles
0     500   1000 kilometers
```

Integrated Technology

eEdition
- Interactive Maps
- Interactive Visuals
- Starting with a Story

INTERNET RESOURCES
Go to **ClassZone.com** for
- WebQuest
- Homework Helper
- Research Links
- Internet Activities
- Quizzes
- Maps
- Test Practice
- Current Events

MUSLIM WORLD

661 Umayyads come to power and establish their capital in Damascus.

711 Umayyads begin their conquest of Spain.

750 Abbasids overthrow the Umayyads. (Abbasid mosque)

600   700   800

WORLD

690 Empress Wu Chao rules in her own name in China.

800 ◄ Pope crowns Charlemagne Holy Roman Emperor.

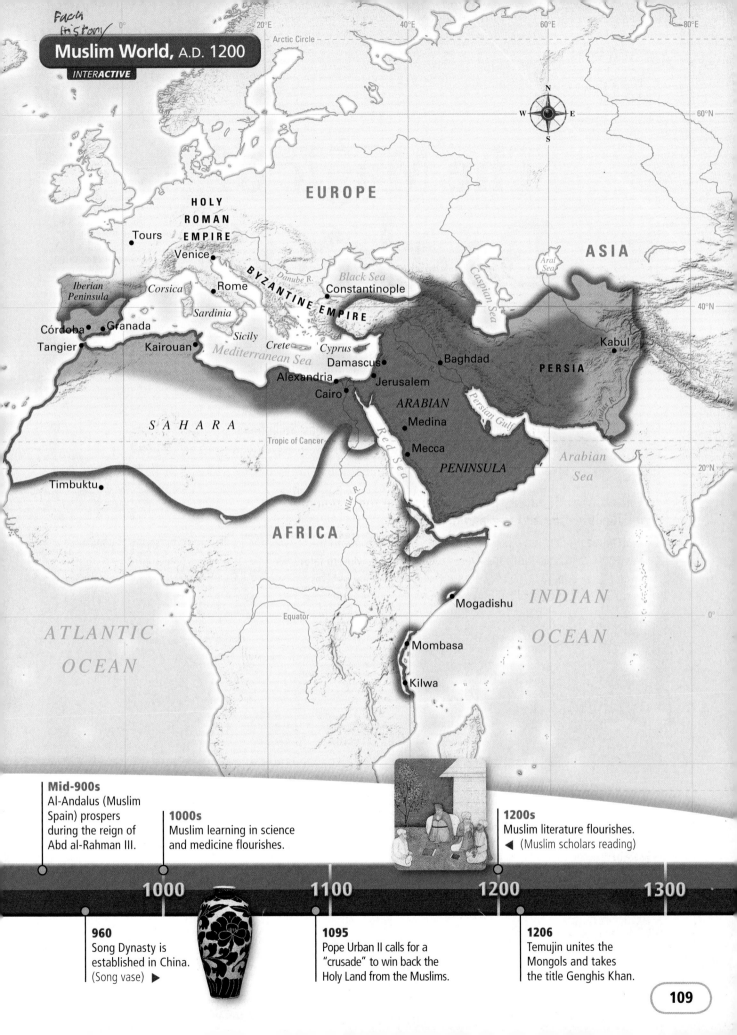

Facts History

Muslim World, A.D. 1200
INTERACTIVE

EUROPE

HOLY
ROMAN
EMPIRE

Tours

Venice

Iberian Peninsula

Corsica

Rome

BYZANTINE EMPIRE

Danube R.

Black Sea

Constantinople

ASIA

Aral Sea

Caspian Sea

Córdoba

Granada

Tangier

Kairouan

Sardinia

Sicily

Crete

Cyprus

Damascus

Alexandria

Jerusalem

Cairo

ARABIAN

Baghdad

PERSIA

Kabul

Mediterranean Sea

S A H A R A

Tropic of Cancer

Medina

Mecca

Red Sea

PENINSULA

Persian Gulf

Arabian Sea

Nile R.

Timbuktu

AFRICA

Equator

INDIAN

Mogadishu

OCEAN

ATLANTIC

OCEAN

Mombasa

Kilwa

Mid-900s
Al-Andalus (Muslim Spain) prospers during the reign of Abd al-Rahman III.

1000s
Muslim learning in science and medicine flourishes.

1200s
Muslim literature flourishes.
◄ (Muslim scholars reading)

1000 **1100** **1200** **1300**

960
Song Dynasty is established in China. (Song vase) ▶

1095
Pope Urban II calls for a "crusade" to win back the Holy Land from the Muslims.

1206
Temujin unites the Mongols and takes the title Genghis Khan.

The Magic of Baghdad

CALIFORNIA STANDARDS

Reading 3.2
Students identify events that advance the plot and determine how each event explains past or present action(s) or foreshadows future action(s).

Background: Muslim civilization developed along with the remarkable growth of its cities. Many great Muslim cities, such as Damascus, had existed for centuries. Others, such as Cairo, began as army camps. They were set up to guard Muslim rulers in newly conquered lands. Still others were planned to be great capitals by Muslim rulers. As you read the following story, imagine that you're living in one of the greatest of these capital cities—Baghdad.

An early map of Baghdad shows the system of canals between the Tigris and Euphrates rivers that provided the city with water. ▶

You are a student living in the magnificent city of Baghdad. You only recently left your village to come live with your uncle. His apartment is in a neighborhood in the Round City at the very heart of Baghdad. He told you that the residential areas of the Round City were built for the caliph and his family. Years ago, however, they moved to grand palaces on the outskirts of Baghdad. Now the Round City is a collection of neighborhoods just like the one you live in.

As you stand on the balcony of your uncle's apartment, you look out over your neighborhood. It's certainly very different from your village. There's a market where you can buy everything from carpets to oranges. It's not unusual to see merchants from half a world away selling their goods there. You've seen silks and porcelain from China, spices and dyes from India, gold and ivory from Africa, and furs and live falcons from Russia.

For you, however, the most amazing thing about the neighborhood is the gardens. It almost never rains in Baghdad, but practically every courtyard has a small garden. Most consist of an ornamental fountain and reflecting pool surrounded by an incredible display of colorful flowers. It seems to you that the splashing of the water from the fountains is the music of everyday life in Baghdad.

Your uncle often tells you that the neighborhood has everything you need and that you really don't have to leave it. But you're not so sure. From your uncle's balcony you can see the roofs of buildings beyond your neighborhood. You decide to take a look at the rest of Baghdad.

What do you think the rest of Baghdad will look like?

Reading & Writing

1. READING: Plot The plot of a story is the sequence of events in the story. With a partner, identify the various events that make up the plot in the story. Explain how the decision at the end of the story foreshadows future actions. (To foreshadow means to give an indication or suggestion of future events.)

2. WRITING: Narration Write a paragraph describing what you think you will find on your journey through the rest of Baghdad. After you have finished, read the chapter to learn more about Baghdad and other great Muslim cities.

CALIFORNIA STANDARDS Writing 2.1
Write fictional or autobiographical narratives.

111

Lesson 1

▶ MAIN IDEAS

❶ Government The Umayyads expanded Muslim rule to the east and westward into Europe.

❷ Government The Umayyads built a unified empire based on a strong government, a common language, and a common coinage.

❸ Government By 750, religious and political differences caused the Muslim Empire to split.

▶ TAKING NOTES

Reading Skill: Finding Main Ideas

Identifying the main ideas in a passage will help you understand key historical events. As you read each section of this lesson, look for essential information on the main ideas. Record this information in a chart like the one shown below.

Umayyad Expansion	Unifying the Empire	Umayyad Downfall

 Skillbuilder Handbook, page R2

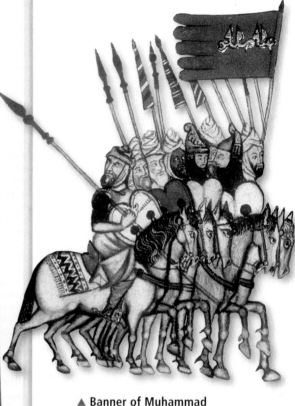

▲ **Banner of Muhammad**
This illustration from a Spanish manuscript shows Muslim soldiers carrying the banner of Muhammad.

CALIFORNIA STANDARDS

7.2.4 Discuss the expansion of Muslim rule through military conquests and treaties, emphasizing the cultural blending within Muslim civilization and the spread and acceptance of Islam and the Arabic language.

CST 1 Students explain how major events are related to one another in time.

CST 3 Students use a variety of maps and documents to identify physical and cultural features of neighborhoods, cities, states, and countries and to explain the historical migration of people, expansion and disintegration of empires, and the growth of economic systems.

The Expansion of Muslim Rule

TERMS & NAMES
Iberian Peninsula
bureaucracy
Abd al-Malik

Build on What You Know You might have seen on the television news that when a leader dies or resigns, a power struggle follows to determine his or her successor. After Muhammad died, several groups fought for control of the Muslim world. In 661, the Umayyad family won this power struggle. The Umayyads built a great empire with Damascus (located in present-day Syria) as its capital.

Expansion Under the Umayyads

1 ESSENTIAL QUESTION What lands did the Umayyads add to the Muslim Empire?

Once the Umayyads had taken control, they began to conquer new lands. In less than 100 years, their empire spanned parts of three continents—Asia, Africa, and Europe.

Expansion to the East Under the Umayyads, the Muslim Empire expanded. When they took power in 661, the empire's eastern boundary extended into Persia. (See the map on the next page.) They quickly pushed that border farther eastward into Central Asia. At first, Umayyad armies staged hit-and-run raids, attacking such cities as Bukhara (boo•KAHR•uh) and Samarkand. These were the region's major trading centers. Soon, however, occasional raids turned into organized campaigns for conquest. By the early 700s, the Umayyads had taken control of much of Central Asia.

Connect to Today

The Great Mosque, Damascus The magnificent Great Mosque was originally built by the Umayyads. ▼

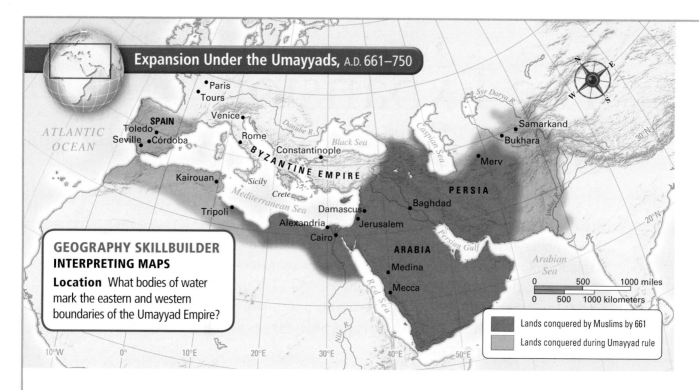

Expansion Under the Umayyads, A.D. 661–750

GEOGRAPHY SKILLBUILDER
INTERPRETING MAPS
Location What bodies of water mark the eastern and western boundaries of the Umayyad Empire?

Lands conquered by Muslims by 661

Lands conquered during Umayyad rule

Westward Expansion The Umayyads also expanded the empire to the west. By 710, they controlled the whole of North Africa from the Nile River to the Atlantic Ocean. The following year, they moved northward across the Mediterranean Sea into the **Iberian Peninsula**. The Iberian Peninsula is the southwestern tip of Europe where the modern nations of Spain and Portugal are located. Using military force and treaties, they took control of nearly all of the peninsula.

From strongholds in Spain, Muslim forces launched raids ever deeper into Europe. However, Christian forces stopped their advance in 732 at the Battle of Tours. (See the map above.) Over the next few years, Muslim forces retreated back to Spain.

REVIEW How did the Umayyads expand the Muslim world?

forced lanched raids ever deeper into eroroupe

Uniting Many Peoples

2 **ESSENTIAL QUESTION** How did the Umayyads build a unified empire?

By the early 700s, the Umayyads controlled a huge empire that covered many lands. As a result, Umayyad leaders needed to take steps to unite and govern the many peoples of this far-flung empire.

Umayyad Government The Umayyads patterned their government on the bureaucracy used in the lands they won from the Byzantine Empire. A **bureaucracy** is a system of departments and agencies that carry out the work of the government. Umayyad caliphs, through this bureaucracy, ruled the entire empire from their capital city of Damascus.

Vocabulary Strategy

The **suffix** –*cracy* means "government" and "rule." It comes from a Greek word that means "strength" or "power."

To rule the different provinces of the empire, the caliphs appointed Muslim governors called emirs (ih•MEERZ). These emirs relied on local clan leaders to help them govern. Working with local leadership helped the Umayyads win support in lands far from Damascus.

A Common Language and Coinage At first, language served as a barrier to unity in the empire. People in different parts of the empire spoke their own languages. **Abd al-Malik** (uhb•DUL muh•LIHK), who became caliph in 685, solved this problem. He declared Arabic the language of government for all Muslim lands. Having a common language for government helped people throughout the empire communicate more easily with other regions. Even so, most Muslims still spoke their own languages in everyday life.

Around 700, Abd al-Malik further unified the empire by introducing a common coinage. Coins were engraved with Arabic quotations from the Qur'an. The coins helped the spread and acceptance of Islam and the Arabic language. They also made commerce among the different parts of the empire much easier.

The Pilgrimage Muslims from across the empire made the pilgrimage, or hajj, to Mecca. On the hajj, pilgrims shared their languages and cultures. In addition, they brought knowledge of the Arabic culture and Umayyad rule back to their homelands. So the pilgrimage helped bring about the blending of many different cultures.

The Hajj This Persian painting shows a caravan of pilgrims on the road to Mecca. ▼

REVIEW How did the Umayyads unify the scattered Muslim states? idk

The Overthrow of the Umayyads

③ ESSENTIAL QUESTION What caused the Muslim Empire to split?

The Umayyads conquered many new lands and brought Islam to large numbers of people. By the mid-700s, however, the Umayyads faced major challenges to their rule.

Rising Protests Some Muslims felt that the Umayyads did not take their duties as leaders of Islam seriously. They accused the Umayyads of being too interested in living a life of luxury and holding on to power. Over time, different groups throughout the empire began to protest Umayyad rule.

The Abbasids One group, the Abbasids (uh•BAS•IHDS), gained support from other Muslims who opposed the Umayyads. By 750, these combined forces had taken power. According to some historians, the Abbasids invited Umayyad leaders to a meeting to talk about peace. At that meeting, the Umayyads were murdered.

Only one prominent Umayyad, Abd al-Rahman (uhb•DUL rahk•MAHN), escaped this ambush. He fled to Spain. There, he re-established the Umayyad dynasty. After this, the Muslim Empire was permanently split into eastern and western sections.

REVIEW Why did the Umayyads lose power?

Lesson Summary

- The Umayyads rose to control all Muslims and create a huge empire.
- Umayyad caliphs created a large bureaucracy to serve the far-flung Muslim lands.
- Religious and political differences among Muslim groups eventually ended Umayyad rule.

Why It Matters Now . . .

Muslims continue to learn the Arabic language in order to practice their religion, as they did in Umayyad times.

Gold Coin The inscription on this coin is the Muslim declaration of faith: There is no God but Allah, and Muhammad is his Prophet. ▼

1 Lesson Review

Homework Helper
ClassZone.com

Terms & Names

1. Explain the importance of

   Iberian Peninsula   bureaucracy   Abd al-Malik

Using Your Notes

Finding Main Ideas Use your completed chart to answer the following question:

2. What was the greatest accomplishment of the Umayyads? Give reasons for your answer. (7.2.4)

Umayyad Expansion	Unifying the Empire	Umayyad Downfall

Main Ideas

3. How did the Umayyads bring new lands into the Muslim Empire? (7.2.4)

4. How did the Umayyads unite the many lands and peoples of the Muslim Empire? (7.2.4)

5. What were some of the problems that triggered the Umayyads' downfall? (7.2.4)

Critical Thinking

6. **Comparing** How did the policies of the Muslims toward conquered lands compare with other empire builders such as the Romans? (CST 1)

7. **Drawing Conclusions** What role did religion play in the expansion of the Muslim Empire? (7.2.4)

Activity

Making a Map Take out the map that you began in Chapter 2. Then use the maps on pages 114 and 120 to draw in the boundaries of the Umayyad and Abbasid empires at their height. (Framework)

Make a Travel Brochure

Goals: To identify the expansion of Muslim rule under the Umayyads; to work in a small group to create a travel brochure or tour guide of the Umayyad Empire

Materials & Supplies

- books on Arab and Muslim history
- examples of tour guides and travel brochures
- old magazines ready for recycling
- scrap paper
- pens
- scissors
- construction paper
- glue stick

Prepare

1. Research the growth of the Umayyad Empire in this textbook and in books on Arab and Muslim history.

2. Look at examples of tour guides and travel brochures.

Do the Activity

1. With other group members, decide what you want to include in your travel brochure. Items you might consider include introductory materials, maps, time lines, short biographies, and pictures and sketches. Don't forget that the brochure needs a title.

2. On scrap paper, create a working layout of your tour guide.

3. Create the various items you want to include in the guide.

4. Assemble the items for your tour guide on a piece of construction paper. Use glue sticks to ensure that all the pieces are securely attached.

Follow-Up

Based on the materials you gathered for your guide, write a one-sentence summary about the Umayyad Empire.

Extension

Making a Presentation Display your guide for the class. Explain why you included the various items in the guide, noting how they add to people's understanding of the Umayyad Empire.

CALIFORNIA STANDARDS

7.2.4 Discuss the expansion of Muslim rule through military conquests and treaties, emphasizing the cultural blending within Muslim civilization and the spread and acceptance of Islam and the Arabic language.

Lesson 2

▶ MAIN IDEAS

1 **Government** The Abbasids built a powerful empire with Baghdad as their capital.

2 **Culture** Muslim culture under the Abbasids was highly advanced.

3 **Government** Internal revolts and external challenges led to the decline of Abbasid rule.

▶ TAKING NOTES

Reading Skill: Forming and Supporting Opinions

After reading this lesson, you will be asked to form and support an opinion about Abbasid culture. To prepare, use a cluster diagram like the one below to record information on developments in Abbasid culture.

Abbasid Advances

 Skillbuilder Handbook, page R22

▲ **Abbasid Falconer** This 12th-century ivory carving shows an Abbasid falconer. Hunting with falcons was a favorite pastime of the Abbasids.

A Golden Age in the East

TERMS & NAMES

standing army

Baghdad

golden age

calligraphy

Omar Khayyam

faction

Build on What You Know After the collapse of Umayyad control, the Muslim Empire was split into eastern and western sections. (See the map on the next page.) In the east, the Abbasids built a new empire where Muslim culture flourished.

used policy of inconclusion to persuade people.

Abbasid Rule

1 ESSENTIAL QUESTION How did the Abbasids build a powerful empire?

Like the Umayyads, Abbasid rulers looked for ways to strengthen their control and to hold their empire together.

Abbasid Power The Abbasids held on to power, first and foremost, through force. They built a huge **standing army**. A standing army is a fighting force that is maintained in times of peace as well as in times of war. The Abbasids stationed army units at military posts throughout the empire. So wherever and whenever trouble broke out, the Abbasids could quickly send soldiers to put it down.

The Abbasids also used a policy of inclusion to persuade people throughout the empire to accept their rule. All Muslims, whether Arab or non-Arab, were equal, they declared. The Abbasids went further and encouraged Christians and Jews to serve in the government. This way, they made sure that the most talented people would be involved in running the empire.

Early Baghdad This illustration shows what the Abbasid capital, Baghdad, and the Tigris River looked like in the late 700s. ▼

A New Capital The Abbasids also strengthened their power by moving their capital. Their most loyal supporters lived far to the east of the Umayyad capital of Damascus. To be closer to their power base, the Abbasids made **Baghdad** their new capital in 762. Located on the Tigris River, Baghdad lay on old east-west trade routes. It was, as one Abbasid caliph said, "a marketplace for the world."

In a very short time, Baghdad became one of the world's major trading centers. Baghdad's merchants visited not only lands in the Muslim Empire but also China, India, Northern Europe, and Africa. They brought back with them precious metals and stones, silk and other fabrics, ivory, spices, furs, and porcelain. These goods filled the tables in Baghdad's many markets.

A Prosperous City As trade increased, Baghdad prospered and grew. By the early 800s, the city had a population of more than 900,000 people. The need to feed and clothe everyone helped to transform the area around Baghdad from desert to garden. Workers repaired and expanded an ancient network of irrigation canals. Farmers used the newly irrigated land to grow such staples as rice, sugar cane, and cotton. They also grew a variety of fruits and vegetables ranging from apricots to artichokes.

Industry flourished under the Abbasids too. In small workshops in and around Baghdad, craftspeople made leather goods, textiles, carpets, ironwork, and perfumes. Merchants from far and wide readily paid top prices for these goods.

REVIEW How did the Abbasids make sure that they held onto power?

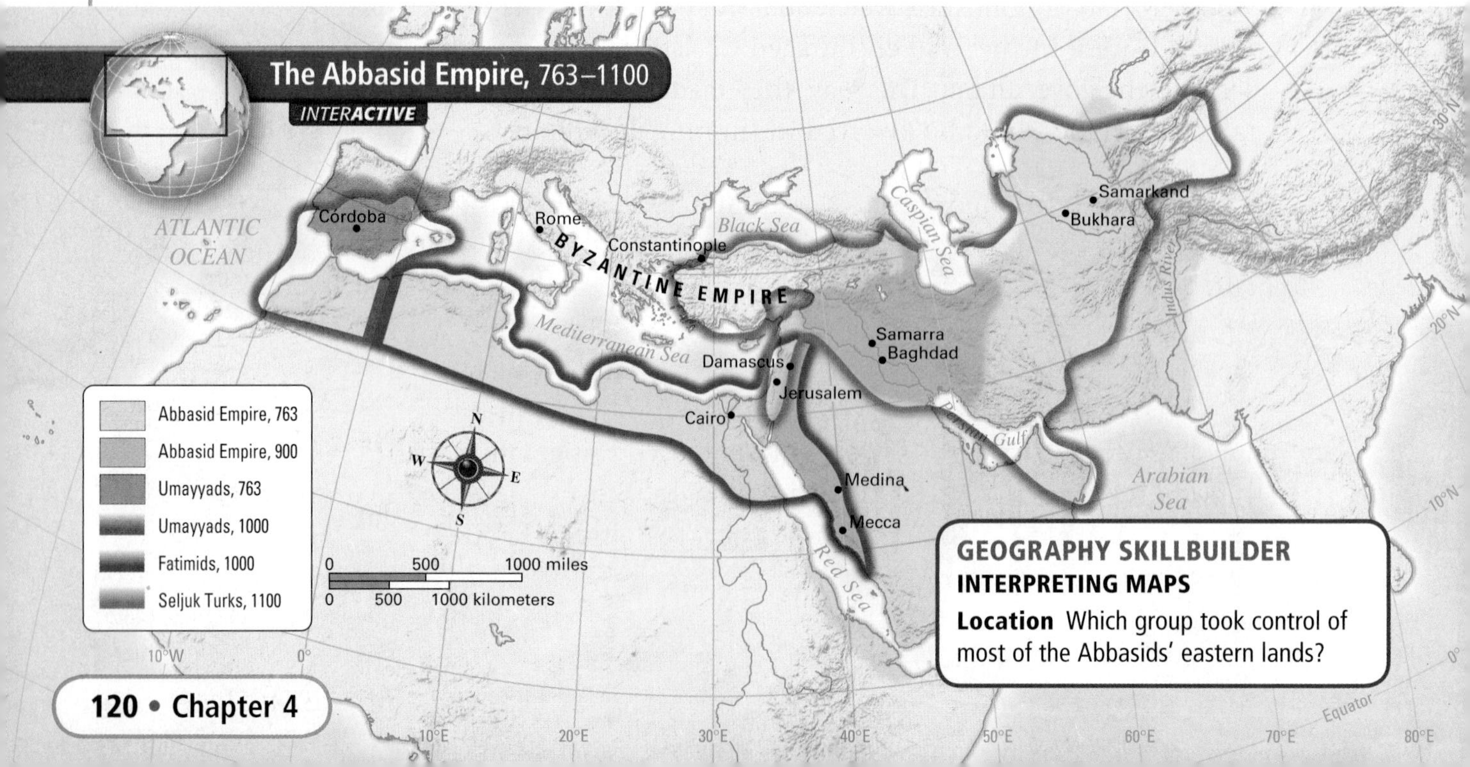
The Abbasid Empire, 763–1100
INTERACTIVE
ATLANTIC OCEAN
Córdoba
Rome
Constantinople
Black Sea
BYZANTINE EMPIRE
Caspian Sea
Samarkand
Bukhara
Indus River
Mediterranean Sea
Damascus
Samarra
Baghdad
Jerusalem
Cairo
Persian Gulf
Arabian Sea
Medina
Mecca
Red Sea
Abbasid Empire, 763
Abbasid Empire, 900
Umayyads, 763
Umayyads, 1000
Fatimids, 1000
Seljuk Turks, 1100
N
S
E
W
0 500 1000 miles
0 500 1000 kilometers
10°W
0°
10°E
20°E
30°E
40°E
50°E
60°E
70°E
80°E
30°N
20°N
10°N
0°
Equator

GEOGRAPHY SKILLBUILDER
INTERPRETING MAPS
Location Which group took control of most of the Abbasids' eastern lands?

▲ Decorated box with hunting scene

Muslim Art		Christian Art
Art should praise Allah but not imitate his human creations.	**Philosophy**	Art should illustrate God's glory.
Decorative shapes and patterns, plants, and flowers	**Subjects**	Biblical scenes and religious figures
Avoidance of human forms; sometimes animals are shown	**Restrictions**	Rarely depicted anything except religious subjects; little everyday life
Art decorated buildings, objects, and manuscripts.	**Display**	Art took such forms as mosaic tiles or wood carvings.

▲ Portrait of Saint Nicholas

Abbasid Advances

2 ESSENTIAL QUESTION What cultural advances were made by the Abbasids?

This brisk economy made the Abbasids very rich. Some wanted to display their wealth. So they began to support the arts and learning. As a result, in the years after 800, Muslim culture enjoyed a golden age. A **golden age** is a period during which a society or culture is at its peak.

Art and Design Most Muslims thought that it was wrong to use the human form in art. Such images, they believed, took people's attention away from their faith. Many religious leaders also felt that people might be encouraged to worship these images rather than God. As a result, Muslim art emphasized plant life and geometric patterns. Abbasid artists became famous for stunning designs using tile, pottery, and wood. One particular design, the *arabesque*, showed the intertwined stem, leaves, and flowers of a plant.

Muslim art also often used Arabic script. Arabic was very special to Muslims because it was the language of the Qur'an. Many Muslim artists became very skilled at **calligraphy**, or the art of fine handwriting. The Abbasids employed calligraphers to decorate everything from buildings to swords and armor. When used as decoration, calligraphy often became so fancy that the words were almost unreadable.

Visual Vocabulary

arabesque

Bookmaking Muslims used calligraphy extensively in books. In the 750s, the Abbasids learned how to make paper from the Chinese. By the early 800s, Baghdad had become a major papermaking center.

Paper was much better for making books than the parchment used in the Middle East and Europe. As books became more widely available, people became interested in all kinds of learning. In the 830s, the Abbasids opened the House of Wisdom in Baghdad to meet the demand for knowledge. It housed books on all subjects from many parts of the world. Scholars there translated into Arabic works by such ancient Greek thinkers as Aristotle and Plato.

Literature Muslims soon developed literature of their own. *The Thousand and One Nights* quickly became a favorite with readers in Baghdad. It mixed stories about life in the Abbasid court with tales of adventure and fantasy. A later European edition added stories that were not part of the medieval Arabic collection. Some of these later additions, such as "Sindbad the Sailor," remain well known today. (For another example of Muslim literature, see pages 126–129.)

Poetry flourished during the Abbasid period. A poetic form called the quatrain was especially popular among people in Persia. This is a four-line poem in which the first, second, and fourth lines rhyme. A Persian-born Muslim named **Omar Khayyam** (OH•mahr ky•yahm) was a master of this form. (See Primary Source feature below.)

P **Primary Source Handbook**

See the excerpt from *The Rubaiyat of Omar Khayyam,* page R40.

Primary Source

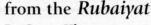

Background: In the *Rubaiyat,* Omar Khayyam (1048–1131) explored such themes as religious faith and worldly pleasure. These two poems take very different views of life.

from the *Rubaiyat*
By Omar Khayyam
Translated by Edward FitzGerald

12 A Book of Verses underneath the Bough,
A Jug of Wine, a Loaf of Bread—and Thou
Beside me singing in the Wilderness—
O, Wilderness were Paradise enow[1]!

71 The Moving Finger writes; and, having writ,
Moves on: nor all thy Piety[2] nor Wit[3]
Shall lure it back to cancel half a Line,
Nor all your Tears wash out a Word of it.

1. **enow:** enough.
2. **Piety:** goodness, devotion.
3. **Wit:** cleverness.

DOCUMENT–BASED QUESTION
How do the moods of these two poems compare? What do you think this says about Omar Khayyam's view of life?

Mathematics and Astronomy Muslim scholars of the Abbasid period borrowed and built upon the ideas of ancient Greeks, Egyptians, and Indians. For example, al-Khwarizmi (al•KWAHR•ihz•mee), who was born in Baghdad around 780, borrowed the numerical system and zero from Indian scholars. His work resulted in the Arabic numbering system that is still used in most of the world today. Al-Khwarizmi also published a set of mathematical calculations titled *Hisab al-jabr.* Roughly translated, this title means "the addition of one thing to another." *Al-jabr* is the origin of the word *algebra.*

In addition to being a poet, Omar Khayyam was a great mathematician. He drew on Greek ideas to further the work of al-Khwarizmi. He also wrote an examination of Greek studies on geometry. Khayyam applied his knowledge of mathematics to astronomy to develop a very accurate calendar. Astronomers' work often had a practical use. For example, an astronomer named al-Biruni fixed the direction of Mecca from any point on Earth. This enabled Muslims everywhere in the empire to fulfill the requirement to pray while facing Mecca.

▲ **Aristotle Teaching** Ancient Greek thinkers, such as Aristotle, had a huge influence on Muslim learning. In recognition of this, Muslim artists often portrayed them in a Muslim setting.

Medicine Muslim doctors, like other Muslim scholars, improved upon the discoveries of earlier scientists. Al-Razi, a Persian-born doctor, used old studies to help him identify and describe diseases such as smallpox and measles. Medical scholars also wrote books that combined ancient works with recent Muslim discoveries. For example, the Persian doctor Ibn Sina wrote the *Canon of Medicine* around 1000. This detailed work organized all known medical knowledge. It even described mental conditions such as "love sickness"! Ibn Sina's work remained an important medical reference book for more than 600 years.

The Abbasids set up hospitals throughout their empire. Unlike hospitals in most other parts of the world, these medical centers treated poor people who couldn't pay. The hospital in Baghdad also served as a teaching center. There, young doctors learned to practice medicine by actually attending to patients.

REVIEW How did Muslim scholars advance world civilization?

The Decline of the Abbasids

3 ESSENTIAL QUESTION What challenges led to the decline of Abbasid rule?

Factions, or opposing groups, challenged Abbasid rule as early as the mid-800s. But many of the Abbasids' problems were of their own making.

Poor Leadership Some Abbasid caliphs were fond of easy living. As a result, they ignored their government responsibilities. Also, they did little to protect merchants from attacks by bandits. This badly hurt trade, which was a major source of caliphs' wealth. Because of this, the Abbasid caliphs raised taxes. People soon tired of the Abbasids' selfish behavior.

Fatimid Revolt One group, the Fatimids, challenged Abbasid rule. The Fatimids claimed descent from Fatima, a daughter of Muhammad, and were Shi'a Muslims. The Abbasids, in contrast, followed the Sunni branch of Islam. So the Fatimids had major religious differences with the Abbasids. They especially disliked the Abbasids' fancy lifestyle. They thought Muslims should live simply.

The Fatimids drove the Abbasids out of what today is Egypt and Tunisia. They set up their own caliphate there, with their capital in Cairo. By the late 960s, they controlled much of North Africa.

The Seljuk Turks The more opposition the Abbasids faced from within their empire, the more open they were to attacks from outside. In 1055, one of these attacks succeeded. The Seljuk Turks from Central Asia captured Baghdad. The Seljuk leader became ruler of the empire. However, he allowed the Abbasid caliph to remain as a religious leader.

Seljuk Expansion
This illustration from an 11th-century manuscript shows a clash between Byzantine and Seljuk cavalries. ▼

hello

Over time, the Seljuks converted to Islam. They also began to expand the lands under their control. (See the map on page 120.) In 1071, they captured Jerusalem. By the late 1090s, they were threatening the Byzantine capital, Constantinople. In response, the Christian countries of Europe launched several wars to drive the Seljuks back. (You'll read more about these wars, called the Crusades, in Chapter 10.)

The Seljuk-Abbasid Empire also faced a challenge from the east. In 1258, a Central Asian tribe called the Mongols overran Baghdad. They destroyed the city and killed the Abbasid caliph. The Abbasid dynasty died with him.

REVIEW Why did Abbasid rule come to an end?

Lesson Summary

- The Abbasids strengthened central control of the Muslim Empire and made Baghdad a great city.
- For more than 200 years, Muslims led the world in scholarship and science.
- Internal and external challenges led to the decline of the Abbasids.

Why It Matters Now . . .

Muslim scholars provided the foundation for much of the mathematical and scientific knowledge that we take for granted today.

---

2 Lesson Review

Homework Helper
ClassZone.com

Terms & Names

1. Explain the importance of

standing army	golden age	Omar Khayyam
Baghdad	calligraphy	factions

Using Your Notes

Forming and Supporting Opinions Use your completed cluster diagram to answer this question:

2. Which Abbasid cultural advance do you think was most important for life today? Why? (7.2.6)

Main Ideas

3. How did Abbasid caliphs strengthen their control over the empire? (7.2.4)

4. What were some of the influences that led to developments in Abbasid culture? (7.2.6)

5. What challenges did Abbasid caliphs face that made it difficult to hold their empire together? (7.2.4)

Critical Thinking

6. Understanding Effects How did trade contribute to the growth of Abbasid power? (7.2.5)

7. Drawing Conclusions How did the wealth that brought the Abbasids power also lead to their downfall? (7.2.5)

Activity

Writing a Poem Look again at the Primary Source feature on page 122. Write two quatrains about people or events discussed in this lesson. Try to use different moods in your poems. (7.2.6)

Literature CONNECTIONS

The Cadi and the Fly

by Al-Jahiz

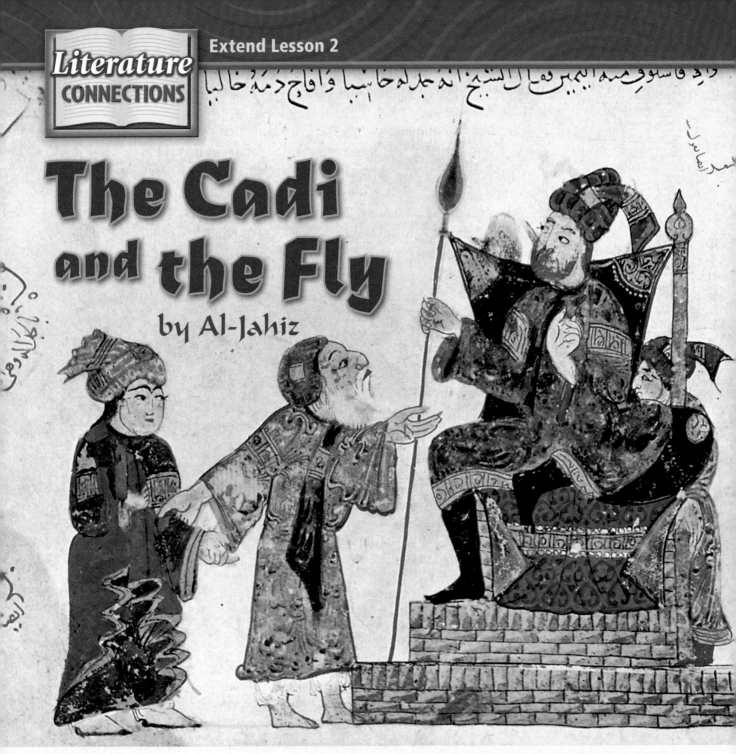

Background: The Golden Age of the Muslim Empire brought an explosion of learning. Mathematicians, scientists, and doctors made great progress in understanding the physical world. Literature, too, enjoyed great popularity. Writers created stories, essays, and poetry to express feelings, teach morals, and discuss scholarly topics.

The writer of this story, al-Jahiz, was one of the greatest writers in classical Arabic literature in the late 700s. He wrote about 200 books during his lifetime. The subjects covered such things as Arabic grammar, zoology, and poetry. In this story, *The Cadi and the Fly* (a cadi is a judge), al-Jahiz teaches a lesson about human weakness.

CALIFORNIA STANDARDS

Reading 3.3 Analyze characterization as delineated through a character's thoughts, words, speech patterns, and actions; the narrator's description; and the thoughts, words, and actions of other characters.

7.2.6 Understand the intellectual exchanges among Muslim scholars of Eurasia and Africa and the contributions Muslim scholars made to later civilizations in the areas of science, geography, mathematics, philosophy, medicine, art, and literature.

There can never have been a magistrate [judge] as sedate [calm], composed, dignified, impassive [emotionless], self-controlled or precise in his movements as a cadi we had at Basra called 'Abd Allah Ibn Sawwar.

He used to say the morning prayer at home, though he lived quite near the mosque, and then go to his court, where he would wrap his robes around him and sit down without supporting himself on anything as he did so. He sat bolt upright and stock still, neither turning round in his seat, opening his coat, crossing his legs, or leaning on either arm of the chair; he was like a statue.

He would remain thus until the noon prayer compelled [forced] him to rise then sit down again and take up the same posture until the time of the afternoon prayer; having accomplished that, he would remain motionless until sunset, when he would get up, say his prayers, and sometimes (what am I saying? often, rather) return to his seat and deal with a multitude of deeds, contracts, and miscellaneous documents. Then he would say his evening prayer and go home. If the truth be told, he never once got up to go to the lavatory during the whole of his tenure [time] of office: he did not need to, since he never felt like a drink of water or other beverage. Such was his routine all the year round, winter and summer, whether the days were long or short. He never so much as lifted his hand or inclined his head, but limited himself to moving his lips.

REVIEW How would you describe 'Abd Allah Ibn Sawwar's behavior?

One day, when his assessors [tax collectors] and the public had taken their place beside him, in front of him and in the gallery, a fly settled on his nose. It lingered there awhile, and then moved to the corner of his eye. He left it alone and endured its biting, just as he had armed himself with patience when it settled on his nose, neither twitching his nostrils, shaking his head, or waving it away with a finger. However, since the fly was becoming really persistent, causing him acute pain and moving towards a spot where it was beyond bearing, he blinked his eyelid. The fly did not go away. This persistence drove him to blink repeatedly, whereupon the fly moved away until the eyelid stopped moving, then returned to the corner of the eye even more fiercely than before and stuck its sting into an already sore spot. The cadi's patience was weakening and his irritation growing: he blinked harder and more rapidly.

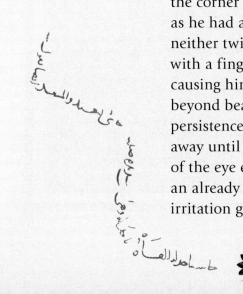

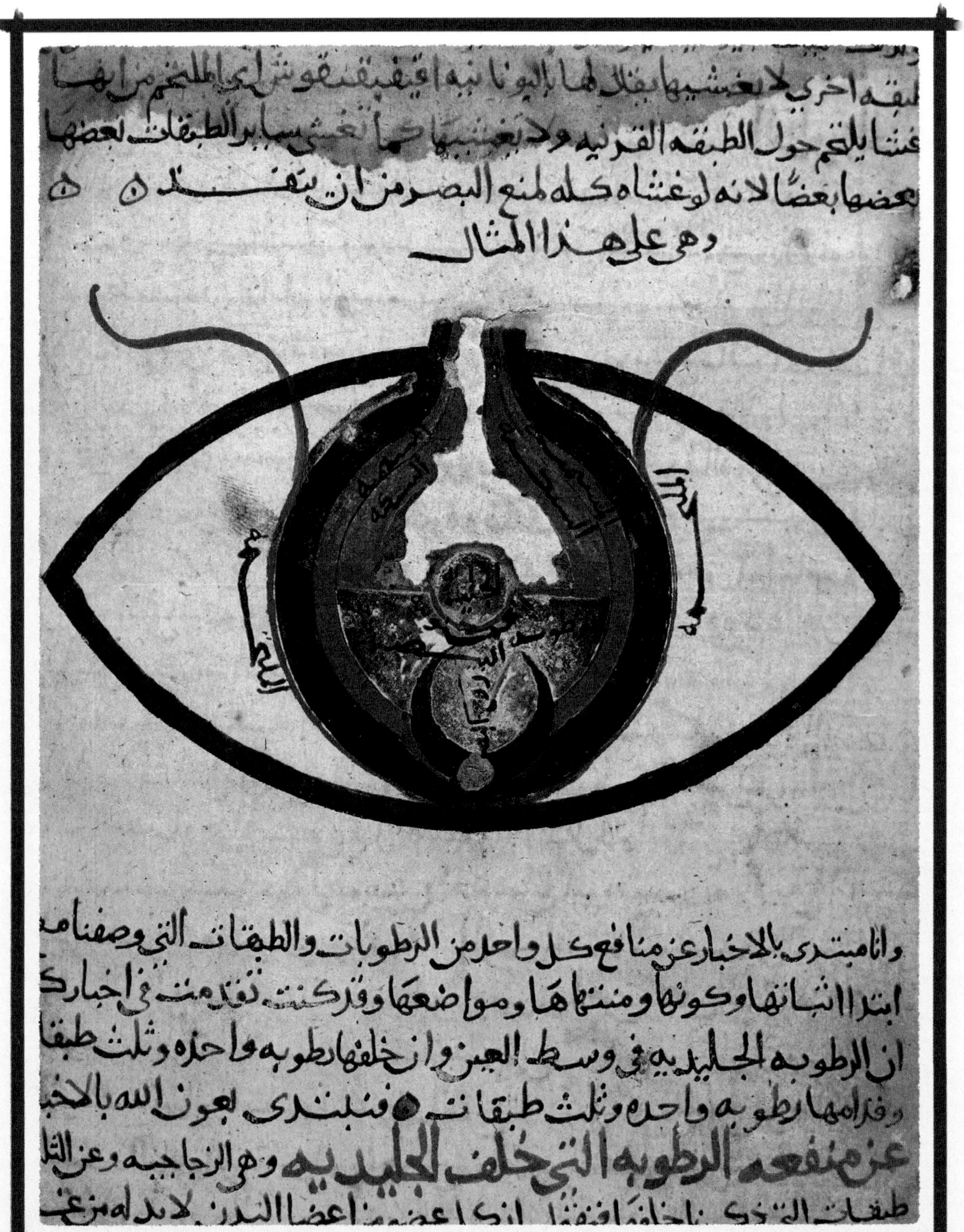

لقه اخرى لا يغشيها يقال لها البونانيه اعفيقتقونراي الملتحم من بها

عشايلتحم حول الطبقه القرنيه ودبغشيها جما بغشى سائر الطبقات لعضها

بعضها بعضا لانه لوغشاه كله لمنع البصر من ان يتفذ ه

وهى على هذا المثال

والانا ابتدى بالاخبار عن منافع كل واحد من الرطوبات والطبقات التى وصفنامع

ابتدا شانها وكونها ومنتها ومواضعها وتركينت تفدمت فى اخبارك

ان الرطوبه الجليديه فى وسط العين وان خلفها رطوبه واحده وثلث طبقا

وقدامها رطوبه واحده وثلث طبقات فنبتدى بعون الله بالاخبا

عن منفعه الرطوبه التى خلف الجليديه وهى الزجاجيه وعن الث

طبقات التى بازائها فافنا ان اعطم اعضا البدن لابد له من غ

The fly went away for a moment, then settled again and became so persistent that our cadi, his endurance [patience] completely at an end, was reduced to driving it away with his hand: Everyone in court was watching this pretending not to see it. The fly went away until he dropped his hand, then returned to the charge and compelled him to protect his face with the hem of his sleeve, not once but several times.

REVIEW What was unusual about 'Abd Allah Ibn Sawwar's behavior when the fly bothered him?

The magistrate realized that no detail of this scene was escaping his assessors and the public. When he caught their eye, he exclaimed: "I swear the fly is more persistent than the cockroach and more presumptuous [conceited] than the crow! God forgive me! How many men are infatuated [in love] with their own persons! But God acquaints them with their hidden weakness! Now I know I am but a weakling, seeing that God's most feeble creature has vanquished and confounded me!" Then he recited this verse: "And if the fly should rob them of aught [anything], the gods of the idolaters would be unable to restore it to them. Worshipper and idol are both powerless [Qur'an, 22:72-73]."

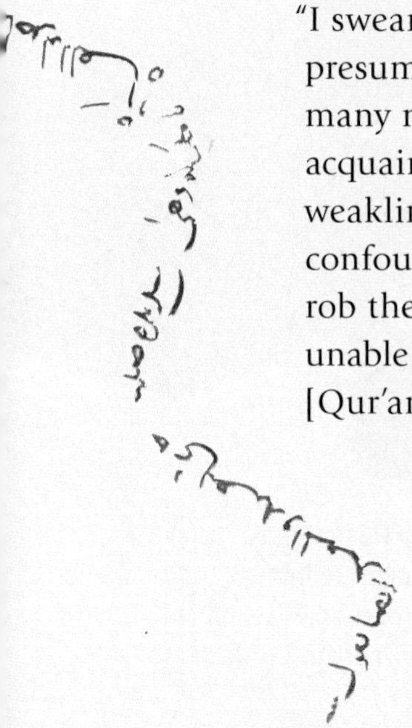

Reading & Writing

1. **READING: Characterization** Identify the ways in which the writer was able to draw a picture of the judge's behavior. Give examples from the story to support your interpretation.

2. **WRITING: Response to Literature** This story is an example of a moral tale. Write a paragraph about what lesson you think the writer was trying communicate to the reader.

CALIFORNIA STANDARDS Writing 2.2
Write responses to literature.

Lesson 3

MAIN IDEAS

1 **Government** The Umayyads created a strong Muslim kingdom, al-Andalus, on the Iberian Peninsula.

2 **Geography** Córdoba, the capital of al-Andalus, became a thriving economic and cultural center under the Umayyads.

3 **Culture** Al-Andalus enjoyed a flowering of culture and learning in the 1000s and 1100s.

TAKING NOTES

Reading Skill:
Identifying Issues and Problems

Learning how people responded to problems in history can help identify solutions to today's problems. Use a chart like the one below to note the issues and problems that Abd al-Rahman III faced when he came to power and the ways he responded to them.

Issues and Problems	Responses
Internal revolts	
Attacks from Christian forces to the north	
Threats from North Africa	

 Skillbuilder Handbook, page R28

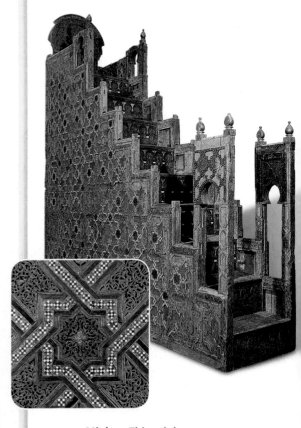

▲ **Minbar** This minbar, where Muslim religious leaders preached, was made by craftworkers in Córdoba.

CALIFORNIA STANDARDS

7.2.4 Discuss the expansion of Muslim rule through military conquests and treaties, emphasizing the cultural blending within Muslim civilization and the spread and acceptance of Islam and the Arabic language.

7.2.5 Describe the growth of cities and the establishment of trade routes among Asia, Africa, and Europe, the products and inventions that traveled along these routes (e.g., spices, textiles, paper, steel, new crops), and the role of merchants in Arab society.

7.9.7 Describe the Golden Age of cooperation between Jews and Muslims in medieval Spain that promoted creativity in art, literature, and science, including how that cooperation was terminated by the religious persecution of individuals and groups (e.g., the Spanish Inquisition and the expulsion of Jews and Muslims from Spain in 1492).

Muslim Rule in Spain

TERMS & NAMES
al-Andalus
Córdoba
Abd al-Rahman III
mercenary

Build on What You Know Only Abd al-Rahman escaped the Abbasid massacre of Umayyad leaders in 750. He fled to the Iberian Peninsula. There he began to build a kingdom that would match the Abbasid Empire in culture and wealth.

The Return of the Umayyads

1 **ESSENTIAL QUESTION** How did the Umayyads create a strong Muslim kingdom on the Iberian Peninsula?

When Abd al-Rahman arrived in Spain, he found a divided land. Various Muslim factions fought for control. However, no single group held on to power for very long. Abd al-Rahman quickly took action to unite all these groups.

Uniting Muslim Spain Abd al-Rahman already had a following in Spain—the people still loyal to the Umayyads. He strengthened his position by making treaties with other Muslim groups. When he felt strong enough, he attacked the ruling factions and defeated them. In 756 he declared himself emir of **al-Andalus**—Muslim Spain. He made **Córdoba** his capital.

A Muslim Stronghold When Abd al-Rahman declared himself emir of al-Andalus, Muslims controlled practically all of the Iberian Peninsula. ▼

Defending Muslim Spain
News of Abd al-Rahman's success quickly spread east to Abbasid lands. Many Umayyad loyalists headed westward to Spain. Their arrival in al-Andalus greatly strengthened Abd al-Rahman's government and army.

Abd al-Rahman faced several internal revolts during his reign. Also, he had to fight off threats from outside forces. However, none of these threats seriously challenged his rule. When Abd al-Rahman died in 788, al-Andalus was strong and united.

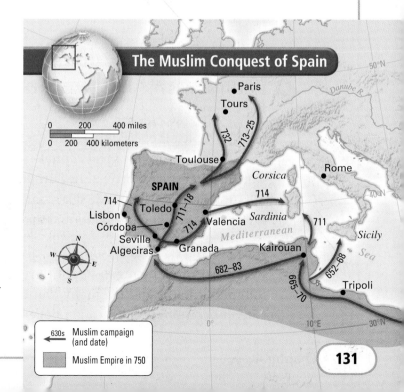

The Muslim Conquest of Spain

Paris
Tours
732
713–25
Toulouse
Rome
Corsica
SPAIN
714
714
Lisbon
Toledo
711–18
Córdoba
Valencia
Sardinia
711
Seville
714
Granada
Mediterranean
Sicily
Algeciras
Kairouan
Sea
682–83
659–70
652–68
Tripoli

0   200   400 miles
0   200   400 kilometers

630s Muslim campaign (and date)
Muslim Empire in 750

A Great Leader

Al-Andalus reached the height of its power some 125 years later during the reign of the eighth emir, **Abd al-Rahman III**. When he came to power in 912, al-Andalus faced many problems. Rebel groups throughout the land challenged the government's authority. Christian armies regularly launched attacks on the northern border. In the south, Muslim opponents threatened to invade from North Africa.

However, Abd al-Rahman III was determined to preserve Umayyad power. He built a huge standing army. Many of the soldiers were non-Muslims from all over Europe. Some were **mercenaries**, or soldiers paid to fight.

Over the next few years, Abd al-Rahman III put down all internal revolts. He then pushed the Christians back from his northern border. He strengthened the southern border by taking control of the northwestern tip of North Africa. By 929, he was so sure of his power that he declared himself caliph of Córdoba. He wanted everyone to know he was ready to challenge the power of the Abbasid and Fatimid caliphs.

▲ **Abd al-Rahman III**
This picture shows Abd al-Rahman III (seated on the left) receiving a representative of Holy Roman Emperor Otto I.

REVIEW What changes did the Umayyads bring to Spain?

The Glory of Córdoba

2 ESSENTIAL QUESTION What was the basis for Córdoba's greatness under the Umayyads?

Soon, people all over Europe and the Muslim world knew of Abd al-Rahman III and his great capital city, Córdoba. By 1000, Córdoba was the largest city in Western Europe. Its population stood at about 500,000 people. That made it several times larger than other major European cities such as London, Paris, or Rome.

A City of Wonders Córdoba truly was a splendid city. Its streets were paved and, by night, were lit by lamps. A water system fed the 900 public baths and the many fountains located around the city. Citizens could wander through dozens of beautiful gardens.

An Economic Center All this splendor was made possible by Córdoba's prosperous economy. The city had hundreds of workshops that produced silk, leather, carpets, paper, weapons, and crystal glass. All of these goods were in great demand throughout Europe. And merchants traveling overland and by sea carried them all of the way to Central Asia and India.

Farming flourished in the countryside around Córdoba. Water wheels irrigated the fields. Farmers grew rice, figs, cherries, apricots, peaches, cotton, and olives. They sold their products at the more than 4,000 markets scattered throughout the city.

A Great Cultural Center Córdoba also was a major center for culture and learning. By the late 900s, the city had 70 libraries. The largest of these had about 400,000 books. (In contrast, most European Christian libraries of the time only had a few hundred manuscripts.) Muslim scholars translated many books into Latin. These books often found their way to Europe, where Christian scholars eagerly studied them.

The caliphs of Córdoba were anxious to outshine their Abbasid rivals. They actively encouraged scholars to leave Baghdad for al-Andalus. These new arrivals brought fresh ideas and different approaches to learning with them. They also added to Córdoba's reputation as one of the world's great cities.

REVIEW Why was Córdoba a great city during Umayyad rule?

The Great Mosque, Córdoba The Great Mosque, one of the largest houses of worship in the world, could hold 52,000 people for services. ▼

A Golden Age in the West

3 **ESSENTIAL QUESTION** What cultural developments took place in al-Andalus in the 1000s and 1100s?

The atmosphere of learning in Córdoba helped create a golden age for culture throughout al-Andalus. Scholars there made important contributions to the study of mathematics, astronomy, geography, medicine, and philosophy.

Mathematics, Astronomy, and Geography The scholars of al-Andalus built on or extended the work of earlier mathematicians, such as al-Khwarizmi. They often put their mathematical learning to practical use. For example, they employed mathematics to create accurate calendars. They also developed tables that showed the location of the sun and other planets at various times of the year. Other scholars made the study of astronomy easier. They built precision instruments for viewing the skies. They also constructed a planetarium with model planets that moved.

Some scholars were more interested in Earth than the skies. They wrote geographic studies of various regions, including Spain, North Africa, and the Arabian peninsula. Al-Idrisi made perhaps the greatest contribution to the study of geography. In 1154, he completed an encyclopedia of geographic knowledge. It contained about 70 maps and descriptions of the geography of many world regions. He based his work mostly on the travels he had taken when he was a young man.

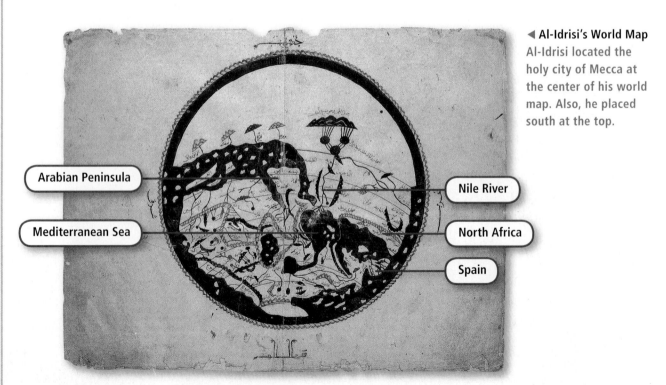

◄ **Al-Idrisi's World Map**
Al-Idrisi located the holy city of Mecca at the center of his world map. Also, he placed south at the top.

Arabian Peninsula

Mediterranean Sea

Nile River

North Africa

Spain

Al-Zahrawi (936–1013)

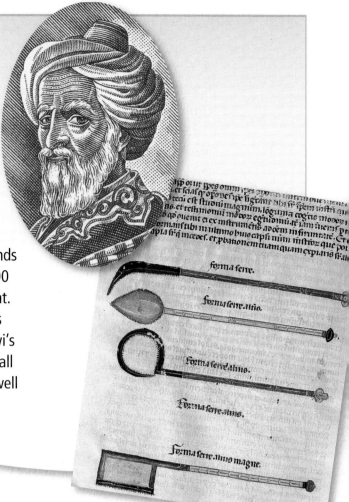

Al-Zahrawi was born, lived, and worked near Córdoba. He became famous for the medical encyclopedia he wrote. This encyclopedia covered everything from the description of diseases to how to prepare and administer medicines.

The most important part of the encyclopedia dealt with surgery. This section described many different kinds of operations. It also included illustrations of about 200 surgical instruments, some of which are shown at right.

Over the years, European scholars translated parts of the encyclopedia into Latin. As a result, al-Zahrawi's work became required reading for medical students all over Europe. It remained a part of medical training well into the 1500s.

Medicine and Philosophy Doctors in al-Andalus borrowed heavily from their counterparts in Baghdad. However, they also made important contributions of their own. Some doctors wrote about the doctor-patient relationship. One such study suggested that doctors should be kind and understanding. It encouraged them to accept patients' criticisms and insults without complaint. This study also suggested that doctors show respect for their patients by keeping themselves clean and behaving with dignity. Other medical scholars wrote about ways to treat diseases. For example, one suggested that changes in diet always should be tried before medicines or other kinds of treatment.

The greatest doctor of the time was al-Zahrawi (al•zah•RAH•wee). He was interested in all aspects of medicine. In the late 900s, he published a 30-volume medical encyclopedia that covered everything from surgery to caring for, repairing, and replacing teeth. He even included entries on how to raise children. (See the History Makers feature above.)

Many doctors were all-around scholars. Ibn Rushd, for example, worked as a doctor. However, he was better known as a philosopher. His studies of Plato and Aristotle were considered his most important work. Latin translations of these studies helped reintroduce classical Greek philosophy to Europe.

A Golden Age for Jews Jews had lived in Spain since Roman times. They often faced persecution. Under the Umayyads, however, they were welcomed, not rejected. Some Jews held high government offices. Samuel ha-Nagid, for example, served as the first minister to the Muslim leader of Granada. Others acted as advisers to Muslim rulers. Hasdai ben Shaprut served as Abd al-Rahman III's personal doctor. He also advised the caliph on other issues, including foreign affairs. For example, he helped the caliph to negotiate peace treaties with several Christian kingdoms.

In this welcoming atmosphere, Spanish Jews flourished. A Sephardic (suh•FAHR•dihk), or Spanish-Jewish, culture with its own language—Ladino—developed. (*Sephardic* comes from the Hebrew word meaning "Spain.") Jews who faced persecution in Christian lands flocked to al-Andalus to enjoy this freedom. They contributed greatly to the golden age of al-Andalus.

▲ **Barcelona Haggadah** This decorated passage is from a Haggadah—a book that tells the story of the Jewish Exodus from Egypt—made in Spain.

A Great Scholar Among the many Jewish scholars of al-Andalus, Maimonides (MY•MAHN•uh•DEEZ) stands above all others. He was born in 1135 to a family that had lived in Córdoba for many years. When he was young, the Almohads (AL•moh•HADZ)—a group of Muslims from North Africa—seized control of the city. Unlike the Umayyads, the Almohads did not allow non-Muslims to practice their own religions. Rather, they demanded that everyone living in Córdoba convert to Islam. Maimonides and his family refused and, after a while, fled to North Africa. They eventually settled in Cairo. There, Maimonides became known as a great writer, doctor, and philosopher.

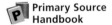 **Primary Source Handbook**

See the excerpt from *The Itinerary of Benjamin of Tudela*, page R39.

Maimonides wrote about and taught many subjects, including religion, science, and medicine. His best-known work, *The Guide for the Perplexed*, was published in 1190. In it, he tried to show that religious faith could be supported by the study of philosophy. His work influenced both Muslim and Christian thinkers.

The Decline of Al-Andalus By the time of Maimonides' death in 1204, al-Andalus had begun to fall apart. Different Muslim factions fought for control. Other Muslim groups broke away and formed their own smaller kingdoms. Christians in the north took advantage of this disarray and launched attacks. By the 1240s, they had pushed as far south as Córdoba and Seville. As you'll read in Chapter 10, over the next 250 years Christian forces slowly regained control of the entire Iberian Peninsula.

REVIEW What contributions to learning did scholars of al-Andalus make?

Lesson Summary
- The Umayyad dynasty that was driven out of Baghdad established the kingdom of al-Andalus on the Iberian Peninsula.
- Córdoba became a major city under Umayyad rule.
- Culture flourished in al-Andalus in the 1000s and 1100s.

Why It Matters Now . . .
Al-Andalus served as a meeting place for the cultures of Southwest Asia, North Africa, and Europe. Europeans regained knowledge of Greek and Roman civilizations through Muslim scholars.

3 Lesson Review

Homework Helper
ClassZone.com

Terms & Names
1. Explain the importance of

al-Andalus	Abd al-Rahman III
Córdoba	mercenary

Using Your Notes
Identifying Issues and Problems Use your completed chart to answer the following question:
2. How did Abd al-Rahman III hold on to power? (7.2.4)

Issues and Problems	Responses
Internal revolts	
Attacks from Christian forces to the north	
Threats from North Africa	

Main Ideas
3. What helped the Umayyads to succeed after losing power to the Abbasids? (7.2.4)
4. What economic and agricultural activities took place in and around Córdoba? (7.2.5)
5. Why were the 1000s and 1100s a golden age for al-Andalus? (7.9.7)

Critical Thinking
6. **Making Inferences** Why do you think Abd al-Rahman III declared himself caliph of Córdoba? (7.2.4)
7. **Comparing and Contrasting** How are Córdoba and Baghdad similar? How are they different? (7.2.5)

Activity **Internet Activity** Use the Internet to research the Great Mosque (also known as the Mezquita) in Córdoba. Use your findings to create a four-page visual essay on the mosque. (7.2.5)
INTERNET KEYWORDS: *Córdoba, Great Mosque, Mezquita*

Connect to Today
Extend Lesson 3

Research Links
ClassZone.com

The Legacy of the Muslim Golden Age

Purpose: To learn about Muslim contributions to science

During the Muslim golden age, scholars in Baghdad and Córdoba made important contributions to the development of astronomy, mathematics, and medicine. These developments had a huge impact on learning in Europe. In many ways, the achievements of the Muslim golden age laid the groundwork for advances in the European Renaissance and Scientific Revolution. Those advances greatly influence the way we live today.

CALIFORNIA STANDARDS
7.2.6 Understand the intellectual exchanges among Muslim scholars of Eurasia and Africa and the contributions Muslim scholars made to later civilizations in the areas of science, geography, mathematics, philosophy, medicine, art, and literature.

Observatories

▶ **Past** Muslims were among the first to establish observatories. These are buildings designed and equipped for studying the stars and planets. Some of these observatories were quite advanced. They were filled with precision instruments invented or designed by Muslim scientists. Astronomers, like those shown at the right, used these instruments to plot the location and movements of the planets.

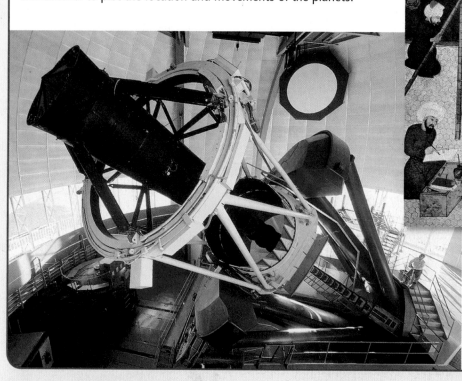

◀ **Present** Astronomers want to discover the nature of the outer limits of the solar system. They work in observatories equipped with high-powered telescopes and advanced computers.

Medicine

▶ **Past** Muslim doctors established new methods of treating illness. First they tried to get patients to change their behavior. If this failed to solve the problem, doctors next tried drugs and other medicines. (At right, doctors prepare medicines.) They viewed drastic measures such as surgery as a last resort.

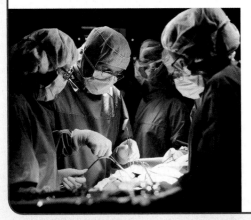

◀ **Present** Surgery is a far more common procedure. However, many doctors also advise patients to change their diet or exercise habits to treat and prevent illness.

Mathematics

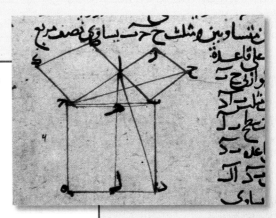

▶ **Past** Muslim mathematicians borrowed the number zero and the decimal system from Indian scholars and introduced them to the West. They also developed Arabic numerals, which made all kinds of calculations simpler. The work of al-Khwarizmi led to the development of algebra as an area of study. Muslim interest in astronomy also led to the development of trigonometry.

▼ **Present** The Arabic number system and algebra are still very much part of the study of mathematics. Also, astronomers still use trigonometry to measure distances in space and on land.

Activities

1. **TALK ABOUT IT** How did religion contribute to Muslim developments in astronomy? (Think about the Five Pillars of Islam as you answer this question.)

2. **WRITE ABOUT IT** What do you think is the most important contribution that Muslims made to science, medicine, and mathematics? Write a paragraph explaining your choice. (Writing 2.4)

▶ **VISUAL SUMMARY**

Great Muslim Empires

The Umayyad Empire 661–750 (7.2.4)

- Established new capital at Damascus
- Extended empire from the Indus Valley in the south to the Iberian Peninsula in the west
- Set up a central bureaucracy in Damascus to govern their vast empire
- Attempted to unify the varied peoples of the empire by establishing a common language for government and common coinage
- Overthrown by the Abbasids in 750
- Re-established dynasty in a western empire in Spain; ruled for another 300 years

The Abbasid Empire 750–1258 (7.2.4)

- Seized the eastern section of the Muslim Empire from the Umayyads
- Maintained control through force and a policy of inclusion—using all able people regardless of their background
- Established new capital at Baghdad, which soon became one of the world's major cities
- Oversaw a golden age of Muslim culture, with notable developments in mathematics and medicine
- Lost power because of internal revolts and poor government
- Collapsed after invasions by Seljuk Turks and Mongols

▶ **TERMS & NAMES**

Explain why the words in each set below are linked with each other.

1. **bureaucracy** and **Abd al-Malik**
2. **Baghdad** and **golden age**
3. **al-Andalus** and **Córdoba**

▶ **MAIN IDEAS**

The Expansion of Muslim Rule (pages 112–117)

4. What areas did the Umayyads add to the Muslim Empire? (7.2.4)
5. How did a common language, coinage system, and religious practices help to unify the peoples of the Umayyad Empire? (7.2.4)

A Golden Age in the East (pages 118–129)

6. What mathematical and medical developments did Muslims make during the Abbasid period? (7.2.6)
7. Why did the Abbasids eventually lose control of the Muslim Empire? (HI 2)

Muslim Rule in Spain (pages 130–139)

8. How did the Umayyads create a powerful kingdom in Spain? (7.2.4)
9. What economic and cultural activities took place in Córdoba? (7.2.5)

CRITICAL THINKING Big Ideas: Geography

10. IDENTIFYING ISSUES AND PROBLEMS
What challenges did the vast size and diversity of the Muslim Empire present Muslim rulers? (7.2.4)

11. UNDERSTANDING CAUSE AND EFFECT
How did the arrival of people from other lands affect al-Andalus? (7.9.7)

12. MAKING INFERENCES How did al-Andalus serve as a meeting place for cultures? (7.2.6)

ALTERNATIVE ASSESSMENT

1. WRITING ACTIVITY Imagine that you are a scholar working at the House of Wisdom in Baghdad. Write a letter to friends living in another part of the Muslim world, encouraging them to come and study or work at the House of Wisdom. (7.2.6)

2. INTERDISCIPLINARY ACTIVITY— ARCHITECTURE Use books or the Internet to research the common features in the design of mosques. Use your findings to create an illustrated essay on mosque architecture. (7.2.4)

3. STARTING WITH A STORY
 Review the way you ended the story "The Magic of Baghdad." Now that you have read the chapter, think of ways that you might change your description of Baghdad. Rewrite your description to incorporate these changes. (7.2.5)

Technology Activity

4. DESIGNING A WEB SITE
Research other Muslim centers in Spain. Use your findings to design a Web site titled "The Muslim Legacy in Spain— Cities." The home page should include some introductory material and links to pages for each of the cities. City pages should include annotated pictures that illustrate the Muslim legacy. (7.2.5)

Research Links
ClassZone.com

Reading Charts The chart below shows some similarities between the Arabic and Spanish languages. Use the chart and your knowledge of world history to answer the questions that follow. (7.2.4)

Arabic and Spanish Words	
Arabic	**Spanish**
al-Andalus (Muslim Spain)	Andalusia (region in southern Spain)
al-ruzz (rice)	arroz (rice)
al-sukkar (sugar)	azúcar (sugar)
al-zayt (olive oil)	aceite (olive oil)
al-suffah (raised platform)	sofá (couch)

1. Based on information in the chart, what do you think the French word *sucre* means?
A. rice   C. olive oil
B. sugar   D. couch

2. Which of the following is the best alternative title for the chart?
A. A Cultural Connection
B. A Word Puzzle
C. The Arabs in Spain
D. The Spanish Influence

Test Practice
ClassZone.com

Additional Test Practice, pp. S1–S33

Writing About History

Summaries of Reading Materials:
A Summary of Unit 2

Writing Model
ClassZone.com

CALIFORNIA STANDARDS
Writing 2.5 Write summaries of reading materials.

Purpose: To write a portion of a study guide for Unit 2
Audience: Your classmates

Unit 2 covers more than 600 years of history. It would take libraries of books to learn all about this period. Yet after reading this unit, you no doubt have a good idea of the rise of Islam and Muslim states. This is possible because history writers summarize, or condense, information.

Summaries are short versions of texts, written in the summary writers' own words. Summaries keep the main ideas and the reflecting underlying meaning, but not the surface details. Summaries are shorter than the original works.

▲ Al-Zahrawi and surgical instruments

Organization & Focus

The class will divide into six groups, one for each lesson in the unit. Your group should divide up the text in your lesson so that each member has about the same amount of text. Each group member will then write a summary of his or her portion. All the summaries will be put together to make a study guide for this unit.

Identifying Purpose and Audience As you work, remember that you are writing your summary to help your classmates study Unit 2. With this in mind, ask yourself what may be especially important to know for a test. Include this information in your summary.

Reading for Main Idea To begin working on your summary, read your portion of the text. Focus on the main ideas. You can often find these in the topic sentences of paragraphs. When you have found the main idea of a paragraph, rewrite it as a complete sentence in your own words.

Evaluating Details Most of the details and examples included in the original text will not be part of your summary. Evaluate the details carefully to determine if any are important enough to include.

The chart below shows a summary of part of the History Makers feature on page 135. The main ideas are highlighted in yellow and some important details are highlighted in green. Compare the original with the summary.

Original	Summary
Al-Zahrawi was born, lived, and worked near Córdoba. He became famous for the medical encyclopedia he wrote. This encyclopedia covered everything from the description of diseases to how to prepare and administer medicines. The most important part of the encyclopedia dealt with surgery. This section described many different kinds of operations. It also included illustrations of about 200 surgical instruments.	Al-Zahrawi, from Córdoba, became famous for his medical encyclopedia. It included information about diseases, medicines, operations, and surgical instruments.

Research & Technology

Summarizing is a useful skill for research. When you take notes from a source, you are summarizing that source. You are restating main ideas **in your own words** and selecting important details.

Outlining and Drafting After you have stated the main ideas and important details in your own words, organize them into an outline. Then draft a smoothly flowing summary that includes transitions between ideas.

 Technology Tip Prepare your summary on a word processor so that it can be pasted into your group's lesson summary.

Evaluation & Revision

At your next group meeting, read all the summaries in order. Add transitions as necessary between summaries to make the entire lesson summary flow smoothly.

Self-Check

Does my summary

☐ include just main ideas and important details?

☐ cover the material in less space than the original?

☐ consist of my own words?

☐ reflect underlying meaning, not surface details?

Publish & Present

Help create a neat, error-free version of your group's lesson summary. Then add the lesson summary to an electronic file that contains the other groups' summaries. When the unit study guide is complete, print it out and use it to prepare for a test or another unit-ending activity.

UNIT 3

African Civilizations

Interact with History ▶

Cairo, Egypt 1324

You are an Egyptian citizen witnessing the caravan of Mansa Musa, king of Mali. He has traveled across much of Africa on a pilgrimage to the holy city of Mecca.

What can you learn about Mali by observing Mansa Musa's caravan?

WebQuest
ClassZone.com

Mali had a lot of gold. Mansa Musa brought 80 camels each loaded with 300 pounds of gold. In addition, he had 500 slaves who each carried a six-pound staff of solid gold.

Why might Mansa Musa have brought so much gold with him?

Mansa Musa's caravan included 60,000 people. About 12,000 of them were his personal servants.

How would the arrival of 60,000 people affect the places they visited?

Mali was a wealthy empire, but Cairo was the greatest city of Africa or Europe in the early 1300s. Around 500,000 people lived there, and it was an important trading city.

Why might news about Mansa Musa's caravan spread so quickly from Cairo?

West Africa

Before You Read: Anticipation Guide

Write "agree" or "disagree" next to each statement in your notebook. After you've read the lesson, review the statements and see if you have changed your mind.

- West African kingdoms traded gold for salt.
- Muslim learning influenced West African governments.

Big Ideas About West Africa

Economics Societies trade the surplus goods that they produce to obtain goods they lack.

The West African empires of Ghana, Mali, and Songhai grew through trade. They were located between areas of gold and salt production. They traded their gold for salt from the Muslim empires to the north.

Integrated Technology

eEdition
- Interactive Maps
- Interactive Visuals
- Starting with a Story

INTERNET RESOURCES
Go to **ClassZone.com** for
- WebQuest
- Homework Helper
- Research Links
- Internet Activities
- Quizzes
- Maps
- Test Practice
- Current Events

AFRICA

500s
Trans-Saharan trade is increasingly conducted by camel caravans. (camel with saddle) ▶

500

1076
Muslim forces conquer Ghana.

1000

WORLD

618
◀ The Tang Dynasty is established in China. (water container in the form of a duck)

c. 1000
The Inca civilization develops in South America.

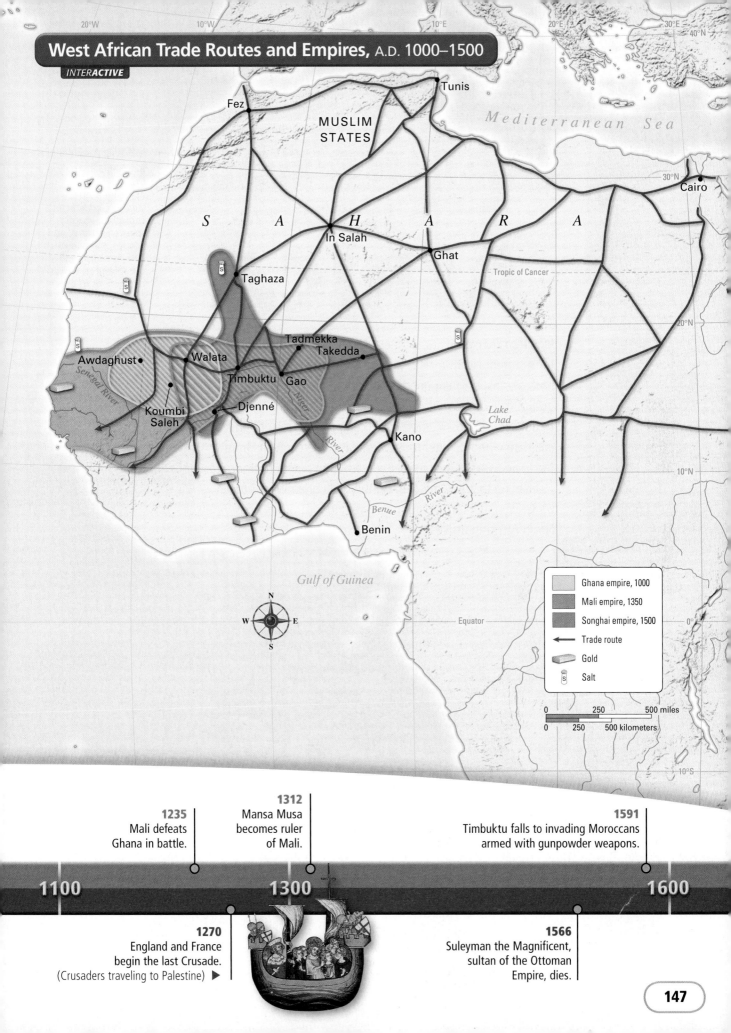

West African Trade Routes and Empires, A.D. 1000–1500

INTERACTIVE

Legend:
- Ghana empire, 1000
- Mali empire, 1350
- Songhai empire, 1500
- Trade route
- Gold
- Salt

0 — 250 — 500 miles
0 — 250 — 500 kilometers

1235
Mali defeats Ghana in battle.

1312
Mansa Musa becomes ruler of Mali.

1591
Timbuktu falls to invading Moroccans armed with gunpowder weapons.

1100

1300

1600

1270
England and France begin the last Crusade.
(Crusaders traveling to Palestine) ▶

1566
Suleyman the Magnificent, sultan of the Ottoman Empire, dies.

TRADING GOLD IN AFRICA

CALIFORNIA STANDARDS

Reading 3.3 Analyze characterization as delineated through a character's thoughts, words, speech patterns, and actions; the narrator's description; and the thoughts, words, and actions of other characters.

Background: For centuries, West Africans traded gold for salt from North Africa. Traders from both regions usually had to transport their goods across deserts. They moved in groups called caravans. Camels were often used in caravans to transport goods. Camels could carry a lot of weight and could go without water for several days. The caravans from North and West Africa met at agreed-upon places to trade.

Imagine that it is the 14th century. You are a West African trader camping for the night and waiting for traders from North Africa to arrive.

Gold was an important West African trade good. ▶

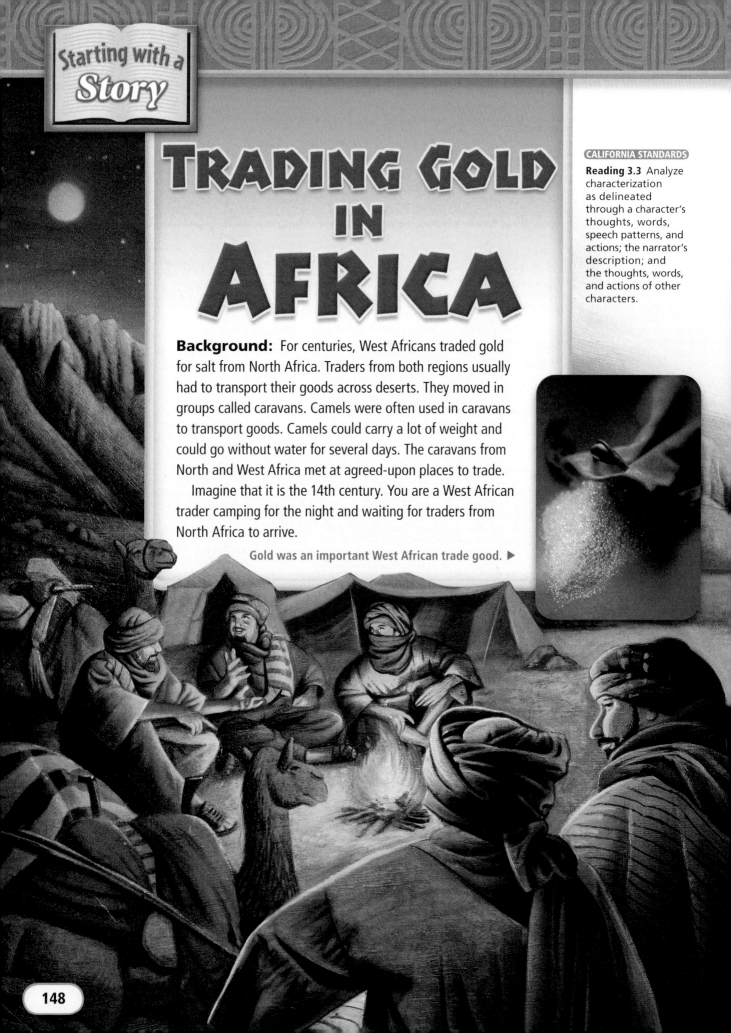

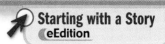

ou are a trader from West Africa. This is your first trip with a caravan. Tomorrow the caravan will meet Saharan nomadic traders, called Berbers, from North Africa. You and your fellow traders are worried that you might not receive enough salt for the gold you brought. Getting salt is profitable for you and important for your king. West Africa has little salt, and people need salt to live.

Around the campfire, the caravan master describes what he expects to happen tomorrow.

"First will come the faint tinkling of the bells that are attached to the harnesses of the camels. The Berbers will lead in a long row of camels carrying slabs of salt." The caravan master points to you and says, "You will help carry the bags of gold we will trade into the courtyard."

The next day, the traders inspect each other's goods. As they do this, you see a Berber boy take something from one of his sacks and eat it. You wonder what it is. He notices you and gestures toward the sack. Bending over, you look in the sack and see that it is filled with a fruit called dates. You take one and eat it. It's delicious! You then take a cola nut from one of your sacks and hand it to the boy. He takes it and smiles.

Then something amazing occurs. As the goods are traded, one of the Berbers makes scratchlike marks on parchment. People say your own king has scholars who can record events by using similar marks called letters. But you have never seen it being done. What could these stranger's marks mean?

As the caravan packs up to leave, you remember all the interesting things that happened on the trip.

What have you learned from your first trip with a caravan?

Reading & Writing

1. **READING: Characterization** How are the Berbers characterized in this story? Use examples from the text to support your answer.

2. **WRITING: Persuasion** Imagine you are a West African trader who wants to convince someone to invest in trade with North Africa. Write a paragraph describing why your trade with North Africa is important.

CALIFORNIA STANDARDS **Writing 2.4**
Write persuasive compositions.

▶ **MAIN IDEAS**

1 **Culture** Strong family relationships and agriculture shaped life for most people in West Africa.

2 **Government** Powerful kings helped expand trading networks that included slavery.

3 **Culture** Oral traditions preserved the history of West African village societies.

▶ **TAKING NOTES**

Reading Skill: Summarizing

When you summarize, you restate something in fewer words. In Lesson 1, summarize each of the main sections using a chart like the one below.

Section	Summary
Village life in West Africa	
Trade and regional commerce	
The oral tradition in West Africa	

 Skillbuilder Handbook, page R3

▲ **Ceremonial Pot** This Nigerian pot depicts a snake, a common element in this style of pottery.

CALIFORNIA STANDARDS

7.4.1 Study the Niger River and the relationship of vegetation zones of forest, savannah, and desert to trade in gold, salt, food, and slaves; and the growth of the Ghana and Mali empires.

7.4.2 Analyze the importance of family, labor specialization, and regional commerce in the development of states and cities in West Africa.

7.4.5 Describe the importance of written and oral traditions in the transmission of African history and culture.

West African Culture and Daily Life

TERMS & NAMES

kinship

clan

labor specialization

griot

Build on What You Know Think about your society's structure: its government, economy, and the role of family and friends. You might be surprised to learn that many of the same structures were important to West African societies too.

Village Life in West Africa

1 ESSENTIAL QUESTION What role did families play in West African society?

From 300 to 1500, powerful empires controlled much of West Africa. However, the rulers of these empires did not greatly affect the daily lives of their people. In fact, most West Africans dealt with their rulers only for court cases and taxes. Many people felt a greater sense of loyalty to their village—and to their family.

The Importance of Family Family relationships were important in West Africa. A connection among people by blood, marriage, or adoption is called **kinship**. Kinship groups formed the government of many African societies. In kinship groups, decisions were often made by a council of the eldest members. Members of kinship groups felt strong loyalty to each other. Kinship groups with a common ancestor formed larger groups called **clans**. Clans usually followed the same rules. For example, in some clans, members were not allowed to marry one another.

African Villagers The Niger River (shown below) was, and still is, an important communication and transportation route, and source of food for many West Africans. ▼

151

Connect to Today

◄ **Family Gathering**
These women in the modern West African country of Guinea Bissau are inspecting the bride's gifts before her wedding.

Work In West African villages, the way of life for most people centered on farming. Women prepared food, cared for the children, made pottery, worked in the fields, and brought water to the village. Men looked after large animals—such as cattle or camels—cleared land for farming, and built houses and fences. Children were often responsible for gathering firewood, helping their fathers tend the flocks, and helping their mothers clean their home.

Some people focused on specific types of work, a process known as **labor specialization**. Labor specialization led to a diverse West African economy. Most people practiced an economy based on farming. Others specialized in the herding of animals. Metalworking was a specialization that required great skill. Iron technology allowed Africans to create stronger agricultural tools and weapons. As a result of this technology, the population grew and became wealthier. Finally, some people traded goods within West Africa and with other regions, such as North Africa.

REVIEW What does labor specialization mean?

Trade and Regional Commerce

2 ESSENTIAL QUESTION How did trading develop in West Africa?

West African kingdoms began to grow through trade. As trading centers expanded, so did the need for control of trade.

Cities and States Develop By A.D. 300, population growth and trade had led to the formation of West African cities such as Djenné (jeh•NAY). Then gold mining and a trade in slaves led to more contact with North Africa. As regional and international trade increased, the expanding cities became even more important as centers of trade. They also became centers of politics, religion, and education.

Trade between West and North Africa continued to grow. West Africans received salt, cloth, and metal wares from North Africans. In return, West Africans traded gold, slaves, ivory, and cattle hides.

Rise of Kings As West African societies developed complex trade systems, some powerful individuals called kings gained control of this system. Many people were loyal to the king because he kept trade running smoothly. In addition, kings often played an important role in the religious life of the people. By performing the proper prayers and rituals, kings were expected to help bring rain, to make the land fertile, and to bring prosperity to their people.

REVIEW What was the relationship between kings and trade in West Africa?

The Oral Tradition in West Africa

3 ESSENTIAL QUESTION What is oral history?

For centuries, West Africa had no written language. As a result, early West Africans did not record a written history. Instead, they recorded their culture using oral history.

Storytellers West Africans passed on their history and cultural values through a rich collection of stories about people and spiritual forces of the natural world. The storytellers, or **griots** (gree•OHS), often used music in their stories.

The stories entertained and educated. A clan's or kinship group's history was passed on through the griots. West Africans believed their departed ancestors watched over them. They thought that their ancestors could help the living communicate with the creator of the universe. Griots were often part of religious rituals in which people appealed to ancestors for favor and protection. The griots were important in the transmission of African history.

Modern Griots
These male and female griots, or storytellers, use music to help tell their story. ▼

INTER*ACTIVE*

Stories and Community While the most famous griots sang for kings and other powerful people, they also entertained and instructed common villagers. Griots acted out various characters in a story, and the audience often participated.

The cultures you will read about in the rest of this chapter all had strong oral traditions. In fact, griots are still an important part of West African culture. Anthropologists have made an effort to write down the oral traditions of West Africa. But the griot's performance and sense of community created is difficult to capture in written versions.

REVIEW Why were oral traditions important in West Africa?

Lesson Summary
- Kinship groups and farming shaped the lives of West Africans.
- Trade with North Africa brought wealth to West Africa where kings rose to power by controlling trade.
- Oral tradition preserved the history and culture of West Africans.

Why It Matters Now . . .
Many West Africans today still place a strong emphasis on their kinship group, and through storytelling children learn the stories of their ancestors.

1 Lesson Review

Homework Helper
ClassZone.com

Terms & Names

1. Explain the importance of

    kinship   clan   labor specialization   griot

Using Your Notes

Summarizing Use your completed chart to complete the following exercise:

2. Summarize the role of trade in West Africa. (7.4.2)

Section	Summary
Village life in West Africa	
Trade and regional commerce	
The oral tradition in West Africa	

Main Ideas

3. What formed the basis for government in many African societies south of the Sahara? (7.4.2)

4. How did trade help cities and states develop? (7.4.1)

5. What role did oral tradition play in West African societies? (7.4.5)

Critical Thinking

6. **Contrasting** How might the West African oral tradition be different from written tradition? (7.4.5)

7. **Drawing Conclusions** How did West African farmers' ability to grow more food encourage labor specialization? (7.4.2)

Activity

Telling a Story Tell a story about your family or a friend, or about the history of your society to your class. (7.4.5)

Play Mancala

Goal: To learn an ancient African game that was popular with families in all levels of society

Materials & Supplies

- one egg carton
- scissors
- 48 game pieces (these can be anything small, such as buttons, pebbles, paper clips, and so on)

CALIFORNIA STANDARDS
7.4.2 Analyze the importance of family, labor specialization, and regional commerce in the development of states and cities in West Africa.

Prepare

Cut off the top of an egg carton and cut it in half. Place one half under each end of the egg carton to form a tray. This tray is called the kahala. Each player's kahala is on his or her right.

Do the Activity

1 **Set Up** Choose a partner. Each player puts four pieces in each of their bins, leaving the kahalas empty.

2 **Playing the Game** As the first player, pick up the four pieces from one of your bins. Moving to the right, drop one piece in each bin you come to. When you finish placing pieces, your turn is over.

- If you reach your kahala, place a piece in it.

- If the last piece you place is in the kahala, you get another turn.

- If you still have pieces in your hand after placing one in your kahala, place them in your opponent's bins from right to left.

- If you reach your opponent's kahala with pieces, skip it, and continue placing pieces in your bins from left to right.

3 **How the Game Ends** The game ends when all of one player's bins are empty. The other player puts his or her remaining pieces into his or her kahala. The player with the most pieces in his or her kahala wins.

Player 2 Kahala

6	• 1
5	2
4	3
3	4
2	5
1 •	6

Player 1 Kahala

Follow-Up

Use library resources to find games from other ancient cultures.

Extension

Comparing and Contrasting Compare a game from another culture with Mancala. Write a paragraph about their similarities and differences.

▶ MAIN IDEAS

1 **Geography** The people of West Africa built empires using the wealth gained from trade in resources such as gold and salt.

2 **Economics** Ghana's empire was built on trading gold. It also benefited from cultural contact with foreign traders.

3 **Belief Systems** Muslim traders brought Islam to Ghana. Islam greatly influenced Ghana's development.

▶ TAKING NOTES

Reading Skill: Finding Main Ideas

The main idea is a statement that summarizes the most important point of a section. In Lesson 2, find supporting details for each main idea using a chart like the one below.

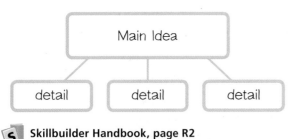

S Skillbuilder Handbook, page R2

▲ **Bronze Sculpture** This modern West African sculpture was made using an ancient technique known as lost wax process.

CALIFORNIA STANDARDS

7.4.1 Study the Niger River and the relationship of vegetation zones of forest, savannah, and desert to trade in gold, salt, food, and slaves; and the growth of the Ghana and Mali empires.

7.4.3 Describe the role of the trans-Saharan caravan trade in the changing religious and cultural characteristics of West Africa and the influence of Islamic beliefs, ethics, and law.

7.4.4 Trace the growth of the Arabic language in government, trade, and Islamic scholarship in West Africa.

The Empire of Ghana

TERMS & NAMES
vegetation zone
Sahara
savannah
Ghana
Almoravids

Build on What You Know What made an empire strong? Rome had mighty armies, while the Byzantine Empire had wealth from trade. In this lesson, you will learn about the West African empire of Ghana and what made it powerful.

West Africa's Geography Fuels Empires

1 ESSENTIAL QUESTION What are the three vegetation zones in West Africa?

West Africa's geography supported a strong trade system—a system that led to an empire.

Geography of West Africa West Africa has three vegetation zones: desert, grasslands, and forests. A **vegetation zone** is a region that has certain types of plants. Soil and climate determine what plants grow in a vegetation zone. For example, a desert has a dry climate. Only plants that need little water grow there.

The northern section of West Africa is part of a large desert called the **Sahara**. The middle section of West Africa is a **savannah** (suh•VAN•uh). *Savannah* is the name for grassland in a tropical region. It is flat, grassy, and has scattered trees. Forests make up the southern region of West Africa.

The Niger (NY•juhr) River runs across West Africa. For centuries, the river has been a key route for transportation, communication, and trade. Part of the river floods each year, producing good soil for farmland. The Niger River formed part of the southern border of Ghana's empire. And south of Ghana, major gold deposits could be found. (See the map on page 147.)

The Sahara This photograph of the Sahara shows how few plants can survive in this region. ▼

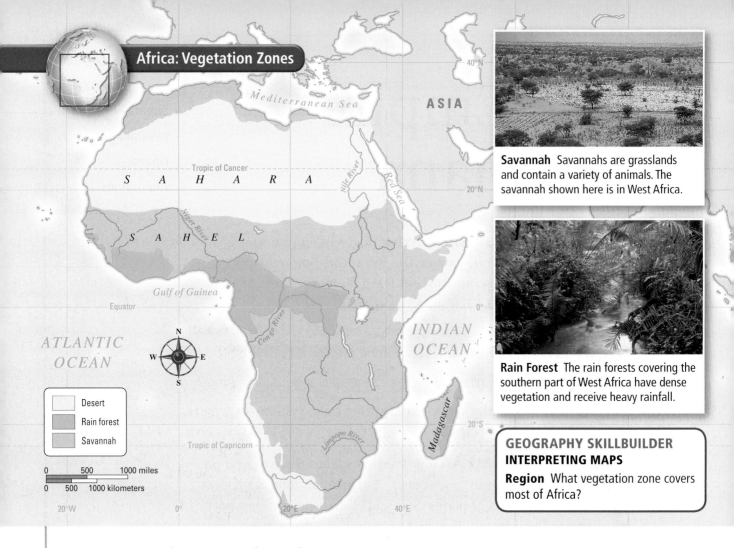

Africa: Vegetation Zones

Savannah Savannahs are grasslands and contain a variety of animals. The savannah shown here is in West Africa.

Rain Forest The rain forests covering the southern part of West Africa have dense vegetation and receive heavy rainfall.

Desert
Rain forest
Savannah

0   500   1000 miles
0   500   1000 kilometers

GEOGRAPHY SKILLBUILDER
INTERPRETING MAPS
Region What vegetation zone covers most of Africa?

Trade Across the Sahara Each vegetation zone in West Africa has certain types of resources. The Sahara has rich deposits of salt. Crops, such as millet, grow well on the savannah, and the land is also good for raising cattle. The southern forests hold large amounts of gold.

People in the savannah and forests of West Africa had gold but very little salt. People in North Africa had salt, but they wanted gold. As a result, a trans-Saharan trade of gold and salt developed. *Trans-Sahara* means "across the Sahara." People in the Sahara would mine salt and trade it for the gold mined in the forests of West Africa.

Food and slaves were also traded. People in the desert traded dried fruits for West African crops. Because parts of North Africa lacked sources of labor, some West Africans enslaved people, such as captured soldiers, and traded them for goods.

To trade between the Sahara, the savannah, and the forest, people had to move goods across the desert. That trade became much easier once camels were used, beginning around A.D. 300. Camels could cover great distances with little food or water. They often traveled in groups called caravans. Camel caravans helped increase trans-Saharan trade.

> **Vocabulary Strategy**
>
> The word *trans-Sahara* is made up of the name of the desert with the **prefix** *trans-* added to it. One of the meanings of the prefix *trans-* is "*across.*" So "trans-Sahara" could also be said as "across the Sahara."

REVIEW What trade goods are found in the different vegetation zones?

The Growth of Ghana's Empire

2 **ESSENTIAL QUESTION** Besides goods, what can trade bring to a region?

Many people farmed the region between the Sahara and the forests of southern West Africa. These people called their king *Ghana*. Eventually, the region itself came to be known as **Ghana**. The people here played an important role in the trade of gold and salt.

The Foundation of the Empire The northern part of Ghana bordered the Sahara. More and more goods began to flow through this area. Salt and other goods arrived there after crossing the Sahara. Gold, enslaved people, and food reached Ghana from the south. The people of Ghana supervised the trading. They also kept the source of the gold a secret. In this way, they could limit the amount of gold traded. Making the gold scarce increased its value.

The king of Ghana gained wealth by taxing trade. Using the wealth gained from this taxation, Ghana quickly expanded into an empire. It conquered surrounding lands. The people living in the conquered lands were forced to give a tribute, or payment, to Ghana's king.

Cities in Ghana became thriving trade centers. The city of Koumbi Saleh was Ghana's capital and the center of the empire. Before the 1200s, it was the greatest city in West Africa. It had a population of more than 15,000 people.

Religious and Cultural Changes Most of the people who traded salt and other goods across the Sahara were a group called the Berbers. Berbers came from North Africa, practiced Islam, and often spoke Arabic. They raised camels and established the trade routes to West Africa. In Chapter 4, you read about the Umayyads, an Arab group who conquered North Africa and worked with the Berbers to trade with West Africa.

North African trade caravans crossing the Sahara brought more than just trade goods to West Africa. Berber traders introduced written language (Arabic) and brought Islam to West Africa. Some kings of Ghana converted to Islam and used the Arabic language in their government. Islamic scholars also came to West Africa. Both the Arabic language and Islam had a major and lasting influence on the empires of West Africa.

REVIEW Who brought Islam and written language to West Africa?

Salt Caravan This African trader travels with camels loaded down with a key product in the trans-Saharan trade—salt. ▼

Islam and Ghana

3 **ESSENTIAL QUESTION** In what ways did Islam influence Ghana?

Many rulers and most of the upper class of Ghana eventually converted to Islam. However, most of the common people kept their traditional beliefs.

Influence of Islamic Beliefs Some of Ghana's kings converted to Islam but still practiced certain aspects of their traditional religion. For example, in Ghana's traditional religion, kings were descended from the ancestors who settled Ghana. This ancestry gave the king the right to rule. Most people accepted this belief. So if the king rejected the traditional religion, he would lose his claim to the throne.

Still, Islam strongly influenced Ghana's rulers. Muslims' use of written language helped them gain positions of power in Ghana's government. Many Muslims advised the king on how to best run the empire.

Much of Ghana's upper class, most of whom lived in cities and were involved with government and trade, converted to Islam. They learned Arabic in order to study the Muslim holy book called the Qur'an. As a result, Islamic ethics, or beliefs in what is right and wrong, also influenced Ghana. For example, in Ghana's legal system, only men could inherit property. But under Islam, women had certain property rights when their fathers died. People in Ghana had to follow either traditional law or Islamic law, or find some way of combining the two.

The Great Mosque
The Great Mosque in modern Djenné has Islamic features such as minarets and West African features such as mud bricks. ▼

Ghana Under Attack Islam's influence, however, could not stop Ghana's decline. A Muslim group called the **Almoravids** came to power in North Africa during the 11th century. They wanted other Muslims to follow the Almoravid interpretation of Islam. In addition, most Almoravids were camel herders who envied the great wealth of Ghana. With these two motivations, the Almoravids declared war on Ghana. The war weakened Ghana's trade network. Under attack and with trade weakened, Ghana began to crumble. In 1076, the Almoravids seized the capital city of Koumbi Saleh.

REVIEW What led to Ghana's decline?

Lesson Summary

- The geography of West Africa supported the development of a strong trade network.
- The empire of Ghana was built on controlling the trade of gold and salt within its borders.
- Islam strongly influenced the empire of Ghana.

Why It Matters Now . . .

Today Islam continues to win new converts in West Africa. The modern nation of Ghana takes its name from the ancient empire.

---

2 Lesson Review

Homework Helper
ClassZone.com

Terms & Names

1. Explain the importance of

| vegetation zone | savannah | Almoravids |
| Sahara | Ghana | |

Using Your Notes

Finding Main Ideas Use your completed chart to answer the following question:

2. What details support the main idea "Ghana's empire was built on trading gold"? (7.4.1)

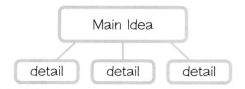

Main Ideas

3. What resources were traded in Ghana's empire? (7.4.1)

4. What did the trans-Saharan caravans bring to Ghana other than trade goods? (7.4.3)

5. Why did some of Ghana's kings continue to practice aspects of their traditional religion after the arrival of Islam? (7.4.3)

Critical Thinking

6. **Understanding Effects** What effect do you think Islam had on the education of the people of Ghana who converted to this religion? Explain. (7.4.4)

7. **Making Inferences** Why were common people in Ghana less likely to convert to Islam? (7.4.3)

Activity

Planning a Trading System List items you own that you would be willing to trade. Then list items you want to trade for. Make sure that items on both lists are of similar value. (7.4.1)

SAHARA
desert mining
coastal production
Niger River
Gulf of Guinea

Producing Salt

Purpose: To learn about salt production in Africa at the time of the empires of Ghana and Mali

Salt production in the coastal regions of West Africa might have looked much like the scene shown here. In fact, this method of salt production is still used in parts of Africa. It is hard and exhausting work.

Farther into the deserts of West Africa, salt deposits were mined directly out of the ground. In cities like Taghaza, where building materials were scarce, salt bricks were used to construct buildings.

Evaporation Process

A Pouring the Water Pits were filled with salt water from the ocean. The water evaporated and left behind salt.

B Harvesting the Salt The salt, which was still damp, was removed from the pit. Then the salt was transported to a shaping and drying area. Once hardened, the salt was ready for transport.

Mining Process

C Digging Up the Salt Ancient seas once covered the Sahara. When they evaporated, they left behind salt. The salt hardened over time and could be mined as you see here. Great blocks were hauled out of the mines and then split into slabs.

D The Trade Caravan The salt slabs were loaded onto camels along with other provisions the caravan needed. If you look carefully, you can see that the men of the caravan were well armed in case they ran into bandits on the trade route. Muslim traders brought more than salt to West Africa. They also brought their religion and culture, which had a great influence on West African kingdoms.

CALIFORNIA STANDARDS
7.4.1 Study the Niger River and the relationship of vegetation zones of forest, savannah, and desert to trade in gold, salt, food, and slaves; and the growth of the Ghana and Mali empires.

Activities

1. **TALK ABOUT IT** Why is a dry climate helpful for the evaporation process?

2. **WRITE ABOUT IT** Pick one of the steps shown and write a paragraph about what might be needed to do that job. (Writing 2.2)

Lesson 3

MAIN IDEAS

1 **Economics** Mali expanded and built upon Ghana's trading network to establish its empire.

2 **Government** Problems such as weak rulers and rebellious subjects led to Mali's decline.

3 **Government** Songhai was a powerful African empire that promoted Islam and learning.

TAKING NOTES

Reading Skill: Comparing and Contrasting

Comparing and contrasting means finding the similarities and differences between things that share some common elements. In Lesson 3, compare and contrast the empires of Ghana, Mali, and Songhai using a chart like the one below.

	Ghana	Mali	Songhai
Trade			
Religion			
Decline			

 Skillbuilder Handbook, page R4

▲ **Terracotta sculpture** Terracotta is the type of clay used to make this sculpture. This sculpture was made around the 14th century in Mali, West Africa.

CALIFORNIA STANDARDS

7.4.1 Study the Niger River and the relationship of vegetation zones of forest, savannah, and desert to trade in gold, salt, food, and slaves; and the growth of the Ghana and Mali empires.

7.4.3 Describe the role of the trans-Saharan caravan trade in the changing religious and cultural characteristics of West Africa and the influence of Islamic beliefs, ethics, and law.

7.4.4 Trace the growth of the Arabic language in government, trade, and Islamic scholarship in West Africa.

The Empire of Mali

TERMS & NAMES

Mali

Sundiata

Timbuktu

Mansa Musa

Songhai

Askia Muhammad

Build on What You Know As you read in Lesson 2, Ghana used trade to develop into a powerful empire. After Ghana's decline, the empires of Mali and Songhai followed the same pattern of using trade to gain power and grow.

Mali Builds on Ghana's Foundation

1 ESSENTIAL QUESTION How could Mali build on Ghana's empire?

In about 1240, the empire of **Mali** formed in the southern area of what had been Ghana's empire (see the map on page 147). It was founded by the Malinke (muh•LIHNG•kee) people. The Malinke were led by a great chief named **Sundiata** (sun•JAH•tah).

Sundiata Comes to Power Sundiata organized a powerful army and captured the former capital of Ghana. He expanded his empire beyond Ghana's old borders, reestablished the gold-salt trade, and expanded trade routes.

Sundiata developed the city of **Timbuktu** as a center of trade and culture. Timbuktu was on the Niger River where the desert and savannah vegetation zones met. Later, Timbuktu became a famous center of Islamic scholarship. Sundiata also supported the development of food crops, cotton farming, and cotton weaving. He balanced his Islamic beliefs with his traditional religious beliefs—much like the kings of Ghana had. Sundiata was very popular with his people and is still considered a hero by the Malinke people of West Africa.

Savannah This modern village in the West African savannah is similar to what a village in Mali might have looked like. ▼

Mansa Musa Expands the Empire After Sundiata's death, the rulers of Mali continued to expand the empire. In 1312, Mali's most famous king, **Mansa Musa**, came to power. Mansa Musa was a devoted Muslim. However, he allowed his subjects to practice other religions.

Mansa means "king" in the Malinke language, and *Musa* is Arabic for *Moses*. So Mansa Musa could also be called King Moses.

In 1324, Mansa Musa began a pilgrimage to Mecca, fulfilling one of the Five Pillars of Islam. On his pilgrimage, Mansa Musa brought 12,000 slaves, 80 camels, and 300 pounds of gold. Mansa Musa rode on horseback. In front of him were 500 slaves, each dressed in silk and carrying a gold staff.

Mansa Musa's pilgrimage greatly impressed those who saw the caravan. More merchants wanted to travel to the empire of Mali and trade increased. West African gold also enriched Europe and provided financial support for the European Renaissance, which you will read about in Chapter 13.

Mansa Musa returned to Mali with an architect and Arab scholars from Egypt. The architect designed the Sankore mosque in Timbuktu. Religious scholars taught history, theology, and law in Timbuktu. The city also attracted some of the best poets and artists in Africa and Southwest Asia.

Mansa Musa continued to expand the empire's borders until his death around 1332.

▲ **Mansa Musa**
Mansa Musa became emperor of Mali in 1312. He made a famous pilgrimage to Mecca.

P Primary Source Handbook
See the excerpt from *The Chronicle of the Seeker,* page R41.

REVIEW What were the effects of Mansa Musa's pilgrimage?

Decline of Mali

2 ESSENTIAL QUESTION How did weak rulers lead to Mali's decline?

After Mansa Musa's death, his descendants argued about who should be the next ruler of Mali. This internal fighting greatly weakened the empire. Eventually, Timbuktu was raided and burned.

Internal Problems Newly conquered regions of Mali's empire began to rebel. In the east, the **Songhai** people gradually gained strength around their homeland near the great bend of the Niger River. The main Songhai city in the region, Gao, was captured by Mali in 1325. About 40 years later, the Songhai were powerful enough to lead the city of Gao to independence from Mali.

from *Travels in Asia and Africa*

By Ibn Battuta
Translated by H. A. R. Gibb

Background: Ibn Battuta (below) was a famous Muslim traveler. In this passage from his travels, he recalls his impression of the justice system in Mali.

They [the people of Mali] are seldom unjust, and have a greater abhorrence[1] of injustice than any other people. Their sultan shows no mercy to anyone guilty of the least act of it. There is complete security in their country. Neither traveler nor inhabitant in it has anything to fear from robbers or men of violence. . . . They are careful to observe the hours of prayer, and assiduous[2] in attending them in congregations, and in bringing up their children to them.

1. **abhorrence:** looking upon with a feeling of disgust.
2. **assiduous:** work hard at.

DOCUMENT–BASED QUESTION
What might a traveler like Ibn Battuta have learned by traveling through Mali?

External Problems In the north, Berber nomads seized much of Mali's territory and captured Timbuktu in 1433. Berbers are descendants of the pre-Arab inhabitants of North Africa. In the south, bandits began to raid trading caravans and military outposts.

By 1500, rebels and invaders had reduced Mali's territory to the original area occupied by the Malinke people. Mali was no longer a strong empire.

REVIEW What internal problems led to the decline of Mali's empire?

The Empire of Songhai

3 ESSENTIAL QUESTION What benefits did a strong leader bring to Songhai?

As you just read, the Songhai city of Gao declared its independence from Mali around 1365. Over the next several decades, the Songhai tried unsuccessfully to form a kingdom.

Songhai Expands Since 1433, the Berbers had controlled Timbuktu. In 1468, Muslim leaders of the city asked the Songhai king, Sunni Ali, to help overthrow the Berbers. Sunni Ali captured Timbuktu, drove out the Berbers, and killed many people who lived in the city. Soon Sunni Ali established a reputation as a powerful, harsh leader. He went on to conquer neighboring lands. After a seven-year siege, he captured the trading city of Djenné.

Askia Muhammad The Songhai empire expanded greatly under Sunni Ali's rule. When he died in 1492, his son was declared the ruler. However, a leader named **Askia Muhammad** wanted to seize the throne. He and his followers felt that Sunni Ali did not practice Islam correctly. In 1493, Askia Muhammad defeated Sunni Ali's son and became the ruler of the Songhai empire.

Askia Muhammad took control of the salt mines to the north and expanded Mali's other borders. Soon the Songhai empire covered an area larger than the empire of Mali had.

Askia's Organization Askia Muhammad's greatest achievement was organizing the government of this vast empire. He began by dividing Songhai into provinces. He then put a governor in charge of each province. He also appointed people as directors of finance, agriculture, army, and navy. In addition, Askia Muhammad set up an organized tax system.

Under Askia Muhammad's rule, Islam spread throughout the empire. He sent Muslim scholars into areas that had little contact with the Islamic religion. These scholars converted many people in the cities to Islam. But in rural areas, Islamic beliefs continued to blend with traditional religious practices. For example, West Africans believed in mischievous spirits who played tricks on people. This was mixed with the Muslim belief in *djinn*, or "genies," such as the one who appeared in Aladdin's lamp in *The Thousand and One Nights*.

History Makers

Askia Muhammad: King of Songhai

Under Askia Muhammad's leadership, Songhai became a well-run empire and a center of trade and learning. But by 1519, Askia Muhammad was a half-blind old man.

In 1528, his son removed him from the throne and declared himself king. The son sent Askia Muhammad to an island that was "infested with mosquitoes and toads." While on this island, Askia Muhammad heard about his children fighting each other for control of the Songhai empire. In 1537, one of his sons brought Askia Muhammad back to Gao. The following year, Askia Muhammad died. His tomb still stands and is one of the most respected shrines in West Africa.

An artist's portrayal of what Askia Muhammad might have looked like ▶

Songhai Falls Askia Muhammad's son removed his father from the throne. (See History Makers on page 168.) The rulers of Songhai after Askia were weak. During the 1580s, the army of Morocco raided the Songhai salt mines. Then, in 1591, Moroccan forces captured Timbuktu and Gao. Soon after that, the Songhai empire collapsed. Even so, most West Africans, living in kinship groups in agricultural villages, continued their lives much as before.

REVIEW What was Askia Muhammad's greatest achievement?

Lesson Summary

- Mali expanded and developed into a powerful empire.
- Internal and external problems caused the empire of Mali to collapse.
- Songhai developed into a powerful, well-organized African empire that promoted Islam and learning.

Why It Matters Now . . .

West Africans later suffered greatly from the slave trade to the Americas and the colonization of their continent by Europeans. Today Africans take pride in the great achievements of the cultures of West Africa and the empires of Ghana, Mali, and Songhai.

---

3 Lesson Review

Homework Helper
ClassZone.com

Terms & Names

1. Explain the importance of

Mali	Timbuktu	Songhai
Sundiata	Mansa Musa	Askia Muhammad

Using Your Notes

Comparing and Contrasting Use your completed chart to answer the following question:

2. What did Ghana, Mali, and Songhai have in common? (7.4.1)

	Ghana	Mali	Songhai
Trade			
Religion			
Decline			

Main Ideas

3. Why did Mansa Musa's pilgrimage impress people? (7.4.1)

4. What external factors weakened the Mali empire? (7.4.1)

5. How did Askia Muhammad spread Islam? (7.4.4)

Critical Thinking

6. **Forming and Supporting Opinions** Do you think Askia Muhammad was a successful ruler? Explain your answer. (7.4.4)

7. **Making Inferences** What might have been another reason for Mansa Musa's pilgrimage, other than religion? (7.4.3)

Making a Time Line Make a time line that shows the main events during the decline of the Mali empire. List a date for each event. Start with Mansa Musa's death. (CST 2)

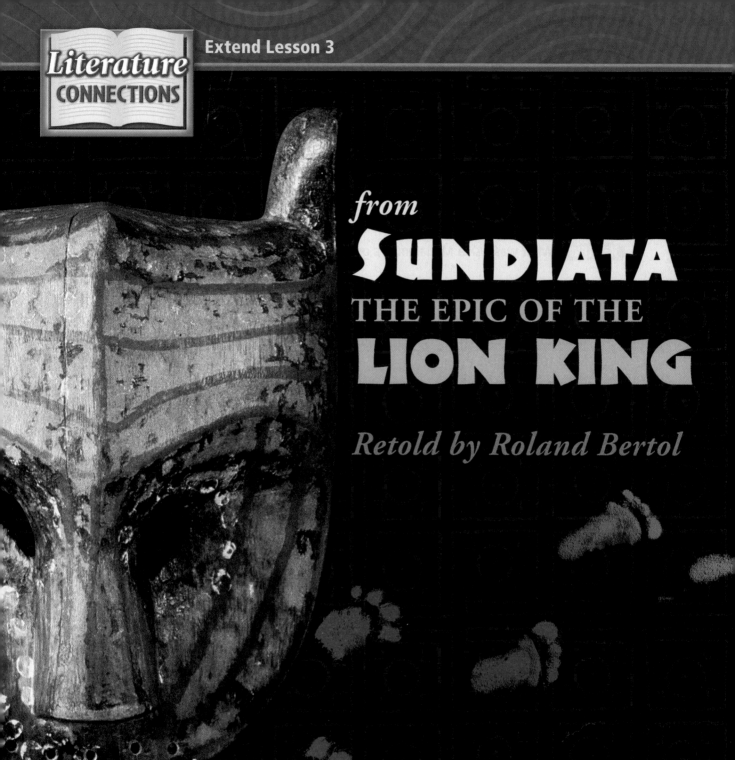

Literature CONNECTIONS

from
SUNDIATA
THE EPIC OF THE
LION KING

Retold by Roland Bertol

Background: Sundiata founded the empire of Mali. He became known as "the lion king." The story of his life is a favorite West African oral tradition. This selection is from one retelling of his life. Sundiata is seven years old and cannot use his legs. The evil Sumanguru, King of Sosso, has killed 10 of his brothers. His 11th brother, Kalabamba Diokunto, has come to power, but he is weak. Farakurun and Kekotonki are men of the village who discuss the prophecy that Sundiata would become the king that would lead their city of Niani to freedom.

CALIFORNIA STANDARDS
Reading 3.3 Analyze characterization as delineated through a character's thoughts, words, speech patterns, and actions; the narrator's description; and the thoughts, words, and actions of other characters.

ust then a lookout on the crumbling wall called out: "He comes. The Master comes. Sound the drums of honor."

Followed by his men, Sumanguru was coming across the grasslands for his monthly share of the harvest and many cattle besides.

"Did you say, 'He comes'?" cried Kalabamba Diokunto from within his hut. Soon he was rushing along the streets crying, "Bring out your fairest children so that the Master may choose."

Farakurun clenched his gnarled hands and looked down at the ground beneath his feet. "You are no King, but an insect," he muttered darkly. . . .

Sumanguru marched into town to the sound of drums. The people trembled and Sumanguru smiled.

"You are early this month. The harvest is not yet in, Master," stammered Kalabamba Diokunto as he looked down at Sumanguru's feet. He did not dare look higher than that, from fear of the terrible eyes.

REVIEW Why was Kalabamba afraid of Sumanguru?

Suddenly, Sumanguru placed his heavy hands upon Kalabamba's shoulders and smiled. "Dear Kalabamba, why call me 'Master'? Call me brother instead. Say it. Say 'Brother' to me and I will call you brother also."

"Bro—Brother . . ." stammered the King.

"Louder, louder, Brother. Let all Niani hear that we are brothers, that it may rejoice at your good fortune."

"Brother!" said Kalabamba Diokunto. "Brother." And now the foolish King began to strut about like a rooster displaying his feathers. "You, Kekotonki." He pointed at that unhappy man. "I have heard you whispering behind my back, saying evil things. We shall settle this when my brother is gone."

This photograph of the area around Sundiata's homeland reveals the sparse vegetation of the region. ▼

"Good, Brother. Make them cringe in terror, for that is the only joy there is," shouted Sumanguru.

"And you also, Farakurun, for you are a useless old man!" Now Kalabamba Diokunto wagged his head from side to side and laughed.

But Sumanguru wearied of his game. "Kill him," he said and Kalabamba Diokunto fell under the knives.

"Where," Sumanguru now asked, "is the twelfth and last son of Nare-Famakan, that unfortunate ruler?"

Kekotonki pointed mutely to Sundiata . . . who still lay in the dust beside his mother's feet.

Sumanguru strode up to him and looked down. "How old are you, future King of all Niani?" he demanded.

"He is seven," replied Kekotonki.

"Let him speak for himself!" snarled the King of Sosso. "I have just made him a King."

"He has never spoken."

"Then let him stand before me."

"He cannot stand."

So Sumanguru crouched beside the boy. "I have come to pay my respects, O King of Niani. I grieve the loss of your fine brothers and their deaths sadden me."

REVIEW Does Sumanguru respect Sundiata?

Sundiata looked into the terrible eyes of Sumanguru. "I will walk now," said the boy, and they were the first words he had ever spoken. He struggled to rise but his knees would not hold him up and he slipped back into the dust.

"A stick, get him a stick," ordered Farakurun. A stunned villager gave his walking stick to the outstretched hands of the boy. Again, Sundiata struggled to rise, leaning on the stick, but the stick broke under his weight.

"You," shouted Farakurun to one of his assistants, "get me a bar of iron. Quickly."

Sundiata was a member of the West African Malinke people. This sacred hut is cared for by modern Malinke holy men. ▼

The bar of iron was brought. The boy took it in his arms and propped it in the ground. Again he struggled to rise but the bar twisted and bent in half, and still Sundiata did not rise.

"In my shop you will find a rod of iron which three men cannot lift with ease. Go fetch it," ordered the smith. Soon, struggling men returned with the heavy bar and rolled it to the foot of the boy. Effortlessly, Sundiata propped it up and struggled to rise. And the rod twisted and bent in half, and still Sundiata did not rise.

REVIEW What is the significance of Sundiata bending the iron rod?

"What sorcery is this?" muttered Sumanguru to himself. Everybody was silent. Nobody dared to move. Sweat poured out of Sundiata in a flood, and still he lay in the dust, his useless legs stretched out before him.

"I know," shouted Kekotonki. "Bring him the scepter of the kings."

The thin reed, symbol of Niani's power, was brought to the child. The scepter weighed no more than a hollow gourd [a vine like a pumpkin or squash], yet Sundiata grasped it in his hands and rose from his prison of earth.

Now, on shaking limbs, Sundiata smiled up at Sumanguru the Accursed and said: "I am glad you grieve the loss of my brothers, who were dear to me also. Yet more will you sorrow in time to come."

Sumanguru backed away, then laughed. "We will meet again later. . . . There are other regions for me to conquer."

Sumanguru left the city of Niani and returned to his castle, shaken.

Reading & Writing

1. **READING: Characterization** Based on the characterization of Sundiata in this story, what kind of leader do you think Sundiata will be?

2. **WRITING: Response to Literature** This is an oral tradition that combines fact and fantasy. Write a paragraph about which parts of this story you think are fact and which parts are fiction. Explain why.

CALIFORNIA STANDARDS Writing 2.2
Write responses to literature.

▶ **VISUAL SUMMARY**

West African Empires

Geography (7.4.1)
- West Africa had a good availability of natural resources: gold and salt.
- The Sahara was a challenge for traders.

Economics (7.4.1, 7.4.2)
- West Africa traded with Muslim North Africa.
- Gold and salt made the empires wealthy.

Belief Systems (7.4.3, 7.4.4)
- Muslim traders brought Islam to West Africa.
- West Africa had a mix of native religions and Islam.

Culture (7.4.2, 7.4.5)
- Oral tradition preserved history and culture.
- Family structures were very important.

Government (7.4.2, 7.4.4)
- Individual power came from strong kinship ties.
- Muslim scholarship heavily influenced West Africa.

▶ **TERMS & NAMES**

Explain why the words in each set below are paired with each other.

1. **kinship** and **clan**
2. **vegetation zone** and **savannah**
3. **Mali** and **Sundiata**
4. **Songhai** and **Askia Muhammad**

▶ **MAIN IDEAS**

West African Culture and Daily Life (pages 150–155)
5. What is the relationship of kinship groups and clans? (7.4.2)
6. How did cities grow in West Africa? (7.4.2)
7. What do West African oral traditions preserve? (7.4.5)

The Empire of Ghana (pages 156–163)
8. How did West Africa's vegetation zones affect what trade goods were available? (7.4.1)
9. How did trans-Saharan trade caravans influence Ghana's religion and culture? (7.4.3)
10. What influence did Islam have on the kings of Ghana? (7.4.3)

The Empire of Mali (pages 164–173)
11. How did Mali build on Ghana's empire? (7.4.1)
12. What role did Timbuktu play in Mali's empire? (7.4.4)
13. How did Askia Muhammad organize the government of Songhai? (7.4.4)

CRITICAL THINKING Big Ideas: Economics

14. **ANALYZING ECONOMIC ISSUES** What effect did keeping the source of West African gold secret have on its price? (7.4.1)

15. **COMPARING AND CONTRASTING** How did trade help empires, such as Ghana and Rome, develop? Give examples. (7.4.1)

16. **MAKING INFERENCES** What economic advantage did Songhai gain by expanding its territory to the north? (7.4.1)

ALTERNATIVE ASSESSMENT

1. **WRITING ACTIVITY** Imagine you are a merchant in North Africa who sees Mansa Musa's pilgrimage to Mecca. Write a paragraph that describes this pilgrimage. Use the Internet and your library to research your document. (7.4.2)

2. **INTERDISCIPLINARY ACTIVITY— GEOGRAPHY** Pull out the world map you created in Chapter 2 and add the empires of Ghana and Mali to it. Use the map on page 147 to help you. (7.4.1)

3. **STARTING WITH A STORY** Review your response to the question about what you learned with the trading caravan. After reading the chapter, what other things might you have learned? (7.4.3)

Technology Activity

4. **CREATING A MULTIMEDIA PRESENTATION** (7.4.1) Use the Internet or the library to find information about the vegetation zones of West Africa. Create a multimedia presentation comparing the different vegetation zones. Include the following points:
   • which zone covers the most land
   • the different plant and animal life

Research Links
ClassZone.com

Reading a Map Use your knowledge of West Africa and the map below to answer the questions. (7.4.1)

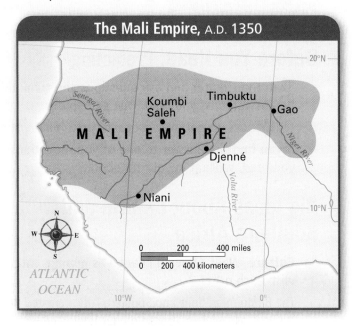

The Mali Empire, A.D. 1350

1. **Which city would have depended more on camel caravans than on water transportation?**

   A. Gao
   B. Djenné
   C. Koumbi Saleh
   D. Niani

2. **Under good conditions, an Arabian camel transporting a single person can travel a maximum of 180 miles in a day. How long would it take a camel and its rider to travel from Timbuktu to Koumbi Saleh?**

   A. about 1 day
   B. about 2 days
   C. about 3 days
   D. about 4 days

Test Practice
ClassZone.com

Additional Test Practice, pp. S1–S33

Before You Read: Predicting

Skim the chapter and ask questions you think might be answered as you read. One example is:

What role did gold play in creating powerful kingdoms?

If you find the answer to one of your questions as you read, write it in your notebook.

Big Ideas About Central and Southern Africa

Culture Ways of living change as humans interact with each other.

The Bantu migrations into Southern Africa created new cultures. Meanwhile, African groups interacted with Muslims and Europeans through trade. This brought new ways of life and ideas to each culture.

 Integrated Technology

eEdition
- Interactive Maps
- Interactive Visuals
- Starting with a Story

 VIDEO *Ancient Africa*

INTERNET RESOURCES

Go to **ClassZone.com** for
- WebQuest   • Quizzes
- Homework Helper   • Maps
- Research Links   • Test Practice
- Internet Activities • Current Events

c. 1000
Great Zimbabwe emerges.
◄ (conical tower at Great Zimbabwe)

AFRICA

800   1000

WORLD

843
Treaty of Verdun divides European empire built by Charlemagne.

1095
Muslims and Europeans begin series of battles called the Crusades.
◄ (Crusades battle scene)

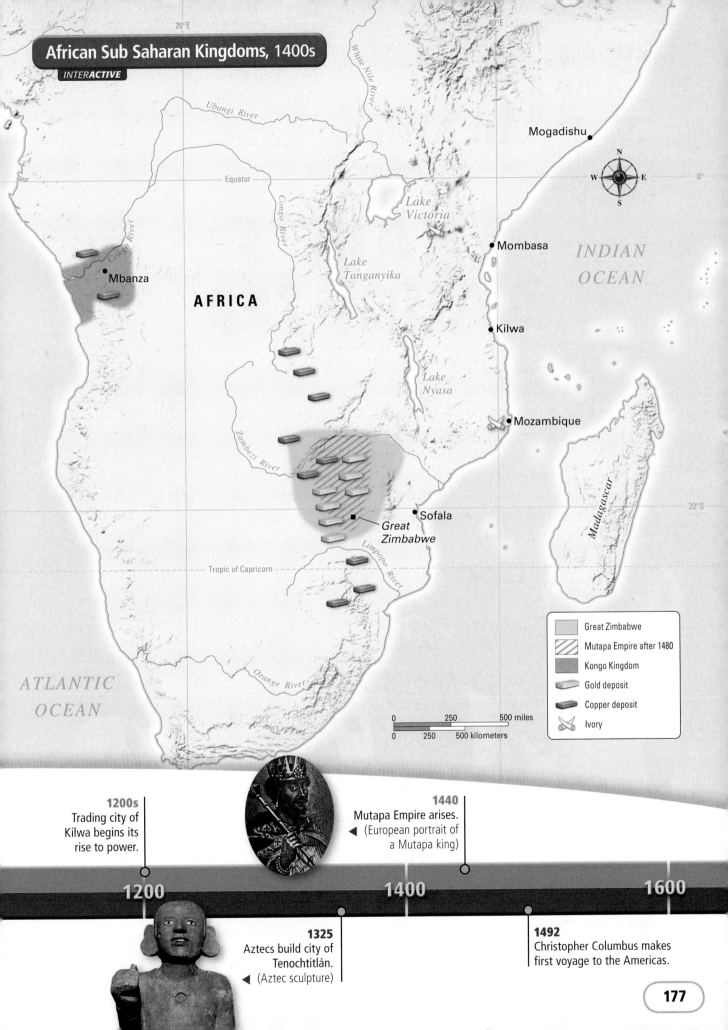

African Sub Saharan Kingdoms, 1400s

INTER*ACTIVE*

White Nile River

Ubangi River

Equator

Congo River

AFRICA

• Mbanza

Congo River

Lake Victoria

Mogadishu •

• Mombasa

INDIAN OCEAN

Lake Tanganyika

Lake Nyasa

• Kilwa

Zambezi River

Mozambique •

Great Zimbabwe

• Sofala

Limpopo River

Tropic of Capricorn

Madagascar

20°S

Orange River

ATLANTIC OCEAN

N
W E
S

	Great Zimbabwe
	Mutapa Empire after 1480
	Kongo Kingdom
	Gold deposit
	Copper deposit
	Ivory

0   250   500 miles
0   250   500 kilometers

1200s
Trading city of Kilwa begins its rise to power.

1440
Mutapa Empire arises.
◄ (European portrait of a Mutapa king)

1200

1400

1600

1325
Aztecs build city of Tenochtitlán.
◄ (Aztec sculpture)

1492
Christopher Columbus makes first voyage to the Americas.

An African Tale:
THE
SNAKE'S
DAUGHTER

CALIFORNIA STANDARDS
Reading 2.4
Identify and trace
the development
of an author's
argument, point of
view, or perspective
in text.

Background: As you read in Chapter 5, stories played an important role in many African cultures. Oral tradition is the passing on of history and ideas through storytelling. For societies that did not use a written language, storytelling served as a way to preserve the past and promote values and beliefs. In many of these stories, animals were the main characters. The following story is taken from an African tale titled *Tshiama, the Snake's Daughter*.

Historic African clothing called kente ▶

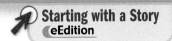

Tshiama was the python's daughter. She was very beautiful. Many animals in the forest wanted to marry her. There was one problem, however. Any animal that wished to marry her had to ask her father's permission. The old python was big and mean and could squeeze the life out of anyone who angered him. He caused great fear throughout the forest.

One day, the buffalo told the animals that he would go see the old python. "I'm not afraid," he declared. "After all, I am stronger than most pythons."

So the buffalo went before the python and asked to marry his daughter. The snake raised his body high in the air and glared at the buffalo. The buffalo turned around and ran all the way home.

A short time later, the leopard announced that he would visit the old python. "I don't scare so easily," he said. But when he encountered the giant snake, he, too, turned and ran home.

Some time after that, the tiny groundhog told everyone that he would see the python. The rest of the animals all laughed at him. He was one of the smallest creatures in the forest, they told him. He most certainly would run away upon seeing the giant snake.

The groundhog ignored the other animals. He set out one day for the python's home in the rocks. The groundhog called out to the great snake and announced that he wished to marry his daughter. The python rose into the air and hissed at the tiny creature.

The groundhog thought about running home. However, he stood his ground and repeated why he had come. The old python was impressed. He told the groundhog that he had the biggest heart and the most courage of any animal in the forest. And he gave the groundhog his permission to seek his daughter's hand in marriage.

What qualities does this tale promote?

Reading & Writing

1. **READING: Point of View** Discuss with your classmates what argument or point the author of this tale is trying to make.

2. **WRITING: Response to Literature** Write a paragraph explaining what values you think were important to the tellers of this story.

CALIFORNIA STANDARDS **Writing 2.2**
Write responses to literature.

▶ **MAIN IDEAS**

1 **Geography** Bantu-speaking people spread out across central and southern Africa to create new cultures.

2 **Economics** African coastal city-states established profitable trade relationships with Arab traders.

3 **Culture** Islam had a great influence on the culture and government of East Africa.

▶ **TAKING NOTES**

Reading Skill: Categorizing

Categorizing means grouping similar things together. As you read about the establishment of coastal trading cities in East Africa, use a graphic like the one below to categorize ways that Islam influenced the region.

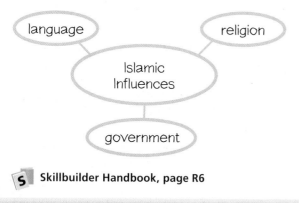

language

religion

Islamic Influences

government

S **Skillbuilder Handbook, page R6**

▲ **Kuba Mask** This wooden mask was made by a craftsperson in the Kuba kingdom in southern Africa. The Kuba were part of a larger group known as the Bantu-speaking peoples.

CALIFORNIA STANDARDS

7.2.4 Discuss the expansion of Muslim rule through military conquests and treaties, emphasizing the cultural blending within Muslim civilization and the spread and acceptance of Islam and the Arabic language.

7.2.5 Describe the growth of cities and the establishment of trade routes among Asia, Africa, and Europe, the products and inventions that traveled along these routes (e.g., spices, textiles, paper, steel, new crops), and the role of merchants in Arab society.

CST 3 Students use a variety of maps and documents to identify physical and cultural features of neighborhoods, cities, states, and countries and to explain the historical migration of people, expansion and disintegration of empires, and the growth of economic systems.

The Growth of Coastal Trading Cities

▶ **TERMS & NAMES**

Bantu migrations

Kilwa

Swahili

Build on What You Know What things do you trade? Perhaps you and your friends exchange CDs or DVDs. Consider why people trade things as you learn in this chapter about the growth of trade between Africa and other parts of the world.

The Land and Its People

1 ESSENTIAL QUESTION What were the Bantu migrations?

Central and southern Africa are vast regions. Because they are so large, they have a great variety of geographic features.

A Diverse Geography Huge tropical rain forests cover much of central Africa. Such forests are home to thousands of species of colorful birds. In southern Africa, immense grasslands are more common. Elephants, giraffes, lions, zebras, and many other animals live in the grasslands.

The human geography of central and south Africa is also diverse. The peoples of these regions belong to hundreds of different ethnic groups. Many groups have their own languages, customs, and religions. However, many of these different peoples come from a single group known as the Bantu speakers.

African Landscape
A lion stands proudly amid the grass in southeastern Africa. ▼

Bantu Influences The Bantu speakers are a group of African peoples who speak one of the more than 450 Bantu languages. The first Bantu speakers probably lived near the present-day border of Nigeria and Cameroon in west-central Africa.

Starting sometime around 1000 B.C., the many different Bantu-speaking groups began moving south and east through Africa. This movement, called the **Bantu migrations**, began one of the most important migrations in history. About 1,500 years after the migrations began, the Bantu speakers reached the southern tip of Africa.

Bantu speakers adapted to new habitats as they moved throughout the continent. They exchanged ideas and intermarried with the people they met. Such interactions gradually led to cultural blending.

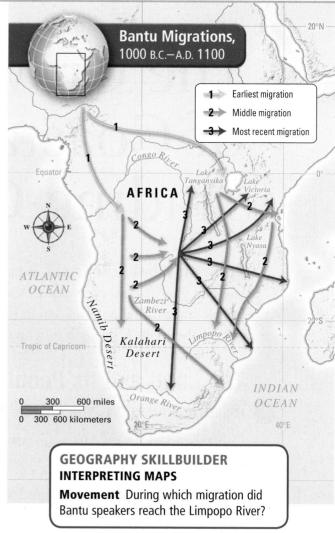

Bantu Migrations, 1000 B.C.–A.D. 1100

1 ➤ Earliest migration
2 ➤ Middle migration
3 ➤ Most recent migration

GEOGRAPHY SKILLBUILDER
INTERPRETING MAPS
Movement During which migration did Bantu speakers reach the Limpopo River?

REVIEW What was the result of migrations by Bantu-speaking groups?

Coastal City-States Emerge

2 ESSENTIAL QUESTION How did Africans and Arabs interact?

By 1100, large numbers of Bantu-speaking peoples had migrated across central Africa toward the eastern coast. In East Africa, the Bantu speakers established farming villages as well as lively trading outposts.

Coastal Trade Routes East African merchants participated in trade across the Indian Ocean. They exchanged goods with traders from Arabia, Persia, and India. Persian traders brought Asian manufactured goods to Africa and African raw materials to Asia.

Kilwa By the 13th century, a network of trading towns and city-states dotted the coast of East Africa. (A city-state is a city and its surrounding lands functioning as an independent political unit.) One of the most important of these was the coastal city-state of **Kilwa**. Settlers from Arabia and Persia founded Kilwa in the late 10th century. The city-state prospered because it was as far south on the coast as a ship from India

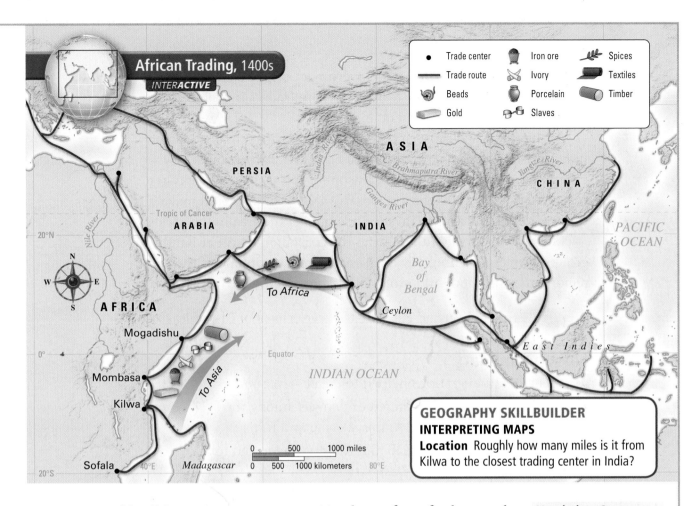

African Trading, 1400s
INTERACTIVE

Legend:
- ● Trade center
- ── Trade route
- Beads
- Gold
- Iron ore
- Ivory
- Porcelain
- Slaves
- Spices
- Textiles
- Timber

ASIA

PERSIA

CHINA

Brahmaputra River

Yangtze River

Indus River

Ganges River

Tropic of Cancer

ARABIA

INDIA

PACIFIC OCEAN

20°N

Nile River

To Africa

AFRICA

Bay of Bengal

Mogadishu

Ceylon

Equator

0°

Mombasa

To Asia

INDIAN OCEAN

East Indies

Kilwa

GEOGRAPHY SKILLBUILDER
INTERPRETING MAPS
Location Roughly how many miles is it from Kilwa to the closest trading center in India?

Sofala

40°E

Madagascar

0   500   1000 miles
0   500   1000 kilometers

80°E

20°S

---

could sail in one *monsoon* season. Merchants from farther south had to send their goods to Kilwa, where Asian merchants could buy them. Kilwa grew very influential in the late 1200s.

REVIEW What factors helped Kilwa become wealthy and powerful?

The Influence of Islam

3 ESSENTIAL QUESTION What influence did Arabs have on culture and government in East Africa?

Kilwa was one of several African trading states with Arabic ties. As trade across the Indian Ocean increased, Arab traders settled in numerous East African port towns. As a result, coastal Africans borrowed some aspects of Arab culture.

Cultural Influence One result of the cultural interaction between Arabs and Africans was the creation of a new language, known as **Swahili**. Swahili developed as a Bantu language that borrowed many words from the Arabic language. Arabs also introduced their religion, Islam, in East Africa. The majority of Africans living along the coast kept their traditional religious beliefs. Even so, many chose to convert to Islam. Africans who converted to Islam tended to be middle-class townspeople who were involved in the Indian Ocean trade.

Vocabulary Strategy

Use context clues to figure out the meaning of *monsoon*. Monsoons are strong seasonal winds that help push boats back and forth across the Indian Ocean.

Influence in Government Government officials and wealthy merchants also tended to be Muslims. These leaders introduced Islamic ideas about government and law.

As they grew and prospered, these coastal towns remained largely independent. The city-states along the East African coast made few efforts to join together. The main reason for this was that the city-states competed with each other for trade. This lack of unity would make it easier for the Europeans to invade and conquer the area in the 1500s.

Meanwhile, further inland from the coastal cities, other Bantu groups were establishing powerful empires based on one of the region's most precious and profitable resources: gold.

REVIEW How did Muslims influence the development of East Africa?

Lesson Summary

- The Bantu migrations helped to create new cultures.
- Indian Ocean trade fostered exchanges among the peoples of East Africa, Arabia, Persia, and India.
- Interaction between Arab and African traders led to the spread of Islam in East Africa.

Why It Matters Now . . .

More than one-third of Africans today are Muslims.

---

1 Lesson Review

Terms & Names

1. Explain the importance of

Bantu migrations   Kilwa   Swahili

Using Your Notes

Categorizing Use your completed graphic to answer the following question:

2. Which Africans tended to practice Islam? (7.2.4)

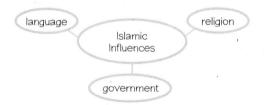

Main Ideas

3. Where did the migrations of Bantu-speaking peoples begin? (CST 3)

4. What was the main trade route among the people of East Africa, Arabia, Persia, and India? (7.2.5)

5. What is the origin of the Swahili language? (7.2.4)

Critical Thinking

6. Understanding Cause and Effect How did the establishment of trade affect coastal villages in East Africa? (7.2.5)

7. Making Inferences What do the trade items imported by East Africa suggest about its societies? (7.2.5)

Activity **Internet Activity** Use the Internet to find statistics about trade in the Indian Ocean today. Then present your information in a chart, table, or other graphic. (7.2.5)

INTERNET KEYWORD: *Indian Ocean trade*

Create an African Mask

Materials & Supplies
- cardboard
- ruler
- scissors
- paint, colored paper, yarn, glitter, feathers, and other decorations
- white glue
- hole puncher
- 1/4" elastic, about 8" long

Goal: To learn how culture was transmitted in nonwritten ways by making an African mask

Prepare

Think about the way that many African cultures used masks—for religious ceremonies, funerals, and theatrical performances. African masks often depicted spirits and family members who passed away and gave the person wearing it the powers of the spirits or ancestors it represented.

Do the Activity

1 Cut the cardboard into a rough oval shape slightly larger than your face.

2 Have a classmate measure the distance between your eyes. Use the measurement to create eye holes on your mask.

3 Make a triangular hole for your nose and an oval hole for your mouth.

4 Decorate the mask in any way you like using the materials provided.

5 Punch holes on either side of the mask and tie on the elastic. Then try on your mask.

▲ **African Mask** Painted wood and straw mask by Kuba craftsperson

Follow-Up

Write a brief description of what your mask represents and what it is used for. Display your mask with your description.

Extension

Researching Ceremonial Masks Search the Internet to find other cultures that used ceremonial masks.

CALIFORNIA STANDARDS
REP 1 Students frame questions that can be answered by historical study and research.

Lesson 2

▶ **MAIN IDEAS**

1 **Government** A Bantu-speaking group known as the Shona built a strong empire in southeastern Africa.

2 **Economics** Great Zimbabwe gained power by controlling the trade of gold.

3 **Government** After the fall of Great Zimbabwe, the Shona people carved out another powerful empire in its place.

▶ **TAKING NOTES**

Reading Skill: Comparing and Contrasting

Comparing and contrasting involves finding similarities and differences between two or more things in order to understand them better. As you read the lesson, use the graphic below to take note of the similarities and differences between Great Zimbabwe and the Mutapa Empire.

Great Zimbabwe	Mutapa Empire

 Skillbuilder Handbook, page R4

Connect to Today

▲ **Modern Zimbabwe** This woman is a member of the Bantu-speaking Ndebele group that lives in Zimbabwe. The modern African nation takes its name from the civilization that thrived there centuries ago.

CALIFORNIA STANDARDS

7.2.5 Describe the growth of cities and the establishment of trade routes among Asia, Africa, and Europe, the products and inventions that traveled along these routes (e.g., spices, textiles, paper, steel, new crops), and the role of merchants in Arab society.

7.4.5 Describe the importance of written and oral traditions in the transmission of African history and culture.

REP 4 Students assess the credibility of primary and secondary sources and draw sound conclusions from them.

Empires Built on Gold and Trade

TERMS & NAMES

Shona

Great Zimbabwe

Great Enclosure

Mutapa

Build on What You Know What comes to mind when you think about gold? You might think of a ring or a necklace or something else precious and valuable. Like our societies today, the groups living in and around southern Africa centuries ago placed a high value on gold. Some of these civilizations used their control of gold to become wealthy and powerful.

Rise of the Shona Civilization

1 ESSENTIAL QUESTION What was Great Zimbabwe?

During the ninth century, a Bantu-speaking people called the **Shona** settled in the valley of the Limpopo River in southern Africa. By 1000, they had moved onto an area of rich farmland between the Zambezi and Limpopo rivers. There, the Shona established a thriving empire.

Shona Empire The empire that the Shona carved out of the grasslands of southern Africa consisted of numerous zimbabwes, or settlements encircled by large stone walls. The term *zimbabwe* comes from a Shona phrase, *dzimba dza mabwe*, which means "houses of stone." The ruins of about 150 such structures are scattered throughout present-day southern African countries of Botswana, Mozambique—and Zimbabwe, which takes its name from these historic settlements.

Zambezi River The Zambezi River is the fourth largest river in Africa. It winds through the southern part of the continent for about 1,700 miles. ▼

187

Great Zimbabwe The largest of these settlements was known as **Great Zimbabwe**. It was the center of the Shona empire. The city and surrounding area covered more than 100 acres and had a population of 10,000 to 20,000 people. Geography played an important role in Great Zimbabwe's rise. The region was surrounded by huge plains that the Shona used for farming and cattle raising. In addition, Great Zimbabwe was located near key trade routes.

The Great Enclosure There were three main sections of Great Zimbabwe: the Valley Ruins, the Hill Complex, and the Great Enclosure. The **Great Enclosure** is the largest and most significant of these sections. Archaeologists think it likely that the Great Enclosure was used as a home for kings and queens.

From the air, the Great Enclosure looks like a giant necklace. Its outer wall is about 820 feet around and rises as high as 36 feet. An inner wall runs along part of the outer wall. The two walls form a narrow passageway that leads to the mysterious 33-foot high *conical* tower. At one time, the enclosure contained elaborate buildings constructed of *daga*—brick made from mud and clay.

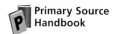

Primary Source Handbook

See the excerpt from a Description of Great Zimbabwe, page R42.

Vocabulary Strategy

By examining the first part of *conical*, you can determine that it might be associated with a cone. *Conical* means shaped like a cone.

The Great Enclosure

1. The ruins of the Great Enclosure stand as an enduring symbol of Great Zimbabwe. The maximum diameter of the Great Enclosure is about the length of a football field. In some areas, the enclosure's walls are about 18 feet thick.

2. Scholars believe that kings and queens lived within the Great Enclosure, while farmers and workers lived outside.

3. The purpose of the conical tower remains a mystery. It may have represented a giant grain bin meant to symbolize good harvests. Some also believe that residents built the tower as a form of religious worship.

SKILLBUILDER
INTERPRETING VISUALS
What conclusions can you draw about Great Zimbabwe society from the ruins at the Great Enclosure?

Shona builders cut stone blocks for the Great Enclosure's walls from the granite hills around the city. They carved the blocks with such precision that nothing was needed to hold them in place. Many of the Great Enclosure's walls are as smooth as a modern brick wall. The most elaborate walls probably date from the 14th and 15th centuries.

REVIEW What role did geography play in the growth of Great Zimbabwe?

Gold Brings Great Wealth

2 **ESSENTIAL QUESTION** How did Great Zimbabwe grow wealthy and powerful?

In time, Great Zimbabwe became an influential center of wealth and power. This wealth and power came in large part from the trade routes that passed through the city. The key product that traveled along these routes was gold.

Gold and Trade Gold was one of the most prized materials among Africans and other peoples of the world. It was one of the main goods traded between Africa and the lands of India and China. Great Zimbabwe did not actually mine and produce gold. However, it stood between the gold-producing regions to the west and the trading cities along the eastern coast.

As a result, Great Zimbabwe's leaders could tax traders who traveled the routes. They could also demand gold payments from the region's less powerful leaders. The city's key location soon made it the center of an international gold trading system. Scholars estimate that during the peak of the gold trade, travelers were carrying more than 2,000 pounds of the precious metal through Great Zimbabwe every year.

Decline of Great Zimbabwe During the 15th century, Great Zimbabwe began to decline. Historians disagree about why the city weakened. Some say that drought and the overuse of land by cattle caused a shortage of resources that led people to leave. Others argue that people left in order to take advantage of shifting trade networks. Whatever the reason, Great Zimbabwe was abandoned by 1500.

REVIEW How did Great Zimbabwe gain control of the gold trade?

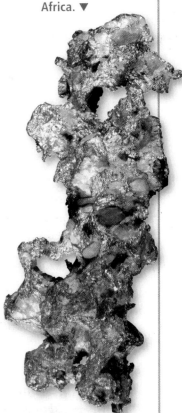

Gold Specimen This piece of gold was taken from an old mine in southern Africa. ▼

A New Kingdom Emerges

③ ESSENTIAL QUESTION What empire followed the one at Great Zimbabwe?

As Great Zimbabwe fell, an empire known as Mutapa arose nearby and also grew strong by controlling the trade of gold.

Mutota the Conqueror According to Shona oral tradition, a man named Mutota left Great Zimbabwe around 1440 and traveled north. He was searching for a new source of salt, which had become scarce in the southern areas. (Salt, as you have read, helps to protect water loss and is thus an important part of our diet.) Along the way, he found a valley with fertile soil, good rainfall, and ample wood. There, he founded a new state that eventually would replace Great Zimbabwe.

Mutota became the leader of an army, which he used to take control of the surrounding lands. The conquered people called Mutota *Mwene Mutapa*, or the "Great Pillager." **Mutapa** became the name for both the kingdom and its rulers. By the time of Mutota's death, the Mutapa Empire controlled most of what is now Zimbabwe. Mutota's son extended Mutapa control north to the Zambezi River and east to the Indian Ocean coast.

Comparisons Across Cultures

Oral Tradition

The story of Mutapa's founding as an empire was an example of oral tradition, or the telling of stories from generation to generation. As you have learned, oral tradition was an important part of the culture in many African groups. These stories helped to preserve the past, explain events, and promote values and beliefs.

Such storytelling played a similarly significant role among the native groups of North America. Oral tradition was particularly important to the groups known as the Plains Indians. And as in Africa, the peoples of the Plains memorized and told these tales to strengthen and preserve their culture.

A Native American elder tells a tale to children. ▶

The Mutapa Empire The people of Mutapa were a Shona group related to the people of Great Zimbabwe. The Mutapa Empire, like Great Zimbabwe, got much of its wealth and power by controlling the gold trade.

As powerful as it was, the Mutapa Empire would not last. In the 16th century, a European people known as the Portuguese would seize control of the area. As you will read, Portugal was just one of the European nations that would later conquer the lands of Africa. Meanwhile, as the Mutapa Empire thrived, so did another civilization in west-central Africa known as the Kongo, which you will read about in the next lesson.

REVIEW How did the Mutapa Empire gain its wealth and power?

Lesson Summary

- The Shona people created a thriving empire in southern Africa, centered around Great Zimbabwe.
- Control of gold-trading routes made Great Zimbabwe rich and powerful.
- After the fall of Great Zimbabwe, the Shona people built another powerful empire known as Mutapa.

Why It Matters Now . . .

The pre-colonial civilizations at Great Zimbabwe and Mutapa are today a great source of pride to nations in southern Africa.

---

2 Lesson Review

Homework Helper
ClassZone.com

Terms & Names

1. Explain the importance of

Shona   Great Enclosure
Great Zimbabwe   Mutapa

Using Your Notes

Comparing and Contrasting Use your completed graphic to answer the following question:

2. What similarities did Great Zimbabwe and the Mutapa Empire share? (7.2.5)

Great Zimbabwe	Mutapa Empire

Main Ideas

3. Where was the center of Shona civilization? (CST 3)

4. What factors might have led to the decline of Great Zimbabwe? (HI 2)

5. According to oral tradition, how did the Mutapa Empire begin? (7.4.5)

Critical Thinking

6. **Evaluating Information** What role did gold play in the rise to power of Great Zimbabwe and the Mutapa Empire? (7.2.5)

7. **Making Inferences** What do the characteristics of the Great Enclosure say about how the people of Great Zimbabwe viewed their rulers? (HI 5)

Activity

Creating a Book Cover Use library resources to find a story from Africa's oral tradition. Briefly examine the story and draw what you think would be an appropriate book cover for the story. (7.4.5)

Drawing Conclusions from Sources

Goal: To read a secondary source and draw conclusions about the civilization of Great Zimbabwe

CALIFORNIA STANDARDS
REP 4 Students assess the credibility of primary and secondary sources and draw sound conclusions from them.

Learn the Skill

Drawing conclusions means analyzing what you have read in order to understand its meaning. To draw conclusions from a source, look closely at the facts. Combine the facts with what you learn by inferring, or determining any deeper meanings. Then use your common sense and experience to draw conclusions about what the facts mean.

S See the Skillbuilder Handbook, page R25.

Practice the Skill

1 Read the passage on the right to understand all of the facts, or statements that can be proven true. Some facts are labeled for you.

2 Use the facts to make inferences. An inference is not stated directly in the text. It is what you figure out from the facts presented to you.

3 Make a graphic organizer. Using a graphic such as the one shown below can help you understand the relationship between facts and inferences. The graphic lists some of the key facts from the passage you just read and the inference you can draw from each of these facts.

4 Based on your inferences, you can draw a conclusion about the subject.

Example:

3

GREAT ZIMBABWE			
FACTS ⬇	Builders at Great Zimbabwe cut stones for their buildings so that they fit perfectly together.	Some burial sites at Great Zimbabwe contained precious items. Others were more plain and simple.	Some items found in burial sites came from distant lands.
INFERENCES ⬇	The people of Great Zimbabwe were skilled builders who used advanced techniques.	Different levels of wealth and importance existed in the society.	Great Zimbabwe was part of a wide trading network.
CONCLUSION	The society at Great Zimbabwe was technologically advanced and highly structured.		

The following passage describes the civilization of Great Zimbabwe in southern Africa. Use the strategies listed under Practice the Skill to help you draw conclusions based on the facts in the passage.

The Ruins of Great Zimbabwe

① The ruins of Great Zimbabwe include many large stone structures. The builders cut the stones from nearby granite hills so that they fit together perfectly.

Part of the ruins includes a complex that sat at the bottom of a steep hill. It is believed to have been the home of the ruling family. The stone walls of this structure are about 18 feet thick and rise as high as 36 feet. **①** The remains of a nearby royal burial site include gold, copper, glass beads, pottery, and cloth. **①** Some of these items came from distant lands.

Despite the presence of these impressive stone structures, most houses at Great Zimbabwe were made of mud bricks. These homes belonged to ordinary workers. **①** Burial sites found near these homes were much more simple and plain.

▲ **Great Zimbabwe** Two girls walk past a towering wall among the ruins at Great Zimbabwe.

Apply the Skill

Turn to pages 53–54 in Chapter 2, Lesson 2. Read "Internal Weaknesses Threaten Rome." As you read, draw conclusions based on the facts. Make a diagram like the one on page 192 to organize the facts, inferences, and conclusions about the passage.

Lesson 3

▶ MAIN IDEAS

1 **Government** A Bantu-speaking group settled along the west coast of southern Africa and established the Kongo kingdom.

2 **Culture** Kongo developed a strong trading relationship with the Portuguese, which brought great changes to the kingdom.

3 **Culture** Kongo became increasingly involved in the slave trade, which eventually caused turmoil and instability in the kingdom.

▶ TAKING NOTES

Reading Skill:
Understanding Cause and Effect

A cause is an action that makes something happen. An effect is the event that results from a cause. As you read Lesson 3, use a chart such as the one shown here to identify the causes and effects of interaction between Kongo and Portugal.

Causes	Effects

 Skillbuilder Handbook, page R26

▲ **Kongo Figure** This wooden sculpture portrays a leader of the Kongo kingdom.

CALIFORNIA STANDARDS

7.11.2 Discuss the exchanges of plants, animals, technology, culture, and ideas among Europe, Africa, Asia, and the Americas in the fifteenth and sixteenth centuries and the major economic and social effects on each continent.

CST 3 Students use a variety of maps and documents to identify physical and cultural features of neighborhoods, cities, states, and countries and to explain historical migration of people, expansion and disintegration of empires, and the growth of economic systems.

HI 1 Students explain the central issues and problems from the past, placing people and events in a matrix of time and place.

The Kongo Kingdom

TERMS & NAMES
Kongo
Mbanza
Afonso I

Build on What You Know In this lesson, you will read about a kingdom that rose to power in central Africa and became one of the first African civilizations to interact with Europeans. As you will learn, the two groups came into conflict over the issue of slavery.

A Kingdom Arises on the Atlantic

1 ESSENTIAL QUESTION How did the Kongo kingdom begin?

As you read earlier, many Bantu-speaking groups migrated from west-central Africa throughout the southern part of the continent. This process started sometime around 1000 B.C. During the 14th century, a Bantu-speaking people known as the Kongo settled along the western coast of Africa and established a mighty kingdom known as **Kongo**.

The Growth of Kongo The Kongo settled just north of the mighty Congo River, which flowed for nearly 3,000 miles before emptying into the Atlantic Ocean. The Kongo took advantage of the area's fertile soil, iron and copper ore, good fishing, and the transportation possibilities of the Congo River. By the 15th century, the Kongo had moved south of the Congo River and imposed their rule over the region's inhabitants. The territory they now held became known as the Kongo kingdom.

The Mighty Congo The Congo River is the second longest river in Africa after the Nile River. It is a major transportation route for the people of central Africa. ▼

195

The Kongo Kingdom The center of the Kongo kingdom was its capital city, **Mbanza**. From there, the Kongo rulers established a highly organized kingdom. The village was the basic political unit of the kingdom. A group of villages made up a district. Districts were grouped together into six provinces. The king appointed leaders known as governors to rule each province.

The king was also in charge of the Kongo economy. The kingdom's people mined iron and copper for their own use and for trade. They also produced pottery and clothing. The king required the provinces to pay taxes every six months. The provinces often made their payments with cowrie shells, a colorful seashell used for money in Kongo.

REVIEW How was the Kongo kingdom organized?

Kongo and Portugal

2 **ESSENTIAL QUESTION** How did interaction affect Kongo and Portugal?

As the Kongo kingdom thrived, great changes were taking place throughout the world. In Europe, the 1400s marked the beginning of an Age of Exploration. As you will learn in later chapters, this was a time when European expeditions sailed the oceans to explore new lands.

Portugal, a small country located west of Spain on the Atlantic Ocean, led the way. In the early 1480s, Portuguese explorers sailed down the western coast of Africa and encountered the Kongo kingdom. This interaction would bring many changes and eventually great difficulties for Kongo.

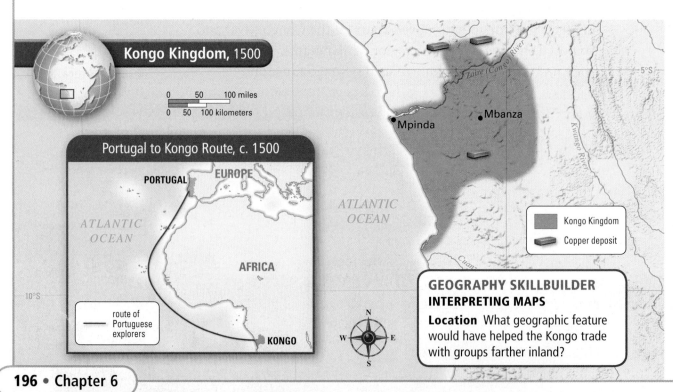

Kongo Kingdom, 1500

0   50   100 miles
0   50   100 kilometers

Portugal to Kongo Route, c. 1500

PORTUGAL   EUROPE

ATLANTIC OCEAN

AFRICA

route of Portuguese explorers

KONGO

ATLANTIC OCEAN

Zaire (Congo) River

5°S

Mpinda   Mbanza

Kwango River

Kwanzo River

Cuanza

Kongo Kingdom
Copper deposit

10°S

N
W   E
S

GEOGRAPHY SKILLBUILDER
INTERPRETING MAPS
Location What geographic feature would have helped the Kongo trade with groups farther inland?

Cultural Interaction Initial relations between the Portuguese and Kongo people were good. The two groups quickly engaged in active trade. Kongo offered copper, iron, and ivory to Portugal. In return, the Portuguese provided guns, horses, and various manufactured goods.

The leaders of Kongo also were receptive to the Christian religion practiced by the Portuguese. As the two groups traded goods, the Portuguese began sending missionaries to the Kongo kingdom. Missionaries are people who travel to other lands seeking to gain converts to their faith.

The Rule of Afonso Portuguese influence in Kongo increased when Nzinga Mbemba became ruler of the kingdom in 1506. The new king took the European name **Afonso I** and sought to copy many Portuguese ways. He made Roman Catholicism the official religion of Kongo. He also gave the capital of Mbanza a Portuguese name, São Salvador.

In addition, Afonso altered Kongo's political system to reflect European traditions. He appointed dukes and counts and required them to wear Western-style clothing. Afonso learned to read and write Portuguese and sent many of his subjects to get an education in Portugal.

As much as Afonso and his people admired the Portuguese, their good relationship did not last. What eventually drove the two groups apart more than anything else was the growing desire among the Portuguese to use Africans as slaves.

REVIEW How did Afonso increase Portugal's influence in Kongo?

History Makers

Afonso I (? – about 1543)

Afonso used his ties with the Portuguese to try to strengthen his kingdom. In one letter to Portugal's king, he requested doctors for the "many and different diseases which put us very often in such a weakness."

However, Afonso's willingness to provide slaves ultimately ruined his good intentions. As the Portuguese hauled away more and more Africans, Kongo and the surrounding region suffered. Afonso eventually tried to stop it. "Merchants daily seize our subjects," he wrote the Portuguese ruler. "So great, Sir, is their corruption . . . that our country is being utterly depopulated." His pleas for a halt, however, did little good.

An artist's interpretation of King Afonso▶

Kongo and the Slave Trade

3 **ESSENTIAL QUESTION** What were the causes and effects of the slave trade between Kongo and Portugal?

Kongo had begun supplying the Portuguese with enslaved Africans early in their trade relationship. The Portuguese wanted slaves to work on the overseas lands that they had conquered. In return for providing enslaved Africans, Kongo rulers received European goods they desired. However, Portugal's demand for slave labor continued to grow. This led to increasingly strained relations with the Kongo kingdom.

Growth of Slavery As Portugal interacted with Kongo, Portuguese sailors continued their voyages of exploration. In the 1470s, the Portuguese had claimed the island of São Tomé off the west coast of Africa. There, they established huge sugar fields in order to satisfy Europe's growing desire for sugar. These fields required the labor of many workers. As a result, the Portuguese pressured Kongo for more and more African slaves.

The growth of the slave trade began to drain the population of West Africa. As a result, Afonso eventually voiced his opposition to the practice. He urged the Portuguese king to stop. However, his pleas did little good. By the time Afonso died in 1543, the Portuguese were enslaving thousands of Africans each year. The relationship between Kongo and Portugal had begun as a trading partnership that benefited both sides. However, the increasing slave trade eventually caused this relationship to collapse. In 1561, the Kongo kingdom cut itself off from Portugal.

Enslaved Africans
This engraving shows a group of Africans being forcibly led away to slavery. ▼

The Kingdom Struggles The Kongo kingdom experienced a period of instability after Afonso's death. Beginning in the late 1560s, Kongo forces went to war with a neighboring kingdom. Then they had to battle an invasion by a nearby group called the Jaga. Unable to win, the Kongo asked the Portuguese for help. With the aid of Portuguese troops, the Kongo were able to fight off the Jaga. The kingdom slowly regained its stability during the early 1600s.

REVIEW What event weakened Kongo after the death of Afonso?

Lesson Summary
- During the 14th century, a Bantu-speaking group established the Kongo kingdom.
- The arrival of the Portuguese had a strong impact on the economy, religion, and politics of the Kongo.
- The slave trade caused the collapse of relations between the Kongo kingdom and Portugal.

Why It Matters Now . . .
The African slave trade continued and led to the enslavement of Africans around the world. Their descendants are part of the population in numerous countries.

3 Lesson Review

Homework Helper
ClassZone.com

Terms & Names

1. Explain the importance of

    Kongo   Mbanza   Afonso I

Using Your Notes

Understanding Cause and Effect Use your completed chart to answer the following question:

2. What was an economic effect of the interaction between Kongo and Portugal? (7.11.2)

Causes	Effects

Main Ideas

3. What role did the location of Kongo play in its interaction with the Portuguese? (CST 3)

4. How did the early relations between Kongo and Portugal benefit both groups? (7.11.2)

5. How did the slave trade hurt relations between the Kongo kingdom and Portugal? (7.11.2)

Critical Thinking

6. **Making Inferences** What did the organization of their kingdom say about the Kongo people? (HI 1)

7. **Understanding Cause and Effect** How did Portuguese culture influence the Kongo kingdom? (7.11.2)

Activity   **Making a Map** Using the map on page 196, sketch the boundaries of the Kongo kingdom on the world map you have created. Then use the map on pages A6–A7 of the Atlas to determine what country or countries occupy this area today. (CST 3)

The Timeless Appeal of Gold

Purpose: To learn more about the continuous appeal of gold, one of Africa's most valuable resources

What things do you consider to be expensive? A DVD player? A new car? How about gold? These days, a mere ounce of gold can cost as much as $400! Compare that with an ounce of silver, which costs less than $10. As you read in the previous two chapters, gold was greatly valued throughout Africa and the world. Today this precious metal remains highly prized around the globe.

Mining Gold

▶ **Past** As you have learned, the large deposits of gold throughout Africa brought great wealth and power to kingdoms in the west and south. Back then, miners used picks and other light tools to dig the gold from the land.

▼ **Present** Gold remains a key resource of Africa. In fact, Africa is the world leader in gold production. Modern miners in Africa and elsewhere use powerful drills to dig out gold thousands of feet underground.

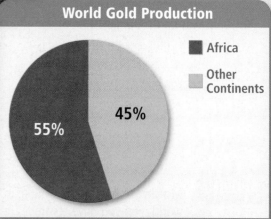

World Gold Production

- Africa
- Other Continents

55%

45%

Source: *Encyclopaedia Britannica Online*

The Gold Trade

▼ **Past** Early Africans used this brass weight to weigh gold powder for trading.

▲ **Present** Gold is now bought and sold on the open market in places such as stock exchanges. Gold has several qualities that make it desirable. Both its color and brightness are highly appealing. It is nearly impossible to break or destroy, and it easily forms into nearly any shape.

A Symbol of Greatness

Present Gold represents more than just something of great wealth. It has also come to symbolize high achievement and outstanding performance. For example, first-place finishers in many athletic events receive gold medals. In addition, winners of the annual U.S. film honors take home Academy Award statuettes coated in gold.

Activities

1. **TALK ABOUT IT** Based on the images shown here, how has the mining and trading of gold changed over the centuries?

2. **WRITE ABOUT IT** Write a paragraph explaining why you agree or disagree that gold should be a symbol of greatness in a particular field. (Writing 2.4)

VISUAL SUMMARY

Central and Southern Africa

Geography (CST 3)
- The great Bantu migrations created many new societies across southern Africa.
- African groups built thriving civilizations along rivers and sea coasts.

Economics (7.2.5)
- Africans in coastal settlements established thriving overseas trade networks.
- Kingdoms such as Great Zimbabwe and Mutapa grew wealthy by controlling the trade of gold.

Government (HI 1)
- The Shona people established the Great Zimbabwe and Mutapa kingdoms.
- A Bantu-speaking group built the Kongo kingdom.

Culture (7.2.5)
- Trade with the East brought Arab culture to numerous societies in eastern Africa.
- Kongo began trading with Portugal and soon adopted many Portuguese ways.

TERMS & NAMES

Explain why the words in each set below are linked with each other.

1. **Kilwa** and **Swahili**
2. **Shona** and **Great Zimbabwe**
3. **Kongo** and **Afonso I**

MAIN IDEAS

The Growth of Coastal Trading Cities (pages 180–185)

4. What did East Africans export in the Indian Ocean trade? (7.2.5)
5. How did the language of Swahili develop? (7.2.4)

Empires Built on Gold and Trade (pages 186–193)

6. How was gold central to the growth of Great Zimbabwe and Mutapa? (7.2.5)
7. How did the Mutapa Empire begin, according to oral tradition? (7.4.5)

The Kongo Kingdom (pages 194–201)

8. How did Portugal influence Kongo's political system? (7.11.2)
9. What caused relations between Kongo and Portugal to grow strained? (HI 1)

CRITICAL THINKING Big Ideas: Culture

10. **UNDERSTANDING CAUSE AND EFFECT** What impact did interaction with Arab traders have on East African societies? (7.2.4)

11. **EVALUATING INFORMATION** How did Great Zimbabwe use its influence over neighbors to its benefit? (HI 1)

12. **FORMING AND SUPPORTING OPINIONS** Did European interaction benefit Kongo or not? Explain. (7.11.2)

ALTERNATIVE ASSESSMENT

1. **WRITING ACTIVITY** Imagine that you are a governor of a Kongo province. The Kongo king has ordered you to begin calling yourself a duke and to wear Portuguese clothing. Write a paragraph expressing support or opposition to this order. (7.11.2)

2. **INTERDISCIPLINARY ACTIVITY—MATH** Use resources such as the Internet to determine the price of an ounce of gold today. Then choose five of your favorite things to buy (compact discs, baseball cards, and so on). Create a table that displays how many of each you could buy with an ounce of gold. (REP 1)

3. **STARTING WITH A STORY**
 Review the tale from the beginning of the chapter. Then discuss with the class whether you think such stories are a good way to teach lessons and promote ideas. (7.4.5)

Technology Activity

4. **MAKING A MULTIMEDIA PRESENTATION** (CST 3) Use the Internet or the library to research the Bantu migrations. Work with a partner to make a multimedia presentation of the journey.
   - Include maps and images.
   - Cite your sources.

 **Research Links**
ClassZone.com

Using a Time Line Use the time line below to answer the questions. (CST 1)

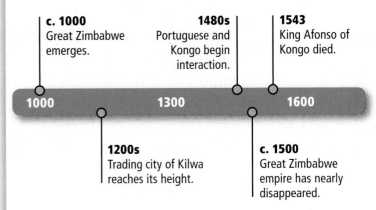

c. 1000 Great Zimbabwe emerges.

1480s Portuguese and Kongo begin interaction.

1543 King Afonso of Kongo died.

1200s Trading city of Kilwa reaches its height.

c. 1500 Great Zimbabwe empire has nearly disappeared.

1. **Roughly how long did the civilization of Great Zimbabwe last?**
   A. 250 years
   B. 500 years
   C. 750 years
   D. 1,000 years

2. **Which of the following took place closest to the time that Portugal and Kongo began interacting?**
   A. Great Zimbabwe arose.
   B. Kilwa reached its height of power and prestige.
   C. Great Zimbabwe disappeared.
   D. King Afonso of Kongo died.

 **Test Practice**
ClassZone.com

Additional Test Practice, pp. S1–S33

Writing About History

Persuasive Writing:
A Proposal for a New Trade Route

CALIFORNIA STANDARDS
Writing 2.4 Write
persuasive compositions.

Purpose: To convince the ruler of a city-state on Africa's eastern coast to finance the development of a trade route to Mali

Audience: The ruler of Kilwa

Persuasive writing is writing whose purpose is to convince another person to adopt your opinion or position. It can take a variety of forms, such as letters to the editor, formal essays, articles, and proposals. Historians use persuasive writing to propose interpretations of history and support them with facts and examples. People in public life—leaders and community members—use persuasive writing to advance ideas and actions they believe in.

▲ A trade caravan in Africa

Organization & Focus

In Unit 3, you read about the Ghana, Mali, and Songhai empires of West Africa, which controlled the gold-salt trade across the Sahara. You also studied the city-states on Africa's eastern coast, which traded across the Indian Ocean. Imagine you are a trader in Kilwa in the 1200s. You have heard of the wealth of Mali, far away. Your assignment is to write a proposal to the ruler of your city-state convincing him to finance you as you develop a trade route to Mali.

Identifying Purpose and Audience Your purpose is to use evidence to persuade another person to adopt your proposal. Your audience is the ruler of your city-state. As you develop an argument for why the ruler should finance a new trade route, keep in mind the ruler's interests. What would he hope to gain from a new trade route?

Finding Supporting Evidence Review Chapters 5 and 6 to find reasons to support your proposal of the trade route. Pay attention to the maps. Read and take notes on the descriptions of Mali on pages 165–167 and Kilwa on pages 182–183. Look for the products each society produced and the goods they traded. Try to anticipate any concerns the ruler might have about financing a trade route. Also, find details to show that the benefits of the trade route will outweigh the costs.

Research & Technology

Good persuasive writing depends on strong evidence. Use facts to convince your ruler of your plan. Do additional research to find out what products West Africa has to offer your city-state. Use technology to find this information. The chart below explains how.

Technology Tip Check with your librarian to find out what electronic services your local library has.

Using Technology in Research			
• Most libraries have electronic card catalogs. You can search these by author, title, or subject to find information in a number of ways.	• Some libraries have access to online databases of magazine articles, such as Infotrac, which are searchable in the same way.	• Search engines can help you locate thousands of sources of information on the World Wide Web.	• Electronic encyclopedias on CDs contain a wealth of information. Many encyclopedias are also online and have links to Web sites for additional information.

Outlining and Drafting Make an outline showing the three main parts of your proposal. The **introduction** should grab the ruler's interest and state your recommendation. The **body** of your proposal should offer facts and examples in support of your recommendation. Present your supporting arguments in order of importance, saving the most important argument for last. The body of your proposal should also show how to overcome any potential problems. The **conclusion** should tie together the ideas in the rest of the proposal and make a final strong appeal to the ruler and his interests.

Evaluation & Revision

When you have finished the first draft of your proposal, exchange papers with a classmate. Compare and contrast your arguments with his or hers. Rework your proposal as needed to make your arguments as strong as possible. Then edit your work to make it free of errors.

Self-Check

Does my proposal

- [ ] show an awareness of my audience and purpose?
- [ ] have an introduction stating my recommendation and making a strong appeal?
- [ ] contain well-organized and convincing evidence?
- [ ] have a strong conclusion with a final appeal?

Publish & Present

Make a neat final copy of your proposal. Prepare a cover for it, decorated with images from the cultures of Africa. If possible, read your proposal to your classmates and display it on a bulletin board.

Asian Civilizations

Interact with History ▶

The Great Wall of China, A.D. 1400
You are a guard on the Great Wall charged with protecting Ming China. Suddenly, a flurry of Mongol fireballs shatters the peaceful morning. A Mongol attack is beginning.

How will you repel the attack?

WebQuest
ClassZone.com

The Chinese built a signal fire on top of the nearest watchtower to warn of a Mongol attack.

What is another way the Chinese might have warned each other of an attack?

The Chinese constructed the wall on the tops of hills and mountains to make it even more difficult to overcome.

Why might building the wall on mountain peaks make it more difficult to attack?

To make rockets, the Chinese stuffed gunpowder into bamboo tubes. Sometimes they mixed stones, lead pellets, and broken pottery with the gunpowder.

What might be some of the advantages of a rocket in warfare?

Chapter 7

China Builds an Empire

Before You Read: K-W-L

The K-W-L approach will help you recall prior knowledge and develop a plan for learning new information. Consider the following questions as you read this chapter:

- What do you already know about China?
- Study the map and time line on these pages. What do they tell you about China's lands and its people?
- What do you want to learn about China?

Big Ideas About Ancient China

Belief Systems People adopt new beliefs that give meaning to life.

Belief systems, such as Confucianism and Daoism, arose in ancient China. The Buddhist religion also became widely practiced. These belief systems had a powerful effect on Chinese society and government.

Integrated Technology

eEdition
- Interactive Maps
- Interactive Visuals
- Starting with a Story

The Mongol Empire

INTERNET RESOURCES
Go to **ClassZone.com** for
- WebQuest
- Homework Helper
- Research Links
- Internet Activities
- Quizzes
- Maps
- Test Practice
- Current Events

CHINA

300s
Buddhism flourishes in China and spreads to Korea.
(sculpture of Buddha) ▶

618
Li Yuan founds Tang Dynasty.
(Tang horse sculpture) ▶

200   400   600

WORLD

610
Muhammad begins preaching Islam.
◀ (Qur'an)

Physical Geography of Present-Day China

INTERACTIVE

KAZAKHSTAN

Altai Shan

RUSSIA

MONGOLIA

Amur R.

Great Khingan Mountains

Manchurian Plain

KYRGYZSTAN

TIAN SHAN

GOBI DESERT

NORTH KOREA

SOUTH KOREA

40°N

▲ *Kongur Mt. 25,325 ft. (7,719 m)*

Taklimakan Desert

Kunlun Shan

Qinghai Hu

Huang He (Yellow R.)

Grand Canal

Yellow Sea

PLATEAU OF TIBET

C H I N A

North China Plain

30°N

Chang Jiang

Yangtze R.

East China Sea

H I M A L A Y A S

NEPAL

▲ *Gongga Shan 24,790 ft. (7,556 m)*

BHUTAN

Brahmaputra R.

INDIA

Xi Jiang (West R.)

TAIWAN

Taiwan Strait

Tropic of Cancer

MYANMAR

VIETNAM

20°N

Elevation	
13,100 ft.	(4,000 m)
6,600 ft.	(2,000 m)
3,280 ft.	(1,000 m)
650 ft.	(200 m)
0 ft.	(0 m)
Below sea level	

▲ Mountain peak

LAOS

Hainan

South China Sea

PHILIPPINES

THAILAND

0   250   500 miles
0   250   500 kilometers

N W E S

70°E 80°E 90°E 100°E 110°E 120°E 130°E 140°E

960
Song Dynasty is established. (Song vase) ▶

1405–1433
Zheng He makes several voyages.

1000   1200   1400   1600

1095
European Christians begin First Crusade to capture the Holy Land.

1325
The Aztecs build Tenochtitlán. (Aztec ornament) ▶

The Fall of Luoyang

CALIFORNIA STANDARDS
Reading 3.2 Identify events that advance the plot and determine how each event explains past or present action(s) or foreshadows future action(s).

Background: In the past, you may have learned about the Han Dynasty, which ruled China from 206 B.C. to A.D. 220. As you may recall, China often had conflicts with enemy invaders from the northwest. One group of those invaders was the Xiongnu (shyung•noo).

When the Han Dynasty fell, China broke apart into smaller kingdoms. The lack of a strong central government to organize defenses put China in greater danger from invaders. As you read the following story, imagine you are living during those dangerous times.

Soldiers on horseback were a favorite subject of Han artists. ▶

Y ou are a Chinese merchant in A.D. 311. You're very proud of the city where you live—Luoyang (lwoh•yahng). Your grandfather told you that the city used to be the Han capital. It still has palaces and temples. Students from all over the country flock to the university there. Hundreds of thousands of people live in Luoyang. The walled city has survived tough times, such as peasant revolts, civil wars, and even the fall of a dynasty.

Since the Han Dynasty fell, Luoyang has had many different governments. Some of your friends wonder who is going to rule your city next, but you're too busy to worry about it. You tell your friends, "Rulers come and go, but merchants and farmers make sure that life goes on." Most of the time, you go about your daily work and never think about the government at all.

Today, while you are selling porcelain in the market, you hear pounding hooves and shrill screams down the street. A man shouts, "Xiongnu!" Your heart leaps in terror. The Xiongnu are fierce nomadic warriors on horseback who have attacked China many times in the past. Now they have broken through the city's walls!

WHISH! An arrow flies by your head. You duck under the table holding your porcelain. Delicate teapots and bowls crash to the ground and shatter. Quickly, you crawl away and run down an alley until you see an outhouse. You crawl into the sewage pit and hide there all night. The stench is terrible.

The next day, you learn that the Xiongnu have killed thousands of people and destroyed your beautiful city. It looks like a garbage dump. Instead of riding away, the Xiongnu have decided to stay and start a new dynasty.

What do you think will happen to China now?

Reading & Writing

1. **READING: Plot** The first stage of the plot of a story is the exposition. In it, characters and setting are introduced and background information is provided. With a partner, identify the information provided in the exposition to this story. As you read other stories in this book, note how the exposition is used to "set the scene."

2. **WRITING: Response to Literature** How do you predict the story will continue? Write a paragraph describing what Xiongnu rulers might be like.

CALIFORNIA STANDARDS Writing 2.2
Write responses to literature.

211

▶ **MAIN IDEAS**

① **Government** The Han Dynasty, China's strong central government, fell in A.D. 220. A period of conflict followed.

② **Belief Systems** China went through major changes in its belief systems.

③ **Government** In 589, the Sui Dynasty reunified China. In 618, the Tang Dynasty took over China.

▶ **TAKING NOTES**

Reading Skill:
Understanding Cause and Effect

Following causes and effects will help you understand why events occurred. In Lesson 1, look for the effects of each event listed in the chart. Record the effects on a chart of your own.

Causes	Effects
The Han Dynasty falls.	
Buddhism becomes widely practiced.	
The Sui and Tang dynasties reunify China.	

 Skillbuilder Handbook, page R26

▲ **Han Watchtower** The Han often placed pottery models of buildings, like the military watchtower above, in tombs. These models provided the deceased with shelter and protection in the afterlife.

TERMS & NAMES
nomad
Confucianism
Buddhism
Daoism
reunify

Reunifying China

Build on What You Know What words would you use to describe the country of China? Does your list include the words huge and powerful? In this chapter, you will learn that China was a huge and powerful country 1,500 years ago.

Fall of the Han Dynasty

1 ESSENTIAL QUESTION What happened after the Han Dynasty fell in A.D. 220?

The Han Dynasty, founded in 206 B.C., was a period of progress and prosperity for China. In time, however, political struggles, social problems, and a widening gap between rich and poor weakened the Han Dynasty. It fell in A.D. 220.

Conflict and Chaos A time of great disorder followed. Various kingdoms fought among themselves. Invading nomads from the north crossed the Mongolian Plateau into northern China. (A **nomad** is a person who moves from place to place.) Floods, droughts, and food shortages also plagued the land.

Despite these troubles, Chinese culture survived. In the north, the invading nomads eventually settled down and adopted Chinese customs. In the south, good harvests and growing trade helped people to prosper. Even so, most Chinese people led difficult lives.

REVIEW What were the effects of the fall of the Han Dynasty on China?

The Himalayas This great mountain range provided a barrier to protect China from invasion from the southwest. ▼

Changes in Belief Systems

2 **ESSENTIAL QUESTION** What changes took place in China's belief systems?

The turmoil after the fall of the Han Dynasty led to major changes in China's belief systems.

Confucianism For centuries, the Chinese had looked to Confucianism (kuhn•FYOO•shuh•nihz•uhm) for comfort and guidance. **Confucianism** is a belief system based on the ideas of Confucius (551–479 B.C.). He was a scholar who taught moral virtues and ethics—ideas of right and wrong. In his teachings, Confucius emphasized these principles.

Vocabulary Strategy

The suffix *-ism* refers to an action, a process, or a practice. Confucianism is the practice of Confucius' teachings.

- Use right relationships to produce social order.
- Respect family and older generations.
- Educate individuals and society.
- Act in morally correct ways.

Confucianism Influences Chinese Life Confucianism affected many aspects of Chinese government and society. For example, Confucius taught that people could advance in life through education. An emphasis on education helped to produce an efficient, well-trained set of government officials.

Confucius' ideas also influenced society. He thought society should be organized around five basic relationships. A code of conduct governed these relationships. For example, one relationship was between ruler and subject. Confucius taught that the ruler should be virtuous and kind. The subject should be loyal and obey the law. Other relationships were based on the family. Confucius wanted children to have respect for their parents and older generations. Around A.D. 200, however, Confucianism began to lose its influence as the Han Dynasty lost power.

The Spread of Buddhism As Confucianism lost influence, many Chinese turned to Buddhism. **Buddhism** is a religion that started in India and is based on the teachings of Siddhartha Gautama (sihd•DAHR•tuh GOW•tuh•muh) (c. 566–486 B.C.). Siddhartha was known as the Buddha, or "Enlightened One."

Buddha This huge seated Buddha, located in caves about 150 miles west of Beijing, was carved in the fifth century A.D. ▶

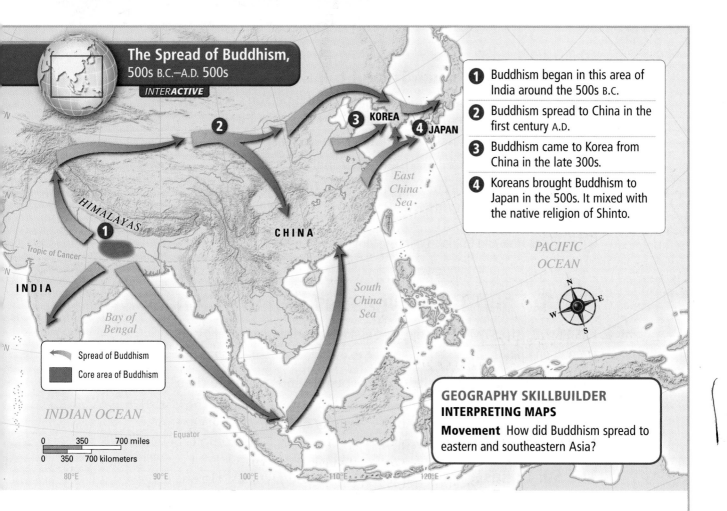

The Spread of Buddhism, 500s B.C.–A.D. 500s
INTERACTIVE

HIMALAYAS

Tropic of Cancer

INDIA

Bay of Bengal

CHINA

East China Sea

KOREA

JAPAN

South China Sea

PACIFIC OCEAN

INDIAN OCEAN

Spread of Buddhism
Core area of Buddhism

0   350   700 miles
0   350   700 kilometers

Equator

80°E   90°E   100°E   110°E   120°E

1 Buddhism began in this area of India around the 500s B.C.

2 Buddhism spread to China in the first century A.D.

3 Buddhism came to Korea from China in the late 300s.

4 Koreans brought Buddhism to Japan in the 500s. It mixed with the native religion of Shinto.

GEOGRAPHY SKILLBUILDER
INTERPRETING MAPS
Movement How did Buddhism spread to eastern and southeastern Asia?

Buddhism teaches the following principles:

- Suffering is a part of life.
- The reason people suffer is that they are too attached to material possessions and selfish ideas.
- By living in a wise, moral, and thoughtful way, people can eventually learn to escape suffering.

During the first century A.D., missionaries and traders carried Buddhist teachings to China, as the above map shows. Over time, the religion spread into Korea and Japan too. Buddhism became widely practiced after the Han Dynasty fell. Buddhist teachings helped people endure the suffering that followed the dynasty's collapse.

Influences on Confucianism Confucianism began to enjoy a rebirth in the 600s. However, gradual changes began to take place in Confucian thought. Buddhism and Daoism caused some of these changes. **Daoism** is a belief system that seeks harmony with nature and with inner feelings. Daoism began in China in the 500s B.C.

Since the Han Dynasty, Confucianism had mostly been a set of social ethics and political principles. Later, during the Song Dynasty, Confucian thinkers blended Buddhism and Daoism into Confucianism. As a result, Confucianism broadened its outlook.

A Change in Confucian Thought This new Confucianism was greatly concerned with human behavior and a person's relationship with the universe. It emphasized the following principles:

- Morality is the highest goal a person can reach.
- This morality can be achieved through education.
- Education can occur through books, observation, or interaction with other wise people.

REVIEW How did China's belief systems change?

The Sui and Tang Dynasties Reunify China

3 ESSENTIAL QUESTION How did the Sui and Tang dynasties reunify and strengthen China?

After the fall of the Han, the Chinese people endured more than 350 years of chaos and conflict. Finally, the Sui (sway) Dynasty (581–618) reunified China and brought order. **Reunify** means to bring a group together after it has been divided.

The Sui Dynasty Yang Jian founded the Sui Dynasty. He was a general in the army of the Zhou (joh), the rulers of northern China. In 581, he took power by killing the heir to the Zhou throne—his grandson. He then massacred 59 royal princes. By 589, he had conquered the south and reunified China. He declared himself first emperor of the Sui Dynasty. Later he became known as Wendi.

The Great Wall Wendi rebuilt parts of the Great Wall to keep out invaders. This section of the wall winds through the mountains northwest of Beijing. ▼

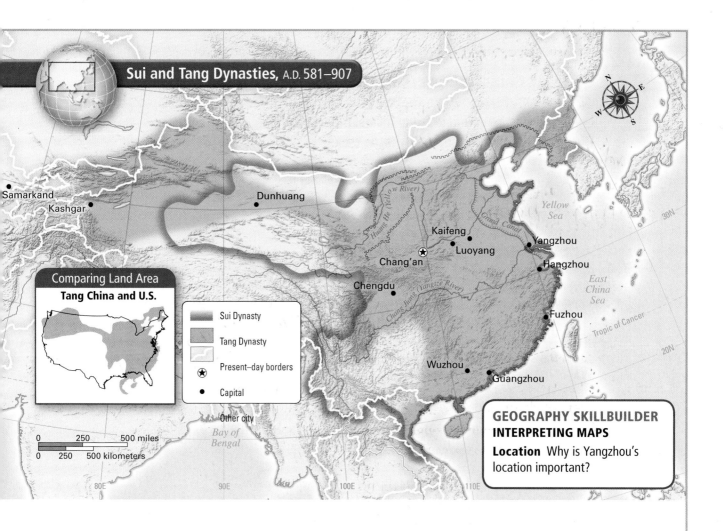

Samarkand
Kashgar
Dunhuang
Kaifeng
Huang He (Yellow River)
Grand Canal
Yangzhou
Chang'an
Luoyang
Hangzhou
Chengdu
Chang Jiang (Yangtze River)
Yellow Sea
East China Sea
Fuzhou
Tropic of Cancer
Wuzhou
Guangzhou
Bay of Bengal
30N
20N

Comparing Land Area
Tang China and U.S.

Sui Dynasty
Tang Dynasty
Present–day borders
★ Capital
• Other city

0 250 500 miles
0 250 500 kilometers

80E   90E   100E   110E

GEOGRAPHY SKILLBUILDER
INTERPRETING MAPS
Location Why is Yangzhou's location important?

Wendi Reunifies China During his rule, Wendi did many things to make the Chinese feel more unified. He restored old political traditions that reminded the Chinese of their glorious past. For example, on taking the throne he accepted the traditional Chinese imperial gifts of red doors for his house and a robe with a red sash.

Wendi also reduced conflict by allowing people to follow their own belief systems. Although he was a Buddhist, he encouraged Daoist beliefs and practices. As you read earlier, Confucianism also enjoyed a rebirth during this time. For example, candidates for government jobs once again had to take a civil service examination. The examination carried out Confucius's belief that a government had to be built on the skill of its people.

Wendi also began public works projects. He rebuilt portions of the Great Wall, which you learned about on pages 206–207. He also started the building of the Grand Canal. It connected the Huang He (Yellow River) and Chang Jiang (Yangtze River), linking northern and southern China. Thousands of peasants labored five years to dig the Grand Canal. Nearly half of them died during the project.

Wendi and his successor, Yangdi, raised taxes to pay for all these projects. In time, the Chinese people grew tired of high taxes, and they revolted. As a result, the dynasty fell after only 37 years.

China Builds an Empire • 217

Cycle of Chinese Dynasties

Chinese dynasties rose and fell in a similar pattern. Historians call this pattern the dynastic cycle.

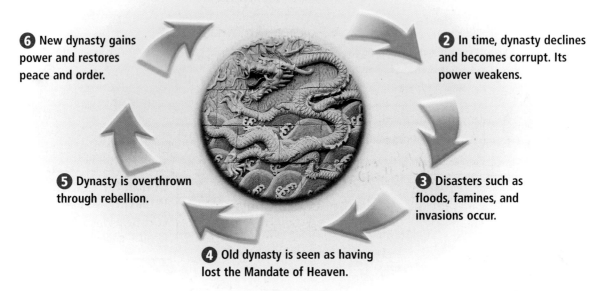

1 New dynasty is considered to have the Mandate of Heaven, or the approval of heaven.

2 In time, dynasty declines and becomes corrupt. Its power weakens.

3 Disasters such as floods, famines, and invasions occur.

4 Old dynasty is seen as having lost the Mandate of Heaven.

5 Dynasty is overthrown through rebellion.

6 New dynasty gains power and restores peace and order.

The Tang Dynasty Although the Sui Dynasty lasted only a short time, it set the foundation for the Tang Dynasty. The Tang Dynasty started in 618 and ruled for nearly 300 years. During this period, China expanded its borders on all sides. In addition, Tang emperors expanded the network of roads and canals to bring the country together. Such a large empire needed many officials to manage it. So the Tang emperors fully adopted the Confucian ideas of how government should be run. The Tang government system was one of the most advanced and complex in the world at the time.

Tang Emperors Taizong (ty•johng) helped his father, Gaozu (gow•joo), to found the Tang Dynasty. Taizong seized the throne in 626 after killing his two brothers and all ten of his brothers' sons. Even though Taizong used violence to rise to power, many Chinese considered him a fair and just leader. For example, he did not overburden peasants with high taxes. He also took some lands from the rich to give to peasants.

In 690 Wu Zhao (woo jow) declared herself emperor. She was the only woman to occupy the throne of China. She proved to be a capable leader. One of her greatest achievements was the reconquest of Korea. (China had ruled Korea earlier, in the 660s and the 670s.) She did not leave power until 705, when she was more than 80 years old.

Another great Tang emperor, Xuanzong (shwahn•zung), came to power in 712. He ruled for more than 40 years. During his reign, Chinese literature and art reached great heights. The Tang period is best known for its masterful and lively poetry. (See the Primary Source feature on page 228.) Also, Tang sculptures of graceful horses were greatly desired trade items.

In the next lesson, you will learn more about the development of the Chinese empire. In addition, you will learn about agricultural, technological, and commercial developments in China.

REVIEW What methods did the Sui and Tang dynasties use to reunify and strengthen China?

Lesson Summary

- Confucianism helped shape Chinese beliefs about social morals and political principles.
- Buddhism spread throughout East Asia because it helped people during difficult times.
- The Sui and Tang dynasties reunited China and brought a new sense of national identity.

Why It Matters Now . . .

In Asia today about 10 percent of the population follows Confucianism and Buddhism.

1 Lesson Review

Homework Helper
ClassZone.com

Terms & Names

1. Explain the importance of

| nomad | Buddhism | reunify |
| Confucianism | Daoism | |

Using Your Notes

Understanding Cause and Effect Use your completed chart to answer the following question:

2. How did the fall of the Han Dynasty affect the spread of Buddhism? (7.3.1)

Causes	Effects
The Han Dynasty falls.	
Buddhism becomes widely practiced.	
The Sui and Tang dynasties reunify China.	

Main Ideas

3. Why did Buddhism spread throughout China and other Asian countries? (7.3.1)

4. How did Confucianism influence Chinese society and government? (7.3.3)

5. What actions by Sui and Tang emperors helped unify China? (7.3.2)

Critical Thinking

6. **Comparing and Contrasting** Compare the role of families and older generations in Confucianism and in West African culture. (7.3.3)

7. **Making Generalizations** How did Wendi view peasants? Provide examples to support your generalizations. (7.3.1)

Activity **Creating an Illustrated Chart** Review the information about the teachings of Confucius in this lesson. Create a chart that shows the basic ideas of what Confucius taught. Use drawings to illustrate the teachings. (7.3.3)

Identifying Issues and Problems

Goal: To use a reading selection to identify issues and problems that developed in China during a period of much disorder

CALIFORNIA STANDARDS
HI 1 Students explain the central issues and problems from the past, placing people and events in a matrix of time and place.

Learn the Skill

To explain issues and problems from the past, you must first identify the problem and then look for the effects of the problem. Then you will want to see if the problem was solved. Studying how people solved problems in the past can help you learn ways to solve problems today.

S See the Skillbuilder Handbook, page R28.

Practice the Skill

1 Read the passage at right. Look for the main idea or issue by reading the title or topic sentence. Ask yourself what might be a problem connected with the main idea.

2 Look for causes. Ask yourself what events might be linked with the problem. In this case, internal and external fighting caused China's disorder.

3 Determine effects. Think about which groups of people might be affected by the problem. Remember that there may be more than one effect. Look for cue terms such as *so, because,* or *as a result.* One effect of China's disorder was the fall of the Han dynasty.

4 Make a graphic organizer. Using a graphic organizer can help you understand the issues and problems. The graphic organizer below shows what problems resulted because of disorder in China.

Example:

4

PROBLEM
Disorder in China

EFFECT
Traditional values of Confucius were not practiced.

EFFECT
Suffering people looked for a way to deal with hardships.

SOLUTION
Teachings of Buddhism helped deal with the hardships of disorder.

LONG-TERM EFFECT
Buddhism spread.

In the passage below, the author discusses what happened in China during a time of much disorder. Look for the problem and the effects it had on the people. Remember that sometimes there are several effects. Then see if you can find the solution to the problem.

❶ *China Faces Disorder*

❷ Military battles against outsiders and fights between insiders caused much disorder in China. ❸ As a result, the Han Dynasty fell apart around 220 A.D. People were upset because the traditional values of Confucius were no longer practiced. They felt their world was collapsing. ❸ Because of this, they began looking for a belief system to help them deal with their suffering. The teachings of Buddhism helped them live with the hardships they experienced. ❸ As a long-term effect, Buddhism became widely practiced in China.

▲ **Buddha** This sculpture of the Buddha shows him with Chinese features. Many Chinese turned to the teachings of the Buddha during troubled times.

Apply the Skill

Read the paragraph on page 217 about the building of the Grand Canal in China. Use what you have learned to identify the issues and problems connected with the Grand Canal. Create a graphic organizer to show these issues and problems.

MAIN IDEAS

1 **Government** The Tang Dynasty built a powerful imperial state. This efficient government continued under the Song Dynasty.

2 **Economics** Tang and Song China had a strong economy based on trade and farming.

3 **Science and Technology** Under the Tang and Song, the Chinese developed technologies that influenced the world.

TAKING NOTES

Reading Skill: Finding Main Ideas

As you read each section of Lesson 2, look for essential information about the main ideas. Record this essential information on a cluster diagram like the one shown below.

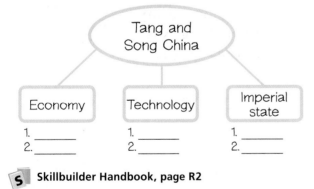

Tang and Song China

Economy	Technology	Imperial state
1. _____	1. _____	1. _____
2. _____	2. _____	2. _____

S Skillbuilder Handbook, page R2

▲ **Court Dress** This pottery figurine shows how women at the Tang court dressed.

CALIFORNIA STANDARDS

7.3.2 Describe agricultural, technological, and commercial developments during the Tang and Song periods.

7.3.5 Trace the historic influence of such discoveries as tea, the manufacture of paper, woodblock printing, the compass, and gunpowder.

7.3.6 Describe the development of the imperial state and the scholar-official class.

Framework Students should analyze the economic foundations of this society in the conversion of the jungle regions of the Yangtze valley into productive rice paddies.

Advances Under the Tang and Song

TERMS & NAMES

imperial

bureaucracy

scholar-official

wood-block printing

movable type

porcelain

Build on What You Know As Lesson 1 explained, the Sui Dynasty reunited China. In 618, the Tang Dynasty succeeded the Sui. The Tang rulers faced the task of keeping the recently reunified China together. They also wanted to hold onto their newly gained power.

Building the Imperial State

1 ESSENTIAL QUESTION How was the Chinese government organized under the Tang and Song dynasties?

Ruling a vast country like China was a difficult task. To rule more efficiently, the Tang rulers developed an imperial state. **Imperial** means related to an empire.

The Tang used several ideas they had learned from the Sui Dynasty to set up this organized, well-run government. For the most part, Tang central and local government and military organization followed Sui models. In addition, the Tang used the Sui tax system. They even made the Sui capital—the city of Ch'ang-an on the Wei River—their capital. (See the map on page 217.) Ch'ang-an was important because it was located on major trade routes.

Calligraphy This document shows one skill that all Chinese government officials had—calligraphy. The ability to write Chinese characters was the sign of an educated person. ▼

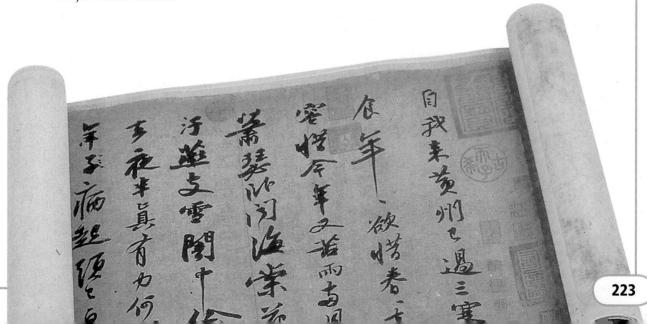

Chinese Government The Tang government was like a pyramid. An emperor ruled at the top, and many people served in various levels below him. The emperor's chief advisers served him directly. They were the second-highest level of the pyramid.

Below those advisers was the bureaucracy. A **bureaucracy** is a government that is divided into departments. Each department in China was in charge of a certain area, such as taxes, agriculture, or the army. This political system ruled all of China. Local governments throughout China had to report to the central bureaucracy.

A Law Code Tang rulers created a new code of law. It listed all of the laws of China so that the same laws would be used everywhere. This new code proved highly effective. China used it from about 624 until the late 1200s.

Scholar-Officials The Tang needed to educate people to work in the bureaucracy. For many jobs in the bureaucracy, people had to take an exam given by the government. The Han and Sui dynasties had also given exams to job seekers, but the Tang rulers greatly expanded the system. The state exam tested knowledge of Confucian ideas, poetry, and other subjects. The test was long and difficult. Most people who took it failed.

A person who passed the state exam could become a **scholar-official**, an educated person with a government position. Almost all scholar-officials came from the upper class. Most wealthy people had relatives who worked in government. In China, relatives often helped each other get jobs. Also, only rich people could afford the education needed to pass the test.

The Song Dynasty After the Tang, the Song Dynasty ruled from 960 to 1279. The Song Dynasty expanded and improved the exam system. It set up more schools and changed the exam to cover more practical subjects. More people took the exams, passed them, and got government jobs. Even so, most officials continued to come from rich families with political influence.

> **REVIEW** What were the features of the Chinese government during the Tang and Song dynasties?

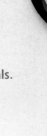

Confucius Confucius taught a system of ethics and morals. Chinese rulers thought that people who studied these ideas made good government officials. ▶

▲ **State Exams** This illustration from a 17th-century history of China shows scholars taking the state exam in front of a Song emperor, who is dressed in yellow.

Prosperity from Trade and Farming

2 ESSENTIAL QUESTION On what was China's economy based during the Tang and Song periods?

Under Tang and Song rule, China's economy grew. In fact, China became the wealthiest and most developed nation in the world. One factor in this growth was an improved transport system.

Changes in Travel and Trade The Tang and Song governments built many roads and waterways. This transportation system helped tie the Chinese empire together.

Better transportation improved trade. Traders used the new roads to move grain, tea, and other goods. Along the roads were inns in which travelers could stay. Mounted messengers and runners carried government mail on the roads. This improved communication.

Waterways were just as important. The government repaired old canals and built new ones to link major rivers. The resulting network of waterways provided an efficient way to move goods and people.

Trade was also improved by several technological developments. These developments included gigantic ships powered by both oars and sails. Such ships made sea voyages faster and safer. The development of the magnetic compass, too, improved travel on the open seas.

Terraced Rice Fields

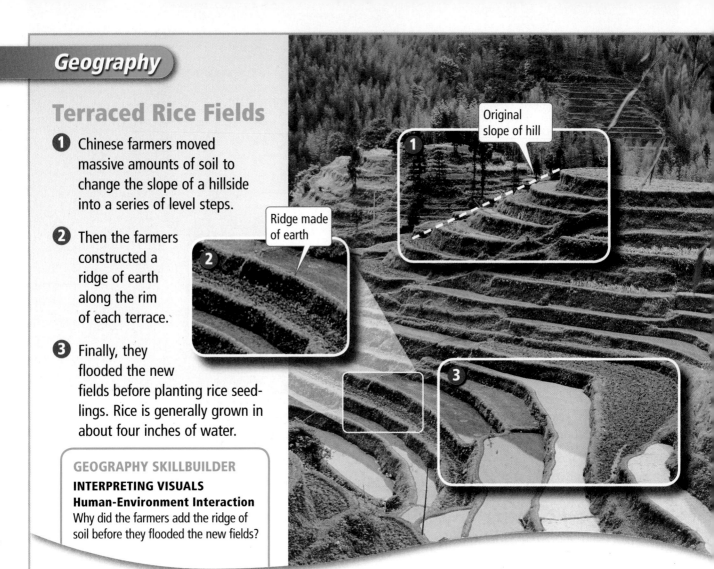

1 Chinese farmers moved massive amounts of soil to change the slope of a hillside into a series of level steps.

2 Then the farmers constructed a ridge of earth along the rim of each terrace.

3 Finally, they flooded the new fields before planting rice seedlings. Rice is generally grown in about four inches of water.

Original slope of hill

Ridge made of earth

GEOGRAPHY SKILLBUILDER
INTERPRETING VISUALS
Human-Environment Interaction
Why did the farmers add the ridge of soil before they flooded the new fields?

Changes in Agriculture Around A.D. 1000, Chinese farmers began planting a new type of rice from Southeast Asia. This rice ripened faster than the type they had used before. With the new rice, farmers could raise two or even three crops a year instead of one. The food supply expanded rapidly, allowing the population to grow to about 100 million.

During Tang and Song times, the Chinese turned areas of the Chang Jiang valley into productive rice paddies, or fields. Farmers used pumps and canals to drain water from marshes. They built terraces on hillsides and used elaborate irrigation systems to water them. By changing their environment, the Chinese farmers gained cropland. Additional land enabled them to grow more rice.

These changes and a mild climate allowed southern China to grow more rice than the people in that region needed. Farmers sold the extra rice to merchants, who shipped it by canal to imperial centers in northern China. Having extra food meant that fewer people needed to work as farmers. As a result, more people could work in trade.

Changes in Commerce By the Song period, trade was thriving in China. Barges and cargo ships carried goods on canals and rivers and along the coastline of China. They also brought Chinese foods and other products to foreign lands, such as Korea and Japan.

The growth of trade led to a rapid expansion in the use of money, in the form of coins, to pay for goods. However, large numbers of coins were heavy and difficult to carry. To solve this problem, Tang and Song governments began to print paper money. They were the first governments in history to do so.

▲ **Chinese Money** The Chinese developed the first paper money in the world.

As trade increased, more people became merchants. China's merchant class lived mainly in cities and towns, where most private trade took place. The cities grew and prospered. By the Song period, China had a few cities with populations of about 1,000,000 people. In contrast, Paris, one of Europe's largest cities, had only 150,000 people at the time.

REVIEW What brought about the change to a money economy during China's Tang and Song dynasties?

A Time of Brilliant Achievements

3 ESSENTIAL QUESTION What technological advances were made under the Tang and Song dynasties?

The Tang and Song dynasties were among the most creative periods in China's long history. Poetry and art, in particular, flourished during this time.

A Golden Age for Poetry and Art Three Tang writers—Li Bai, Du Fu, and Wang Wei—are considered among the greatest Chinese poets of all time. Li Bai wrote about life's pleasures. In his poetry, Du Fu praised orderliness and Confucian values. And Wang Wei wrote of the beauty of nature and the briefness of life. (To read one of Wang Wei's poems, see the Primary Source feature on the next page.)

Tang artists produced beautiful pottery figurines. During Song times, landscape painting became an important art form. Song painters used only black ink—in every shade from pale grey to the darkest black. As one Song artist noted, "Black is ten colors." Today, Tang pottery figurines and Song landscape paintings can be found in museums around the world.

Background: Wang Wei (shown below) who lived from 699 to 759, was one of the great poets of the Tang Dynasty. This poem is about his experiences as a scholar-official. It describes what happened after he disagreed with the emperor.

"On Being Demoted and Sent Away to Qizhou"
By Wang Wei

How easy for a lowly official to offend
and now I'm <u>demoted</u>[1] and must go north.
In my work I sought <u>justice</u>[2]
but the wise emperor disagreed.
I pass houses and roads by the riverside
and villages deep in a sea of clouds.
Even if one day I come back,
white age will have invaded my hair.

---

1. **demoted:** forced to take a lower-ranking job.
2. **justice:** moral rightness, fairness.

DOCUMENT–BASED QUESTION
According to this poem, what problems did scholar-officials sometimes face?

Technological Progress In addition, the Tang and Song periods were a time of exciting advances in technology. Because the Chinese loved learning, they looked for better ways to support scholarly study and spread traditional ideas. They developed methods to manufacture paper in large quantities. Paper was easier to write on than other materials, such as silk cloth.

The Chinese also invented **wood-block printing**. Printers carved wooden blocks with enough characters to print entire pages. Later, printers created **movable type**. The Chinese used paper and printing to make the first printed books. This allowed them to record their knowledge in a permanent form.

Historic Influence Chinese technology shaped history in China and the West in many different ways.

- The technology of paper-making spread to the Arab world in the 700s and later to Europe.
- The Chinese invented gunpowder, which they used for fireworks. Later, gunpowder changed warfare by making deadly new weapons possible.
- The Chinese made the first magnetic compass, which spread to Europe. Compasses helped make the European Age of Exploration possible.

Visual Vocabulary

movable type: a small block of metal or wood with a single raised character. Movable type can be used more than once and rearranged to spell different words.

The Chinese influenced daily life by exporting porcelain and tea to the world. **Porcelain** is a hard white ceramic often called china. People desired porcelain for its beauty. It became one of China's most valuable exports.

For centuries, the Chinese used tea as a medicine. During the Tang Dynasty, it became a popular drink. Later, traders brought tea from East Asia to Europe.

REVIEW What were some key Chinese inventions or products that had a great influence on the world?

Lesson Summary

- Imperial China was run by a bureaucracy filled with scholar-officials.
- Improvements in agriculture and transportation helped make China one of the most powerful countries in the world.
- Chinese inventions such as the compass, gunpowder, and paper shaped the history of other world regions.

▲ **Tang Tea Cup** The designs on this Tang tea cup show a Persian influence.

Why It Matters Now . . .

Chinese inventions, such as porcelain and paper money, are a part of everyday life in the 21st century.

---

2 Lesson Review

 **Homework Helper** ClassZone.com

Terms & Names

1. Explain the importance of

| imperial | scholar-official | movable type |
| bureaucracy | wood-block printing | porcelain |

Using Your Notes

Finding Main Ideas Use your completed cluster diagram to answer the following question:

2. What are two examples of technology developed during the Tang and Song dynasties? (7.3.2)

Main Ideas

3. Who served as China's scholar-officials? (7.3.6)
4. How did farming change in Tang and Song China? (7.3.2, Framework)
5. What were the historic influences of tea, printing, paper, gunpowder, and the compass? (7.3.5)

Critical Thinking

6. **Making Inferences** Why do you think the Song Dynasty tried to make the exams cover more practical subjects? (7.3.2)
7. **Understanding Cause and Effect** How did the use of a new type of rice in China affect China's relationship with foreign lands? (7.3.2)

Activity **Making a Map** Using the map on page 209 as a model, make an outline map of China. Then reread the section "Changes in Agriculture" on page 226. In what river valley did the Chinese create new rice fields? Put that river on your map. (7.3.2)

CALIFORNIA STANDARDS

7.3.2 Describe agricultural, technological, and commercial developments during the Tang and Song periods.

7.3.5 Trace the historic influence of such discoveries as tea, the manufacture of paper, wood-block printing, the compass, and gunpowder.

The Chinese Legacy

Purpose: To learn about Chinese contributions to science and culture

Many Chinese inventions are still a part of our lives today. The compass, the wheelbarrow, and the umbrella are only a few of the many Chinese inventions that people still use. Some of these inventions were the result of solving a problem. Others may simply have been an accident.

Seismoscope

▶ **Past** A Chinese scientist invented an accurate seismoscope (a machine to record the occurrence of earthquakes) in A.D. 132. It was a bronze vase with eight dragons around the outside.

▼ **Present** We use seismographs that are capable of not only recording earthquakes but also measuring their magnitude.

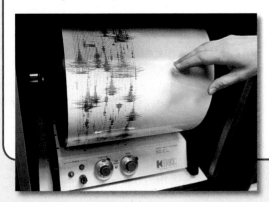

Each dragon held a ball in its mouth. When the ground shook, one ball would fall into the mouth of a frog.

Seeing which frog held the ball made it possible to tell the direction of the earthquake.

Paper Currency

Past Paper money came into use in China in the A.D. 800s. It was called "flying cash." It was used for goods bought in distant regions.

▶ **Present** Businesses accept paper money in payment for goods all over the world.

Testing

Past The Chinese used testing to fill positions in the government. To prevent cheating, candidates were searched when they entered the testing room. The candidates' names did not appear on their tests; they were each identified by a number.

▶ **Present** The federal government uses civil service exams to fill government positions. Schools use tests to show that their students have learned required material.

Fireworks

Past Over 1,000 years ago, a Chinese cook created a black powder that exploded when it was lit by fire. The powder was placed inside bamboo tubes. When the tubes were lit, they made a loud noise. The result was firecrackers!

▼ **Present** This technology is now used for gunpowder and weapons—as well as for fireworks used in celebrations like this one.

Activities

1. **TALK ABOUT IT** Why do you think paper money became popular?

2. **WRITE ABOUT IT** Which of the inventions shown on these two pages are solutions to a problem? Choose an invention and write a paragraph identifying the invention and telling how the invention solved a problem. (Writing 2.3)

MAIN IDEAS

1 **Government** The Mongols built a vast empire stretching from Europe to China.

2 **Government** The Mongols kept some features of the Chinese form of government but did not let Chinese officials have important jobs.

3 **Economics** The Mongols encouraged and increased trade and foreign contacts.

TAKING NOTES

Reading Skill:
Explaining Chronological Order and Sequence

Ordering events in the correct chronological order can help you see how they are related. As you read about Mongol China, record major events on a time line like the one shown below.

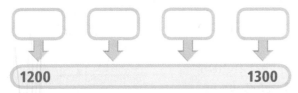

1200   1300

S Skillbuilder Handbook, page R15

▲ **Mongol Passport** The Mongols issued passports for officials on government business in other countries or for important foreign visitors. The passport stated that the bearer was protected by the emperor.

CALIFORNIA STANDARDS

7.3.3 Analyze the influences of Confucianism and changes in Confucian thought during the Song and Mongol periods.

7.3.4 Understand the importance of both overland trade and maritime expeditions between China and other civilizations in the Mongol Ascendancy and the Ming Dynasty.

CST 2 Construct various time lines of key events, people, and periods of the historical era they are studying.

Framework Foreign merchants such as Marco Polo were given special privileges and high office.

The Mongol Empire

TERMS & NAMES

Genghis Khan

Kublai Khan

Mongol Ascendancy

Marco Polo

Build on What You Know As you read in Lesson 1, nomads from the north invaded China when the Han Dynasty fell. In the 1200s, outsiders once again invaded China. This time, the invaders were the Mongols.

The Mongol Invasion

1 ESSENTIAL QUESTION How did the Mongols build a vast empire that stretched from Europe to China?

The Mongols were fierce nomadic warriors who lived in the vast plains to the northwest of China. In the 1200s, they invaded and conquered China.

A Great Leader The Mongols lived in independent family groups called clans. These clans were joined together into several tribes, which were independent of each other. But around 1206 a strong leader named Temujin (TEHM•yuh•juhn) united the Mongol tribes. He fought and defeated all his rivals for leadership one by one. By doing so he became the khan, or ruler, of all the Mongols. He took the name **Genghis Khan** (JEHNG•gihs KAHN), which means "universal ruler." Genghis organized the Mongol warriors into a mighty fighting force and began a campaign of conquest. He invaded northern China, then moved west across Central Asia.

Throughout history, nomadic people often had a military advantage against settled people. Settled people tried to defend their cities and towns. Nomads, however, moved quickly, looked for weak spots, attacked, and moved on. This helped them succeed at war. By 1221, the Mongols had conquered all of Central Asia.

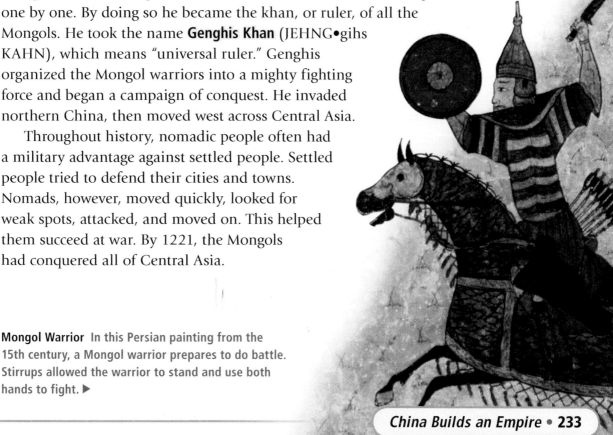

Mongol Warrior In this Persian painting from the 15th century, a Mongol warrior prepares to do battle. Stirrups allowed the warrior to stand and use both hands to fight. ▶

The Mongol Empire When Genghis died in 1227, his son, Ogadai (OH•goh•DAY), took power. Ogadai captured the rest of northern China. He also extended Mongol rule as far west as Russia and Persia.

The Mongol Empire was divided into four large parts called khanates. A different descendant of Genghis ruled each part. **Kublai Khan** (KOO•bly KAHN), Genghis's grandson, took power in the Chinese part of the empire in 1260. At that time, southern China was still under Song control. Kublai's forces finally defeated the Song in 1279. The Mongols now controlled all of China and would rule until 1368.

REVIEW What regions did the Mongol leaders conquer?

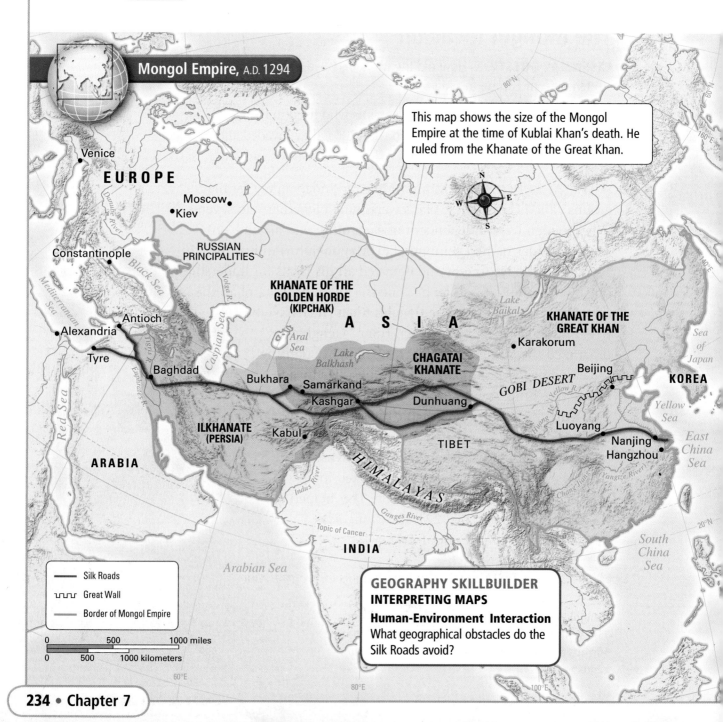

Mongol Empire, A.D. 1294

This map shows the size of the Mongol Empire at the time of Kublai Khan's death. He ruled from the Khanate of the Great Khan.

Venice

EUROPE

Moscow
Kiev

Constantinople

RUSSIAN
PRINCIPALITIES

**KHANATE OF THE
GOLDEN HORDE
(KIPCHAK)**

A S I A

Lake
Baikal

**KHANATE OF THE
GREAT KHAN**

Karakorum

Sea
of
Japan

Antioch

Alexandria

Aral
Sea

Lake
Balkhash

**CHAGATAI
KHANATE**

Tyre

Baghdad

Bukhara
Samarkand
Kashgar

Dunhuang

GOBI DESERT

Beijing

KOREA

Yellow
Sea

**ILKHANATE
(PERSIA)**

Kabul

TIBET

Luoyang
Nanjing
Hangzhou

East
China
Sea

ARABIA

HIMALAYAS

Indus River

Ganges River

Chang Jiang (Yangtze River)

Tropic of Cancer

INDIA

Arabian Sea

South
China
Sea

Silk Roads

Great Wall

Border of Mongol Empire

| 0 | 500 | 1000 miles |
| 0 | 500 | 1000 kilometers |

**GEOGRAPHY SKILLBUILDER
INTERPRETING MAPS
Human-Environment Interaction**
What geographical obstacles do the Silk Roads avoid?

Mongol Government

2 **ESSENTIAL QUESTION** What features of the Chinese form of government did the Mongols adopt?

Kublai Khan was the first ruler in 300 years to control all of China. The Mongols were also the first foreign power to rule China. Kublai ruled China for 15 years and died in 1294.

Learning to Rule The Mongols did not have much experience with government. The Chinese, on the other hand, had a long history of organized government. So Kublai kept many aspects of Chinese rule. He built his capital at Beijing in traditional Chinese style and declared himself emperor. He also founded a new dynasty—the Yuan (YOO•ahn) Dynasty. These steps were familiar to the Chinese and made it easier for Kublai to control China.

Maintaining Control Kublai kept features of the Chinese form of government, but he made sure that the Chinese politicians didn't gain too much power. He did this to keep control of China in Mongol hands. He ended the civil-service examination system for choosing officials. Instead, he gave the important government jobs to Mongols or to trusted foreigners. Chinese officials were given only minor jobs with little or no power.

Even so, the influence of Confucian thought remained strong during Mongol rule. Mongol officials adopted Confucian approaches to government. In addition, Kublai appointed Confucian scholars to educate the sons of the Mongol nobility.

Despite differences with the Chinese, Kublai Khan was a capable leader. He worked to rebuild China after years of warfare. He restored the Grand Canal and extended it 135 miles north to Beijing. And he built a paved highway that connected Bejing and Hangzhou. These land and water routes allowed for easy travel between north and south. He also made changes that helped promote trade and contacts with the rest of the world.

REVIEW How did the Mongols maintain control of China?

Opening China to the World

3 **ESSENTIAL QUESTION** How did the Mongols encourage trade?

During Kublai Khan's rule, China became more open to the outside world. The Mongols developed a thriving sea trade and welcomed visitors from foreign lands.

Kublai Khan (1215–1294)

Kublai Khan was the Great Khan, the leader of all Mongol people. He gained this title in 1260 and named himself emperor of China around 1279.

Unlike most Mongols, Kublai was interested in Chinese culture. He lived in high style in lavish Chinese palaces and supported the work of Chinese artists.

At the same time, Kublai remained loyal to his Mongol roots. To remind him of home, he planted grass from the northern plains in his palace garden at Beijing. He also honored his ancestors in Mongolian style. Every August he performed a special ritual, scattering horse milk on the ground and calling out the name of his grandfather, Genghis Khan.

Trade Routes One way that the Mongols encouraged trade was by making trade routes safer. In the past, China sometimes closed overland trade routes because of warfare and banditry. Now, the Mongols controlled all of Central Asia. This period of Mongol control is known as the **Mongol Ascendancy**. Mongol control made overland travel safe.

Caravans moved along the Silk Roads, ancient trade routes stretching from China to the Black Sea. (See the map on page 234.) Merchants took silks, porcelain, tea, and other goods to western Asia and Europe. The merchants brought back new foods, plants, and minerals. The Mongols also encouraged sea trade. Ships crossed the Indian Ocean and South China Sea to reach Chinese ports such as Guangzhou (gwahng•joh) and Fuzhou (foo•joh). There, merchants did a lively trade in goods from both East and West.

Foreign Contacts Trade brought increased contact with foreign peoples and cultures. People from Arabia, Persia, and India frequently visited Mongol China. Even missionaries and diplomats from as far away as Europe made the long trip. These visitors helped tell the rest of the world about Chinese civilization.

The most famous European visitor during this period was **Marco Polo**. Polo was a young trader from Venice, Italy. He traveled

Vocabulary Strategy

ascendancy: dominance in position or power. *Ascendancy* comes from the Latin **root word** *scandere,* "to climb." For example, a sports team climbs to first place by defeating its competitors. If successful, that team has ascendancy.

the Silk Roads to China with his father and uncle. He arrived around 1275 and stayed for 17 years. Polo became an assistant to Kublai Khan and traveled throughout China on government missions. He later published a book about his adventures. Polo's book was a great success, but many Europeans found his vivid descriptions of China hard to believe. In the next lesson you will learn how the Chinese overthrew the Mongols.

P **Primary Source Handbook**
See the excerpt from *The Travels of Marco Polo*, page R43.

> **REVIEW** How did the Mongols promote Chinese contact with the rest of the world?

Lesson Summary

- The Mongols built an enormous empire stretching from China to Europe.
- The Mongols adopted some features of the Chinese style of government.
- The Mongols increased foreign trade, especially along the Silk Roads to Western markets.

Why It Matters Now . . .

The contacts between Mongol China and the Arab and Western worlds spread important ideas and trade goods. Because of this, many Chinese inventions can be found worldwide today.

3 Lesson Review

Homework Helper
ClassZone.com

Terms & Names

1. Explain the importance of

Genghis Khan	Mongol Ascendancy
Kublai Khan	Marco Polo

Using Your Notes

Explaining Chronological Order and Sequence Use your completed time line to answer the following question:

2. What were the main events of the Mongol conquest of China? (CST 2)

1200   1300

Main Ideas

3. How did the Mongols gain power? (7.3.3)

4. How did the Mongols control China's government? (7.3.3)

5. What was the Mongol policy toward trade and foreign contacts? (7.3.4)

Critical Thinking

6. **Making Inferences** Why do you think Kublai Khan did not want Chinese to fill important government jobs? (7.3.3)

7. **Forming and Supporting Opinions** Was Mongol rule good or bad for China? Explain your opinion. (7.3.3)

Activity **Internet Activity** Use the Internet to research the inventions that Marco Polo brought back from China. Create a poster showing these inventions. Write captions for the inventions pictured. (7.3.3)
INTERNET KEYWORDS: *Marco Polo, inventions*

Lesson 4

MAIN IDEAS

1 **Government** Chinese rebels overthrew Mongol rule and started the Ming Dynasty.

2 **Economics** At first, Ming emperors encouraged trade and exploration, but they later became less interested in maintaining relations with the outside world.

3 **Government** The Qing Dynasty ruled for almost 300 years. It was China's last dynasty.

TAKING NOTES

Reading Skills:
Forming and Supporting Opinions

After reading this lesson, you will be asked to form and support an opinion about China's ocean voyages. To prepare, use a web diagram like the one shown below to record information about the voyages.

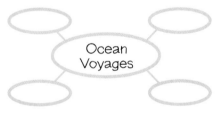

Ocean Voyages

S **Skillbuilder Handbook, page R22**

▲ **Emperor's Robe** This robe was worn by a Qing emperor for special events. Its golden color and dragon designs were symbols of the emperor's power.

CALIFORNIA STANDARDS

7.3 Students analyze the geographic, political, economic, religious, and social structures of the civilizations of China in the Middle Ages.

7.3.4 Understand the importance of both overland trade and maritime expeditions between China and other civilizations in the Mongol Ascendancy and Ming Dynasty.

7.3.5 Trace the historic influence of such discoveries as tea, the manufacture of paper, wood-block printing, the compass, and gunpowder.

A Return to Chinese Rule

TERMS & NAMES
Forbidden City
maritime
tribute
Zheng He
Manchus

Build on What You Know The Chinese were a proud people with a long history of great achievements. Many did not like being ruled by the Mongols.

Overthrowing the Mongols

1 **ESSENTIAL QUESTION** How was the Ming Dynasty established?

After Kublai Khan's death in 1294, Mongol rule slowly weakened. In 1368 a rebel army led by Zhu Yuanzhang (joo yoo•ahn•jahng) overthrew the Mongol emperor.

The First Ming Emperor Zhu Yuanzhang established the Ming Dynasty and became its first emperor under the name Hongwu (hung•woo). He encouraged Confucianism and brought back the state exams. To help trade, he rebuilt roads and canals. In addition, he rebuilt and extended the Great Wall to improve China's defenses. Hongwu also helped farmers by lowering taxes and providing them with land.

In addition to these positive steps, Hongwu began to increase his personal power. He did away with the position of prime minister and took control of all government offices. He made all decisions himself without consulting his advisers. He also set up a secret service to spy on his people. And he had tens of thousands of people arrested for treason and killed.

Connect to Today

Forbidden City The Forbidden City, built mostly during the Ming Dynasty, is one of China's leading tourist attractions. ▼
INTERACTIVE

Yongle's Rule Hongwu died in 1398. He had chosen his grandson to succeed him. Not everyone supported this decision, however. A struggle for power began. After nearly five years of fighting, Yongle (yung•law)—one of Hongwu's sons—won victory. He declared himself emperor in 1403.

Yongle, like his father, was a strong, capable leader. Under his leadership, the Ming Dynasty reached the height of its power. One of his greatest achievements was the enlarging of the capital city at Beijing. A great complex of palaces and temples, surrounded by 35-foot-high walls, stood at the center of the city. In time, this collection of buildings became known as the **Forbidden City** because commoners and foreigners were not allowed to enter it. (See the photograph on the previous page.) The Forbidden City symbolized Yongle's, and China's, power and might.

Yongle wanted not just China but also the rest of the world to know of his greatness. This desire led to another of his great achievements.

REVIEW What improvements did the Ming emperors make in China?

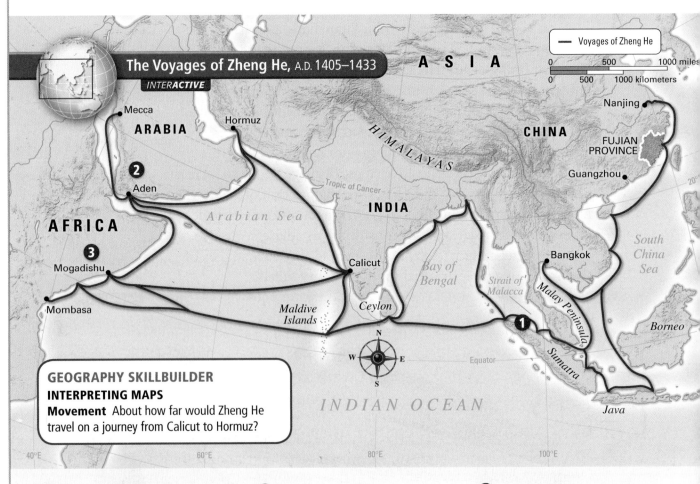

The Voyages of Zheng He, A.D. 1405–1433
INTERACTIVE

Voyages of Zheng He

0   500   1000 miles
0   500   1000 kilometers

GEOGRAPHY SKILLBUILDER
INTERPRETING MAPS
Movement About how far would Zheng He travel on a journey from Calicut to Hormuz?

❶ In the Strait of Malacca, Zheng He fought a deadly battle with pirates. The Chinese won, burning ten pirate ships and capturing seven others.

❷ The sultan of Aden gave the Chinese lions, zebras, ostriches, and a giraffe. He also gave them gold belts and a gold hat covered with jewels.

❸ Near Mogadishu, the Chinese used gunpowder explosives to force a town to surrender. Local rulers feared the Chinese would conquer the African coast.

	Zheng He's Voyages	Columbus' Voyages
Date	Zheng He began his voyages in 1405.	Columbus began his voyages in 1492.
Ship	Zheng He's largest ships were more than 400 feet long.	Columbus' largest ship, the *Santa Maria*, was about 100 feet long.
Crew	One of Zheng He's ships could carry up to 1,000 people.	Columbus' first voyage totaled about 90 people on three ships.
Results	China decided in the 1430s to end its maritime voyages and focus more on its northern borders.	The Europeans continued their voyages and established colonies.

Trade and Overseas Voyages

2 **ESSENTIAL QUESTION** How did China's relations with the outside world change under the Ming emperors?

In the early 1400s, Yongle sent a series of maritime expeditions to other civilizations. **Maritime** means "related to the sea."

The Voyages of Zheng He Yongle wanted to extend Chinese influence and win tribute from other countries. **Tribute** is a payment made by one country to another as a sign of respect. To achieve this goal, Yongle built a great fleet of ships for exploration.

China completed seven long voyages between 1405 and 1433. Admiral **Zheng He** (juhng huh) led the fleet. He had as many as 300 ships and nearly 28,000 crew members. Zheng He sailed around Southeast Asia to India, Arabia, and Africa. (See the map opposite.) He returned with tribute that included gold and jewels. China's foreign trade and reputation grew because of his voyages.

A Change of Policy By the 1430s, Yongle and Zheng He had died. Most Confucian officials thought the government gained little from trade and contact with foreigners. They were more concerned with threats of invasion from Central Asia. So the Ming government ended the maritime voyages and banned the building of seagoing ships.

China did not remain isolated, however. Chinese merchants expanded trade with the rest of Southeast Asia. In addition, European ships were traveling to China by the early 1500s. The Chinese traded silk, tea, and porcelain for a variety of Western goods, including silver.

> **Vocabulary Strategy**
>
> **maritime:** relating to the sea. The Latin word for the sea is *mare*. *Mare* is the **root word** of *maritime*. Other words based on *mare* are *marina* and *marine*.

REVIEW How did China's policies change after the 1430s?

The Last Dynasty

3 **ESSENTIAL QUESTION** How was the Qing Dynasty established?

The Ming Dynasty declined after almost 300 years in power. Weak rulers, high taxes, and poor harvests led to rebellion. To the northeast of China was a region called Manchuria. The people were known as the **Manchus**. In 1644, the Manchus took advantage of Ming weaknesses and conquered China. They started the Qing (chihng) Dynasty.

Like the Ming rulers, the Manchus allowed some trade. But in general, they limited foreign contacts and tried to restrict foreign influence in China. The Qing Dynasty, China's last, endured until 1911.

REVIEW How did the Manchus gain power?

Lesson Summary

- The Ming Dynasty restored China to a great empire.
- The Ming Dynasty greatly expanded overland trade and maritime voyages.
- After the 1430s, China focused on its northern borders.

Why It Matters Now . . .

Today the Chinese government still tries to limit foreign influence in political and economic affairs.

---

4 Lesson Review

Homework Helper
ClassZone.com

Terms & Names

1. Explain the importance of

Forbidden City	tribute	Manchus
maritime	Zheng He	

Using Your Notes

Forming and Supporting Opinions Use your completed web chart to answer the following question:

2. Did the voyages of Zheng He benefit the Ming Dynasty? Explain. (7.3.4)

Ocean Voyages

Main Ideas

3. What changes did the Ming rulers bring to China? (7.3)

4. Why did Yongle support ocean voyages? (7.3.4)

5. How did trade change under Manchu rule? (7.3.4)

Critical Thinking

6. **Comparing and Contrasting** How did Mongol and Ming trade policies after the death of Yongle compare? (7.3.4)

7. **Explaining Historical Patterns** How were the invasions by the Mongols and the Manchus similar? (7.3)

Activity **Writing Interview Questions** Review the information about the voyages of Zheng He. Create a series of questions you would ask him about his travels for either a newspaper or television interview. (7.3.4)

Make a Compass

Goals: To understand the Chinese invention of the magnetic compass and its historic influence; to work with a partner to create a model compass and explain the compass's importance

Prepare

Research the development of the compass in books on exploration or Chinese history.

Do the Activity

1 Unbend a paper clip and straighten it. Rub one end of the paper clip on a magnet until it is magnetized. Using the marking pen, mark the magnetized end. Stick the paper clip through the piece of foam or cork. Turn the ends slightly upward.

2 Fill the bowl with water. Float the paper clip on the water. The clip will turn so that the magnetized end points north.

3 Carefully place the bowl on the map near China. Follow the route of Zheng He by slowly moving the bowl south toward the islands of Indonesia. Then slide the bowl toward the Indian Ocean. Finally, move the bowl to the coast of Africa. Now return the bowl to China following the route you took to reach Africa.

Follow-Up

What did you notice about the movement of the compass needle as you moved the bowl?

Extension

Writing a Paragraph Write a paragraph explaining how the compass would have helped people to make a long sea voyage.

Materials & Supplies
- paper clip
- magnet
- marking pen
- piece of foam or cork
- bowl
- water
- desktop size world map

▲ **Magnetic Compass**
The Chinese characters around the rim of this compass give directions.

CALIFORNIA STANDARDS
7.3.5 Trace the historic influence of such discoveries as tea, the manufacture of paper, wood-block printing, the compass, and gunpowder.

VISUAL SUMMARY

Early Dynasties

Tang Dynasty (618–907) (7.3)
- Expanded Chinese territory
- Used state exams to choose officials
- Created a law code

Song Dynasty (960–1279) (7.3)
- Built a network of roads and canals
- Expanded trade
- Oversaw advances in technology

Yuan Dynasty (1279–1368) (7.3)
- Kept Chinese out of power
- Ended state exams
- Encouraged foreign trade

Ming Dynasty (1368–1644) (7.3)
- Sponsored Zheng He's voyages; then limited foreign trade
- Restored state exam system
- Rebuilt Great Wall of China

Qing Dynasty (1644–1911) (7.3)
- Tried to restrict foreign influence
- Was China's last dynasty

TERMS & NAMES

Explain why the words in each set below are linked with each other.

1. **Confucianism** and **Buddhism**
2. **bureaucracy** and **imperial**
3. **Kublai Khan** and **Mongol Ascendancy**
4. **maritime** and **Zheng He**

MAIN IDEAS

Reunifying China (pages 213–221)

5. What was the main reason Buddhism spread from China to Korea and Japan? (7.3.1)
6. What did the Sui and Tang dynasties accomplish? (7.3.1)

Advances Under the Tang and Song (pages 222–231)

7. How did the imperial state and the scholar-official class develop? (7.3.6)
8. How did Chinese inventions influence the world? (7.3.5)

The Mongol Empire (pages 232–237)

9. How did Kublai Khan change China? (7.3.4)
10. What kind of government did the Mongols establish in China? (7.3.3)

A Return to Chinese Rule (pages 238–243)

11. How did Yongle try to extend Chinese influence in the world? (7.3.4)
12. How did the Ming rulers after Yongle relate to the world outside China? (7.3.4)

CRITICAL THINKING Big Ideas: Belief Systems

13. **MAKING INFERENCES** After the collapse of the Han Dynasty, why did many Chinese turn from Confucianism to Buddhism? (7.3.1)
14. **FORMING AND SUPPORTING OPINIONS** Explain whether Confucian morals were upheld in the development of the scholar-official class. (7.3.6)
15. **EVALUATING INFORMATION** How did Confucianism change during Song and Mongol times? (7.3.3)

ALTERNATIVE ASSESSMENT

1. **WRITING ACTIVITY** Imagine that you are an adviser to the emperor of China in A.D. 1000. The emperor has asked you to write a paragraph summarizing the reasons the network of roads and canals in the country should be expanded. Write your paragraph using information from the chapter. (7.3.2)

2. **INTERDISCIPLINARY ACTIVITY—MATH** Use books or the Internet to research the abacus. The abacus is a computing machine that has been used in China since Tang and Song times. Create a display showing what an abacus looks like and explaining how it is used to do calculations. (7.3.2)

3. **STARTING WITH A STORY**

 Review the way you ended the story "The Fall of Luoyang." Now that you've read the chapter, would you end the story differently? If so, how? (7.3.1)

Technology Activity

4. **PLANNING A VIRTUAL FIELD TRIP** Use the Internet to research the Forbidden City. Work with a partner to plan a virtual field trip of the city. Include Web sites that explore the city's many gates, palaces, and gardens. (7.3.6)

   • Create an itinerary for the trip.
   • Include any maps or graphics.
   • Write questions and answers to accompany each Web site.

Research Links
ClassZone.com

Reading Maps The 1,794-km-long Grand Canal is the longest artificial waterway in the world. Use the map and your knowledge of world history to answer the questions. (7.3.2)

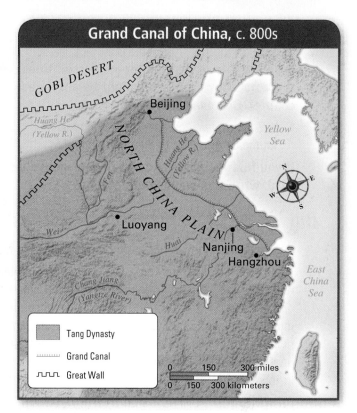

Grand Canal of China, c. 800s

Tang Dynasty
Grand Canal
Great Wall

1. **What is the southernmost port on the Grand Canal?**

   A. Beijing
   B. Luoyang
   C. Nanjing
   D. Hangzhou

2. **Which rivers are connected by the Grand Canal?**

   A. Huang He and Wei
   B. Wei and Chang Jiang
   C. Chang Jiang and Huang He
   D. Wei, Chang Jiang, and Huang He

Test Practice
ClassZone.com

Additional Test Practice, pp. S1–S33

Chapter 8

Japan, Korea, and Southeast Asia

Before You Read: Predicting

Scan the title of the chapter and lesson titles. Write three questions you think might be answered in the chapter. One example is:

How are Japan, Korea, and the kingdoms of Southeast Asia alike in their geography?

If you find the answer to one of your questions as you read, write it down in your notebook.

Big Ideas About East and Southeast Asia

Geography Many geographic factors influence history.

The closeness of Japan, Korea, and mainland Southeast Asia to China influenced their development. China has been one of the world's largest and most powerful countries for much of the past 5,000 years. Its ideas, culture, and even political control spread into neighboring regions. India, another powerful country in Asia, also extended its culture in the area.

Integrated Technology

eEdition
- Interactive Maps
- Interactive Visuals
- Starting with a Story

INTERNET RESOURCES
Go to **ClassZone.com** for
- WebQuest
- Homework Helper
- Research Links
- Internet Activities
- Quizzes
- Maps
- Test Practice
- Current Events

EAST AND SOUTHEAST ASIA

500s Khmers establish kingdom in Southeast Asia.

593 Prince Shotoku begins his rule in Japan. ▶

935 Koryu dynasty controls Korea.

400 600 800

WORLD

570 Muhammad is born in Mecca.

800 Charlemagne crowned Holy Roman Emperor by pope. (Charlemagne's crown) ▶

East and Southeast Asia, A.D. 1100

100°E 120°E 140°E

N W E S

Sea of Japan

KORYO (KOREA)

Yellow Sea

JAPAN

Heian (Kyoto)

Huang He (Yellow River)

Kaifeng

Grand Canal

SONG CHINA

Chang Jiang

(Yangtze River)

Hangzhou

East China Sea

PACIFIC OCEAN

40°N

Taiwan

Tropic of Cancer

DAI VIET

Hainan

20°N

KHMER

Angkor

South China Sea

Philippines

0   250   500 miles
0   250   500 kilometers

1192
First shogun comes
to power in Japan.
(Yoritomo Minamoto) ▶

1428
Vietnamese drive out
Chinese invaders.

1603
Tokugawa Shogunate
begins in Japan.

1200   1400   1600   1800

1076
Ghana Empire in West Africa
conquered by Muslims.

1492
Columbus makes first
voyage to the Americas.
(replicas of the ships of Columbus) ▶

The EDUCATION of a SAMURAI

CALIFORNIA STANDARDS
Reading 3.4
Identify and analyze recurring themes across works. (e.g., the value of bravery, loyalty, and friendship; the effects of loneliness).

Background: You may have heard about the samurai warriors of Japan. Japanese lords used these well-trained fighters to defend their lands against enemies. *Samurai* means "one who serves." Some samurai were prepared from birth to become warriors. Usually, their fathers and grandfathers were also samurai.

Future samurai received a special education. They trained in fighting skills. But the most important lesson was learning the warrior code, or bushido (BUSH•ih•DOH). This code of honor emphasized loyalty and bravery above all else.

As you read, imagine you are in Japan in the 1300s. You are watching a 15-year-old boy complete the final day of his training to become a samurai.

Mask worn by actor portraying a samurai in Japanese noh drama, 1300s ▶

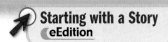

Tomorrow, Yoro will go through the ceremony to become a samurai. He will receive his first sword, the samurai's most important weapon. But today he must rise early to complete the final day of training. As he has done each day before, Yoro will learn the skills of a warrior and how to live by the warrior's code of honor, bushido. His first act is to report to the master, who himself was a famous samurai.

Then, Yoro practices riding a horse and shooting a bow. A samurai rides into battle on horseback. Next comes unarmed fighting skills, for it is possible to lose your weapons in battle. Yoro finishes his morning by practicing wrestling and jujitsu (a self-defense skill like modern judo) with other pupils. In the afternoon, the master gives instruction on one of the samurai's most important skills—sword fighting. Over the years, Yoro has developed strength, speed, and accuracy.

Finally, as his last day as a student ends, Yoro studies meditation, or mental exercises. Being a samurai requires more than skill at using weapons. It is not enough to train the body. You must also prepare the mind. A samurai must always be alert. Life depends on it!

From tomorrow onward, Yoro must be ready to fight for his lord at any moment. Death in service to the lord is a great honor. Still, the students have been taught by a Buddhist monk not to rush to sacrifice their lives. The monk cautions, "What is your purpose? . . . If you are in such reckless haste to seek death at the hands of the enemy, who is there to succeed you?" Yoro's commitment is to serve—in life as long as he can, in death if necessary. Tomorrow that service begins!

How important do you think the warrior code was to the Japanese?

Reading & Writing

1. **READING: Theme** Identify and analyze the themes you see at work in this story about warriors and their code of honor.

2. **WRITING: Response to Literature** Imagine you are a Japanese youth training to become a samurai. Consider the code of honor you must follow. Write a short essay explaining how important it is to live by the warrior code.

CALIFORNIA STANDARDS **Writing 2.2**
Write responses to literature.

249

Lesson 1

MAIN IDEAS

1 **Geography** Japan's development was influenced by its landforms, its climate, and its closeness to China and Korea.

2 **Government** Prince Shotoku wrote Japan's first constitution and also brought Chinese culture to Japan.

3 **Culture** The Japanese developed distinctive family and social structures.

TAKING NOTES

Reading Skill: Summarizing

When you summarize, you restate a paragraph, passage, or chapter in fewer words. In Lesson 1, summarize each of the main sections using the chart below.

Section	Summary
The effect of geography on Japan	
Early Japanese society	
The reign of Prince Shotoku	

 Skillbuilder Handbook, page R3

▲ **Floating Shinto Gate**
Shrines where Shinto believers worship are marked by a gate, or *torii*. Shinto is the traditional religion of Japan.

CALIFORNIA STANDARDS

7.5.1 Describe the significance of Japan's proximity to China and Korea and the intellectual, linguistic, religious, and philosophical influence of those countries on Japan.

7.5.2 Discuss the reign of Prince Shotoku of Japan and the characteristics of Japanese society and family life during his reign.

HI 2 Students understand and distinguish cause, effect, sequence, and correlation in historical events, including the long- and short-term causal relations.

Land of the Rising Sun

Build on What You Know How would you be affected by a bigger and stronger neighbor? Japan, the much smaller island neighbor of China, would feel Chinese influence for centuries.

The Effect of Geography on Japan

1 ESSENTIAL QUESTION How was Japan's development influenced by its landforms, its climate, and its closeness to China and Korea?

According to legend, Japan was formed from drops of water. The drops fell from a jeweled spear that a god had dipped into the ocean. Each drop formed one of the four large and more than 4,000 small mountainous islands that make up Japan.

Landforms and Climate Japan is located 120 miles off the coast of Asia. In some ways, it is a difficult place in which to live. Only 15 percent of the land is flat enough for farming. Volcanoes, earthquakes, tidal waves, and hurricanes are a constant danger. Also, the islands have few natural fuels such as coal and oil.

But Japan has advantages too. It has a mild climate with plenty of rain. So, rice grows well there. Because Japan is an island, the ocean provides abundant fish for food. It also provides protection from invasion. This is a form of defense that mainland civilizations of East Asia, like China and Korea, did not have.

The ancestors of most Japanese came from East Asia in the 300s B.C. Because of Japan's separation from the mainland, fewer immigrants moved there than to other places.

Mount Fuji This cone-shaped, dormant volcano is one of Japan's most widely recognized symbols. ▼

251

Nature Inspires Japanese Culture Japan's many mountains and frequent rainfall have resulted in lush green lands. Japanese culture often expresses a love of this natural beauty. One form of expression is the traditional religion known as **Shinto**. *Shinto* means "way of the gods." It is based on respect for nature and ancestors. According to Shinto, rocks, trees, rivers, and other natural objects are often home to divine spirits. One of Japan's most honored objects is Mount Fuji, its tallest mountain, shown on the previous page.

Japan's Influential Neighbors—China and Korea

Japan's closest neighbors are China and Korea. Both countries influenced Japan, but the powerful Chinese civilization had the strongest impact. (See chart at right and map on page 276.) China, in fact, gave Japan its name. The Chinese referred to the islands to the east as "the land of the rising sun," which is *Nippon* in Japanese. Nippon is what the Japanese call their country.

Chinese Influences on Japan	
Areas of Influence	**How Japan Adapted Chinese Influences**
Religion	Combined Buddhism with traditional Shinto rituals
Government	Adopted principles of Confucianism for Japanese government
Writing System	Used Chinese characters to stand for additional ideas and sounds in language
Arts	Employed Chinese techniques and themes, especially in landscape painting
Agriculture	Adapted Chinese wet-field rice cultivation to Japan's island environment

REVIEW What areas of Japanese culture were influenced by China?

Early Japanese Society

2 ESSENTIAL QUESTION What was the structure of early Japanese society?

Early Japan was divided into clans. These were families of people who were related by blood or marriage. Clans often fought one another for land. Land was the main source of wealth and power because so little of it was available for cultivation.

Structure of Japanese Society Japanese society remained organized around large and powerful clans for centuries. Each clan was led by a few powerful nobles. They were the only people in Japan known by both a family name and an individual name. Most Japanese were common workers. They usually lived in villages and farmed or fished. Some had special skills, such as making pottery or weaving cloth. Some people in Japan were enslaved. Slaves were usually forced to cook, clean, or take care of the house of a noble.

The Shinto religion was a strong unifying force in Japanese society. For example, noble families and their workers and slaves all honored the same divine spirits and ancestors.

Japan's Emperors In the 400s, the Yamato clan of central Japan established itself as the most powerful clan. Japan's first emperors came from Yamato families. According to tradition, members of the Yamato clan were descendants of the sun goddess. Emperors are considered to be human, but because of this tradition, the Japanese also treat them as divine, which means godlike. The emperor claimed to rule, but military leaders usually held the real power. Rivals within the Yamato clan fought one another to gain this power.

Since Japan rarely changed emperors, the country appeared very stable. If a child succeeded to the throne, a **regent** was appointed. This official would rule until the child was old enough. One of Japan's most important regents was **Prince Shotoku** (SHOH•toh•KOU).

REVIEW Who held real power in early Japanese society?

The Reign of Prince Shotoku

3 ESSENTIAL QUESTION What role did Prince Shotoku play in Japanese history?

Prince Shotoku was asked by his aunt, Empress Suiko (SWEE•koh) the first woman to be ruler, to act as her regent. Shotoku held power from 593 to 622.

Shotoku Introduces Chinese Culture

Prince Shotoku was impressed by Chinese culture. He encouraged the Japanese to learn from their powerful neighbor. Shotoku sent Japanese scholars and artists to China to study Chinese society. He also welcomed skilled workers from China to Japan.

Shotoku opened a Japanese embassy in China. An **embassy** is an office of a government in another country. He created guidelines for Japanese leaders that were based on Confucian principles, such as hard work and obedience to authority. (See Chapter 7, Lesson 1.) These guidelines are known as the Seventeen Article Constitution.

Prince Shotoku The seventh-century Japanese regent is shown with his two sons. ▶

Shotoku Promotes Buddhism An aspect of Chinese culture that impressed Shotoku was Buddhism. With his support, it began to spread quickly in Japan. At first, Buddhism challenged Shinto, the traditional Japanese belief system. But Buddhism was based on the teachings of the Buddha, who was born in India, not Japan. So Shotoku's support of Buddhism met opposition. Eventually, most Japanese blended the religions. They accepted Buddhism but shaped it according to traditional Japanese customs. They also continued to practice Shinto. As people adopted Buddhism, they became more aware of other aspects of Chinese culture.

REVIEW What was the most lasting effect of Shotoku's reign?

▲ **Early Japanese Warrior** This red earthenware sculpture shows a warrior of the time of Prince Shotuku.

Lesson Summary

- Japan's island location and its proximity to China and Korea affected its development.
- Japanese emperors reigned but had little power.
- Prince Shotoku introduced Chinese culture to Japan.

Why It Matters Now . . .

Japanese society continues to adapt influences from other cultures. This type of creative borrowing is a common theme in history.

Lesson Review

Homework Helper
ClassZone.com

Terms & Names

1. Explain the importance of

Shinto	Prince Shotoku
regent	embassy

Using Your Notes

Summarizing Use your completed chart to answer the following question:

2. What is important about the geography of Japan? (7.5.1)

Section	Summary
The effect of geography on Japan	
Early Japanese society	
The reign of Prince Shotoku	

Main Ideas

3. Why was Japan influenced by its closeness to China? (7.5.1)

4. How did Prince Shotoku change Japan? (7.5.2)

5. What was the structure of society like during Prince Shotoku's reign? (7.5.2)

Critical Thinking

6. **Understanding Cause and Effect** How did geography affect the diet of people in Japan? (HI 2)

7. **Making Inferences** Why would the Yamato clan's claim to be descended from the sun goddess affect its power? (HI 2)

Activity

Writing a Letter Imagine you are living in Japan under the rule of Prince Shotoku. Write a letter to him describing your reaction to the influence of China on Japanese culture. (7.5.1)

Make a Poster

Goal: To understand Japanese society and family life in the seventh century by creating a poster that shows various aspects of life during the period

Materials & Supplies
- poster board
- markers
- scissors
- glue stick
- construction paper
- magazines
- books or Internet research on Japan

Prepare

1. Read the information on life in Japan on pages 251 to 254 of this chapter. Research seventh-century Japan in books or on the Internet.

2. Pay special attention to the images in this chapter and those found in your research.

Do the Activity

1. Select four or five aspects of Japanese life that you would like to show, such as activities of daily life.

2. Make a rough sketch of your poster design on a separate sheet of paper.

3. Draw illustrations for each aspect, or cut out appropriate visuals and glue them to the poster. You may use a combination of both drawn and applied visuals.

4. Write a brief explanatory sentence below each aspect of Japanese life that you are showing.

Follow-Up

How well does the poster you produced show life in Japan during the seventh century?

Extension

Making a Presentation Show your poster to the class. Explain why you selected the aspects of Japanese life that are illustrated on your poster.

CALIFORNIA STANDARDS
7.5.2 Discuss the reign of Prince Shotoku of Japan and the characteristics of Japanese society and family life during his reign.

MAIN IDEAS

1 **Religion** The Japanese adopted the forms of Buddhism that best met their needs.

2 **Culture** The Japanese developed unique forms of literature and drama.

3 **Culture** The Japanese arts reflected a love of natural beauty.

TAKING NOTES

Reading Skill: Categorizing

Sorting information into groups helps you understand patterns in history. In Lesson 2, look for three categories of Japanese culture and details about each one. Record the information on a web diagram like the one below.

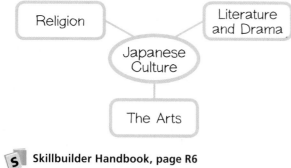

S **Skillbuilder Handbook, page R6**

▲ **The Buddha** This wooden sculpture from the 1100s shows the Buddha as a "healer," with a medicine jar in his left hand.

CALIFORNIA STANDARDS

7.5.4 Trace the development of distinctive forms of Japanese Buddhism.

7.5.5 Study the ninth and tenth centuries' golden age of literature, art, and drama and its lasting effects on culture today, including Murasaki Shikibu's *Tale of Genji*.

HI 2 Students understand and distinguish cause, effect, sequence, and correlation in historical events, including the long- and short-term causal relations.

Growth of Japanese Culture

TERMS & NAMES
Zen
noh
kabuki
Lady Murasaki Shikibu
haiku

Build on What You Know As you learned, Japan was influenced by Chinese culture. But the genius of the Japanese was their ability to adapt foreign customs and ideas to meet their own needs. A very important Chinese influence was Buddhism.

Japanese Forms of Buddhism

① ESSENTIAL QUESTION How did the Japanese adapt Buddhism?

Buddhism began in India in the 500s B.C. It was based on the teachings of Siddhartha Gautama. (See Chapter 7.) Buddhism spread to China and then Korea. It arrived in Japan in the A.D. 500s.

Buddhism Spreads in Japan Because Buddhism had the support of Prince Shotoku, it spread rapidly in Japan. It did not replace Japan's ancient Shinto religion, but was practiced alongside it. Buddhism had a powerful influence on Japanese culture. It was popular first with the nobility and later with the common people. The Buddhist belief that peace and happiness could be gained by leading a life of virtue and wisdom appealed to many.

Different forms, or sects, of Buddhism developed in Japan over the centuries. Tendai Buddhism focused on the intensive study of texts. Shingon attracted followers who appreciated its complex rituals. Amida, or Pure Land, included a belief that people might have salvation in a pure land after their death. Zen held that something precious and divine exists in each person.

Connect to Today

Zen Garden These gardens of rocks and gravel provide peaceful surroundings. ▼

Zen Buddhism Some Buddhist sects flourished while others died out. The Japanese adopted the forms whose beliefs and practices best met their preferences and needs. Beginning in the 1100s, **Zen** became more and more common. It put emphasis on self-discipline, simplicity, and meditation. In fact, the word *Zen* means "meditation." Followers believed that quiet reflection was more useful than performing ceremonies or studying scriptures. In some ways, Zen was very simple. It focused on the individual's attempt to achieve inner peace rather than on the idea of salvation.

As a major school of Buddhism, Zen had a great influence on Japanese culture. Samurai favored it because they thought it would give them inner peace and help them in battle. Some artists liked its combination of simplicity and boldness. They reflected these qualities in drawings by using just black ink and making strong, dark lines. Zen later spread to other countries and became popular in the West.

REVIEW How was Japanese society affected by Buddhism?

A Golden Age of Literature and Drama

2 ESSENTIAL QUESTION What is unique about Japanese literature and drama?

A great period of literature in Japanese history began in the 800s. People today still read diaries, essays, and novels written at this time.

Japanese Writing Systems Another aspect of China's culture that Japan adopted was its writing system. By about 400, the Japanese had begun using Chinese characters to write Japanese words. Like the Chinese, the Japanese used characters to stand for specific objects, actions, or ideas. (See the illustration on page 260.) Later, they also used characters to stand for certain sounds. These characters worked like letters or syllables in English.

Today Japanese writing includes both letters and characters. While Japanese writing was influenced by China, its language is related to that of Korea. You will read about Korea in Lesson 4.

Japanese Drama Japan's long tradition of drama dates back to the 600s. It began with people performing Shinto dances at religious shrines. Then, in the 1300s, actors developed a special type of drama called **noh**. Noh plays were often retellings of legends and folktales. Actors wore painted wooden

Kabuki Actor
This kabuki actor is dressed as a warrior. ▼

Background: Lady Murasaki's book, *The Tale of Genji*, provides detailed descriptions of Japanese customs and values. It is an excellent primary source for historians.

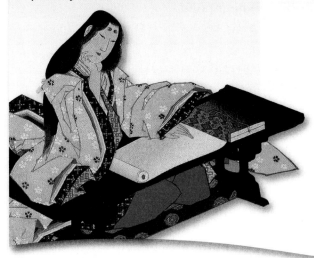

from *The Tale of Genji*

By Lady Murasaki Shikibu
Translated by Edward G. Seidensticker

The royal excursion[1] to the Suzaki palace took place toward the middle of the Tenth Month. . . . On the day of the excursion the emperor was attended by his whole court, the princes and the rest. The crown prince too was present. Music came from boats rowed out over the lake, and there was an infinite[2] variety of Chinese and Korean dancing. Reed and string and drum echoed through the grounds.

---

1. **excursion:** short trip.
2. **infinite:** immeasurably great or large.

> **DOCUMENT–BASED QUESTION**
> How can you tell from this excerpt that Japan was influenced by other cultures?

masks to show various emotions and used gestures, costumes, and music to tell the story. Most noh actors were men. The plays were performed for both upper classes and common people.

In the early 1600s, another style of drama called **kabuki** (kuh•BOO•kee) developed. It combined melodramatic singing and dancing with elaborate costumes and heavy makeup. This type of drama was more informal than noh. Its themes often dealt with common people. Kabuki was, and still is, performed by men. Both noh and kabuki remain popular today.

 Primary Source Handbook
See the excerpt from *The Tale of Genji*, page R44.

The Tale of Genji

In the early 800s, Japan ended diplomatic relations with China. Some Japanese leaders felt they had learned enough from the Chinese. China's influence remained, but Japan developed its own cultural traditions. This was especially true in literature. One of Japan's finest writers was **Lady Murasaki Shikibu** (MOO•rah•SAH•kee SHEE•kee•BOO). She lived at the emperor's court in the early 1000s.

Murasaki wrote *The Tale of Genji*, a book about the life of a prince in the imperial court. Her book is important in the development of literature. Earlier books in Japan and elsewhere either retold old myths or were collections of stories. *Genji* is a long, realistic story focused on one individual. These characteristics make it the world's first important novel.

Japanese Poetry Japanese poets often wrote about the sadness of rejected love or the beauty of nature. Some of the most popular Japanese poems are very short compared with the poetry of other countries. One shorter form of poetry is called **haiku**. It has just 17 syllables—three lines of 5, 7, and 5 syllables. Matsuo Basho, who lived in the 1600s, was a great haiku poet. He wrote poems that had the quiet, reflective spirit of Zen, such as this one about a pond.

> *An old silent pond . . .*
> *Into the pond a frog jumps,*
> *splash! Silence again.*

REVIEW What new forms of literature and drama did the Japanese develop?

Distinctive Japanese Arts

3 ESSENTIAL QUESTION What themes are reflected in Japanese arts?

Two themes often expressed in Japanese literature and drama are simplicity and a love of natural beauty. These themes also appear in many forms of Japanese art.

Calligraphy and Painting Like the Chinese, the Japanese wrote with brushes and ink on paper. They considered writing a way to express beauty. Calligraphy is the art of beautiful writing. Each character is painted in a set order of brush strokes. But calligraphers vary the shapes and sizes of characters to suggest different meanings.

Brush painting with ink on paper scrolls and silk began in the 600s. Typical Japanese designs are very detailed. They depict landscapes, historical events, and daily life. Sometimes a short description is written on the art itself. (See painting on page 267.)

Visual Vocabulary

Japanese calligraphy: This is the character for the word *eternal.*

◀ **The Scholarly Arts** These Japanese gentlemen are practicing what the Chinese called the four scholarly arts— chess, lute playing, calligraphy, and painting.

Flower Arranging and Gardening The art of flower arranging was another tradition that Buddhists brought to Japan. People emphasized simple arrangements. They tried to highlight the natural beauty of flowers. Bonsai is the art of growing miniature trees or shrubs in small pots or trays.

Landscape gardeners also tried to create places that would show the beauty of nature. Zen-inspired gardens (shown on page 257) are designed to help people think quietly. These gardens are arranged with rocks and pathways and few flowers or trees. Gardening and flower arranging remain important art forms in Japan today.

Bonsai Tree Most bonsai trees are two inches to three feet tall and are kept small by cutting and shaping. ▼

REVIEW How did Japanese culture reflect an interest in natural beauty?

Lesson Summary

- Several forms of Buddhism were adopted in Japan, and Zen became one of the most popular.
- Noh, kabuki, and haiku are distinctive forms of drama and literature that developed in Japan.
- Japanese art shows a love of natural beauty.

Why It Matters Now . . .

The Japanese adopted ideas and developed distinctive cultural practices that are an important part of Japanese life today.

---

2 Lesson Review

Homework Helper
ClassZone.com

Terms & Names

1. Explain the importance of

Zen	kabuki	haiku
noh	Lady Murasaki Shikibu	

Using Your Notes

Categorizing Use your completed web diagram to answer the following question:

2. What is one statement that characterizes the development of Japanese culture? (7.5.5)

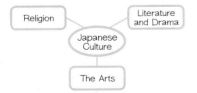

Main Ideas

3. Why did the Japanese adapt different forms of Buddhism? (7.5.4)

4. How was Japanese literature unlike that of other countries? (7.5.5)

5. How does Japanese art reflect a love of natural beauty? (7.5.5)

Critical Thinking

6. **Making Generalizations** Why did Zen Buddhism appeal to many Japanese? (7.5.4)

7. **Understanding Cause and Effect** How might Japan's culture have developed differently without Chinese influence? (HI 2)

Activity

Writing Poetry Write a haiku about a topic in nature. Use the pattern of syllables described on page 260. (7.5.5)

Reader's THEATER

The Siege of
Chihaya Castle

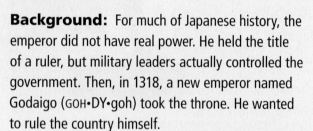

Background: For much of Japanese history, the emperor did not have real power. He held the title of a ruler, but military leaders actually controlled the government. Then, in 1318, a new emperor named Godaigo (GOH•DY•goh) took the throne. He wanted to rule the country himself.

The military government, called the bakufu (BAH•koo•foo), fought Godaigo's attempts to exercise power. In 1332, about 1,000 of the emperor's troops were trapped inside Chihaya (chee•HAH•yah) Castle. An army of 10,000 bakufu soldiers was camped outside. A warrior chieftain named Kusunoki Masashige (KUS•un•OH•kee MAHS•ah•SHEE•geh) led the emperor's troops.

CALIFORNIA STANDARDS

7.5.6 Analyze the rise of a military society in the late twelfth century and the role of the samurai in that society.

Samurai Armor Samurai warriors wore elegant iron-plated armor. ▼

Cast of Characters

Narrator

Kusunoki: commanding general of emperor's troops

Satsuma: (saht•SOO•ma) an important samurai officer

Yukio: (YUK•ee•oh) a samurai captain

Samurai 1

Samurai 2

Samurai 3

Narrator: Satsuma, Yukio, and General Kusunoki walk along the top of the outer wall of Chihaya Castle. Banners have been erected along the top of the wall. The banners whip violently in the harsh wind.

Kusunoki: Good evening, Satsuma. I see the men have returned from their raid.

Satsuma: Yes, General, the raid has been a great success. As you ordered, we stole the bakufu banners and put them up on our walls. Now the bakufu are challenged to come get them. Their shame is great.

Kusunoki: Their shame will not win us the battle. We have upset them, yes. But they still outnumber us ten to one. Unless we find a way to lower the odds, the shame of defeat will be ours, not theirs.

Satsuma: But General, how can this happen without losing the lives of many of our men?

Kusunoki: By not using our men to fight them.

Yukio: I don't understand.

Kusunoki: Yukio, I want the samurai of your battalion to make dolls.

Yukio: (*astonished*) Dolls, General?

Kusunoki: Yes, life-sized dolls made out of straw. Have the samurai clothe them well—with armor, shields, and helmets—as befits our best troops.

Yukio: Uh . . . yes, general.

Satsuma: I have a feeling some new trickery awaits our enemy.

Narrator: Several samurai put armor on the straw dolls.

(continued)

◄ **Fortified Castles**
Castles, like Himeji Castle shown here, were mainly built for defense. So they were usually located on rocky cliffs.

Samurai 1: Will someone tell me why we are putting our best armor and weapons on straw dummies?

Samurai 2: I don't know. I just do as I am told.

Samurai 1: There are nearly 30 of them. And we have to finish in an hour.

Samurai 3: You should not complain so. Have you forgotten how, at the Battle of Akasaka, Kusunoki had us build a false outer wall for the castle? When our enemy attacked, the wall fell upon them and killed many. No doubt this is some new strategy of the general's to defeat our foes.

Narrator: During the night, some of the emperor's troops sneak out from the castle and place the straw soldiers in a grove of trees at the foot of the castle. At dawn, the mist begins to lift. Kusunoki and Satsuma stand on the outer wall and observe the battlefield.

Kusunoki: Are the archers ready?

Satsuma: Yes, General.

Kusunoki: Now we will let our enemy's desire to avenge the stolen banners work against them. Have the archers shout a great battle cry.

Narrator: About 500 archers near the inside of the gate shout boldly, "If you want your banners back, come to get them!" Hearing this challenge, the bakufu forces think the emperor's troops are coming out of the castle to fight. Anxious to remove the shame of having had their banners stolen, they rush wildly toward the castle.

Kusunoki: Have the archers go out the gate and form a line in front of the castle.

Narrator: The archers do as they are ordered.

Kusunoki: Fire one volley!

Narrator: The archers shoot a volley of arrows at the bakufu. Enraged, the bakufu charge at the archers.

Kusunoki: Archers, retreat.

Narrator: The archers move back to the castle. By now, the bakufu are close to the castle walls. They see the shadowy figures of the armor-clad straw soldiers among the trees in the grove. They think they are real. Anxious to slaughter their enemies, they rush in that direction—moving close to the base of the castle wall.

Kusunoki: Hurl the rocks!

Narrator: In the grove, the bakufu troops realize they have attacked a bunch of straw men. Suddenly, the emperor's troops hurl large boulders from the top of the wall down upon the bakufu. The boulders crush more than 300 soldiers. About 500 more are severely injured.

Satsuma: (*excitedly*) Look! The enemy is starting to panic and turn back. General, you have outfoxed them once more. We have killed many of the bakufu troops.

Kusunoki: Yes, I doubt they will try anything so foolish again. Now they will probably place the castle under a long siege. But thousands of their troops will be sitting here during the siege instead of fighting elsewhere. This means the bakufu army will be weaker in other parts of Japan. This will greatly help our emperor.

Narrator: The long siege at Chihaya Castle did help the emperor. Kusunoki and his troops held out long enough to allow the emperor's forces to defeat the weaker bakufu forces.

Eventually, the emperor regained his power. But his rule was short-lived.

Three years later, an important warrior wanted the emperor to name him the shogun, or chief general of the military government. The emperor refused, and the warrior led an attack against the emperor. Kusunoki loyally supported the emperor to the end. But the emperor was defeated, and the warrior ruled Japan as shogun.

Samurai warriors attack on horseback. ▼

Activities

1. **TALK ABOUT IT** What qualities of a good leader did Kusunoki have?

2. **WRITE ABOUT IT** Before the bakufu forces attacked Chihaya Castle, Kusunoki's troops stole the bakufu banners. Write a scene in which Kusunoki and his officers are planning how to steal the banners. Remember that Kusunoki often used trickery. (Writing 2.1)

► **MAIN IDEAS**

1 **Government** The emperor of Japan grew weaker, and noble families gained power.

2 **Government** The rising power of the samurai led to military government in Japan.

3 **Government** Military leaders ruled Japan for centuries.

► **TAKING NOTES**

Reading Skill:
Explaining Chronological Order and Sequence

To explain chronological order and sequence means to put events in order based on the time they happened. As you read about Japan during the age of the samurai and shoguns, record major events on a time line like the one shown.

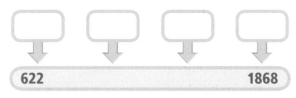

622   1868

S **Skillbuilder Handbook, page R15**

▲ **Samurai Armor** A warrior's armor was usually made of iron, leather, and copper. The helmets were often beautifully decorated.

CALIFORNIA STANDARDS

7.5.3 Describe the values, social customs, and traditions prescribed by the lord-vassal system consisting of *shogun*, *daimyo*, and *samurai* and the lasting influence of the warrior code throughout the twentieth century.

7.5.6 Analyze the rise of a military society in the late twelfth century and the role of the samurai in that society.

HI 2 Students understand and distinguish cause, effect, sequence, and correlation in historical events, including the long- and short-term causal relations.

Samurai and Shoguns

TERMS & NAMES

daimyo

samurai

vassal

shogun

Tokugawa Shogunate

Build on What You Know As you read in Lesson 1, an emperor ruled Japan. But wealthy noble families often held the real power. Nobles would battle one another to gain the power the emperors no longer had.

Nobles Gain Power

1 ESSENTIAL QUESTION Who lost power in Japan?

Japan remained strong and united after Prince Shotoku's rule ended with his death in 622. It was a time of relative peace. The emperor still headed the central government. But he was only a figurehead—someone who appeared to have power but did not. In the 800s, wealthy nobles of the Fujiwara (FOO•jee•WAH•ruh) clan, or family, became the real rulers of Japan. They remained Japan's most powerful family for 300 years.

The Central Government Grows Weak During the 1100s, the power of the central government and the Fujiwaras declined. The government was running out of money. It began to lose authority over larger landholders. These estate owners, called **daimyo** (DY•mee•OH), paid no taxes to the government. They also had their own private armies of trained warriors called **samurai** (SAM•uh•RY), whom you read about in Starting with a Story.

◄ **A Noble's Household**
This fan-shaped illustration shows servants performing daily chores in a noble's household in the 1100s.

◀ **Samurai in Combat**
Samurai loyal to the Minamoto family attacked and burned a palace associated with the Taira clan in 1159.

Feudalism Begins in Japan Daimyo hired samurai warriors both to protect themselves and to attack other daimyo. Powerful families, such as the Taira and the Minamoto, had large armies of samurai. Daimyo often fought among themselves to try to gain more land to increase their wealth and power.

As the power of the daimyo increased, the central government weakened and lawlessness increased. Small landowners wanted protection. To win the aid of a more powerful lord, they pledged their loyalty to that lord. Often, their loyalty included military service. A person who received land and protection from a lord in return for loyalty was called a **vassal**. This lord-vassal system increased the power of large landowners. It also marked the start of feudalism in Japan. This was a system of local rule similar to ancient China and medieval Europe. (You will read about European feudalism in Chapter 9.)

REVIEW Why did power shift from the central government to the nobles?

The Rise of a Military Society

②ESSENTIAL QUESTION How did Japan become a military society?

While nobles fought among themselves, the emperor remained in office. But the emperor no longer held real power. This continued the pattern begun early in Japan's history.

The Emperor and the Shoguns Now military leaders called **shoguns** had taken control. *Shogun* means "supreme commander of the army." A shogun ruled on the emperor's behalf. But usually his own interest came first. Minamoto Yoritomo (MIH•nah•MOH•toh YOH•ree•TOH•moh) became the first shogun in 1192. As shogun, he led more than just the army—he ruled the country. Japan would be under a shogunate, or military government, for nearly 700 years.

The Samurai and the Warrior Code Samurai were fearsome warriors. They vowed to fight for their lord, even if it meant that they could not protect their own family. Dying an honorable death was more

important to them than a long life. Women in warrior families learned to handle weapons to protect their families from bandits when the men were away fighting. At this time, women had higher status than at earlier times. Some inherited land. A few even became samurai.

Samurai lived by an unwritten code of honor called *bushido*. This warrior code called for honor, loyalty, and bravery. It was similar to the chivalry code followed by knights in medieval Europe. Samurai pledged to show respect for the gods and generosity toward the poor. Zen Buddhism was an important aspect of their lives. Samurai values and traditions continued to appeal to the Japanese into the 1900s.

REVIEW Who held power in Japan's military society?

Japanese Society
INTER**ACTIVE**

SKILLBUILDER
INTERPRETING VISUALS
What activities do you see being performed? At what level does production of goods take place?

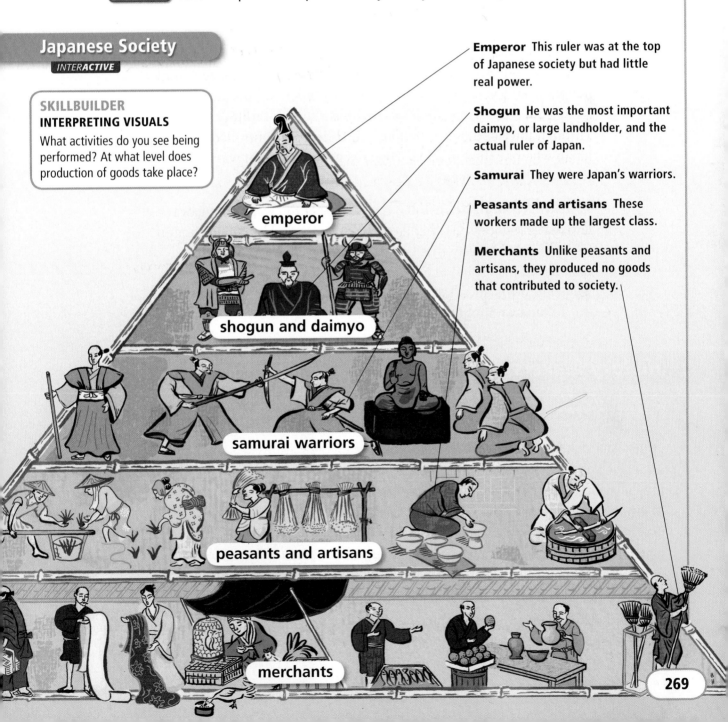

Emperor This ruler was at the top of Japanese society but had little real power.

Shogun He was the most important daimyo, or large landholder, and the actual ruler of Japan.

Samurai They were Japan's warriors.

Peasants and artisans These workers made up the largest class.

Merchants Unlike peasants and artisans, they produced no goods that contributed to society.

emperor

shogun and daimyo

samurai warriors

peasants and artisans

merchants

Three Powerful Warriors Unify Japan

3 **ESSENTIAL QUESTION** How did powerful military leaders unify Japan?

A succession of three strong military leaders helped to unify the country. They ended the fighting between rival daimyo.

Oda Nobunaga In the mid-1500s, a daimyo named Oda Nobunaga (OH•dah• NOH•boo•NAH•gah) began to reunite Japan. He was a fierce warrior who recognized the importance of the guns European traders had introduced into Japan. His soldiers were the first Japanese to use guns in battle and defeated armies that were many times larger than his own. Through wars and negotiations, Nobunaga won control of nearly half of Japan before his death in 1582.

Toyotomi Hideyoshi Shortly after Nobunaga died, his best general, Toyotomi Hideyoshi (TOH•yoo•TOH•mee HEE•deh•YOH•shee), took his place. Hideyoshi was born a peasant. Under Nobunaga, he had risen from a common soldier to become a superb military leader. Through force and political alliances, Hideyoshi controlled all of Japan when he died in 1598. Then his generals fought wars among themselves to rule Japan.

Tokugawa Ieyasu In 1603, the winner of the wars, Tokugawa Ieyasu (TOH•goo•GAH•wah EE•yeh•YAH•soo), was named shogun. He founded a dynasty that held power in Japan until 1868. He established his capital at Edo, later called Tokyo. The rule of Ieyasu and his successors in the Tokugawa family was called the **Tokugawa Shogunate**.

History Makers

Tokugawa Ieyasu (1543–1616)

Conflict surrounded Tokugawa Ieyasu most of his life. When he was two, his mother was separated from the family because of fighting between the families of his mother and father. When he was six, his father was murdered. As an adult, Ieyasu was often in battles, first as a warrior and then as a military leader.

When he became ruler, Ieyasu wanted to make the country peaceful and stable. He had studied history and concluded that only a strong, united government could bring peace and stability.

When Ieyasu became shogun, Japan had growing ties with Europe. Traders and missionaries brought Western ideas and goods to Japan. But Ieyasu and his successors worried about changes foreign influence would bring to Japan. So they drove out foreign merchants and missionaries. They banned Christianity and executed Japanese Christians. They also forbade the Japanese to leave Japan and ended nearly all foreign trade.

In the mid-1600s, Japan went into a period of isolation, or separation from the world, which would last until the 1850s.

Samurai Sword A samurai sword was not only a weapon but was often a work of a swordsmith's artistry. ▼

REVIEW What was the result of the unification of Japan?

Lesson Summary

- As Japan's central government grew weak, violence increased and noble families hired samurai for protection.
- Japan had a military government for centuries.
- In the mid-1500s, three powerful military leaders began to unite Japan.

Why It Matters Now . . .

Japan remains a strongly united country today. It continues to limit immigration and control the country's dealings with foreigners.

---

3 Lesson Review

Homework Helper
ClassZone.com

Terms & Names

1. Explain the importance of

   daimyo   vassal   Tokugawa Shogunate
   samurai   shogun

Using Your Notes

Explaining Chronological Order and Sequence Use your completed time line to answer the following question:

2. What event would you consider the most important in Japan's history during this period? Why? (HI 2)

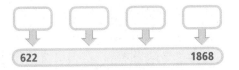

622   1868

Main Ideas

3. Why did the emperor lose power in the 1100s? (7.5.3)

4. What caused the rise of military government in Japan? (7.5.6)

5. What was the structure of Japanese feudal society? (7.5.3)

Critical Thinking

6. **Making Inferences** Why do you think the values of the samurai code appealed to the Japanese for centuries? (7.5.6)

7. **Summarizing** How did Japanese attitudes toward foreigners change in the 1600s and why? (HI 2)

Activity   **Internet Activity** Use the Internet to research the code of the samurai. Create a poster using simple images with labels to show the main principles. (7.5.3)
INTERNET KEYWORD: *samurai code*

Research Links
ClassZone.com

Himeji
Castle   **JAPAN**

An Inside Look at Himeji Castle

Purpose: To learn about castle life in 16th- and 17th-century Japan

A samurai warrior in 16th- and 17th-century Japan probably lived in the large castle of the lord, or daimyo, he served. It might have looked like Himeji Castle, shown here. Daimyo built castles primarily for defense, but they also served as a center to administer the lord's estate.

These castles, and the towns that were built around them, housed servants, soldiers, officials, and the samurai's families. As shown below, many different activities dominated castle life at this time.

A **Soldiers** As a soldier living in the castle, you were always ready to protect it. During periods of peace, you spent much of your time training on the castle grounds.

B **Scribes** As a scribe, you wrote letters and also made sure that a messenger delivered them to other samurai and to the emperor.

C **Samurai Wives** As the wife of a samurai, you educated your daughters and taught them manners. However, you might also have commanded the castle's soldiers while your husband was away.

D **Entertainment** You and your family might have enjoyed the talents of musicians.

E **Servants** If you were a servant at this time, you spent your days preparing food, cleaning rooms, washing clothes, and keeping the castle in good order.

CALIFORNIA STANDARDS

7.5.3 Describe the values, social customs, and traditions prescribed by the lord-vassal system consisting of *shogun, daimyo,* and *samurai* and the lasting influence of the warrior code in the twentieth century.

Activities

1. **TALK ABOUT IT** What types of activities are taking place in this castle in medieval Japan? Which people are performing the activities?

2. **WRITE ABOUT IT** Choose one of the activities shown and write a brief dialogue between the people in that scene. (Writing 2.1)

Lesson

4

▶ **MAIN IDEAS**

1 **Culture** Korea was independent for much of its history, but it adopted many elements of the culture of China.

2 **Government** Vietnam was one of several small kingdoms that developed on the mainland of Southeast Asia in the shadow of China.

3 **Culture** The Khmer Empire prospered between two powerful neighbors, China and India.

▶ **TAKING NOTES**

Reading Skill: Comparing and Contrasting

Comparing and contrasting involves finding similarities and differences between two or more things in order to better understand them. Use a chart like this one to compare and contrast accomplishments of the kingdoms discussed in this lesson.

Korea	Vietnamese Kingdoms	Khmer Empire
1.	1.	1.
2.	2.	2.
3.	3.	3.
4.	4.	4.

S **Skillbuilder Handbook, page R4**

▲ **Ancient Korean Map** This Korean map of the world dates from the 17th century. It was based on a Chinese map. The enlarged area shows what Koreans believed to be East Asia.

CALIFORNIA STANDARDS

7.3.1 Describe the reunification of China under the Tang Dynasty and reasons for the spread of Buddhism in Tang China, Korea, and Japan.

CST 1 Students explain how major events are related to one another in time.

HI 1 Students explain the central issues and problems from the past, placing people and events in a matrix of time and place.

HI 2 Students understand and distinguish cause, effect, sequence, and correlation in historical events, including the long- and short-term causal relations.

Korea and Southeast Asia

TERMS & NAMES

Koryo

celadon

Nam Viet

Khmer Empire

Angkor Wat

Build on What You Know As you read earlier in this chapter, Japan's development was significantly influenced by China. Japan was not alone, though, in feeling the influence of more powerful neighbors. Smaller kingdoms in Korea and Southeast Asia rose in the shadow of China to the north and India to the west.

An Independent Korea

1 **ESSENTIAL QUESTION** Why did Korea adopt many elements of the culture of China?

Korea is one of the world's oldest nations. According to legend, it was founded in the 2300s B.C. Korea developed independently of China but was influenced by Chinese culture. Throughout their history, the Koreans borrowed Chinese practices and ideas. Like Japan, they adapted them to meet their own needs.

Geography of Korea Korea is a peninsula. It extends from northern China, on the Asian mainland. (See map on page 276.) Only a river separates Korea from its much larger neighbor to the north. So movement between the two countries has been easy throughout history. Korea is also close to the islands of Japan. Chinese culture sometimes spread to Japan by way of Korea.

Korean Painting Korean warriors on horseback hunt deer and tigers in this fifth-century tomb mural. ▼

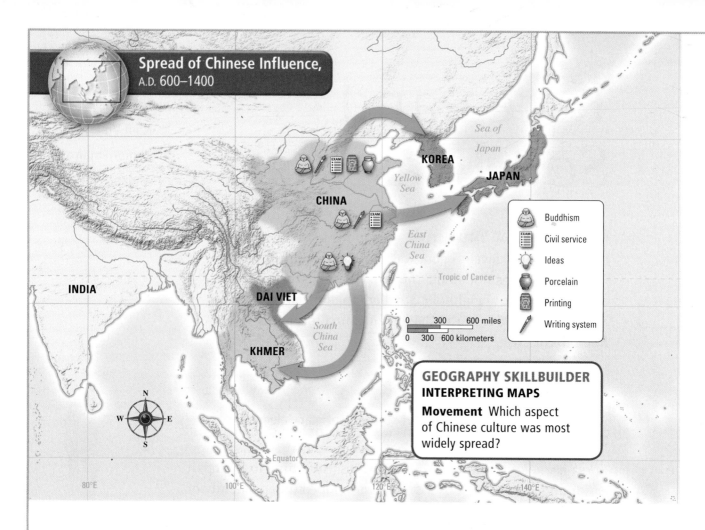

Spread of Chinese Influence, A.D. 600–1400

KOREA

JAPAN

Sea of Japan

Yellow Sea

CHINA

East China Sea

Tropic of Cancer

INDIA

DAI VIET

South China Sea

KHMER

Equator

Buddhism	
EXAM	Civil service
Ideas	
Porcelain	
Printing	
Writing system	

0   300   600 miles
0   300   600 kilometers

N W E S

80°E   100°E   120°E   140°E

GEOGRAPHY SKILLBUILDER
INTERPRETING MAPS
Movement Which aspect of Chinese culture was most widely spread?

Founding Korean Kingdoms Korea's first inhabitants were probably nomads from the north. They lived in clans. In 108 B.C., Chinese of the Han Dynasty invaded northern Korea. The Koreans resisted and won back most of the lost territory by 75 B.C. During the next 700 years, three main kingdoms formed in Korea. These kingdoms fought wars for supremacy of the Korean peninsula.

The Silla kingdom in the southeast conquered the other two kingdoms during the 600s. As it did, it also drove out the remaining Chinese. Silla united Korea for the first time. But soon Silla nobles were fighting among themselves for power. Peasants, too, rebelled. These conflicts caused Silla to collapse in 935. A kingdom called **Koryo** replaced it. The name Korea evolved from this kingdom's name.

China Influences Korea The Koryo rulers modeled their government after China's. Koreans also learned rice cultivation, papermaking, and printing from the Chinese. In addition, they adapted Chinese artistic styles, including a method for making pottery. In fact, Korea became famous for its **celadon** (SEHL•uh•DAHN), pottery that has a bluish-green glaze. (See photograph on page 279.) Koreans also learned about and adopted two belief systems from China: Confucianism and Buddhism. Buddhism was adopted first by the nobles and later by the common people. It then spread from Korea to Japan.

Resisting Foreign Invaders Korea remained united and
independent for centuries. But it had to struggle to be free of foreign
control. In the 1200s, the Mongol conquerors of China invaded the
kingdom. They controlled Korea until their empire in China collapsed
in the late 1300s. In 1392, the powerful Yi family established a
new Korean dynasty called the Choson Dynasty. It turned back an
invading army from Japan in the late 1500s. The Choson Dynasty
ruled Korea for more than 500 years.

REVIEW What influences shaped Korea's development?

Vietnamese Kingdoms

2 **ESSENTIAL QUESTION** What role did China play in the development
of Vietnamese kingdoms?

Mountains separate the mainland peninsula of Southeast Asia from
China to the north. (See map on pages 246–247.) So movement
between the two regions was mostly by sea or along coastal plains.
Chinese soldiers, merchants, and missionaries followed these routes
as they brought China's culture to Vietnam and other regions.

The Kingdom of the Viets The Viets were a people who lived
just south of China in what is now Vietnam. In 111 B.C., the Chinese
Empire conquered their kingdom, called **Nam Viet**. At first, China's
rule was not harsh. Mostly, Chinese rulers wanted to use the region's
ports on the South China Sea. Chinese trading ships needed places to
stop on the way to and from India and the islands of Southeast Asia.

Soon, though, China's rulers began to force the Vietnamese
to adopt their culture. For example, they required them to speak
Chinese and to wear Chinese clothes. They also forced them to follow
the principles of Confucianism and Daoism. But many Vietnamese
resisted these efforts.

Driving Out the Chinese In A.D. 40,
Trung Trac, a noblewoman whose husband
had been killed by the Chinese, and her
sister, Trung Nhi, led a rebellion against
China's rule. Their forces were successful
at first but were later overpowered. The
Vietnamese rebelled several times during
the next few centuries. But at the same
time, they continued to adopt elements of
Chinese culture, including Buddhism. In
the 900s, China's Tang Dynasty weakened,
and the Vietnamese broke free.

The Trung Sisters
The Trung sisters
ruled briefly as
co-queens after
they drove out the
Chinese. ▼

Dai Viet In 939, the Vietnamese established an independent kingdom called Dai Viet. In the 1200s, Mongols who had conquered China attacked Dai Viet. Three times, the Vietnamese turned back the invaders. But the fighting left the kingdom weakened. In 1407, Chinese soldiers of the Ming Dynasty invaded the kingdom. The Vietnamese eventually drove them out in 1428 and returned to ruling themselves. Dai Viet then strengthened its position by seizing Champa, a rival kingdom to the south.

REVIEW How was Vietnam shaped by outside influences?

The Khmer Empire

3 ESSENTIAL QUESTION How was the Khmer Empire able to prosper between two powerful neighbors?

The most powerful and longest-lasting kingdom on the mainland of Southeast Asia was the **Khmer Empire**. It was centered in what is today Cambodia. (See map on page 247.) The culture of Khmer was significantly influenced by its western neighbor India, as well as by its northern neighbor China.

The Khmers A people known as the Khmers established a kingdom on the mainland peninsula in the 500s. It prospered mainly because of its successful cultivation of rice. Peasant farmers built excellent irrigation systems to help them grow rice. They also developed better seeds that may have allowed them to grow three crops a year.

The Khmers learned rice farming from the Chinese. But India had a stronger cultural influence on the Khmers. They took ideas about rule by a god-king, a writing system, and forms of religion—Hinduism and Buddhism—from India.

Angkor Wat
The temple at Angkor Wat is considered the masterpiece of Khmer architecture. ▼

Angkor Era In the late 800s, the Khmer ruler began to build a new capital at Angkor. Several temples were constructed here. The most famous formed a complex known as **Angkor Wat**, built in the 1100s. It still exists and covers nearly one square mile. It is the largest religious structure in the world. The temples honored the Hindu god Vishnu. Buddhist statues were added later.

The Khmer Empire reached its peak in the 1200s. It declined under attack from neighboring empires. In 1431, Angkor fell to the Thais, a people from what is now Thailand.

REVIEW How did the Khmers adapt to outside influences?

Lesson Summary

- Korea developed independently from China but borrowed and adapted many aspects of its culture.
- Vietnam was invaded and influenced by China for much of its history.
- The Khmer Empire was influenced by India.

Why It Matters Now. . .

China and India are the two most populous nations in the world, with more than one billion people each. They remain powerful cultural influences on their Asian neighbors and countries around the globe.

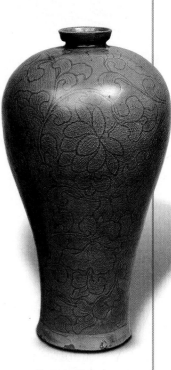

▲ **Korean Celadon Vase** Celadon pottery was developed during the Koryo dynasty. It is highly prized.

---

4 Lesson Review

Homework Helper
ClassZone.com

Terms & Names

1. Explain the importance of

Koryo	Nam Viet	Angkor Wat
celadon	Khmer Empire	

Using Your Notes

Comparing and Contrasting Use your completed chart to answer the following question:

2. What common themes do you notice about Korea, Vietnam, and Khmer? (HI 1)

Korea	Vietnamese Kingdoms	Khmer Empire
1.	1.	1.
2.	2.	2.
3.	3.	3.
4.	4.	4.

Main Ideas

3. How did developments in China affect its influence on Korea and the kingdoms of Southeast Asia? (7.3.1)

4. What was a recurring theme in the history of the Vietnamese people? (CST 1)

5. Where did Buddhism spread from China? (7.3.1)

Critical Thinking

6. **Making Inferences** What role did geography play in the early development of mainland Southeast Asia? (HI 1)

7. **Comparing and Contrasting** How are the histories of Korea and the kingdoms of Southeast Asia similar? different? (HI 2)

Activity

Making a Map Take out the map that you began in Chapter 2. Then use the map on page 247 to draw the boundaries of China, Japan, Korea, Dai Viet, and Khmer. (Framework)

VISUAL SUMMARY

Japan, Korea, and Southeast Asia

Land of the Rising Sun (7.5.1)
- Japan is a country of over 4,000 mountainous islands.
- Distinctive family and social structures developed.
- Prince Shotoku promoted Chinese influence.

Growth of Japanese Culture (7.5.4)
- Shintoism and Buddhism became important religions.
- Unique forms of literature and drama were created.
- The arts reflected a love of natural beauty.

Samurai and Shoguns (7.5.6)
- Noble families began to gain power.
- Emperor and central government were weakened.
- Military society developed with the shogun as real ruler.
- Japan unified under Tokugawa Shogunate in 1603.

Korea and Southeast Asia (7.3.1)
- Region was influenced by China and India.
- Korea was founded in 2300s B.C.
- Vietnamese drove out Chinese invaders several times.
- Khmer Empire established in what is today Cambodia.

TERMS & NAMES

Explain why the words in each set below are linked with each other.

1. **regent** and **Prince Shotoku**
2. **noh** and **kabuki**
3. **daimyo** and **shogun**
4. **Khmer Empire** and **Angkor Wat**

MAIN IDEAS

Land of the Rising Sun (pages 250–255)

5. How was the diet of people in Japan influenced by its location? (7.5.1)
6. Why was Prince Shotoku's support for Buddhism important? (7.5.2)

Growth of Japanese Culture (pages 256–265)

7. What are the forms of Buddhism that became popular in Japan? (7.5.4)
8. Why is haiku unlike other forms of poetry? (7.5.5)

Samurai and Shoguns (pages 266–273)

9. What powers did the emperor and the shogun each have during the period of military government? (7.5.3)
10. How did the loss of tax revenue bring about military government? (7.5.6)

Korea and Southeast Asia (pages 274–279)

11. What was the relationship between China and Korea before the rise of the Koryo kingdom? (HI 2)
12. What cultures influenced the Khmer kingdom? (7.3.1)

CRITICAL THINKING Big Ideas: Geography

13. **MAKING INFERENCES** How do you think Japan's history would be different if it were part of the Asian mainland? (7.5.1)
14. **SUMMARIZING** What role did Japan's island location play in its development? (7.5.1)
15. **EXPLAINING GEOGRAPHIC PATTERNS** How did China's geography affect its ability to spread such ideas and influences as Buddhism to other regions? (7.3.1)

ALTERNATIVE ASSESSMENT

1. **WRITING ACTIVITY** Select an individual mentioned in this chapter whom you would most like to meet. You might select a person named in this chapter or a person from a group described in this chapter. Write one paragraph explaining why you selected this person. (Writing 2.4)

2. **INTERDISCIPLINARY ACTIVITY—ART** Use books or the Internet to research Japanese calligraphy. Find an example to share with the class. Describe what the calligrapher was writing about. Explain how the calligrapher tried to make the writing beautiful. (REP 4)

3. **STARTING WITH A STORY** Review the essay you wrote telling why living by a code of honor is or is not important. Now that you have read the chapter, would you answer the question in a different way? If so, how? (Writing 2.4)

Technology Activity

4. **ESTABLISHING E-MAIL CORRESPONDENCE** Select one of the countries studied in this chapter—Japan, Vietnam, Korea, or Cambodia. Create a list of questions to ask Japanese, Korean, Vietnamese, or Cambodian students. Work with your teacher to establish e-mail correspondence with the students. Some areas of inquiry to consider:
- facts about their country
- information about their daily lives
- their knowledge of the United States (REP 1)

Research Links ClassZone.com

Reading Maps Japan is composed of four large and more than 4,000 small mountainous islands. Use the map and your knowledge of world history to answer the questions. (7.5.1)

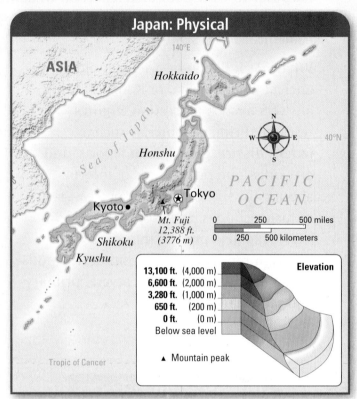
Japan: Physical

1. **What is the largest of the Japanese islands?**
   A. Hokkaido   C. Honshu
   B. Kyushu   D. Shikoku

2. **Which physical factor was most responsible for Japan's isolation?**
   A. It was composed of nearly 4,000 islands.
   B. The islands were mountainous.
   C. Only one of the four major islands was large.
   D. It was separated from the Asian mainland by a large body of water.

Test Practice ClassZone.com

Additional Test Practice, pp. S1–S33

Writing About History

Research Reports:
Young People in Ancient Asia

CALIFORNIA STANDARDS
Writing 2.3 Write
research reports.

Purpose: To write a research report on what life was like for young people in an ancient Asian culture

Audience: Your classmates

What was it like to be a 12-year-old in ancient China, Japan, or Korea? Finding answers to such a question requires research. Primary sources—such as letters, diaries, government reports, and artworks—are rich sources of information about daily life. Secondary sources—such as history books, encyclopedias, and Web sites—can also provide information. A **research report** is a composition that pulls together information from several primary and secondary sources.

▲ Learning calligraphy in Japan

Organization & Focus

Your assignment is to write a 500- to 700-word research report on the lives of young people in one of the Asian cultures covered in this unit. Your report should have an introduction, a body, and a conclusion, plus a **bibliography**—a list of the sources used in preparing the report.

Choosing a Topic Skim Chapters 7 and 8, looking for aspects of Chinese, Japanese, Korean, or Southeast Asian history that interest you. When you have chosen a culture to write about, be sure to limit your topic to a certain time period. A suitably limited topic might be "Chinese young people during the Tang Dynasty."

Identifying Purpose and Audience Imagining yourself in history is a powerful way to appreciate past events. Vivid details can help readers to imagine themselves in the past. Your purpose, then, is to research the lives of young people and explain their lives in a way that helps your classmates—your audience—connect to history.

Research & Technology

Create a list of questions to guide your research. These might include: "What amusements did young people have?" and "How were they educated?"

Use these tools in your research process.

Technology Tip Your word processor will automatically place your footnotes properly. Use the instruction manual or help feature to learn how to do this.

In the Library	Online
1. Use the card catalog, either traditional or electronic, to find books.	1. Use search engines to find Web sites on your topic.
2. Refer to the *Readers' Guide to Periodical Literature* for magazine articles.	2. Use available databases of information. Ask your librarian for recommendations.
3. Refer to encyclopedias.	3. Use electronic encyclopedias with links to the World Wide Web.

Taking Notes Take notes from your sources. At the top of each note, write a heading, such as "Education." Write down key ideas in your own words. If you find a well-written phrase or sentence you want to use, record it in quotation marks. Keep track of each source, including title, author, publisher, date, and page number or Web address. You will need these for your bibliography.

Outlining and Drafting The headings on the note cards will help you group them into categories. Use your categories and notes to outline your report. As you write your report, whenever you use a quotation or fact from a source, credit the source in a footnote or in-text citation.

Evaluation & Revision

Share your first draft with a reader. Let your reader's reaction and your own rereading guide your revision. You might need to add, take out, replace, or move information.

Prepare your bibliography. Use a language arts textbook, such as McDougal Littell's *Language Network*, or a school handbook to find the correct form for each type of source.

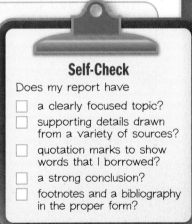

Self-Check

Does my report have

- [ ] a clearly focused topic?
- [ ] supporting details drawn from a variety of sources?
- [ ] quotation marks to show words that I borrowed?
- [ ] a strong conclusion?
- [ ] footnotes and a bibliography in the proper form?

Publish & Present

After editing your report, prepare a final copy. If possible, present your report to the class. After all the presentations, discuss the similarities and differences of life in different cultures and at different times.

UNIT 5

Medieval Europe

Interact with History ▶

Siege of a Castle, A.D. 1000
Your mission is to conquer an enemy castle. It won't be easy. The castle defenders are waiting along the castle walls, ready to strike back. You march up with all of the soldiers and equipment you think you need. You then finalize the invasion plans with your men and begin your attack.

How will you take over the castle?

WebQuest
ClassZone.com

Large, mobile wooden towers gave attacking forces a closer shot at the enemy and enabled troops to jump over the castle wall.

What might be a way for castle defenders to combat this weapon?

Attackers used such weapons as a trebuchet, which slung heavy rocks at the enemy.

What might be the advantages and disadvantages of using long-range weapons?

Castle defenders repelled attackers by
shooting arrows and dumping boiling
water and oil on those who got too close.

**What made trying to capture a
castle so difficult?**

Feudal Europe

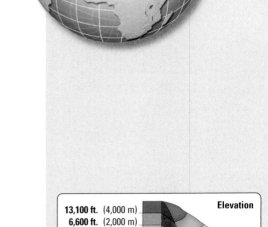

Before You Read: Anticipation Guide

Copy the statements below in your notebook. Write "agree" or "disagree" next to each one. After you have read the chapter, look over the statements again.

- Political disorder and constant warfare led to the development of feudalism in Europe.
- Feudal manors relied on trade with each other.
- European and Japanese feudalism were the same.

Big Ideas About Feudal Europe

Culture Many societies rely on family roles and social classes to keep order.

After the fall of Rome, a political and social system called feudalism developed in Europe. Feudal society was divided into well-defined classes. At the top were kings and wealthy landowners. At the bottom were peasants, many of whom worked for the landowners.

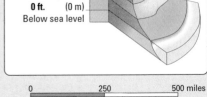

Elevation	
13,100 ft.	(4,000 m)
6,600 ft.	(2,000 m)
3,280 ft.	(1,000 m)
650 ft.	(200 m)
0 ft.	(0 m)
Below sea level	

```
0          250         500 miles
0     250       500 kilometers
```

Integrated Technology

eEdition
- Interactive Maps
- Interactive Visuals
- Starting with a Story

INTERNET RESOURCES
Go to **ClassZone.com** for
- WebQuest
- Homework Helper
- Research Links
- Internet Activities
- Quizzes
- Maps
- Test Practice
- Current Events

EUROPE

500

700

511
Frankish ruler Clovis dies.
(portrait of Clovis) ▶

768
Charlemagne becomes king of the Franks.

WORLD

527
Justinian becomes emperor of Byzantine Empire.

661
Umayyad Caliphate begins rule of Muslim empire.

Europe, A.D. 1000
INTERACTIVE

KINGDOM OF NORWAY

FINLAND

KINGDOM OF SWEDEN

North Sea

KINGDOM OF DENMARK

Baltic Sea

IRELAND

ENGLAND

Elbe River

Vistula River

Oder River

DUCHY OF POLAND

Thames River

English Channel

HOLY ROMAN EMPIRE

Rhine River

Seine River

Danube River

Loire River

ALPS

KINGDOM OF HUNGARY

ATLANTIC OCEAN

FRANCE

KINGDOM OF BURGUNDY

Po River

KINGDOM OF CROATIA

Danube River

Adriatic Sea

SERBIA

Bay of Biscay

Apennines

BULGARIA

KINGDOM OF LEON

Pyrenees

Corsica

Duero River

Balearic Sea

CALIPHATE OF CORDOBA

Iberian Peninsula

Sardinia

Tyrrhenian Sea

Sicily

Mediterranean Sea

900s
Outside invasions spur development of feudalism.
◄ (painting of a Viking ship)

1095
First Crusade pitting Christians against Muslims begins.

900

1100

960
Song Dynasty begins in China.
(Song sculpture of a child) ▶

Becoming a Knight

CALIFORNIA STANDARDS

Reading 3.4 Identify and analyze recurring themes across works (e.g., the value of bravery, loyalty, and friendship; the effects of loneliness).

Background: As you will learn in this chapter, knights were skilled warriors who fought for and protected the powerful landowners who ruled much of Europe during the Middle Ages. Knights began their training early in life. During their mid-teens, they served as squires. Squires acted as aides to knights. They also learned how to use many different weapons and how to handle a horse during combat. After about five years of service, a squire became a knight. This event took place during a special ceremony—often in a church.

Knight's helmet ▶

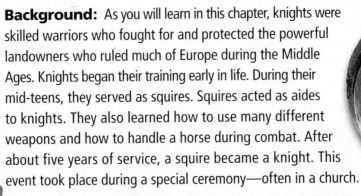

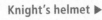

The teenage boy sits in a chapel, and he can hardly contain his excitement. In a few hours, his days as a squire will end. He is about to become a knight. Soon his family and friends will arrive. They will all watch as the knight this boy has served for years lays his sword on the boy's shoulder and declares him ready for knighthood.

As he waits for the ceremony to begin, he considers everything he has been through to get here. He learned to follow a code of conduct that required knights to show loyalty to the nobles they served and to protect the weaker members of society.

During his years as a squire he also trained long and hard to use a sword and ride a horse. His knight, Sir Robert, recently let him join him on one of his missions. The two of them set out to capture several bandits that had been terrorizing the area.

As the boy rode through thick forestland, the bandits suddenly attacked. The squire's horse reared up on its hind legs. He fought hard to control the animal. Sir Robert swiftly swung his sword. One bandit fell to the ground and then another. However, a third bandit rushed Sir Robert and raised his sword to strike. The boy regained control of his horse and rammed the attacking bandit. The bandit fell to the ground and ran off.

After this episode, the boy truly felt ready to become a knight. But as the moment approaches, he is feeling more and more nervous. He knows there will be many more battles and challenges ahead. Will he be up to facing them?

What have you learned that will help you become an outstanding knight?

Reading & Writing

1. **READING: Theme** Discuss the ways in which a knight was expected to be brave and loyal.

2. **WRITING: Summary** Write a paragraph explaining what qualities you think were necessary to be a knight. After you are finished, read the chapter to learn more about the life of knights and how they were expected to act.

CALIFORNIA STANDARDS Writing 2.5
Write summaries of reading materials.

▶ MAIN IDEAS

1 **Geography** Climate, topography, and other geographic features helped bring about the feudal way of life in Europe.

2 **Belief Systems** Despite the upheaval in Europe, Christianity survived and spread.

3 **Government** Feudalism provided a social and political structure during the Middle Ages.

▶ TAKING NOTES

Reading Skill: Categorizing

Categorizing involves grouping similar things together. As you read about the beginning of the Middle Ages and feudalism in Lesson 1, use a chart like the one shown here to record details that help explain the role that each group played in the feudal structure.

Lords	Vassals	Serfs

S Skillbuilder Handbook, page R6

▲ **Clovis I** One of the more powerful kingdoms in Europe was built by the Franks. Their early leader was Clovis I.

CALIFORNIA STANDARDS

7.6.1 Study the geography of Europe and the Eurasian land mass, including their location, topography, waterways, vegetation, and climate and their relationship to ways of life in Medieval Europe.

7.6.2 Describe the spread of Christianity north of the Alps and the roles played by the early church and by monasteries in its diffusion after the fall of the western half of the Roman Empire.

7.6.3 Understand the development of feudalism, its role in the medieval European economy, the way in which it was influenced by physical geography (the role of the manor and the growth of towns), and how feudal relationships provided the foundation of political order.

The Development of Feudalism

TERMS & NAMES
Middle Ages
Charlemagne
monastery
feudalism
lord
serf

Build on What You Know What comes to mind when you think of the Middle Ages? Perhaps it is knights in armor and fierce sword battles. Or maybe you picture large stone castles, where kings and queens and other nobles lived. In this chapter, you will learn about these aspects of the Middle Ages. You will also learn about a new political, economic, and social system known as feudalism that developed during this period.

Setting of Medieval Europe

1 ESSENTIAL QUESTION What changes occurred in Europe after the fall of Rome?

The collapse of Rome in the late fifth century ushered in a roughly 1,000-year period (500–1450) known as the **Middle Ages**. This time is also known as the medieval period, from the Latin words *medium* (middle) and *aevum* (age). During much of the Middle Ages, Europe contained many small kingdoms that often fought one another.

The European Continent The continent of Europe occupies about one-fifth of what is known as the Eurasian land mass. As its name indicates, the Eurasian land mass, or Eurasia, is the continuous stretch of land that includes Europe and Asia.

Roman Ruins The famous Roman road the Appian Way is one of many Roman ruins that still stands centuries after the empire's fall. ▼

Topography and Waterways Major geographic features make up Europe's general boundaries. Europe borders the Atlantic Ocean on the west and the Arctic Ocean to the north. The Mediterranean Sea serves as Europe's southern boundary. In the east, Europe is separated from Asia by the Ural Mountains.

The topography, or landforms, of Europe is diverse. (See map on page 289.) Rugged mountain ranges, such as the Apennines and the Alps, run across southern Europe. Much of northern and western Europe is a series of plains and farmland.

Meanwhile, rivers wind their way through many regions of Europe. The longest river in Europe is the Volga. It begins near Moscow, Russia, and runs 2,293 miles southeast into the Caspian Sea. Many smaller rivers and streams flow throughout Europe. As a result, river travel has long played a key role in trade and communications throughout the continent.

Climate and Vegetation The climate patterns of Europe vary across the continent. Northern Europe experiences cold winters, while southern Europe has mild winters and hot and often dry summers. Most of Europe receives plenty of rainfall. As a result, there is much forest and farmland.

Generally mild weather and dependable rainfall have enabled agriculture to thrive throughout Europe. In the warmer weather of the Mediterranean region, for example, farmers of Medieval Europe could grow citrus fruits. Meanwhile, crops such as wheat and barley thrived in the climate of western Europe.

The abundance of forests, farmland, and rivers played a key role in shaping ways of life in Medieval Europe. As you will learn, Europe would become home to many small kingdoms and small estates that thrived on their own. This was due in large part to the favorable climate and topography, which allowed people to take and produce much of what they needed from the land.

European Landscape
The Moselle River valley in Germany highlights many of Europe's geographic features, including mountains, rivers, and lush land. ▼

Cultural Changes The political and cultural landscape of Europe changed greatly after the fall of Rome. The Romans no longer ruled the region by unifying its many different groups under one government. Instead, numerous Germanic kingdoms dominated the lands that had once been ruled by a mighty empire.

The Germanic groups that occupied Europe after the fall of Rome brought great cultural changes to the continent. The Romans, as you recall, had a highly developed government. They believed that the state was more important than the individual. The Romans also emphasized learning.

The Germanic peoples, on the other hand, had little notion of a state. Unlike the Romans, Germanic people lived in small communities and maintained order through unwritten rules and traditions. As a result, they did not develop large governments or trade systems. In addition, they did not emphasize learning scholarly works.

Learning and Trade Decline The educated middle class all but disappeared during the Middle Ages. Most schools ceased to exist. Eventually, few people could read or write Latin. Europeans mostly forgot about the great achievements of the ancient Greeks and Romans in the arts and learning.

As trade throughout Europe disappeared, so did many cities. Most city dwellers made their living by trading goods. The lack of trade prompted many of them to move to the country, where they made their living by farming.

REVIEW What role did geography play in shaping medieval society in Europe?

Changes to Europe after the Fall of Rome
Decline in the size and power of governments
Reduction in long-distance trade
Decline in learning and devotion to Greek and Roman culture
Disappearance of cities and rise of rural villages and farms
Growth of numerous Germanic kingdoms

▲ **Germanic Cup** This cup lined with gemstones belonged to the Germanic group the Franks.

Christianity Grows and Spreads

2 ESSENTIAL QUESTION What factors helped Christianity to grow and spread?

One institution that survived the fall of Rome was the Christian Church. Many German rulers and their subjects converted to Christianity. These conversions helped to spread Christianity throughout Europe. As you recall from Chapter 2, a group of Germanic people called the Franks established one of the more powerful kingdoms in Europe during the Middle Ages. The Franks and their powerful leaders played a significant role in strengthening Christianity north of the Alps in the lands of northern and western Europe.

Clovis and the Franks In 486, a Frankish leader named Clovis invaded Roman Gaul (now France). He defeated the last great Roman army in Gaul. Clovis then went on to defeat other weaker Germanic groups. By 507, his kingdom stretched west from the Rhine River to the Pyrenees Mountains. Around this time, Clovis converted to Christianity. In time, most of his subjects became Christians.

The Rule of Charlemagne Clovis died in 511. Some two centuries later, in the early 700s, a powerful leader named Charles Martel became ruler of the Franks. Charles expanded the Frankish kingdom through military conquest. Charles Martel's son, Pepin the Short, became the next king of the Franks. Pepin ruled until his death in 768. His son Charles, also known as **Charlemagne** (SHAHR•luh•MAYN), then took over the kingdom.

Charlemagne built a European empire greater than any known since ancient Rome. By 800, the powerful Frankish king ruled much of western Europe. Charlemagne created a highly organized and well-run empire. He established new laws to help keep order in the kingdom. In addition, he enlisted powerful landholders known as counts to govern the many different regions of the empire. Charlemagne often traveled throughout the kingdom to ensure that the counts ruled justly.

Under the leadership of Charlemagne, Christianity grew stronger across Europe. Charlemagne spread Christianity through his conquests. A deeply religious man, he also encouraged and sometimes forced his subjects to become Christians.

History Makers

Charlemagne (742?–814)

Charlemagne certainly looked and acted like the powerful ruler of a large kingdom. He was tall and strong and enjoyed physical activities, especially swimming. He normally instructed his nobles and friends to swim with him. In addition, he also thrived on little sleep. He was said to wake up four or five times a night—often waking those around him to finish a task or give him reports.

Charlemagne also showed an interest in scholarly matters, including astronomy. However, one thing may have kept him from learning more. Historians speculate that like many others during the Middle Ages, the mighty Frankish king may have been unable to read.

The Growth of Monasteries While powerful rulers helped to spread Christianity, devoted worshipers did the same. During the Middle Ages, religious structures known as monasteries arose across Europe. **Monasteries** were places where religious followers called monks practiced a life of prayer and worship. In monasteries, monks studied Christian works and made copies of the Bible. By doing so, they preserved and promoted the ideas and beliefs of Christianity.

▲ **French Monastery** A monastery dating back to the 12th century sits amid a field of lavender in Vaucluse Province, France.

REVIEW Who was Charlemagne, and how did he strengthen Christianity?

Feudalism: A New Social Order

3 **ESSENTIAL QUESTION** What was feudalism and how did it work?

After Charlemagne's death in 814, his son, Louis I, became emperor. When Louis died, his three sons fought each other for control of the kingdom. They all signed a treaty in 843 that divided the empire into three parts. This split caused the Frankish kingdom to grow weak and unstable. The decline of Frankish rule led to disorder across Europe.

Various groups of people took advantage of this disorder. Scandinavian pirates, called Vikings, terrorized coastal villages. Muslims raided coastal areas in Italy and southern France. A group known as the Magyars attacked towns throughout central Europe. Beginning in the mid-800s, Europe became a place of constant conflict and warfare.

The Emergence of Feudalism This unstable and violent period led to the creation of a political and social system known as **feudalism**. Feudalism emerged largely as a way for kings and nobles to hold onto their land and power amid so much warfare.

Feudalism was based on an agreement between two groups of nobles—lords and vassals. A **lord** was a powerful noble who owned land. Lords gave pieces of their land to lesser nobles called vassals. These plots of land were called fiefs. In return for the land, the vassal owed his lord service in his court and army. Many vassals were warriors known as knights. Thus, they fought on behalf of the lord. Other vassals hired knights to defend the lord and his property. Vassals also paid taxes to their lord in return for their fief.

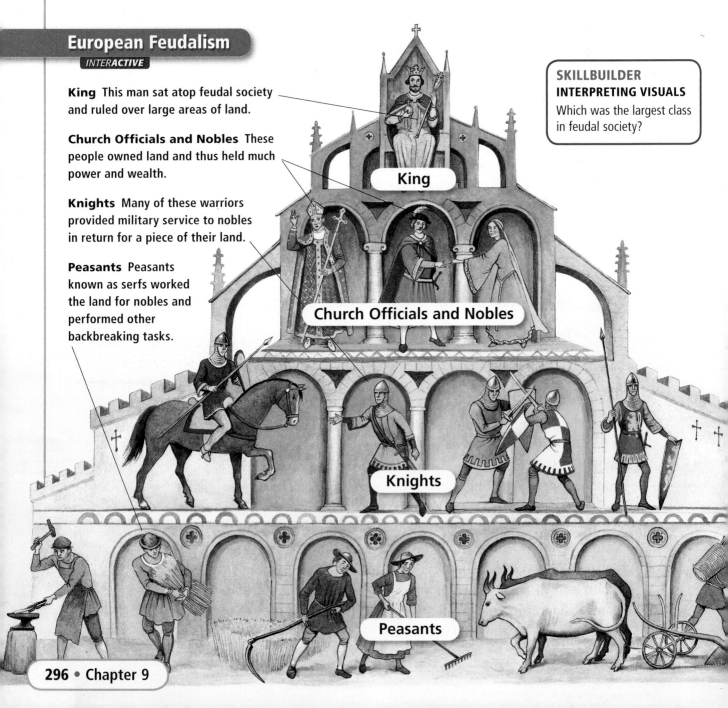

European Feudalism
INTERACTIVE

King This man sat atop feudal society and ruled over large areas of land.

Church Officials and Nobles These people owned land and thus held much power and wealth.

Knights Many of these warriors provided military service to nobles in return for a piece of their land.

Peasants Peasants known as serfs worked the land for nobles and performed other backbreaking tasks.

King

Church Officials and Nobles

Knights

Peasants

> **SKILLBUILDER**
> **INTERPRETING VISUALS**
> Which was the largest class in feudal society?

The Feudal Structure Feudal society was highly structured. The king ruled at the top of society. Next came wealthy landowners and high-ranking church members. Serving below them were the knights. At the bottom of society were the peasants. Most peasants were **serfs**. Serfs were people who lived and worked on the land belonging to a lord or a vassal. In return, the nobles granted them shelter and protection.

Feudalism created a new political structure in Europe. Europe became home to many small kingdoms and estates ruled by kings and powerful nobles. In the next lesson, you will learn more about everyday life in Europe during the feudal age.

REVIEW What role did serfs play in feudalism?

Lesson Summary

- The Germanic invasions transformed Europe.
- Kings and monasteries helped to spread Christianity.
- Warfare and the constant threat of invasion led to the development of feudalism in Europe.

Why It Matters Now . . .

The strength and popularity of Christianity today is due in part to all of the efforts to promote the religion during the Middle Ages.

---

1 Lesson Review

Homework Helper
ClassZone.com

Terms & Names

1. Explain the importance of

Middle Ages	monastery	lord
Charlemagne	feudalism	serf

Using Your Notes

Categorizing Use your completed chart to answer the following question:

2. Which group held the least amount of power? (7.6.3)

Lords	Vassals	Serfs

Main Ideas

3. How did geography help shape the way of life in Europe during the Middle Ages? (7.6.1)

4. What role did monasteries play in strengthening Christianity? (7.6.2)

5. What role did vassals play in the structure of feudalism? (7.6.3)

Critical Thinking

6. **Understanding Cause and Effect** How did warfare and the constant threat of invasion in Europe help lead to the creation of feudalism? (7.6.3)

7. **Making Inferences** The Middle Ages is sometimes called the "Dark Ages." Why do you think this is so? (REP 5)

Activity

Creating a Diary Entry Use library resources to explore the life led by monastery monks. Use the information to create a diary entry for a day in the life of a monk. (7.6.2)

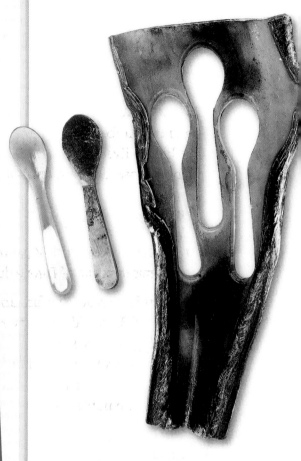

Lesson 2

▶ MAIN IDEAS

1 **Economics** The manor system provided an economic structure in Europe during the Middle Ages.

2 **Culture** During the Middle Ages, knights were highly valued for their military skills.

3 **Culture** During the Middle Ages, towns gradually reappeared and thrived.

▶ TAKING NOTES

Reading Skill: Comparing and Contrasting
Comparing and contrasting means finding similarities and differences between two or more things. Use a chart like the one below to highlight the differences between life on a manor and life in a town.

```
            Middle Ages

   Manor Life        Town Life
   1. _____         1. _____
   2. _____         2. _____
```

S **Skillbuilder Handbook, page R4**

▲ **Animal Horn Spoons**
Residents of Medieval Europe ate meals with spoons sculpted from animal horns.

CALIFORNIA STANDARDS

7.6.1 Study the geography of Europe and the Eurasian land mass, including their location, topography, waterways, vegetation, and climate and their relationship to ways of life in Medieval Europe.

7.6.3 Understand the development of feudalism, its role in the medieval European economy, the way in which it was influenced by physical geography (the role of the manor and the growth of towns), and how feudal relationships provided the foundation of political order.

CST 3 Students use a variety of maps and documents to identify physical and cultural features of neighborhoods, cities, states, and countries and to explain the historical migration of people, expansion and disintegration of empires, and the growth of economic systems.

Daily Life in Medieval Europe

TERMS & NAMES

manor

knight

chivalry

guild

Build on What You Know During the Middle Ages, feudalism formed the basis of European society. But what was it like to live in the feudal system? In this lesson, you will read about how the main classes of feudal society lived.

The Manor System

1 ESSENTIAL QUESTION What role did the manor system play in the economic structure of Europe during the Middle Ages?

As you have read, warfare and political disorder characterized much of Europe during the Middle Ages. In the absence of strong central governments, Europe became little more than a series of kingdoms and lands held by high-ranking nobles. In such a setting, there was little trade or commercial interaction. Instead, the lands held by the nobles became the center of most economic activity.

The Role of the Manor The main part of a noble's land was called a **manor**. The center of a manor was the house where the lord and his family lived. Often the manor house was a fortified building or castle. Surrounding the manor house was the lord's estate. Much of the estate consisted of farmland.

Dover Castle Dover Castle, one of the more fortified castles of the medieval period, sits along the famous Cliffs of Dover in southern England. ▼

299

Geography and the Manor System

The geography of Europe played a key role in the development of self-contained manors. Plenty of rainfall and mild temperatures created good conditions for farming. In addition, numerous streams and lakes offered fresh water and fish. In short, the land provided nearly everything the manor needed.

Such a way of life could not develop in other places. For example, the Arabian peninsula had a hot, dry climate that did not support agriculture. Shown here is a chart comparing the farmable land in four present-day and similarly-sized countries, two in Europe and two in drier regions.

SKILLBUILDER
INTERPRETING VISUALS
Which country has the second-greatest amount of farmable land?

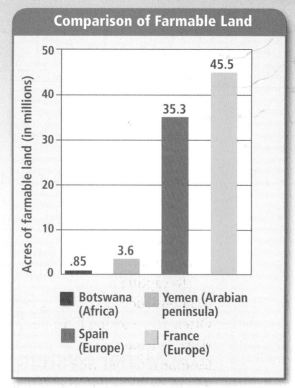

Comparison of Farmable Land

Acres of farmable land (in millions)

- Botswana (Africa): .85
- Spain (Europe): 35.3
- Yemen (Arabian peninsula): 3.6
- France (Europe): 45.5

Source: *The Statesman's Yearbook,* 2004

Manor Life and the Economy As Lesson 1 explained, peasants called serfs lived and worked on the manor. The serfs farmed the land, which formed the economic basis of the manor system. Serfs were said to be "bound to the soil." This meant that they were considered part of the property. They remained on the land if a new lord acquired it.

Feudalism and manor life had a powerful effect on the medieval European economy. The land on a manor supplied residents with most of the things they needed. As a result, most activity—from farming to woodworking to wine making—took place on the manor. Manors became worlds unto themselves, and few people ever left the property.

REVIEW Why did residents of the manor rarely have to leave?

The Age of Chivalry

2 ESSENTIAL QUESTION What was chivalry?

As you learned in Lesson 1, **knights** were often vassals, or lesser nobles, who fought on behalf of lords in return for land. During the Middle Ages, conflict often broke out between various lords. Many times, they settled a quarrel simply by attacking each other. To do their fighting, lords relied on knights, who were skilled horse riders and fighters.

Knighthood and Chivalry Knights were not merely professional fighters. They were expected to live by a code of honor known as **chivalry**. They had to demonstrate a strong religious faith and a willingness to defend the Catholic Church. They were also expected to protect women and the weak. In addition, knights were supposed to fight against injustice and show courage in every battle they fought. The battles that knights and other warriors fought ranged from bloody open field skirmishes to grueling attacks on castles.

To capture a castle, lords and knights used weapons such as battering rams and catapults. Often an attacking force put a castle under siege. During a siege, an army tries to prevent food or supplies from entering a castle. Its goal was to slowly starve the people inside and force them to surrender.

REVIEW How was a knight expected to act under the honor code of chivalry?

The Growth of Towns

3 ESSENTIAL QUESTION What was town life like during the Middle Ages?

Around A.D. 1000, town life began to return to Europe. This was due in large part to the fact that a number of lords became increasingly powerful. They brought peace and stability to numerous regions. As a result, people felt more safe and secure. Merchants began to travel more freely and trade their goods. Wherever merchants settled, builders and other tradespeople gathered around them.

Town Life Most medieval towns were dirty, cramped, and busy places. In the center of town were the market square and a cathedral. The streets were narrow, filthy, and usually not paved. After a rain, streets turned to mud that was often knee-deep. Most of the houses were made out of wood and easily caught fire. As a result, entire towns often burned down. In France, between 1200 and 1225, the city of Rouen burned down six times!

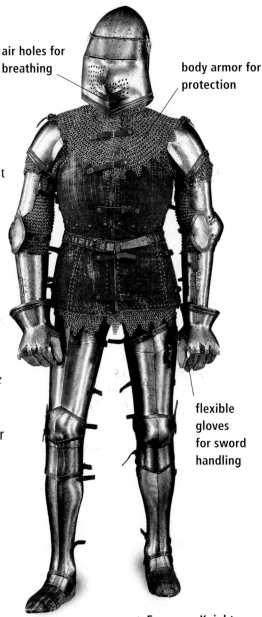

air holes for breathing

body armor for protection

flexible gloves for sword handling

▲ **European Knight** Knights often wore a suit of armor to protect themselves in battle. These suits made it difficult to move quickly—the average suit weighed around 65 pounds!

The Guilds In towns, people with the same occupation formed groups called **guilds**. Many guilds were formed by tradespeople, such as goldsmiths, bakers, weavers, and dyers. Guilds made rules that controlled the quantity and quality of production. The guilds watched out for their members and worked to make sure everyone found employment.

The formation of the guilds was one of the many unique aspects of life in Medieval Europe. However, a feudal society developed thousands of miles away in Japan that showed both similarities and differences to the way of life in Europe.

REVIEW What led to the growth of towns in Medieval Europe?

Lesson Summary

- The manor system shaped the economy in feudal Europe.

- During an age marked by warfare and fighting, knights became a highly valued group in society.

- As warfare declined and trade increased, town life reappeared during the Middle Ages.

Why It Matters Now . . .

Today people who share an occupation often form groups known as unions. Unions help their members gain better wages and working conditions.

---

2 Lesson Review

Homework Helper
ClassZone.com

Terms & Names

1. Explain the importance of

    manor   knight   chivalry   guild

Using Your Notes

Comparing and Contrasting Use your completed chart to answer the following question:

2. What was the main economic activity in each setting? (7.6.3)

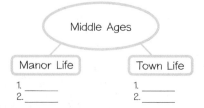

Main Ideas

3. How were serfs an important part of the manor system? (7.6.3)

4. Why were knights highly valued in medieval society? (HI 2)

5. Why did tradespeople form guilds? (7.6.3)

Critical Thinking

6. **Identifying Issues and Problems** Do you think the lack of long-distance trade hurt society during the early Middle Ages? Explain. (7.6.3)

7. **Drawing Conclusions from Sources** What were the benefits and drawbacks of town life in Medieval Europe? (HI 1)

Activity

Making a Map Using the map on page 287 as a reference, draw the major mountain ranges and rivers of Europe on the world map you have created. (7.6.1)

Debate the Life of a Knight

Goal: To debate the following historical issue: Did the benefits of being a knight outweigh the drawbacks?

Materials & Supplies
- research materials on the life of knights
- note cards
- pens or pencils

Prepare

1. Review Lesson 2, "Daily Life in Medieval Europe," on pages 299–302. Examine the age of chivalry and the life that medieval knights led.

2. Use books and the Internet to learn more about the rewards and difficulties of being a knight.

1. Life of a knight too risk-filled

A.

B.

C.

1. Knights enjoyed a rewarding life.

A.

B.

C.

Do the Activity

1. Review your research and decide which positions you favor.

2. List the arguments that support your opinion. Make a note card for each argument. Include any quotations or evidence.

3. Organize your note cards so the arguments are in a logical order. Then write an outline of a speech stating your position and supporting arguments.

4. Hold a class debate. First, all the students who saw too many drawbacks to being a knight should give their speeches. Then all students who believed that the benefits outweighed the drawbacks should speak.

Follow-Up

Discuss as a class which group made the better case.

Extension

Researching Debaters often try to prove their opponent is wrong by using evidence to weaken their opponent's arguments. Research to find evidence that disproves the arguments of the other side.

Life on a Medieval Manor

Purpose: To learn about daily life on a manor in feudal Europe

During much of the Middle Ages, the manor served as the center of life for many people in Europe. Two well-defined classes lived alongside each other on the manor—the wealthy lord or vassal and his family and the poor peasants, or serfs.

EUROPE

A

A Hard Labor The main job of the serfs was to farm the land. Rain or shine, they worked in the fields every day except Sundays and holy days. Serfs had to give most of what they farmed to their lord.

B The Manor House The lord of the manor lived with his family in a large house that was often built of stone. They lived a comfortable and leisurely life compared with the serfs'. Among other things, they hosted large dinners consisting of many meats.

C The Serf Home Most serfs lived in small, damp huts made of wood and mud. The ground often served as the floor. Each hut usually had only one bed, which was made out of piles of leaves or straw. Families did their cooking in the hut over a fire on the floor. Most peasants survived on a simple vegetable stew and stale bread.

D Recreation Lords and their families liked to spend much of their leisure time hunting in the woods on their property. Serfs, meanwhile, engaged in more simple forms of recreation. A popular game among younger serfs was knucklebones. It was played much like marbles—except the pieces were the various tiny and round bones of farm animals.

CALIFORNIA STANDARDS

7.6.3 Understand the development of feudalism, its role in the medieval European economy, the way in which it was influenced by physical geography (the role of the manor and the growth of towns), and how feudal relationships provided the foundation of political order.

Activities

1. **TALK ABOUT IT** How did home life for the serfs and their lord differ?

2. **WRITE ABOUT IT** Imagine you are leading a group of fellow serfs to ask your lord to consider improving your conditions. Write several paragraphs describing your life and steps the lord might take to improve it. (Writing 2.4)

▶ MAIN IDEAS

1 **Government** European and Japanese feudalism shared similar political structures and social values.

2 **Culture** Despite similarities, feudal Europe and Japan showed key cultural differences.

3 **Culture** Aspects of feudal culture still exist in present-day Europe and Japan.

▶ TAKING NOTES

Reading Skill: Comparing and Contrasting

As you read about similarities and differences between European and Japanese feudalism, use a chart like the one below to compare the main political, social, and cultural characteristics of each land.

	Political	Social	Cultural
Europe			
Japan			

 Skillbuilder Handbook, page R4

▲ **European Women** Women in Medieval Europe, shown here spinning thread, enjoyed fewer rights than women in Medieval Japan.

CALIFORNIA STANDARDS

Framework To understand what was distinctive about European culture during this period, students should compare Western Europe with Japan during the High Middle Ages. They will see that the two cultures had aspects in common: a feudal, lord-vassal system, with military leaders (shogun), great lords (daimyo), and knights (samurai). Both feudal societies emphasized personal loyalty to the lord, military skills, a strict code of honor, self-discipline, and fearlessness in battle. Students will also see striking differences in cultural values, religious beliefs, and social customs, including women's roles.

REP 4 Students assess the credibility of primary and secondary sources and draw sound conclusions from them.

Feudalism in Europe and Japan

▶ TERMS & NAMES

bushido

epic poem

Build on What You Know If you recall your reading from Chapter 8, you know that the Europeans and Japanese developed a similar type of feudal society at roughly the same time. As you will learn, these two cultures did indeed share many characteristics. However, they differed in a number of significant ways as well.

Similar Societies

1 ESSENTIAL QUESTION What similarities did the feudal societies in Europe and Japan share?

Japanese and European feudalism shared a number of similarities—both in political structure and in social values.

Two Feudal Systems Both the European and Japanese feudal systems developed as a result of a weak central government. The Japanese emperor had no real power. After the Frankish king Charlemagne died in 814, most European kings did not have much power either. Because strong central governments did not exist, individual landowners were able to gain power in both regions. In Europe, these landowners were called lords. In Japan, they were called daimyo (DY•mee•OH).

Japanese Castle A lasting symbol of both Medieval Europe and Medieval Japan was the castle. This castle from feudal Japan still stands in Kobe, Japan. ▼

Similar Structures Both lords and daimyo had many peasants working for them. Farming was the main economic activity on both European and Japanese estates. In addition, the governments and landowners of both regions relied on professionally trained soldiers for protection. These soldiers were called knights in Europe. In Japan, they were known as samurai. In addition, both Europe and Japan had strong military leaders. As you recall, these military leaders were known as shoguns in Japan.

Similar Values In the feudal systems of both Japan and Europe, personal loyalty was greatly valued. The military skills of both knights and samurai were also highly valued. As you read in Lesson 2, knights were expected to follow a code of behavior known as chivalry. According to this code, knights were kind to the weak, loyal to their lord, and courageous in battle. The samurai code of behavior was known as **bushido**. According to this code, samurai were generous, fearless in battle, and above all, loyal to their daimyo, or lord.

> **REVIEW** What values did both the European and Japanese feudal cultures admire?

iron plate to protect against neck stabbing

belt for holding sword

bow for slinging arrows

▲ **Samurai Warrior** Like knights, samurai dressed for ultimate protection during battle.

Cultural Differences

2 ESSENTIAL QUESTION How did European and Japanese feudalism differ?

Although the feudal systems of Japan and Europe had many similarities, they also were different. Among the key differences were those involving religion, literature, and the role of women.

Religion Both knights and samurai were expected to be deeply religious. However, the two groups of warriors practiced different religions. Knights were Christians. Christianity is based on the life and teachings of Jesus Christ. As you read in Chapter 8, samurai practiced ancient Shintoism as well as a form of Buddhism known as Zen. Buddhism is based on the teachings of the Buddha.

Haiku

One of the most noted Japanese haiku writers was Matsuo Basho. Here is one of the many haikus he wrote.

As I ride my horse
Through cold rice-fields my shadow
Creeps along the ground.

◀ Matsuo Basho

from *Beowulf*

Translated by Burton Ruffel

The epic poem *Beowulf* tells the story of a hero who battles the evil Grendel and other monsters. Below is a small excerpt from the poem.

My people have said, the wisest, most knowing
And best of them, that my duty was to go to the Danes'
Great king. They have seen my strength for themselves,
Have watched me rise from the darkness of war,
Dripping with my enemies' blood. I drove
Five great giants into chains, chased
All of that race from the earth. I swam
In the blackness of night, hunting monsters
Out of the ocean, and killing them one
By one; death was my errand and the fate
They had earned. Now Grendel and I are called
Together, and I've come.

> **DOCUMENT–BASED QUESTION**
> What is the subject of each poem?

Literature The literature in feudal Europe and Japan also differed. Poetry thrived in both Medieval Europe and Medieval Japan. However, the types of poetry that gained popularity in each land were anything but similar. Poetry called haiku became popular in feudal Japan. Haiku are short poems that follow a common pattern (three lines with five, seven, and five syllables per line). Most haiku deal with nature.

In Europe, the epic poem became popular. An **epic poem** is a long poem usually about warriors or heroes. The poems often include legends and myths and heroes with superhuman qualities. Famous European epics include *Beowulf* and *The Song of Roland*.

Lyric poetry was also a significant part of European literature. These poems resemble songs. Most lyric poetry praises women and ideal love. Poet-musicians called troubadours usually wrote such poems.

Women in Europe While lyric poetry praised women, the role of women in feudal Europe was limited. Medieval women, for example, often had no say in whom they married. The woman's father and future husband often made this decision. In addition, women were expected to stay at home. They were trained in household chores, such as sewing, spinning, weaving, and farming.

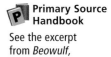

Primary Source Handbook

See the excerpt from *Beowulf*, page R45.

Women in Japan Women in feudal Japanese society enjoyed more equal status with men. In samurai families, women were allowed to inherit part of the family's estate. Women could also join Buddhist convents. In addition, they were expected to live up to the values of honor and courage. Often women were trained in the martial arts. In fact, some women became samurai and fought alongside their husbands. Gradually, however, the role of women became more restricted.

REVIEW How did the main styles of poetry in Medieval Europe and Japan differ?

Legacies of Feudalism

3 ESSENTIAL QUESTION What lasting legacy did feudal society leave in Europe and Japan?

Both feudal Europe and Japan left legacies. Aspects of the feudal culture can be seen today in Japan and Europe. For example, Japanese weddings are usually based on a Shinto ceremony. The Shinto religion was widely practiced in Medieval Japan. Haiku continues to be a popular form of poetry in Japan. Also, many Japanese today have a strong sense of duty and loyalty to the family. These attitudes are the legacy of the old code of bushido.

The ideals of loyalty and honor also remain strong in Europe—especially within the military. Another legacy of the European Middle Ages is surnames, or family names. Many European family names have medieval origins. For example, during the Middle Ages, a person took a family name from his or her job. Family names such as Baker, Carpenter, Cook, and Taylor (tailor) are still common today.

Summary of European Feudalism		
Political	**Economic**	**Social**
• Kings and large landowners rule in place of central governments.	• Most people live and work in a rural setting on farms or manors. • Manors provide residents with much of what they need and become the center of economic and social life.	• Society becomes highly structured, with kings at the top followed by nobles, knights, and peasants. • Age of chivalry emerges as knights become highly valued and respected for their loyalty and military skills.

▲ Knight's shield

Many medieval structures, such as churches and castles, still stand in Europe. So do key institutions from this era. One of the most powerful institutions during this time was the Catholic Church. In the next chapter, you will learn more about the power of the Church during the Middle Ages. You will also learn about key political and military events of the Middle Ages—and how the institutions of Medieval Europe gave way to new institutions.

REVIEW What impact did the code of bushido have on Japan?

Lesson Summary

- The feudal system of Japan and the feudal system of Europe shared similar structures and values.

- The two feudal systems differed in many ways. These differences can be seen in the areas of religion, literature, and the role of women.

- The impact of both Japanese and European feudalism is still felt today.

Why It Matters Now . . .

From attitudes toward the family to family names, a number of cultural aspects from the Middle Ages still influence Europe and Japan today.

3 Lesson Review

Homework Helper
ClassZone.com

Terms & Names

1. Explain the importance of
   bushido   epic poem

Using Your Notes

Comparing and Contrasting Use your completed chart to answer the following question:

2. In which society did women enjoy greater freedom? (Framework)

	political	social	cultural
Europe			
Japan			

Main Ideas

3. How were the codes of bushido and chivalry similar? (Framework)

4. What were the main cultural differences between feudal Europe and feudal Japan? (Framework)

5. What cultural traditions have survived from the Middle Ages in Japan? (Framework)

Critical Thinking

6. **Understanding Cause and Effect** How did the political structure help to bring about feudalism in Europe and Japan? (Framework)

7. **Forming and Supporting Opinions** Did Japanese or European feudalism leave a more lasting legacy? Explain. (Framework)

Activity **Internet Activity** Use the Internet to learn about other works of epic poetry. Conduct further research on a poem that interests you and present your findings in a brief speech. (Framework)
INTERNET KEYWORD: *epic poetry*

Comparing and Contrasting

Goal: To determine from a passage the similarities and differences between feudalism in Europe and Japan

CALIFORNIA STANDARDS
REP 4 Students assess the credibility of primary and secondary sources and draw sound conclusions from them.

Learn the Skill

Comparing means looking at similarities and differences between two or more things. Contrasting means examining only the differences between them. Historians compare and contrast events, personalities, and beliefs in order to better understand them.

S See the Skillbuilder Handbook, page R4.

Practice the Skill

1 Read the passage on the opposite page. Look for aspects of feudal society in Europe and Japan that may be compared and contrasted.

2 To find similarities, look for clue words indicating that two things are alike. Clue words include *both*, *each*, *like*, *as*, and *similarly*.

3 To contrast, look for clue words that show how two things differ. Clue words include *by contrast*, *however*, *except*, and *yet*.

4 Making a Venn diagram like the one below will help you identify similarities and differences between two things. In the separate ovals, list the characteristics of each subject not shared by the other. In the overlapping area, list characteristics shared by both subjects. This Venn diagram identifies the similarities and differences between feudalism in Japan and Europe.

Example:

4 JAPAN
- Warriors called samurai
- Favored haiku poetry
- Women had many rights

BOTH
- Breakdown in central government
- Rise of powerful landowners
- Reliance on skilled warriors

EUROPE
- Warriors known as knights
- Favored epic poetry
- Women had few rights

The paragraph below examines some of the similarities and differences between Japanese and European feudalism. As you read, look for the clue words to help you compare and contrast these two cultures.

Japanese and European Feudalism

1 Japanese and European feudalism showed both similarities and differences. **2** In both societies, feudalism developed as a result of a breakdown in the central government and the rise to power of individual landowners. Fierce warriors who fought on behalf of the powerful landowners played a key role in **2** each society. In Europe, these warriors were known as knights. In Japan, they were called samurai.

Some of the most notable differences between the two cultures could be seen in the areas of literature and the role of women. In Japan, a short poem known as the haiku was popular. **3** By contrast, Europeans preferred the long narrative style of epic poetry.

Meanwhile, the Japanese provided many rights to women. In Europe, **3** however, women had few rights or privileges.

▲ Japanese samurai

▼ European knight

Apply the Skill

Turn to page 214 in Chapter 7, Section 1. Read "Changes in Belief Systems." Make a Venn diagram showing the similarities and differences between Confucianism and Buddhism.

VISUAL SUMMARY

Feudal Europe

Culture (7.6.3)
- Feudalism brought great cultural changes to Europe. Aspects of European feudalism were similar to feudalism in Japan.

Economics (7.6.3)
- Trade declined as warfare and disorder spread across Europe. Instead, manors became the center of most economic and production activity.

Belief Systems (7.6.2)
- Powerful leaders and the work done at monasteries helped to spread Christianity.

Geography (7.6.1)
- Europe had many rivers and much farmland. This enabled feudal manors to produce much of what they needed. As a result, the manor system grew and thrived.

Government (7.6.3)
- Europe came under the rule of small kingdoms and large landowners.
- The landowners aligned with lords and knights to help create order. This relationship became the foundation of feudalism.

TERMS & NAMES

Explain why the words in each set below are linked with each other.

1. **Middle Ages** and **feudalism**
2. **lord** and **serf**
3. **knight** and **chivalry**

Use the following terms in their own sentence.

4. **bushido**
5. **epic poem**

MAIN IDEAS

The Development of Feudalism (pages 290–297)

6. How did the geography of Europe help promote the growth of a rural way of life? (7.6.1)
7. What helped Christianity to continue spreading after the fall of the Roman Empire? (7.6.2)

Daily Life in Medieval Europe (pages 298–305)

8. What factors made the manor the center of the European economy during the Middle Ages? (7.6.3)
9. What were the characteristics of a medieval town? (7.6.3)

Feudalism in Europe and Japan (pages 306–313)

10. What were similarities and differences between Japanese and European feudalism? (Framework)
11. In what way did women in feudal Japan enjoy more rights than women in feudal Europe? (Framework)

CRITICAL THINKING Big Ideas: Culture

12. **COMPARING AND CONTRASTING** How did culture during the Middle Ages and in the Roman Empire differ? (7.6.3)

13. **DETECTING HISTORICAL POINTS OF VIEW** How might a serf and a noble differ in their view of feudal society? (7.6.3)

14. **DRAWING CONCLUSIONS FROM SOURCES** What conclusions can you draw about European and Japanese culture based on their similarities and differences? (Framework)

ALTERNATIVE ASSESSMENT

1. **WRITING ACTIVITY**—Imagine you are a medieval woman in Europe who has just learned about the life of women in feudal Japan and the rights they enjoy. Write a brief speech encouraging greater rights for women in Europe. (REP 5)

2. **INTERDISCIPLINARY ACTIVITY— ARCHITECTURE** Use books and the Internet to learn more about castle architecture. Based on your research, draw a sketch of your own castle. (7.6.3)

3. **STARTING WITH A STORY**
 Review the story you read about becoming a knight. Now that you have learned more about what it took to be a knight, why do you think someone would want to lead such a dangerous and duty-filled life? (7.6.3)

Technology Activity

4. **CREATING A MULTIMEDIA PRESENTATION** Work with a partner to make a multimedia presentation about the various commercial, religious, and social activities that took place in medieval towns. Include

- drawings and Internet photos
- possible trade objects (7.6.3)

Research Links
ClassZone.com

Reading Graphs The following graph shows the growth of villages in one region of present-day Germany during the Middle Ages. Use the information and your knowledge of history to answer the questions. (7.6.3)

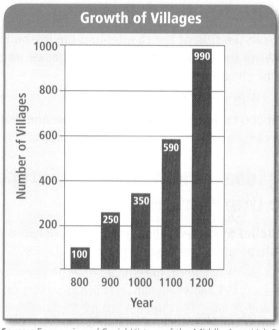

Growth of Villages

Source: *Economic and Social History of the Middle Ages Vol. 2*

1. **Between which years did the number of villages grow the most?**
   A. 800–900
   B. 900–1000
   C. 1000–1100
   D. 1100–1200

2. **How many new villages emerged between 800 and 1200?**
   A. 350
   B. 590
   C. 890
   D. 990

Test Practice
ClassZone.com

Additional Test Practice, pp. S1–S33

Chapter 10

Medieval Europe and the Ottoman Empire

Before You Read: Predicting

Scan the title of the chapter and the lesson titles. Write three questions you think might be answered in the chapter. One example is

What were the Crusades?

If you find the answer to one of your questions as you read, write it down in your notebook.

Big Ideas About Medieval Europe and the Ottoman Empire

Belief Systems Belief systems and religions may shape governments and society.

In Medieval Europe, the Catholic Church became as powerful as any individual kingdom and filled important social and political roles. The Crusades against Muslim Palestine were a result of the influence of religion and politics. The Ottoman Empire was also shaped by religion.

Integrated Technology

eEdition
- Interactive Maps
- Interactive Visuals
- Starting with a Story

VIDEO *A History of the Middle Ages*

INTERNET RESOURCES
Go to **ClassZone.com** for
- WebQuest
- Homework Helper
- Research Links
- Internet Activities
- Quizzes
- Maps
- Test Practice
- Current Events

1209
The Franciscans, founded by Francis of Assisi, are recognized by the pope.
◀ (St. Francis)

EUROPE

1000   1100   1200

WORLD

1000s
The Yoruba people of Ife in Africa produce detailed sculptures.
◀ (Ife terra cotta sculpture)

1127
The northern Song Dynasty in China collapses.

Europe and the Ottoman Empire, c. 1500
INTERACTIVE

ATLANTIC OCEAN

Arctic Circle

NORWAY

SCOTLAND

IRELAND

SWEDEN

North Sea

ENGLAND

DENMARK

London

Baltic Sea

RUSSIAN PRINCIPALITIES

Paris

HOLY ROMAN EMPIRE

LITHUANIA-POLAND

FRANCE

Augsburg

OTTOMAN EMPIRE

HUNGARY

VENICE

PAPAL STATES

Belgrade

Danube River

Black Sea

PORTUGAL

Madrid

Rome

NAPLES

OTTOMAN EMPIRE

Constantinople

SPAIN

Adriatic Sea

Aegean Sea

Mediterranean Sea

0   250   500 miles
0   250   500 kilometers

Political border in 1500

1337
Hundred Years' War begins.

1347
A devastating plague reaches Europe.

1453
The Hundred Years' War ends.

1520
Suleyman I becomes sultan of the Ottoman Empire. ▶

1300

1400

1500

1325
The Aztec establish their capital city in what is today Central Mexico.
◀ (Aztec mask)

1464
Songhai Empire begins in West Africa.

317

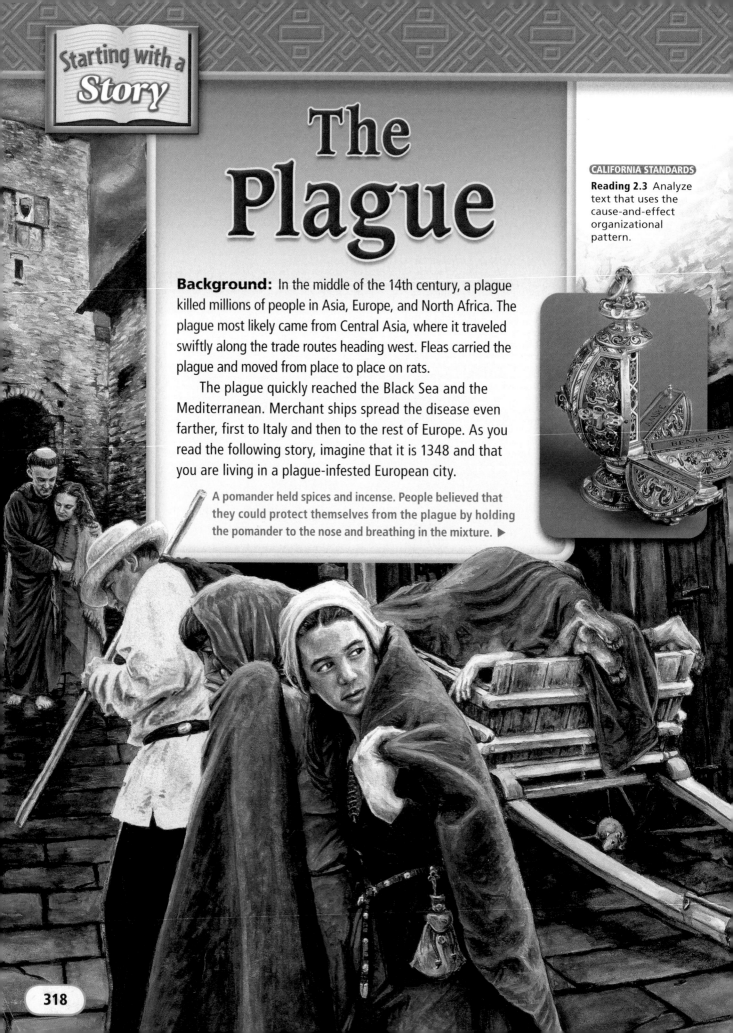

The Plague

CALIFORNIA STANDARDS
Reading 2.3 Analyze text that uses the cause-and-effect organizational pattern.

Background: In the middle of the 14th century, a plague killed millions of people in Asia, Europe, and North Africa. The plague most likely came from Central Asia, where it traveled swiftly along the trade routes heading west. Fleas carried the plague and moved from place to place on rats.

The plague quickly reached the Black Sea and the Mediterranean. Merchant ships spread the disease even farther, first to Italy and then to the rest of Europe. As you read the following story, imagine that it is 1348 and that you are living in a plague-infested European city.

A pomander held spices and incense. People believed that they could protect themselves from the plague by holding the pomander to the nose and breathing in the mixture. ▶

The year 1348 has been filled with misery for everyone I know. Just last week, my best friend Claire's aunt died. It was hard for me to listen to her description of her aunt's death. Claire said her aunt's armpits had suddenly swelled up. She said they were truly awful to look at—that some of her swellings were as big as apples. After that, black and blue splotches appeared on her arms and legs. They called for a doctor, but he said he could do nothing. Claire's aunt was dead within three days. I hate to say it, but her death was hardly unusual. It seems like the plague has killed half the people in my town.

My parents have done their best to lend a hand to Claire's family. They help look after the children and see to the cooking and cleaning. They also made arrangements for the funeral. It was difficult to find people willing to take part, but a few close friends did come. I suppose we were lucky that anyone at all came. Nowadays, many of the dead have neither family nor friends to see to their burial. They die alone in their houses, and only the smell of their decaying bodies tells neighbors of their passing. In Siena, where we live, townspeople have begun digging large ditches where the corpses of such people are hastily buried.

My Siena was once an orderly and beautiful city. But the plague has killed many of the town's authorities, and many others have fled. My father has taken steps to protect us from the plague. He nailed thick boards over our windows. He also forbade us to bathe. He says that if our pores are clogged, the disease might have more trouble getting into our bodies. My parents have talked about leaving the city. But they decided, for now anyway, that we should stay and help Claire's family.

What do you think will happen to your community because of the plague?

Reading & Writing

1. **READING: Cause-and-Effect** Understanding effects is an important part of historical study. With a partner, discuss the effects of the plague as described in this story.

2. **WRITING: Narration** If a plague hit your town today, would you stay to help people or would you leave? Write a personal letter to a friend that explains your decision.

CALIFORNIA STANDARDS **Writing 2.1**
Write fictional or autobiographical narratives.

▶ MAIN IDEAS

1 **Belief Systems** The Catholic Church was very influential because of its structure and leadership.

2 **Government** Monarchs and popes struggled with each other for control of society.

3 **Belief Systems** The Catholic Church took a leading role in education as well as religion.

▶ TAKING NOTES

Reading Skill: Summarizing

Summarizing is restating a passage in fewer words, including only the main ideas and most important details. In Lesson 1, summarize each of the main sections using a chart like the one below.

Section	Summary
Power of the Church	
Conflict Between Monarchs and the Papacy	
The Church and Society	

 Skillbuilder Handbook, page R3

▲ **St. James Cathedral, Compostela, Spain** The Church was an important part of life in the Middle Ages. Many Christian pilgrims came to this cathedral. The cathedral is said to contain the body of St. James, one of the apostles of Jesus.

CALIFORNIA STANDARDS

7.6.4 Demonstrate an understanding of the conflict and cooperation between the Papacy and European monarchs (e.g., Charlemagne, Gregory VII, Emperor Henry IV).

7.6.8 Understand the importance of the Catholic church as a political, intellectual, and aesthetic institution (e.g., founding of universities, political and spiritual roles of the clergy, creation of monastic and mendicant religious orders, preservation of the Latin language and religious texts, St. Thomas Aquinas's synthesis of classical philosophy with Christian theology, and the concept of "natural law").

The Role of the Catholic Church

TERMS & NAMES
clergy
Pope Gregory VII
Emperor Henry IV
religious order
Francis of Assisi
Thomas Aquinas

Build on What You Know Is there one type of church in your area, or are there many different churches? In all of Medieval Europe, Catholicism was the dominant religion.

Power of the Roman Catholic Church

1 ESSENTIAL QUESTION Why was the Catholic Church so powerful?

From the 11th through 15th centuries, some aspects of feudalism could still be found in Europe. For example, nobles still ruled much of the countryside. However, both the Roman Catholic Church and European monarchies, such as those of France and England, were increasing their power. The Church and European monarchies were also trying to centralize political and religious authority.

Church Organization The Roman Catholic Church needed strong organization to efficiently serve laypeople, or its worshipers. This service included providing people with the sacraments (SAK•ruh•muhnts). These were religious ceremonies, such as baptism, in which a member received the grace of God.

The Church had many different levels of leadership among the **clergy**, or people given priestly authority by the Church. The pope was the spiritual and political leader of the Church. His office was called the Papacy. Below him were the various ranks of the clergy, shown in the illustration on the following page.

Notre Dame Cathedral, Paris, France Notre Dame was built in the Middle Ages and is an outstanding example of Gothic architecture. The exterior supporting structures are called flying buttresses. ▼

Political Role of the Clergy The men who filled important positions in the church had strong social and political ties to Europe's nobility. In fact, local princes were also often bishops. Many nobles and religious leaders had gone to school together. As a result, European nobles and Church leaders had much in common, and they often supported one another.

Many Church officials helped European political leaders run their kingdoms. For example, local priests kept records of births and deaths in their parish, or area served by their church. Monarchs needed this information to more effectively run their kingdoms.

Clergy in the Roman Catholic Church
INTER**ACTIVE**

Pope The pope was the spiritual and political leader of the Church.

Cardinals and Bishops Cardinals helped the pope run the Church. The bishops ran the dioceses, areas with several churches.

Priests Priests ran individual churches and administered the sacraments—including communion, matrimony, and baptism—to most Catholics.

Monks and Nuns Monks and nuns lived in isolated communities. They learned to read Latin, grew their own food, and copied and translated religious texts.

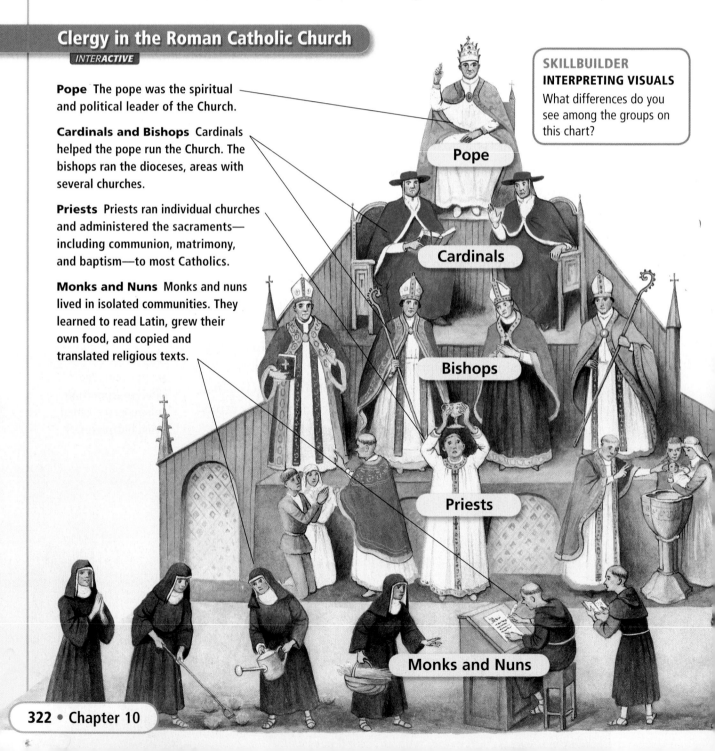

Pope

Cardinals

Bishops

Priests

Monks and Nuns

SKILLBUILDER
INTERPRETING VISUALS
What differences do you see among the groups on this chart?

The Church also had great wealth, which made it an even more powerful institution. The Church earned income from property it owned. The wealth of the pope was greater than that of any individual European monarch. Also, the Papacy's authority was often greater than that of kings and emperors. The pope's power caused many monarchs to cooperate with the Church, but it also caused conflict.

REVIEW What was the structure of the Church in the Middle Ages?

Conflict Between Monarchs and the Papacy

2 **ESSENTIAL QUESTION** Why did monarchs and popes struggle with each other for control of society?

For a long time, Church leaders and European monarchs and nobles saw that it was in their best interest to cooperate with each other. But they eventually came into conflict. In the 11th century, a dispute between **Pope Gregory VII** and **Emperor Henry IV** reached a crisis point.

One Cause of Conflict The Holy Roman Empire, which began around 962, included much of central and western Europe. Holy Roman Emperor Henry IV had built up political power by appointing Church officials. Monarchs such as Henry IV relied on literate and efficient Church officials to help run their kingdoms. They wanted as much control over those officials as possible. In 1075, Pope Gregory said that laypeople—including Henry IV— could no longer appoint people to Church offices.

The Outcome The pope's decision made Henry furious. He called together the bishops that supported him. Together, they declared the pope's election invalid. Pope Gregory responded by excommunicating, or banishing, Henry from the Church for violating the pope's order. He told Henry's subjects that he was no longer emperor, and they did not have to obey him.

Many nobles and church officials then turned against Henry. Henry cleverly chose to ask the pope to forgive him. Some accounts say that to seek forgiveness, Henry stood barefoot for three days in the snow outside the castle where the pope was staying. As a priest, Gregory had to forgive Henry. Henry regained his title and control over his subjects, but conflict between European monarchs and the Papacy would continue.

REVIEW Why was appointing Church officials important to Henry IV?

Emperor Henry IV Seeks Forgiveness Emperor Henry kneels before Countess Matilda as Pope Gregory, dressed in red, looks on. Matilda is persuading the pope to forgive Henry. ▼

The Church and Society

3 **ESSENTIAL QUESTION** How did the Catholic Church support education?

The medieval Church played a dominant role in education. Religious orders were the Church's most important educational institutions.

Religious Orders A **religious order** is a group of people who live by rules specific to their order. Monastic orders are religious orders that largely separate themselves from the rest of society to focus on prayer and service to God—a Christian ideal. Men who joined monastic orders were called monks. They lived in monasteries. Women who joined monastic orders were called nuns, and they lived in convents. Nuns in the convents often had great control over their daily lives, something very few women outside the convents had.

Friars formed another type of religious order. They traveled to preach the word of God. Friars were mendicants. That is, they owned nothing and primarily lived by begging. Franciscans were the most important mendicant order. **Francis of Assisi**, an Italian, founded this order in the early 1200s. He called on his followers to live without property and serve as teachers, healers, and friends to all living things. The Church later named him a saint.

▲ Benedictine Monastery, Normandy, France The Benedictines are a religious order. Each Benedictine monastery sets its own rules, which makes Benedictines different from other religious orders.

The Founding of Universities Schools were established at cathedrals, the center of power for bishops. As you read earlier, students of these schools were usually the sons of European nobles who often became religious or political leaders. As the cities grew, these cathedral schools expanded as early forms of universities. Instructors taught their students in Latin. The Church was also an intellectual institution that worked to preserve the Latin language and religious texts.

Scholars studied classical philosophers. Muslim scholars preserved and interpreted ancient Greek texts, lost for centuries in the West. Church scholars translated the texts into Latin and made them available at the new universities. But some Church officials worried that some classical ideas went against Church teachings about faith.

In the mid 1200s, an Italian scholar named **Thomas Aquinas** (uh•KWY•nuhs) began studying the writings of a Greek philosopher named Aristotle. Aquinas argued that classical philosophy could exist in harmony with Christian faith and natural law, which he said came from God and was about moral behavior. His work is a synthesis, or combination, of classical philosophy with Christian theology. He is remembered as a great religious scholar. You will read more about reason and faith during the European Renaissance in Chapter 13.

REVIEW How did universities develop?

Lesson Summary

- The Church as a political institution in Medieval Europe was powerful and organized.
- Church leaders and monarchs came into conflict when they could not agree on who had authority.
- The Church was a powerful intellectual institution in Medieval Europe that helped establish universities.

Why It Matters Now . . .

Teachers at medieval universities developed a new teaching method using lectures and textbooks—a method that is still used in universities today.

1 Lesson Review

Homework Helper
ClassZone.com

Terms & Names

1. Explain the importance of

clergy	religious order
Pope Gregory VII	Francis of Assisi
Emperor Henry IV	Thomas Aquinas

Using Your Notes

Summarizing Use your completed chart to answer the following question:

2. Why did Pope Gregory VII and Emperor Henry IV come into conflict? (7.6.4)

Section	Summary
Power of the Church	
Conflict Between Monarchs and the Papacy	
The Church and Society	

Main Ideas

3. Why was the Roman Catholic Church so powerful in Medieval Europe? (7.6.8)

4. Why did Pope Gregory VII excommunicate Emperor Henry IV? (7.6.4)

5. Why is Thomas Aquinas important? (7.6.8)

Critical Thinking

6. **Drawing Conclusions** Why might Church leaders and Europe's traditional nobility have cooperated for so long? (7.6.4)

7. **Comparing and Contrasting** What were the similarities and differences between priests and monks or nuns? (7.6.8)

Activity

Creating a Brochure Research to learn more about life in a medieval monastery. Create a brochure that shows the activities performed by the monastery's inhabitants. Include descriptions of each activity. (7.6.8)

Lesson 2

MAIN IDEAS

1 **Government** Religious and political motives led the Christians to begin a series of wars to conquer Palestine.

2 **Government** Muslim armies gradually recaptured territory lost during the First Crusade.

3 **Culture** The Crusades, including the reconquest of Spain and Portugal, had a lasting effect on European culture.

TAKING NOTES

Reading Skill:
Explaining Chronological Order and Sequence

Putting things in chronological order helps you understand how different events relate to one another. For Lesson 2, draw a time line like the one below and fill in events as you read.

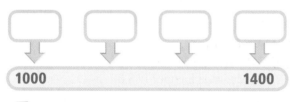

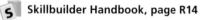

1000   1400

S Skillbuilder Handbook, page R14

▲ **St. Peter's Castle** This castle was built by Christian Crusaders, and is now a museum in modern Turkey.

CALIFORNIA STANDARDS

7.6.6 Discuss the causes and course of the religious Crusades and their effects on the Christian, Muslim, and Jewish populations in Europe, with emphasis on the increasing contact by Europeans with cultures of the Eastern Mediterranean world.

7.6.9 Know the history of the decline of Muslim rule in the Iberian Peninsula that culminated in the Reconquista and the rise of Spanish and Portuguese kingdoms.

Framework The expulsion of the Jews and Muslims in Spain in 1492 should be noted.

The Crusades

TERMS & NAMES

Seljuk Turk

Crusade

Saladin

Reconquista

Inquisition

Build on What You Know In Chapter 4, you read about how the **Seljuk Turks** took control of Palestine and came into conflict with Orthodox Christians of eastern Europe. In Lesson 2, you will read more about that conflict.

Battle for Palestine

1 **ESSENTIAL QUESTION** Why did the Christians begin a series of wars to conquer Palestine?

The **Crusades** were military expeditions from Christian Europe to Palestine between the 11th and 13th centuries. They had a lasting impact on European politics and society.

Causes of the Crusades European Christians began the Crusades for several reasons. Jerusalem and the area around it was, and still is, sacred to Christians, Jews, and Muslims. Christians called this area the Holy Land. The Seljuk takeover of Jerusalem in 1071 made Christian pilgrimages to the Holy Land nearly impossible.

Additionally, European feudal princes often used success in warfare as one way to gain power. As a result, many princes were eager to go on the Crusades. European merchants were also willing to finance the Crusades because they might gain access to the rich trade routes that connected with Asia to the east.

Finally, Seljuk forces attacked the Byzantine Empire. The Byzantine emperor asked the pope for help. By 1096, the pope responded, and the First Crusade began (see map below).

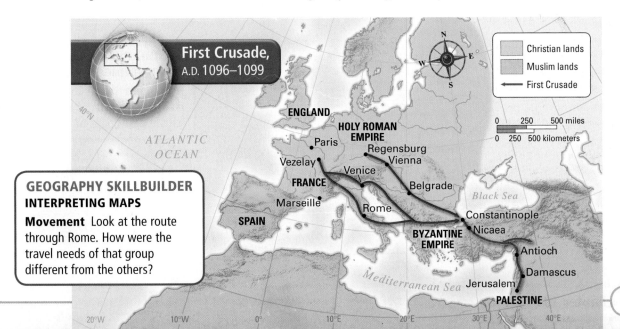

First Crusade, A.D. 1096–1099

Christian lands
Muslim lands
First Crusade

0   250   500 miles
0 250 500 kilometers

ATLANTIC OCEAN

ENGLAND

HOLY ROMAN EMPIRE

Paris

Regensburg

Vezelay

Vienna

FRANCE

Venice

Belgrade

Marseille

Rome

Black Sea

SPAIN

Constantinople

BYZANTINE EMPIRE

Nicaea

Antioch

Damascus

Mediterranean Sea   Jerusalem

PALESTINE

GEOGRAPHY SKILLBUILDER
INTERPRETING MAPS
Movement Look at the route through Rome. How were the travel needs of that group different from the others?

The First Crusade In 1096, several European armies started out for the Byzantine capital of Constantinople. From there they planned to attack Palestine. Many Crusaders did not take enough supplies. Tens of thousands died on the way, and many were captured and enslaved. Still, a large Crusader force was prepared to attack Palestine.

Christian forces captured the cities of Nicaea and Antioch, and in 1099, they captured Jerusalem. They divided the conquered land into four Crusader states: Edessa, Antioch, Tripoli, and Jerusalem.

REVIEW What were the results of the First Crusade?

Muslims Return to Power

2 ESSENTIAL QUESTION How successful were Muslim armies after the First Crusade?

The Second Crusade (1147–1149) began after Muslim Turks recaptured the Crusader state of Edessa in 1144. A French army and a German army went on the Crusade. They marched separately to Palestine and were weakened by a difficult journey. Muslim forces defeated the Crusaders at Damascus.

Christians kept control of the other Crusader states. They survived in part because of continued disagreements among the Muslim leadership. But the Muslim disagreements ended in the late 1100s with the rise of Salah-al-Din, a Muslim political and military leader.

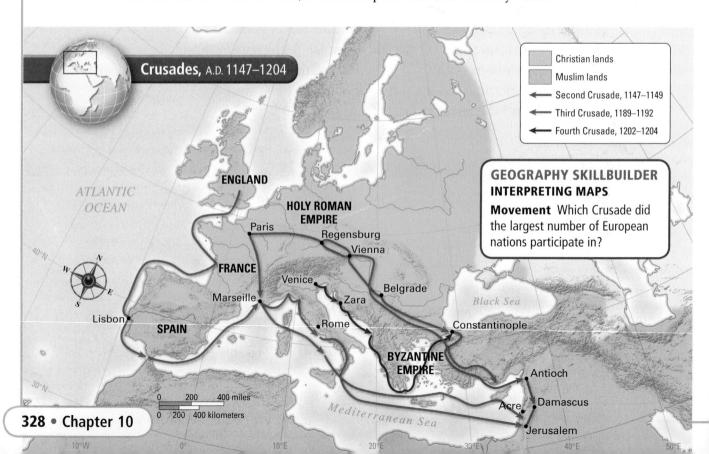

Crusades, A.D. 1147–1204

Christian lands
Muslim lands
⟵ Second Crusade, 1147–1149
⟵ Third Crusade, 1189–1192
⟵ Fourth Crusade, 1202–1204

GEOGRAPHY SKILLBUILDER
INTERPRETING MAPS
Movement Which Crusade did the largest number of European nations participate in?

ATLANTIC OCEAN

ENGLAND

HOLY ROMAN EMPIRE

Paris

Regensburg

Vienna

FRANCE

Venice

Belgrade

Marseille

Zara

Black Sea

Lisbon

Rome

Constantinople

SPAIN

BYZANTINE EMPIRE

Antioch

0 200 400 miles
0 200 400 kilometers

Acre

Damascus

Mediterranean Sea

Jerusalem

Saladin's Rise to Power Salah-al-Din was known to Europeans as **Saladin** (SAL•uh•dihn). As a young man, Saladin was more interested in studying Islam than warfare. But he eventually joined an uncle who was a military leader in Syria. Saladin went with a Syrian army to defend Egypt against the Crusaders. After the war, he took over the Egyptian government. Saladin began to unify Muslims in the region, and then he turned his attention to the Crusaders still in Palestine.

In 1187, Saladin gathered a large force to attack the Crusader states. Saladin's forces won many victories and recaptured Jerusalem. It did not take long for news of Saladin's victories to reach Europe.

The Third Crusade After the fall of Jerusalem, the pope called for another Crusade. Some of Europe's most powerful leaders went on the Third Crusade (1189–1192). Among them was the English king Richard the Lion-Hearted. Richard became the Crusaders' leader because of his courage and skill in battle. The Crusaders were successful at first, but they did not achieve their main goal of retaking Jerusalem. In 1192, Saladin and Richard agreed to a truce. Jerusalem would remain under Muslim control. However, in return, Saladin agreed to allow Christian pilgrims to visit the city's holy places.

The Fourth Crusade The truce did not last, and a Fourth Crusade (1202–1204) was launched. To pay the Italian traders who were transporting them, the Crusaders agreed to attack the Byzantine city of Zara. The Crusaders then sacked Constantinople to put a political ally in charge of the Byzantine Empire. The pope was furious with the Crusaders for attacking Christian cities, but he could not stop them. The Crusaders did not continue the Crusade. The Byzantine Empire was further weakened as a result of the Fourth Crusade.

REVIEW What was the key to the success of the Muslim armies?

Muslims Recapture Palestine

3 **ESSENTIAL QUESTION** What were some effects of the Crusades on Europe?

Europe began more Crusades, but by 1270, the Muslims had driven the Crusaders out of Palestine, and the wars ended. The Crusades did not have a permanent effect on Muslims in Palestine. People's daily lives continued much as they had before the Crusades.

But Christian traders remained in Palestine, and European pilgrims continued to visit their religion's Holy Land. Both the traders and the pilgrims maintained a cultural exchange with the Turkish, Arab, Persian, and African cultures present in the region.

Effects of the Crusades European contact with the cultures of the Eastern Mediterranean grew during the Crusades. Crusaders brought back Asian goods, resulting in increased trade. These goods included spices, furs, cloth, cane sugar, rice, and different fruits. Increased trade across the Mediterranean helped European towns to grow and made the role of urban merchants more important.

Another legacy of the Crusades was rising Christian hostility toward Jews. More and more Christians believed that all non-Christians were their enemy. On their way to Palestine, some Crusaders massacred European Jews and continued the killing in Palestine. After the Crusades, Jews were expelled from England in 1290 and from France in 1306 and again in 1394. Many of these Jews moved to eastern Europe.

Muslims, however, allowed Jews and Christians to live in peace in most cases. Many Crusaders who stayed in Palestine came to respect Muslims, but Christian intolerance toward Jews continued.

The Reconquista Muslim leaders drove the Crusaders out of Palestine. But in Spain just the opposite occurred. Here, it was Christian armies that drove out the Muslim rulers. This reconquest is called the **Reconquista** (reh•kawn•KEES•tah) in the Spanish language.

In the early 700s, Muslims had conquered the Iberian Peninsula, which includes present-day Spain and Portugal (see the map below). In Chapter 4, you read about how Spain experienced a golden age of cooperation among Muslims and Jews during this period.

By the 1000s, however, Muslim unity on the peninsula broke down. Spanish and Portuguese kingdoms rose to defeat Muslim forces. King

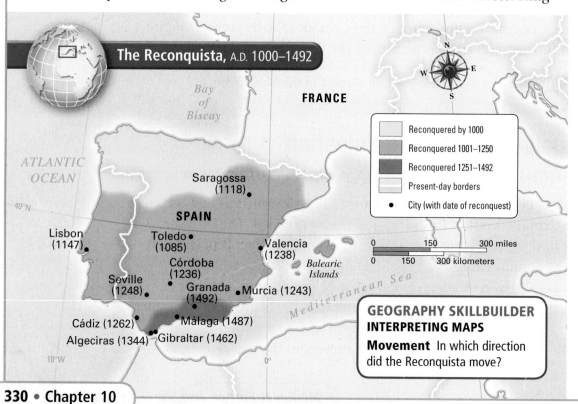

The Reconquista, A.D. 1000–1492

FRANCE

Bay of Biscay

ATLANTIC OCEAN

40°N

Reconquered by 1000
Reconquered 1001–1250
Reconquered 1251–1492
Present-day borders
• City (with date of reconquest)

SPAIN

Saragossa (1118)

Lisbon (1147)

Toledo (1085)

Valencia (1238)

Córdoba (1236)

Balearic Islands

Seville (1248)

Granada (1492)

Murcia (1243)

0   150   300 miles
0   150   300 kilometers

Cádiz (1262)

Málaga (1487)

Algeciras (1344) Gibraltar (1462)

Mediterranean Sea

10°W   0°

GEOGRAPHY SKILLBUILDER
INTERPRETING MAPS
Movement In which direction did the Reconquista move?

Ferdinand and Queen Isabella unified Spain through military and religious authority. Their armies captured cities, and their Church officials used a court to punish people opposed to Church teachings. This court, which was used throughout Europe, was called the **Inquisition**. Many Jews and Muslims in Spain and Portugal were tortured and executed by the Inquisition. In 1492, Ferdinand and Isabella completed the Reconquista by forcing out the last Muslim rulers and their followers and many Jews as well.

REVIEW How are the Crusades and the Reconquista related?

Lesson Summary

- Christian Europe launched Crusades from 1096 to 1270 to take control of the Holy Land from Muslims.
- Under Saladin, Muslims regained much territory lost during the First Crusade.
- Crusaders failed to take control of the Holy Land, but the Reconquista in Spain was successful.

Why It Matters Now . . .

Some present-day Christians and Muslims look back to the period of the Crusades in an effort to understand tensions between the West and the Middle East today.

---

2 Lesson Review

Homework Helper
ClassZone.com

Terms & Names

1. Explain the importance of

Seljuk Turk	Saladin	Inquisition
Crusade	Reconquista	

Using Your Notes

Explaining Chronological Order and Sequence Use your completed time line to answer the following question:

2. When did the first Christian armies head for the Holy Land? (7.6.6)

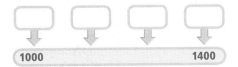

1000   1400

Main Ideas

3. What economic effects did the Crusades have on Europe? (7.6.6)

4. What impact did the Crusades have on the Jewish population of Europe? (7.6.6)

5. Why were the Spanish and Portuguese kingdoms able to start taking back territory? (7.6.9)

Critical Thinking

6. **Understanding Causes** What motivated the Crusaders to attack Palestine? (7.6.6)

7. **Understanding Effects** How did the Crusades impact the Christian, Muslim, and Jewish populations in Europe? (7.6.6)

Activity

Making a Poster Research to learn more about the Crusades. Make a poster that shows how the Crusades changed life in Europe. (7.6.6)

► MAIN IDEAS

1 **Culture** Disease devastated Asia, Africa, and Europe in the early to mid-1300s.

2 **Science and Technology** Military technology during the Hundred Years' War became deadlier.

3 **Government** The Hundred Years' War helped to end feudalism.

► TAKING NOTES

Reading Skill: Finding Main Ideas

Finding a main idea means finding a statement that explains the main point of a lesson and the details to support it. Use a chart like the one below to list each main idea provided and the details from the lesson that support it.

Main Idea

S Skillbuilder Handbook, page R2

▲ **The Crossbow**
Crossbows like the one shown here were deadly on medieval battlefields. They could pierce light armor and had a range of up to 1,000 feet.

CALIFORNIA STANDARDS

7.6 Students analyze the geographic, political, economic, religious, and social structures of the civilizations of Medieval Europe.

7.6.7 Map the spread of the bubonic plague from Central Asia to China, the Middle East, and Europe and describe its impact on global population.

HI 2 Students understand and distinguish cause, effect, sequence, and correlation in historical events, including the long- and short-term causal relations.

Plague and the Hundred Years' War

TERMS & NAMES

bubonic plague

Hundred Years' War

Joan of Arc

longbow

Build on What You Know The Crusades you read about in Lesson 2 began the decline of feudalism in Europe. In Lesson 3, you will learn about a series of crises—including the plague that you read about in the opening story—that further weakened feudalism in Europe.

The Plague

1 ESSENTIAL QUESTION How did disease affect the world in the 1300s?

Before the end of the century, the plague had killed tens of millions of people in Europe, North Africa, and western Asia. In Europe, about one-third of the total population was killed.

Spread of the Disease The plague that struck western Eurasia in the mid-1300s is called **bubonic plague**. Its victims experienced severe chills, fever, convulsions, and vomiting. Victims also developed dark spots on their skin and swollen glands. A person infected with the bubonic plague was usually dead within a few days. The plague of the 1300s became known as the Black Death.

The Plague One of the symptoms of the plague was dark spots on the skin, evident in this painting from the period. ▼

The Spread of the Plague

Scholars believe the plague spread from Central Asia. It moved by land along trade routes from Asia to Europe. It also moved along sea routes. In October 1347, a trading ship brought the disease to Italy. The disease then traveled rapidly north. By the following spring, the plague had spread to France, Germany, and as far north as England.

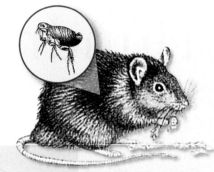

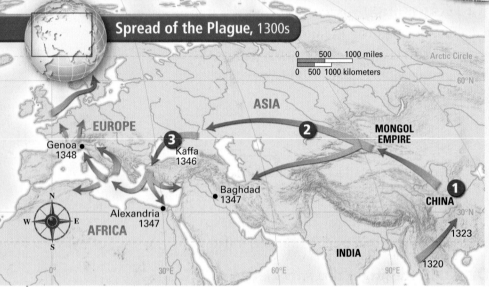

Spread of the Plague, 1300s

0   500   1000 miles
0   500 1000 kilometers

ASIA

EUROPE

Genoa 1348

3 Kaffa 1346

2

MONGOL EMPIRE

Baghdad 1347

Alexandria 1347

AFRICA

INDIA

CHINA

1

1323

1320

Arctic Circle

60°N

30°N

1 The plague probably spread from Central Asia, but it is impossible to know for certain.

2 Rats carrying infected fleas traveled with merchants along trade routes.

3 Italian merchants unknowingly brought the plague to Europe.

SKILLBUILDER
INTERPRETING VISUALS
How did the plague travel from Asia to Europe?

Global Impact of the Plague The massive loss of life caused by the plague had a major impact on Asia, North Africa, and Europe. Christians and Muslims reacted differently to the plague. Christians often saw the plague as a punishment for sin. By comparison, Muslims saw the plague as testing their faith in God. Regardless of their faith, the plague had killed 20 to 30 million people by 1400.

For a short time, wars stopped and trade declined. Some landowners were ruined by a shortage of labor. However, this was followed by economic recovery for some people. For example, European workers were so scarce that those able to work could demand higher pay for their labor. The shortage of labor and higher wages weakened feudalism because workers began to migrate in search of higher wages.

In Europe, the hostility toward Jews that developed during the Crusades continued during the bubonic plague. Jews were often accused of causing the plague by poisoning water wells. They were driven out of many German towns during the plague.

REVIEW How did the plague affect the size of Europe's population?

The Hundred Years' War

2 ESSENTIAL QUESTION Who fought in the Hundred Years' War?

In the 1300s, England and France faced not only the plague but frequent warfare as well. Between 1337 and 1453, England and France fought each other in the **Hundred Years' War**. It was actually a series of wars—not one continuous battle.

Background for the War William, Duke of Normandy, was from the Norman region of France. He claimed to be the rightful king of England. In 1066, William captured England in what is called the Norman invasion. He became known as William the Conqueror and tied the nobility of France with the nobility of England. Over the years, tensions grew over who had the right to rule either region.

Years of Battle Those tensions reached a crisis point in the early 1300s. England claimed territory in the southwest of France. France was supporting Scotland's fight against England. There was also debate about rights to sea travel in the English Channel. Fighting began when the king of France tried to take the territory claimed by England in southern France. The English king responded by claiming that he was the rightful king of France. In 1337, England attacked France.

The English had several victories. In 1428, the English attacked Orleans, one of France's last major strongholds. A French peasant girl known as **Joan of Arc** led the French to victory. By 1453, the French had driven the English from France and ended the war.

History Makers

Joan of Arc (c. 1412–1431)

Joan of Arc was born a peasant in Domrémy, France, around 1412. She was a devoted Catholic. When she was about 13, she believed that religious visions were urging her to fight the English during the Hundred Years' War. In 1429, she went to Charles, the French heir to the throne. Charles often prayed alone, but Joan knew what he said. Convinced her visions were divine, Charles made her a knight. In May 1429, Joan led the French to victory in the battle against the English at Orleans.

A year after the victory at Orleans, Joan was captured by allies of England. She was eventually executed in 1431. She became a national heroine in France and was declared a saint by the Catholic Church in 1920.

New Weapons New weapons changed warfare in Europe and around the world. A **longbow** shot arrows that could penetrate a knight's armor. Europeans also took advantage of new gunpowder weapons. Gunpowder technology came from China, but Europeans developed the technology into a major instrument of war. The longbow and gunpowder weapons could easily defeat knights. Over the next 300 years, the development of gunpowder weapons would greatly change the intensity and organization of warfare.

REVIEW What new weapons were used in the Hundred Years' War?

Early Modern Europe Emerges

3 **ESSENTIAL QUESTION** How did social and political structures of Medieval Europe change?

For centuries, many European societies followed the feudal structure you learned about in Chapter 9. Over time, however, European feudalism broke down and signaled the end of the Middle Ages.

Social and Political Structures European trade and towns grew throughout the Middle Ages. People kept moving from the country to towns seeking their fortune. Towns required stability to make business and trade more reliable. Stronger monarchies could provide that stability. As a result, towns increasingly became centers of support for monarchies, and monarchies in turn expanded their power.

Monarchies gained even more strength after the Hundred Years' War. For example, the French monarchy no longer had to worry about an English claim to their throne. The French monarchy would eventually become the best example of an absolute monarchy under King Louis XIV (1643–1715). With guidance from skilled councilors, Louis would make France the most powerful nation in Europe.

Europe in Transition	
Medieval Europe	**Early Modern Europe**
weaker monarchies	stronger monarchies
powerful nobility	weaker nobility
mostly agricultural	rising importance of trade
common people loyal to local rulers	common people loyal to the king
knights were a fearsome weapon	gunpowder weapons make knights obsolete

New Ideas For many historians, the end of the Middle Ages began with the development of large nations that had powerful central governments run by kings. As the Middle Ages came to an end, scholars continued the study of classical texts begun by men such as Thomas Aquinas, whom you read about in Lesson 1. New ideas about learning, science, and art developed in Italian cities. The new ideas spread along European trade routes. This new era is called the Renaissance, and you will read more about it in Chapter 13.

REVIEW How did life change during the Middle Ages?

Lesson Summary

- During the 14th century, the plague killed about one-third of Europe's population.
- Deadlier weapons were developed during the Hundred Years' War.
- The Hundred Years' War helped weaken the social and political structures of feudalism.

▲ **Hundred Years' War** In this detail from a 15th-century painting, you can see some of the firearms that would change warfare forever.

Why It Matters Now . . .

In today's world, our health is still challenged by the spread of epidemic diseases, such as HIV/AIDS. Our security is also challenged by powerful new military technologies, such as nuclear weapons.

---

3 Lesson Review

🔍 **Homework Helper**
ClassZone.com

Terms & Names

1. Explain the importance of

bubonic plague	Joan of Arc
Hundred Years' War	longbow

Using Your Notes

Finding Main Ideas Use your completed chart to answer the following question:

2. What were the effects of the plague on European society? (7.6.7)

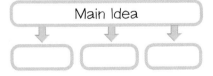

Main Ideas

3. How were European Jews treated during the plague? (7.6.7)

4. What were two causes of the Hundred Years' War? (7.6)

5. How did political structures change during the Middle Ages? (7.6)

Critical Thinking

6. **Making Inferences** How might the longbow and gunpowder technology have changed what weapons were used on medieval battlefields? (7.6)

7. **Making Predictions** What result might a plague as devastating as the one in the mid-1300s have on North America today? (HI 2)

Activity **Internet Activity** Use the Internet to research Joan of Arc. Write a two-page biography that explains the central issues and problems she faced. (HI 1)

INTERNET KEYWORD: *Joan of Arc*

Epidemics

Purpose: To learn more about how diseases like the bubonic plague have affected people throughout history

An epidemic is an outbreak of a disease that infects a large number of people. An epidemic covering a large land area is called a pandemic. The Black Death was a pandemic because it spread through the territory from eastern Asia to western Europe. Epidemic diseases have been, and continue to be, a powerful force in human history.

On these pages you will read about past and present ideas about infection, prevention, and treatment. Remember that doctors from past historical periods could only apply the knowledge available to them. Their medical practices may seem strange to us today, but our medical practices may seem strange to people 1,000 years from now.

CALIFORNIA STANDARDS

7.6.7 Map the spread of the bubonic plague from Central Asia to China, the Middle East, and Europe and describe its impact on global population.

Method of Infection

▼ **Past** Over the centuries, people have had different ideas about how humans are infected by disease. Often, a disease was thought to be the result of a demon or evil spirits—a belief still held by many people around the world. The men in the engraving below are beating themselves as a punishment for sin. Sins were thought to be the cause of some illnesses.

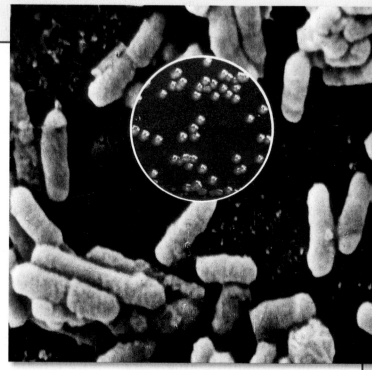

▲ **Present** Modern scientists discovered that microscopic germs and viruses cause diseases. Even before these germs and viruses were identified, however, many scientists had predicted their existence.

Prevention

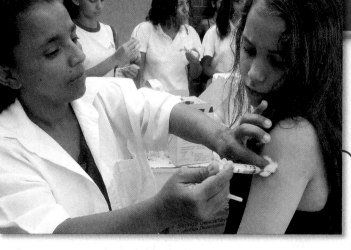

▶ **Past** To prevent infection from diseases, people have tried many things over the centuries. This doctor from the Middle Ages understood, as we do today, that close contact with people infected by the plague could spread the disease. His mask was filled with herbs thought to prevent disease.

▲ **Present** Inoculations (ih•NOHK•yuh•LAY•shuhns) can prevent people from getting specific types of diseases. They are an important part of modern medicine that medieval doctors did not have. Today, children usually get inoculations to prevent diseases.

Treatment

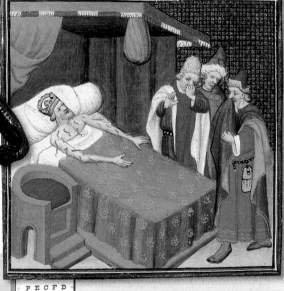

▶ **Past** Bloodletting, or bleeding, was a treatment often used for a variety of illnesses. Blood might be drained directly from the patient, or blood-sucking leeches might be attached to the patient. Medicines developed from natural ingredients have been used by doctors for centuries.

▼ **Present** Modern doctors use medicines developed from natural and chemical sources that are targeted to attack a specific disease or to treat specific symptoms.

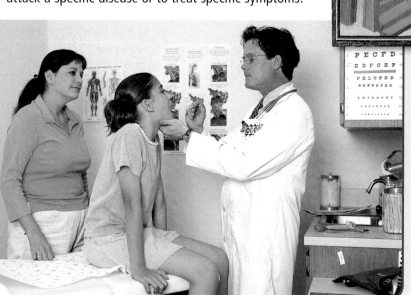

Activities

1. **TALK ABOUT IT** What are some epidemics you have heard about?

2. **WRITE ABOUT IT** Write a paragraph predicting how our knowledge of infections and treatment of diseases will be different in 500 years. (Writing 2.1)

Lesson

4

▶ **MAIN IDEAS**

1 **Government** New ideas in law developed in medieval England.

2 **Government** New political ideas changed the structure of England's government.

3 **Government** The legal and political changes in medieval England influenced later democratic thought and representative institutions.

▶ **TAKING NOTES**

Reading Skill: Making Generalizations

Making generalizations means to make broad judgments based on information. In Lesson 4, list the details for the different sections in a chart like the one below. Then write a general statement about the section.

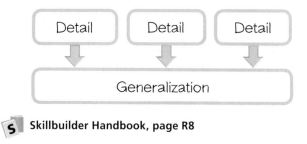

| Detail | Detail | Detail |

↓ ↓ ↓

| Generalization |

S **Skillbuilder Handbook, page R8**

▲ **King John's Coat of Arms**
This is King John's coat of arms before he took the throne. A coat of arms is a set of symbols used to identify a family or individual. They were developed in early Medieval Europe primarily to identify each other on the battlefield.

CALIFORNIA STANDARDS

7.6 Students analyze the geographic, political, economic, religious, and social structures of the civilizations of Medieval Europe.

7.6.5 Know the significance of developments in medieval English legal and constitutional practices and their importance in the rise of modern democratic thought and representative institutions (e.g., Magna Carta, parliament, development of habeas corpus, an independent judiciary in England).

HI 3 Students explain the sources of historical continuity and how the combination of ideas and events explains the emergence of new patterns.

Changes in Government and Economics

Build on What You Know In Lesson 3, you read about events that weakened European feudalism. In this lesson, you will study legal and constitutional practices of England from the 12th and 13th centuries that are still important today.

The English Government

1 **ESSENTIAL QUESTION** What were some of the new ideas about government in England?

The legal practices of medieval England are the foundations of many modern legal practices.

Common Law King Henry II (1154–1189) brought consistency to England's legal system by sending royal judges to every part of the country. In the early 1100s, court decisions were based on local customs and previous rulings. This was called common law, and it meant the decisions in one part of England could be different from those in another part of England. The decisions of the new royal judges, however, were intended to apply to all of England. The royal laws made it more likely that people all over England would receive equal treatment.

King John King John is shown here signing the Magna Carta, a document that would influence governments for many years to come. ▼

Independent Courts The royal judges were meant to be independent from local politics. However, they were not independent from the royal government. English medieval courts were very different from courts today. For example, U.S. courts are independent from the other parts of the government. This is called an independent judiciary, which you will read more about later in this chapter.

Magna Carta In 1199, the youngest of Henry II's sons, John, came to power. **King John** fought, and lost, many wars. The wars weakened England financially. Many barons, members of England's nobility, grew tired of John's policies. They told John that he must recognize their rights. They listed these rights in a document called the **Magna Carta** and forced John to sign it in 1215.

P **Primary Source Handbook**
See the excerpt from the Magna Carta, page R46.

The Magna Carta guaranteed the protection of the law and trial by jury. It also guaranteed that the king could not collect money from the nobles without their approval. Ordinary English people did not immediately benefit from the Magna Carta. The Magna Carta did, however, set an example for later democratic developments in England and around the world. In Chapter 16, you will read more about how the Magna Carta influenced later democratic thought.

REVIEW How did new legal practices develop in England?

Primary Source

Background: The Magna Carta (detail shown below) was first drafted in 1215. Some of the ideas it contains can be found in the U.S. Constitution—written nearly 575 years later.

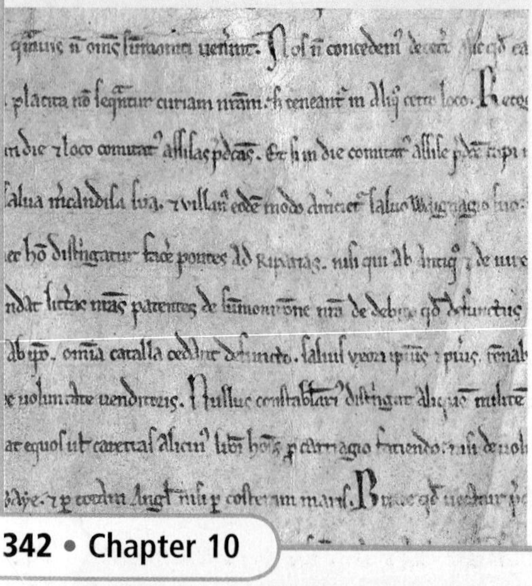

from the Magna Carta (1215)
Translated by Claire Breay

For a trivial offence, a free man shall be fined only in proportion to the degree of his offence, and for a serious offence correspondingly, but not so heavily as to deprive him of his livelihood.

No free man shall be seized or imprisoned, or stripped of his rights or possessions, or outlawed or exiled . . . in any other way, nor will we proceed with force against him, or send others to do so, except by the lawful judgment of his equals or by the law of the land.

To no one will we sell, to no one deny or delay right or justice.

DOCUMENT–BASED QUESTION
The U.S. Constitution states that "No person shall . . . be deprived of life, liberty, or property, without due process of law." How is this similar to the Magna Carta quotation above?

Representative Institutions

2 **ESSENTIAL QUESTION** How did new ideas in politics change the government of England?

Political practices of medieval England are seen by some historians as the foundation of modern representative governments.

A New Governing Body An important step toward representative government came in 1264. English nobles removed King Henry III from the throne after he broke an agreement with them. They replaced him with a group of representatives, which would later be called a **parliament**. The parliament included nobility, high-ranking church officials, and representatives from cities and towns.

Henry's son Edward I took back the throne in 1265, but he did not get rid of Parliament because he needed its political support. In 1295, a parliament was assembled that is widely considered the first truly representative parliament. It is known as the Model Parliament. Representatives from every county, district, and city were assembled. Edward called for parliaments throughout his reign. By the time he died in 1307, Parliament was an important part of English politics. But Parliament's powers were still not totally clear.

Vocabulary Strategy

The **root** of the word *parliament* is *parler*, which is the French word for "to talk."

Edward I's Parliament This page from a 14th-century manuscript shows England's King Edward I supervising his newly formed parliament. ▼

Parliament's Powers Parliament formed two houses, or groups, to govern the country: the House of Commons and the House of Lords. Parliament would eventually control the collection of taxes. As a result, it could limit the power of the English monarchy. Parliament was also eventually able to introduce and pass laws. The king could not declare new laws without Parliament's approval.

Parliament's power grew slowly. The changes mentioned above took centuries to develop. Wars were even fought over the question of Parliament's authority. But the legal and constitutional practices of medieval England would be a guide to later political thinkers.

REVIEW How did Parliament limit the power of the king?

Rise of Modern Democratic Thought

3 **ESSENTIAL QUESTION** What are some modern legal or political ideas that have their roots in medieval England?

Independent judiciaries, citizens' rights, and democratic forms of government did not exist in medieval England as we know them today. Like Parliament, developing these ideas and institutions would take centuries. During their development, however, the legal and constitutional practices of medieval England often became a guide.

Independent Judiciaries Independent judiciaries have developed around the world. In many countries, the courts are independent from other branches of government and can make sure there is a balance of power. For example, the courts can prevent government from passing laws that violate the rights of citizens.

One legal right that probably started in medieval England is **habeas corpus**. This is the right people have to not be imprisoned unlawfully. In modern courts, habeas corpus requires authorities to provide legal proof for why a person is being imprisoned.

Rights listed in the Magna Carta mainly affected English nobles. Later politicians expanded the Magna Carta's use. For example, the barons said that King John must consult them when he needed money. Centuries later, English parliaments argued that this meant the king could not ask for taxes without Parliament's agreement.

Connect to Today

England's Parliament
The English parliament is still officially led by a monarch. Queen Elizabeth II, seated, is shown in the middle of this photograph. ▼

Representative Government A government elected by the people to represent their interests is a representative government. Representative governments that try to include all members of society are a relatively recent development. A majority of English men could not vote for members of Parliament until the 1800s. In the United States, women could not vote until 1920, and many African Americans were effectively prevented from voting through the 1960s. When reading history, it is important to remember that developments often occurred over tens, hundreds, or even thousands of years.

REVIEW Why are independent courts important to some modern governments?

Lesson Summary

- In medieval England, new legal developments established a pattern for the rule of law.
- Political developments in medieval England laid the foundation for representative government.
- Later democratic ideas and institutions used the legal and political changes of medieval England as a guide.

Why It Matters Now . . .

Many of the legal and political ideas that exist today have their foundation in medieval England.

4 Lesson Review

Homework Helper
ClassZone.com

Terms & Names

1. Explain the importance of

| King John | parliament |
| Magna Carta | habeus corpus |

Using Your Notes

Making Generalizations Use your completed chart to answer the following question:

2. What is one general statement you can make about government in medieval England? (7.6.5)

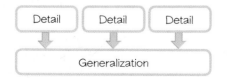

Detail → Detail → Detail → Generalization

Main Ideas

3. How did the decisions of England's royal judges help bring equality to English law? (7.6.5)

4. How did the English Parliament become the model for future representative institutions? (7.6.5)

5. Give an example of a modern legal or political idea that can be traced back to medieval England. (7.6)

Critical Thinking

6. **Making Inferences** Why might the development of modern democratic thought have taken so long? (HI 3)

7. **Drawing Conclusions** How did the changes in medieval England's government affect ordinary people? (HI 3)

Activity

Giving an Oral Report Research to learn more about common law in the United States. Then write a short description of its main features and read the description aloud to the class. (7.6.5)

The Barons Confront King John

Background: In 1215, several English feudal barons felt that their ruler, King John, was treating them unfairly. After driving him from the English capital of London, they confronted him at a meadow called Runnymede with a written agreement to protect their rights. A written protection of rights had never been produced in English history.

CALIFORNIA STANDARDS

7.6.5 Know the significance of developments in medieval English legal and constitutional practices and their importance in the rise of modern democratic thought and representative institutions (e.g., Magna Carta, parliament, development of habeas corpus, an independent judiciary in England).

Cast of Characters

Kirby: Squire for William Marshal and narrator

King John: Ruler of England

William Marshal: Earl of Pembroke and an unhappy baron

Stephen Langton: Archbishop of Canterbury, England's top religious leader

Fulk FitzWarin: Former baron, now an outlaw sometimes called Robin Hood

Kirby: Hail fellows well met! I am Kirby, squire to William Marshal. My lord is here at Runnymede with dozens of other knights of the crown. They are very unhappy with our monarch, King John. The barons have presented him with an agreement with 63 provisions for better treatment. If he doesn't sign it, there will be trouble.

King John: It is indeed a pleasure to be here with all my fine nobles together in the spirit of friendship.

Marshal: Your majesty, let's be honest. We have been chasing you all over England for a month. Now there is no escape. You must meet our conditions.

King John: I am always happy to hear the concerns of my worthy vassals. I realize I have asked for more military service from you and for more money to protect England. But I am your king, and I must do what I feel is necessary to protect the kingdom.

Marshal: We may be scattered in all corners of your realm, but we know the truth of the matter. You know as well as we do that your armies have faced humiliating defeats. And you have violated the established custom of consulting us about raising the money to finance your wars. You also sell royal positions to the highest bidder and demand outrageous fees from those who lose cases in your courts.

Langton: We also insist that you do not imprison people or take their property without a fair trial. Remember when you stole the estates of the Canterbury monks and deported them from England?

King John: Ah, my archbishop, that was just a misunderstanding. I let them return. And I gave the property back to the church.

Langton: You sold it back.

King John: Hmm . . . I can see that my esteemed vassals are in ill humor today. I think these differences can be resolved very easily. I promise I will not seek more money.

Marshal: Your grace, we have seen that promise broken many times before. We demand that you formally recognize our complaints and observe the customs of this land. And we want it in writing. All of this is outlined in the document we've presented to you.

(continued)

King John of England (ruled 1199–1216) ▶

◀ Reproduction of the Magna Carta

King John: What did you call that document again?

Langton: The Magna Carta, your majesty. That's Latin for "Great Charter." This will be one of the most important agreements in history, and you will be remembered as the wise king who made it possible.

King John: Now, now, my baron. There's no need to be so formal about this. Perhaps I've been somewhat harsh on the English nobles lately. But that's no reason to change how things have been for hundreds of years. What is good for the king is good for the kingdom. How can I defend England against enemies if I can't make my own decisions?

Marshal: Your grace, we will honor our pledge to fight for you. But if we are to risk our lives for England, we want a voice in the most important decisions. And we want an agreement in writing. Now will you please sign the Magna Carta?

King John: (*angrily*) Let me remind you, I am your king!

FitzWarin: That can be changed, your majesty.

King John: (*laughing nervously*) Why it's Fulk FitzWarin, my childhood friend! Do you remember how we enjoyed playing chess as young boys?

FitzWarin: You broke the chessboard over my head. And when we grew up, you gave my family's estate and title to my enemy.

King John: And how did you try to regain my favor? Any of you? By raising an army and causing unrest throughout England! You question my authority and demand that I submit to your . . . your Magna Carta! I could stick your heads on poles above the gates of London!

FitzWarin: Begging your majesty's pardon, I think that right now, the opposite is true. It's your head that is on the block.

Marshal: Your grace, we want to resolve this peacefully. If you recognize our demands, we will remain your faithful servants. Otherwise, we are prepared to remove you from power.

King John signing the Magna Carta ▶

King John: All right, all right. I can see you will not rethink your traitorous position. I'll sign this Magna Carta. Bring it forth, and I'll apply my royal seal, and we can be done with this unpleasant business.

Marshal: You are indeed a wise king. History will remember you as a great leader. We will return with it immediately, your majesty.

King John: Those fools! I am the king. I do not answer to my nobles, they answer to me. Nobody can bind me to a piece of paper. I'll live with their Magna Carta for a year or two. Then I'll make them pay for their treachery! I'll find a way to make sure they all suffer. I'll see that FitzWarin is captured and put to a painful death. Soon this Magna Carta business will be forgotten, and I will bring the barons into line. If I can't, I'll find a way to get rid of all of them.

Kirby: My good people, I have had the chance to see into the future, and I know this is not true. The nobles did not forget the Magna Carta. When King John refused to honor it, they rose against him once more. He had not a moment of peace until he died the next year. The ideas of the Magna Carta lived on. Such rights as trial by jury and citizens represented in government became an important part of English law. They were also a foundation for the U.S. Constitution. This scene in history is ended, and I bid you a fond farewell.

Activities

1. **TALK ABOUT IT** Discuss with a partner what you think would happen if King John had refused to sign the Magna Carta.

2. **WRITE ABOUT IT** Research one of the historical figures (not Kirby, because he is fictional) in this story, and write a one-page biography about that person. (Writing 2.3)

MAIN IDEAS

1 **Government** The Ottoman Empire had an efficient government and legal system for much of its history.

2 **Government** The Ottomans controlled a vast empire that included parts of Africa, Asia, and Europe.

3 **Culture** Conquered peoples, women, and slaves had a remarkable degree of freedom.

TAKING NOTES

Reading Skill: Finding Main Ideas

A main idea is usually followed by sentences that support it. For each of the numbered main ideas above, list at least one sentence that supports it in a chart like the one below.

Main Idea	Supporting Sentence
1	
2	
3	

 Skillbuilder Handbook, page R2

▲ **Suleyman's Court** This Ottoman painting shows Suleyman in his court with two European prisoners who are being brought before him. Suleyman ruled the Ottoman Empire at the height of its power.

CALIFORNIA STANDARDS

Framework Islam spread to the area known today as Turkey, where, in the fourteenth century, the Ottoman Turks began gradually to absorb other Turkish tribes and to establish control over most of Asia Minor. In 1453 they captured Constantinople, the seat of the Byzantine Empire, and expanded into Christian Europe until nearly 1700. In studying the social structure of the Ottoman Empire, students should give attention to the role of women; the privileges of its conquered peoples; slavery; the political system; and the legal code.

HI 1 Students explain the central issues and problems from the past, placing people and events in a matrix of time and place.

The Ottoman Empire

TERMS & NAMES

Osman

divan

Suleyman I

janissary

Build on What You Know In Lesson 2, you read about the Seljuk Turks who fought the Crusaders. In the 1300s, a new Turkish group rose to become even more powerful.

An Emerging Power

1 ESSENTIAL QUESTION How did the Ottomans structure their empire?

After the Crusades, Mongol warriors conquered the Seljuks. However, a new Turkish leader named Osman rose to power.

Osman Founds an Empire In the early 1300s, **Osman** founded the Ottoman Empire in Asia Minor. This is the Asian part of present-day Turkey. The name of the empire comes from the Arabic form of Osman: Uthman (uth•MAHN). The Ottomans would control a vast territory (see the map on page 353).

The sultan was the head of the imperial system. Beneath the sultan was an imperial council called the **divan**. The divan advised the sultan. A grand vizier headed the divan and was the sultan's main adviser. Across the empire, military leaders, religious authorities, and large estate owners helped run local affairs. These layers of government allowed the Ottomans to manage and govern their lands effectively.

The Blue Mosque in Istanbul Muslim architects built elaborate mosques in Constantinople after the Ottomans conquered the capital. ▼

New Leadership In 1520, **Suleyman I** (SOO•lay•MAHN) became sultan of the empire. Under Suleyman, the Ottomans produced great art, architecture, and literature. Because of his achievements people often called him "Suleyman the Magnificent." However, people within the empire called him "The Lawgiver" because he organized a legal code that would become famous.

The Legal Code As Muslims, the Ottomans followed Islamic law. But there were topics not fully covered by Islamic law—criminal law and taxation, for example. So the sultans passed laws to address such situations. Suleyman organized these laws into a legal code that could effectively govern the vast and expanding empire.

REVIEW Why was Suleyman's law code important to the Ottomans?

The Empire Expands

2 ESSENTIAL QUESTION What regions did the Ottomans expand into?

Ottoman sultans expanded their territory into many different regions and made their empire one of the most powerful in the world.

Eastern and Southern Expansion The Ottomans captured much of Southwest Asia and northern Africa. This included Syria, Arabia, Persia, Palestine, and Egypt. The Ottomans controlled the cities of Mecca and Medina—considered the holiest cities of Islam.

End of the Byzantine Empire In 1453, the Ottomans conquered the Byzantine capital of Constantinople and brought the Byzantine Empire to an end. The Ottomans changed the name of Constantinople to Istanbul and made it their own capital. By 1525, Suleyman was attacking Hungary and Austria, which the powerful Hapsburg dynasty controlled.

The Hapsburgs were a German family that ruled much of central Europe. They were bitter enemies of France. As a result, when Suleyman attacked Hapsburg Hungary and Austria, France allied with Suleyman. In 1529, Suleyman's armies reached the outskirts of Vienna, Austria. But Suleyman had to withdraw when he could not supply his armies.

REVIEW How far did the Ottomans expand into Europe?

Expansion Through Force An Ottoman army attacks a city with rifles and artillery in this 14th-century painting. ▼

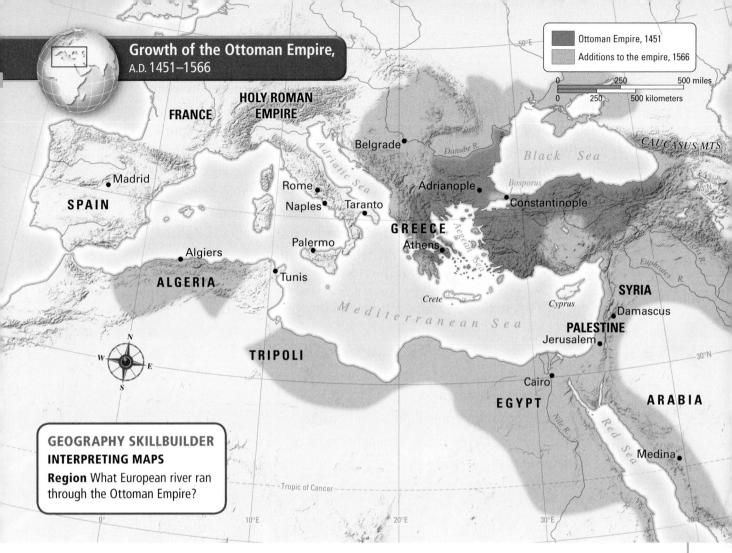

Growth of the Ottoman Empire,
A.D. 1451–1566

| | Ottoman Empire, 1451 |
| | Additions to the empire, 1566 |

0   250   500 miles
0   250   500 kilometers

FRANCE

HOLY ROMAN EMPIRE

Belgrade

Danube R.

Black Sea

CAUCASUS MTS

Madrid

Rome

Adriatic Sea

Adrianople

Bosporus

Constantinople

SPAIN

Naples   Taranto

GREECE

Aegean Sea

Athens

Algiers

Palermo

Tunis

ALGERIA

Crete

Cyprus

SYRIA

Damascus

Mediterranean Sea

PALESTINE

Jerusalem

Euphrates R.

TRIPOLI

Cairo

Nile R.

EGYPT

Red Sea

ARABIA

30°N

Medina

Tropic of Cancer

0°   10°E   20°E   30°E

GEOGRAPHY SKILLBUILDER
INTERPRETING MAPS
Region What European river ran through the Ottoman Empire?

Life in the Ottoman Empire

3 **ESSENTIAL QUESTION** What was the Ottoman policy toward Christians?

Many different peoples lived in peace under the Ottoman Empire.

Privileges of Conquered Peoples Following Islamic law, the Ottomans granted freedom of worship to Christians and Jews living within their empire. Christians and Jews were allowed to establish their own communities, called millets. As long as residents of millets remained loyal and paid their taxes, the sultan allowed them to follow their own religions, speak their own languages, and govern themselves.

Slaves The Ottoman rulers developed a system of slave soldiers and officials. They enlisted limited numbers of slaves from the people they conquered. Some of these slaves filled important positions in the Ottoman Empire. Slaves also made up the elite of the Ottoman army known as the **janissaries**, who, beginning soon after the corps was founded, were forcibly drafted as youths and came mainly from Christian families. The janissaries and the rest of the Ottoman army were highly organized and used advanced gunpowder weapons. This helped the Ottomans expand their empire.

Women in the Empire The situation of women under Ottoman rule depended on their social class and where they lived. However, Islamic law gave women the right to own and inherit property, and to file for divorce. In the country, women worked with men farming and herding. In the cities, women often worked in markets and workshops. Women of the sultan's court received an education, but their lives were limited to the palaces. Some court women were very powerful, especially the mothers of the sultans. The sultans' fortunes, however, slowly declined over the next three centuries, while powerful European monarchies were on the rise.

REVIEW How were women treated in the Ottoman Empire?

Lesson Summary

- The Ottoman Empire was run by an efficient state and legal organization.
- The Ottomans controlled a huge empire.
- Slaves and women were an active part of society in the Ottoman Empire.

Why It Matters Now . . .

The Ottoman Empire was a powerful Muslim state. Today no single Muslim government is as powerful as the Ottoman Empire once was.

5 Lesson Review

Homework Helper
ClassZone.com

Terms & Names

1. Explain the importance of

   Osman   Suleyman I
   divan   janissary

Using Your Notes

Finding Main Ideas Use your completed chart to answer the following question:

2. What rights did women have in the Ottoman Empire? (Framework)

Main Idea	Supporting Sentence
❶	
❷	
❸	

Main Ideas

3. How did Suleyman's legal code help sultans run the Ottoman Empire? (HI 1)

4. On which three continents did the Ottoman Empire claim territory? (HI 1)

5. Why did the Ottomans allow Christians and Jews to organize into millets? (Framework)

Critical Thinking

6. **Forming and Supporting Opinions** Why was the Ottoman Empire so powerful? (Framework)

7. **Making Inferences** Why might Christian France have helped the Muslim Ottomans in their fight against the Christian Hapsburgs? (HI 1)

Activity

Making a Map Use the map on page 353 to help you add the geographic boundaries of the Ottoman Empire to the world map you drew in Chapter 2. (Framework)

Trade with Your Neighbor

Goal: To understand trade during the Middle Ages between Europeans and cultures of the Eastern Mediterranean world

Materials & Supplies
- construction paper cut into 35 3"x 3" squares
- pen or pencil
- scissors

Prepare

Use this chapter and other books to research trade and bartering during the Middle Ages.

Do the Activity

1. Pair with a classmate. One of you will be a European merchant, and the other an Arab merchant. The European merchant gets 17 squares, and the Arab merchant gets 18 squares.

2. Goods with high demand have more value. The European merchant should write on 4 squares "timber, high demand," on 5 squares "fur, medium demand," and on 8 squares "wool, low demand."

3. The Arab merchant should write on 3 squares "gold, high demand," on 6 squares "spices, medium demand," and on 9 squares "cotton, low demand."

4. In at least three transactions, trade goods with each other. The goal for each merchant is to trade as many goods as he or she can and end up with the most value.

5. Keep a record of each transaction that includes the goods traded, the amount of each good, and the demand for each good.

TIMBER
High Demand

Follow-Up

Did you find keeping a record of each transaction helpful? Explain.

Extension

Each merchant should tell the class what goods he or she acquired in the trade. The class should then decide which merchant ended up with the most value.

CALIFORNIA STANDARDS

7.6.6 Discuss the causes and course of the religious Crusades and their effects on the Christian, Muslim, and Jewish populations in Europe, with emphasis on the increasing contact by Europeans with cultures of the Eastern Mediterranean world.

► **VISUAL SUMMARY**

Medieval Europe and the Ottoman Empire

Belief Systems (7.6.8)
- The Catholic Church was a political, educational, and religious institution.

Culture (7.6.6, Framework)
- The Crusades increased cultural interaction.
- Ottoman stability brought cultural exchange.

Science and Technology (7.6)
- Military technology advanced during the Hundred Years' War.

Government (7.6.5, 7.6.6, Framework)
- The Crusades and the Hundred Years' War weakened feudalism.
- Origins of representative government developed in England.
- Ottomans threatened Europe.

► **TERMS & NAMES**

Explain why the words in each set below are linked with each other.

1. **religious order** and **Francis of Assisi**
2. **Reconquista** and **Inquisition**
3. **Hundred Years' War** and **Joan of Arc**
4. **King John** and **Magna Carta**
5. **Osman** and **Suleyman I**

► **MAIN IDEAS**

The Role of the Catholic Church (pages 320–325)
6. Why did Church officials often have great political power? (7.6.4)
7. What role did monastic orders play in the Church? (7.6.8)

The Crusades (pages 326–331)
8. How did the Crusades begin? (7.6.6)
9. How were Jews affected by the Crusades? (7.6.6)

Plague and the Hundred Years' War (pages 332–339)
10. What effect did the bubonic plague have on Europeans? (7.6.7)

Changes in Government and Economics (pages 340–349)
11. How did the Magna Carta contribute to the growth of democracy? (7.6.5)
12. How did the English Parliament lay the foundation for future representative institutions? (7.6.5)

The Ottoman Empire (pages 350–355)
13. How did the Ottomans manage their empire? (Framework)

CRITICAL THINKING
Big Ideas : Belief Systems

14. **ANALYZING POLITICAL ISSUES** How did the Catholic Church become so politically powerful? (7.6.8)

15. **COMPARING AND CONTRASTING** Were the religious motivations behind the Christian Crusades similar to or different from the motivations of the later Muslim Ottomans? Explain. (7.6.6)

16. **UNDERSTANDING EFFECTS** What effect did Islamic law have on Ottoman society? (Framework)

ALTERNATIVE ASSESSMENT

1. **WRITING ACTIVITY** Write a paragraph describing what you think life was like in the Ottoman Empire. (Framework)

2. **INTERDISCIPLINARY ACTIVITY—ART** Research weapons used during the Hundred Years' War. Create a series of trading cards detailing those weapons and their impact. (7.6)

3. **STARTING WITH A STORY**

    Review your response to the question about the plague. Now that you've read the chapter, would you answer this question differently? If so, how? (7.6.7)

Technology Activity

4. **CREATING A MULTIMEDIA PRESENTATION** (7.6.9)
Use the Internet or the library to research the Spanish Inquisition. Work with a partner to make a multimedia presentation that answers these three questions:
   - When did the Inquisition begin and end?
   - What were its practices and techniques?
   - What impact did it have?

Research Links
ClassZone.com

Interpreting Primary Sources The primary source below is an Ottoman description of the conquered Hungarians. Use the primary source to answer the questions. (Framework)

Primary Source

Though [the Hungarians] have lost their power, they still have fine tables [serve good meals], are hospitable to guests, and are capable cultivators of their fertile land. Like the Tartars [Mongol horsemen], they ride wherever they go with a span [a pair] of horses, with from five to ten pistols, and with swords at their waists. Indeed, they look just like our frontier soldiers, wearing the same dress as they, and riding the same thoroughbred horses. They are clean in their ways and in their eating, and honor their guests.

From *The Muslim Discovery of Europe*
By Bernard Lewis, page 155

1. **How does the Ottoman author feel about the Hungarians?**

   A. He dislikes them.
   B. He respects them.
   C. He fears them.
   D. He envies them.

2. **What seems to be the most important trait of the Hungarians to the Ottoman author?**

   A. that the Hungarians were farmers
   B. that the Hungarians rode horses
   C. that the Hungarians made good food
   D. that the Hungarians respected guests

 **Test Practice**
ClassZone.com

Additional Test Practice, pp. S1–S33

Writing About History

Fictional Narratives:
A Medieval Tale

Writing Model
ClassZone.com

CALIFORNIA STANDARDS
Writing 2.1 Write fictional or autobiographical narratives.

Purpose: To write a fictional narrative about someone in the Middle Ages

Audience: Your classmates

The Canterbury Tales was written in the 1300s by the poet Geoffrey Chaucer. It tells of several pilgrims on their way to a shrine in Canterbury. These pilgrims are a knight, a squire, a cook, a nun, a monk, and others. To pass the time on the journey, they have a storytelling contest. *The Canterbury Tales* is the collection of their stories. Each of these stories, and the bigger story of the pilgrims' journey, is a **fictional narrative,** or made-up story.

◀ Medieval women spinning thread

Organization & Focus

Your assignment is to write a fictional narrative about a medieval character to become part of a class collection of stories, similar to *The Canterbury Tales*. Remember that the plot of a narrative often has five parts:

- **Beginning**—description of the setting and start of the action
- **Conflict**—either between people or within a character's feelings
- **Rising action**—complication to the conflict
- **Climax**—turning point that changes the action
- **Denouement**—resolution of the conflict

Choosing a Topic Review Chapters 9 and 10. With a small group of classmates, create a list of possible characters by taking note of every occupation and social role mentioned in the chapters.

- From the list of characters, choose the one you most want to write about.
- Choose a setting, or time and place, for your story.
- Think of a plot that your character might find himself or herself in.
- Decide what other major and minor characters your story needs.

Identifying Purpose and Audience Your purpose is to write a story about the Middle Ages. Your audience is your classmates and others who might read the collection, such as your family. Not everyone is familiar with medieval times, so include any necessary information about what life was like then.

Finding Details Use a time line like the one below to create your plot. In the boxes, write the events of your story in the order they happen.

In the column beneath each event, list vivid details about the event. Such details include descriptions of actions, sensations, and emotions.

BEGINNING	CONFLICT	RISING ACTION	CLIMAX	DENOUEMENT
event				
details				

Outlining and Drafting Referring to the events and details in your time line, draft your story. Remember this advice for writers: show, don't tell. Instead of saying that a character is happy or sad, show that emotion through dialogue and descriptions of expressions and gestures.

Research & Technology

Details that appeal to the five senses bring stories to life. What kinds of clothes would your characters wear? What might they eat? Asking questions like these and finding answers in a library or online will give you details to make your story seem real.

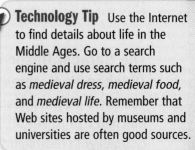

Technology Tip Use the Internet to find details about life in the Middle Ages. Go to a search engine and use search terms such as *medieval dress, medieval food,* and *medieval life.* Remember that Web sites hosted by museums and universities are often good sources.

Evaluation & Revision

Ask a friend to read your first draft to see if it seems like a completed story. Note any weaknesses that your friend finds and decide how to correct them.

After you have made revisions based on your friend's comments, read your story again. This time make sure you have chosen vivid words.

Self-Check

Does my fictional narrative have

- [ ] a definite setting?
- [ ] a consistent point of view?
- [ ] lifelike major and minor characters?
- [ ] a good plot, with rising action, a turning point, and a denouement?

Publish & Present

Make a neat final copy of your story to be included in the class collection of tales. With your classmates, think of a title. If possible, participate in the publishing by working on the front and back cover design, the table of contents, or the illustrations within the book.

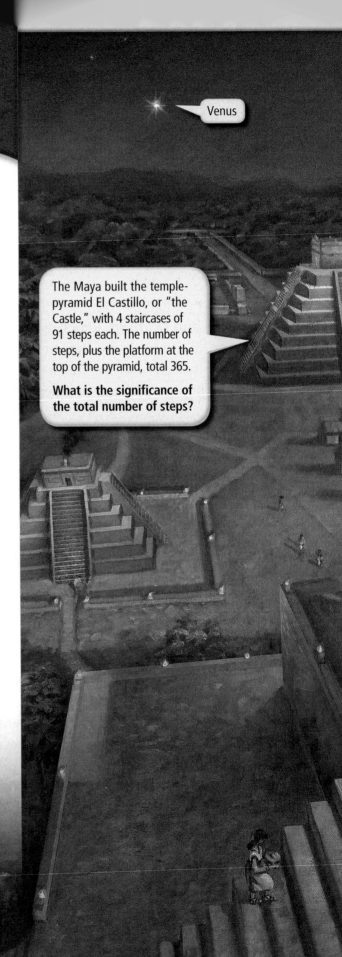

Civilizations of the Americas

Interact with History ▶

The Caracol Observatory, Chichén Itzá, about A.D. 1000
You are a Mayan priest in the city of Chichén Itzá (chee•CHEHN ee•TSAH) charged with recording the movement of the planets. This evening, you note that Venus rises in the western sky. You know that this means trouble for your people.

Why might observing the planets be important to the Mayans?

WebQuest
ClassZone.com

Venus

The Maya built the temple-pyramid El Castillo, or "the Castle," with 4 staircases of 91 steps each. The number of steps, plus the platform at the top of the pyramid, total 365.

What is the significance of the total number of steps?

Tracking the location of Venus was important to the Maya. They thought that its appearance in certain places in the sky signaled the coming of disasters, like war.

What actions might the Maya take based on their observations of Venus?

Mayan priests observed the sun, the moon, Venus, and other planets from the Caracol Observatory. They used their observations to construct very accurate calendars.

Why might the Maya want an accurate calendar?

Before You Read: K-W-L

The K-W-L approach will help you recall prior knowledge and develop a plan for learning new information. Consider the following questions as you read this chapter:

- What do you already know about early Mesoamerica?
- Study the map and time line on these pages. What do they tell you about early Mesoamerica?
- What do you want to learn about early Mesoamerica?

Big Ideas About Early Mesoamerica

Culture Many societies rely on family roles and social classes to keep order.

The development of agriculture in Mesoamerica allowed many societies to begin to produce food surpluses. This meant that some people could focus on tasks other than farming. The resulting division of labor led to the development of a class system. The upper levels of this system—rulers and nobility—established law and order in society.

Integrated Technology

eEdition
- Interactive Maps
- Interactive Visuals
- Starting with a Story

INTERNET RESOURCES
Go to **ClassZone.com** for
- WebQuest
- Homework Helper
- Research Links
- Internet Activities
- Quizzes
- Maps
- Test Practice
- Current Events

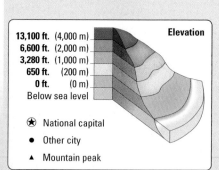

Elevation	
13,100 ft.	(4,000 m)
6,600 ft.	(2,000 m)
3,280 ft.	(1,000 m)
650 ft.	(200 m)
0 ft.	(0 m)
Below sea level	

⊛ National capital

● Other city

▲ Mountain peak

MESOAMERICA

1200s B.C.
Olmec civilization emerges.
(Olmec jade figurine) ▶

500s B.C.
Zapotecs complete the city of Monte Albán.

1200 B.C.   750 B.C.   500 B.C.   250 B.C.

WORLD

750 B.C.
Greek city-states flourish.

509 B.C.
Rome becomes a republic.

334 B.C.
Alexander the Great builds his empire. ▶

Present-Day Mexico and Central America: Physical

INTER*ACTIVE*

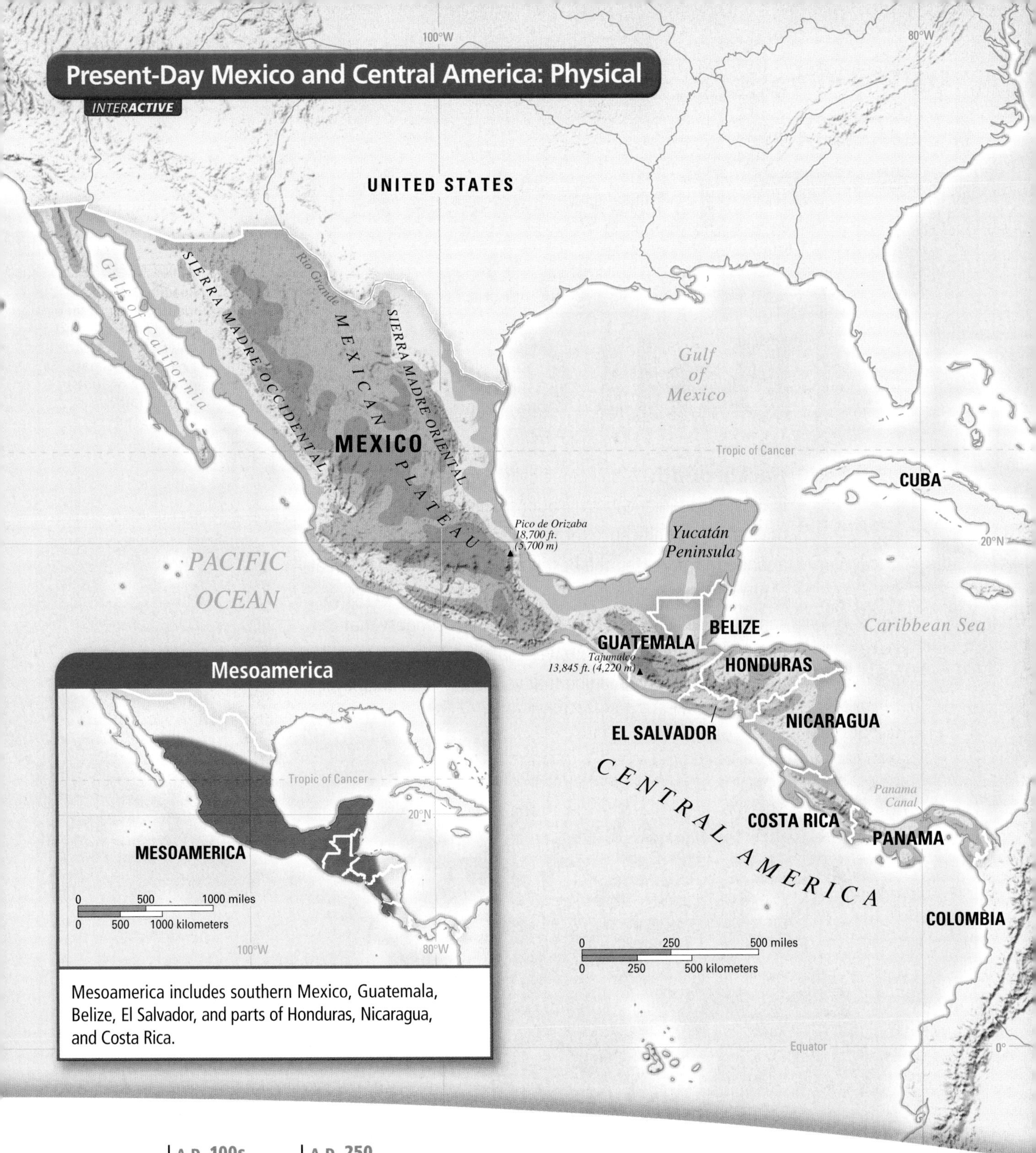

UNITED STATES

Gulf of California

SIERRA MADRE OCCIDENTAL

Rio Grande

SIERRA MADRE ORIENTAL

M E X I C A N   P L A T E A U

MEXICO

Pico de Orizaba
18,700 ft.
(5,700 m) ▲

PACIFIC
OCEAN

*Gulf
of
Mexico*

Tropic of Cancer

CUBA

20°N

*Yucatán
Peninsula*

BELIZE

GUATEMALA
Tajumulco
13,845 ft. (4,220 m) ▲

HONDURAS

Caribbean Sea

EL SALVADOR

NICARAGUA

C E N T R A L   A M E R I C A

*Panama
Canal*

COSTA RICA

PANAMA

COLOMBIA

Equator

0°

100°W

80°W

Mesoamerica

Tropic of Cancer

20°N

MESOAMERICA

| 0 | 500 | 1000 miles |
| 0 | 500 | 1000 kilometers |

100°W

80°W

Mesoamerica includes southern Mexico, Guatemala,
Belize, El Salvador, and parts of Honduras, Nicaragua,
and Costa Rica.

| 0 | 250 | 500 miles |
| 0 | 250 | 500 kilometers |

A.D. 100s
Teotihuacán
becomes a
major city.

A.D. 250
Classical period of
Maya begins.
(Mayan pyramid) ▶

A.D. 800s
Maya begin to
abandon their cities.

A.D. 900
Classical period
of Maya ends.

B.C. | A.D. | A.D. 250 | A.D. 500 | A.D. 750 | A.D. 1000

A.D. 300
Kingdom of Aksum
emerges in East Africa.
(Aksumite stele) ▶

A.D. 618
Tang Dynasty
comes to power
in China.

A.D. 912
Muslim kingdom of
al-Andalus thrives during the
rule of Abd al-Rahman III.

363

Take Me Out to the Ball Game!

CALIFORNIA STANDARDS
Reading 3.2
Identify events that advance the plot and determine how each event explains past or present action(s) or foreshadows future action(s).

Background: A ball game called *pok-a-tok* was played in most Mesoamerican civilizations. This game seemed to have special significance for the Maya. It was hugely popular, and the Maya treated the best players like heroes. The great players also grew rich from the game. But fame and riches came at a price. Some Mayan inscriptions suggest that members of the losing team were sacrificed. As you read the following story, imagine that you're a Mayan ballplayer about to step onto the *pok-a-tok* court.

The hoop at the ball court in Chichén Itzá is 20 feet above the ground. ▶

The crowd goes wild when you and other players step onto the stone court. Only nobles like you can play. You wear your finest jewelry and a headdress made of bright parrot feathers.

Sometimes you play the game as a sport. At other times, like today, you play for religious reasons. In these special games, you and your fellow ballplayers act out an ancient battle between the gods of the day and the night. Today the stakes are high. The losing captain pays with his life. His blood ensures that the gods will continue to let the sun shine. Without the sun, the crops will die. Without food, the Mayan people will die too.

To win, you and your teammates must shoot a rubber ball through a stone ring. But this isn't easy. The ring hangs some 20 feet over your head. The solid rubber ball weighs over 5 pounds. And you can't use your hands or your feet. You must hit the ball off padding on your hips, wrists, elbows, chest, or waist.

You take a breath and start to play. After a really long time, your team finally takes control of the ball. As the ball flies your way, you drop to one knee and use your chest to force it through the stone ring. Victory is yours!

Once again the Mayan people have cheated death. The blood of the defeated captain will keep the sun shining. You wonder, will the Maya always be so fortunate?

Why do you think the ball game is so important to the Maya?

Reading & Writing

1. **READING: Plot** The plot is a sequence of events in the story. Usually, each event is caused by an event that came before it. With a partner, identify the various events that make up the plot of this story.

2. **WRITING: Narration** Imagine you're a Mayan teacher. Write an information sheet to give to your students explaining the rules and the meaning of the *pok-a-tok* game.

CALIFORNIA STANDARDS Writing 2.1
Write fictional or autobiographical narratives.

▶ **MAIN IDEAS**

1 **Geography** Mesoamerica has a variety of landforms.

2 **Geography** Climates in Mesoamerica vary from tropical to dry.

3 **Geography** Geographic diversity caused Mesoamerica to have a variety of natural resources and crops.

▶ **TAKING NOTES**

Reading Skill: Finding Main Ideas

Identifying main ideas in a passage will help you understand what you read. As you read each section of Lesson 1, look for essential information on the main ideas. Record this information in a chart like the one shown below.

▲ **Mesoamerican Farming Tools** Mesoamerican farmers used hand tools with heads made of stone and metal to clear and prepare the land for planting.

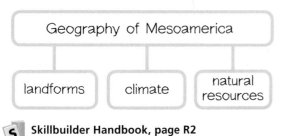

Geography of Mesoamerica

| landforms | climate | natural resources |

S **Skillbuilder Handbook, page R2**

CALIFORNIA STANDARDS

7.7.1 Study the locations, landforms, and climates of Mexico, Central America, and South America and their effects on Mayan, Aztec, and Incan economies, trade, and development of urban societies.

CST 3 Students use a variety of maps and documents to identify physical and cultural features of neighborhoods, cities, states, and countries and to explain the historical migration of people, expansion and disintegration of empires, and the growth of economic systems.

REP 3 Students distinguish relevant from irrelevant information, essential from incidental information, and verifiable from unverifiable information in historical narratives and stories.

Geography and Agriculture in Mesoamerica

TERMS & NAMES

Mesoamerica

Yucatán Peninsula

elevation

slash-and-burn agriculture

maize

cacao

Build on What You Know What is the landscape like in the area where you live? Are there high mountains? Or do you live in a lowland area? Are there any volcanoes nearby? As you'll read in this lesson, Mesoamerica has all these different landforms.

Landforms of Mesoamerica

1 **ESSENTIAL QUESTION** What landforms are found in Mesoamerica?

Rugged highlands, coastal lowlands, and smoking volcanoes are just some of the physical features that have shaped life in Mesoamerica.

Location and Landforms **Mesoamerica**, or Middle America, lies between the present-day United States and South America. It includes the southern part of Mexico and much of Central America. (See the map on page 363.)

Mesoamerica is a land of varying elevations. A central spine of mountains runs through much of the region. In the north, the mountain range divides into two. A section called the Mexican Plateau separates these two highland areas. On each side of the mountains, narrow coastal plains run along the Pacific Ocean and the Caribbean Sea and Gulf of Mexico. In some places, the plains widen into broad lowlands such as the **Yucatán Peninsula**. The Yucatán stretches into, and divides, the Caribbean Sea and the Gulf of Mexico.

Pacaya Volcano
Located in southern Guatemala, Pacaya is one of the world's most active volcanoes. ▼

Volcanoes Volcanoes have had a huge effect on the landscape of Mesoamerica. When a volcano erupts, it spits out streams of lava, or melted rock, and clouds of ash. In time, the lava and ash build up to form huge conelike mountains. In Mesoamerica, some of these volcanic mountains are well over 10,000 feet high. More than a dozen of them are still active. (See the photograph on page 367.) That means they can erupt at any time. But most have been dormant, or inactive, for hundreds of years. The craters of a few of these dormant volcanoes have filled with water, forming vast highland lakes.

REVIEW What is the landscape like in Mesoamerica?

Climate and Vegetation

2 **ESSENTIAL QUESTION** How do climates vary in Mesoamerica?

The climate of Mesoamerica ranges from hot and humid in much of the south to desertlike conditions in the far north. Such a difference means diverse growing conditions for plants.

Wet and Dry Climates Much of Mesoamerica lies in the *Tropics*. This area stretches from the tropic of Cancer (about 23° north latitude) to the tropic of Capricorn (about 23° south latitude). Generally, the climates here are hot and wet. Daytime temperatures stay above 80°F for most of the year. A little over 80 inches of rain falls every year. The heat and moisture of this tropical climate give rise to rain forests, where various trees and plants flourish. In the lowland areas, where less rain falls, the rain forest gives way to rich grasslands with a few trees and bushes.

Visual Vocabulary

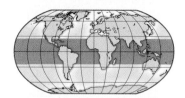

the Tropics

In the northern section of Mesoamerica, the climate is still very hot. However, very little rain falls there. Much of this area is covered with grasses with an occasional bush or shrub. Some parts of the north get so little rain that they are considered to be deserts.

Elevation and Climate One of the greatest influences on climate in Mesoamerica is **elevation**, or the height of the land above sea level. The higher land is, the cooler the climate becomes. Under normal conditions, the temperature drops by about 3.5°F for every 1,000 feet you rise. And growing conditions change as climate changes. The Geography feature on the next page shows the main elevation and climate zones in Central America and the different plants that grow in each zone.

REVIEW What is the link between elevation and climate?

Geography

Elevation and Climate in Central America

Climate and vegetation vary according to elevation. This diagram shows the main climate zones, as defined by elevation, in Central America. The different natural vegetation and crops found in each zone are also shown.

1 Tierra Helada (Very Cold Land)

2 Tierra Fria (Cold Land)

3 Tierra Templada (Temperate Land)

4 Tierra Caliente (Hot Land)

GEOGRAPHY SKILLBUILDER

INTERPRETING VISUALS
Human-Environment Interaction
Which zones are the most productive for growing crops?

4,000 feet elevation

Tierra Helada (Very Cold Land)

Natural Vegetation	Modern Land Use
mountain grasses, mosses	animal grazing

3,000 feet elevation

Tierra Fria (Cold Land)

Natural Vegetation	Modern Land Use
cloud forest (forest near mountain peaks with almost constant cloud cover)	wheat, potatoes

2,000 feet elevation

Tierra Templada (Temperate Land)

Natural Vegetation	Modern Land Use
wet forest	corn, beans, squash, cotton, coffee

1,000 feet elevation

Tierra Caliente (Hot Land)

Natural Vegetation	Modern Land Use
dry forest	cacao, bananas, sugar cane

Geography Shapes Mesoamerican Life

3 ESSENTIAL QUESTION How has geographic diversity affected the natural resources and crops found in Mesoamerica?

The landforms and climate of Mesoamerica provided the region with a variety of natural resources. These natural resources helped to shape the way that early peoples of the region lived.

Natural Resources The highlands of what is now Guatemala supplied Mesoamericans with jade and obsidian, a black volcanic glass. People carved small figures from jade and made razor-sharp weapons from obsidian. They also found seashells and shark's teeth in the coastal regions. Mesoamericans used these for jewelry.

Mesoamericans also made use of the animals found in the region. They especially prized the colorful feathers of a bird called the quetzal (keht•SAHL). The quetzal was sacred to many Meso-americans. They often used the feathers from these birds to decorate their clothing and headdresses.

Agriculture and Cities

The development of agriculture made the production of surpluses possible and led to the development of urban societies.

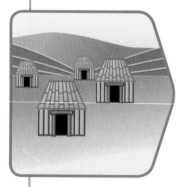

1 Agriculture leads to settled villages.

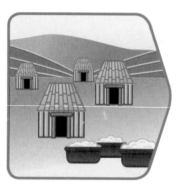

2 As agriculture improves, surpluses of food crops such as corn are produced. This encourages population growth and larger villages.

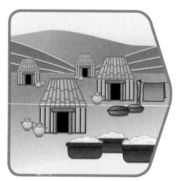

3 Surpluses also mean that not everyone has to raise food. Some people begin specializing in other kinds of work, such as weaving.

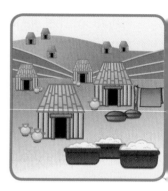

4 Food surpluses and specialized skills lead to the growth of cities.

Agriculture Mesoamericans farmed all kinds of land. Some of it was good for farming, such as the floodplains of rivers or the slopes of volcanic mountains. In both places the soil was fertile—favorable for growing crops. Other areas, such as the rain forests, were not so good for farming. To work these lands, Mesoamericans used a method called **slash-and-burn agriculture**. Farmers cleared the land by cutting down trees. Then they burned the fallen trees and used the ashes to fertilize the soil. Finally, they planted crops on the cleared land. After a few years, they abandoned this land and moved on to another part of the rain forest.

Mesoamericans grew a variety of crops, including **maize**—a type of corn—beans, peppers, and squash. They used maize to make many types of foods such as the tortilla, a kind of flat bread. In addition, Mesoamericans grew cacao. **Cacao** is a type of tree that grows well in moist, hot tropical climates. Mesoamericans used the beans from this tree to make a chocolate drink. The beans also were a prized trading item.

Geography and Trade Mesoamericans looked outside of their local areas for many luxury goods. Jade and obsidian were mostly found only in mountain areas. Seashells came from the coastal areas. Trade developed as Mesoamericans began to exchange their local goods for goods found in other regions.

Mesoamericans traded goods over great distances by water. Using dugout canoes, they traveled the few navigable rivers in the region. They also ventured into open waters, traveling along the Pacific, Caribbean, and Gulf coasts. The Mesoamericans also carried on an overland trade, lugging the goods on their backs. Such heavy human labor was necessary because they had not developed the wheel and no horses or oxen were available to use as pack animals.

Trade goods were not the only items that moved along these routes. Knowledge also spread, carried by traders all over the region. This sharing and blending of ideas helped to create a common culture throughout Mesoamerica.

REVIEW How did the geography of Mesoamerica encourage trade?

Lesson Summary

- Mesoamerica has a variety of landforms.
- Mesoamerica has a variety of climates.
- Geographic diversity caused Mesoamerica to have a variety of natural resources and crops.

Why It Matters Now . . .

Chocolate, made from the cacao bean, has become one of the world's most popular foods.

1 Lesson Review

Homework Helper
ClassZone.com

Terms & Names

1. Explain the importance of

Mesoamerica	slash-and-burn agriculture
Yucatán Peninsula	maize
elevation	cacao

Using Your Notes

Finding Main Ideas Use your completed chart to answer the following question:

2. What are the major geographic features of Mesoamerica? (7.7.1)

Geography of Mesoamerica

landforms   climate   natural resources

Main Ideas

3. What landforms are found in Mesoamerica? (7.7.1)

4. What types of climate does Mesoamerica have? (7.7.1)

5. How did Mesoamericans prepare the rain forest for farming? (7.7.1)

Critical Thinking

6. **Making Inferences** Mesoamericans did not use pack animals to transport goods. How do you think overland trade would have been affected if Mesoamericans did have pack animals? (7.7.1)

7. **Drawing Conclusions** Why do you think Mesoamericans used slash-and-burn agriculture? (7.7.1)

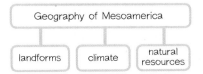
Activity   **Internet Activity** Use the Internet to research what role chocolate played in the lives of Mesoamericans. Write and illustrate a report on chocolate in early Mesoamerica.   (REP 3)
INTERNET KEYWORDS: *chocolate, Mesoamerica*

Lesson

2

▶ **MAIN IDEAS**

1 **Geography** Because of geographic advantages for agriculture, the Olmec developed one of the earliest civilizations in the Americas.

2 **Culture** The Olmec developed a sophisticated culture that influenced later civilizations.

3 **Culture** Through trade, Olmec culture spread throughout Mesoamerica and had a lasting influence.

▶ **TAKING NOTES**

Reading Skill: Summarizing

Summarizing information, which involves restating main ideas and important details in fewer words, will help you understand materials that you read. As you read Lesson 2, record information on the major features of Olmec civilization in a graphic organizer like the one shown below.

▲ **Jaguar** The jaguar is native to Mesoamerica. Its importance to the Olmec is seen in the many jaguarlike sculptures and figurines they made.

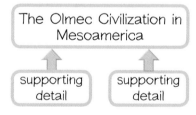

```
          The Olmec Civilization in
                  Mesoamerica

         ↑                    ↑
  supporting            supporting
    detail                detail
```

 Skillbuilder Handbook, page R3

CALIFORNIA STANDARDS

7.7 Students compare and contrast the geographic, political, economic, religious, and social structures of the Meso-American and Andean civilizations.

HI 2 Students understand and distinguish cause, effect, sequence, and correlation in historical events, including long- and short-term causal relations.

CST 2 Students construct various time lines of key events, people, and periods of the historical era they are studying.

The Olmec Civilization

TERMS & NAMES
Olmec
alluvial soil
elite
glyph
mother culture

Build on What You Know Mesoamerica has a variety of landforms, climates, plants, and natural resources. In this lesson you will learn how these geographic elements led to the development of the Olmec civilization.

An Early American Civilization

1 ESSENTIAL QUESTION Why were the Olmec able to develop one of the earliest civilizations in the Americas?

About 3,000 years ago, a group of people called the **Olmec** lived along the Gulf Coast in what is now southern Mexico. They settled near rivers and began to farm. This activity helped them to develop the first major civilization in Mesoamerica.

A Productive Land The area where the Olmec lived received a lot of rain. In the rainiest months, the rivers often flooded. When the floodwaters subsided, they left a layer of **alluvial soil** on the land near the rivers. This soil, deposited by flowing water, was very fertile.

The Olmec soon realized that the flat lands near rivers were good for growing crops. In time, farming began to thrive in the region. As a result, the food supply increased and became more reliable. With a steady food supply, the Olmec population grew.

A steady food supply also meant that some people could focus on tasks other than farming. Some became potters or weavers, while others became priests or teachers. This division of labor was accompanied by another important development—the growth of cities.

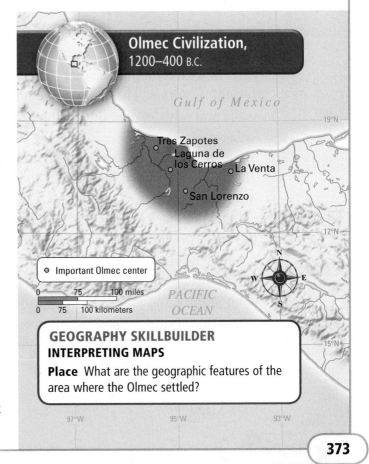

Olmec Civilization, 1200–400 B.C.

Gulf of Mexico

19°N

Tres Zapotes
Laguna de los Cerros
La Venta
San Lorenzo

17°N

● Important Olmec center

0 75 100 miles
0 75 100 kilometers

PACIFIC OCEAN

15°N

GEOGRAPHY SKILLBUILDER
INTERPRETING MAPS
Place What are the geographic features of the area where the Olmec settled?

97°W 95°W 93°W

Olmec Cities As the Olmec population grew, so did their farming villages. Some of these villages developed into cities. By 1150 B.C., the Olmec had built the city now called San Lorenzo. (See the map on the previous page.) The center of the city contained raised mounds and huge stone monuments used for religious ceremonies. San Lorenzo also had plazas—large open areas—which probably were used as trade centers. In addition, there were housing areas, where Olmec priests and rulers lived.

To the east of San Lorenzo, another huge Olmec city, now called La Venta, began to grow around 900 B.C. Within 100 years, it had replaced San Lorenzo as the center of the Olmec civilization. Like San Lorenzo, La Venta served as a religious and trade center.

REVIEW What impact did an increased and more reliable food supply have on the Olmec?

Olmec Culture

2 ESSENTIAL QUESTION What kind of culture did the Olmec develop?

Much of how the Olmec lived remains a mystery. However, based on archaeological evidence, historians have formed some ideas about Olmec culture. These ideas continue to develop and change as more evidence is found.

Olmec Society and Daily Life Most Olmec were farmers and fishers. They lived in villages near rivers. They may have built their houses on top of earthen mounds. Each mound probably held several dwellings. These buildings most likely had mud or wooden walls and roofs made out of palm leaves. The Olmec villagers' main task was to provide food for all. They grew maize, beans, squash, and peppers. They also caught fish and turtle, and hunted deer.

Most Olmec city-dwellers were from the **elite**, an upper class of priests and nobles who ruled Olmec society. These people lived in large stone houses. They wore jewelry and fancy clothes. Some commoners, who were mostly laborers and craftworkers, also lived in the cities. Their houses were smaller and made of wood or mud. In general, their clothes were very plain.

Olmec Stone Head
This stone head, located at La Venta, stands about 6 feet tall. Some heads are more than 10 feet tall and weigh as much as 20 tons. ▼

Olmec Glyph

Some historians believe that a recently discovered Mexican clay cylinder suggests that the Olmec may have invented the glyph writing used in many Mesoamerican civilizations. **Glyphs** are pictures that represent words, syllables, or sounds.

One of the glyph symbols is the name "3 Ajaw," which might be a date or the name of a king. Rulers of Mesoamerican civilizations traditionally took their names from the date on which they were born.

The clay cylinder seal probably was inked and rolled on cloth or animal skins to create a continuous pattern.

The cylinder has a design showing a bird with glyph symbols coming from its beak.

DOCUMENT–BASED QUESTION
Some historians believe that the pattern produced by the seal was used to show the king's authority. How might these glyphs express a ruler's power?

Historians know that the Olmec played a ball game like the one you read about on pages 364–365. In fact, the Olmec may have invented the game. The huge ball courts built by the Olmec suggest that the game was popular with spectators.

Olmec Art and Learning In the remains of San Lorenzo and other Olmec cities, archaeologists have discovered several huge stone heads. Each head has a flat face, thick lips, and staring eyes. What these heads represent and why the Olmec built them are a mystery. They may be monuments to Olmec rulers or famous ballgame players.

The Olmec made the heads out of basalt (buh•SAWLT), a kind of volcanic rock. They transported these huge rocks from quarries more than 50 miles away. How the Olmec managed to accomplish this feat remains unknown. They did not have the wheel or pack animals.

The Olmec also made small sculptures out of jade. Other Olmec art included pottery and cave paintings.

The Olmec used an early form of glyph writing to record events, dates, and to tell stories. (See the Primary Source feature above.) The Olmec were also incredible astronomers. They developed a calendar that was amazingly accurate for its time.

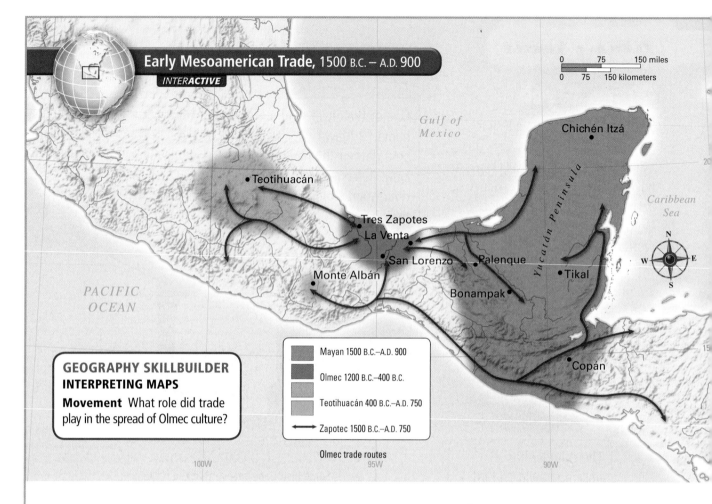

Early Mesoamerican Trade, 1500 B.C. – A.D. 900

INTER**ACTIVE**

Gulf of Mexico

Chichén Itzá

Teotihuacán

Tres Zapotes

La Venta

San Lorenzo

Palenque

Monte Albán

Bonampak

Tikal

Caribbean Sea

Yucatán Peninsula

PACIFIC OCEAN

Copán

GEOGRAPHY SKILLBUILDER
INTERPRETING MAPS
Movement What role did trade play in the spread of Olmec culture?

Mayan 1500 B.C.–A.D. 900

Olmec 1200 B.C.–400 B.C.

Teotihuacán 400 B.C.–A.D. 750

Zapotec 1500 B.C.–A.D. 750

Olmec trade routes

Religion The Olmec worshiped several gods. The chief god was the jaguar. They probably believed that the jaguar god brought rain. The Olmec also worshiped a fire god and a corn god. These gods were sometimes represented as a jaguar and sometimes as other animals.

As you read earlier, the Olmec built large mounds in the centers of their cities. Later, they replaced these mounds with pyramids. The Olmec probably used the pyramids as religious centers.

REVIEW How was Olmec society organized?

The Olmec Legacy

3 **ESSENTIAL QUESTION** Why did Olmec culture have a lasting influence in Mesoamerica?

Historians believe that the Olmec did not focus on warfare and conquest. Instead, they influenced other cultures mainly through trade.

Prosperous Trade Most Olmec cities served as trade centers. The Olmec mainly traded for luxury items needed by the elite. These items included precious stones, iron ore, and obsidian. Knowledge and ideas also were exchanged at these trade centers. As a result, the Olmec culture spread throughout much of Mesoamerica.

A Lasting Influence Around 500 B.C., the Olmec began to abandon their cities. The reason for this remains unclear. By 400 B.C., the Olmec civilization had largely disappeared. Even so, it had a huge impact on Mesoamerica.

Many historians consider the Olmec civilization the mother culture of Mesoamerica. A **mother culture** is a way of life that strongly influences later cultures. Olmec culture and customs shaped succeeding Mesoamerican cultures, such as the Zapotec, the people of Teotihuacán, the Aztec, and especially the Maya.

REVIEW Why is Olmec civilization considered a mother culture?

Zapotec Jaguar Head
The Zapotec, like the Olmec, worshiped the jaguar god. In this sculpture, another god is emerging from the mouth of the jaguar god. ▼

Lesson Summary

- The Olmec developed a thriving civilization that included cities.
- The Olmec developed notable art and a complex religion.
- Olmec culture shaped later Meso-american civilizations.

Why It Matters Now . . .

Today the peoples of Mexico and Central America are still influenced by Olmec culture.

---

2 Lesson Review

Homework Helper
ClassZone.com

Terms & Names

1. Explain the importance of

Olmec	elite	mother culture
alluvial soil	glyph	

Using Your Notes

Summarizing Use your completed graphic organizer to answer the following question:

2. How do the features of Olmec civilization compare with those of a typical civilization? (7.7)

```
The Olmec Civilization in
Mesoamerica
    ↑           ↑
supporting   supporting
 detail       detail
```

Main Ideas

3. What type of human-made structures did San Lorenzo contain? (7.7)

4. What gods did the Olmec most likely worship? (7.7)

5. How did trade help to spread Olmec culture? (HI 2)

Critical Thinking

6. Making Inferences Why do you think the jaguar god, or rain god, was the most important one for the Olmec? Explain. (7.7)

7. Forming and Supporting Opinions How do you think the Olmec transported the huge heads they created without using pack animals or the wheel? Give reasons for your answer. (7.7)

Creating a Diagram Conduct research to find information about Olmec pyramids. Use your findings to create an annotated diagram that shows what an Olmec pyramid looked like. (7.7)

Explaining Chronological Order and Sequence

CALIFORNIA STANDARDS
CST 2 Students construct various time lines of key events, people, and periods of the historical era they are studying.

Goal: To read a passage and understand the relationship of events that led to the rise and fall of the Olmec civilization

Learn the Skill

Sequence is the order in which events follow one another. Historians need to figure out the order in which things happened so they can understand how events are related to one another. They try to see causes, effects, and other connections. Exact dates place events in the framework of the passage of time. Understanding the chronological order, or their order in time, will help you learn how events are related.

S See the Skillbuilder Handbook, page R15.

Practice the Skill

1 Look for clue words about time as you read the passage on the next page. These are words such as *first, next, later, before, after, finally,* and *ago.* In a passage about a person's life, the words *born* and *died* signal the beginning and end of the story.

2 Check for specific dates provided in the text.

3 Look for phrases that link two events together to help you find an exact date. To know by what year La Venta became the center of Olmec civilization, subtract 100 from 900.

4 Notice events that came before something to understand possible causes. Seeing what happened afterward helps you find effects.

5 Use a time line like the one below to help you put the events in a passage in the right sequence. Look for the earliest date to know how to mark the beginning and latest to mark the end of the time line.

Example:

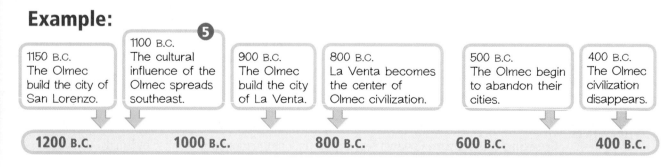

1150 B.C.
The Olmec build the city of San Lorenzo.

1100 B.C.
The cultural influence of the Olmec spreads southeast.

900 B.C.
The Olmec build the city of La Venta.

800 B.C.
La Venta becomes the center of Olmec civilization.

500 B.C.
The Olmec begin to abandon their cities.

400 B.C.
The Olmec civilization disappears.

1200 B.C.   1000 B.C.   800 B.C.   600 B.C.   400 B.C.

The following passage describes the rise and fall of the Olmec civilization. Use the strategies listed under Practice the Skill to help you follow the sequence of events.

The Rise and Fall of the Olmec

About 3,000 years **1** ago, a group of people called the Olmec lived along the Gulf Coast in what is now southern Mexico. At **1** first, they settled near rivers. They obtained much of their food from fishing. **1** Later, the Olmec began to farm. **4** This activity helped them to develop the first major civilization in Mesoamerica.

By **2** 1150 B.C., the Olmec had built the city now called San Lorenzo, located near the Chiquito River. The center of the city contained raised mounds and huge stone monuments, which were used for religious ceremonies.

Starting around **2** 1100 B.C., the cultural influence of the Olmec began to spread southeast. By **2** 900 B.C., the Olmec had built another huge city to the east of San Lorenzo. This city is now called La Venta. **3** Within 100 years, it had replaced San Lorenzo as the center of the Olmec civilization.

A 100-foot-high mound dominated the center of La Venta. Near the mound, the Olmec built several tombs, probably for their rulers. Like San Lorenzo, La Venta served as a religious and trade center.

Around **2** 500 B.C., the **4** Olmec began to abandon their cities. The reason for this remains unclear. Many historians believe that invaders destroyed the Olmec cities. Whatever the reason, the Olmec civilization had largely disappeared by **2** 400 B.C.

▲ **Olmec Priest**
This sculpture from La Venta shows an Olmec priest making an offering.

Apply the Skill

Turn to pages 327–328 in Chapter 10, Lesson 2. Read "Battle for Palestine" and "Muslims Return to Power." Make a time line like the one at left to show the sequence of events in these passages.

▶ MAIN IDEAS

1 **Geography** Mayan civilization rose in what is now Mexico and Central America.

2 **Culture** Mayan society was divided into classes. Each class had its own way of life.

3 **Culture** From about A.D. 250 to 900, known as the Classical period of Mayan civilization, the Maya built great cities, produced beautiful art, and made important advances in learning.

▶ TAKING NOTES

Reading Skill: Framing Historical Questions

Framing questions helps focus your reading. In a chart, write several questions on the Mayan civilization, such as the one shown here, that you would like answered. As you read Lesson 3, record in the chart any answers that you find.

Questions	Answers
Where was the Mayan civilization located?	

 Skillbuilder Handbook, page R18

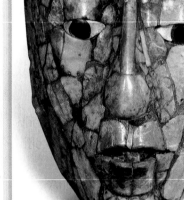

▲ **Mayan Burial Mask** This mask, made of jade and seashells, covered the face of the dead King Pacal of Palenque.

CALIFORNIA STANDARDS

7.7.2 Study the roles of people in each society, including class structures, family life, warfare, religious beliefs and practices, and slavery.

7.7.3 Explain how and where each empire arose and how the Aztec and Incan empires were defeated by the Spanish.

7.7.4 Describe the artistic and oral traditions and architecture in the three civilizations.

7.7.5 Describe the Meso-American achievements in astronomy and mathematics, including the development of the calendar and the Meso-American knowledge of seasonal changes to the civilizations' agricultural systems.

The Mayan Civilization

TERMS & NAMES
Maya
stele
Pacal II
codex

Build on What You Know The Olmec served as the mother culture for civilizations that developed later in Mesoamerica. One of these, the Maya, was strongly influenced by the Olmec.

Birth of a Civilization

1 ESSENTIAL QUESTION Where did Mayan civilization arise?

The **Maya** consist of groups of Mesoamerican peoples who speak various forms of the Mayan language. Their culture can be traced as far back as 2000 B.C.

Lands of the Maya Around 1500 B.C., the Maya began to establish villages in the highlands and lowlands of Mesoamerica. (See the map on the following page.) Most of their highland villages were located in what is now southern Guatemala. This mountainous region contained many minerals. In general, this area had a dry, cool climate.

The lowland villages of the Maya were located in what is now northern Guatemala, Belize, and the Yucatán Peninsula in southern Mexico. The Yucatán lowlands tended to be hot and dry. Hot, humid rain forests covered the lowlands farther to the south. This area had fertile soil that was good for farming.

Beginnings of the Maya The development of Mayan society was similar to the development of Olmec society. As farming thrived in the Mayan homelands, the Maya were able to grow more food. With more food, the Maya became healthier and their population grew. In time, some Mayan farming villages grew into great cities.

REVIEW Where did the Maya establish villages?

Connect to Today

A Guatemalan Market These Mayan women are selling blankets woven in centuries-old traditional designs. ▼

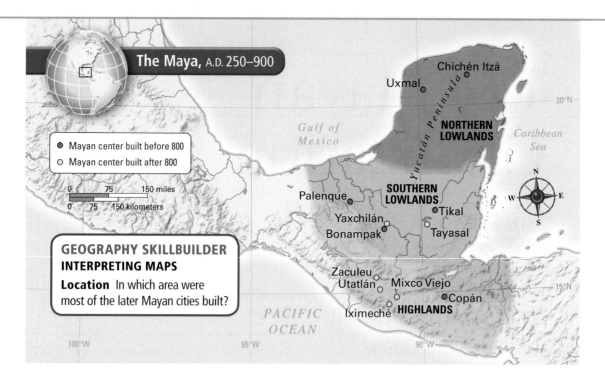

The Maya, A.D. 250–900

- Mayan center built before 800
- Mayan center built after 800

0   75   150 miles
0   75   150 kilometers

Chichén Itzá
Uxmal
Gulf of Mexico
NORTHERN LOWLANDS
Caribbean Sea
Yucatán Peninsula
20°N
SOUTHERN LOWLANDS
Palenque
Yaxchilán
Bonampak
Tikal
Tayasal
Zaculeu
Utatlán
Mixco Viejo
Copán
Iximeché HIGHLANDS
15°N
PACIFIC OCEAN
100°W   95°W   90°W

GEOGRAPHY SKILLBUILDER
INTERPRETING MAPS
Location In which area were most of the later Mayan cities built?

Mayan Life

2 ESSENTIAL QUESTION Into what social classes was Mayan society divided?

Because the Maya produced a food surplus, some people could focus on tasks other than farming. Some became craftspeople. Others became priests or teachers. This division of labor resulted in the development of a class system.

Class Structures Mayan society consisted of four broad social classes. These were the ruling class, the nobility, peasants, and slaves.

The ruling class consisted of kings and their families. Kings governed each of the Mayan cities. Kings also performed the religious duties of priests. The nobility probably included scholars, architects, and merchants. They were educated and wealthy. Many historians believe that Mayan warriors were mostly nobles. Peasants included farmers and laborers. They made up the vast majority of the population. Slaves were mostly criminals and people captured in war. Orphaned children sometimes became slaves.

Peasant Farmers Most Mayan peasants worked as farmers. Farm families lived in small villages near the big cities. Their homes were simple buildings made of mud or wooden poles with roofs of palm leaves or grass. Mayan farmers grew maize, beans, squash, chili peppers, avocados, pineapples, and cacao. Maize was the most important crop. In fact, the Maya believed that they had been created out of maize.

Mayan farmers used a variety of techniques to grow their crops. In the rain forests, they used slash-and-burn agriculture. In the highlands, they increased the land available for farming by building terraces. (See the Geography feature on page 226, which shows terrace farming in China.) In drier areas, they dug irrigation canals that carried water from streams and rivers to their fields. Some Mayan farmers still use these techniques today.

The Nobility Mayan noble families led very different lives from the peasants. Nobles lived in houses built of stone with plastered walls. Often the walls were decorated with *murals*—paintings applied directly to walls. Nobles wore fancy clothes, such as jaguar skins and headdresses decorated with colorful feathers. They also wore jewelry crafted out of jade and shells.

In addition, nobles ate much better than peasants. In fact, some foods were reserved for the nobility. For example, only nobles were allowed to drink chocolate.

Religious Beliefs The Maya worshiped more than 160 gods and goddesses. The main god was called ItzamNá. The Maya believed that this god created the world. They also worshiped a sun god, a moon goddess, and the gods of death, war, rain, and maize. The Maya often represented these gods as animals.

To get help from the gods, the Maya fasted, prayed, and offered sacrifices. Most of these sacrifices were animals, such as turkeys or deer. Occasionally, the Maya made human sacrifices. In addition, the Maya expected their rulers to communicate with the gods on their behalf. Unlike the ancient Egyptians, who looked forward to life after death, the Maya viewed the afterlife as an unhappy existence.

Visual Vocabulary

mural

Mayan Artistic Traditions Mural The Maya decorated the walls of buildings with murals that portrayed religious ceremonies, battles, or other important events from their history. ▼

Religious Ceremonies The Maya had many religious festivals and ceremonies. Ruler-priests performed many of these ceremonies on platforms on top of pyramids. However, one important ceremony, the ball game that you read about on pages 364–365, was performed in a ball court. While the ball game was often just a sporting competition, sometimes it had religious meaning. On such occasions, it was played to honor great Mayan heroes. It was also played to celebrate important events from Mayan history.

REVIEW What were the four classes that made up Mayan society?

Glory and Decline

3 ESSENTIAL QUESTION What cultural developments did the Maya achieve during the Classical period of their civilization?

The Maya reached their peak roughly during the years between A.D. 250 and 900. During this time, which was known as the Classical period, the Maya built an advanced civilization that included large cities.

Great Cities The Maya built more than 40 cities, including Copán, Tikal, Palenque (pah•LEHNG•keh), Bonampak, and Chichén Itzá. Mayan cities were notable for their magnificent architecture. Each one contained palaces, plazas, ball courts, and pyramids topped by temples. Many cities also had large stone monuments called **steles** (STEE•leez). On these monuments, the Maya carved glyphs that represented important dates and great events.

History Makers

Pacal II of Palenque (603–683)

Pacal II was one of the greatest Mayan kings. He took the throne of the city of Palenque in 615 at the age of 12, and ruled for nearly 70 years. During his reign, Palenque reached the height of its power.

Interestingly, Pacal almost did not become king. Pacal's mother, Lady Zac-Kuk, ruled Palenque as queen. However, according to Mayan tradition, only the son of a king could become king. But Pacal declared that his mother was the living image of the First Mother, a goddess who created the Maya. In other words, Pacal claimed that he was the son of a goddess. With this declaration, Pacal secured his right to the throne.

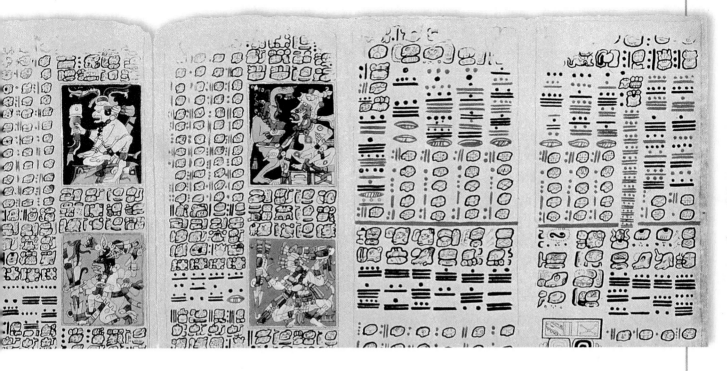

Cities and Warfare

A king governed each Mayan city and its surrounding area. (The History Makers feature on the previous page is about Pacal II, one of the greatest Mayan kings.) Sometimes kings declared war on neighboring cities. They did this to gain political or economic advantage. For example, if a king won a war, he would gain control of important trade routes. A victory might also win him tribute from other cities.

Advances in Learning

The Maya developed a complex writing system that used glyphs. The Maya carved glyphs on buildings and wrote them on bark paper. This paper was screen-folded to form a type of book called a **codex**. Few of these books still exist. The most famous is the *Popol Vuh* (poh•POHL VOO). It tells the Mayan story of the creation.

The Maya developed a mathematical system based on the number 20. The Maya did not represent numbers in the same way as we do today. They used a dot to represent 1 and a bar to represent 5. The Maya combined these symbols to show other numbers. Also, the Maya were one of the first people to use the zero.

By using their math system, the Maya made great advances in astronomy. For example, they accurately predicted eclipses of the sun and charted the orbit of the planet Venus. The Maya also used mathematics to produce a very accurate calendar system. This system helped the Maya identify the best times to plant seeds and harvest crops. It also helped Mayan kings make important political decisions, such as when to go to war. Finally, the calendar system enabled the Maya to keep very precise records of events.

▲ *Dresden Codex*
These pages from the *Dresden Codex* contain astronomical calculations, including predictions of eclipses of the sun and of the movement of Venus.

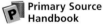 **Primary Source Handbook**
See the excerpt from the *Popul Vuh*, pages R47–48.

A Mysterious Downfall Beginning in the 800s, the Maya began to abandon their cities in the southern lowlands. At the same time, their population declined sharply. The reasons for these events remain a mystery. Overfarming may have damaged the environment. This may have led to food shortages and famine. Other possible reasons include disease, warfare among the cities, and peasant revolts.

Whatever the cause, Mayan civilization in the southern lowlands began to decline. Some Maya went to the northern lowlands and highland areas, where they built new cities. By the 1400s, however, these cities had been abandoned too.

REVIEW What advances did the Maya achieve in record keeping?

Lesson Summary

- The Maya settled in Mesoamerica, where they began to develop their civilization.
- Mayan society had four classes—rulers, nobility, peasants, and slaves.
- The Maya built great cities, crafted beautiful art, and made advances in math, science, and record keeping.

Why It Matters Now . . .

More than 800,000 Maya live in Mesoamerica today.

---

3 Lesson Review

Homework Helper
ClassZone.com

Terms & Names

1. Explain the importance of

    Maya   stele   Pacal II   codex

Using Your Notes

Framing Historical Questions Use your completed chart to answer the following question:

2. What was unique about Mayan civilization? (7.7.2)

Questions	Answers
Where was the Mayan civilization located?	

Main Ideas

3. How and where did Mayan society develop? (7.7.3)

4. What did the Maya do to get help from the gods? (7.7.2)

5. How was Mayan mathematics different from math today? (7.7.5)

Critical Thinking

6. **Making Inferences** Why might Mayan kings use warfare to gain prestige? (7.7.2)

7. **Understanding Cause and Effect** How do you think overfarming could have led to the downfall of the Maya? Explain your answer. (HI 2)

Activity

Writing a Newspaper Article Imagine that you are a reporter visiting a Mayan city. Write a short article that describes the city's architecture. (7.7.4)

Count the Mayan Way

Goal: To use the Mayan number system; to create and solve math problems

Prepare

Research the Mayan number system in encyclopedias, on the Internet, and in books about the Maya.

The Maya used a seashell for zero, a dot for 1, and a bar for 5. They used combinations of these symbols to form other numbers. ▼

Do the Activity

1. Familiarize yourself with the Mayan number system by studying the symbols to the right.

2. Working with a few other students, create ten math problems using the Mayan number system. Include addition, subtraction, multiplication, and division problems. Make sure that the answer to each problem does not exceed 20.

3. Write the problems neatly on a piece of paper, making sure to leave blank spaces for their solutions.

4. Trade your problems with another group and try to solve that group's math problems with your group members. Hand back your answers for marking.

Follow-Up

Based on your research and the math problems you solved, is the Mayan number system easier or harder to use than our own? Write a one-sentence explanation.

Extension

Create a Wall Chart Using a piece of poster board, make a wall chart for the class showing how the Maya represented the numbers 0 through 20. Write a caption explaining how the Mayan number system, based on multiples of 20, is different from our own system, based on multiples of 10.

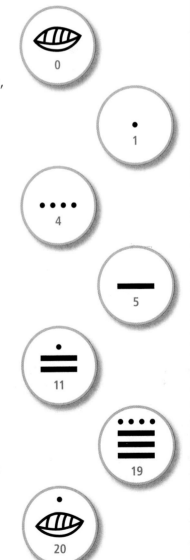

CALIFORNIA STANDARDS

7.7.5 Describe the Mesoamerican achievements in astronomy and mathematics, including the development of the calendar and the Meso-American knowledge of seasonal changes to the civilizations' agricultural systems.

The Mayan Legacy

Purpose: To learn about contributions of the Mayan civilization

Some aspects of Mayan culture continue to play a part in everyday life today. Few people go through a week without eating a meal that contains either corn or chocolate. The Maya helped to perfect both of these foods. And the Maya ball game is reflected in sports, such as soccer and basketball.

CALIFORNIA STANDARDS
7.7 Students compare and contrast the geographic, political, economic, religious, and social structures of the Meso-American and Andean civilizations.

Corn

Past Corn—or maize—was a staple, or basic, crop of the Maya. They began growing it about 4,000 years ago. Maize was essential to Mayan civilization. The Maya even called themselves "People of the Maize."

▼ **Present** ▶ Corn is an important part of many people's diets today. Mexicans use corn flour to make a flat bread called a tortilla (below to the right), just as the Maya did centuries ago. (The painting to the right by Mexican artist Diego Rivera shows the traditional method of making tortillas.)

Ball Games

▶ **Past** The Maya took part in a complicated ball game that had religious significance. It was played in large ball courts. Some of these were nearly twice the size of a modern football field. The rules of the ball game remain something of a mystery. However, the goal was to propel a hard rubber ball through a hoop high on the court wall—without using the hands or feet. (The figurine to the right shows a Mayan ball player.)

◀ **Present** Throughout the world, people play many different ball games. Some, such as soccer, restrict the use of the hands.

Chocolate

▶ **Past** Chocolate was very important to the Maya. It was considered so valuable that only nobles, priests, and warriors could drink it. Instead of eating chocolate in solid form, the Maya drank it from pots like the one shown to the right. Archaeologists have found a 2,600-year-old Mayan pot that still contains traces of the chocolate drink.

◀ **Present** Today people enjoy chocolate bars and candy as well as chocolate drinks. The modern chocolate-making process remains basically the same as that used by the Maya.

Activities

1. **TALK ABOUT IT** Why do you think chocolate was so highly valued by the Maya?

2. **WRITE ABOUT IT** What do you think is the most important contribution the Maya made to modern life? Write a paragraph supporting your choice. (Writing 2.4)

VISUAL SUMMARY

Cultural Connections
The Olmec and the Maya

Geography (7.7.1)
- Settled in similar areas of Mesoamerica
- Used slash-and-burn agriculture

Belief Systems (7.7.2)
- Worshiped many gods, most of which were represented in animal form
- Probably used cities as religious centers

Government (7.7.2)
- Were governed by ruler-priests

Economics (7.7.1)
- Depended on agriculture and trade

Culture (7.7.2, 7.7.4)
- Built great cities
- Divided society into several social classes
- Used glyph writing
- Produced magnificent sculptures and other works of art

Science & Technology (7.7.5)
- Developed a very accurate calendar

TERMS & NAMES

Explain why the words in each set below are linked with each other.

1. **Mesoamerica** and **Yucatán Peninsula**
2. **maize** and **cacao**
3. **Olmec** and **mother culture**
4. **stele** and **codex**

MAIN IDEAS

Geography and Agriculture in Mesoamerica (pages 366–371)

5. What landforms and climates dominated Mesoamerica? (7.7.1)
6. What farming methods did Mesoamericans use? (7.7.1)

The Olmec Civilization (pages 372–379)

7. What made the development of Olmec civilization possible? (7.7)
8. What impact did Olmec culture have on Mesoamerica? (7.7)

The Mayan Civilization (pages 380–389)

9. In what ways was the life of Mayan nobles different from the life of Mayan peasants? (7.7.2)
10. What types of human-made structures were often found in Mayan cities? (7.7.4)

CRITICAL THINKING Big Ideas: Culture

11. **UNDERSTANDING CAUSE AND EFFECT** How did social classes develop in Mesoamerica? (HI 2)
12. **FINDING MAIN IDEAS** How do you think the social classes of the Maya helped to keep order in their society? (7.7.2)
13. **MAKING GENERALIZATIONS** What was the relationship between religion and politics for the Maya? (7.7.2)

ALTERNATIVE ASSESSMENT

1. **WRITING ACTIVITY** Conduct research on Mayan glyph writing. Use your findings to design a stele that tells about a recent event in the news. Write a brief explanation of the stele, noting what the glyphs mean and why you selected them. (7.7.4)

2. **INTERDISCIPLINARY ACTIVITY— MATH** Use the Internet and library resources to learn about how the Mayan calendar system worked. Use your findings to write a report about the Mayan calendar, noting the role that Mayan mathematics had in its development. Include illustrations in your report. (7.7.5)

3. **STARTING WITH A STORY**

Review the information sheet that you wrote on Mayan *pok-a-tok*. Then use books and the Internet to learn about the Mayan ball game. As you research, think of ways that you might change or add to your information sheet. Rewrite your information sheet to incorporate these changes and additions. (7.7.2)

Technology Activity

4. **CREATING A GRAPHIC ORGANIZER** Use the Internet, library resources, and this textbook to research the geography of Mesoamerica. Create a graphic organizer that provides information on the landforms, climate, and natural resources of Mexico and Central America. Include the following for both Mexico and Central America:
   - Descriptions for each category
   - Images to illustrate these descriptions (7.7.1)

Research Links
ClassZone.com

Analyzing Secondary Sources Use the paragraph below and your knowledge of world history to answer the questions that follow. (7.7.5)

Secondary Source

The full knowledge of the Maya calendar must have been guarded by the ruling elite, since it was undoubtedly a source of great power. . . . One might assume, however, that even the poorest farmer had some knowledge of the basic system, by which to guide his family's daily life.

From *The Ancient Maya.*
By Robert J. Sharer, p. 559.

1. **Why do the writers think the ruling elite guarded knowledge of the Mayan calendar?**
   A. because this knowledge would have confused the general population
   B. to stop people from other cultures from stealing this knowledge
   C. because this knowledge was a source of great power
   D. to prevent others from using this knowledge against them

2. **Which statement is supported by information in the paragraph?**
   A. The Mayan population at large knew nothing about the calendar.
   B. The ruling elite wanted all the Maya to have knowledge of the calendar.
   C. The calendar was of little interest to the Mayan population at large.
   D. Most Maya had some knowledge of how the calendar worked.

Test Practice
ClassZone.com

Additional Test Practice, pp. S1–S33

Later American Civilizations

Before You Read: Preview Map

Create a chart like the one below to help you see at a glance what the chapter is about. Refer to your chart as you read.

What is the title?	Later American Civilizations
What is the Big Idea?	
What were these civilizations?	
Where were they located?	

Big Ideas About Later American Civilizations

Belief Systems Belief systems and religions may shape governments and societies.

Two large empires rose in the Americas at about the same time. The Aztec empire developed in the Valley of Mexico in Mesoamerica. The Incan empire arose in South America. Religion was very important in the everyday lives of the Aztecs and Inca.

Integrated Technology

eEdition
- Interactive Maps
- Interactive Visuals
- Starting with a Story

VIDEO
Ancient Inca

INTERNET RESOURCES
Go to **ClassZone.com** for
- WebQuest
- Homework Helper
- Research Links
- Internet Activities
- Quizzes
- Maps
- Test Practice
- Current Events

THE AMERICAS

987
Toltecs make Tula in the Valley of Mexico their capital. (warrior statue) ▶

900   1000   1100

WORLD

939
Kingdom of Dai Viet founded in Southeast Asia.

1099
Christians and Muslims battle at Ascalun during the First Crusade. ▶

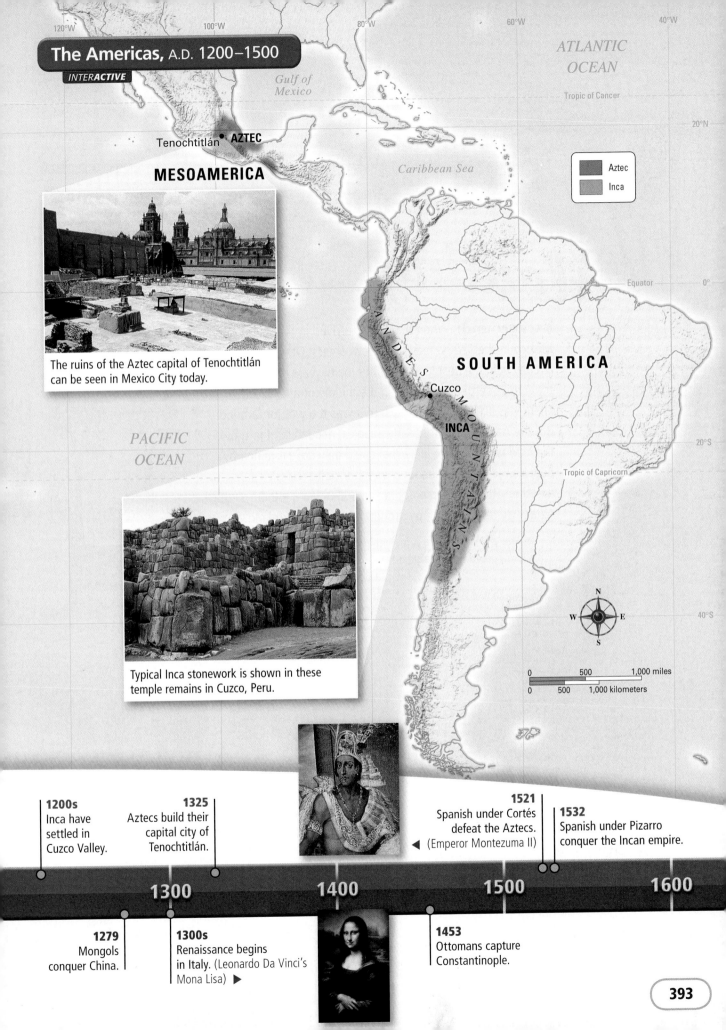

The Americas, A.D. 1200–1500

INTERACTIVE

ATLANTIC OCEAN

Gulf of Mexico

Tenochtitlán • **AZTEC**

MESOAMERICA

Caribbean Sea

Tropic of Cancer

20°N

| | Aztec |
| | Inca |

The ruins of the Aztec capital of Tenochtitlán can be seen in Mexico City today.

SOUTH AMERICA

Equator   0°

Cuzco

INCA

PACIFIC OCEAN

20°S

Tropic of Capricorn

Typical Inca stonework is shown in these temple remains in Cuzco, Peru.

N / W E / S

40°S

| 0 | 500 | 1,000 miles |
| 0 | 500 | 1,000 kilometers |

1200s
Inca have settled in Cuzco Valley.

1325
Aztecs build their capital city of Tenochtitlán.

1521
Spanish under Cortés defeat the Aztecs.
◄ (Emperor Montezuma II)

1532
Spanish under Pizarro conquer the Incan empire.

1300   1400   1500   1600

1279
Mongols conquer China.

1300s
Renaissance begins in Italy. (Leonardo Da Vinci's Mona Lisa) ►

1453
Ottomans capture Constantinople.

393

Turning Swamps into Floating Gardens

CALIFORNIA STANDARDS
Reading 2.3 Analyze text that uses the cause-and-effect organizational pattern.

Background: When the Aztecs arrived in the Valley of Mexico in the 1200s, they were newcomers. Other peoples already held the best land. So, after many years of wandering, the Aztecs settled on islands in the middle of a large lake. There was little land, and much of it was too wet for farming. But the Aztecs, like most early peoples, needed land to grow the food necessary for life. What could they do? From nearby peoples, they learned about *chinampas* (chee•NAHM•pahs), or so-called "floating gardens." Imagine that you are there as the Aztecs try to turn swampy ground into usable farmland.

▶ The *chinampas* did not really float because wooden stakes were placed in the lakebed.

wooden stake

fresh mud

dirt and vegetation

canal

lakebed

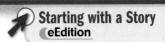

*C*ozuma (koh•ZOO•muh) is an Aztec farmer. Like everyone else, he worries about having enough food in his new home. The Aztec settlement does not have enough land. But he has heard about a strange way to farm—on water! "The Aztecs may not have good land, but they have plenty of water," Cozuma tells his chief. The chief is doubtful but is willing to let Cozuma and others try to build some *chinampas*, which were raised garden beds.

Cozuma and several other farmers begin building five *chinampas* by weaving large rafts from reeds. The work is hard, and the sun is hot. But the thought of famine drives them all. When they finish, each *chinampa* is huge—about 300 feet long and 15 to 30 feet wide.

Together, Cozuma and the others dig ditches for canals. Then they float the large rafts onto the water. Next, they drive wooden stakes through the rafts, deep into the lakebed, to keep them still. Then they cover the *chinampas* with three layers of soil. There is rich mud from the lake bottom, dirt and plant matter, and fresh mud. Each layer has different nutrients to help plants grow. They also plant trees to keep the soil from washing away.

Now the time to plant the seeds has come. On each *chinampa*, Cozuma and his fellow farmers carefully bury seeds for corn and beans. As Cozuma moves along the rows, the floating gardens feel strange beneath his feet. But he gets used to it. During the growing season, he will tend the gardens. He has to weed them but not water them. The lake water constantly washes through the *chinampas*, keeping the soil moist.

The chief arrives to inspect their work. Cozuma can only hope that green shoots will soon appear to prove that the idea works.

How might the *chinampas* benefit the Aztecs?

Reading & Writing

1. **READING: Cause and Effect** Identifying causes and effects can help you understand why events happen. With a partner, identify the causes and effects of the various events in this story.

2. **WRITING: Persuasion** Write a few paragraphs telling whether or not the *chinampas* will be successful. Include details to support your opinion.

CALIFORNIA STANDARDS Writing 2.4
Write persuasive compositions.

▶ MAIN IDEAS

① **Geography** The Aztecs developed an agricultural society and founded a great empire in the Valley of Mexico.

② **Government** The Aztecs had a highly structured society, with authoritarian rulers.

③ **Culture** The Aztecs made advances in art, architecture, and astronomy.

▶ TAKING NOTES

Reading Skill:
Explaining Chronological Order and Sequence

Sequence is the order in which events follow one another. Use a "chain of events" diagram to identify the sequence of events in the rise and fall of the Aztec empire.

```
┌─────────────────┐
│     Event 1     │
└─────────────────┘
         ↓
┌─────────────────┐
│     Event 2     │
└─────────────────┘
         ↓
┌─────────────────┐
│                 │
└─────────────────┘
```

 Skillbuilder Handbook, page R15

▲ **Aztec God Quetzalcoatl**
Quetzalcoatl, whose name means "feathered serpent," was the important god of wind. Quetzalcoatl was sometimes pictured as a serpent.

CALIFORNIA STANDARDS

7.7.1 Study the locations, landforms, and climates of Mexico, Central America, and South America and their effects on Mayan, Aztec, and Incan economies, trade, and development of urban societies.

7.7.2 Study the roles of people in each society, including class structures, family life, warfare, religious beliefs and practices, and slavery.

7.7.3 Explain how and where each empire arose and how the Aztec and Incan empires were defeated by the Spanish.

7.7.4 Describe the artistic and oral traditions and architecture in the three civilizations.

7.7.5 Describe the Meso-American achievements in astronomy and mathematics, including the development of the calendar and the Meso-American knowledge of seasonal changes to the civilizations' agricultural systems.

The Aztecs

Build on What You Know Did you ever have to look for a new place to live? Well, the Aztecs did in the 1200s. And they turned their new home into the greatest empire of Mesoamerica.

Aztecs Settle in Central Mexico

1 ESSENTIAL QUESTION How did the Aztecs adapt to the Valley of Mexico?

The Aztecs were nomadic hunters and gatherers. They lived in what is now the northwest desert of Mexico. In the late 1200s, they began to move south. Eventually, they came upon the Valley of Mexico, a mountain basin about 7,500 feet above sea level.

Settling in the Valley of Mexico When the Aztecs arrived in the Valley of Mexico, there was no major power in the region. A people called the Toltecs had ruled there from about 900, but they had lost control in the late 1100s. Now the region contained a number of small city-states ruled by various peoples.

These city-states held the most fertile land. So the Aztecs had to settle for what was left. A legend says that the Aztec sun and war god told them they would find a new home where they saw an eagle sitting on a cactus. In 1325, they found such a place. It was a small island in a large lake (later called Lake Texcoco). There they built the city of **Tenochtitlán** (teh•NOHCH•tee•TLAHN), or Place of the Prickly Pear. (See story on pages 404–407.) This is the site of Mexico City today.

The Aztecs now had a land of their own. As they adapted to the land, they also adapted to their neighbors. They carved out a place for themselves as paid warriors for local rulers.

Aztec Capital
Tenochtitlán was built on an island in Lake Texcoco in the Valley of Mexico.▼

Teotihuacán

Valley of Mexico

Lake Texcoco

Tenochtitlán

Adapting to the Land The lands around Tenochtitlán were swampy. The lake was in a valley surrounded by high mountains, with little level land for farming. There also was little wood or stone nearby for building. But the Aztecs adapted. They learned to construct *chinampas,* or raised garden beds, on the lake. (See pages 394–395.) The *chinampas* enabled them to grow many crops, including corn, squash, and chili peppers. They also hunted animals that lived in and around the lake.

▲ **Tenochtitlán Markets** This mural shows goods of all kinds—including foods, textiles, and building materials—being traded in the busy markets of Tenochtitlán.

With a plentiful food supply, the population of Tenochtitlán grew. Soon, the Aztecs spread out from the island to new communities on the lakeshore. At its height, between 200,000 and 400,000 people may have lived in the urban area of Tenochtitlán.

Trade was important to the Aztec economy. The Aztecs traded for goods they could not get locally, especially wood and stone for building. They dug canals to provide routes into the city for canoes loaded with trade goods. Aztec builders also engineered bridges and causeways to tie the city to the mainland.

Building an Empire As the years passed, the Aztecs made alliances with some city-states and used their warrior skills to conquer others. By the early 1500s, their empire stretched from the Gulf of Mexico to the Pacific Ocean and from the Valley of Mexico to what is now Guatemala. (See map on page 393.) Between 6 and 12 million people lived under Aztec rule. From the peoples they conquered, the Aztecs demanded *tribute.* This forced payment took the form of goods such as corn, gold, and jade.

Vocabulary Strategy

The word *tribute* has **multiple meanings.** It can mean "a forced payment in goods or labor." It also can refer to something given or said to show great respect.

REVIEW How did the Aztecs build a powerful empire?

Aztec Society and Beliefs

2 ESSENTIAL QUESTION What was the structure of Aztec society?

As the Aztecs' power grew, their society became more complex. It was organized into tightly structured groups, or classes.

Aztec Class Structure Three main classes formed Aztec society—the nobles, the intermediate class, and the commoners. Each class was divided further. At the top was the emperor, who belonged to the noble class. His power came from control of the military and was supported by Aztec religious beliefs. The emperor lived a life of luxury.

As in most societies, the nobles made up the smallest class but held the most power. They owned large estates and ran the government and the military. Priests, too, came from the noble class. Below the nobles was an intermediate class. Merchants and skilled artisans made up this group.

Most people in Aztec society were in the third class, the commoners. Some commoners were landowning farmers, fishers, craftspeople, and soldiers. Also included were landless workers, or serfs, who labored in the fields of the nobles and could not move off the land.

Enslaved persons were at the very bottom of this class. They were usually prisoners of war. Slaves worked at many different tasks. In all classes, women's roles were restricted.

▲ **Aztec Eagle Warrior**
This life-size statue shows a high-ranking warrior wearing a birdlike helmet, feathered sleeves, and claws.

Family Life and Religious Practices The Aztecs lived in family groups in large land-based communities. Most men farmed their own or nobles' lands. The women cooked the meals, tended the children, and did other domestic chores. Boys began formal education at about age 10. They learned about religion and were taught fighting skills. As in many societies, girls were usually taught at home.

Aztec life was dominated by religion. It was central to the daily lives of all members of society. The Aztec religion was based mainly on the worship of agricultural gods. Aztecs believed in about 1,000 gods.

Priests in the temples used a complex calendar to set the times for many public religious ceremonies each year. The most important ceremonies were held to ask the gods for a good harvest. Humans, usually war prisoners, were sometimes sacrificed to the gods. Families also worshiped at small altars in their homes.

▲ **Montezuma and Cortés** The Aztec emperor and the Spanish leader exchanged gifts at their first meeting in 1519.

Aztec Warriors and Warfare

To the Aztecs, war was a sacred duty. Territory and peoples had to be conquered for the empire to expand. Most boys had begun intensive training to become warriors by 15. In battle, the Aztecs were fearsome. During an attack, they might kill everyone in an enemy village who was not a warrior. The warriors would be taken as prisoners to be used as slaves or human sacrifices.

Fall of the Aztec Empire

As the empire's population grew, so did the need for farmland. The emperor and the nobles also demanded more tribute. To meet these needs, the Aztecs were almost always at war.

The empire was at its height in 1502 when a new emperor, **Montezuma II**, came to power. He demanded more tribute and victims for sacrifice. His harsh treatment and endless demands for tribute caused bitter hatred among Aztec subjects. Some began to rebel. Montezuma tried to repair the damage by asking for less tribute. But unrest had weakened Aztec power.

In 1519, a Spanish expedition led by **Hernán Cortés** (ehr•NAHN kawr•TEHZ) arrived in the Aztec empire. It was seeking gold and glory for Spain. Montezuma met with Cortés in the hopes of avoiding war. But he was soon taken prisoner. He was later killed in the fighting between the Aztecs and the Spaniards.

The Spanish eventually were victorious. Diseases brought by the Europeans weakened the Aztecs. The invaders also had superior weapons, including muskets and body armor, and the help of thousands of rebels. In 1521, Cortés conquered Tenochtitlán. The capital's fall signaled the end of the Aztec empire.

P **Primary Source Handbook**
See the excerpt from an Aztec Account of the Conquest of Mexico, page R49.

REVIEW Why did the Aztec empire fall?

The Cultural Legacy of the Aztecs

③ ESSENTIAL QUESTION What cultural advances did the Aztecs make?

The Aztecs had a rich culture that produced distinctive works of art and architecture. They also made advances in astronomy.

Art and Architecture Thanks to discoveries by archaeologists, we know that the Aztecs built huge and unique structures. Visitors to Tenochtitlán and other Aztec cities would have marveled at the temples, palaces, and city walls. Evidence of Aztec achievements in building can still be seen in Mexico City. The Spanish built the city over Tenochtitlán, but part of the Great Temple remains.

Along with the remains of the temple and other buildings, archaeologists have also found everyday objects. These include gold beads, pottery, and stone urns. Aztec artisans also produced beautiful feather headdresses, stone sculptures, and jewelry set with precious stones.

The Aztec Codices The Aztecs' writing system did not represent the sounds of their spoken language. Instead, they used pictures and symbols, called glyphs, to represent words and ideas. The Aztecs collected their writings in books called codices. Each codex was made of a long folded sheet of bark or deerskin, filled with colorful pictures showing details of Aztec life. Historians have learned much about the Aztecs from these records.

Primary Source

Aztec Codices

Aztec codices are illustrated books. Brightly painted pictures cover both sides of these long folded sheets of bark or deerskin. Each codex illustrates scenes from Aztec life or contains official government records. There once were hundreds of these codices, but many were destroyed. The panel at right shows the funeral of a noble (wrapped in a cloth). His family prepares him for the afterlife.

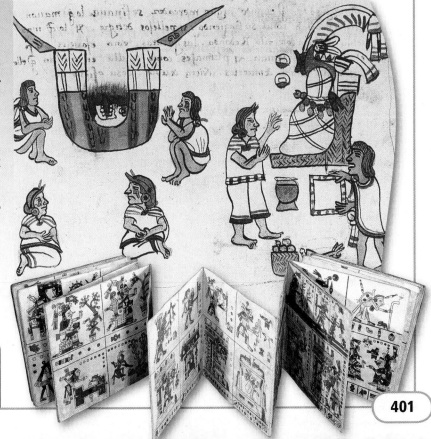

DOCUMENT–BASED QUESTION
How might you tell from the picture that the deceased was a noble?

Advances in Astronomy To predict planting and harvesting times, early peoples studied movements of the sun, stars, and planets. They used this information to make calendars. The Aztecs created two calendars—one for farming and one for religion. The farming calendar let them know when to plant and to harvest crops. The religious calendar was used to plan religious ceremonies. An Aztec calendar stone dug up in Mexico City in 1790 includes information about the months of the year and pictures the sun god at the center.

Aztec Calendar Stone
This calendar stone is 12 feet wide and weighs 25 tons. ▼

REVIEW What was the Aztecs' cultural legacy?

Lesson Summary

- The Aztecs adapted to the environment of the Valley of Mexico and built an empire there.
- The Aztecs' harsh treatment of their subjects weakened their empire and made it easier for the Spanish to conquer them.
- The Aztecs made contributions in art, architecture, and astronomy.

Why It Matters Now . . .

The Aztecs ruled much of what is now Mexico and built their capital where Mexico City, one of the world's largest cities, now stands.

---

1 Lesson Review

Homework Helper
ClassZone.com

Terms & Names

1. Explain the importance of

   Tenochtitlán   Montezuma II   Hernán Cortés

Using Your Notes

Explaining Chronological Order and Sequence Use your completed "chain of events" diagram to answer the following question:

2. How do you think the Aztecs were able to build a large empire so quickly? (7.7.3)

Event 1
↓
Event 2
↓

Main Ideas

3. What challenges did the Aztecs face when they settled in the Valley of Mexico? (7.7.1)

4. How did the rule of Montezuma II cause unrest among the peoples of the Aztec empire? (7.7.2)

5. What were the purposes of the two Aztec calendars? (7.7.5)

Critical Thinking

6. **Drawing Conclusions** Why are Aztec codices important to historians? (7.7.4)

7. **Understanding Causes and Effects** How were the Aztecs able to develop large urban centers, such as Tenochtitlán? (7.7.1)

Activity **Internet Activity** Research the *chinampas*, or "floating gardens." Then make a cross-sectional diagram of a *chinampa*, with labels showing its features. (7.7.1)
INTERNET KEYWORD: *chinampas*

Create a Picture Story

Goal: To create a picture story in order to understand how early peoples in the Americas communicated with picture writing systems

Materials & Supplies
- white construction paper
- colored pencils or markers
- book on glyphs
- Internet research on glyphs

Prepare

❶ Reread the information on the Aztecs in this lesson.

❷ Carefully study various types of picture symbols in books and Internet sources. The Aztecs used picture symbols, or glyphs, to represent people, animals, objects, events, and ideas.

Do the Activity

❶ Decide on a simple event or idea from this lesson that you could communicate with picture symbols.

❷ Determine how many and what kinds of picture symbols you will need to show the event or idea. Keep their design simple.

❸ On a piece of paper, draw the picture symbols in a way that tells your story or idea.

▲ Glyphs from an Aztec codex

Follow-Up

❶ How well do your images show the idea or event that you wanted to communicate?

❷ How well did the early peoples of the Americas get their ideas across through picture stories?

Extension

Making a Presentation Show your picture story to the class. See if your classmates are able to understand the idea or event before you give an explanation.

CALIFORNIA STANDARDS
7.7.4 Describe the artistic and oral traditions and architecture in the three civilizations.

Literature CONNECTIONS

The Eagle on the Prickly Pear

Retold by John Bierhorst

Background: "The Eagle on the Prickly Pear" is the legend of the founding of Tenochtitlán, the capital city of the Aztecs, in 1325. According to this legend, the Mexicans [Aztecs] received a command from the god Huitzilopochtli (WEE•tsuh•loh•POHCH•tlee). He told them, "Go where the cactus grows, on which the eagle sits happily." There they should build themselves a homeland. After almost 200 years of wandering, they found their new home in the Valley of Mexico. It is now the site of Mexico City.

CALIFORNIA STANDARDS
Reading 3.2 Identify events that advance the plot and determine how each event explains past or present action(s) or foreshadows future action(s).

Having escaped from Colhuacan,[1] the Mexicans [Aztecs] began wandering over the marshy islands in the middle of the lake, stopping briefly at a spot where one of their daughters, Corn Blossom, gave birth to a baby called Jug Boy, and the place is still known as Childbirth.

At another place they stopped to build a sweat bath for Corn Blossom, the mother of Jug Boy, and gave it the name Bath. Then all the Mexicans took baths and camped for a while. From there two elders, Cuauhcoatl (KWOW•koh•AHT•uhl) and the priest Axolohua (ahk•soh•LOH•wuh), went into the reeds to a spot now known as Reeds and Rushes, hunting for a place to settle permanently; and here they saw a great many wonderful things, all of which had been predicted by Huitzilopochtli, who had told them exactly what they would find. This spot, he had said, would be his fortress and his home. Suddenly they saw that the cypress trees were white.

And the willow trees were white.

And the reeds were white.

And the rushes were white.

And the frogs that lived in the water were white.

And the fish were white.

And the snakes were white.

And just ahead they saw a jumble of crags and caverns, and those that lay to the east were the ones called Fire Water and Water Burn. Those on the north, all jumbled, were the ones called Blue Water and Parrot-colored Water. When they saw all this, they wept.

"Here must be the place," they cried. "Now we have seen what our god was telling us about when he sent us on our way and said, 'In the reeds you will see many things.' Now we have seen them and his words have come true. Let us go back to camp and wait for him to tell us what will happen next."

REVIEW What were the Mexicans looking for as they began their journey?

---

1. **Colhuacan** (kohl•WAH•kahn): a city-state in the Valley of Mexico.

That night Huitzilopochtli appeared to Cuauhcoatl in a dream, saying, "Cuauhcoatl, you have seen everything that was in the reeds. But listen, there is something more you haven't seen, and I want you to go find it. It is a prickly pear, and on top of it you will see an eagle, contentedly eating, and sunning himself. You will be pleased because it comes from Copil's[2] heart. You were the one who threw it from the shore when we were at Chapultepec.[3] It fell beside the crags at Reeds and Rushes and began to grow, and now it is called *tenochtli*. It is where our home and our fortress will be, where we will wait for intruders and meet them with chest and shoulders, arrow and shield.

"This is Mexico, this is Tenochtitlán, where the eagle screams, spreads his wings, and eats, where the fish flies, where the snake rustles.

2. **Copil** (koh•PEEL): Aztec god whose heart was thrown into the lake and from which a prickly pear grew.
3. **Chapultepec:** a hill near Lake Texcoco.

▼ **This illustration shows Aztecs performing various activities around Tenochtitlán.**

"This is Mexico, this is Tenochtitlán. And many things will be done."

"Your heart is generous," said Cuauhcoatl. "Now all the elders must hear what you have told me," and the next day he called the Mexicans together and revealed his dream. Immediately they returned to the edge of the caverns at Reeds and Rushes, and as they passed through the reeds, there in front of them was the prickly pear with the eagle perched on top, contentedly eating, his claws punching holes in his prey. When he saw the Mexicans in the distance, he bowed to them.

The eagle's nest was all of precious feathers, cotinga and roseate spoonbill, and there were quetzal[4] plumes. Scattered around were the heads, claws, and bones of the different birds the eagle had killed.

The voice of the spirit said, "Mexicans, this is the place." And with that they all wept. "We are favored," they said. "We are blessed. We have seen where our city will be. Now let us go rest."

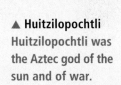

▲ **Huitzilopochtli**
Huitzilopochtli was the Aztec god of the sun and of war.

REVIEW How did the Mexicans know they had found the site for their settlement?

---

4. **cotinga . . . roseate spoonbill . . . quetzal:** birds native to Mexico.

Reading & Writing

1. **READING: Plot** Think about the ideas you see at work in this story. With a partner, discuss why the Mexicans [Aztecs] took the actions that they did.

2. **WRITING: Summaries** Write, in your own words, a brief description of the plot of this Aztec legend.

CALIFORNIA STANDARDS Writing 2.5
Write summaries of reading materials.

MAIN IDEAS

1 **Geography** The Inca adapted their way of life to the mountainous terrain found throughout their empire.

2 **Government** The Inca developed a complex society that placed the government in control of most aspects of life.

3 **Culture** The Inca developed a unique system of record keeping and built a wide-ranging system of roads.

TAKING NOTES

Reading Skill: Categorizing

To categorize is to sort people, objects, ideas, or other information into groups. Use a web diagram like the one below to record information about the Inca empire.

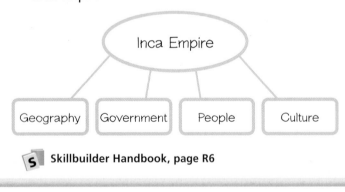

Inca Empire

| Geography | Government | People | Culture |

S **Skillbuilder Handbook, page R6**

▲ **Llama Figurine** Llamas were important to the Inca. The Inca used them as beasts of burden, made cloth from their wool, and even sometimes ate them as food. An Incan artisan made this silver llama figurine.

CALIFORNIA STANDARDS

7.7.1 Study the locations, landforms, and climates of Mexico, Central America, and South America and their effects on Mayan, Aztec, and Incan economies, trade, and development of urban societies.

7.7.2 Study the roles of people in each society, including class structures, family life, warfare, religious beliefs and practices, and slavery.

7.7.3 Explain how and where each empire arose and how the Aztec and Incan empires were defeated by the Spanish.

7.7.4 Describe the artistic and oral traditions and architecture in the three civilizations.

7.7.5 Describe the Meso-American achievements in astronomy and mathematics, including the development of the calendar and the Meso-American knowledge of seasonal changes to the civilizations' agricultural systems.

The Inca

TERMS & NAMES

Pachacuti

chasqui

Francisco Pizarro

quipu

Build on What You Know In Lesson 1, you learned how the Aztecs built Mesoamerica's greatest empire. Now you will read about a people who created an important empire in South America about the same time—the Inca.

Geography of a Mountain Empire

1 ESSENTIAL QUESTION How did the Inca adapt their way of life to the mountainous terrain of their homeland?

The Inca learned to live in the high and rugged terrain of the Andes Mountains in what is now Peru. They also conquered a huge territory to create one of the largest empires in the Americas.

A Land of Diverse Terrain The central Andes are a region of geographic extremes. Tropical rain forests cover areas of the north. In the center, green and fertile valleys are surrounded by some of the highest mountains in the world. A highland plateau with a dry, cool climate lies between two mountain ranges.

In the 1100s, the Inca began to travel north from the highland plateau. Sometime before 1200, they settled in a fertile mountain valley more than 11,000 feet above sea level. There they founded their capital city, Cuzco (KOOZ•koh). *Cuzco* is a Quechua (KEHCH•wuh) word meaning "navel" or "center." Quechua is the language of the Inca. In the wide, green Cuzco Valley, the Inca created a small kingdom. The valley took its name from the city.

Connect to Today

Machu Picchu The ruins of the Incan city of Machu Picchu are located between two peaks of the Andes Mountains. ▼

Pachacuti Founds an Empire By the early 1400s, the Inca had slowly expanded their rule over neighboring peoples. They controlled the valley and nearby areas. Some peoples peacefully accepted Inca rule. Others were conquered. In 1438, the ninth Incan ruler, **Pachacuti** (PAH•chah•KOO•tee), came to power. Under his rule, the Inca conquered all of Peru and moved into surrounding lands. Pachacuti's son and grandson continued his conquests during their reigns.

By 1500, the Inca governed an empire that extended 2,500 miles along the west coast of South America. It included parts of what is now Colombia, Ecuador, Peru, Bolivia, Chile, and Argentina. About 12 million people lived in the empire.

Governing the Empire Unlike the Valley of Mexico, the Andes did not have suitable sites for large cities or enough farmland to support urban societies. Cities the size of Tenochtitlán did not develop in the Incan empire. For example, the mountain settlement at Machu Picchu probably never held more than 1,000 people. Cuzco may have had as few as 25,000, although the total population of the Cuzco Valley may have been about 100,000.

The rough terrain and varied peoples also made governing the empire difficult. But the Inca were talented organizers and administrators. They took several steps to unify the lands and peoples under their rule. They divided their subjects into family groups for easier control. Subjects also had to learn to speak Quechua language and worship the Incan gods. But mostly the Inca, like the Aztecs, let conquered peoples follow their traditional ways.

History Makers

Pachacuti (c. 1391–1473)

The Incan leader Pachacuti's name means "Earth Mover" or "Great Transformer." He was the emperor's younger son and, as such, was not in line to become ruler. But in 1438, during an attack on Cuzco, Pachacuti's father and older brother fled. Pachacuti, who was a gifted soldier, took control and saved the city. Then he made himself the new Incan ruler.

During his 33-year reign, Pachacuti began the expansion of Incan territory. He also reorganized the government and built a grand capital at Cuzco. He is considered the greatest Incan ruler.

Daily Life in the Empire

The geography of the Andes made life challenging for the peoples of the empire. Farming was difficult because much of the land was high and steep. Incan farmers had to cut flat terraces into the sides of mountains to get the most out of their land. (See the Geography feature on page 226.) They also developed irrigation systems to bring water to their fields.

The Incan farmer usually grew one or more crops, such as corn and potatoes, and raised animals. There were higher areas too cold and too dry for crops. On these, the Inca grazed llamas and alpacas. These are small animals related to the camel. They were an important source of wool and, sometimes, meat. However, meat usually was scarce. So there was little of it in the Incan diet.

Inca Empire, A.D. 1438–1525

Chan Chan

PACIFIC OCEAN

Machu Picchu
Cuzco

Lake Titicaca

Atacama Desert

Equator   0°

20°S

Tropic of Capricorn

80°W

Growth of Incan Empire	
	Under Pachacuti, 1438–1471
	Added by 1525

GEOGRAPHY SKILLBUILDER
INTERPRETING MAPS
Human-Environment Interaction What physical features stopped the east-west expansion of the Incan empire?

Communication, like farming, was difficult. But the Inca met the challenge. They improved roads that had been built by earlier peoples and constructed new ones. Along these mountain highways, runners called **chasquis** (CHAHS•kees) carried messages up and down the length of the empire. (See the Daily Life feature on pages 416–417.)

Keeping the roads in good repair took much time and work. So the Incan government required its subjects to perform a number of days of labor each year. Much of this labor duty was spent building and repairing roads and bridges.

The Inca had a moneyless economy. Trade was in the form of barter, or exchanges of goods and services. Products included food, clothing, and pottery. But trade was very limited. Most of it was local and took place during the harvest season. Any trade between regions was controlled by the emperor.

REVIEW How important was the extensive road network to the success of the Incan empire?

Incan Society and Beliefs

2 **ESSENTIAL QUESTION** How did Incan society develop?

The government controlled much of life in the empire. Little happened without the permission of the Incan ruler in Cuzco.

Incan Class Structure Incan society had two main groups—nobles and commoners. Unlike the Aztecs, the Inca did not make slaves of prisoners of war. Nobles ran the government, controlled the army, and enjoyed a rich style of life. Aside from the artisans, who had a slightly higher social position, most commoners were farmers. Those who lived along the coast were fishermen. Commoners did all of the basic work. This included growing crops for themselves, the priests, the nobles, and the emperor. Most people stayed in the class they were born in for life.

The Incas' organizational skills helped the government meet the daily needs of every subject. But this meant that the government also tightly controlled nearly all aspects of Incan life. Through chiefs, the government regulated what was going on in even the smallest villages. It decided who would farm, who would trade goods, who would be soldiers, and even who could marry.

Religious Beliefs and Practices For the most part, the Incan people accepted the control of their emperor. They believed that he was divine, the son of their most important god—Inti, god of the sun. Incan society was based on agriculture, and the sun was seen as the source of life.

The Inca built many temples to worship their gods. The priests in the temples played a central role in Incan life. They performed daily prayers and rituals. They made animal sacrifices for a good harvest. Human sacrifice was rare. Only in a crisis, such as a long drought, might humans be sacrificed.

If the emperor needed to make a decision, priests performed special rites that they believed let them read the future. Often, these rites were held before a battle to look for signs telling who would win.

Warfare and the Mighty Incan Army The Incan army was the most powerful force in the Andes. Nearly 200,000 strong, it was so frightening that the emperor often had only to

▲ **Sacrificial Knife**
This gold knife from about 1100 to 1300 was probably used by an Incan priest in a sacrifice during a religious ceremony.

ask neighboring peoples to join the empire. A chief would accept the emperor's "invitation" just to avoid a battle he knew he would lose.

Most soldiers were commoners. They were mainly Incan farmers who were performing their required government service. But some were people from conquered territories. The officers were always Incan nobles. The soldiers drilled regularly and were well equipped with bone-tipped spears and arrows, lances, clubs, and slings.

The Inca Fall to the Spanish

Other Andean peoples could not defeat the Inca. But like the Aztecs, the Inca would be no match for invading Spaniards, who rode horses, wore metal armor, and carried steel swords and muskets.

The Incan Empire had been weakened by unrest. A leader named Atahualpa (AH•tuh•WAHL•puh) had won the throne by defeating his brother in a bitter civil war that began about 1527. Thousands of Inca were killed in battle or put to death. The war was just ending when the Spanish explorer **Francisco Pizarro** and his troops arrived at an Incan port on the South American coast in 1532.

Pizarro sent a message to Atahualpa requesting a meeting. When the Incan emperor arrived, he was taken prisoner by the Spanish. Later, Pizarro had him executed. After Atahualpa's death, the Incan empire began to fall apart. The Spaniards moved on to Cuzco. Conquered peoples took this opportunity to rebel against their Incan masters.

By 1535, the Spanish controlled most of the Incan lands. They enslaved many. Eventually, millions of Inca died of diseases brought by the Europeans. The last Incan ruler was defeated in 1572, and the Incan empire ceased to exist.

REVIEW What caused the fall of the Incan Empire?

Spanish Conquest This is a 19th-century recreation of the day Pizarro (on horseback) and his troops captured the Incan emperor Atahualpa (in white at center right) in a surprise attack in 1532. ▼

The Cultural Legacy of the Inca

3 **ESSENTIAL QUESTION** What advances did the Inca make in science, technology, and the arts?

The Inca ruled a vast territory for more than a hundred years. During that time, they also made advances in engineering, art, and medicine. Aspects of their rich culture survive today.

A Civilization Without Writing

Unlike the Aztecs, the Inca did not have a system of writing. Yet they were still able to run a large government and control trade. A mathematical, or counting, tool called the **quipu** (KEE•poo) helped them do this.

A quipu was a cord with knotted strings of various lengths tied to it. The color and length of a string stood for what was being counted. The knots represented a number of items. This tool allowed the Inca to keep track of trade goods, the distribution of troops, and the populations of their territories.

The Inca were also able to preserve their history and legends—partly through oral tradition and partly through the use of another type of quipu. It had symbols that stood for ideas and events tied to the strings. Some still use the quipu today.

Quipu The quipu was a knotted string device (see inset) used for counting purposes. ▼

Road Builders and Artisans

The Inca were gifted builders. Like the ancient Romans, they built a huge network of highways. About 14,000 miles of roads crisscrossed the empire. The Inca built tunnels through hills and bridges across rivers. Their road system allowed the rulers at Cuzco to send troops quickly wherever they were needed. In addition, they moved food and trade goods over the roads.

Incan buildings were marvels of engineering. The Inca built forts, palaces, and temples from huge stone blocks put together without mortar. Many Incan structures still stand.

The Inca were also talented artisans. They fashioned beautiful jewelry and figurines out of precious metals such as gold. Incan weavers used wool from alpacas to weave intricately designed cloth. The people of the Andes today still practice both these crafts.

Incan Medical Advances The Spanish in Peru were impressed by Incan medicine. They recorded that Incan medical practices were as advanced as those in Europe, if not more so in some ways. In fact, the Inca developed medical knowledge that is still valuable. By studying sick people and local plants, they created very effective medicines, including quinine to cure fevers. Also, Incan surgeons performed blood transfusions and even an early form of brain surgery.

▲ **Early Surgery**
This Incan skull shows evidence of a surgical procedure called trepanning.

REVIEW What was the cultural legacy of the Inca?

Lesson Summary

- The Inca developed ways to live in and to rule a vast region of mountainous terrain.
- Most Inca lived highly regulated lives under the supreme rule of an emperor.
- The Inca created a record-keeping system, built a vast road network, and made medical advances.

Why It Matters Now . . .

Incan influence is still present in Ecuador, Peru, Columbia, Bolivia, Argentina, and Chile.

2 Lesson Review

Homework Helper
ClassZone.com

Terms & Names

1. Explain the importance of

| Pachacuti | Francisco Pizarro |
| *chasqui* | quipu |

Using Your Notes

Categorizing Use your completed web diagram to answer the following question:

2. What is one statement that characterizes the government of the Inca empire? (7.7.2)

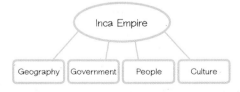

Main Ideas

3. Describe the geography of the central Andes and how it affected agriculture. (7.7.1)

4. What classes made up Incan society, and what were their roles? (7.7.2)

5. What were quipus, and what were their purposes? (7.7.5)

Critical Thinking

6. **Drawing Conclusions** What are some of the disadvantages when a culture passes its history on orally? (7.7.4)

7. **Comparing** How was the Spanish conquest of the Inca different from the Spanish conquest of the Aztecs? How was it similar? (7.7.3)

Activity **Drawing a Diagram** Find out more about the construction methods of the Inca. Draw a diagram showing how huge blocks of stones can be fitted together without mortar. Write a caption explaining your diagram. (7.7.4)

Runners on the Royal Road

Purpose: To learn how *chasquis*, the speedy Incan runners, provided a communication system for the far-flung Incan empire

If you were a subject of the Incan empire in the 15th century, you knew about the *chasquis* who carried messages along the "royal road." The Incan road system wound through the Andes and along the coast from one end of the empire to the other. It connected all major cities. It allowed the Incan ruler in Cuzco to keep in contact with the empire. The roads were also essential for trade.

The *chasquis* were young men trained from an early age to run at high altitudes. Each one's job was to run as fast as he could for a mile and a half and then pass a message to another runner.

A **Emperor's Message** The Incan ruler in Cuzco might order a *chasqui* to take a message whose final destination was a coastal city. Usually, messengers carried imperial orders or news. The message might be verbal or be carried on a quipu.

B **Arrival Announced** A *chasqui* blew on a conch shell to let the next runner know he was coming. Many roads were connected by rope bridges over gorges or rivers, as shown here.

C **Message Passed** Runners were posted at way stations about a mile and a half apart. A fresh runner left as soon as the incoming runner passed on the message.

D **Destination** The final runner delivered the emperor's message to an army officer in a coastal city: "Your troops are needed in Cuzco!" Another messenger then began the return journey with the reply. Messages could travel 125 to 150 miles in a day.

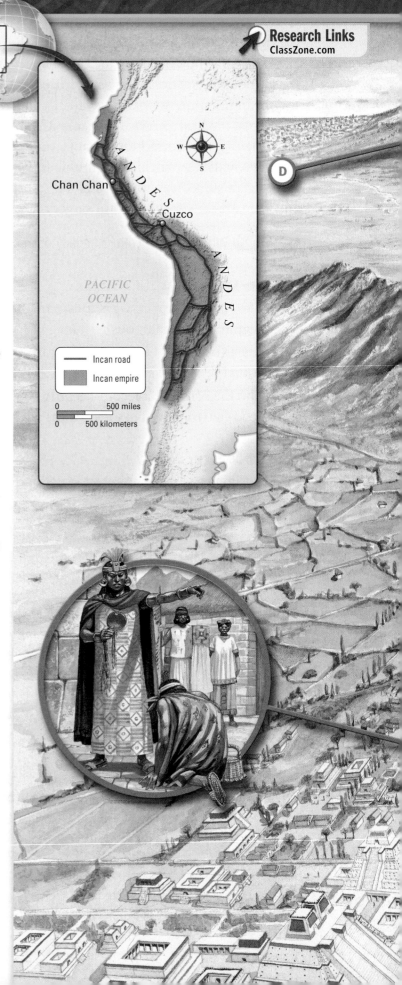

Chan Chan

Cuzco

PACIFIC OCEAN

ANDES

Incan road
Incan empire

0   500 miles
0   500 kilometers

Activities

1. **TALK ABOUT IT** What types of activities are taking place along the Incan road system? Who are the people performing the activities?

2. **WRITE ABOUT IT** Choose one of the activities shown in the illustration and described in the text. Write a brief dialogue between people in that scene. (Writing 2.1)

VISUAL SUMMARY

Later American Civilizations

Geography (7.7.1)
- Aztecs settled in the Valley of Mexico.
- The Inca settled in the Cuzco Valley (now in Peru).

Government (7.7.3)
- The Aztecs established the most powerful empire in Mesoamerica.
- Brilliant rulers and a strong army helped the Inca create an empire.

Economy (7.7.1)
- Aztecs built *chinampas* to gain farmland.
- Tenochtitlán was a major Aztec trading center.
- The Incan economy was based on farming and barter.

Science and Technology (7.7.5)
- The Aztecs made advances in architecture and astronomy.
- The Inca built a huge road network and made advances in medicine.

Belief Systems (7.7.2)
- Religion was important to both Aztecs and Inca.
- Each believed in many gods.

TERMS & NAMES

Explain why the words in each pair below are linked with each other

1. **Montezuma II** and **Hernan Cortés**
2. **Pachacuti** and **Francisco Pizarro**
3. *chasqui* and **quipu**

MAIN IDEAS

The Aztecs (pages 396–407)

4. How did the Aztec empire develop? (7.1.1)
5. How did the geography of the Valley of Mexico affect the farming techniques of the Aztecs? (7.7.1)
6. What were the main classes of Aztec society? (7.7.2)
7. What factors contributed to the fall of the Aztec empire? (7.7.3)

The Inca (pages 408–417)

8. What were the main accomplishments of Pachacuti? (7.7.3)
9. How was daily life in the Incan empire different from that in the Aztec empire? (7.7.2)
10. How important was the road system to life in the Incan empire? (7.7.1)
11. In what ways were the Inca a technologically advanced civilization? (7.7.5)

CRITICAL THINKING Big Ideas: Belief Systems

12. **Understanding Cause and Effect** In what ways do you think religion made it easy or difficult for the Aztecs to rule their empire? (7.7.2)
13. **Finding Main Ideas** How important was religion in the daily life of the Inca? (7.7.2)
14. **Making Inferences** Why do you think the Inca made conquered peoples adopt the Incan religion? (7.7.2)

ALTERNATIVE ASSESSMENT

1. **WRITING ACTIVITY** Find out more about Montezuma II and Hernán Cortés. Write an imaginary dialogue between them, in which the two leaders compare their cultures and the actions they took. (Writing 2.1)

2. **INTERDISCIPLINARY ACTIVITY—MATHEMATICS** With a small group of classmates, use the Internet and the library to find out more about how quipus worked. Then create your own quipu system, using strings tied into series of knots. Present your work to the class. (7.7.5)

3.  **STARTING WITH A STORY** Review the essay you wrote about the effect of the *chinampas*. Now that you have read the chapter and seen the results, would you answer the question in a different way? If so, how? (Writing 2.4)

Technology Activity

4. **DESIGNING A WEB PAGE**
   Using the Internet or the library, research a building, person, or event discussed in Chapter 12. Use the material to design a Web page about your subject. (7.7.3)
   - Decide on your subject.
   - Include a title for your page.
   - Create an outline that organizes your information.
   - Make a sketch that shows the layout of your Web page.

Research Links
ClassZone.com

Interpreting Charts The Aztec and Incan populations dropped dramatically in the 16th century. Use the chart and your knowledge of world history to answer the questions. (7.7.3)

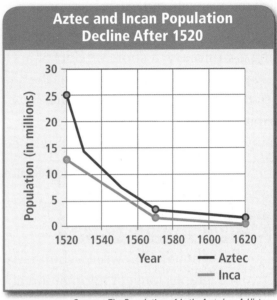

Aztec and Incan Population Decline After 1520

Source: *The Population of Latin America: A History*

1. **During what time period after 1520 did the Aztec population show its sharpest drop?**
   A. 1520–1540
   B. 1540–1560
   C. 1560–1580
   D. 1580–1600

2. **What reason best explains the dramatic decline in the Aztec and Incan populations?**
   A. Nomadic peoples moved out of the empires.
   B. Earthquakes caused widespread death and destruction.
   C. The Spanish arrived, bringing warfare, disease, and enslavement.
   D. Crop failures led to massive starvation.

 **Test Practice**
ClassZone.com

Additional Test Practice, pp. S1–S33

Writing About History

Summaries of Reading Materials:
American Civilizations

 **Writing Model**
ClassZone.com

CALIFORNIA STANDARDS
Writing 2.5 Write summaries of reading materials.

Purpose: To summarize the information in Unit 6

Audience: Yourself and your classmates

On page 407, you had a chance to practice writing a **summary,** a short version of a text, expressed in your own words. The ability to summarize helps you learn new information. It is also a skill you can use in many other kinds of writing you will do in school.

The Aztec god Quetzacoatl ▶

Organization & Focus

Your assignment is to write a summary, at least five paragraphs long, of information about American civilizations. Write at least one paragraph summarizing each lesson in this unit.

Identifying Purpose and Audience You have several purposes for writing this summary. One is to learn and remember the information in Unit 6. Another is to practice summarizing. Whenever you take notes or draft a composition in the future, you will use summarizing.

   If you were writing just for yourself, you wouldn't have to use complete sentences and formal paragraphs. But you are also writing to help your classmates learn. When you write for an audience other than yourself, using correct form helps to make your ideas clear.

Reading for Main Ideas Use the section headings in each lesson to find main ideas. For example, the headings in Chapter 12, Lesson 1, are "Aztecs Settle in Central Mexico," "Aztec Society and Beliefs," and "The Cultural Legacy of the Aztecs." Each heading tells the main topic of a section. Scan the material under the heading to see what point is made about the topic. Then write one or more complete sentences restating that main idea in your own words.

Evaluating Details Evaluate details carefully to determine which are important enough to include. Remember to include the facts, numbers, and dates that are necessary for the main idea to make sense.

Outlining and Drafting Use the lesson titles in Unit 6 as the outline for your unit summary. You have already restated the main ideas of the lessons. Now use those sentences to write a smoothly flowing draft. Add transitions to keep the links between ideas clear.

Research & Technology

Summarizing helps you get to the core of a subject. As you do so, you can often see areas that you would like to know more about. After you finish a draft of your summary, review it for topics that interest you. From those, develop a few questions to guide future research. Record those questions in your notebook.

> **Technology Tip** To keep track of the main ideas you want to remember, highlight them with your word processor's highlighting tool. Use the help menu or user's manual to learn how to do this.

Evaluation & Revision

Read over your summary. Did you include all the main ideas in the unit? Did you include an appropriate amount of detail? One way to check is to compare your summary with the visual summaries on pages 390 and 418. Do you see anything you should add?

When revising, make sure your summary has unity, coherence, and emphasis (explained in the chart below).

Unity	All of the parts relate clearly to the whole. There is no information or idea that doesn't belong.
Coherence	The parts hold together well. They are in a logical order, and they are connected with transitional words and phrases. Key words are repeated to help readers make connections.
Emphasis	The most important ideas are clearly presented as being important. The summary covers equally important topics in about the same amount of detail.

Both individual paragraphs and your whole summary should be checked for unity, coherence, and emphasis and then revised as needed.

> **Self-Check**
> Does my summary
> ☐ cover all lessons in Unit 6?
> ☐ include just main ideas and only a few important details?
> ☐ have smooth transitions between sentences and paragraphs?
> ☐ consist of my own words?
> ☐ reflect underlying meaning, not surface details?

Publish & Present

Create a neat, error-free version of your summary and print it out. Then, if you want, create an illustrated cover page for it. When you have finished, share your summary with your classmates.

UNIT 7

European Renaissance and Reformation

Interact with History ▶

Building the Duomo, c. 1420
You are a project manager overseeing the construction of the Duomo, a new cathedral in Florence, Italy. It will be like nothing else you have helped build before. Painters, sculptors, and architects everywhere are experimenting with bold new styles and designs. They plan to use these new ideas in creating the cathedral.

What makes new designs and styles appealing?

WebQuest
ClassZone.com

Builders of this period have developed new technology to help them lift heavy equipment and more easily maneuver materials around the construction site.

How might this new technology aid in building large structures?

This new age has placed a great value on artistic beauty. As a result, the cathedral will be decorated with detailed paintings and sculptures.

What effect might these additions have on visitors to the cathedral?

The designer of the dome is Filippo Brunelleschi, who is using new styles and designs to create an awe-inspiring cathedral.

What difficulties might arise in creating such a structure?

This statue by 15th-century Italian sculptor Luca della Robbia is located in the Duomo.

This stained glass window from the Duomo depicts the Nativity, or the birth of Jesus. The window was created by Italian artist Paolo Uccello.

Chapter 13
The Renaissance

Before You Read: Predicting

Scan the main headings in each lesson. Then write three questions you hope to answer based on the headings. One example is:

What advances were made in art during the Renaissance?

If you find the answer to one of your questions as you read, write it in your notebook.

Big Ideas About the Renaissance

Science and Technology New inventions and techniques change the way people live.

During the Renaissance, painters, writers, and architects used new styles and techniques to create powerful and influential works. In addition, Renaissance scholars and inventors made key breakthroughs that changed the way of thinking in many fields.

★ Renaissance centers

Political border in 1500

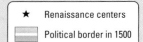

0   125   250 miles
0   125   250 kilometers

Integrated Technology

eEdition
- Interactive Maps
- Interactive Visuals
- Starting with a Story

 VIDEO *Everyday Life in the Renaissance*

INTERNET RESOURCES
Go to **ClassZone.com** for
- WebQuest   · Quizzes
- Homework Helper   · Maps
- Research Links   · Test Practice
- Internet Activities · Current Events

EUROPE

1300s
Renaissance begins in Italian cities.

mid-1400s
Johann Gutenberg invents the printing press.
◄ (page from Gutenberg Bible)

1300   1400

WORLD

1325
Aztecs build city of Tenochtitlán in Central Mexico.
◄ (mask of Aztec rain god)

1453
Ottoman Turks capture Constantinople.

Renaissance Europe, c. 1500

INTERACTIVE

SCOTLAND

NORWAY

SWEDEN

North Sea

DENMARK

ENGLAND

Oxford ★
London ★

Hamburg ★

FLANDERS
Antwerp ★
Ghent ★ ★ Brussels
Frankfurt ★

Paris ★

HOLY ROMAN
EMPIRE

Munich ★

FRANCE

SWITZERLAND
Geneva ★

Lyon ★

Milan ★   Venice ★

VENICE

PORTUGAL

PAPAL
STATES

Florence ★

Adriatic Sea

Madrid ★

Barcelona ★

Lisbon ★

SPAIN

Rome ★

NAPLES

Seville ★

Valencia ★

Mediterranean Sea

This painting of the Angel Annunciate is part of a larger work called the Ghent Altarpiece by artist Jan Van Eyck.

The *Pieta* is one of the many masterpieces by painter and sculptor Michelangelo.

1504
Michelangelo unveils his famous sculpture *David*.
◄ (upper half of *David*)

1564
English writer William Shakespeare is born.
◄ (portrait of Shakespeare)

1500

1600

1467
"Warring States" period begins in Japan. (samurai on horseback) ►

1587
Shah Abbas I begins rule of Safavid Empire.

425

A Fierce Competition

CALIFORNIA STANDARDS

Reading 3.3
Analyze character-ization as delineated through a character's thoughts, words, speech patterns, and actions; the narrator's description; and the thoughts, words, and actions of other characters.

Background: You are about to explore a period in history known as the Renaissance. This was a time of remarkable artistic achievement in Europe. The atmosphere in many cities was one of great creativity and competition as artists worked to achieve fame and fortune.

To achieve success, Renaissance artists often relied on patrons. A patron was a person who provided money and support to an artist. Many patrons were rich merchants or bankers. Some religious and political leaders were also patrons. Imagine you are an artist trying to win over a patron and break out of the crowd.

Famous patron Lorenzo de Medici ▶

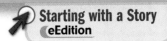

It is just before sunrise, and you are already hard at work in your small art studio above a busy street in the city of Florence, Italy. All around you are brushes and paint cans. You have been working on the painting in front of you for months, and now it all comes down to this: a wealthy banker is on his way to see your work.

He is looking for an artist to paint portraits of his family. You know that many other artists are competing against you for this position. You need this job to support yourself. Your money is running low.

You can't ask your family for more money. They are just simple farmers who live in a small village many miles away. They already gave you most of their savings so you could go to Florence and become an artist. If you gain the patronage of this banker, your family's faith in you will be justified. You could become a wealthy artist and help your family.

The moment of the banker's arrival nears. You walk back and forth in front of the painting looking for any flaws. The painting depicts Helen of Troy, a heroine of a Greek epic poem called the *Iliad*. You have heard that the banker likes ancient Greek writings.

You eventually decide that Helen's eyes do not shine enough. You quickly grab the smallest brush you can find. For the next hour you painstakingly work to achieve the look you want. Suddenly, you hear footsteps coming up the stairs. You look over the painting. Is it good enough? Will the banker like it? Soon you will know the answer.

Why do people value art so highly?

Reading & Writing

1. **READING: Characterization** What personal traits do you think were necessary to become a successful Renaissance artist?

2. **WRITING: Summarize** Based on what you read, write a paragraph summarizing the relationship between artists and patrons during the Renaissance.

CALIFORNIA STANDARDS Writing 2.5
Write summaries of reading materials.

1

▶ MAIN IDEAS

1 **Culture** Key events brought an end to the Middle Ages and feudal life.

2 **Economics** Toward the end of the Middle Ages, trade flourished. This brought new goods and ideas to an increasing number of people.

3 **Belief Systems** The movement known as humanism stressed the importance of individuals and encouraged human achievement.

▶ TAKING NOTES

Reading Skill: Categorizing

When you categorize, you sort things into groups with similar characteristics. Use a chart like the one shown below to describe the new ways of thinking brought on by humanism.

Impact of Humanism	
Old Thinking	New Thinking
king and Church most important	

S Skillbuilder Handbook, page R6

▲ **Marco Polo** The Italian trader Marco Polo helped to build trade between Europe and Asia with his journeys across the Silk Roads.

CALIFORNIA STANDARDS

7.8.1 Describe the way in which the revival of classical learning and the arts fostered a new interest in humanism (i.e., a balance between intellect and religious faith).

7.8.3 Understand the effects of the reopening of the ancient "Silk Road" between Europe and China, including Marco Polo's travels and the location of his routes.

CST 3 Students use a variety of maps and documents to identify physical and cultural features of neighborhoods, cities, states, and countries and to explain the historical migration of people, expansion and disintegration of empires, and the growth of economic systems.

Origins of the Renaissance

Build on What You Know The *arts* refers to a broad range of cultural activities and creations. Consider your favorite movies or music. They are all part of the arts. So too are painting, sculpture, literature, and architecture. In this chapter, you will learn about one of the most significant periods of artistic advancement in Western history.

European Society Changes

1 **ESSENTIAL QUESTION** What events helped bring an end to feudalism and the Middle Ages?

As you read in Chapter 10, a number of key events took place in Europe during the late Middle Ages. They included the growth of nations, the onset of a deadly plague, and the Hundred Years' War. All of these events combined to bring an end to feudal society.

The Rise of Nations Under feudalism, numerous small kingdoms ruled Europe. This began to change with the development of England and France as nations during the 1100s and 1200s.

As you recall, William the Conqueror led a group known as the Normans in conquering all of England. In France, the nobles who ruled Paris gradually increased their power and territory until they ruled much of the land. Eventually, England and France became unified countries under a single government or ruler. As a result, individual lords and landowners lost much of their power.

Monastery Ruins
As the Middle Ages ended, so did the use of many monasteries across Europe— including this one in Yorkshire, England. ▼

End of Medieval Institutions The feudal way of life also suffered a setback with the onset of a widespread plague and the Hundred Years' War during the 1300s. The deadly plague led to a large population decline throughout Europe. This meant that there were fewer serfs to work the land. As a result, the feudal system weakened.

Meanwhile, the Hundred Years' War between England and France spelled an end to the age of chivalry. The war featured the use of the longbow, which could penetrate armor from a long distance. This new weapon quickly made knights and their hand-to-hand style of fighting all but useless.

REVIEW What role did the plague and the Hundred Years' War play in the decline of feudalism?

The Expansion of Trade

2 ESSENTIAL QUESTION What effect did the reopening of the Silk Roads have on Europe?

As the feudal system faded, cities throughout Europe continued to grow. This was due in large part to the expansion of trade and the development of a strong merchant class. As you recall from Chapters 9 and 10, Europe experienced a revival of trade during the late Middle Ages. The main reason for the growth of trade was a gradual decline in warfare and invasion. As a result, traders once again felt safe to travel long distances.

Mongol Tile This star-shaped tile came from the Mongol Empire that Marco Polo visited. ▼

The Silk Roads Reopen Perhaps the most notable example of the return of long-distance trade was the reopening of the Silk Roads. The **Silk Roads** were an ancient trade route that connected Europe with China. After the fall of Rome, many viewed the roads as too dangerous. As a result, the nearly 5,000-mile route saw little use.

The rise of the Mongol Empire brought security to the region, which led to an increase in trade along the Silk Roads during the early 1200s. Then, in 1271, an Italian trader named Marco Polo started a journey along the route. Eventually, he reached China.

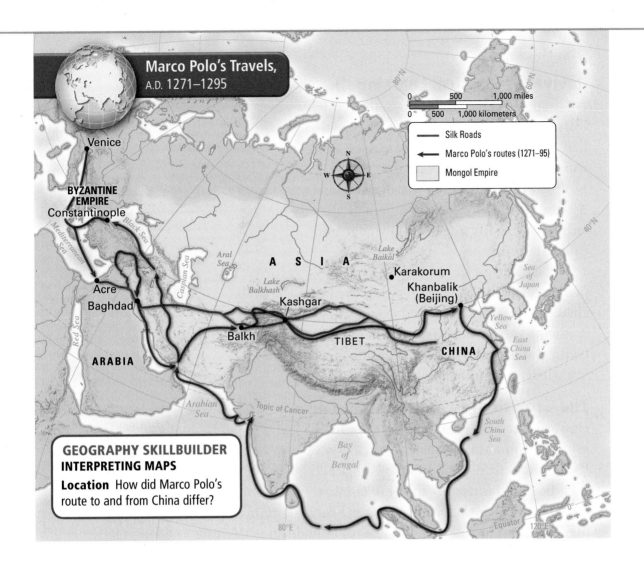

Marco Polo's Travels, A.D. 1271–1295

0   500   1,000 miles
0   500   1,000 kilometers

— Silk Roads
← Marco Polo's routes (1271–95)
▢ Mongol Empire

Venice

BYZANTINE EMPIRE
Constantinople

Mediterranean Sea

Black Sea

Acre

Baghdad

Red Sea

ARABIA

Arabian Sea

Caspian Sea

Aral Sea

Lake Balkhash

Kashgar

Balkh

TIBET

A S I A

Lake Baikal

Karakorum

Khanbalik (Beijing)

CHINA

Sea of Japan

Yellow Sea

East China Sea

South China Sea

Bay of Bengal

Tropic of Cancer

Equator

GEOGRAPHY SKILLBUILDER
INTERPRETING MAPS

Location How did Marco Polo's route to and from China differ?

After 24 years, Polo returned to Italy with tales of great riches from Asia. He wrote about the many places he visited in China, ". . . no fewer than a thousand carriages and packhorses loaded with raw silk, make their daily entry; and gold tissues and silks of various kinds are manufactured to an immense extent."

The success of Polo's journey encouraged European merchants to increase their trade with Asia. This growth of trade with Asia opened Europeans up to a host of new goods and ideas.

REVIEW How did Marco Polo contribute to the growth of European trade?

New Ways of Thinking

③ ESSENTIAL QUESTION What is humanism?

The events of the late Middle Ages had a great effect on many Europeans. Those who survived the years of plague and war wanted to celebrate and enjoy life. Meanwhile, the growth of trade introduced more people to new goods and ideas. As a result, new attitudes spread across Europe and helped to create new ways of thinking.

Revival of Classical Learning The end of the Middle Ages brought the return of learning in Europe. As you recall, education had declined during the Middle Ages. This was due largely to the fact that war and political instability had disrupted society. By the 1200s, however, people had grown eager once again to gain knowledge and understanding.

To achieve greater knowledge, many people turned to the past. They revived the classical ideas of Greece and Rome. They studied a variety of texts from these earlier civilizations in the hopes of gaining greater knowledge and fulfillment.

The Growth of Humanism
The study of classical texts and ideas led to a movement known as humanism. **Humanism** is a way of thought that focuses on human beings and their potential for achievement. It stresses the study of such classical subjects as history, grammar, literature, and philosophy. The goal of humanism is to create well-rounded individuals and encourage people to achieve all they could in life.

The early leader of the humanist movement was an Italian poet and scholar named Petrarch. He was one of the first thinkers to stress the value of classical learning, or the teachings of Greece and Rome. He worked to find and restore the works of many important Greek and Roman writers. In fact, scholars believe that such significant Latin writers as Cicero and Livy might be unknown today if Petrarch had not dug up their lost works buried in monastery libraries.

Humanist Thought
Humanism stressed the importance of the individual. This way of thinking differed greatly from that of medieval times—which placed kings and institutions such as the Church above everything else. Humanism also promoted a greater balance between intellect and religious faith. Humanist thinkers stressed the importance of leading a Christian life. However, they challenged people to think for themselves and not blindly accept church orders. They also taught that people could enjoy life and still be good Christians. This teaching differed from earlier beliefs that one had to avoid life's pleasures in order to please God.

▲ **Humanist Leader**
The early humanist leader Petrarch helped to preserve the work of classical writers such as Livy, an example of whose writing is shown here.

A New Age of Creativity Humanism helped to strengthen the growing desire among people to experiment, explore, and create. Indeed, in the wealthy cities of Italy such activities had already begun. In the next lesson, you will read about an explosion of creativity, learning, and discovery that began on the Italian peninsula and gradually spread throughout Europe. This movement is known as the Renaissance, and it touched nearly every aspect of life. It signaled the end of the Middle Ages and the beginning of a new era.

REVIEW How did the ideas of humanism differ from the beliefs of the Middle Ages?

Lesson Summary

- A number of factors combined to bring about an end to the Middle Ages and the feudal way of life.
- An increase in trade and the reopening of the Silk Roads brought new goods and ideas to more people.
- Humanism stressed the importance of individuals and encouraged human achievement.

Why It Matters Now . . .

Humanist ideas continue to encourage humans to make advances in all areas of society.

---

1 Lesson Review

 **Homework Helper** ClassZone.com

Terms & Names

1. Explain the importance of

 Silk Roads   humanism

Using Your Notes

Categorizing Use your completed chart to answer the following question:

2. How did humanism differ from earlier beliefs about the place of individuals in society? (REP 5)

Impact of Humanism	
Old Thinking	New Thinking
king and Church most important	

Main Ideas

3. What were the key factors that led to the decline of feudalism? (HI 1)

4. What two regions did the Silk Roads connect? (CST 3)

5. What was the main goal of humanism? (7.8.1)

Critical Thinking

6. **Drawing Conclusions from Sources** How did the reopening of the Silk Roads contribute to new ways of thinking among Europeans? (7.8.3)

7. **Making Inferences** How did the teachings of humanism weaken the power of the Church? (7.8.1)

Activity **Making a Map** Using library resources, draw an annotated map of Marco Polo's journey on the world map you have created. Include several call-outs from his stops that you found most interesting. (7.8.3)

Lesson 2

▶ MAIN IDEAS

1 **Economics** Wealthy patrons provided financial support to fuel the Renaissance.

2 **Culture** During the Italian Renaissance, artists and writers made many advances in the arts and learning.

3 **Science and Technology** The Renaissance witnessed the development of new artistic and engineering techniques.

▶ TAKING NOTES

Reading Skill: Finding Main Ideas

Finding main ideas and the details to support them helps you determine the key points of a lesson. Use a graphic like the one below to list achievements in various artistic fields.

```
Painting ── Main Idea: ── Engineering
            Renaissance
            Achievement
                │
            Literature
```

S **Skillbuilder Handbook, page R2**

▲ **Moses** The statue *Moses* is a famous work by Renaissance artist Michelangelo. With its graceful pose and powerful features, the sculpture highlights Michelangelo's unique ability to give the stone a sense of movement and life.

CALIFORNIA STANDARDS

Framework Examination of masterpieces such as Michelangelo's *Moses* and Dürer's *The Four Horsemen of the Apocalypse* will demonstrate the powerful vision of these artists as well as the power of art to communicate ideas.

7.8.2 Explain the importance of Florence in the early stages of the Renaissance and the growth of independent trading cities (e.g., Venice), with emphasis on the cities' importance in the spread of Renaissance ideas.

7.8.5 Detail advances made in literature, the arts, science, mathematics, cartography, engineering, and the understanding of human anatomy and astronomy (e.g., by Dante Alighieri, Leonardo da Vinci, Michelangelo di Buonarroti Simoni, Johann Gutenberg, William Shakespeare).

The Italian Renaissance

TERMS & NAMES
Renaissance
patron
perspective
Leonardo da Vinci
Michelangelo

Build on What You Know A creative person is someone who is good at using imagination and insight to excel at something or to produce new things. People can be creative in many ways. Some are creative writers or artists. Others are creative with music or computers. Still others show creativity in the areas of math or science. Consider the area in which you are creative. Then learn about an era of great creativity in Europe.

The Renaissance Begins in Italy

1 ESSENTIAL QUESTION What factors helped make Italy the birthplace of the Renaissance?

As you just read, Europe experienced a growth of cities and trade along with an increased focus on learning and human achievement. All of this led to a movement of great creativity in art, writing, and thought. This movement is known as the **Renaissance**.

The term *Renaissance* means "rebirth." It refers to the rebirth of classical art and learning that took place during this time. However, Renaissance writers and artists also created new styles and ways of thinking. The Renaissance lasted from about 1300 to 1600. The Renaissance began in Italy and then spread to all of Europe.

View of Florence
This painting depicts a river scene in Florence, Italy, one of the centers of the early Renaissance. ▼

Growth of Independent Trading Cities

The Renaissance began in Italy for several reasons. For one thing, Italy had been the center of the Roman Empire. As a result, artists and writers of Italy did not have to go far to revive the styles from this classical period.

Another advantage for Italy was its cities. Many of the trade routes that developed between Europe and Asia during this period went through northern Italy. As a result, several large urban centers developed in the region. They included Florence, Venice, and Milan. Cities became the main places for exchanging different goods and ideas. Thus, they were ideal locations for creating new styles and for spreading Renaissance ideas.

▲ **Classical Era Reborn** This painting (*The School of Athens*) of famous Greek thinkers by Renaissance artist Raphael shows an appreciation of the classical period.

Florence Shines

One of the most important and influential cities of the early Renaissance was Florence. Florence is located in northern Italy along the Arno River. Florence gained importance as a center of banking and clothing production. The growth of banking brought Florence great wealth.

By the early 1300s, Florence had a population of around 120,000—making it one of the largest cities in Europe. Among those who made Florence their home were talented artists and writers. Many of those who made notable contributions to the Renaissance lived and worked in Florence.

One reason that Florence and other Italian cities produced such influential artists and writers was that the ruling class actively supported the arts. A wealthy merchant class developed in many Italian cities. Many of its members became influential leaders. For example, a powerful banking family, the Medici, ruled Florence during the Renaissance. The Medici and other wealthy families became **patrons** of the arts. This meant that they encouraged artists to create and supported them financially. Such support enabled artists to work full-time on creating their masterpieces.

REVIEW What made Florence an early center of the Renaissance?

Advances in the Arts

2 ESSENTIAL QUESTION In what areas did Renaissance figures make notable achievements?

Renaissance artists broke from the past in several key ways. During the Middle Ages, art and literature often dealt with religious matters. Renaissance artists focused on portraying humans in realistic ways. In addition, Renaissance writers and painters experimented with new styles and techniques that resulted in unique works. Many of these works are still celebrated today for their beauty and realism.

New Techniques To be sure, Renaissance artists continued to portray many religious subjects. But these subjects were shown in a more realistic manner. To accomplish this, Renaissance artists moved away from the flat, two-dimensional style of painting that characterized medieval art. Instead, they used a technique known as **perspective**. This technique produced the appearance of three dimensions in works of art. As a result, they looked more realistic.

Perspective in Art

To create perspective, artists run parallel lines away from the viewer until they appear to meet at a spot on the horizon called the vanishing point.

Drawing people in the foreground larger than those in the background helps to give the painting a three-dimensional appearance.

◀ *The Marriage of the Virgin* (1504), Raphael

SKILLBUILDER
INTERPRETING VISUALS
Where does the central activity of the painting take place? How do you know?

Leonardo da Vinci (1452–1519)

Aspects of da Vinci's most famous painting, *Mona Lisa*, remain a mystery. Critics continue to wonder what the woman with the slight smile is thinking. Even more mysterious is the fact that da Vinci painted the work for a wealthy merchant but kept it by his side until his death.

Michelangelo (1475–1564)

Michelangelo was known to eat little while working and sleep on a cot near his painting or sculpture. His famous painting on the ceiling of the Sistine Chapel in Rome consists of a series of scenes from the Bible. It took him from 1508 to 1512 to complete the work.

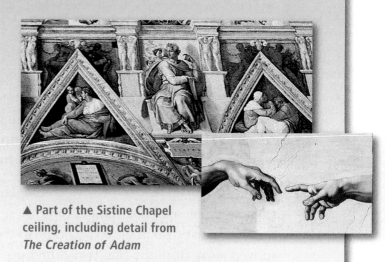

◄ *Mona Lisa* is thought to be a portrait of 24-year-old Lisa Gherardini. She was married to a wealthy Florentine merchant, who paid da Vinci to paint her picture.

▲ Part of the Sistine Chapel ceiling, including detail from *The Creation of Adam*

Leading Figures Three artists dominated the Italian Renaissance. They were **Leonardo da Vinci**, **Michelangelo**, and Raphael. Leonardo da Vinci was born outside the village of Vinci, near Florence, in 1452. He was trained as a painter. However, he excelled in several subjects, including astronomy, geometry, and anatomy. As a painter, he created many masterpieces, including *The Last Supper* and the *Mona Lisa*.

Michelangelo di Buonarroti Simoni was born in the Italian village of Caprese in 1475. He was trained mainly as a sculptor. Michelangelo completed many great works, including the sculpture *Moses* (1516) for the tomb of Pope Julius II. The works of Michelangelo were known for conveying intense feelings and portraying a sense of power. One of his greatest masterpieces was not a sculpture but a huge painting. It was painted on the ceiling of the Sistine Chapel in Rome.

Raphael was born in Urbino, Italy, in 1483. As a young man, he moved to Florence. There he studied the works of great artists including da Vinci. One of Raphael's most famous works was titled *The School of Athens* (see page 436).

Other Influential Artists Other Renaissance painters made their mark on the movement. A painter from Venice named Titian used bright colors and broad strokes to set his work apart from other artists'. He produced several masterpieces, including *Crowning with Thorns*. Sandro Botticelli was a significant painter from Florence. His works are known for their delicate colors, flowing lines, and overall poetic feeling. His paintings were generally not as realistic as those of other Renaissance artists.

Architecture and Engineering The Renaissance also witnessed breakthroughs in building techniques. One of the most influential architects of this period was Filippo Brunelleschi. He is perhaps best known for designing and building large domes for churches. One of his most famous domed cathedrals is the Duomo in Florence. He also developed techniques for raising construction materials onto various structures and buildings.

Renaissance Writers Writers broke new ground during the Renaissance. Like painters and sculptors of the time, writers focused on portraying the real life of individuals. An Italian author named Dante Alighieri wrote many poems and nonfiction works. His greatest masterpiece was the long poem *The Divine Comedy*. It focused on spiritual development and life after death.

During the 1200s and 1300s, many European scholars preferred to write in Latin. However, Dante often wrote in Italian. Influenced by Dante's example, other Renaissance writers also began to use their native language instead of Latin.

Cervantes Many great literary works were produced during the Renaissance. Among the notable literary figures of this era was the Spanish writer Cervantes. His most famous work was the novel *Don Quixote*. It tells the story of a landowner who imagines that he is a knight and goes on many adventures.

Primary Source Handbook

See the excerpt from the *Inferno*, pages R50–51.

Primary Source Handbook

See the excerpt from *Don Quixote*, pages R53–54.

Connect to Today

The Duomo Brunelleschi's creative work with dome architecture can be seen in the Duomo, a cathedral in Florence. ▼

Machiavelli Another influential writer was Niccolò Machiavelli. In 1513, he published his most famous work, *The Prince*. The book takes a realistic look at the world of politics and analyzes how to gain and hold political power.

Primary Source Handbook

See the excerpt from The Prince, page R52.

REVIEW In what ways did Renaissance works differ from those of earlier periods?

Life During the Renaissance

3 ESSENTIAL QUESTION What groups made up the different social classes in Renaissance Italy?

The Renaissance benefited mainly the upper class. In general, only wealthy people had time to study classical texts and examine humanist ideas. Most members of the middle and lower classes were not well educated. As a result, most of them did not take part in Renaissance activities. Over time, however, Renaissance ideas gradually spread to more of the population as more people became educated.

The Upper Class The upper class of Renaissance Italy consisted of nobles and wealthy merchants. The men of this class worked to become sophisticated and well-rounded. They learned to appreciate Renaissance art and literature. They also sought to master the various fields of classical study. Their goal was to achieve greatness in many areas. Today, we refer to a man who excels in many aspects of life as a "Renaissance man."

Upper-class women also sought to become well-rounded. Many of them received an education and developed an appreciation for the arts. Some became accomplished artists and writers themselves. The Italian poet Vittoria Colonna, for example, emerged as a notable and respected Renaissance writer. She exchanged many letters and sonnets with Michelangelo.

However, women gained few social or political rights during the Renaissance. Wealthy women mainly stayed at home. They went out only to the market or to church. Their main duties in life remained overseeing the education of their children and supervising servants.

Renaissance Women As this painting by an anonymous Dutch artist shows, upper-class women in the Renaissance were expected to engage in artistic activities. ▼

Other Classes The vast majority of people in Renaissance Italy were not wealthy. Many were middle-class citizens who made a modest living as tradespeople or as merchants. An even larger number of people were poor. These people made up the lower class. They often worked as laborers.

The ideas and breakthroughs of the Renaissance did not reach most of the poor. However, the movement did spread. In the next lesson, you will learn how the Renaissance gradually moved north and influenced the rest of Europe.

REVIEW Why did the Renaissance influence mainly the upper class?

Lesson Summary

- The Renaissance first developed in Italy, which was home to large and thriving cities.
- The Italian Renaissance gave rise to great achievements in the arts.
- The Renaissance influenced mainly the upper class of society.

Why It Matters Now . . .

The artistic and literary styles that emerged during the Renaissance continue to influence society today.

▲ **Peasant Life** This detail of *Peasants' Dance* by Renaissance artist Pieter Bruegel the Elder shows peasants relaxing.

---

2 Lesson Review

Homework Helper
ClassZone.com

Terms & Names

1. Explain the importance of

| Renaissance | perspective | Michelangelo |
| patron | Leonardo da Vinci | |

Using Your Notes

Finding Main Ideas Use your completed graphic to answer the following question:

2. Which achievement do you consider to be the most significant? Why? (7.8.5)

Main Ideas

3. How did Italy's cities help to make it the birthplace of the Renaissance? (7.8.2)

4. What three artists dominated the Italian Renaissance? (7.8.5)

5. What are the characteristics of a "Renaissance man"? (7.8.5)

Critical Thinking

6. Evaluating Information Do you think the Renaissance could have occurred without the presence of large cities? Explain. (7.8.2)

7. Comparing and Contrasting How did the focus and style of Renaissance art differ from that of the Middle Ages? (7.8.5)

Activity **Internet Activity** Use the Internet to locate a work by one of the artists mentioned in this lesson. Then write a paragraph describing why it interests you. (7.8.5)
INTERNET KEYWORD *Renaissance art*

Connect to Today
Extend Lesson 2

Renaissance Advances

Purpose: To learn about the scientific and technological achievements of the Renaissance

The new ways of thinking that helped drive the Renaissance touched not only the arts. As you have read, Leonardo da Vinci made advances in a variety of fields. The work of da Vinci and other Renaissance thinkers helped to pave the way for continued progress in a number of scientific and technological areas.

CALIFORNIA STANDARDS

7.8.5 Detail advances made in literature, the arts, science, mathematics, cartography, engineering, and the understanding of human anatomy and astronomy (e.g., by Dante Alighieri, Leonardo da Vinci, Michelangelo di Buonarroti Simoni, Johann Gutenberg, William Shakespeare).

Cartography

▶ **Past** Cartography, or mapmaking, became more scientific during the Renaissance. This map from 1489 shows how Europeans began understanding more about the world around them.

▼ **Present** Global Positioning Systems (shown here) can tell drivers their exact location. These devices get their information from satellites orbiting Earth.

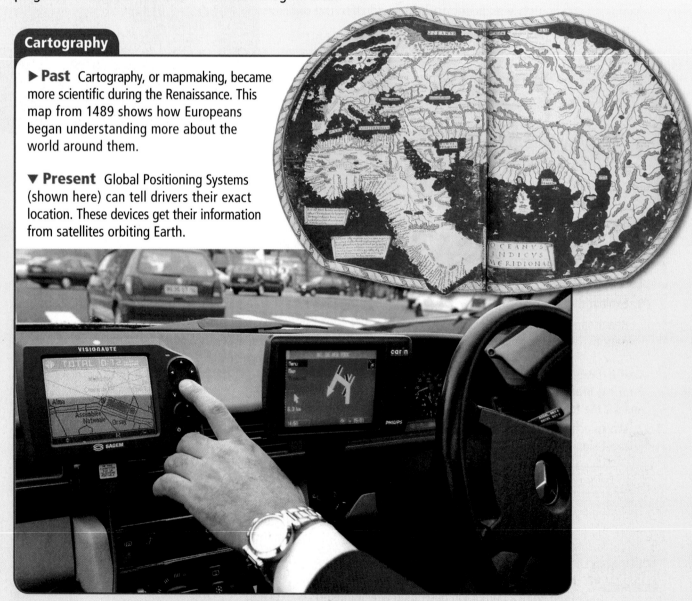

Human Anatomy

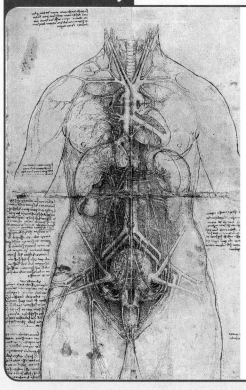

◄ **Past** As this drawing by da Vinci shows, Renaissance scholars attempted to learn more about how the human body worked. Among their discoveries was that the heart pumps blood throughout the body.

▶ **Present** Doctors use magnetic resonance imaging (MRI) to get a detailed look inside the body. MRIs use magnetic fields to create two-dimensional and three-dimensional images of the body's tissue.

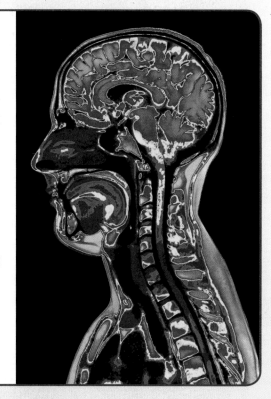

Engineering

▶ **Past** Da Vinci designed plans for many inventions, including flying machines. This drawing by da Vinci was based on his understanding of various scientific principles.

▼ **Present** Da Vinci's design is recognized as an ancestor of the modern helicopter.

Activities

1. **TALK ABOUT IT** Which Renaissance idea do you think had the greatest impact on the technology that followed it?

2. **WRITE ABOUT IT** Write a paragraph explaining which of the modern tools described above you consider most important and why. (Writing 2.4)

MAIN IDEAS

1 **Geography** The ideas of the Italian Renaissance spread to northern Europe.

2 **Culture** The Northern Renaissance produced its share of significant art, literature, and learning.

3 **Science and Technology** The invention of the printing press helped to spread Renaissance ideas throughout Europe.

TAKING NOTES

Reading Strategy: Evaluating Information

Evaluating information may involve organizing the material in order to better understand its main idea. As you read about the Northern Renaissance, use a chart like the one below to highlight the contributions made by each individual.

Albrecht Dürer	William Shakespeare	Johann Gutenberg

 Skillbuilder Handbook, page R23

▲ **Theater Costume** This outfit resembles one worn by actors during the Northern Renaissance in England, where plays were a popular form of entertainment.

CALIFORNIA STANDARDS

7.8.4 Describe the growth and effects of new ways of disseminating information (e.g., the ability to manufacture paper, translation of the Bible into the vernacular, printing).

7.8.5 Detail advances made in literature, the arts, science, mathematics, cartography, engineering, and the understanding of human anatomy and astronomy (e.g., by Dante Alighieri, Leonardo da Vinci, Michelangelo di Buonarroti Simoni, Johann Gutenberg, William Shakespeare).

REP 4 Students assess the credibility of primary and secondary sources and draw sound conclusions from them.

Framework Examination of masterpieces such as Michelangelo's *Moses* and Dürer's *The Four Horsemen of the Apocalypse* will demonstrate the powerful vision of these artists as well as the power of art to communicate ideas.

The Renaissance Spreads

TERMS & NAMES
William Shakespeare
Elizabethan Age
Johann Gutenberg
printing press
vernacular

Build on What You Know What do you know about William Shakespeare? You probably think of him as a writer from long ago. Did you know that he wrote the love story *Romeo and Juliet*? Or that a number of his works have been remade as modern movies that you may have seen? In this lesson, you will learn more about William Shakespeare and other notable artists from the Northern Renaissance.

The Renaissance Moves North

1 ESSENTIAL QUESTION What factors helped the Renaissance spread north?

During the late 1400s, Renaissance ideas began to spread north from Italy to countries such as France, Germany, Spain, and England. This was due in large part to cultural interaction, the growth of towns, and support from the region's powerful rulers.

Growth of Cities The growth of cities across northern Europe aided the spread of the Renaissance. In 1453, the destructive Hundred Years' War between England and France ended. As a result, life changed for many people. Trade expanded and cities grew rapidly. Renaissance ideas made their way to these cities and influenced large numbers of people. The growth of cities also helped to create a wealthy merchant class. Like the merchants in Italy, these wealthy businesspeople were eager to sponsor artists and writers.

Town Life The growth of Ghent (in what is today Belgium) and other cities across northern Europe helped spread the Renaissance throughout the region. ▼

445

▲ **Patron Monarch** An example of a monarch who supported the arts was Francis I of France (*left*). He had Italian artists and architects rebuild and decorate his castle at Fontainebleau (*above*).

Role of Monarchs The governments of northern Europe also stepped forward to support the arts. Italy was not a unified country but a collection of powerful and independent cities. However, England and France were unified countries ruled by powerful monarchs. Many of these rulers took an interest in the arts. They viewed artistic achievement as a source of pride for their country. As a result, they purchased paintings and provided financial support to many artists and writers.

Cultural Interaction The Italian artists who led the Renaissance eventually interacted with painters and writers throughout the rest of Europe. In the late 1400s, a war broke out between kingdoms in Italy. As the fighting dragged on, many Italian artists fled to the safety of northern Europe. There, they shared their new styles and techniques. In addition, artists from northern Europe traveled to Italy and learned all they could. They then brought Renaissance ideas back to their homelands.

REVIEW How did northern European monarchs encourage the Renaissance?

Northern Artists and Writers

2 **ESSENTIAL QUESTION** How did the Northern and Italian Renaissance differ?

The Northern Renaissance produced a second wave of talented painters, writers, and scholars. They made significant advances in the arts and learning. The Northern Renaissance and the Italian Renaissance differed in several ways. For one thing, northern European scholars did not study the classics as much as Italian scholars did. In addition, northern artists created works that were much more detailed in their presentation of everyday life.

German and Flemish Painters One figure who stood out for his realistic and detailed works was the German artist Albrecht Dürer. He is considered by many to be the greatest German Renaissance artist. Besides paintings, Dürer also created many woodcuts. A woodcut is a painted image produced from a wood carving. One of the most famous of his woodcuts is *The Four Horsemen of the Apocalypse* (1498). It portrays death, war, plague, and famine—four forces that the Bible states will appear at the end of the world.

▲ *The Four Horsemen of the Apocalypse* Dürer's famous woodcut presents a frightening image.

Jan Van Eyck and Pieter Bruegel (BROY•guhl) the Elder were two great Flemish painters. The term *Flemish* describes the people from a region of northwest Europe called Flanders (now in Belgium). Van Eyck often worked for wealthy patrons. His paintings contain minute details and bright colors. Many of these details have deeper meanings. For example, in one of his paintings, a single high window in a room represents a single God. Some of his more famous paintings are *Annunciation* and *Giovanni Arnolfini and his Bride*.

The paintings of Pieter Bruegel the Elder often show everyday scenes such as peasants dancing or children playing. Like other artists during the Northern Renaissance, Bruegel painted detailed works.

Northern Writers Talented writers also helped to shape the Northern Renaissance. The most famous of these northern writers was **William Shakespeare**. He was born in 1564 in Stratford, England. During the late 1580s, he moved to London, where he pursued a career in theater. Shakespeare soon became one of the more popular playwrights in England. He wrote comedies, tragedies, and history plays. His best-known works include *A Midsummer Night's Dream*, *Romeo and Juliet*, and *Hamlet*.

The works of Shakespeare show that he had a strong understanding of human nature. Because of this, his plays still speak to people today. His works continue to be performed throughout the world.

Background: The plays of William Shakespeare still speak to modern audiences. For example, *Romeo and Juliet* has been made into 34 different film versions. In this excerpt, Romeo reveals his feelings for Juliet as he watches her stand at her window.

from *Romeo and Juliet*
By William Shakespeare

. . . The brightness of her cheek would shame those stars
As daylight doth a lamp; her eyes in heaven
Would through the airy region stream so bright
That birds would sing and think it were not night.
See how she leans her cheek upon her hand!
O, that I were a glove upon that hand,
That I might touch that cheek!

◄ Claire Danes and Leonardo DiCaprio starred in the 1996 film *William Shakespeare's Romeo + Juliet.*

DOCUMENT–BASED QUESTION
What two features of Juliet does Romeo admire in this excerpt?

The Elizabethan Age Shakespeare wrote during a time in England known as the **Elizabethan Age**. The period was named after Queen Elizabeth I. She ruled from 1558 to 1603. Elizabeth promoted the Renaissance spirit in England. She was well educated and spoke several languages. She also wrote poetry. In addition, she showed great support for artists and writers.

REVIEW What qualities did the paintings of many northern artists have?

Advances in Science and Technology

3 ESSENTIAL QUESTION What Renaissance advances occurred outside the arts?

The advances made during both the Italian and Northern Renaissance occurred not just in the arts. Scholars and thinkers of this age made breakthroughs in a variety of fields, including mathematics, science, and technology.

Math and Science Renaissance scholars left their mark on a number of academic fields. In mathematics, for example, thinkers advanced the study of algebra by introducing the use of letters in algebraic equations. Meanwhile, Renaissance scientists developed new theories about the universe. They also developed a greater understanding of the minerals and metals that made up Earth's surface.

Visual Vocabulary

$x + y^2 = 6$
algebra

Scholars also made advances in the science-related areas of anatomy—the study of the human body—and cartography, or mapmaking. (See the Connect to Today feature on p. 442.) As they learned more about the world around them, Europeans created more accurate maps. They also increased their study of anatomy in order to learn more about the human body. Scientists, for example, first dissected a human body for educational purposes in 1315.

The Printing Press Renaissance Europe saw many technological advances as well. The most significant technological advancement was the invention of the printing press. This invention built on earlier Chinese technology known as wood-block printing. Under this technique, a printer carved a word or a letter on a wooden block. The printer then rolled ink on the block and used it to print on paper.

The Printing Press

A person could copy a single book in about five months.

5 months

A printing press could produce 500 books in the same amount of time.

5 months

During the mid-1400s, a German named **Johann Gutenberg** used movable type to invent a printing press. The **printing press** was a machine that pressed paper against a full tray of inked movable type. Gutenberg used his machine to print a complete version of the Bible in 1455. The book became known as the Gutenberg Bible.

The Impact of Printing The printing press had a huge impact on European society. Before, printers had to spend many months handwriting copies of books. Now, they could produce hundreds of copies quickly. As a result, books became cheap enough for many people to buy. The availability of so many books encouraged more people to learn how to read. It also helped spread new ideas more quickly than ever.

In addition, the printing press encouraged more authors to write in the **vernacular**, or their native language. Before this, most authors wrote mainly in Latin—the language of ancient Rome and the well educated. Now, many more people wanted to read works in their own language. As a result, authors wrote to readers in their everyday language. Printers across Europe produced works such as the Bible in the vernacular. This allowed people to interpret the Bible for themselves and draw their own conclusions about religious teachings.

The Renaissance Spirit The printing press, more than anything else, fueled the spread of Renaissance ideas. As you recall, these ideas were based on the humanist principles that people should think for themselves and work to achieve their potential.

These were the ideas that fueled so many advances in art and thought during this period. These ideas also led people to take a more critical look at the institutions around them, including the Church. In Chapter 14, you will read how Renaissance ideas helped to spark a major religious reform movement throughout Europe.

REVIEW What effects did the printing press have on European society?

Lesson Summary

- The growth of cities and the support of monarchs contributed to the spread of Renaissance ideas.
- The Northern Renaissance produced many great artists, writers, and scholars.
- Printing and the use of the vernacular helped to spread Renaissance ideas and increase learning.

Why It Matters Now . . .

Printing is used everywhere in today's world, including in books, Web sites, and newspapers.

---

3 Lesson Review

Terms & Names

1. Explain the importance of

   William Shakespeare   printing press
   Elizabethan Age   vernacular
   Johann Gutenberg

Using Your Notes

Evaluating Information Use your completed chart to answer the following question:

2. Who made the most lasting contribution to the Renaissance? Explain. (7.8.5)

Albrecht Dürer	William Shakespeare	Johann Gutenberg

Main Ideas

3. Why does Shakespeare's work remain popular today? (7.8.5)

4. What advances were made in math and science during the Renaissance? (7.8.5)

5. What effect did translating the Bible into the vernacular have? (7.8.4)

Critical Thinking

6. **Drawing Conclusions** How did the printing press help strengthen the Renaissance movement? (7.8.4)

7. **Forming and Supporting Opinions** Do you consider the artistic or the scientific advances of the Renaissance more important? Explain. (7.8.5)

Activity **Analyzing Renaissance Art** Examine various paintings, sculptures, and buildings done during the Renaissance. Choose one of your favorite works and identify features that reflect Renaissance ideas and styles. (REP 4)

Create a Quiz Show

Goal: To learn more about the achievements of the Renaissance

Materials & Supplies
- sheet of paper
- note cards
- marker or thick pen
- wristwatch

Prepare

Divide into groups of four and then into two teams of two. The two teams will compete to see who can answer questions about the achievements of the Renaissance in the fastest time.

Do the Activity

1 Work with your teammate to create seven questions about achievements of the Renaissance as well as about key figures of the period. One team should draw its questions from Lesson 2 and the other team from Lesson 3.

2 Write an answer to each of your questions and then have the teacher review your work. Make any revisions that the teacher suggests.

3 Write each question on one side of a note card. Write the answer to the question on the other side of the card.

4 One member of your team should then read the questions to the opposing team. The other member should time how long it takes for each answer. Teams may consult the text to find answers to the questions.

5 Record the times on a sheet of paper and then work with your partner to answer the questions from the other team.

Follow Up

Review with your partner the one or two questions with which you had the most difficulty.

Extension

Quizzing the Class Determine your two most challenging questions and put them before the class to answer.

CALIFORNIA STANDARDS

7.8.4 Describe the growth and effects of new ways of disseminating information (e.g., the ability to manufacture paper, translation of the Bible into the vernacular, printing).

7.8.5 Detail advances made in literature, the arts, science, mathematics, cartography, engineering, and the understanding of human anatomy and astronomy (e.g., by Dante Alighieri, Leonardo da Vinci, Michelangelo di Buonarroti Simoni, Johann Gutenberg, William Shakespeare).

North Sea

ENGLAND
London

English Channel

FRANCE

Life at the Globe Theater

Purpose: To learn about daily life in Renaissance England

A large part of cultural life in Renaissance London revolved around an open-air playhouse known as the Globe Theater. The theater was built in 1599 and took its name from its circular design. Members from every class of society filled the theater to socialize and watch the latest plays. The Globe was home to most of the plays of William Shakespeare.

A The Playwrights The Globe playwrights were often involved in the production of their plays. Shakespeare also acted in some of them. He even tried to keep his plays from being printed so no other theater could perform them!

B The Lords' Rooms Special rooms above the stage were reserved for the wealthiest members of society. These rooms were well furnished and comfortable and held no more than four people.

C The Actors The Globe actors often worked for little money and without much rehearsal. During Elizabethan times, women were not allowed to act. As a result, younger or inexperienced actors usually played the female roles.

D The Yard Members of the lower class paid a penny to stand in the "yard" and watch the plays. They sometimes showed their displeasure with a play by throwing apple cores and other food items at the actors.

CALIFORNIA STANDARDS

7.8.5 Detail advances made in literature, the arts, science, mathematics, cartography, engineering, and the understanding of human anatomy and astronomy (e.g., by Dante Alighieri, Leonardo da Vinci, Michelangelo di Buonarroti Simoni, Johann Gutenberg, William Shakespeare).

Activities

1. **TALK ABOUT IT** How was the experience of attending a play at the Globe different for the upper and lower classes?

2. **WRITE ABOUT IT** Write a paragraph explaining why you think the Globe was a true symbol of the Renaissance. Consider what took place there and who attended. (Writing 2.4)

► **VISUAL SUMMARY**

The Renaissance

Culture (7.8.5)
The Renaissance witnessed many advances in the arts.

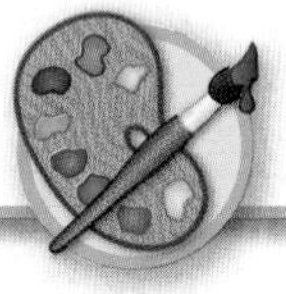

Geography (7.8.2)
- The Renaissance began in the cities of Italy.
- Renaissance ideas eventually spread north to all of Europe.

Belief Systems (7.8.1)
- Humanism stressed the importance and power of individuals.
- Humanist beliefs helped to start the Renaissance.

Economics (7.8.2)
- The growth of cities helped the Renaissance spread.
- Wealthy patrons provided financial support to many artists.

Science & Technology (7.8.5)
- Renaissance scholars made advances in math and science.
- A key technological advancement was the invention of the printing press.

► **TERMS & NAMES**

Explain the contribution that each individual made to the Renaissance.

1. **Leonardo da Vinci**
2. **Michelangelo**
3. **William Shakespeare**
4. **Johann Gutenberg**

► **MAIN IDEAS**

Origins of the Renaissance (pages 428–433)
5. How did the reopening of the Silk Roads affect Europe? (7.8.3)
6. How did humanism try to strike a balance between human intellect and faith? (7.8.1)

The Italian Renaissance (pages 434–443)
7. What role did cities play in the spread of Renaissance ideas? (7.8.2)
8. Why did many Renaissance paintings look more realistic than earlier works? (7.8.5)

The Renaissance Spreads (pages 444–453)
9. What advances in art and science occurred during the Renaissance? (7.8.5)
10. What were the effects of the printing press on European society? (7.8.4)

CRITICAL THINKING
Big Ideas: Science and Technology

11. EVALUATING INFORMATION How might the ideas of humanism have helped lead to advances in human anatomy? (7.8.1)

12. MAKING INFERENCES Why might describing Leonardo da Vinci as solely a Renaissance artist be incomplete? Give examples. (7.8.5)

13. UNDERSTANDING CAUSE AND EFFECT What effect did the printing press have on the dissemination of information? (7.8.4)

ALTERNATIVE ASSESSMENT

1. WRITING ACTIVITY Write a paragraph explaining any similarities and differences you see between the invention of the printing press and the Internet. (7.8.4)

2. INTERDISCIPLINARY ACTIVITY—SCIENCE Consider a question about how your body works. For example, what do your lungs do? What is the role of your liver? Research your question and summarize your findings in a paragraph. (7.8.5)

3. STARTING WITH A STORY Review the story "A Fierce Competition." Explain what you think drove so many artists and writers to create during the Renaissance. (7.8.5)

Technology Activity

4. CREATING A GRAPHIC ORGANIZER Use the Internet, library, and this chapter to research more about any five people mentioned in the text. Create a graphic organizer that includes the following information about each individual:
- Country of origin
- Years lived
- Type of artist
- Major works (7.8.5)

Research Links
ClassZone.com

Interpreting Visuals The following detail is from the painting *The Birth of Venus* by Renaissance artist Botticelli. Use the image and your knowledge of history to answer the questions. (7.8.5)

1. What feature of Venus does Botticelli attempt to make most noticeable?

A. ears
B. hair
C. eyes
D. mouth

2. The detailed and lifelike facial features of Venus are a characteristic of which term?

A. realism
B. Stoicism
C. feudalism
D. humanism

Test Practice
ClassZone.com

Additional Test Practice, pp. S1–S33

Chapter 14

The Reformation

Before You Read:
Previewing Key Concepts

The red titles throughout the chapter tell you what the text below them will be about. Rewrite these titles as questions that can be answered as you read. The first one is done for you.

What was the Great Schism?

Watch for the answers to your questions as you read.

Big Ideas About the Reformation

Government New ideas and beliefs can challenge a government's authority, leading to change.

During the Reformation, reformers split from the Catholic Church. The split changed Christianity and politics in Europe. Many Protestant churches practiced self-government. This influenced later democratic practices and ideas of federalism.

Integrated Technology

eEdition
- Interactive Maps
- Interactive Visuals
- Starting with a Story

INTERNET RESOURCES
Go to **ClassZone.com** for
- WebQuest
- Homework Helper
- Research Links
- Internet Activities
- Quizzes
- Maps
- Test Practice
- Current Events

EUROPE

1305
Clement V becomes pope.

1378
The Great Schism divides the Catholic Church.

1417
The Council of Constance ends the Great Schism.

1300

1400

WORLD

1324
Mansa Musa, king of Mali, begins a pilgrimage to Mecca.

1368
◄ Hongwu founds the Ming Dynasty in China. (stoneware Buddha figurine from Ming Dynasty)

Christianity in Europe, A.D. 1600
INTERACTIVE

ATLANTIC OCEAN

SCOTLAND

IRELAND

ENGLAND
· London

North Sea

NORWAY

SWEDEN

DENMARK

Baltic Sea

PRUSSIA

POLAND–LITHUANIA

NETHERLANDS

Wittenberg ·

HOLY ROMAN

Worms ·

EMPIRE

Augsburg ·

Nantes ·

FRANCE

Geneva ·

· Trent

Avignon ·

PAPAL STATES

Adriatic Sea

OTTOMAN EMPIRE
(Islamic & Greek Orthodox)

PORTUGAL

Madrid ·

SPAIN

Corsica

Rome ·

NAPLES

Sardinia

Sicily

Mediterranean Sea

Legend:
- Church of England
- Calvinist
- Lutheran
- Roman Catholic

0   125   250 miles
0   125   250 kilometers

1492
◄ King Ferdinand and Queen Isabella drive the last Muslim rulers out of Spain.

1517
Martin Luther presents his Ninety-Five Theses.

1545
Catholic Church leaders meet at the Council of Trent to define church doctrine.

1500

1600

1453
The Ottomans capture Constantinople.

1556
Akbar becomes sultan of the Mughal Empire. (Akbar's Panch Mahal palace in India) ▶

Starting with a Story

Printing Challenging IDEAS

CALIFORNIA STANDARDS

Reading 2.3 Analyze text that uses the cause-and-effect organizational pattern.

Background: During the 1500s, reformers risked the anger of Church officials by raising questions about the Roman Church's authority. To help spread their ideas, the reformers used the new printing technologies that had developed during the 1400s. As you read the following story, imagine that you worked for a printer in those difficult times.

Blocks with individual letters were used to assemble words. The letters are backwards so they will print in the correct direction. ▶

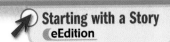

This morning, as you inked the type in the printing press, you saw the master printer examine a freshly printed sheet of paper. It looked like a long list of sentences. When you asked him what it was, he said, "Ninety-five theses." "What are theses?" you responded. According to the master, theses are just ideas. Apparently, some professor wrote them down because he wanted to discuss them with his students. Simple enough, you thought to yourself.

But the other apprentices in the shop seemed to do an awful lot of grumbling about the work. A few seem angry to have anything to do with it. Late in the afternoon, you get the chance to ask them why they're angry. You are surprised when they tell you that the list being printed is going to get the shop in big trouble. Johann, one of the apprentices, explains that a lot of the theses are about how it isn't right for the Church to be selling indulgences, or pardons for sins. Johann explains that the pope himself had ordered the sale of indulgences.

Everybody knows that the pope is the leader of the Catholic Church. And when you think of it, you don't know anybody who isn't a Christian. You wonder what will happen to someone who dares to question the pope's authority. You feel a wave of fear when you think about how people who have insulted the pope have been excommunicated, or kicked out of the Church.

Strangely, not everyone in the shop was afraid. Some of the older apprentices said that they'd seen copies of the same theses made by other shops. Some of them agree that they are tired of the pope's control over what they do and what they believe. You leave the shop at the end of the day very confused and filled with questions.

How might the Ninety-Five Theses affect people in European society?

Reading & Writing

1. **READING: Cause-and-Effect** According to the story, what might be the effects if the print shop prints the theses?

2. **WRITING: Persuasion** Write a one-page persuasive essay explaining why you think the shop should or should not print the theses.

CALIFORNIA STANDARDS **Writing 2.4**
Write persuasive compositions.

MAIN IDEAS

1 **Belief Systems** The Catholic Church was weakened by internal conflict.

2 **Culture** People began to question and speak out against some Church practices.

3 **Belief Systems** Reformation begins as a result of Martin Luther's Ninety-Five Theses.

TAKING NOTES

Reading Skill: Summarizing

When you summarize, restate the passage in fewer words and include only the main ideas and most important details. In Lesson 1, summarize each of the main sections using a chart like the one below.

Section	Summary
The Great Schism	
Criticism of the Church	
Martin Luther confronts the Church	

S Skillbuilder Handbook, page R3

▲ **Pope Clement V and King Philip IV of France** Pope Clement (in the green robe) moved the center of the Church from Italy to France, which was ruled by King Philip (in the red robe).

CALIFORNIA STANDARDS

7.9.1 List the causes for the internal turmoil in and weakening of the Catholic church (e.g., tax policies, selling of indulgences).

7.9.2 Describe the theological, political, and economic ideas of the major figures during the Reformation (e.g., Desiderius Erasmus, Martin Luther, John Calvin, William Tyndale).

CST 1 Students explain how major events are related to one another in time.

Trouble for the Catholic Church

TERMS & NAMES

Great Schism

indulgence

Martin Luther

Protestant

Reformation

Build on What You Know Have you ever disagreed with a friend's behavior and decided to spend less time with that person? In the 1300s and 1400s, many followers disagreed with the Catholic Church—and some left the Church.

The Great Schism

[handwritten: What is the great schism-split between Avigon & rome]

1 **ESSENTIAL QUESTION** How did internal differences weaken the Catholic Church?

The Roman Catholic Church had competing centers of authority from 1378 until 1417. A major cause of the split was the decision of Pope Clement V to move the Catholic government from Rome, Italy, to Avignon (ah•vee•NYAWN), France.

French Popes In the 1300s, the growth of national states weakened the power of the Church. Some monarchs grew powerful enough to force the Church to support their policies.

In 1305, the French king used his political power to have Clement V elected pope. Two years later, the pope moved the center of the Church to Avignon. After the move to Avignon, most of the popes were French. This made other Europeans, and many Church officials, feel that the French king was controlling the pope. This resulted in a struggle for control of the Church.

Connect to Today

The Papal Palace at Avignon, France This palace was used by one of the popes during the Great Schism. ▼

461

A Struggle for Power The Church developed two centers of power—Avignon and Rome. In 1378, the two sides split and elected different popes. The split is known as the **Great Schism** (SKIHZ•uhm). Each pope demanded obedience from the faithful, and excommunicated, or excluded from the Church, the rival pope's followers. This caused confusion and doubt among Christians and weakened the Church.

Healing the Church In 1414, the Holy Roman Emperor summoned a conference to end the schism and reform the Church. Remember that the Holy Roman Empire ruled much of central Europe and was closely associated with the Roman Catholic Church. As a result, the Holy Roman Emperor was very influential. The conference took place in Germany and met from 1414 to 1418. Church officials removed the French pope and persuaded the Roman pope to resign. In 1417, they elected Pope Martin V. He was based in Rome, and began to unify the Church once again.

▲ **Pope Clement VII**
This painting shows the election of Pope Clement VII, the first rival to the pope in Rome during the Great Schism.

REVIEW How did the Great Schism weaken the Church?

Criticism of the Church

2 **ESSENTIAL QUESTION** Why did people begin to question some Church practices?

The efforts of the Church to heal itself strengthened the pope's authority. Even so, the Church fell short in its efforts to reform. There was distrust between Church officials and the pope, and believers were uncertain of the Church's authority. Throughout the 14th and 15th centuries, demands for reform grew more intense.

A Corrupt Church Over the centuries, the medieval Church had become an enormous institution. By some estimates, the Church owned from one-fifth to one-third of all of the lands of Europe. Church leaders needed huge sums of money to maintain such an institution. Critics and reformers were angered by some of the ways in which the Church earned and spent its money.

Many Europeans, especially those who lived outside Italy, disliked paying taxes to the Church in Rome. They were also upset that the Church paid no taxes on its vast landholdings.

Reformers also objected to the sale of indulgences. An **indulgence** is a relaxation of earthly penalty for sin. However, sometimes indulgences were sold as if they were a pardon for sin, and people bought these thinking they could avoid punishment in the afterlife. Reformers were enraged that the hierarchy of the Church appeared to allow people to believe they could buy their way into heaven.

Critics also did not like the way the Church spent money. During the Renaissance, many popes spent large sums supporting the arts and their own personal pleasure. Other Church officials followed their example. People from all levels of society, including nobles, townspeople, and peasants, began to call on the Church to emphasize spiritual over material values.

Reformers Take a Stand During the 14th and 15th centuries, a number of important reformers spoke out against Church practices. In England, a philosopher and priest named John Wycliffe (c. 1330–1384) called for Church reform. He questioned the pope's right to levy taxes and to appoint Church officials without the king's approval.

Martin Luther Martin Luther challenged the Church and began the Reformation. ▼

Dutch priest and scholar Desiderius Erasmus (DEHZ•ih•DEER•ee•uhs ih•RAZ•muhs) (1469–1536), urged people to pursue a true Christian faith. He criticized Church officials for neglecting Christian values. But Erasmus also criticized reformers for trying to divide the Church. As a result, he was not wholly trusted by either side. The work of Erasmus and other Renaissance humanists would have a strong influence on Martin Luther, the man who started the 16th-century movement known as the Reformation.

REVIEW What sort of reforms did critics of the Church demand from the 1300s through the 1500s?

Luther Confronts the Church

3 ESSENTIAL QUESTION Who is credited with beginning the Reformation?

Early Church reformers wanted to improve the Church. They thought the Church was basically a good institution that just needed some improvement. Later reformers, however, saw the Church as a corruption of the original Christian faith. The ideas of one man came to represent this new reform movement. His name was **Martin Luther**.

Background: On October 31, 1517, it is said that Martin Luther posted his theses on the church door of the Castle Church in Wittenberg, an event considered to be the start of the Reformation. Today, this document is known as the Ninety-Five Theses. At right are three of the theses posted by Luther.

from *Disputation of Doctor Martin Luther on the Power and Efficacy of Indulgences*

By Martin Luther
Translated by Adolph Spaeth, L.D. Reed, Henry Eyster Jacobs, et al.

21. Therefore those preachers . . . are in error, who say that by the pope's indulgences a man is freed from every penalty, and saved.

52. The assurance of salvation by letters of pardon is vain,[1] even though . . . the pope himself, were to stake his soul upon it.

68. Yet [indulgences] are in truth the very smallest graces compared with the grace of God and the piety of the Cross.

---

1. **vain:** foolish.

> **DOCUMENT–BASED QUESTION**
> What groups of people might Luther have angered by posting his theses?

Martin Luther

Martin Luther was born in Germany in 1483. He had a good education, and his father wanted him to study law. But in 1505, Luther was caught in a thunderstorm and nearly struck by lightning. Fearing for his life, he vowed to become a monk.

Luther tried to live as the Church instructed. But he still felt that he was a sinner and that an angry God would punish him. Luther's fears led him to think about God as a God of mercy. He came to believe that people could be saved only if they had faith in Christ. As a result, he questioned the idea that salvation could be won through good works.

Luther's Ninety-Five Theses

Luther's ideas led to conflict with the Catholic Church. The conflict began in 1517 in Wittenberg (WIHT•n•BURG), Germany. Church officials were selling indulgences to finance St. Peter's Cathedral in Rome. Luther disapproved and wrote out all his disputes with the Church in his Ninety-Five Theses. The theses were ideas that Luther wanted to debate, such as the selling of indulgences. Luther's ideas included the following:

- The Bible is the only source of religious truth.
- People do not need the clergy to interpret the Bible.
- Salvation can be gained only through faith in Christ.

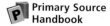

Primary Source Handbook

See the excerpt from the Ninety-Five Theses, page R55.

In 1529, German princes who remained loyal to the Church agreed to unite against Luther's ideas. Princes who supported Luther signed a protest against the agreement. The protest earned them the name *Protestants*. Eventually, **Protestant** became the name for Christians who broke with the Catholic Church during and after the 16th century. Protestants used the term **Reformation** to describe the movement of opposition to the Catholic Church.

REVIEW What were important ideas from the Reformation?

Lesson Summary
- The Great Schism weakened the Church.
- From the 14th through the 16th centuries, many Christians were troubled by the way the Church earned and spent its income.
- At the beginning of the 16th century, Martin Luther unintentionally became the leader of a revolutionary attack on the Roman Catholic Church.

Why It Matters Now . . .
Competition between Catholics and Protestants in Europe caused each to try and spread their version of Christianity throughout the world. Today, Catholics and Protestants are found on every continent.

Treggie

1 Lesson Review

Homework Helper
ClassZone.com

Terms & Names
1. Explain the importance of

Great Schism✓	Martin Luther✓	Reformation✓
indulgence	Protestant	

Using Your Notes
Summarizing Use your completed chart to answer the following question:

2. What was the Great Schism? (7.9.1)

Section	Summary
The Great Schism	
Criticism of the Church	
Martin Luther confronts the Church	

Main Ideas
3. How did the Great Schism weaken the Church? (7.9.1)
4. What were some of the Church practices that reformers spoke out against from the 14th through the 16th centuries? (7.9.1)
5. What were some of the ideas Luther wanted to debate? (7.9.2)

Critical Thinking
6. **Understanding Causes** How did the growing strength of national states affect the papacy? (CST 1)
7. **Drawing Conclusions** How did Luther's ideas about religious truth threaten the Church? (7.9.2)

Activity **Writing a Newspaper Article** The reformer Desiderius Erasmus was influential not only in religious reform but also in educational reform. Research to learn more about Erasmus, then write a brief article about his participation. (7.9.2)

Literature CONNECTIONS

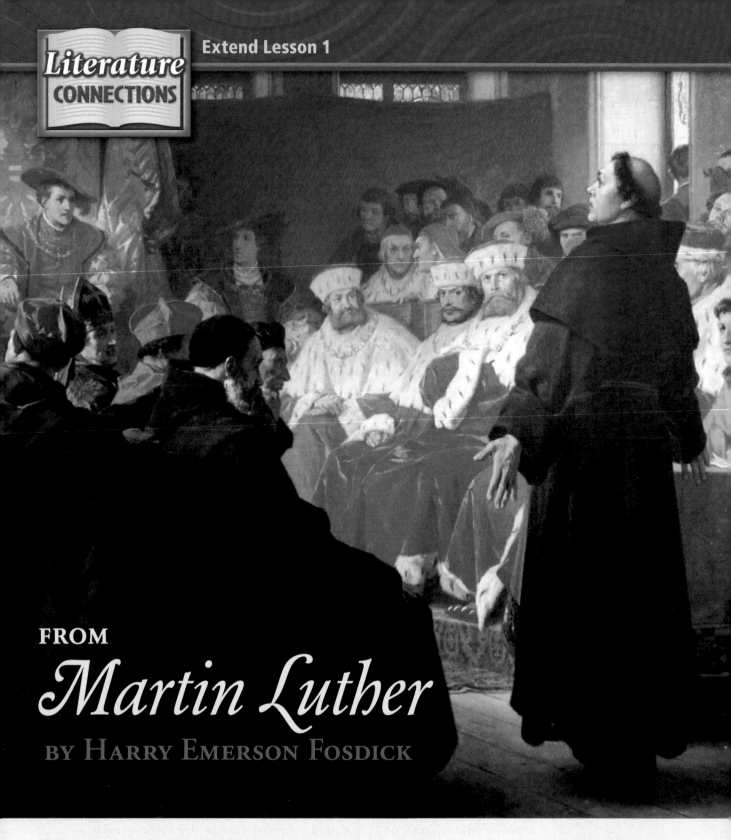

FROM

Martin Luther

BY HARRY EMERSON FOSDICK

Background: Martin Luther found great support after he posted his Ninety-Five Theses in Wittenberg. But he also faced great danger. In 1521, he met with the Holy Roman Emperor and officials from the Catholic Church in the German town of Worms (wurmz). They demanded that Luther take back everything he had written and admit he was wrong. Luther refused. Author Harry Emerson Fosdick describes what happened next in this excerpt from his book *Martin Luther.*

CALIFORNIA STANDARDS

Reading 3.3 Analyze characterization as delineated through a character's thoughts, words, speech patterns, and actions; the narrator's description; and the thoughts, words, and actions of other characters.

So at last [Luther] was condemned in an edict[1] which made him an outlaw for . . . life. To be sure, in the meantime some of the leading princes and noblemen had left Worms, so the edict was signed only by Luther's enemies who had stayed in town. Nevertheless, he stood condemned by the Emperor as well as by the Pope, and he was an outlaw. He was to be arrested wherever found and sent to the Emperor, and it was a crime to read his books or to support and befriend him in any way.

Then Luther disappeared. He simply vanished. Where he was nobody knew. The rumor ran through Germany that he had been murdered. . . .

Luther, however, was not dead. What had happened was this: Luther had slipped out of Worms and had started back toward Wittenberg in his covered wagon. Then one evening, as he and two companions were driving into the woods . . . a party of armed horsemen fell upon them and . . . dragged Luther out and carried him off. Putting him on horseback, they led him around and around through the woods until, late at night, they brought him secretly to Wartburg Castle. There the great doors closed behind him and shut him in.

All over Europe the story went and, of course, almost everyone supposed that Luther's enemies had kidnapped him and perhaps murdered him. On the contrary, the whole scheme had been arranged by Frederick.[2] He was determined to save Luther's life. Against the protests of Luther, who did not like the scheme at all, Frederick had ordered some of his own horsemen to capture Luther and carry him to Wartburg.

So there he was, excommunicated by the Pope and outlawed by the Emperor, and now hidden by his friends in Wartburg Castle with no one for company except the warden[3] and two serving boys.

REVIEW Why did Frederick take Luther to Wartburg Castle?

For nearly a year Luther was kept hidden in Wartburg Castle and its immediate neighborhood. He disguised himself so that no one would recognize him. All monks had shaven heads, but he let his hair grow long and, as well, grew a mustache and a bushy beard, until it was said that his own mother would not know him. He took off his monk's costume and put on the clothes of a knight, wearing a gold chain and carrying a sword. He changed his name to Junker George. He tried to act like a young nobleman and once he went on a two days' hunting expedition with the warden. . . .

▲ **Luther Defends Himself** In this painting, Martin Luther is defending his views before an assembly of Catholic officials.

1. **edict:** an official statement issued by an authority that becomes law.
2. **Frederick:** Frederick III, a very powerful German prince who protected Martin Luther.
3. **warden:** person who handled the castle's affairs.

Altogether he had a miserable year. "I did not want to come here," he wrote, "I wanted to be in the fight." And once he even said, "I would rather burn on live[4] coals than rot here." Luther never liked to be alone. He always needed companions to keep up his spirits. Especially during that year, of all years, when the struggle which he had started was raging all over Germany and his friends and backers were carrying the burden of it, it was maddening to be holed up[5] in lonely seclusion in Wartburg. He had dreadful times of depression. . . . Doubts and fears troubled him. Had he been right? He thought of all the confusion and turmoil he had caused. Was it worth while? Would any good come out of it? He wrote to one friend, "You can believe that I am exposed to a thousand devils in this lazy solitude. . . ."

To be sure, at times he found some peace of mind. . . . He would persuade himself that, since he could not be out in the thick of the struggle, the best thing was to forget it. Once he even wrote to his friend Spalatin, "What is going on in the world I care nothing for. Here I sit in quiet." Anyone who understands Luther, however, will realize that he could not long keep up that kind of bluff. He cared more about what was going on in Germany than he cared about his own life.

REVIEW Why was Luther so upset at having to stay in hiding?

So, despite the fact that he was holed up in Wartburg Castle, he began getting into the struggle by letter. He wrote continually to his friends in Wittenberg, giving advice and begging for all the news.

---

4. **live:** burning.
5. **holed up:** hiding out.

Martin Luther's Study In this room in Wartburg Castle, Luther wrote his German translation of the Bible.

Wartburg Castle Martin Luther was hidden in this castle by German prince Frederick III to protect him from Catholic authorities. ▼

At first he was delighted by what he heard. Things were going very well. His friends missed him but they were forging ahead, and the reformation of the Church was going strongly forward. . . .

Luther's happiness, however, did not last long. The news from Wittenberg began to be troublesome. When Luther had left for Worms, very little had been changed in the day-by-day religious life of the people and in the way the Church's services were run. Even the sale of indulgences had not been altogether stopped. Now, however, changes were taking place thick and fast. . . . This caused an uproar. Some wanted the changes to be made even more rapidly; others were angry and upset because the changes were coming so fast. . . .

So the months went by, with the news from Wittenberg growing ever more disturbing. . . . Violence broke out. The statuary in the churches was destroyed by mobs who denounced the images as idols before which the people prayed. . . . Rioting students broke up church services where they thought changes to the new order of things were not being made fast enough, and once at least they even dragged the priest from the altar. . . .

REVIEW Why had violence broken out in Germany?

Luther could not stand it any longer. Frederick told him he must not come back, but he had to come back. At last the town council in Wittenberg, despite Frederick, invited him back, and back he came. That was one of the bravest things he ever did. He had been excommunicated by the Pope and outlawed by the Emperor, and even Frederick did not see how he could save Luther if he returned. Nevertheless, while he stood in the deadliest danger he ever was in, it was a glad day in Luther's life when he turned his back on Wartburg Castle and headed for home.

Reading & Writing

1. **READING: CHARACTERIZATION** Based on this story, what were Martin Luther's personal qualities? Use examples from the text to support your answer.

2. **WRITING: RESEARCH REPORTS** What happened to Luther when he returned home? Research and write a one-page report explaining Luther's actions. Be sure to document the sources you used for your research.

CALIFORNIA STANDARDS **Writing 2.3**
Write research reports.

▶ MAIN IDEAS

1 **Government** The spread of Luther's ideas changed European politics.

2 **Belief Systems** Different Protestant movements developed quickly throughout Europe.

3 **Belief Systems** The Catholic Church developed new ways to spread its message and counter the spread of Protestantism.

▶ TAKING NOTES

Reading Skill: Finding Main Ideas

The main idea is the most important point of a paragraph or section. Record the main idea and supporting details of each section in Lesson 2 using a diagram like the one below.

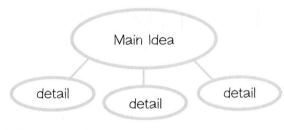

Main Idea

detail   detail   detail

S Skillbuilder Handbook, page R2

▲ **King Henry VIII** As king of England, Henry broke with the Catholic Church when the pope refused to grant him a divorce.

CALIFORNIA STANDARDS

7.9.2 Describe the theological, political, and economic ideas of the major figures during the Reformation (e.g., Desiderius Erasmus, Martin Luther, John Calvin, William Tyndale).

7.9.5 Analyze how the Counter Reformation revitalized the Catholic church and the forces that fostered the movement (e.g., St. Ignatius of Loyola and the Jesuits, the Council of Trent).

HI 2 Students understand and distinguish cause, effect, sequence, and correlation in historical events, including the long- and short-term causal relations.

Reform and Reaction

TERMS & NAMES

John Calvin

predestination

Ignatius of Loyola

Jesuit

Inquisition

Build on What You Know As you read Lesson 2, try to predict how the conflict in the Church will develop, and what the possible outcomes might be.

Luther's Ideas Spread

1 ESSENTIAL QUESTION What were some of the results of Luther's ideas?

Luther's ideas spread quickly. Priests who approved of Luther's ideas preached his message in their churches. Churchgoers, in turn, talked about the new ideas at home, in the streets, and in the universities. Merchants spread Luther's ideas along trade routes.

The Printed Word Printing also became an effective method for spreading Luther's ideas. There were several reasons for this. The printing process was becoming cheaper and, as a result, printing shops more common. Also, more Europeans could read, and printers produced an increasing variety of works in local languages.

For centuries Bibles were only printed in Latin. During Luther's time, however, printers began producing Bibles in local languages. As a result, people could read and interpret the Bible for themselves. The ability of people to interpret the Bible in their own way threatened the Catholic Church's authority.

Church leaders believed that religious teaching had to come to the people through the clergy. They also feared that people would develop their own religious ideas, challenging the authority of the pope and the clergy.

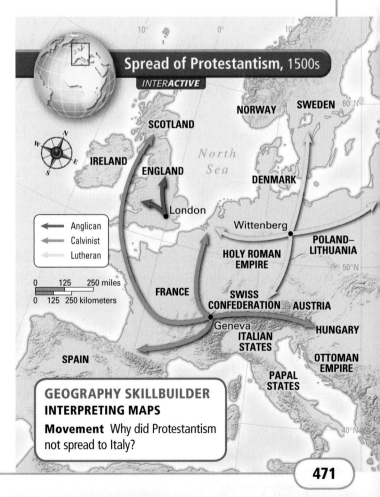

Spread of Protestantism, 1500s
INTERACTIVE

Anglican
Calvinist
Lutheran

0   125   250 miles
0   125   250 kilometers

NORWAY   SWEDEN
SCOTLAND
IRELAND   North Sea
ENGLAND   DENMARK
London
Wittenberg
HOLY ROMAN EMPIRE   POLAND–LITHUANIA
FRANCE   SWISS CONFEDERATION   AUSTRIA
Geneva   ITALIAN STATES   HUNGARY
SPAIN   OTTOMAN EMPIRE
PAPAL STATES

GEOGRAPHY SKILLBUILDER
INTERPRETING MAPS
Movement Why did Protestantism not spread to Italy?

The Peasants' Revolts Peasants across Europe sought more rights during the 1500s. Their complaints for better wages and living conditions were economic and social rather than religious. But many peasants believed Luther's ideas of individual freedom meant that their protests had God's support. As a result, peasants used Luther's ideas to justify revolts. Luther condemned both the peasants for the violent nature of the revolts, and the nobility for the callous disregard for the plight of the peasants.

Religious Wars In the mid 1500s, battles were fought across Europe over religion. Charles V was Holy Roman Emperor as well as king of Austria, Spain, and the Spanish Americas. In 1521, he made Luther an outlaw. But Charles's control over the empire was limited. In Germany, many Lutheran princes went to war against Charles. Germany's Lutheran and Catholic princes eventually met in 1555 and agreed to a peace treaty known as the Peace of Augsburg.

REVIEW Why did religious division have such a dramatic political impact?

The Reformation Grows

2 ESSENTIAL QUESTION What were some of the different Protestant movements that developed throughout Europe?

Luther believed that the Bible was the only source of religious truth. However, people read the Bible in different ways. This led to many different interpretations.

Calvinism John Calvin was a French reformer. His interpretation of the Bible resulted in a type of Protestantism called Calvinism. Calvin argued that Christians could do nothing to earn salvation—God had chosen people for salvation even before they were born. This idea is called **predestination**. According to predestination, if individuals were condemned there was nothing they could do about it.

Calvin himself admitted that such a belief was awful to think about. Even so, he attracted many followers and became one of the most important leaders of the Protestant Reformation. Calvin's ideas spread throughout Europe. (See the map on page 471.)

The Church of England The Reformation in England was different than in the rest of Europe. It started when King Henry VIII wanted to divorce his wife, but the pope would not permit it. As a result, Henry refused to recognize the Catholic Church. Henry founded the Church of England—also called the Anglican Church— which kept most Catholic beliefs but rejected the power of the pope.

John Calvin John Calvin created a Protestant system of belief, called Calvinism, that differed from Martin Luther's. ▼

The Branches of Christianity

This chart shows the evolution and division of some different Christian belief systems.

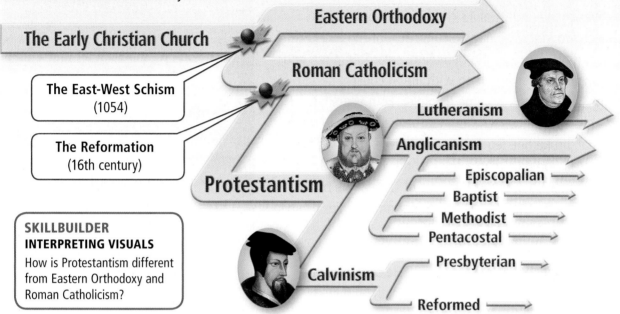

The Early Christian Church

Eastern Orthodoxy

Roman Catholicism

The East-West Schism (1054)

The Reformation (16th century)

Lutheranism

Anglicanism

Protestantism

Episcopalian
Baptist
Methodist
Pentacostal
Presbyterian

Calvinism

Reformed

SKILLBUILDER
INTERPRETING VISUALS
How is Protestantism different from Eastern Orthodoxy and Roman Catholicism?

Some reformers believed the Anglican Church should reject Catholic beliefs and practices completely. One such reformer was William Tyndale. He worked on an English translation of the New Testament. Anglican officials, however, prevented Tyndale from working in England, so he went to Germany. He was eventually captured and executed by Catholic officials for publicly opposing the Catholic Church. The battle within England to keep most Catholic beliefs or to seek more Protestant reform raged on for many years.

REVIEW How did the Reformation affect England?

The Counter Reformation

3 **ESSENTIAL QUESTION** What was the Counter Reformation?

The Catholic Church began new policies to stop the spread of Protestantism. This is sometimes called the Counter Reformation.

The Council of Trent The Council of Trent was a gathering of high-level Church officials. They met between 1545 and 1563 to reform and define the Catholic belief system. They wanted to clarify how Catholic faith differed from Protestantism. For example, Protestants found religious truth in the Bible alone. However, the Council said that truth also came from Church tradition.

Vocabulary Strategy

The word *counter* has **multiple meanings**. Here, the word *counter* means "against."

Ignatius of Loyola (1491–1556)

Ignatius was born into a noble family in northern Spain. He was the youngest of 13 children. At 16, Ignatius started working as a page at the court of the king's chief treasurer. He enjoyed the gambling, sword fighting, and romancing that went along with life at court.

In 1517, Ignatius became a soldier. Four years later, he was hit by a cannonball during a battle with the French. The ball broke one leg and wounded the other. As he recovered, Ignatius read a book about the life of Jesus and another book about the lives of saints. The books convinced him that he should abandon his earlier lifestyle and dedicate himself to God.

After many years of prayer, meditation, and study, Ignatius founded the Society of Jesus. He served as the order's "general" from 1540 until his death on July 31, 1556.

The Jesuits The Council of Trent was just one force that fostered the Counter Reformation. The Church also recognized and supported new religious orders. One of the most important new religious orders was the Society of Jesus, or the **Jesuits** (JEHZH•oo•ihts). The Spaniard **Ignatius of Loyola** formed the Jesuits in the early 1530s.

In some ways, the Jesuits were more like a military unit than a religious order. A strong central authority commanded the order. Jesuits learned obedience and discipline. Their education was based on a balance of faith and reason. They studied the teachings of St. Thomas Aquinas, whom you read about in Chapter 10. They also studied languages so they would have the tools to spread Catholicism across Africa, Asia, and the Americas. Such training allowed the Jesuits to play an active role in supporting the Counter Reformation.

The Inquisition In addition to calling the Council of Trent and supporting the Society of Jesus, the Church also made use of the **Inquisition**. The Inquisition was a court established to investigate people "who wander from the way of the Lord and the Catholic faith." Church officials used intimidation, and sometimes even torture, to get people to confess their sins—including that of being Protestant. The inquisition was used throughout Europe, but the most famous was the Spanish Inquisition.

The papacy also had Church officials create a list of books considered a threat to the Catholic faith. The pope told bishops throughout Europe to collect the forbidden books, which included Protestant Bibles, and burn them. By the end of the 16th century, the Counter Reformation had been largely successful. Reformers had breathed new life into the Church, which began the next century in a powerful position.

REVIEW What tools did the Catholic Church use against the spread of Protestantism?

▲ **The Inquisition** This painting, *Portrait of the Cardinal Inquisitor Don Fernando Niño de Guevara*, is by the famous artist El Greco. The cardinal headed the Spanish Inquisition from 1599 to 1602.

Lesson Summary

- Printing in local languages helped spread Luther's ideas. These ideas sparked revolts and wars.
- New faiths emerged during the 16th century, as people began to interpret the Bible in different ways.
- The Counter Reformation was a movement of internal renewal as well as a response to the spread of Protestantism.

Why It Matters Now . . .

Both Protestant and Catholic churches have widespread influence throughout the world today.

---

2 Lesson Review

Homework Helper
ClassZone.com

Terms & Names

1. Explain the importance of

John Calvin	Ignatius of Loyola	Inquisition
predestination	Jesuit	

Using Your Notes

Finding Main Ideas Use your completed diagram to answer the following question:

2. What caused the Counter Reformation? (HI 2)

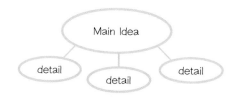

Main Ideas

3. How did peasants use Luther's ideas to support their revolts? (7.9.2)

4. According to John Calvin, what effect did good works have on a Christian's chances for salvation? Explain. (7.9.2)

5. How did the Council of Trent make the Catholic Church stronger? (7.9.5)

Critical Thinking

6. **Drawing Conclusions** What about the Reformation was most threatening to the Catholic Church? (7.9.2)

7. **Making Inferences** What advantages did the Catholic Church have when beginning the Counter Reformation? (7.9.5)

Activity **Internet Activity** Select one historical figure involved in the Reformation or the Counter Reformation. Write a one-page editorial that critiques that figure's point of view. (7.9.2, 7.9.5)
INTERNET KEYWORDS: *Martin Luther, Ignatius of Loyola*

Understanding Cause and Effect

Goal: To understand the cause-and-effect relationships in the growth of Calvinism

CALIFORNIA STANDARDS
HI 2 Students understand and distinguish cause, effect, sequence, and correlation in historical events, including the long- and short-term causal relations.

Learn the Skill

Causes are the events and conditions that lead to an event. Causes happen before the event; they explain why it happened. Effects are the results or consequences of the event. One effect can become the cause of other effects, resulting in a chain of events. Looking at cause-and-effect relationships helps historians see how events are related and why they took place.

 See the Skillbuilder Handbook, page R26.

Practice the Skill

1 Read the passage at right. To identify causes, look for clue words that show cause. These include *because*, *due to*, *since*, and *therefore*. One cause is labeled in the passage.

2 To identify effects, look for results or consequences. Sometimes these are indicated by clue words such as *brought about*, *led to*, *as a result*, and *consequently*. One effect is labeled in the passage.

3 Notice that an effect may be the cause of another event. A chain of causes and effects begins. For example, Calvin's joining of the reform movement in France ultimately led to the spread of his ideas throughout the world.

4 Look for multiple causes and effects. Calvin's flight to Switzerland resulted in the two effects (a, b) labeled at right.

5 Make a cause-and-effect diagram like the one below. Starting with the first cause in a series, fill in the boxes until you reach the end result.

Example:

5 Cause ⇒	Effect/ Cause ⇒	Effect/ Cause ⇒	Effect/ Cause ⇒	Effect/ Cause ⇒	Effect
Luther's ideas spread to France.	Calvin doubts his faith and joins reformers.	The government persecutes reformers.	Calvin flees to Switzerland.	Calvin publishes a book based on Luther's ideas. Geneva becomes a model Protestant community.	Calvinism influences Protestants throughout the world.

In the following passage, the author describes the role of John Calvin in the growth of Protestantism. Use the strategies listed under Practice the Skill to help you see the cause-and-effect relationships.

Calvin and the Spread of Protestantism

John Calvin was only a boy when Luther published his Ninety-Five Theses, yet Luther's ideas changed his life. **1** Luther's writings spread to France while Calvin was a student. **2** As a result, Calvin began to have doubts about his Catholic faith. As a teenager, he had studied to be a priest, but his father decided he should be a lawyer. He **3** joined with others who wanted to reform the church. As the reform movement grew, the government became less tolerant of Protestants. Therefore, Calvin fled to Switzerland.

There, in 1536, **4** (a) he published *The Institutes of the Christian Religion* and (b) established a model Protestant community in Geneva based on his ideas. Because of Luther's influence, Calvin stressed the importance of the Bible and faith alone. However, he also said it was important to live a holy life as a sign of having been saved by God.

From Geneva, the influence of Calvin's writing and preaching spread throughout Europe. His ideas led to the creation of the Reformed churches of France, Switzerland, and the Netherlands and the Presbyterian Church in Scotland. The Puritans in England followed some of Calvin's ideas. Since they were persecuted for their beliefs in England, they brought some Calvinist ideas to the New World.

▲ **John Calvin** Calvin was an influential Protestant reformer.

Apply the Skill

Turn to page 323 in Chapter 10, Lesson 1. Read the passage headed "Conflict Between Monarchs and the Papacy." Make a diagram like the one at left to summarize the causes and effects of the conflict.

▶ MAIN IDEAS

1 **Belief Systems** Protestant and Catholic missionaries worked to find new converts to their religion.

2 **Culture** Missionaries experienced different results and reactions to their efforts.

3 **Government** The Reformation changed the balance of power in Europe, and contributed to the growth of democratic forms in the Americas.

▶ TAKING NOTES

Reading Skill: Comparing and Contrasting

Comparing and contrasting means finding the similarities and differences between two or more things. Use a Venn diagram like the one below to compare and contrast Protestant and Catholic efforts described in Lesson 3. List their differences in the individual ovals and their similarities where the ovals overlap.

Protestant — both — Catholic

S Skillbuilder Handbook, page R4

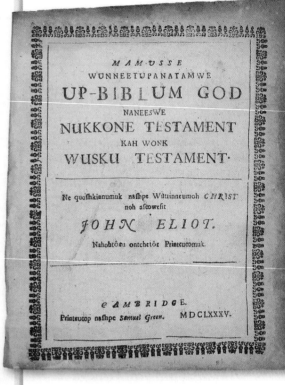

▲ **Algonquin Bible** During the 1650s, Protestant missionary John Eliot translated the Bible into a Native American language known as Algonquin. This is the title page of that translation.

CALIFORNIA STANDARDS

7.9.3 Explain Protestants' new practices of church self-government and the influence of those practices on the development of democratic practices and ideas of federalism.

7.9.4 Identify and locate the European regions that remained Catholic and those that became Protestant and explain how the division affected the distribution of religions in the New World.

7.9.6 Understand the institution and impact of missionaries on Christianity and the diffusion of Christianity from Europe to other parts of the world in the medieval and early modern periods; locate missions on a world map.

Expansion of Christianity

TERMS & NAMES
missionary
convert
Peace of Westphalia
covenant
federalism

Build on What You Know Lesson 2 explained how the Reformation created new Christian religious groups in Europe. In Lesson 3, you will learn about how European Christians spread their belief systems around the world.

The Impact of Missionaries

1 ESSENTIAL QUESTION What did Protestant and Catholic missionaries do in the 16th century?

Many Christian groups send members to foreign countries to do religious work. Such efforts are called missions. A person who goes on missions is called a **missionary**. Sometimes religious groups organize missions to persuade people who do not share their faith to **convert** to, or adopt, their religion. During the 16th century, the Catholic Church put particular emphasis on using missionaries to spread its faith around the world. These missions would have great success in the Americas. But Catholic missions would not do as well in Asia.

Catholic Efforts The Roman Catholic Church frequently relied on its religious orders to do missionary work. After the Council of Trent, the Catholic Church put increasing energy into helping its orders send missions around the world. Franciscans, Dominicans, and Jesuits were among the Catholic orders that performed missionary work.

Searching for Converts This painting shows a missionary preaching to a group of Native Americans in the mid-1600s. ▼

479

Religious Orders as Missionaries The Franciscans, as you read in Chapter 10, began as a mendicant order. That is, they owned nothing and lived by begging. As time went on and the order grew, Franciscans became less strict about owning nothing. Franciscans could then begin to organize missions.

The Dominicans were also mendicants. The Spanish priest St. Dominic founded the order in the 1200s. His original focus was education. But like the Franciscans, the order also performed missionary work. Dominicans were among the first to join the Spanish and Portuguese voyages to the Americas.

The Jesuits also sent members overseas. In fact, the order sent out missionaries shortly after its founding. By 1556, about 1,000 Jesuits were working in Europe, Asia, Africa, and the Americas. By 1626 their number had climbed to more than 15,000.

Protestant Missionaries Until the 19th century, Protestantism spread most successfully by European Protestants settling overseas. Once there, they did little to convert local people. But there were exceptions. For example, the Dutch East India Company sent out missionaries early in the 1600s. English Puritans John Eliot and Roger Williams organized a religious school to train missionaries. England's Society of Friends, or Quakers, also sought converts overseas.

▲ **St. Dominic** This painting of St. Dominic shows him holding a tall cross and a lily: both symbols associated with St. Dominic.

REVIEW Which faith's missionary efforts met with more success and why?

Responses to Christian Missions

2 ESSENTIAL QUESTION Why were there more Catholic missionaries than Protestant missionaries?

Catholic missionaries saw their beliefs as universal—available to everyone. As a result, they spread out around the world and tried to convert all of the new peoples they came into contact with.

Protestants' missionary efforts were limited in this period. However, some English Protestants in North America sought to convert Native Americans. Still, both Catholics and Protestants sought the diffusion of Christianity from Europe to other parts of the world.

Missionaries in Asia European missionaries traveled to Asia with European traders. European traders wanted a direct trade route to eastern Asia. But during the 1500s, goods from East Asia came to Europe through the established Muslim traders in Southwest Asia. As a result, European traders began searching for direct trade routes to eastern Asia, and missionaries went with them.

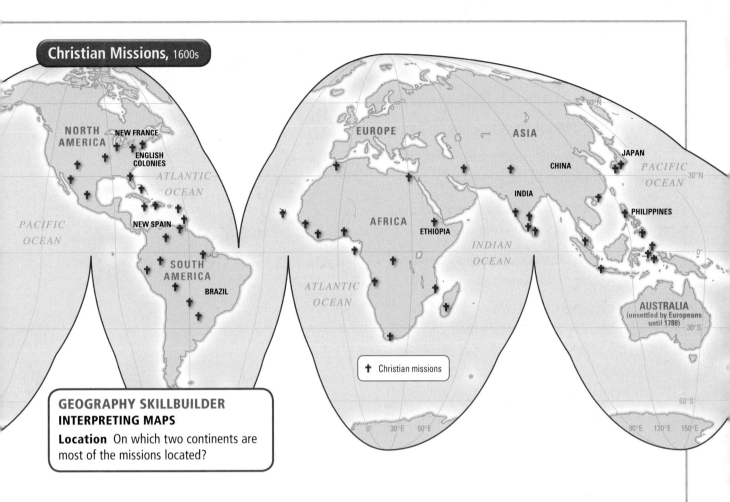

Christian Missions, 1600s

NORTH AMERICA

NEW FRANCE

ENGLISH COLONIES

ATLANTIC OCEAN

NEW SPAIN

PACIFIC OCEAN

SOUTH AMERICA

BRAZIL

EUROPE

ASIA

JAPAN

CHINA

PACIFIC OCEAN

INDIA

PHILIPPINES

AFRICA

ETHIOPIA

INDIAN OCEAN

ATLANTIC OCEAN

AUSTRALIA
(unsettled by Europeans until 1788)

✝ Christian missions

GEOGRAPHY SKILLBUILDER
INTERPRETING MAPS
Location On which two continents are most of the missions located?

Catholic missionaries sought new converts in Asia, but they did not have much success. In fact, there were many more converts to Islam in South Asia than to Catholicism. Catholic missionaries did convert many Japanese people. However, the Japanese military leader forced Japanese Christians to either give up their foreign faith or be killed. Catholic missionaries also had some success in the Spanish Philippines. It would not be until the settlement of the Americas, however, that missionaries would find large numbers of converts.

Catholic Missionaries in the Americas Catholic missionaries often traveled to the Americas with explorers from Europe's Catholic empires. The Portuguese brought Catholicism to Brazil. Catholic missionaries from France settled in the Great Lakes area. By 1700, however, it was Spain that controlled most of the Americas. Spanish explorers claimed territory from California and Florida and deep into South America.

Catholic missionaries worked hard to convert Native Americans. They had success, but many Native Americans did not fully abandon their native religions. Often a blending of cultures occurred. For example, one story describes Mary, the mother of Jesus, appearing to an Aztec peasant. She is called the Virgin of Guadeloupe, and is still important to Mexican Catholics. Still, Catholic missionaries found many new converts, and Catholicism came to dominate Central and South America.

Geography

Distribution of Religions in the Americas

Europeans' religious beliefs influenced the spread of religions in the Americas.

- Spain, Portugal, and France were the main Catholic settlers of the Americas.

- England was the main Protestant country that settled in the Americas.

- Catholics and Protestants controlled the colonies. But African slaves brought Islam to the Americas, and European Jews settled in the Protestant and Catholic communities. Early on, the Americas were places of religious diversity if not tolerance.

> **GEOGRAPHY SKILLBUILDER**
> **INTERPRETING MAPS**
> **Movement** What bodies of water did European Catholics have to sail through?

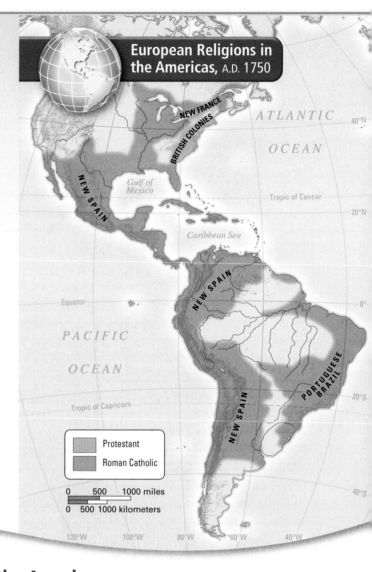

European Religions in the Americas, A.D. 1750

NEW FRANCE
BRITISH COLONIES
ATLANTIC OCEAN
NEW SPAIN
Gulf of Mexico
Tropic of Cancer
Caribbean Sea
Equator
PACIFIC OCEAN
NEW SPAIN
PORTUGUESE BRAZIL
Tropic of Capricorn
NEW SPAIN

40°N
20°N
0°
20°S
40°S

120°W 100°W 80°W 60°W 40°W

Legend:
- Protestant
- Roman Catholic

0   500   1000 miles
0 500 1000 kilometers

Protestant Missionaries in the Americas In 1607, England established the first permanent Protestant settlement in Virginia. English Protestants who were not happy with Anglicanism settled further north in New England. While Protestants established themselves in the Americas, the Catholics controlled more territory and gained many more converts.

> **REVIEW** How were reactions to missionary efforts in Asia different from reactions in the Americas?

Legacy of the Reformation

3 ESSENTIAL QUESTION What effects did the Reformation have on Europe?

The most obvious legacy of the Reformation is the division of western Christianity into Catholicism and Protestantism. Since 1054, all Christians in western Europe belonged to the Catholic Church (see the chart on page 473). By 1700, however, that was no longer true. Europe was divided along religious lines and would never be under one church again.

More Religious Wars Religious wars continued between Catholics and Protestants after the Peace of Augsburg. In 1648, the **Peace of Westphalia** (wehst•FAYL•yuh) brought some stability to Europe. The Peace of Westphalia recognized the permanent division of western Europe into Catholic and Protestant nations.

The skill of France's kings and government officials helped France replace Spain as the leading Catholic power in Europe. Protestant countries such as England, Holland, and, somewhat later, Prussia were gaining power and would again come into conflict with Catholic Spain and France. Europe's religious changes would eventually lead to political changes in the Americas.

Protestantism and Democracy Some historians have suggested that the Protestant practice of church self-government helped the development of democratic practices. For example, John Calvin allowed his followers to share in the governing of the church. They did this through a body of leaders and ministers called a presbytery (PREZ•bih•TEHR•ee). This practice had a strong influence on Puritans and Presbyterians, both of whom settled in English colonies.

Puritans believed that God had voluntarily entered into a **covenant**, or agreement, with people, through which they could be saved. This led to the belief that Christians could agree to join together and voluntarily form a church. This democratic view of church membership would have political results. These same people could join together and voluntarily form a government.

The Mayflower Compact of the Pilgrims reflects this idea. The Pilgrims were a radical branch of the Puritans. A small group of Pilgrims arrived in the Americas in 1620. Before departing their ship they wrote a compact, or agreement, that said their government would make "just and equal laws . . . for the general good of the colony."

Causes and Effects of the Reformation				
	Social	**Political**	**Economic**	**Religious**
Cause	The printing press helped to spread ideas critical of the Church.	Some European leaders saw the pope as interfering in their political affairs through local churches.	People disliked having to pay taxes to the Church in Rome.	Only clergy were allowed to interpret the Bible.
Effect	More people became aware of Protestant belief systems.	By becoming Protestant, European leaders limited the pope's local political influence.	People were more willing to support Reformation ideas that ended these taxes.	Reformers translated the Bible so that people could interpret it for themselves.

Federalism Scholars have also argued that the covenant influenced the development of federalism. **Federalism** is the sharing of power between an organization, such as a church or a government, and its members. In the United States, for example, the national government shares power with the states. The covenants of Calvinist churches allowed the members of a church to share power with the clergy. The practice of sharing power may have influenced plans for organizing governments, such as the U.S. Constitution.

REVIEW How did Protestant ideas influence democratic practices?

Lesson Summary
- Both the Catholic and Protestant churches used missionaries to win converts to their faiths. But the Catholic efforts of the period were much more successful.
- The religious geography of Europe had a great impact on the Americas' religious landscape.
- Protestants' new practices of self-government may have helped the development of democratic practices.

Why It Matters Now . . .
In the year 2000, about 56 percent of U.S. citizens were Protestants and 27 percent were Roman Catholics.

3 Lesson Review

Homework Helper
ClassZone.com

Terms & Names
1. Explain the importance of

missionary	Peace of Westphalia	federalism
convert	covenant	

Using Your Notes
Comparing and Contrasting Use your completed Venn diagram to answer the following question:

2. What are two things Catholic and Protestant missionary efforts had in common? (7.9.6)

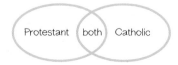

Protestant   both   Catholic

Main Ideas
3. What role did religious missionaries play in the Reformation? (7.9.6)
4. What impact did the Reformation have on the religious geography of the Americas? (7.9.4)
5. How did the Protestants influence the development of democratic practices? (7.9.3)

Critical Thinking
6. **Making Inferences** Why might Catholic missionaries have had more success finding converts than Protestant missionaries did? (7.9.6)
7. **Comparing** Compare the maps on pages 457 and 482. What is the relationship between the distribution of religions in Europe and the Americas? (7.9.4)

Activity **Writing a Research Paper** Research European missionary activity in the Americas. Use your research to write a two-page essay about interaction between European missionaries and Native Americans. (7.9.6)

Communication Across Cultures

Goal: To understand difficulties faced by people trying to communicate who do not speak the same language

Materials & Supplies
- paper
- pens

Prepare

Think about how people throughout history have tried to describe abstract ideas to people who didn't speak their language. (Abstract ideas include concepts such as justice, truth, or loyalty.)

Do the Activity

1 Find a partner. Imagine that you and your partner are from different cultures and speak different languages. One of you picks an abstract idea to communicate and then writes out an explanation of this idea. Then try to communicate the idea to your partner without using words.

2 Your partner then writes down what he or she thinks you are trying to communicate.

3 Compare what each of you wrote down to find out how well the idea was communicated.

4 Reverse roles and repeat the activity.

Follow-Up

1 How do you think people from different cultures who did not speak the same language communicated with each other?

2 Do you think this type of communication was accurate? Explain.

Extension

Write a Research Paper Research how missionaries from the 1500s and 1600s prepared for their work. How did they communicate with people?

CALIFORNIA STANDARDS
7.9.6 Understand the institution and impact of missionaries on Christianity and the diffusion of Christianity from Europe to other parts of the world in the medieval and early modern periods; locate missions on a world map.

▶ **VISUAL SUMMARY**

The Reformation
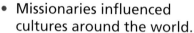

Government (7.9.1, 7.9.3)
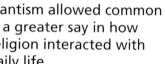
- The Reformation changed the balance of power in Europe.
- Protestants' new practices of church self-government may have helped the development of democratic practices.

Culture (7.9.4, 7.9.6)
- Missionaries influenced cultures around the world.
- Protestantism allowed common people a greater say in how their religion interacted with their daily life.

Belief Systems (7.9.2, 7.9.5)

- Martin Luther began the Reformation.
- Different Protestant movements developed quickly throughout Europe.
- The Counter Reformation was the Catholic Church's effort to stop the spread of Protestantism.

▶ **TERMS & NAMES**

Explain why the words in each set below are linked with each other.

1. **indulgence** and **Martin Luther**

2. **Protestant** and **Reformation**

3. **John Calvin** and **predestination**

4. **St. Ignatius of Loyola** and **Jesuit**

5. **missionary** and **convert**

▶ **MAIN IDEAS**

Trouble for the Catholic Church (pages 460–469)
6. How did the Catholic Church's tax policies weaken the Church? (7.9.1)
7. How did the ideas of reformers John Wycliffe and Desiderius Erasmus differ? (7.9.2)

Reform and Reaction (pages 470–477)
8. Why did William Tyndale translate the Bible into English? (7.9.2)
9. How might the Jesuits' focus on education have contributed to the Counter Reformation? (7.9.5)

Expansion of Christianity (pages 478–485)
10. What areas of Europe remained Catholic, and what areas became Protestant? (7.9.4)
11. How might Protestantism have had an influence on the U.S. Constitution? (7.9.3)

CRITICAL THINKING

Big Ideas: Government

12. **MAKING INFERENCES** In what way did Catholic missionaries help European nations control overseas colonies? (7.9.6)

13. **UNDERSTANDING EFFECTS** Did the religious choices of European leaders affect their political power? Explain. (7.9.4)

14. **ANALYZING POLITICAL ISSUES** How did the structure of some Protestant churches reflect later ideas of federalism? (7.9.3)

ALTERNATIVE ASSESSMENT

1. **WRITING ACTIVITY** Read the Literature Connection on pages 466–469. Write a story about Martin Luther from the point of view of the warden in Wartburg Castle. (7.9.2)

2. **INTERDISCIPLINARY ACTIVITY—ARCHITECTURE**
   Research the type of architecture churches use today and compare that to architectural styles of the past. Write a page about what you discover. (7.9.6)

3. **STARTING WITH A STORY**

   Review your response to the question about how the Ninety-Five Theses might affect European society. Now that you've read the chapter, would you answer this question differently? If so, how? (7.9.2)

Technology Activity

4. **CREATING A GRAPHIC ORGANIZER**
   Use the Internet or the library to research the Reformation and the Counter Reformation. Create an illustrated graphic organizer that compares the two movements. Include

   • a summary of Protestant and Catholic ideas
   • images of the major figures involved in both movements (7.9.2, 7.9.5)

Research Links
ClassZone.com

Reading Primary Sources The primary source below is part of a letter from Martin Luther to Pope Leo X written after Luther's Ninety-Five Theses had spread. Use the primary source to answer the questions. (7.9.2)

Primary Source

It is a miracle to me by what fate it has come about that this single Disputation [the Ninety-Five Theses] of mine should . . . have gone out into very nearly the whole land. It was made public at our University and for our University only, and . . . I cannot believe it has become known to all men. For it is a set of theses, not doctrines or dogmas [religious laws], and they are put, according to custom, in an obscure and enigmatic [confusing] way. . . . If I had been able to foresee what was coming, I should have taken care . . . that they would be easier to understand.

From *Works of Martin Luther.*
Edited and translated by Adolph Spaeth, L.D. Reed, Henry Eyster Jacobs, et al., pages 44–48.

1. **What word best describes Luther's reaction to the spread of his ideas?**
   A. satisfaction
   B. fear
   C. surprise
   D. disappointment

2. **What was Luther's purpose in writing this letter?**
   A. to convince the pope that he wanted to challenge the pope's authority
   B. to convince the pope that he did not write his theses for the general public
   C. to convince the pope that the doctrines of the Catholic Church were wrong
   D. to convince the pope that he was not responsible for the Ninety-Five Theses

Test Practice
ClassZone.com

Additional Test Practice, pp. S1–S33

Writing About History

Persuasive Writing:
An Influential Individual

 **Writing Model**
ClassZone.com

CALIFORNIA STANDARDS
Writing 2.4 Write persuasive compositions.

Purpose: To convince readers that an individual of your choice had a lasting historical impact
Audience: Your classmates, family, and friends

During the era you just studied, many people used persuasion to convince others to accept their viewpoints. For example, humanists challenged religious people to use reason as well as faith, and missionaries converted Native Americans. **Persuasive writing** is writing whose purpose is to convince another person to adopt your opinion or position.

▲ Luther defending his opinions

Organization & Focus

During the Renaissance, the individual was highly prized. Your assignment is to review the many great individuals discussed in Unit 7 and select the one you believe had the biggest impact on history. Then write a persuasive essay that is at least five paragraphs long.

Identifying Purpose and Audience Your purpose is to use facts, examples, and reasons to persuade others to adopt your opinion about which individual had the biggest impact. Your essay will be included in a class magazine about individuals, so your audience will be your classmates, family, and friends. Keep them in mind as you work.

Choosing a Topic Scan Chapters 13 and 14. For each outstanding individual you find, note his or her area of influence, accomplishments, and impact. Record your notes in a chart like the one below.

Individual	Area(s) of Influence	Accomplishments	Impact
Petrarch	learning, the arts	revived classical literature, helped spread humanism	preserved the work of classical writers for future generations

When you've finished, review your notes and decide which individual of the Renaissance or Reformation had the biggest impact on history.

Finding Supporting Evidence You will need to do more than gather evidence about the individual you choose. Also consider which individuals others might choose. Prepare to argue against their choices.

Research & Technology

Use the Internet or a library to find additional sources that discuss your individual and his or her historical impact. In addition to using the individual's name as a search term, you might also find information by using the term *Renaissance* or *Reformation*.

Outlining and Drafting Organize your notes into categories, such as *major works*, *important actions*, and *innovative ideas*. Create at least three categories that show the individual's impact. Decide whether to address opposing views within each category or separately.

Make an outline of your main categories, with subentries for supporting details. This outline will help you draft your essay.

Technology Tip Not all information on the Internet is accurate. Learn to evaluate online sources. For example, museums and encyclopedias are reliable. If you have questions about a source, ask your teacher or librarian.

Evaluation & Revision

To make your essay better, look through magazines. Which articles grab your attention? Note approaches that writers use to keep your interest. These might include starting with a dramatic incident, using an interesting quotation, and vividly describing a scene. Then revise your essay, trying some of those approaches.

Also, remember that you want to convince people to adopt your opinion. Review your essay to eliminate the pitfalls of sloppy arguments. These include:

- Using opinions to support opinions, instead of using solid facts
- Using exaggerated language instead of clear, precise words
- Appealing only to readers' emotions and not to their reason
- Failing to address opposing views

Revise your writing until you are sure you have made the strongest case you can, in the liveliest language possible.

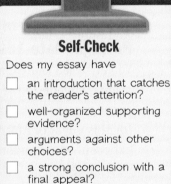

Self-Check

Does my essay have

- [ ] an introduction that catches the reader's attention?
- [ ] well-organized supporting evidence?
- [ ] arguments against other choices?
- [ ] a strong conclusion with a final appeal?

Publish & Present

Help think of a good title for the class magazine. With your classmates, divide up the tasks of binding, illustrating, and reproducing the magazine. Then take turns sharing the finished product with friends and family members.

UNIT 8

Early Modern Europe

Interact with History ▶

The Waterfront of Lisbon, Portugal, late 1500s

You are a sea captain about to leave on a trading voyage to the East Indies. You've spent months organizing and preparing for this voyage. After all of the time and expense, you wonder if the voyage will be a success.

Why would people be willing to take part in trading voyages to distant lands?

WebQuest
ClassZone.com

By the late 1500s, Lisbon, located on the Atlantic Ocean, had become one of Europe's leading port cities. Its harbor was lined with warehouses, merchants' offices, shipyards, and armories.

What features do you think a city needs to be a good port?

The ship carries three guns on either side. These will be used to ward off attacks or to launch assaults on unfriendly ships or ports.

Why might a trading ship be the target of attacks?

The ship's cargo includes linen, wool, iron, and copper. These items will be traded for pepper, nutmeg, cinnamon, or silk.

Why do you think spices are such sought-after trade goods?

491

Chapter
15

Scientific Revolution and the Age of Exploration

Before You Read: Anticipation Guide

Read the statements below and note if you agree or disagree with them. After you've read the lesson, see if you've changed your opinion.

- European exploration and settlement of the Americas, Africa, and Asia had little impact on these regions.
- Colonial rivalries helped to shift the balance of power in Europe.

Big Ideas About the Scientific Revolution and Exploration

Science and Technology New scientific discoveries change human understanding of the world.

Great voyages of exploration and discovery gave rise to a new European worldview. Also, scientific and technological developments changed the way people looked at religion, politics, and culture.

Integrated Technology

eEdition
- Interactive Maps
- Interactive Visuals
- Starting with a Story

Spanish Explorers

ⓘ INTERNET RESOURCES
Go to **ClassZone.com** for
- WebQuest
- Homework Helper
- Research Links
- Internet Activities
- Quizzes
- Maps
- Test Practice
- Current Events

NORTH AMERICA

PACIFIC OCEAN

← Dutch
← English
← French
← Portuguese
← Spanish

| 0 | 500 | 1000 miles |
| 0 | 500 | 1000 kilometers |

EUROPE

1460s
Portuguese gain control of trade along West African coast.

1492
Columbus makes his first voyage to the Americas. ▲

1543
Copernicus publishes heliocentric theory. (model of heliocentric universe) ▶

1500

1550

WORLD

1464
Sunni Ali begins Songhai empire in West Africa.

1520
Suleyman the Magnificent becomes sultan of the Ottoman Empire.

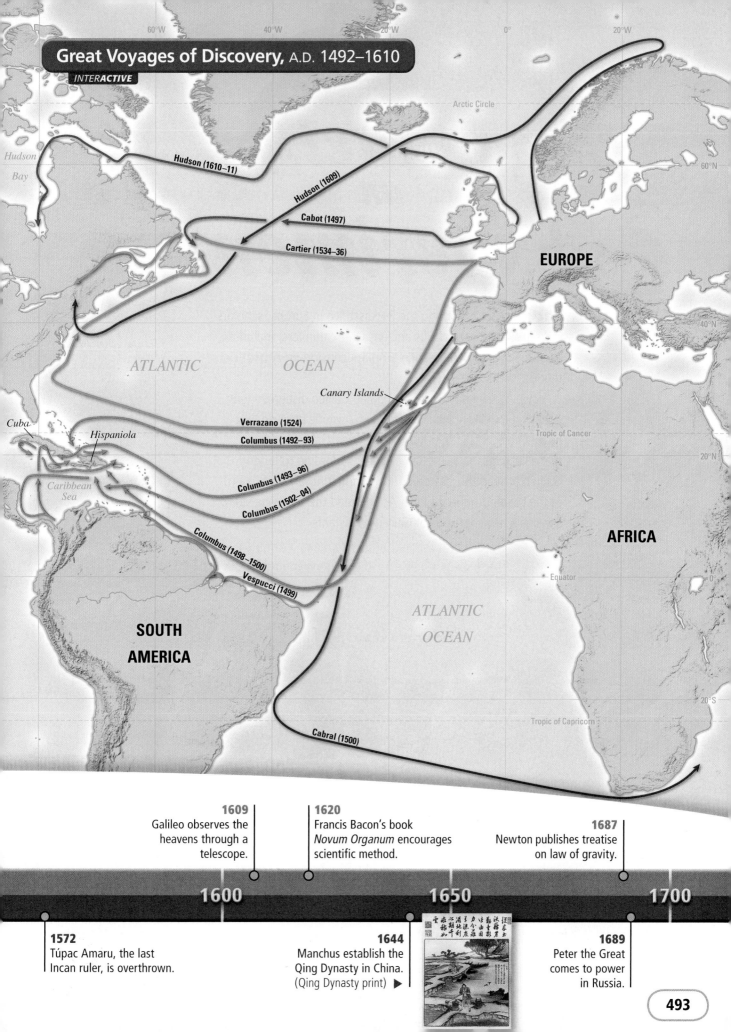

Great Voyages of Discovery, A.D. 1492–1610

INTERACTIVE

Hudson (1610–11)

Hudson (1609)

Cabot (1497)

Cartier (1534–36)

Hudson Bay

EUROPE

ATLANTIC   OCEAN

Canary Islands

Cuba

Hispaniola

Caribbean Sea

Verrazano (1524)

Columbus (1492–93)

Columbus (1493–96)

Columbus (1502–04)

Columbus (1498–1500)

Vespucci (1499)

AFRICA

Tropic of Cancer

Equator

ATLANTIC OCEAN

SOUTH AMERICA

Tropic of Capricorn

Cabral (1500)

Arctic Circle

60°N

40°N

20°N

0°

20°S

1609
Galileo observes the heavens through a telescope.

1620
Francis Bacon's book *Novum Organum* encourages scientific method.

1687
Newton publishes treatise on law of gravity.

1600   **1650**   **1700**

1572
Túpac Amaru, the last Incan ruler, is overthrown.

1644
Manchus establish the Qing Dynasty in China.
(Qing Dynasty print) ▶

1689
Peter the Great comes to power in Russia.

Conducting an Experiment

CALIFORNIA STANDARDS
Reading 3.2 Identify events that advance the plot and determine how each event explains past or present action(s) or foreshadows future action(s).

Background: During the Renaissance in Europe, scholars rediscovered the works of ancient Greek thinkers, including Aristotle. Many Renaissance scholars considered Aristotle's theories to be accurate.

However, an Italian scientist named Galileo disagreed with Aristotle on many points. For example, Aristotle believed that heavier objects fall faster than lighter ones. Galileo claimed that all objects fall at the same speed. According to legend, Galileo proved this statement by conducting an experiment at the Leaning Tower of Pisa. As you read the following story, imagine that you are one of Galileo's assistants.

The tower at Pisa already had a pronounced tilt when Galileo reportedly carried out his experiment. ▶

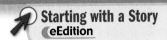

Your arms ache from carrying a heavy cannonball. You are jealous of the other assistant, Lucio, who is carrying a lighter ball. But the pain in your arms is nothing compared with the dread that you feel. After today, your friends, your relatives, and many scholars will probably consider Galileo a fool. They will make fun of you for being his assistant. Galileo has dared to disagree with Aristotle, one of the greatest thinkers of all time. Aristotle stated that heavier objects fall faster than lighter ones. But Galileo claims that all objects, regardless of their weight, fall at the same speed. And he has you and Lucio carrying cannonballs to the Leaning Tower of Pisa to prove his point.

You see the Leaning Tower loom ahead. Galileo walks confidently toward it. A group of well-known scholars have gathered at the tower's base. They laugh mockingly. Ignoring the crowd, Galileo marches directly into the tower. You and Lucio follow. You look up. A steep, spiral staircase winds its way to the top. Galileo tells you not to look up while you climb, or you might lose your balance. You imagine yourself rolling down the stairs, still hanging onto the cannonball. Galileo, Lucio, and you start to climb. The stairs are worn, and occasionally you slip. Finally, you reach the top.

Galileo says to place the cannonballs on the ramp. Then he licks his finger and holds it up to test the wind. The air is calm. Below, the crowd looks up at the three of you. Galileo gives the command. You and Lucio let go of your cannonballs at the same time. The balls drop quickly toward the ground. Plunk. You hear a gasp from the crowd. Galileo smiles knowingly. The balls have hit the ground at the same time.

How do you think people watching your experiment will react?

Reading & Writing

1. **READING: Plot** The second stage of the plot of a story is sometimes called rising action. The events described in this part of the plot tend to build suspense in the story. With a partner, identify how the writer of this story builds suspense. As you read other stories in this book, note how suspense is used.

2. **WRITING: Narration** As you and Lucio head down the stairs after the experiment, you talk about what will happen next. Write a dialogue of this conversation.

CALIFORNIA STANDARDS Writing 2.1
Write fictional or autobiographical narratives.

▶ MAIN IDEAS

1 **Science and Technology** Classical ideas about science and math shaped European thought for centuries.

2 **Science and Technology** Scholars of other cultures preserved the scientific knowledge of Greece and built upon it.

3 **Belief Systems** The Renaissance renewed interest in scientific learning. It also led to a questioning of old beliefs.

▲ **Ptolemy** The ideas of Ptolemy shaped the way Europeans looked at the universe for hundreds of years.

▶ TAKING NOTES

Reading Skill: Explaining Chronological Order and Sequence

Placing events in sequence means putting them in order based on the time they happened. Create a time line like the one below to put events discussed in this lesson in order.

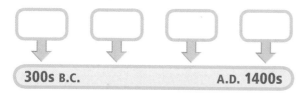

300s B.C.   **A.D. 1400s**

S **Skillbuilder Handbook, page R15**

CALIFORNIA STANDARDS

7.10.1 Discuss the roots of the Scientific Revolution (e.g., Greek rationalism; Jewish, Christian, and Muslim science; Renaissance humanism; new knowledge from global exploration).

7.10.3 Understand the scientific method advanced by Bacon and Descartes, the influence of new scientific rationalism on the growth of democratic ideas, and the coexistence of science with traditional religious beliefs.

HI 2 Students understand and distinguish cause, effect, sequence, and correlation in historical events, including the long- and short-term causal relations.

History of Scientific Thought

▶ **TERMS & NAMES**
rationalism
geocentric theory
harmony
anatomy
dissection

Build on What You Know Have you ever read a book or seen a movie that changed the way you look at things? In this chapter, you will learn how new ideas and discoveries helped to change the way people in Europe viewed the world.

Classical Science

1 **ESSENTIAL QUESTION** How did classical ideas about astronomy, mathematics, and medicine shape European thought?

Between 600 B.C. and A.D. 200, Greek scientists developed many ideas on how the world worked. They used an approach called **rationalism**. In this approach, people use reason, or logical thought, to understand the world.

A Geocentric Universe Aristotle, who lived from 384 to 322 B.C., is considered one of the greatest thinkers of all time. He studied the stars and planets in a rational way. His studies led him to develop the **geocentric theory**. This theory placed Earth at the center of the universe.

Some 500 years later, the work of an astronomer named Ptolemy (TAHL•uh•mee) agreed with and expanded on Aristotle's view. Ptolemy claimed that objects such as the moon and stars move in small orbits of their own. While doing this, they revolve in a bigger orbit around Earth. Aristotle's and Ptolemy's view of the universe proved to be wrong. Even so, scientists accepted it for the next 1,400 years.

Ptolemy's Theory
This 17th-century engraving illustrates Ptolemy's geocentric theory. ▼

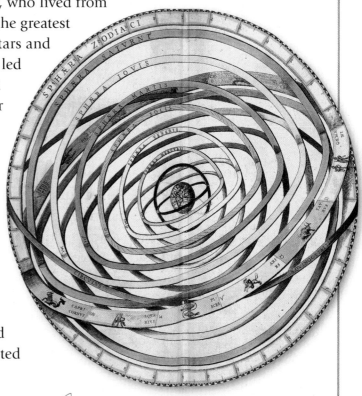

Greek Mathematics In the 500s B.C., a Greek scholar named Pythagoras (pih•THAG•uhr•uhs) tried to explain the universe in mathematical terms. According to his view, all things combine in an agreeable way to form the universe. This idea of things combining well with each other to form a whole is known as **harmony**. Pythagoras' work greatly influenced classical Greek and European philosophy.

About 200 years later, Euclid (YOO•klihd) built on Pythagoras' theories. He studied shapes such as circles and triangles. His work formed the basis of the area of study known as geometry. Euclid's studies are still the basis for courses in geometry today.

Greek Medicine The Greeks also laid the foundations of modern medicine. Hippocrates, who lived in the 400s B.C., believed that doctors would be able to diagnose diseases by observing many cases. This approach strongly influenced later medical practices.

Galen, who lived in the A.D. 100s, focused on **anatomy**, the structure of living things. He gained much of his knowledge through **dissection**, cutting open plants and animals to look at their parts. Galen made many discoveries. For example, he learned that arteries are filled with blood and not air, as was previously believed.

REVIEW How did advances made by the Greeks affect medical practices?

Science in the Middle Ages

2 ESSENTIAL QUESTION What role did Muslim scholars play in preserving classical scientific knowledge?

For centuries after Galen's death, little scientific study took place in Europe. European scholars were more interested in studying religion. Muslim scholars, however, became interested in classical scientific knowledge.

Muslim Scholars Between the mid-700s and mid-1200s, Muslim culture flourished. (See Chapter 4.) Muslim scholars of this time borrowed and advanced the learning of classical Greece and other ancient societies.

For example, al-Khwarizmi, who lived in the late 700s and early 800s, borrowed the numbering system and zero from Indian scholars.

Al-Khwarizmi
Al-Khwarizmi, one of the greatest mathematicians of all time, developed algebra. ▼

His work resulted in the Arabic numbering system that is still used in most of the world today. He also developed the branch of mathematics called algebra. Some 300 years later, a Persian scholar named Omar Khayyam drew on Greek ideas to further the work of al-Khwarizmi. He also wrote a study of Euclid's work on geometry.

Muslim doctors also borrowed ideas from the past and then built on them. In the early 900s, al-Razi, a Persian-born doctor, used classical Greek studies to help him identify and describe diseases. Around 1000, Ibn Sina, another Persian doctor, published the *Canon of Medicine*. This organized all medical knowledge since Aristotle's time. The works of al-Razi and Ibn Sina were used as medical references for hundreds of years.

Jewish and Christian Scholars

From the Muslim world, classical scientific knowledge spread to western Europe. Muslim, Jewish, and Christian scholars in al-Andalus (Muslim Spain) greatly helped this movement of information. Many of them translated Greek and Arabic scientific works into Latin. Christian scholars flocked to Spain to study these works and carried them back to Europe.

▲ **University Class** In time, classical science became part of higher education in Europe. This 14th-century manuscript illustration shows a professor leading a class at a Paris college.

Jewish scholars made other contributions to scientific learning. Maimonides, who lived in the 1100s, wrote about and taught many subjects, including religion, science, and medicine. His work greatly influenced both Muslim and Christian thinkers. Also, the 14th-century Jewish scholar Gersonides (guhr•SAHN•uh•DEEZ) made an instrument to measure the distance between objects in the sky. Using it, he estimated that stars were a huge distance from Earth. Before this discovery, most scholars agreed with Ptolemy that the stars were just beyond the moon.

As scientific knowledge spread through Europe, conflict soon arose between Christianity and science. Christianity stressed viewing the world through faith. Scientists, however, emphasized reason. During the 1200s, Christian scholar Thomas Aquinas tried to show that the two approaches could exist in harmony. (See Chapter 10.) Reason and faith, he argued, both came from God. Later discoveries, however, threatened this harmony between religion and science.

REVIEW How did the contributions of Muslims, Jews, and Christians advance knowledge during the Middle Ages?

The Renaissance Leads to New Ideas

3 ESSENTIAL QUESTION How did the Renaissance affect science?

As you learned in Chapter 13, the work of scholars such as Aquinas gave rise to a new open-mindedness that led to the development of humanism. In turn, humanism helped to launch the period of experimentation, exploration, and creativity known as the Renaissance.

Influence of the Humanists The collapse of the Byzantine Empire in the mid-1400s helped the development of Renaissance thought. At that time, many Byzantine scholars fled to Italy. They brought with them knowledge of classical Greek and Roman literature. This literature formed the basis of humanism.

At about the same time, the invention of the printing press helped to spread humanist ideas across Europe. As more books became available, scholars realized that the classical thinkers did not always agree. Influenced by these findings and by humanistic ideals, European scholars also began to question classical learning. Before long, a new spirit of investigation emerged in Europe.

Influence of Renaissance Artists The revolution in art during the Renaissance also affected scientists. Artists wanted to show their subjects in a realistic way. To do this, they closely observed humans and animals. Some even dissected human corpses. This careful study led to a more accurate scientific knowledge of human anatomy.

Leonardo's "Study of Arms" The Renaissance artist Leonardo da Vinci learned about muscles and tendons through dissection. ▼

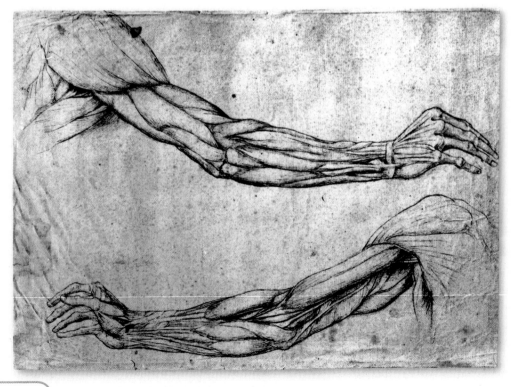

Influence of Global Explorations During the Renaissance, Europeans looked for new routes to Asia. (You'll learn about these voyages of exploration in Lesson 3.) These voyages increased knowledge of Earth's shape, size, and weather. Some of this new knowledge challenged classical ideas. For example, Aristotle thought that the temperature at the equator was too high to support human life. However, explorers found that the temperatures there were high, but the region was still livable.

REVIEW How did humanism influence learning during the Renaissance?

Lesson Summary

- For centuries, European scholars accepted the ideas of ancient Greek scientists without question.
- In the late Middle Ages, translations of Greek and Arabic scientific works helped European scholars rediscover scientific learning.
- The Renaissance revived interest in scientific learning and encouraged the questioning of old beliefs.

Why It Matters Now . . .

The renewed interest in scientific investigation that started during the Renaissance led to the development of modern science.

---

1 Lesson Review

Homework Helper
ClassZone.com

Terms & Names

1. Explain the importance of

rationalism	harmony	dissection
geocentric theory	anatomy	

Using Your Notes

Explaining Chronological Order and Sequence
Use your completed time line to answer the following question:

2. How did scientific knowledge expand during the Middle Ages? (7.10.1)

300s B.C.   A.D. 1400s

Main Ideas

3. How did Aristotle and Ptolemy influence modern scientific thought? (7.10.1)
4. How did Muslims help to preserve classical learning? (7.10.1)
5. How did Renaissance artists and explorers help increase scientific knowledge? (7.10.1)

Critical Thinking

6. **Finding Main Ideas** What impact did learning about classical science have on Christianity? (7.10.3)
7. **Understanding Cause and Effect** Why do you think humanistic ideals encouraged European scholars to question classical learning? (HI 2)

Activity **Drawing a Diagram** Draw a diagram that depicts Ptolemy's view of the universe and another diagram that shows today's view of our solar system. Then write captions that describe how the diagrams are similar and different. (7.10.1)

Lesson
2

▶ **MAIN IDEAS**

1 **Science and Technology** Several scientists developed new ideas based on close observation of the world and precise mathematical calculations.

2 **Science and Technology** New inventions helped scientists make more precise observations and measurements.

3 **Science and Technology** Philosophers proposed a new way to view the universe and to develop scientific theories.

▶ **TAKING NOTES**

Reading Skill: Categorizing

To categorize means to sort information. As you read Lesson 2, take notes about the Scientific Revolution. Use a diagram like the one below to categorize your information.

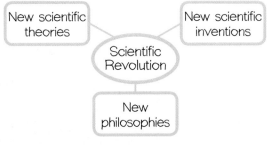

 Skillbuilder Handbook, page R6

▲ **Galileo's Telescope**
Galileo was the first person to use a telescope—an instrument that magnifies distant objects—to study the skies.

CALIFORNIA STANDARDS

7.10.2 Understand the significance of the new scientific theories (e.g., those of Copernicus, Galileo, Kepler, Newton) and the significance of new inventions (e.g., the telescope, microscope, thermometer, barometer).

7.10.3 Understand the scientific method advanced by Bacon and Descartes, the influence of new scientific rationalism on the growth of democratic ideas, and the coexistence of science with traditional religious beliefs.

REP 2 Students distinguish fact from opinion in historical narratives and stories.

The Scientific Revolution

TERMS & NAMES
Scientific Revolution
heliocentric
universal gravitation
scientific method

Build on What You Know Influenced by humanism, scholars began to question classical scientific ideas and Christian beliefs. This new spirit of questioning accepted views of the world became known as the **Scientific Revolution**.

New Scientific Theories

1 **ESSENTIAL QUESTION** What new ideas did scientists develop?

In the 1500s, scholars began to look at old scientific beliefs in a different way. This change led to an explosion of new ideas.

A Heliocentric Universe In the early 1500s, a Polish astronomer named Nicolaus Copernicus (koh•PUR•nuh•kuhs) challenged Ptolemy's geocentric theory. Copernicus reasoned that the stars, Earth, and other planets revolved around the sun, which did not move. This view of the universe is called **heliocentric**, or sun-centered.

Almost 100 years later, German astronomer Johannes Kepler refined and built on Copernicus' theories. He used mathematical laws to prove that the planets did indeed move around the sun. One law showed that the planets revolved in elliptical orbits, and not circular orbits as Copernicus believed. Elliptical orbits are oval in shape.

A Demonstration
In this painting, Galileo shows the ruler of Venice how to use a telescope. ▼

Galileo Challenges Accepted Beliefs The Italian scientist Galileo (1564–1642) made many scientific advances that challenged classical ideas. For example, his observations made with the telescope clearly supported Copernicus' ideas. This, however, brought him into conflict with the Church. Copernicus' view contradicted official Church beliefs that said the universe was geocentric. Church leaders denounced Galileo. They forced him to publicly deny his findings. But Galileo knew he was right, and so did other scientists.

Primary Source Handbook

See the excerpt from *The Starry Messenger*, page R56.

Newton's Universal Law In the late 1600s, the English scientist Sir Isaac Newton combined the ideas of Copernicus, Kepler, and Galileo into one single theory. It stated that all physical objects were affected by the same force—gravity. This natural force tends to draw objects toward each other. Gravity is the force that keeps planets revolving around the sun. It also keeps people from flying off Earth's surface and into space. Since gravity acts on all objects throughout the universe, Newton called his theory the law of **universal gravitation**.

Discoveries in Medicine Some scientists sought to understand the universe. Others wanted to know how the human body worked. In 1628, English physician William Harvey published an accurate description of how blood circulates through the body. He based his findings on human dissections he had performed. His observations showed that the heart, not the liver as Galen believed, pumped blood through living creatures.

Blood Circulation
In this 19th-century painting, William Harvey explains to King Charles I how blood circulates. Below is an illustration from Harvey's study of blood circulation. ▼

REVIEW How did Copernicus' view of the universe differ from Ptolemy's?

New Scientific Inventions

② **ESSENTIAL QUESTION** What new inventions helped scientists make more precise observations and measurements?

In the 1600s and 1700s, scientific investigation was made easier by the invention of such instruments as the microscope, the thermometer, and the barometer.

The Microscope In the 1670s, a Dutch amateur scientist named Anton van Leeuwenhoek (LAY•vuhn•HUK) built a microscope. This brass tube containing curved glass lenses magnified objects between 250 and 300 times. Using the microscope, van Leeuwenhoek observed bacteria, or tiny moving matter, in fluids. He also observed the flow of blood through tiny blood vessels called capillaries.

The Thermometer In the early 1600s, Galileo invented the thermometer, an instrument that measures temperature. Galileo's thermometer was an open glass tube with a bulb containing water at the bottom. The water rose in the tube as it warmed and sank as it cooled. Some 100 years later in 1714, German scientist Gabriel Daniel Fahrenheit (FAR•uhn•HYT) made the first mercury thermometer. He also proposed the first formal temperature measurement system. Fahrenheit's measurement scale showed water freezing at a temperature of 32° and boiling at 212°.

The Barometer In 1643, a friend and supporter of Galileo, Evangelista Torricelli (TAWR•uh•CHEHL•ee), invented the barometer. This instrument measures the pressure of Earth's atmosphere. Later, scientists used the barometer to predict the weather.

Three Scientific Inventions

Microscope

Zacharias Janssen (YAHN•suhn), a Dutch maker of eyeglasses, invented the microscope in 1590. Anton van Leeuwenhoek, however, was the first person to observe microscopic life. A microscope made in the late 1600s is shown here.

Thermometer

A Swedish astronomer, Anders Celsius, created a thermometer measurement scale in 1742 that showed water freezing at 0° and boiling at 100°. One of the first thermometers to use the Celsius scale is shown here.

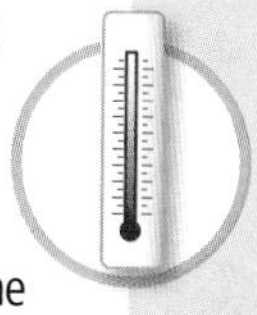

Barometer

The barometer is useful in predicting the weather because it measures changes in air pressure, which signal changes in the weather. Rising air pressure usually indicates good weather. Falling air pressure tends to be a sign of bad weather. A replica of Torricelli's barometer is shown here.

REVIEW Why might instruments such as the microscope and the thermometer be useful to scientists?

Sir Francis Bacon (1561–1626)

For Francis Bacon, science was a hobby. He was a politician. Bacon wanted to incorporate rational thinking into politics and science. His writings helped the English legal system set a world standard for fairness. Bacon was among the first to show that rationalism worked in government as well as in science.

Bacon was determined to pursue his passion for scientific experiments even if it killed him. In the end, it did. Bacon became sick and died after testing a theory that snow can actually insulate against the cold. The theory was later proved true.

The Scientific Method

③ ESSENTIAL QUESTION What new ways of viewing the universe did philosophers propose?

In the 1600s, two philosophers, René Descartes (day•KAHRT) and Francis Bacon, had a huge impact on how scientists studied the world.

Descartes and Rationalism Frenchman René Descartes believed in questioning the opinions of recognized authorities. He also believed that every idea should be doubted until it had been proved through reason. Descartes based his approach on a simple statement: "I think, therefore I am." He argued that God created two realities. The first was physical reality. The other was the mind, or what people think. Descartes claimed that people could use their rational mind to understand the "truths" of the physical world.

Bacon and the Scientific Method Englishman Sir Francis Bacon also believed in using rational, organized thought. However, Bacon felt that scientists should use experiments and observation rather than abstract reasoning to understand the world. This approach, called the **scientific method**, had specific steps.

1. Observing and describing a subject
2. Forming a hypothesis—an unproved assumption about the subject
3. Testing the hypothesis in an experiment
4. Interpreting results to draw a conclusion

The Impact of Scientific Rationalism The ideas of Descartes and Bacon became known as scientific rationalism. By the 1700s, the influence of scientific rationalism had begun to erode the power of the Church. Why did this happen? Scientific rationalism encouraged people to think for themselves instead of relying on church authority.

Some political thinkers applied scientific rationalism to government. For example, political thinker John Locke believed people have the natural ability to be in charge of their own affairs. He viewed this ability as a natural law or right. Such beliefs planted seeds of democracy that soon blossomed in nations such as the United States.

REVIEW What are the four steps involved in the scientific method?

Lesson Summary

- Scientists developed new theories about the universe.
- The invention of new scientific instruments helped to prove new theories and to change some old beliefs.
- The scientific rationalism of Descartes and Bacon had a major impact on religion and politics.

Why It Matters Now . . .

The Scientific Revolution established a rational method of looking at scientific questions that is still used today.

2 Lesson Review

**Homework Helper**
ClassZone.com

Terms & Names

1. Explain the importance of

Scientific Revolution   universal gravitation
heliocentric   scientific method

Using Your Notes

Categorizing Use your completed diagram to answer the following question:

2. What idea or event do you think had the strongest impact on the Scientific Revolution? Explain. (7.10.2)

Main Ideas

3. How do the geocentric and heliocentric theories differ? (7.10.2)

4. What was the importance of the new scientific instruments discussed in this lesson? (7.10.2)

5. How did scientific rationalism affect European religion and politics? (7.10.3)

Critical Thinking

6. **Making Inferences** Why do you think church authorities forced Galileo to deny his ideas on the universe? (7.10.2)

7. **Drawing Conclusions** Why was the law of universal gravitation such an important step in understanding the universe? (7.10.2)

Activity

Creating an Experiment Devise an experiment to test a hypothesis. (For example, a feather holds more weight than a piece of cardboard.) Use the scientific method to conduct research and determine your answer. (7.10.3)

Distinguishing Facts from Opinions

Goal: To differentiate between facts and opinions to understand the role of women in the Scientific Revolution

CALIFORNIA STANDARDS
REP 2 Students distinguish fact from opinion in historical narratives and stories.

Learn the Skill

A fact is a piece of information that can be proved to be true. Statistics, dates, and events are all facts. An opinion, on the other hand, is a belief, feeling, or judgment that someone expresses. An opinion cannot be proved to be true. Being able to tell the difference between facts and opinions is an important part of critical thinking.

S See the Skillbuilder Handbook, page R19.

Practice the Skill

1 Facts: In the passage at right, look for specific names, dates, statistics, and statements that can be proved. Information about history or people's lives such as names, dates, and places can be checked for accuracy in encyclopedias or books by experts in a particular field of study.

2 Opinions: Look for statements that express feelings, beliefs, or judgments. Decide if the opinions belong to the author or to someone else. In this passage, the phrase "some scholars think" signals an opinion.

3 Opinions: Look for judgment words that the writer uses to describe people or events. Judgment words are often adjectives that a writer uses to get readers to feel a certain way.

4 Separate the facts from the opinions and summarize them. Organize these summaries in a chart like the one shown below.

Example:

Facts	**Opinions**
Most women in the 17th century were mainly confined to the role of home and family.	People in the 17th century: Women were not meant to study.
Tycho Brahe was a Danish astronomer. His observatory was called Uraniborg.	Author: Tycho Brahe was brilliant. Women's contributions to science were important.
Sophia Brahe lived between 1556 and 1643. She contributed to her brother's work.	Scholars: Sophia Brahe should get more credit for her work.
The Brahes' work influenced Kepler.	

Scientists in 17th-century Europe started thinking about the world in new ways. They shared their ideas with one another through books and letters. Society supported the work of men as scientists. This passage describes how women were able to take part in the new community of science.

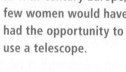

Women Astronomers in the 17th Century

❶ The role of middle-class women in 17th-century Europe was mainly confined to home and family. Few of them had the chance for a good education. ❷ Most people believed that the life of the mind was not suited to women. Yet there were women who were interested in learning. Although they were less famous than Galileo or Kepler, these women made ❸ important contributions to science.

One such woman was ❶ Sophia Brahe (1556–1643). Her older brother Tycho was a ❸ brilliant Danish astronomer. Sophia started helping him when she was ten years old. They worked in his observatory called Uraniborg. Together they recorded accurate positions for the planets. Their writings on the stars and planets formed the basis for Kepler's work. ❷ Some scholars think that Sophia should get more credit for the work she and her brother did together.

▲ **Women and Science**
In 17th-century Europe, few women would have had the opportunity to use a telescope.

Apply the Skill

Select an article from a recent current affairs magazine. Make a chart like the one at left to help you distinguish facts from opinions in the article.

▶ MAIN IDEAS

① **Geography** Seeking an ocean route to Asia, Portugal sent out explorers on sea voyages.

② **Geography** Searching for a new route to Asia, Columbus sailed west across the Atlantic and reached the Americas.

③ **Geography** After Columbus' first voyage, a number of explorers made the trip to the Americas.

▲ **The *Victoria*** This illustration shows explorer Ferdinand Magellan aboard his ship the *Victoria* on his voyage around the world.

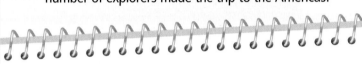

▶ TAKING NOTES

Reading Skill: Summarizing

To summarize is to restate a passage in fewer words. After you read Lesson 3, write a sentence or two summarizing each of the three main sections. Use a chart like the one below to record your summaries. Each summary statement is started for you.

The Age of Exploration
The Portuguese used advances in technology to help . . .
By sailing west across the Atlantic, Columbus . . .
After Columbus' first voyage, several European nations . . .

 Skillbuilder Handbook, page R3

(CALIFORNIA STANDARDS)

7.11.1 Know the great voyages of discovery, the locations of the routes, and the influence of cartography in the development of a new European worldview.

Framework This unit begins with the age of exploration, with special attention given to Spanish and Portuguese explorations in the New World.

CST 2 Students construct various time lines of key events, people, and periods of the historical era they are studying.

The Age of Exploration

TERMS & NAMES

sponsor

caravel

astrolabe

Treaty of Tordesillas

circumnavigate

Build on What You Know Inventions and a spirit of investigation helped bring about many scientific discoveries. In this lesson, you will learn how scientific developments and the desire for wealth led to an age of exploration.

Portugal Leads the Way

1 **ESSENTIAL QUESTION** How did Portugal find an ocean route to Asia?

Since the Middle Ages, Europeans had craved luxury goods, such as silks and spices, from Asia. During this time, Italian and Muslim merchants controlled overland trade between Europe and Asia. Merchants from such countries as Portugal, Spain, England, and France wanted a share of this trade. To do this, these merchants needed to find a sea route to Asia.

Henry the Navigator Portuguese merchants were the first Europeans to establish sea trade with Asia. They were able to do this, in part, because they had government backing. Prince Henry, the son of Portugal's king, was a strong supporter of exploration. He set up a school on Portugal's southwest coast for mapmakers, navigators, and shipbuilders. He also sponsored voyages of exploration. A **sponsor** is a person who gives money for an undertaking, such as a voyage. Even though he rarely boarded a ship, Henry became known as "the Navigator."

Prince Henry's School
The fortress at Sagres (SAH•greesh), at the southwestern tip of Portugal, probably was the location of Prince Henry's navigation school. ▼

511

Technology and Exploration

Technological advances made at Henry the Navigator's school aided Portuguese exploration. Shipbuilders there perfected the **caravel**, a ship designed for long voyages. Caravels had both the square sails used on European ships and the triangular lateen sails used on Arabian ships. Square sails provided caravels with power, and lateen sails permitted quick turns.

Portuguese sailors also borrowed instruments from other cultures. They tracked their direction with a compass, a Chinese invention. The Portuguese also used the astrolabe, which was invented by the ancient Greeks and improved by the Arabs. An **astrolabe** measures the angle of the stars above the horizon. This information helped sailors find their ship's latitude, or the distance north or south of the equator.

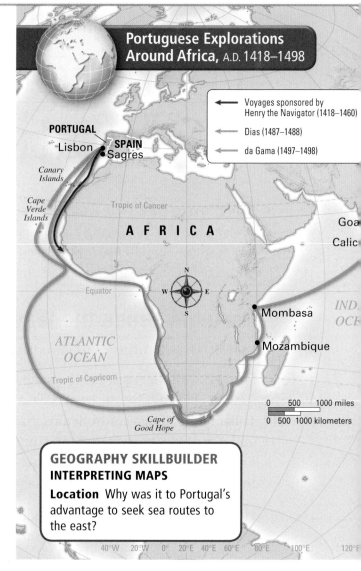

Portuguese Explorations Around Africa, A.D. 1418–1498

→ Voyages sponsored by Henry the Navigator (1418–1460)
→ Dias (1487–1488)
→ da Gama (1497–1498)

PORTUGAL
Lisbon
SPAIN
Sagres
Canary Islands
Cape Verde Islands
Tropic of Cancer
AFRICA
Goa
Calic
Equator
Mombasa
IND. OCE
Mozambique
ATLANTIC OCEAN
Tropic of Capricorn
Cape of Good Hope

0   500   1000 miles
0   500   1000 kilometers

GEOGRAPHY SKILLBUILDER
INTERPRETING MAPS
Location Why was it to Portugal's advantage to seek sea routes to the east?

Reaching India By the time that Henry the Navigator died in 1460, the Portuguese had set up trading posts along Africa's west coast. There they developed a profitable trade for gold, ivory, and slaves. Soon, however, they set their sights beyond Africa.

In 1488, the Portuguese explorer Bartolomeu Dias rounded Africa's southern tip. (See the map on this page.) He then sailed up part of Africa's east coast before returning home. Vasco da Gama extended Dias's route, sailing east all the way to India in 1498. A few years later, the Portuguese set up a trading post in India. Then they continued moving eastward. In time, they set up several trade centers in the Spice Islands—present-day Indonesia.

Overland trade from Asia to Europe tended to be expensive, because cargo had to be loaded and unloaded many times. Sea trade, however, was much cheaper. The cargo did not have to be handled so frequently. As a result, the Portuguese could charge less for spices. For a time, Portugal dominated European trade with Asia.

REVIEW What type of technology aided Portuguese exploration?

Columbus Reaches America

2 ESSENTIAL QUESTION Why did Columbus sail west across the Atlantic, and what did he find?

While the Portuguese headed east to secure trade routes, an Italian navigator named Christopher Columbus looked west. He hoped to find a westward route to the riches of Asia.

Columbus' First Voyage
By studying existing maps and reports, Columbus knew that Earth was round. Because of this, Columbus thought that he could reach Asia sooner if he sailed west instead of east around Africa. However, Columbus miscalculated the distance around Earth. He estimated this distance at only three-quarters as far as it actually was.

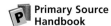
Primary Source Handbook
See the excerpt from the Journal of Christopher Columbus, page R57.

To many people, Columbus' idea of sailing west to get to the east seemed a little strange. The Portuguese rejected it, preferring to continue their search for an eastern route to Asia. Even Spain, which was eager to compete for trade, was skeptical. After six years, however, Columbus convinced Spanish monarchs Ferdinand and Isabella to sponsor his plan.

In early August 1492, Columbus left Spain with three caravels and about 90 men. After almost ten weeks at sea, Columbus'
crew grew restless. They had not seen land for over a month and wanted to return home. Columbus persuaded them to continue. Then, on October 12, a sailor called out *"Tierra, tierra"* [Land, land].

Columbus Lands at Hispaniola This 16th-century engraving shows Columbus landing on the island of Hispaniola during his first voyage. ▼

Columbus' Mistake
Columbus thought this land was India. He even called the people who greeted him and his men *Indios* (Indians). Once again, he was mistaken. He actually had landed on an island in the Caribbean Sea. Columbus explored other islands but did not come across any trade goods. Even so, he was still excited at finding what he thought was a route to Asia. He set up a settlement on the island of Hispaniola and then sailed back to Spain.

Background: Diego Alvarez Chanca, from Seville in Spain, served as surgeon on Columbus' second voyage to the West Indies. He wrote of his experiences in a letter to the town council of Seville. In this excerpt, he describes the animals he saw on the island of Hispaniola.

▲ The site of Isabella, Columbus' first settlement on Hispaniola

from *Letter of Dr. Chanca on the Second Voyage of Columbus*
By Diego Alvarez Chanca

No four-footed animal has ever been seen in this or any of the other islands, except some dogs of various colors, as in our own country, . . . and also some little animals, in color and fur like a rabbit, . . . with long tails, and feet like those of a rat; these animals climb up the trees. . . .

There are great numbers of small snakes, and some lizards, but not many . . . [O]ur men saw an enormous kind of lizard, which they said was as large round as a calf, with a tail as long as a lance, which [islanders] often went out to kill: but bulky as it was, it got into the sea, so that they could not catch it.

DOCUMENT–BASED QUESTION
Why do you think Dr. Chanca wanted to describe the wildlife of the West Indies to people back in Spain?

The Treaty of Tordesillas Ferdinand and Isabella wanted to make sure that Portugal, their trading rivals, did not benefit from Columbus' expedition. The Portuguese feared that if Columbus had found a route to Asia, Spain might claim lands that Portugal had already claimed. In 1494, Spain and Portugal signed the **Treaty of Tordesillas** (TAWR•day•SEEL•yahs). This drew an imaginary line from north to south around the world. (See the map on the opposite page.) Spain could claim all lands west of the line. Portugal could claim all lands to the east. This gave Portugal control of one area in the Americas—present-day Brazil.

Additional Voyages Ferdinand and Isabella were excited with the results of Columbus' first voyage. They sent him on three more journeys west to find mainland India. Although Columbus landed on many islands, he found no proof that he was in Asia. Eventually, Ferdinand and Isabella lost patience with him. Columbus died in 1506, a bitter and lonely man. Right up to his death, he continued to insist that he had reached India. However, people soon realized that Columbus had found a vast land previously unknown to them.

REVIEW What miscalculations did Columbus make?

Exploration After Columbus

3 **ESSENTIAL QUESTION** Which other European countries explored and claimed parts of the Americas?

After Columbus' journeys, several European countries sponsored voyages of exploration to the Americas. Many of the explorers who undertook these expeditions were, like Columbus, searching for a fast route to Asia. Others simply were in search of wealth.

Circling the Globe In 1519, the Spanish sponsored a voyage captained by a Portuguese sailor named Ferdinand Magellan. He set out from Spain with five ships and about 250 men. His goal was to circumnavigate the globe. **Circumnavigate** means to travel completely around the world. Up to this time, no one had accomplished this feat.

Magellan sailed around the southern tip of South America and into the vast waters of the Pacific Ocean. (See the map below.) The ships sailed on for several months without sighting land. Eventually, the ships arrived in the Philippine Islands. There, Magellan was killed in a local war. His crew, under the leadership of Juan Sebastián del Cano, continued on to the Spice Islands and then home. After a nearly three-year voyage, only one ship and 18 of the original crew members made it back to Spain. Still, the expedition had successfully traveled around the world. In addition, it was an economic success. The ship's hold was full of Asian spices.

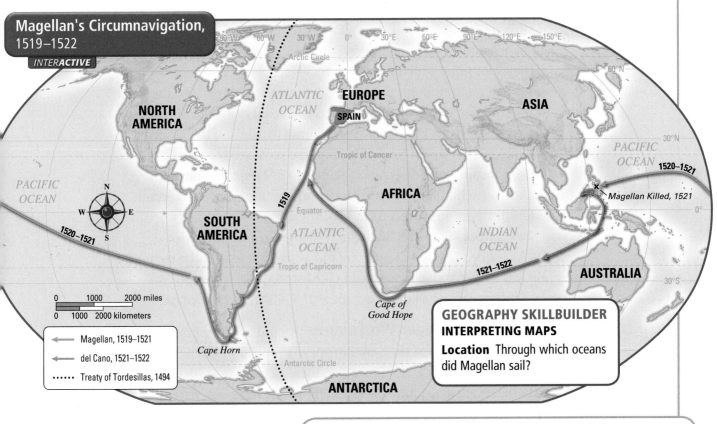

Magellan's Circumnavigation, 1519–1522
INTER**ACTIVE**

GEOGRAPHY SKILLBUILDER
INTERPRETING MAPS
Location Through which oceans did Magellan sail?

→ Magellan, 1519–1521
← del Cano, 1521–1522
······· Treaty of Tordesillas, 1494

Spanish Conquerors In the early 1500s, many Spanish explorers came to the Americas in search of gold. As you read in Chapter 12, Spanish explorer Hernán Cortés conquered the rich Aztec empire in Mexico. Within ten years, Spain had gained control of all of present-day Mexico and Central America. The Spanish enslaved most of the people who lived in these regions.

▲ **Search for Gold**
Francisco Coronado spent two years exploring what today is the southwestern United States in search of gold.

Not long after, Spanish explorer Francisco Pizarro and his soldiers attacked the Incan Empire in South America. They captured and killed the emperor. Soon the Incan Empire collapsed. By 1535, the Spanish controlled most Incan lands. Many Inca became slave laborers in the mines and on the farms that the Spanish set up.

Further Explorations in the North The desire for gold also drew Spanish explorers to travel north. From 1539 to 1542, Hernando de Soto explored territory in the present-day southern United States. In 1540, Francisco Coronado began to search what is now the western United States. However, neither explorer found gold.

The English and French made several attempts to find a shortcut to Asia. They sponsored expeditions to find a Northwest Passage, a legendary water route through northern North America to Asia. In the late 1490s, Italian sailor John Cabot headed two voyages for the English. He claimed coastal lands in present-day eastern Canada and the United States for England. However, he did not find the passage.

In 1524, Giovanni da Verrazzano (VEHR•uh•ZAH•noh), another Italian sailor, searched for the Northwest Passage for France. Although he failed to discover a route to Asia, he did explore what today is New York harbor. Ten years later, the Frenchman Jacques Cartier (kahr•TYAY) sailed about 150 miles inland along Canada's St. Lawrence River. He was sure that this river would take him to Asia. In time, however, Cartier realized that he had not found a Northwest Passage.

Mapmaking and a New Worldview Each discovery made by explorers helped to change the way Europeans looked at the world. Before Columbus' voyages, the European view of the world focused on the Mediterranean Sea and the lands that surrounded it. After

Columbus' explorations, the European worldview stretched from the Americas in the west to the Spice Islands in the east.

Cartographers, or mapmakers, played a leading role in changing this worldview. Maps of the early 1500s began to show two new continents in the west. One mapmaker named these continents "the Americas" after Amerigo Vespucci (vehs•POO•chee). Vespucci was one of the first to explore and map the coasts of this region. An account of his explorations was published under the title *New World*.

REVIEW How did exploration in the Americas change the European worldview?

Lesson Summary

- The Portuguese established trade routes by sea to Africa and Asia.
- Searching for a new route to Asia, Columbus sailed west and reached the Americas.
- Several nations explored North and South America and established claims there.

Why It Matters Now . . .

European exploration and settlement of the Americas had a major impact on the cultures found in the United States today.

---

3 Lesson Review

Terms & Names

1. Explain the importance of

sponsor	astrolabe	circumnavigate
caravel	Treaty of Tordesillas	

Using Your Notes

Summarizing Use your completed chart to answer the following question:

2. How did Columbus' voyages to the Americas affect European exploration? (7.11.1)

The Age of Exploration
The Portuguese used advances in technology to help . . .
By sailing west across the Atlantic, Columbus . . .
After Columbus' first voyage, several European nations . . .

Main Ideas

3. What impact did the work of Henry the Navigator have on Portuguese explorations? (7.11.1)

4. Why do you think many people considered Columbus' plan to be controversial? (7.11.1)

5. What was the importance of Ferdinand Magellan's voyage? (7.11.1)

Critical Thinking

6. Making Inferences Why do you think the Spanish monarchs lost patience with Columbus? Give reasons for your answer. (7.11.1)

7. Drawing Conclusions What impact do you think European exploration and colonization in the Americas had on trade? (Framework)

Activity **Internet Activity** Use the Internet to find information to make a time line titled "The Age of European Exploration." (CST 2)
INTERNET KEYWORD: *exploration*

Life on a Ship

Purpose: To learn about daily life on a 16th-century ship

If you were a sailor in 16th-century Europe, you probably worked on a ship like the one shown here. Life at sea during this time was not easy. Voyages often took months, and sometimes stretched into years. Living quarters were cramped. Food was of poor quality and often in short supply. And violent storms and shipwrecks were a constant threat.

Ⓐ The Ship By the late 1500s, most European ships sailing the oceans were galleons. The typical galleon was between 70 and 100 feet long and about 20 feet wide. It was easy to handle and, when under full sail, very fast.

Ⓑ The Captain The captain usually had a tiny cabin in the stern of the ship. It served as an office as well as living quarters. He kept his maps, charts, and log books there. The charts and logs he kept on the voyage often helped mapmakers draw more accurate maps.

Ⓒ Navigation Sailors used a compass to figure out direction. Plotting the position of the stars and planets with an astrolabe allowed them to determine their latitude. Maps and charts provided them with further information.

Ⓓ Food Some ships carried live pigs and hens on deck to provide fresh eggs and meat. However, the day-to-day diet aboard consisted of hard biscuits, salted meat, and rough wine or beer. The meat often was rotten and the biscuits full of worms.

Ⓔ Living Conditions Aboard ship, ordinary sailors lived in very cramped conditions. They slept wherever they could find space to sling a hammock. Officers' quarters were only slightly better.

CALIFORNIA STANDARDS
7.11.1 Know the great voyages of discovery, the locations of the routes, and the influence of cartography in the development of a new European worldview.

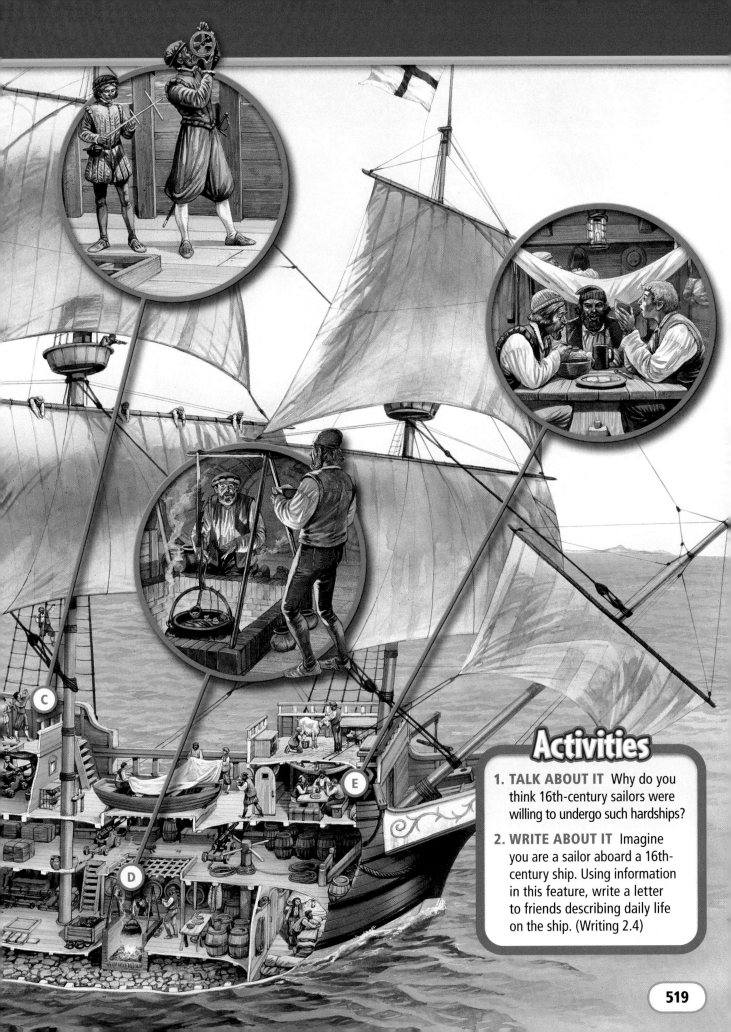

Activities

1. **TALK ABOUT IT** Why do you think 16th-century sailors were willing to undergo such hardships?

2. **WRITE ABOUT IT** Imagine you are a sailor aboard a 16th-century ship. Using information in this feature, write a letter to friends describing daily life on the ship. (Writing 2.4)

MAIN IDEAS

1 **Geography** The Age of Exploration caused ideas, technology, plants, and animals to be exchanged around the world.

2 **Government** Several European countries competed for colonies overseas, both in Asia and the Americas.

3 **Economics** Developments during the Age of Exploration led to the origins of modern capitalism.

TAKING NOTES

Reading Skill: Understanding Cause and Effect

An effect is an event or action that is the result of a cause. In your notebook, draw a chart like the one below. As you read Lesson 4, look for the effects of the causes that are listed.

Results of Exploration	
Causes	**Effects**
The spread of disease between hemispheres	
The defeat of the Spanish Armada	
The establishment of mercantilism	

 Skillbuilder Handbook, page R26

▲ **Coffee** Native to Africa, the coffee tree was taken to the Americas by European settlers. Today the South American countries of Brazil and Colombia lead the world in coffee production.

The Coffee Tree.

CALIFORNIA STANDARDS

7.11.2 Discuss the exchanges of plants, animals, technology, culture, and ideas among Europe, Africa, Asia, and the Americas in the fifteenth and sixteenth centuries and the major economic and social effects on each continent.

7.11.3 Examine the origins of modern capitalism; the influence of mercantilism and cottage industry; the elements and importance of a market economy in seventeenth-century Europe; the changing international trading and marketing patterns, including their locations on a world map; and the influence of explorers and map makers.

Framework The drama of the Spanish galleons and maritime rivalries between Spain and England culminated in the English defeat of the Spanish Armada in 1588; the consequences of that event should be analyzed.

Impact of Exploration

TERMS & NAMES

Columbian Exchange

triangular trade

capitalism

mercantilism

Build on What You Know Seeking wealth and land, European nations began to explore the Americas in the 1500s. In Lesson 4, you will learn about the effects of this exploration.

The Exchange of Goods and Ideas

1 ESSENTIAL QUESTION What did exploration help to spread?

European exploration resulted in the establishment of new trade links between the world's continents. These trade links increased the exchange of ideas and goods throughout the world.

The Columbian Exchange The **Columbian Exchange** was the movement of living things between hemispheres. These living things included people, plants, animals, and diseases. The exchange began after Columbus' voyages to the Americas.

Europeans brought wheat, onions, grapes, sugar cane, and oranges to the Americas. From the Americas, they shipped corn, potatoes, pumpkins, and pineapples. Europeans also brought domestic animals, such as horses. In addition, Europeans brought diseases, such as smallpox and measles, to the Americas. Native Americans had no resistance to these diseases. As a result, the diseases killed about 20 million Native Americans.

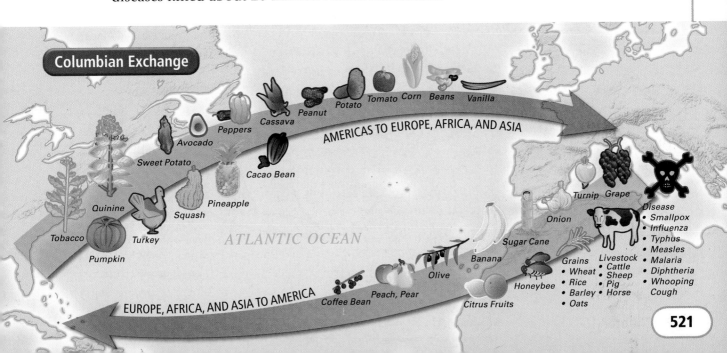

Columbian Exchange

AMERICAS TO EUROPE, AFRICA, AND ASIA

Tobacco, Quinine, Pumpkin, Turkey, Squash, Sweet Potato, Pineapple, Avocado, Cassava, Cacao Bean, Peppers, Peanut, Potato, Tomato, Corn, Beans, Vanilla

ATLANTIC OCEAN

EUROPE, AFRICA, AND ASIA TO AMERICA

Coffee Bean, Peach, Pear, Olive, Banana, Citrus Fruits, Honeybee, Sugar Cane, Onion, Turnip, Grape

Grains
• Wheat
• Rice
• Barley
• Oats

Livestock
• Cattle
• Sheep
• Pig
• Horse

Disease
• Smallpox
• Influenza
• Typhus
• Measles
• Malaria
• Diphtheria
• Whooping Cough

521

Changing International Trade Patterns The links between the continents created by the Columbian Exchange resulted in new international trade patterns. These patterns were based on ocean trade routes that were controlled, for the most part, by Europeans.

Much of the world's trade was fueled by silver mined in the Spanish colonies in Mexico and South America. Silver flowed from the Americas to Europe and then on to China. (See the map below.) In return, Chinese goods such as silks and porcelain went back to Europe. European merchants also used silver to purchase spices from the East Indies and India.

A different kind of trade developed between the Americas, Europe, and Africa. Sugar cane, which grew well in the tropical climate of the West Indies, was processed and then shipped to Europe. The back-breaking labor needed to produce sugar cane was provided by slaves from Africa. Cheap manufactured goods flowed from Europe to pay for enslaved Africans. This **triangular trade** across the Atlantic went on for more than 300 years. In that time, about 10 million enslaved Africans were shipped to the Americas.

The Spread of Culture
Culture and ideas, as well as trade goods, were exchanged between continents. For example, the Spanish and Portuguese launched their voyages of exploration, in part, to spread Christianity. One of the first actions of explorers from these countries was to convert the native populations of the lands they claimed to the Roman Catholic faith. However, these new Christians often stamped their own identity on their faith. They did this by combining their traditional beliefs with Christian beliefs.

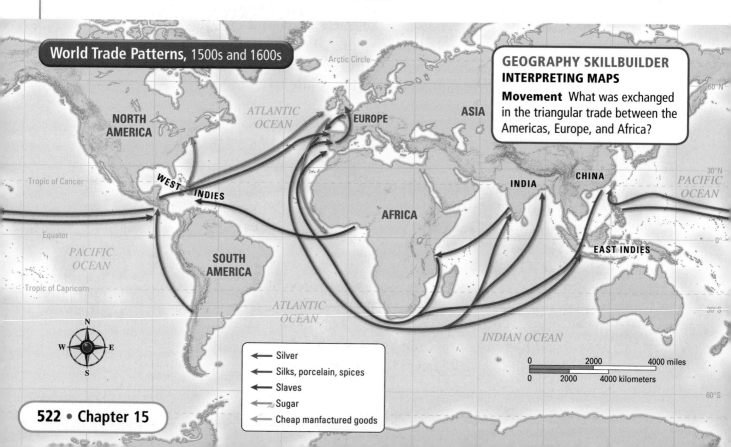

World Trade Patterns, 1500s and 1600s

GEOGRAPHY SKILLBUILDER
INTERPRETING MAPS
Movement What was exchanged in the triangular trade between the Americas, Europe, and Africa?

Legend:
- Silver
- Silks, porcelain, spices
- Slaves
- Sugar
- Cheap manfactured goods

In addition, Europeans often imported cultural practices from other lands. For example, many enjoyed drinking coffee from Arabia, mixed with sugar produced by African slave labor in the Americas.

REVIEW How did the Columbian Exchange affect world trade patterns?

Rivalry for Colonies

2 ESSENTIAL QUESTION What European countries competed for colonies?

As world trade increased, European nations competed for colonies overseas. Colonies provided European nations with raw materials and ready markets.

Portugal and Spain Portugal's eastward voyages of exploration resulted in trading posts in Africa, India, and East Asia. In addition, the Treaty of Tordesillas gave Portugal control of Brazil in South America. (See Lesson 3.)

Spain claimed lands in the Pacific, such as the present-day Philippines. However, the Spanish focused on their colonies in the Americas. Silver and gold mining was especially profitable in Peru and Mexico.

▲ **The Fur Trade**
This 17th-century engraving shows Dutch traders buying furs from Native Americans.

The Dutch Republic and France The Dutch had a presence in the Americas—the colony called New Netherland. However, most Dutch holdings were in the East Indies. Eventually, the Dutch won control of the trade between the East Indies and Europe.

The French, too, hoped to play a part in trade in the East Indies. To this end, they established an outpost in India. Even so, their colonial efforts were more successful in North America. In the early 1600s, they established Quebec in Canada. In time, Quebec became the base of a huge empire that stretched from Canada down the Mississippi River to the Caribbean.

English Colonies Inspired by other European countries, England worked to set up colonies in North America. In 1607, English settlers established Jamestown in Virginia. Other early English colonists included the Pilgrims. They settled in Massachusetts in 1620 to escape religious persecution in England. The English also set up outposts in the Caribbean and India.

The Spanish Armada

England's presence in the Americas brought England into conflict with Spain. Attacks by English sailors on Spanish ships bringing gold from the Americas had angered King Philip II of Spain. Also, England—a Protestant country—had provided support for Protestant subjects who had rebelled against Catholic Spain. So, in 1588, Philip sent an invasion force of 130 ships and 19,000 soldiers against England.

As this Spanish Armada sailed up the English Channel, it came under attack from the English navy. (See the map to the right.) The English ships were faster and better-armed than the Spanish ships. After several days of fighting, the Spanish were completely defeated. This crushing blow seriously weakened Spain. However, Spain continued to be a leading European power because of the great wealth it received from its gold and silver mines in the Americas.

Defeat of the Spanish Armada, 1588

Legend:
- Route of Armada
- Route of English fleet
- Some shipwreck sites
- Spanish possessions

Map labels: SCOTLAND, IRELAND, ENGLAND, London, Dover, Plymouth, Calais, SPANISH NETHERLANDS, FRANCE, SPAIN, Lisbon, To Spain, From Spain, English Channel, North Sea, ATLANTIC OCEAN, 50°N, 40°N, 10°W, 0°, 10°

Scale: 0 100 200 miles / 0 100 200 kilometers

GEOGRAPHY SKILLBUILDER
INTERPRETING MAPS
Movement Why do you think the Spanish sailed north around Scotland instead of back through the English Channel?

REVIEW Which countries had a strong presence in the Americas?

Europe's Economy Changes

3 **ESSENTIAL QUESTION** How did events in the Age of Exploration lead to the development of modern capitalism?

The growth of overseas trade and new wealth from the colonies had a major economic impact on Europe. These factors led to the introduction of new business and trade practices.

Capitalism One development that resulted from colonization and trade was the growth of capitalism. **Capitalism** is an economic system based on private ownership of economic resources and the use of those resources to make a profit. The merchants who invested in successful colonization and trade ventures made enormous profits. Often, they invested this newly gained wealth in business ventures both overseas and at home.

One attractive overseas venture was the chartered company. Such companies held licenses from the government that gave them the sole right to trade in a particular geographic area. At home, some wealthy investors funded industrial ventures. The chief method of manufacturing at this time was the cottage industry. In this system, merchants provided families in the countryside with the raw materials to make a product. The merchants then took the finished products to the cities to sell.

Mercantilism During this time, many European nations adopted a new economic policy called **mercantilism**. The theory behind mercantilism held that a nation's power depended on its wealth. (See the infographic below.) A nation could gain wealth in two ways. First, it could find large deposits of gold and silver. Second, it could obtain gold and silver through a favorable balance of trade. A nation has a favorable balance of trade when it sells more goods than it buys.

Colonies played an important role in mercantilism. In some cases, they provided the home country with a source of gold and silver. In addition, colonies provided the raw materials that the home country used in their cottage industries. Colonies also served as a ready market for manufactured goods.

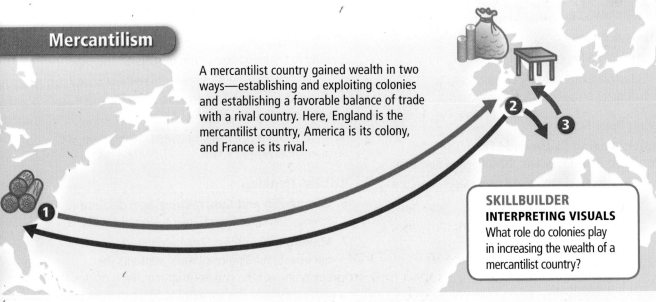

Mercantilism

A mercantilist country gained wealth in two ways—establishing and exploiting colonies and establishing a favorable balance of trade with a rival country. Here, England is the mercantilist country, America is its colony, and France is its rival.

**SKILLBUILDER
INTERPRETING VISUALS**
What role do colonies play in increasing the wealth of a mercantilist country?

1 America produces lumber, the raw material for furniture.

2 England uses American lumber to make furniture. England sells finished furniture to its rival, France, and to America.

3 England gets gold and silver from France. This increases England's wealth and reduces France's wealth.

A Market Economy By the late 1700s, some people felt that governments played too great a role in the economy. The big trading companies owed much of their success to government charters. Also, government mercantilist policies controlled trade between nations. Economists such as Adam Smith argued that the economy should be free of this government interference. He defended his idea of a free economy, or free market, in his book *Wealth of Nations* (1776). If left to work unhindered by government, the market would ensure that economy prospered, he argued. Smith's ideas provided the model for the modern U.S. economic system.

REVIEW What economic developments took place in Europe after the Age of Exploration?

Lesson Summary

- European explorations led to the Columbian Exchange and an increase in international trade.
- European nations competed for colonies.
- The European economy underwent major changes.

Why It Matters Now . . .

Today, as in the days of mercantilism, some groups want to restrict global trade to protect certain jobs and industries from competition.

---

4 Lesson Review

Homework Helper
ClassZone.com

Terms & Names

1. Explain the importance of

Columbian Exchange	capitalism
triangular trade	mercantilism

Using Your Notes

Understanding Cause and Effect Use your completed chart to answer the following question:

2. What effect did the spread of diseases have on Native Americans? (7.11.2)

Results of Exploration	
Causes	Effects
The spread of disease between hemispheres	
The defeat of the Spanish Armada	
The establishment of mercantilism	

Main Ideas

3. How did colonization of the Americas contribute to the development of the slave trade? (7.11.2)

4. Why did Spain send an armada to invade England? (Framework)

5. What is the relationship between colonization and mercantilism? (7.11.3)

Critical Thinking

6. **Comparing and Contrasting** How did Dutch colonization differ from French colonization? (7.11.2)

7. **Making Inferences** Some economists consider the private funding of colonial ventures the beginnings of the capitalist system. Why do you think they hold this view? (7.11.3)

Activity

Making a Map Take out the map that you began in Chapter 2. Then use the map on page 522 to draw in important trade routes of the 1500s and 1600s. (7.11.3)

Hold a Debate

Goal: Debate the following historical issue: "Did the defeat of the Spanish Armada have a significant impact on world history?"

Materials & Supplies
- note cards
- pens or pencils
- sources on the Spanish Armada

Prepare

1. Reread the section "The Spanish Armada" on page 524. Look for the reasons for the defeat of the Spanish Armada and the results of that defeat. Take notes as you read. Use books and the Internet to find more information about the effects of Spanish Armada's defeat.

2. Read the two quotations on this page. They offer different opinions about the effects of the defeat.

> "The widespread [feeling that Philip II] had disregarded professional advice did great damage to his reputation within Spain and, although most of the fleet returned safely, the failure of the Armada also shattered the image of [Spain's unbeatable strength]."
>
> ~ SIMON ADAMS

Do the Activity

1. Review your research and decide whether you think the defeat of the Spanish Armada had a significant impact on world history. List the arguments that support your opinion. Make a note card for each argument. Include any quotations or evidence related to that argument.

2. Organize your note cards so the arguments are in a logical order. Then write an outline of a speech stating your position and supporting arguments.

> "Great as were the effects of the failure of the Armada, they are nevertheless often exaggerated.... Spain seemed within two years of [the defeat] to be nearer to universal domination than ever before.... Spain, though she failed at sea, remained the chief power on land."
>
> ~ J. H. POLLEN

Follow-Up

Hold a class debate. Have students from either side of the issue present their argument. Finally, the class should discuss which side made the better case.

Extension

Preparing Counterarguments Debaters often try to prove their opponent wrong by attacking the opponent's arguments. Research to find evidence to disprove the arguments of the other side.

CALIFORNIA STANDARDS

Framework The drama of the Spanish galleons and maritime rivalries between Spain and England culminated in the English defeat of the Spanish Armada in 1588; the consequences of that event should be analyzed.

Chapter **15** Review

VISUAL SUMMARY

Scientific Revolution and the Age of Exploration

History of Scientific Thought (7.10.1)
- Greek ideas about science and math shaped European thought.
- Muslims preserved Greek knowledge.
- Renaissance thinkers developed new ideas.

The Scientific Revolution (7.10.2)
- Scientists discovered that Earth is not the center of the universe.
- New ideas must be tested through experiments.
- New inventions led to advances in science and exploration.

The Age of Exploration (7.11.1)
- People wanted silks and spices from Asia.
- The Portuguese sailed around Africa to reach Asia.
- Columbus sailed west and located the Americas.

Results of Exploration (7.11.2)
- Goods and ideas were exchanged across the Atlantic Ocean.
- European countries competed for colonies.
- Colonization brought changes to the European economy.

TERMS & NAMES

Explain why the words in each set below are linked with each other.

1. **rationalism** and **harmony**
2. **Scientific Revolution** and **scientific method**
3. **caravel** and **astrolabe**
4. **capitalism** and **mercantilism**

MAIN IDEAS

History of Scientific Thought (pages 496–501)
5. What sources of scientific information were used before the Renaissance? (7.10.1)
6. How did Muslim, Christian, and Jewish thinkers build on ancient Greek knowledge? (7.10.1)

The Scientific Revolution (pages 502–509)
7. How did new scientific instruments improve the accuracy of observations? (7.10.2)
8. What effect did rationalism have on European knowledge and culture? (7.10.3)

The Age of Exploration (pages 510–519)
9. How did Columbus' voyages affect Europeans and Native Americans? (7.11.2)
10. How did voyages of discovery affect European nations' relations with each other? (7.11.1)

Impact of Exploration (pages 520–527)
11. How did the defeat of the Spanish Armada shift the balance of power in Europe? (HI 2)
12. What impact did colonization have on the European economy? (7.11.3)

CRITICAL THINKING
Big Ideas: Science and Technology

13. **UNDERSTANDING CONTINUITY AND CHANGE** How do discoveries by scientists of this era influence scientists today? (7.10.2)
14. **MAKING GENERALIZATIONS** How did scientific and technological developments help to change the European worldview? (7.11.2)
15. **MAKING INFERENCES** What impact do you think early capitalism had on exploration and scientific learning? (7.11.3)

ALTERNATIVE ASSESSMENT

1. WRITING ACTIVITY Choose a voyage described in Lesson 3. Create an advertisement that encourages sailors to join the crew for that voyage. Include information on what country is sponsoring the trip, who is leading it, where the ship is going, and what the voyagers hope to find. (7.11.1)

2. INTERDISCIPLINARY ACTIVITY— SCIENCE Choose an invention described in Lesson 2. Use books or the Internet to find out how that invention has been improved since the Scientific Revolution. Write a paragraph that explains your findings. (7.10.2)

3. STARTING WITH A STORY

Review the dialogue you wrote between you and Galileo's other assistant. Create a newspaper story that describes what happened that day and why it is important. (7.10.2)

Technology Activity

4. CREATING A VIRTUAL MUSEUM
Use the Internet to find out more about the roots of the Scientific Revolution. Work with a partner to create a virtual museum exhibit about this subject. Include

- Important scientific discoveries and technological developments from classical Greece and from Jewish, Muslim, and Christian science
- The impact of the Renaissance on scientific thinking
- Appropriate visual materials
- Documentation of your sources (7.10.1)

Research Links
ClassZone.com

Reading Graphs The bar graph below shows the gold and silver shipped to Spain in the 1500s and 1600s. Use the graph and your knowledge of world history to answer the questions that follow. (7.11.2)

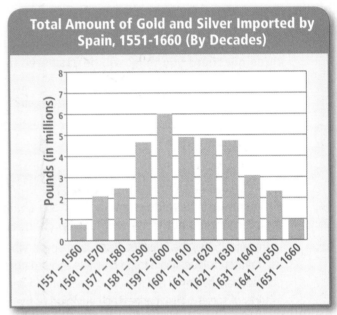

Total Amount of Gold and Silver Imported by Spain, 1551-1660 (By Decades)

Pounds (in millions)

1551–1560, 1561–1570, 1571–1580, 1581–1590, 1591–1600, 1601–1610, 1611–1620, 1621–1630, 1631–1640, 1641–1650, 1651–1660

Source: Earl J. Hamilton, *American Treasure and the Price Revolution in Spain, 1501–1650*

1. During which decade was most gold and silver shipped to Spain?
- A. 1581–1590
- B. 1591–1600
- C. 1601–1610
- D. 1611–1620

2. Which statement best describes Spain's gold and silver imports after 1630?
- A. They rose rapidly.
- B. They increased slightly
- C. They decreased slightly.
- D. They fell rapidly.

Test Practice
ClassZone.com

Additional Test Practice, pp. S1–S33

Chapter 16

The Enlightenment and the Age of Reason

Before You Read: Predicting

Scan the title of the chapter and the lesson titles. Write three questions you think will be answered in the chapter. One example might be

Why was this period called the Enlightenment?

If you find the answer to one of your questions as you read, write it down in your notebook.

Big Ideas About the Enlightenment

Government New ideas and beliefs can challenge a government's authority and lead to change.

In the mid-1500s, the Scientific Revolution began when scientists used reason to question accepted beliefs about nature. In the 1600s, philosophers began to use reason to question old beliefs about aspects of society. This marked the beginning of the Enlightenment, a time that brought great changes to Western civilization.

Integrated Technology

eEdition
- Interactive Maps
- Interactive Visuals
- Starting with a Story

INTERNET RESOURCES
Go to ClassZone.com for
- WebQuest
- Homework Helper
- Research Links
- Internet Activities
- Quizzes
- Maps
- Test Practice
- Current Events

British North American Colonies

Boston

Philadelphia

ATLANTIC OCEAN

EUROPE & NORTH AMERICA

1689
English Bill of Rights is enacted.
◄ (William and Mary)

1690
John Locke publishes *Two Treatises of Government.*

1650

1700

WORLD

1653
Taj Mahal is completed in India.

1661
Emperor Kangxi comes to power in China.

1700s
West African kingdoms grow rich on slave trade.

Cultural Centers, 1700s

INTERACTIVE

0 125 250 miles
0 125 250 kilometers

Uppsala
Stockholm

Copenhagen

Edinburgh
Glasgow

Dublin

North Sea

Oxford Cambridge
London
Greenwich

Berlin

Göttingen
Leipzig

Prague

Kraków

Paris
Orléans Strasbourg

Vienna

ATLANTIC OCEAN

Bordeaux

Toulouse

Turin Padua
Bologna
Florence

Adriatic Sea

Madrid
Barcelona

Lisbon

Rome

Seville

Naples

Mediterranean Sea

Palermo

Baltic Sea

Leading academic centers
Observatories

1750s
Enlightenment reaches
its height in France.
◀ (Voltaire statue)

1762
◀ Catherine the
Great begins her
reign in Russia.

1776
American colonies
declare independence.

1789
*Declaration of
the Rights of Man*
adopted in France.

1750

1800

1722
Safavid dynasty
collapses in Persia.

1773
Ali Bey, ruler of Eygpt,
is killed by rebels.

1788
Britain establishes
a colony in Australia.

Challenging Old Ideas

CALIFORNIA STANDARDS

Reading 3.3 Analyze characterization as delineated through a character's thoughts, words, speech patterns, and actions; the narrator's description; and the thoughts, words, and actions of other characters.

Background: For centuries, European monarchs ruled with absolute power. They claimed their authority came from God. This was called the divine right of kings. Then, in 1689, England adopted the Bill of Rights. It limited the power of the monarch. But other countries in Europe still had rulers with absolute power.

In the mid-1700s, new ideas about government began sweeping through Europe. As you read the following story, imagine that you are hearing a conversation about life at this time. It was a time, called the Enlightenment, when old ways were questioned but new ways were untried. And sometimes supporting new ideas was dangerous.

The Social Contract by Jean Jacques Rousseau ▶

DU CONTRAT
SOCIAL;
OU
PRINCIPES
DU DROIT
POLITIQUE.
Par J. J. ROUSSEAU, Citoyen
de Geneve.

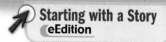

André is a university student in France in 1762. He is sitting in a coffeehouse in Paris, talking to a friend. A strong, rich smell of coffee and a buzz of political conversation reach him from nearby tables. André and his friend Louis begin talking about a new book called *The Social Contract*. It was written by the philosopher Jean Jacques Rousseau (roo•SOH).

Louis attends a Catholic university. He says, "Do you believe it! This Rousseau is challenging the idea that kings have a God-given right to rule. Can you imagine a government in which the king's power is questioned? Can you imagine France without Louis XV?"

Sunlight streams through the coffeehouse windows, and André feels its warmth on his back. "But really, it's an interesting idea," André replies. "Don't you think people have the right to freedom? And if they do, shouldn't that right be the same for all people, rich and poor? Why shouldn't the people have power to choose a government that protects their rights?"

Louis seems impatient. "Well, even if I agreed, how exactly would that happen? You can't just ask the king to stop being king, you know. The nobility won't give up their titles just because Rousseau thinks they should. Are you saying the people should risk their lives to overthrow the king and the nobility?"

Both suddenly look around. They have heard that the coffeehouse has royal spies. The spies hope to catch people who threaten the government and to throw them in jail. André stirs his coffee quietly. He wonders if a political storm is brewing in France. But he is afraid to say more now.

How might these new ideas change the way the French want to be governed?

Reading & Writing

1. **READING: Characterization** What character traits does André show that might represent the spirit of the Enlightenment?

2. **WRITING: Persuasion** Imagine that you have grown up in France in the mid-1700s, governed by an absolute monarchy. The only society you have known is one of unequals—noble and commoner, rich and poor. Write a paragraph explaining how you think you might like to be governed now that you have learned of Rousseau's ideas.

CALIFORNIA STANDARDS Writing 2.4
Write persuasive compositions.

MAIN IDEAS

1 **Culture** The Enlightenment arose from the belief that reason could help people understand their social and political world.

2 **Culture** European philosophers used reason to criticize social and political institutions.

3 **Culture** Women used reason to argue in favor of equal rights and helped spread Enlightenment ideas.

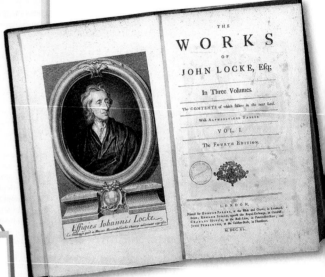

▲ **John Locke** John Locke's many writings influenced Enlightenment thinkers in Europe, as well as the authors of the Declaration of Independence in America.

TAKING NOTES

Reading Skill: Finding Main Ideas

As you read each section of this lesson, look for essential information about the main ideas. Record the information in a cluster diagram like the one shown below.

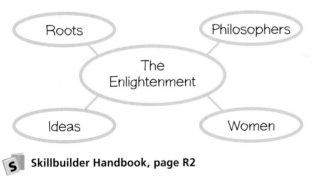

Roots

Philosophers

The Enlightenment

Ideas

Women

S **Skillbuilder Handbook, page R2**

CALIFORNIA STANDARDS

7.11.4 Explain how the main ideas of the Enlightenment can be traced back to such movements as the Renaissance, the Reformation, and the Scientific Revolution and to the Greeks, Romans, and Christianity.

7.11.5 Describe how democratic thought and institutions were influenced by Enlightenment thinkers (e.g., John Locke, Charles-Louis Montesquieu, American founders).

HI 2 Students understand and distinguish cause, effect, sequence, and correlation in historical events, including the long- and short-term causal relations.

The Enlightenment

▶ **TERMS & NAMES**
Enlightenment
natural rights
philosophe
salon

Build on What You Know Have you ever questioned other people's ideas or beliefs? Well, that's what scientists did during the Scientific Revolution. And that's what philosophers would do during the period known as the Enlightenment.

Beginnings of the Enlightenment

1 ESSENTIAL QUESTION Why did the Enlightenment begin?

Scientists found new truths about nature by experimenting and using reason. So philosophers began using reason to seek truths about human nature. Because they wanted to enlighten, or shine a light on, this new way of finding out about the world came to be called the **Enlightenment**. The period also is known as the Age of Reason. The Enlightenment gained so much force in the mid-1700s that it destroyed old beliefs and led to lasting changes in society and government.

Roots of the Enlightenment The respect for reason can be traced back to the ancient Greeks and Romans. Scholars in these classical cultures gained knowledge through observation, logic, and reasoning. They also believed in the worth of the individual.

As Christianity spread during the Middle Ages, faith became more important than reason. But Christianity did introduce the idea that all people were equal in the eyes of God. Equality became a key feature of Enlightenment thought.

Scholars rediscovered the writings of Greece and Rome during the Renaissance. Once again, a person's ability to reason and the importance of the individual were valued. Later, the Reformation appeared to approve the right of an individual to challenge the authority of the Catholic Church to put itself between God and a believer.

Connect to Today

Oxford University
Oxford University, in England, was attended by Enlightenment thinker John Locke in the 1600s. ▼

John Locke (1632–1704)

John Locke's questioning ways began early. "From the time that I knew anything," Locke wrote, "I found myself in a storm." At Oxford University, Locke did not accept the opinions of authorities. He wanted to draw his own conclusions based on his experience and reasoning.

Locke later became an aide to an important government official. He met many men active in public life. He often invited them to debate science or religion. These debates may have led Locke to propose one of the Enlightenment's most revolutionary ideas. He said that humans were not born with basic ideas, as was thought, but learned by experience.

John Locke The English philosopher John Locke set the stage for much of the Enlightenment debate in the late 1600s. Locke did not oppose monarchies. But in his writings, he disagreed with the divine right of kings—the claim that they ruled by the authority of God.

Locke wrote that the power of government came from people, not from God or from a ruler. He believed that people gave their consent to be governed. In return, the government was bound to protect what he called the people's **natural rights**. People were born, Locke said, with the rights to life, liberty, and property. He argued that people had a right to revolt if a ruler failed to protect these rights.

REVIEW What was the Enlightenment, and what were its roots?

European Philosophers

2 ESSENTIAL QUESTION Why did European philosophers use reason to criticize social and political institutions?

Thinkers known as **philosophes** (FIHL•uh•SAHF) which is French for philosophers, began applying the scientific method to social problems. They believed that reason could solve every problem and that society could progress. They challenged old beliefs about power. Both the Church and the absolute monarchs felt threatened. They tried to silence the philosophes. But the philosophes' ideas could not be contained.

Voltaire One of the most brilliant French philosophes was François–Marie Arouet. He was better known as Voltaire (vohl•TAIR), the name he used when writing. Voltaire wrote more than 70 books. In them, he spoke out against religious intolerance and against superstition in the Church. Voltaire was jailed at times for his writings and was later forced to live outside France. Still, he would not give up his ideas. He called for freedom of speech and insisted that each person had a right to liberty.

Montesquieu The Baron de Montesquieu (MAHN•tuh•SKYOO) was another widely read philosophe. Like Locke, he believed liberty was a natural right. Unlike Locke, he opposed absolute monarchs.

Montesquieu also feared that a government could become too powerful. To prevent this, he thought government should be divided into three separate branches. One branch would make the laws. Another would enforce them. A third branch would interpret them. In this way, each branch would keep the others in check. His ideas about the separation of powers became part of the U.S. Constitution.

Rousseau Another philosophe was Jean Jacques Rousseau. In his book *The Social Contract*, he argued that democracy was the best form of government. He stated that people should create governments that would both defend individual rights and protect the good of the whole. He thought people should decide by their votes how they were to be governed. Rousseau opposed absolute monarchs. He also opposed titles of nobility, because he believed that all people were created equal. In time, his ideas stirred people to action—even to revolt.

REVIEW What were some of the important ideas of the philosophes?

Ideas of Enlightenment

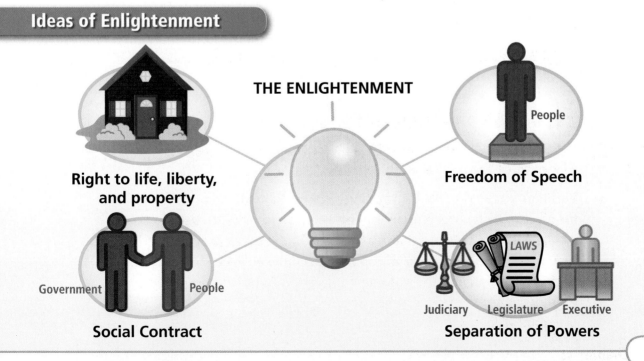

THE ENLIGHTENMENT

Right to life, liberty, and property

Freedom of Speech

People

Government — People

Social Contract

Judiciary — Legislature — Executive

Separation of Powers

LAWS

Women and the Enlightenment

3 ESSENTIAL QUESTION How did women use reason to argue for equal rights?

The philosophes strongly supported the equality of men. But most held traditional views about women. In fact, Rousseau wrote that "woman was specifically made to please man." Some women pursued Enlightenment ideas without challenging the men's traditional views. But other women took up the cause of women's rights.

Women and Salons Some wealthy and talented women in France hosted social gatherings called **salons**. The era's best thinkers and artists participated in the salons. There, men and women discussed and exchanged ideas on an equal basis. For the women present, the salons provided an education that was not available to them anywhere else.

Marie Thérèse Rodet Geoffrin (zhaw•FRAN) was one of the most admired salon hostesses. She knew how to draw out her guests' best ideas. Voltaire and Montesquieu attended her salons. So did leading painters, musicians, playwrights, and scientists. Most guests were of the nobility, but some were not. Foreign visitors were welcome too, for the ideas they brought.

Often the discussions were later written up and published in newspapers as letters to the general public. In this way, many Enlightenment ideas spread beyond the salons.

Education for Women Most women who worked for women's rights focused on social issues, especially education. In 1694, the English writer Mary Astell criticized the lack of educational opportunities for women. In America, Judith Sargent Murray wrote

Salons Spread Ideas Madame Geoffrin *(front row, third from right)* hosted Enlightenment thinkers in her Paris home in the mid-1700s. ▼

in 1784 that women who were deprived of education thought poorly of themselves.

In 1792, Mary Wollstonecraft published *A Vindication of the Rights of Woman.* In this thoughtful essay, she argued that well-educated women would help create enlightened families. She stated that public life would be strengthened by having enlightened families. But few people at the time took her views or those of her predecessors seriously.

REVIEW How did women reformers try to improve women's status?

Lesson Summary

- Enlightenment thinkers believed that human reason could lead to an understanding of all aspects of life.
- Philosophes and other thinkers believed that people had natural rights to life, liberty, and property.
- Women used reason to argue for equal rights and help spread Enlightenment ideas by hosting salons.

Why It Matters Now . . .

The belief that reason is the key that leads humans to understand their social and political world continues to influence thinking today.

▲ **Mary Wollstonecraft** Wollstonecraft had little formal education but taught herself at home by studying books.

---

1 Lesson Review

Homework Helper ClassZone.com

Terms & Names

1. Explain the importance of

Enlightenment	philosophe
natural rights	salon

Using Your Notes

Finding Main Ideas Use your completed diagram to answer the following question:

2. What idea of the Enlightenment do you consider the most important? Why? (7.11.5)

Main Ideas

3. What beliefs regarding reason gave rise to the Enlightenment? (7.11.4)

4. What influence did the philosophes have on the ideas of democracy? (7.11.5)

5. How did women participate in the Enlightenment? (HI 2)

Critical Thinking

6. **Evaluating Information** What was the strongest influence on the Enlightenment? Explain your answer. (HI 2)

7. **Comparing and Contrasting** How were the ideas of Locke, Montesquieu, and Rousseau similar? How were they different? (7.11.5)

Activity

Creating a Poster Select an idea from each Enlightenment philosopher. Turn each into a phrase that could be written on a poster. (7.11.5)

Connect to Today

Extend Lesson 1

Democracy for Women

Purpose: To learn more about the continuing struggle, begun in the Enlightenment, to extend democratic rights to women

Early women reformers wanted change. They demanded that the fundamental human rights called for by Enlightenment thinkers not be limited just to men. In 1791, Olympe De Gouges, a French writer, declared, "Woman is born free and lives equal to man in her rights." Since the Enlightenment, women have been calling for and fighting for equal political, economic, and social rights.

CALIFORNIA STANDARDS

7.11.5 Describe how democratic thought and institutions were influenced by Enlightenment thinkers (e.g., John Locke, Charles-Louis Montesquieu, American founders).

Political Rights

▶ **Past** Early on, women sought the democratic right to express themselves politically and to be heard by those who governed them. In 1789, women who worked in the markets of Paris marched on the palace of King Louis XVI to protest the high cost of bread.

◀ **Present** Today, almost all women can vote. But the struggle for women to win the right to vote, took more than 200 years. In 1994, women in South Africa stood for hours alongside men to cast their ballots in the first all-race election in that country.

Economic Rights

▶ **Past** In the 1700s, most women made clothing, took care of children, and raised crops for their families' food. They received no pay for this work. It was a contribution to the family income.

▶ **Present** Women make up 40 percent of the world's labor force and about 45 percent of that in the United States. But opportunities for women are not the same everywhere. Women are more likely to be managers and professionals in developed countries. However, in all parts of the world, most women still earn less than men.

Educational Rights

▶ **Past** For much of history, girls were denied formal education. Boys were taught skills that would enable them to make a living; girls were trained to be mothers and housekeepers. During the Enlightenment, women reformers saw education as a way to gain equality.

▼ **Present** Women make up the majority of students in colleges and graduate schools in the United States. Educational opportunities for females, though—like those for employment—are not the same everywhere in the world.

Activities

1. **TALK ABOUT IT** What are some other rights that women are seeking to expand?

2. **WRITE ABOUT IT** What do you think is the most important right women must have to gain full equality? Write a paragraph explaining your choice. (Writing 2.4)

Lesson 2

▶ MAIN IDEAS

1 **Government** Inspired by the ideas of the Enlightenment, some European monarchs undertook important reforms.

2 **Culture** Enlightenment ideas helped spark the American Revolution.

3 **Government** Enlightenment ideas continued to influence the United States and the world.

▲ **Philosophers of Democracy** This 18th-century box lid honors three important political thinkers— Voltaire, John Locke, and Benjamin Franklin.

▶ TAKING NOTES

Reading Skill: Summarizing

To summarize is to restate a passage in fewer words. After you read Lesson 2, write a sentence or two summarizing each of the three main sections. Use a chart like the one below to record your sentences.

Democratic Ideas Develop

 Skillbuilder Handbook, page R3

CALIFORNIA STANDARDS

7.11.5 Describe how democratic thought and institutions were influenced by Enlightenment thinkers (e.g., John Locke, Charles-Louis Montesquieu, American founders).

7.11.6 Discuss how the principles in the Magna Carta were embodied in such documents as the English Bill of Rights and the American Declaration of Independence.

HI 3 Students explain the sources of historical continuity and how the combination of ideas and events explains the emergence of new patterns.

Democratic Ideas Develop

▶ **TERMS & NAMES**

enlightened despot

Declaration of Independence

Declaration of the Rights of Man and of the Citizen

Build on What You Know As you have read, Enlightenment ideas were sweeping Europe. Some of the most dramatic changes in history would be required to put these ideas into practice.

Enlightened Monarchs Attempt Reforms

1 ESSENTIAL QUESTION Why did some European monarchs undertake important reforms?

A few European monarchs paid close attention to the political ideas of Enlightenment thinkers. They became **enlightened despots**. A despot is a ruler who has absolute power; enlightened despots wanted to use their power in a just and enlightened way. Frederick II of Prussia, Joseph II of Austria, and Catherine the Great of Russia were the boldest of these rulers.

Frederick II of Prussia Frederick II is also known as Frederick the Great. He ruled Prussia (what is now Poland and northern Germany) with absolute power from 1740 until 1786. But Frederick pleased Enlightenment thinkers when he called himself "the first servant of the state" and made several reforms.

Frederick broadened religious toleration, made the legal system more just, and allowed greater freedom of the press. He also helped improve education and outlawed torture. But Frederick did not see people as equals. He made no reforms to aid serfs, who were the lowest class in feudal society. Also, while he welcomed Catholics into his Protestant kingdom, he did not help Jews, who were oppressed in most German states.

Connect to Today

Frederick's Palace Sansoucci Palace, completed in 1747 and located in Potsdam, was Frederick's summer home. ▼

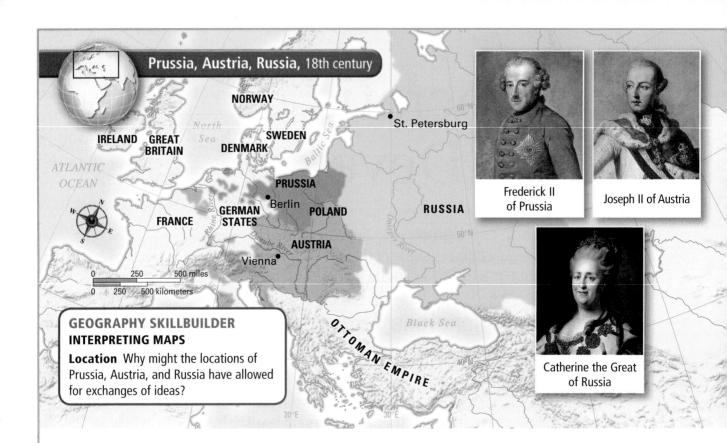

Prussia, Austria, Russia, 18th century

NORWAY

St. Petersburg

IRELAND GREAT
BRITAIN SWEDEN
DENMARK

*North
Sea*

Baltic Sea

ATLANTIC
OCEAN

PRUSSIA
Berlin

GERMAN
FRANCE STATES POLAND

RUSSIA

Rhine River

Dnieper River

Danube River

AUSTRIA

Vienna

60°N

50°N

Black Sea

OTTOMAN EMPIRE

40°N

Frederick II
of Prussia

Joseph II of Austria

Catherine the Great
of Russia

0   250   500 miles
0   250   500 kilometers

20°E   30°E

GEOGRAPHY SKILLBUILDER
INTERPRETING MAPS
Location Why might the locations of
Prussia, Austria, and Russia have allowed
for exchanges of ideas?

Joseph II of Austria In contrast to Frederick, Joseph II of Austria
made widespread reforms. These reforms were based on the
principles of equality and freedom. During his reign, from
1780 to 1790, he abolished *serfdom* and allowed freedom of the
press and freedom of worship, even for Jews.

Like Frederick, Joseph outlawed torture and reformed the
justice system. He also abolished the death penalty. No other
enlightened despot made such sweeping and widespread
changes. But many of these changes were opposed by the
nobles and did not last past Joseph's death.

Catherine the Great of Russia Catherine II, or Catherine
the Great, ruled Russia from 1762 to 1796. She too saw herself as
an enlightened ruler. She studied the ideas of the philosophes.
Early in her reign, she set guidelines for governing based
partly on the ideas of Montesquieu. Catherine also encouraged
scientific farming methods and developed Russia's natural resources.
She opened hospitals and schools, including one for girls, and
supported the arts.

Catherine also had plans to end serfdom. However, when a serf revolt
threatened her rule, she crushed the uprising and changed her views. The
revolt convinced Catherine that she needed the support of the nobles to
keep her throne. So she gave the nobles absolute power over the serfs.

Vocabulary Strategy

Serfdom means being
bound to the land
from one generation
to the next. The word
is formed by adding
the **suffix** -*dom*, which
means "the condition
or state of," to the term
serf, a peasant legally
bound to live and work
on a lord's estate. Other
words using -*dom*
include *officialdom*,
dukedom, and *stardom*.

REVIEW How did enlightened despots try to put Enlightenment ideas
into practice?

Democracy in America

2 ESSENTIAL QUESTION How did Enlightenment ideas help spark the American Revolution?

On a stormy day in June 1752, Benjamin Franklin was conducting an experiment on lightning and electricity in Philadelphia. He was jolted by a spark from a brass key attached to his kite's string. In the 1770s, a different kind of spark led to a political jolt whose impact is still felt. Americans revolted against Great Britain and then created a democracy based mainly on Enlightenment ideas.

American Thinkers Many Americans studied the ideas of the Enlightenment. Some, including Benjamin Franklin and Thomas Jefferson, visited Europe. They even exchanged letters with the philosophes. Franklin and Jefferson believed reason was the key to understanding both the natural and the social orders of the world.

Franklin was a creative inventor and scientist, a witty writer, and an experienced publisher and statesman. Jefferson also had wide interests and a firm belief in an individual's ability to reason. He was a scholar, architect, philosopher, inventor, statesman, and educator. He believed that education was the key to freedom of the mind. Jefferson, like Franklin, helped promote freedom of religion.

Colonial leaders, including Jefferson and Franklin, used Enlightenment ideas about political rights and unjust rule to defend their growing opposition to British rule. In the 1770s, tensions mounted between the colonies and Britain.

Signing the Declaration This painting shows the signing on July 4, 1776. Jefferson is second from the right in the group standing at center. ▼

Revolution and the Declaration of Independence Conflict erupted when Great Britain tried to tax the colonies. The colonists felt they should not have to pay taxes unless they were represented in Parliament. They felt the British government was not protecting their rights. And it was not allowing representation of their interests.

On July 4, 1776, the colonies declared independence from Britain. Jefferson was the principal author of the **Declaration of Independence**. He used his understanding of Enlightenment ideas and his great gifts as a writer to explain the colonies' decision to choose independence.

The declaration begins with an echo of Locke's belief in natural law and human rights when it states that "all men are created equal." It also reflects Locke's thinking when it says that people have the right to form a new government if the old one fails to protect their rights. In addition, the declaration includes a list of violations of the colonists' rights by the British king. In this way, the declaration builds on the democratic principles of the Magna Carta, the first document to limit the power of the sovereign. (See Chapter 10.)

Primary Source Handbook

See the excerpt from the Declaration of Independence, page R59.

REVIEW How does the Declaration of Independence reflect Enlightenment ideas?

Primary Source

Background: The Declaration of Independence was mainly the work of one person—Thomas Jefferson. He was familiar with Enlightenment ideas and used them in the document. It was adopted on July 4, 1776.

from the Declaration of Independence

We hold these truths to be self-evident, that all men are created equal, that they are endowed[1] by their Creator with certain unalienable[2] Rights, that among these are Life, Liberty and the pursuit of Happiness; that, to secure these rights, Governments are instituted among Men, deriving their just powers from the consent of the governed; that whenever any Form of Government becomes destructive of these ends, it is the Right of the People to alter or to abolish it, and to institute new Government.

---

1. **endowed:** provided.
2. **unalienable:** unable to be taken away.

DOCUMENT–BASED QUESTION
How does this passage reflect the ideas of John Locke?

Spread of Democratic Principles

3 ESSENTIAL QUESTION How did Enlightenment ideas continue to influence the United States and the world?

In 1783, the Americans were the victors in the war that followed their declaration of independence. Soon, they would again draw upon Enlightenment ideas. This time, they would create a lasting government that would guarantee the rights and liberties for which the American Revolution was fought. However, women and African Americans would fight for years to have these rights apply to them.

Creating the U.S. Constitution The first government of the United States operated under the Articles of Confederation. But the articles were too weak. In 1787, a convention was called to strengthen the federal government. Some of the nation's best political thinkers gathered in Philadelphia. They included Franklin, George Washington, and James Madison. They debated for months in sweltering summer heat. Finally, they agreed on the U.S. Constitution. Enlightenment ideas were the basis of many of the Constitution's principles.

In 1791, a bill of rights was added. It was modeled after the English Bill of Rights of 1689, which guaranteed basic freedoms to English citizens. The U.S. Bill of Rights gave protection to rights such as freedom of speech, religion, and the press. (See chart below.)

The success of the American Revolution and its ideas gave hope to people elsewhere that a better world was possible. It led to other revolutions and to the creation of other democratic governments.

P Primary Source Handbook
See the excerpt from the English Bill of Rights, page R58.

Development of Democratic Ideas					
Rights	Magna Carta (1215)	English Bill of Rights (1689)	Declaration of Independence (1776)	*Declaration of the Rights of Man . . .* (1789)	U.S. Constitution with the Bill of Rights (1791)
Religious freedom	–	–	–	✔	✔
Natural rights	–	–	✔	✔	–
Free speech	–	–	✔	✔	✔
Right to petition government	–	✔	✔	✔	✔
Trial by jury	✔	✔	✔	✔	✔
No taxation without representation	✔	✔	✔	✔	✔
Protection of the law	✔	✔	✔	✔	✔

The French Revolution In 1789, the French rebelled against the oppressive rule of Louis XVI. They created a revolutionary government. It adopted the ***Declaration of the Rights of Man and of the Citizen***. This document laid out the rights to "liberty, property, security, and resistance to oppression." These rights, like those in the U.S. Constitution, would not be given to women without many years of struggle. Still, the democratic ideas that inspired the American and French revolutions spread widely in the decades that followed.

REVIEW In what ways did the U.S. government use Enlightenment ideas?

Lesson Summary

- Enlightened despots in Europe tried to make reforms without giving up power.
- Americans used Enlightenment ideas to justify their break from Britain.
- The U.S. government is built on Enlightenment ideas and is a model for other democracies.

Inkwell from Independence Hall in Philadelphia ▼

Why It Matters Now . . .

Even today, Enlightenment ideals influence people around the world who are trying to gain and to protect individual rights and freedoms.

---

2 Lesson Review

Homework Helper
ClassZone.com

Terms & Names

1. Explain the importance of

enlightened despot
Declaration of Independence
Declaration of the Rights of Man and of the Citizen

Using Your Notes

Summarizing Use your completed chart to answer the following question:

2. What was the most important legacy of Enlightenment ideas? Explain. (7.11.5)

> Democratic Ideas Develop

Main Ideas

3. How were Prussia, Austria, and Russia affected by Enlightenment thinkers? (7.11.5)

4. How did the Enlightenment thinkers in America influence the shape of modern democracies? (7.11.5)

5. How did the United States' experiment in government affect the spread of democracy? (HI 3)

Critical Thinking

6. Drawing Conclusions Why might it have been easier for Americans than for the French to be the first to put the Enlightenment ideas into action? (7.11.5)

7. Understanding Effects What was the effect of the Magna Carta on the English Bill of Rights and the Declaration of Independence? (7.11.6)

Activity **Internet Activity** Use the Internet to find out more about a political leader mentioned in this lesson. Then write a brief biography of that person. (7.11.5)
INTERNET KEYWORD *leader's name*

Design a Museum Exhibit

Goal: To design a museum exhibit with the title "Democracy Hall of Fame"

> **Materials & Supplies**
> * poster board
> * scissors
> * construction paper
> * markers
>
> **Optional:** Internet research on the Enlightenment

Prepare

1 Consider that the exhibit should highlight the ideas, documents, persons, and events of the Enlightenment that were important in the spread of democratic ideas during the 1600s and 1700s.

2 Reread the information in this chapter on the development and spread of democratic ideas.

3 Use the Internet or books to research the spread of Enlightenment ideas about democracy.

▲ Thomas Jefferson

Do the Activity

1 Work with a small group of classmates.

2 Select the ideas, documents, persons, and events that you would like to highlight, such as the philosophes, the English Bill of Rights, the enlightened despots, and the American Revolution.

3 Make a rough sketch of the exhibit layout.

4 Write a one-page description of the exhibit.

Follow-Up

How well does the exhibit show how democratic ideas and institutions were influenced by Enlightenment thinking?

Extension

Making a Presentation Show your exhibit to the class. Read your description of the elements of democracy that you highlighted in the exhibit.

CALIFORNIA STANDARDS

7.11.5 Describe how democratic thought and institutions were influenced by Enlightenment thinkers (e.g., John Locke, Charles-Louis Montesquieu, American founders).

Reader's THEATER

Adopting a *Bill of Rights*

Background: In the late 1600s, King James II offended many of his subjects by violating English law. Some members of Parliament then asked James's daughter Mary and her husband, William of Orange of the Netherlands, to overthrow James and become king and queen. When they arrived in England, James fled.

Parliament then drew up a declaration of rights in 1689 to limit the monarch's power. It contained ideas first mentioned in the Magna Carta in 1215 and later developed during the Enlightenment. These ideas about people's rights also influenced the American Declaration of Independence and the U.S. Bill of Rights.

CALIFORNIA STANDARDS
7.11.6 Discuss how the principles in the Magna Carta were embodied in such documents as the English Bill of Rights and the American Declaration of Independence.

Cast of Characters

Narrator

Robert: parliamentary page

Edmund: parliamentary page

John Williamson: member of Parliament

Henry Russell: member of Parliament

Richard Ashby: member of Parliament

Speaker of Parliament

Queen Mary: daughter of James II

King William: husband of Mary

Narrator: In early 1689, Parliament met for several weeks to discuss a bill of rights. In a back room of the Parliament building, two 13-year-old pages, Robert and Edmund, sharpen quills for Parliament members to use as pens.

Edmund: This is a long session, that's for sure. It has been going on for well over a week.

Robert: I hear it is very important.

Edmund: Important? That is what they always say. And nothing much comes of it.

Robert: (*seriously*) I think they are trying to decide how to run this country now that King James has fled.

Edmund: And good riddance, I say.

(*Bell tolls.*)

Robert: We must hurry; that bell is for us.

Narrator: Parliament is in session. Members sit in parallel rows of seats. The Speaker sits at the front center of the room. Each member indicates to the Speaker when he wants to talk by half standing. The Speaker then calls the person's name, giving him permission to speak. Robert and Edmund stand off to the side in case they are needed to carry messages to the members of Parliament.

Speaker: John Williamson.

Williamson: We have decided that the monarch's claim to have the power to suspend laws or carry out laws without our consent is illegal. But I suggest that the right to raise money is also important. Whoever controls that right controls the means to gain power.

Speaker: Richard Ashby.

Ashby: Yes, indeed, and I would also mention that the power to raise money, when not controlled, often leads to abuses and places burdens on the people. So I propose that the raising of money by the crown without our permission be illegal.

Speaker: Henry Russell.

Russell: Wait, are we not missing an obvious point? The power of the monarch can be limited only if we limit the monarch's use of an army. I believe that the raising or keeping of a standing army in time of peace ought to be against the law. Unless, of course, Parliament gives its approval.

▼ King James II

551

Robert: (*frowning*) I think a standing army is an army that is permanent, one that is kept during both peace and war. Parliament, you see, does not want monarchs to have their own army.

Edmund: Why not?

Robert: They want to limit the monarchs' power. If the royals do not have an army at their beck and call, they cannot force people to do their will. So they do not get an army unless Parliament agrees to it.

Edmund: But what about this suspending of laws? Do you suppose they are actually going to hang pieces of parchment written with laws from buildings? How are they going to do it? With wires? I guess they want to put them up where everybody can see them. But it's just not practical.

Robert: (*shaking his head*) By "suspending," I think they mean stopping the laws from being enforced. Remember, King James used to do this a lot. Parliament wants to prevent monarchs from stopping the enforcement of laws whenever they like. According to this declaration, monarchs cannot even raise money or taxes without Parliament's say-so. This helps to keep monarchs from taking too much money from common folks like us.

Edmund: Well, if you ask me, I think the gentlemen in Parliament have lost track of their senses.

Robert: Why is that?

Edmund: (*with conviction*) What king or queen is going to put up with this? Why, for hundreds of years the royals have been doing pretty much what they want. And now, all of a sudden, they are going to give up all that power?

(*shouts of agreement and disagreement from members*)

Speaker: Order, order, gentlemen.

Narrator: The day's session is over. As they sweep the floor Edmund and Robert discuss what they heard.

Edmund: This was the strangest meeting I have seen in all my days here. I still cannot make heads or tails of it.

Robert: What do you mean?

Edmund: (*puzzled but with some humor*) Will you tell me what's wrong with keeping a standing army? I'd like to see an army do their job sitting down.

Robert: Well, the gentlemen of Parliament must think William and Mary will accept it.

Edmund: (*smugly*) If they do, then I am the king of England.

Narrator: On April 11, 1689, King William and Queen Mary attend a ceremony held at Westminster Abbey. Edmund and Robert stand off to the side. An official reads the Declaration of Rights to William and Mary, who are seated. Then he asks if they agree to it. This public ceremony is being held only to make official what the monarchs have already agreed to in private. William and Mary confer briefly.

Mary: William, I think the time has come.

William: Yes, it has. (*turning to face officials from Parliament*) We thankfully accept what you have offered us.

Robert: (*whispering to Edmund*) Ha, what do you have to say to that, "your highness?"

Edmund: (*with curiosity*) I wonder what's next?

Narrator: Several months later, Parliament included this declaration in a bill of rights that became the foundation of British law.

◀ **King William and Queen Mary**

Activities

1. **TALK ABOUT IT** What role did the Magna Carta play in efforts by Parliament in 1689 to limit the monarch's power in the English Bill of Rights?

2. **WRITE ABOUT IT** Write a scene in which William and Mary discuss the pros and cons of accepting the Declaration of Rights. (Writing 2.1)

VISUAL SUMMARY

The Enlightenment and the Age of Reason

The Enlightenment (7.11.4)

- People apply the scientific approach to all aspects of society.
- Philosophes propose the use of reason to discover truths.
- Thinkers suggest new ideas about individual rights and the role of government.

Spread of Enlightenment Ideas (7.11.5)

- Enlightenment ideas sweep across Europe.
- Salons help spread Enlightenment thinking.
- Enlightenment thought inspires women to call for reforms.
- Democratic ideas spread to colonial America.

Democratic Ideas in Action (7.11.6)

- Enlightened despots attempt reforms.
- Americans declare independence and create a democracy based on Enlightenment ideas.
- Democratic ideas in the English Bill of Rights become a model for the U.S. Bill of Rights.
- *Declaration of the Rights of Man and of the Citizen* is adopted during the French Revolution.

TERMS & NAMES

For each item below, write a sentence that explains the connections between the given term and the word **philosophes**. Be sure both terms appear in your sentence.

1. **Enlightenment**
2. **natural rights**
3. **salon**
4. **enlightened despot**

MAIN IDEAS

The Enlightenment (pages 534–541)

5. What were the main ideas of the Enlightenment? (7.11.4)
6. What are the natural rights with which people are born, according to John Locke? (7.11.5)
7. How did Locke, Montesquieu, and Rousseau influence the course of democracy? (7.11.5)

Democratic Ideas Develop (pages 542–553)

8. How did enlightened despots try to put the philosophes' ideas into practice? (7.11.5)
9. What influence did the Enlightenment have on the American Revolution? (HI 2)
10. What principles in the Magna Carta were included in the Declaration of Independence? (7.11.6)

CRITICAL THINKING Big Ideas: Government

11. **MAKING GENERALIZATIONS** How was the role of the individual viewed in Christianity? What ideas about that role developed during the Renaissance and the Reformation? (7.11.4)
12. **SUMMARIZING** What changes did Enlightenment thinkers want to make to government? (7.11.4)
13. **MAKING INFERENCES** How did the Declaration of Independence and the U.S. Constitution develop from the Magna Carta and Enlightenment ideas? (7.11.6)

ALTERNATIVE ASSESSMENT

1. **WRITING ACTIVITY** Imagine that you were a guest at the salon of Madame Geoffrin. You took part in a discussion of the ideas of Locke and Rousseau. Write a letter thanking her and recording the discussion you had. (7.11.5)

2. **INTERDISCIPLINARY ACTIVITY—LANGUAGE ARTS** In 1732, the English poet Alexander Pope wrote these lines in his *Essay on Man:*

   Know then thyself, presume not
   God to scan;
   The proper study of Mankind is Man.

   Decide whether these words would or would not be a good slogan for the Enlightenment. Then write a paragraph explaining your decision. (Writing 2.2)

3. **STARTING WITH A STORY**

    Review the answer you gave to the question following the story "Challenging Old Ideas." Would you change your answer now that you have read the chapter? Explain. (Writing 2.4)

Technology Activity

4. **WRITING A VIDEO SCRIPT**

   To protect itself from threatening ideas, the French government banned many political writings. Write a scene for a documentary on the French Revolution, showing how the French used coffeehouses to keep up with new ideas.

   - Use the Internet to research French coffeehouses in the 1700s.
   - Compare how people in the 2000s keep up with news, and discuss whether censorship is still a problem.
   - Include a location, narration, and music in the script. (HI 2)

Research Links
ClassZone.com

Reading Charts Use the chart below to answer the questions. (7.11.5)

Enlightenment Ideas in the U.S. Constitution	
Locke A government's power comes from the consent of the people.	• Preamble begins "We the people of the United States" to establish legitimacy • Creates representative government • Limits government powers
Montesquieu Separation of powers	• Federal system of government • Powers divided among three branches • System of checks and balances
Rousseau Direct democracy	• Public election of president and Congress
Voltaire Free speech, religious toleration	• Bill of Rights providing for freedom of speech and religion

1. **What philosopher's ideas were most responsible for the three branches of the U.S. government?**

   A. Voltaire
   B. Rousseau
   C. Montesquieu
   D. Locke

2. **Which of these Enlightenment ideas refers to individual rights?**

   A. direct democracy
   B. free speech and religious expression
   C. separation of powers
   D. consent of the people

Test Practice
ClassZone.com

Additional Test Practice, pp. S1–S33

Writing About History

Research Reports:
The Roots of Cultural Influence

Writing Model
ClassZone.com

CALIFORNIA STANDARDS
Writing 2.3 Write
research reports.

Purpose: To write a research report on the influence of past cultures on your life

Audience: Your classmates

The year is 1550. A Spaniard sits at his table overlooking his sugar plantation on a Caribbean island. Many cultural influences traveled with this Spaniard when he left Europe for the Americas. For example, he sailed on a ship whose navigation was made possible by centuries of scientific development, tracing back to the Greeks, Chinese, Muslims, and Jews. When he says his prayers at night, he follows a tradition that arose in the Middle East. This Spaniard, like so many people in the world today, has been influenced by a blend of cultures.

▲ A sailor using an astrolabe

Organization & Focus

Your assignment is to write a 500- to 700-word research report explaining how three cultural achievements from the past influence your life. For each achievement, trace how it was developed by the original culture, whether it was changed by other cultures, and how it became part of modern life. Also, explain its importance to you.

Your report should have an introduction that includes a thesis statement telling your main idea, a body of supporting paragraphs to explain and give examples of your main idea, a conclusion that draws meaning from the body, and a bibliography listing your sources.

Choosing a Topic Review this book, looking for cultural achievements that influence life today. The Connect to Today features will be especially helpful. Use the Table of Contents to find them. As you review them, ask yourself which of the featured topics play the biggest role in your life. Choose three, and focus your research on those.

Identifying Purpose and Audience When you see how past events helped shape who you are, you will better understand the importance of history. Your audience is your classmates, and your purpose is to explain to them how modern culture grew out of past achievements.

Research & Technology

Some of the best tools to use in your research are the questions you develop to guide you. There are several different kinds of questions you can ask at different stages of your research. The chart below shows some of these questions, organized by category.

Technology Tip You may want to show the blending of cultural influences in a table. Use the Table menu of your word processor to help you create one.

Getting Started	Looking for Meaning	Finding Supporting Details
• Who? • What? • Where? • Why? • When? • How?	• Why is this important? • Are some things more important than others? Why? • What does this mean? • What is this like or unlike?	• What's a good example? • What information do I need to prove my point? • What background information do I need to know?

The most probing questions are those in the middle column. Simply listing facts makes for a dull report. But when you can use a clearly posed research question to draw your own meaning from the facts, you will have something original and useful to say.

Taking Notes At the top of each sheet of paper or note card, write one of your research questions. Then look for answers in your sources. Record the relevant information about each source for your bibliography.

Outlining and Drafting There are many possible ways to organize your report. Consider discussing the three achievements separately. Decide how to order them, and craft an introduction and a conclusion that link them to a main idea.

Evaluation & Revision

Share your first draft with a reader for feedback. Can your reader tell what you were trying to say? If not, your message is not coming through clearly. If your reader is confused by certain parts of your draft, you should make those parts stronger or clearer.

Self-Check

Does my research report have

☐ supporting details drawn from a variety of sources?

☐ quotation marks to show words I borrowed?

☐ source credits in the proper form?

☐ a bibliography in the proper form?

Publish & Present

Prepare a final copy of your report. If possible, present your report in class. Compare your choices with those of your classmates and discuss the differences.

Reference Section

Skillbuilder Handbook

CONTENTS

1.1 Finding Main Ideas

Learn the Skill

The **main idea** is a statement that summarizes the subject of a speech, an article, a section of a book, or a paragraph. Main ideas can be stated or unstated. The main idea of a paragraph is often stated in the first or last sentence. If it is in the first sentence, it is followed by sentences that support that main idea. If it is in the last sentence, the details build up to the main idea. To find an unstated idea, use the details of the paragraph as clues.

Practice the Skill

The following paragraph examines the bubonic plague that struck parts of Asia, North Africa, and Europe during the 1300s. Use the strategies listed below to help you identify the main idea.

How to Find the Main Idea

Strategy ❶ Identify what you think may be the stated main idea. Check the first and last sentences of the paragraph to see if either could be the stated main idea.

Strategy ❷ Identify details that support the main idea. Some details explain that idea. Others give examples of what is stated in the main idea.

> EFFECT OF THE PLAGUE IN EUROPE
>
> ❶ The bubonic plague had a significant social and economic effect on Europe. ❷ Throughout Europe, the plague created doubts and fears that led to a breakdown in ordinary routines and a loss of order. ❷ In addition, the plague caused a sharp decrease in population. This led to a shortage of labor. As a result, workers could demand higher pay for their labor. Some workers earned as much as five times what they had earned before the plague. ❷ The plague also helped to weaken the power of the Church. Prayers failed to stop the disease, and many priests abandoned their duties.

Make a Chart

Making a chart can help you identify the main idea and details in a passage or paragraph. The chart below identifies the main idea and details in the paragraph you just read.

MAIN IDEA: The plague had a significant social and economic impact on Europe.		
DETAIL: Throughout Europe, the plague created doubts and fears that led to a breakdown in ordinary routines and a loss of order.	DETAIL: The plague caused a sharp decrease in population that resulted in a labor shortage and better wages for workers.	DETAIL: The plague weakened the power of the Church, which could do little to stop the spread of the disease.

Apply the Skill

Turn to Chapter 2, Lesson 2, "Decline and Fall of the Empire." Read "Internal Weaknesses Threaten Rome" and create a chart that identifies the main idea and the supporting details.

1.2 Summarizing

Learn the Skill

When you **summarize,** you restate a paragraph, a passage, or a chapter in fewer words. You include only the main ideas and most important details. It is important to use your own words when summarizing.

Practice the Skill

The passage below describes medical contributions made by doctors in Al-Andalus. Use the strategies listed below to help you summarize the passage.

How to Summarize

Strategy ❶ Look for topic sentences that state the main idea or ideas. These are often at the beginning of a section or paragraph. Briefly restate each main idea in your own words.

Strategy ❷ Include key facts and any names, dates, numbers, amounts, or percentages from the text.

Strategy ❸ Write your summary and review it to see that you have included only the most important details.

> ### DOCTORS IN AL–ANDALUS
>
> ❶ Doctors in Al-Andalus made important contributions to medicine. ❷ Some worked to improve the doctor-patient relationship. They urged doctors to be kind and understanding and encouraged them to accept patients' criticisms and insults without complaint. ❷ Other doctors made breakthroughs in the treatment of certain diseases. The greatest doctor of the time was al-Zahrawi. He was interested in all aspects of medicine. ❷ In the late 900s, al-Zahrawi published a medical encyclopedia that covered everything from surgery to the care of teeth.

Write a Summary

You should be able to write your summary in a short paragraph. The paragraph below summarizes the passage you just read.

> ❸ Doctors in Al-Andalus made important contributions to medicine. Some worked to improve the doctor-patient relationship. Others made advances in the treatment of diseases. The greatest doctor of the time was al-Zahrawi. In the late 900s, he published a medical encyclopedia.

Apply the Skill

Turn to Chapter 13, Lesson 3, "The Renaissance Spreads." Read "Advances in Science and Technology" and write a paragraph summarizing the information.

1.3 Comparing and Contrasting

Learn the Skill

Comparing means looking at the similarities and differences among two or more things. **Contrasting** means examining only the differences among them. Historians compare and contrast events, personalities, behaviors, beliefs, and situations in order to understand them.

Practice the Skill

The following passage describes Roman Catholicism and Eastern Orthodoxy. Use the strategies below to help you compare and contrast these two churches.

How to Compare and Contrast

Strategy 1 Look for two subjects that can be compared and contrasted. This passage compares Roman Catholicism and Eastern Orthodoxy, two Christian churches that have many similarities and differences.

Strategy 2 To find similarities, look for clue words indicating that two things are alike. Clue words include *both*, *together*, and *similarly*.

Strategy 3 To contrast, look for clue words that show how two things differ. Clue words include *however*, *but*, *on the other hand*, and *even so*.

ROMAN CATHOLICISM AND ORTHODOXY

1 In 1054, Christianity split into two branches—the Roman Catholic Church in the West and the Orthodox Church in the East. **2** *Both* churches continued to embrace many of the same principles of Christianity. They based their faiths on the gospel of Jesus and the Bible. The Roman Catholic Church used sacraments such as baptism. **2** *Similarly*, the Orthodox Church also used sacraments. In addition, **2** both churches sought to convert people.

However, each church established its own set of structures and beliefs that set it apart. Roman Catholic services were held in Latin. **3** *On the other hand*, Orthodox services were held in Greek or local languages. In the Catholic Church, the pope claimed authority over all kings and emperors. **3** Under Eastern Orthodoxy, *however*, the emperor ruled over the patriarch, the leader of the Orthodox Church.

Make a Venn Diagram

Making a Venn diagram will help you identify similarities and differences between two things. In the overlapping area, list shared characteristics. In the separate ovals, list characteristics that the two subjects do not share. This Venn diagram is for the passage above.

ROMAN CATHOLICISM
• Services held in Latin.
• Pope claimed authority over rulers.

BOTH
• Converts sought.
• Faith based on the gospel of Jesus and the Bible.
• Sacraments used.

EASTERN ORTHODOXY
• Services held in Greek, other languages.
• Ruler claimed authority over patriarch.

Apply the Skill

Turn to Chapter 3, Lesson 2, "Islam and Muhammad." Read "Connections to Judaism and Christianity." Then make a Venn diagram showing similarities and differences between Islam and Christianity.

1.4 Making Inferences

Learn the Skill

Inferences are ideas that the author has not directly stated. **Making inferences** involves reading between the lines to interpret the information you read. You can make inferences by studying what is stated and using your common sense and previous knowledge.

Practice the Skill

This passage examines the cities of the Maya. Use the strategies below to help you make inferences from the passage.

How to Make Inferences

Strategy ❶ Read to find statements of fact. Knowing the facts will help you make inferences.

Strategy ❷ Use your knowledge, logic, and common sense to make inferences that are based on facts. Ask yourself, "What does the author want me to understand?" For example, from the presence of temples in Mayan cities, you can make the inference that religion was important to the Maya.

> ### MAYAN CITIES
>
> The Maya built more than 40 cities. ❶ Each Mayan city contained pyramids with temples on top of them. Many of the cities also had steles. Steles were large stone monuments. ❶ On these monuments, the Maya carved glyphs that represented important dates and great events. ❶ Mayan cities also contained palaces, plazas, and ball courts. Larger Mayan cities included Copán, Tikal, Palenque, Bonampak, and Chichén Itzá. ❶ A different king governed each Mayan city and the surrounding areas. Sometimes cities fought each other.

Make a Chart

Making a chart will help you organize information and make logical inferences. The chart below organizes information from the passage you just read.

❶ STATED FACTS	❷ INFERENCES
Each Mayan city contained pyramids with temples on top of them.	Religion was important to the Maya.
On these monuments, the Maya carved glyphs that represented important dates and great events.	The Maya believed that history was important.
Mayan cities also contained palaces, plazas, and ball courts.	The Maya were skilled engineers and architects.

Apply the Skill

Turn to Chapter 6, Lesson 2, "Empires Built on Gold and Trade." Read "Rise of the Shona Civilization" and use a chart like the one above to make inferences about the Shona.

1.5 Categorizing

Learn the Skill

To **categorize** is to sort people, objects, ideas, or other information into groups, called categories. Historians categorize information to help them identify and understand patterns in historical events.

Practice the Skill

The following passage discusses the lasting contribution of Roman civilization. Use the strategies listed below to help you categorize information in a passage.

How to Categorize

Strategy ① First, decide what the passage is about and how that information can be sorted into categories. For example, look at the different areas to which Romans made contributions.

Strategy ② Then find out what the categories will be. To determine those areas in which Romans made lasting contributions, look for clue words such as *art, engineering,* and *laws.*

Strategy ③ Once you have chosen the categories, sort information into them. For example, what aspects of Roman engineering remain influential? How did Roman law influence later societies?

> ROME'S LEGACY
>
> ① The Romans made lasting contributions to many areas of society. ② In the area of *art*, the Romans popularized an earlier type of floor art called mosaic. A mosaic is a picture made out of many small, colored tiles or pieces of glass. Examples of mosaics can still be found in churches and government buildings around the world. ② Roman *engineering* styles are also evident today. Countless modern structures make use of styles the Romans pioneered with arches, domes, and vaults. Highway bridges are often built on arches, while the U.S. Capitol consists of a large dome and numerous vault structures. ② One of Rome's most lasting contributions was its system of *laws*. These laws promoted such modern-day principles as equal treatment under the law and the presumption of innocence for those accused of crimes.

Make a Chart

Making a chart can help you categorize information. You should have as many columns as you have categories. The chart below shows how the information from the passage you just read can be categorized.

① LASTING CONTRIBUTIONS OF ROMAN CIVILIZATION		
② Art	Engineering	Law
③ • popularizing of mosaic style	• use of domes, arches, vaults	• principles of equal treatment before the law • innocent until proven guilty

Apply the Skill

Turn to Chapter 15, Lesson 1. Read "New Scientific Theories." Then make a chart like the one above to categorize information about the new scientific theories.

Skillbuilder Handbook

1.6 Making Decisions

Learn the Skill

Making decisions involves choosing between two or more options. Decisions usually have consequences, or results, and sometimes may lead to new problems. By understanding historical decisions, you can learn to improve your own decision-making skills.

Practice the Skill

The passage below explains the decision Henry IV faced when Pope Gregory VII banned lay investiture. Use the strategies below to analyze his decision.

How to Make Decisions

Strategy 1 Identify a decision that needs to be made. Think about what factors make the decision difficult.

Strategy 2 Identify possible consequences of the decision. Remember that there can be more than one consequence to a decision.

Strategy 3 Identify the decision that was made.

Strategy 4 Identify actual consequences that resulted from the decision.

> ### THE POPE'S BAN ON LAY INVESTITURE
>
> Henry IV, the ruler of the Holy Roman Empire, had built his political power by appointing Church officials himself. This practice was called lay investiture. In 1075, Pope Gregory VII banned lay investiture. **1** Henry had to decide how to respond to the pope's ban. **2** If Henry accepted the ban, his political power would be limited. **2** If Henry rejected the ban, he would anger the pope and other church officials. Henry called together the bishops that supported him. **3** Together, they ordered the pope to step down. **4** The pope refused, and many nobles and church leaders turned against Henry. Henry suddenly worried that he might lose his throne. As a result, he decided to seek the pope's forgiveness for his actions.

Make a Flow Chart

A flow chart can help you identify the steps involved in making a decision. The flow chart below shows the decision-making process in the passage you just read.

1 DECISION TO BE MADE: How should Henry IV react to the pope's ban on lay investiture? Should he accept the ban or reject it? →

2 POSSIBLE CONSEQUENCES: Accept the ban and limit his political power. →

2 POSSIBLE CONSEQUENCES: Reject the ban and risk angering nobles and church officials.

3 DECISION MADE: Reject ban by ordering pope to resign. →

4 ACTUAL CONSEQUENCES: Many of the empire's nobles and church officials turn against Henry. He then decides to seek the pope's forgiveness.

Apply the Skill

Turn to Chapter 16, Lesson 2. Read "Revolution and the Declaration of Independence" and make a flow chart to identify a decision and its consequences described in that section.

1.7 Making Generalizations

Learn the Skill

To **make generalizations** means to make broad judgments based on information. When you make generalizations, you should gather information from several sources.

Practice the Skill

The following three passages contain descriptions of how knights lived during the Middle Ages. Use the strategies listed below to make a generalization about these descriptions.

How to Make Generalizations

Strategy ➊ Look for information that the sources have in common. These three sources describe the way of life of knights during the Middle Ages.

Strategy ➋ Form a generalization that describes this way of life in a way that would agree with all three sources. State your generalization in a sentence.

> ### THE LIFE OF KNIGHTS
>
> ➊ As the lord's vassal, a knight's main obligation was to serve in battle. From his knights, a lord typically demanded about 40 days of combat a year.
> –*World History: Patterns of Interaction*
>
> Knights were not merely professional fighters. ➊ They were expected to live by a code of honor known as chivalry. They had to demonstrate a strong religious faith . . . [and] protect women and the weak.
> –*The Medieval World*
>
> In real life, a knight did not always resemble the ideal knight of the minstrels. ➊ His code of honor and loyalty was sometimes applied only to members of his own class.
> –*World Book Encyclopedia*

Make a Chart

Using a chart can help you make generalizations. The chart below shows how the information you just read can be used to generalize about knights.

➊ A knight's main obligation was to serve in battle.	➋ GENERALIZATION Knights were experienced fighters who were chivalrous in their actions, but not always to everyone.
➊ Knights were to follow a code of honor called chivalry.	
➊ Knights often applied their code of chivalry only to members of their own class.	

Apply the Skill

Turn to Chapter 7, Lesson 3. Read "Mongol Government," and study the map on page 234. Also read the History Maker "Kublai Khan" on page 236. Then use a chart like the one above to make a generalization about Kublai Khan.

2.1 Reading a Map

Learn the Skill

Maps are representations of features on the earth's surface. Some maps show political features, such as national borders. Other maps show physical features, such as mountains and bodies of water. By learning to use map elements, you can better understand how to read maps.

Practice the Skill

The following map shows the Reconquista, the effort by Christians to drive the Muslims from Spain. Use the strategies listed below to help you identify the elements common to most maps.

How to Read a Political Map

Strategy ❶ Read the title. This identifies the main idea of the map.

Strategy ❷ Look for the grid of lines that forms a pattern of squares over the map. These numbered lines are the lines of latitude (horizontal) and longitude (vertical). They indicate the location of the area on the earth.

Strategy ❸ Read the map key. It is usually in a box. The key will help you interpret the symbols or colors on the map.

Strategy ❹ Use the scale and the pointer, or compass rose, to determine distance and direction.

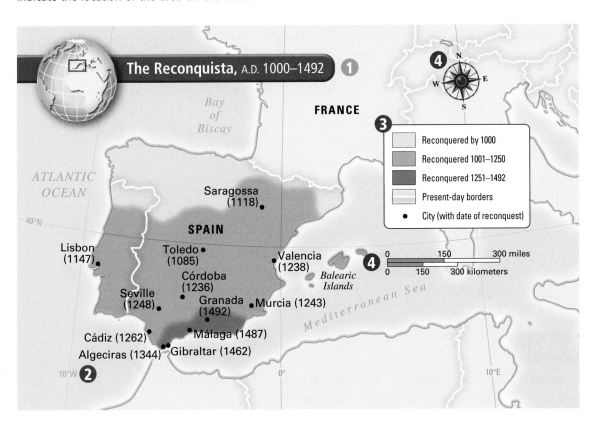

The Reconquista, A.D. 1000–1492 ❶

❹

FRANCE

Bay of Biscay

❸
- Reconquered by 1000
- Reconquered 1001–1250
- Reconquered 1251–1492
- Present-day borders
- ● City (with date of reconquest)

ATLANTIC OCEAN

40°N

SPAIN

Saragossa (1118)

Lisbon (1147)

Toledo (1085)

Valencia (1238)

Córdoba (1236)

Balearic Islands

❹

0   150   300 miles
0   150   300 kilometers

Seville (1248)

Granada (1492)

Murcia (1243)

Mediterranean Sea

Cádiz (1262)

Málaga (1487)

Algeciras (1344) Gibraltar (1462)

10°W ❷

0°

10°E

2.1 Reading a Map (continued)

How to Read a Physical Map

Strategy **1** Read the title.

Strategy **2** Look for the grid of lines.

Strategy **3** Read the map key. (On a physical map, it usually gives information on elevation and sometimes also physical features.)

Strategy **4** Use the scale and the pointer, or compass rose.

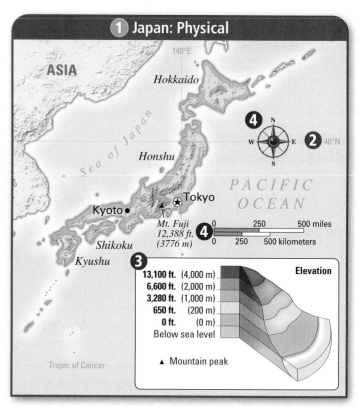

1 Japan: Physical

Make a Chart

A chart can help you organize the information given on a map. The chart below summarizes information about the two maps you just studied.

TITLE	The Reconquista, A.D. 1000–1492	Japan: Physical
LOCATION	"between longitudes 10°W and 0° and latitudes 45°N and 35° N."	"in the Pacific Ocean near longitude 40°N and latitude 140°E"
MAP KEY INFORMATION	colors = areas of Spain reconquered	colors = elevation
SCALE	1 1/4 in. = 300 miles, 3/4 in. = 300 km	1/2 in. = 250 miles, 1/4 in. = 250 km
SUMMARY	The Reconquista moved from north to south and was completed in about 500 years.	Japan is a country composed of four large and many small mountainous islands.

Apply the Skill

Turn to Chapter 11, Lesson 2, "The Olmec Civilization." Read the map entitled "Early Mesoamerican Trade, 1000 B.C.–A.D. 900" and make a chart to identify information on the map.

2.2 Creating a Map

Learn the Skill

Creating a map involves representing geographical information. When you draw a map, it is easiest to use an existing map as a guide. On the map you draw, you can show geographical information. You can also show political information, such as the area covered by empires, civilizations, and countries. In addition, maps can show data on climates, population, and resources.

Practice the Skill

Below is a map that a student created that shows the vegetation zones of Africa. Read the strategies listed below to see how the map was created.

How to Create a Map

Strategy ❶ Select a title that identifies the geographical area and the map's purpose.

Strategy ❷ Draw lines of latitude and longitude using short dashes.

Strategy ❸ Create a key that shows the colors.

Strategy ❹ Draw the colors on the map to show information.

Strategy ❺ Draw a compass rose and scale.

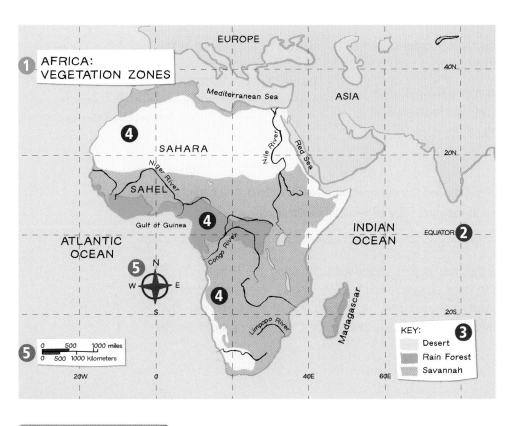

Apply the Skill

Turn to Chapter 2, Lesson 1, "The Rise and Expansion of Rome." Read the section entitled, "Rome Becomes an Empire." Use the information in this passage and the strategies mentioned above to sketch a map of the Roman Empire. Use the map on page 43 as a model for your map.

2.3 Interpreting Charts

Learn the Skill

Charts present information in a visual form. Charts are created by simplifying, summarizing, and organizing information. This information is then presented in a format that makes it easy to understand. Tables and diagrams are examples of commonly used charts.

Practice the Skill

The chart below shows how the Roman Empire compares in size to other civilizations. Use the strategies listed below to help interpret the information in the chart.

How to Interpret a Chart

Strategy ❶ Read the title. It will tell you what the chart is about. Ask yourself what kinds of information the chart shows. For example, does it show chronological information, geographic patterns and distributions, or something else?

Strategy ❷ Read the headings to see how the chart is organized. In this chart, information is organized by dates and size of each civilization.

Strategy ❸ Study the data in the chart to understand the facts that the chart was designed to show.

Strategy ❹ Summarize the information shown in each part of the chart. Use the title to help you focus on what information the chart is presenting.

❶ **Size of Selected Civilizations**

❷ Civilization	Dates	Size (est.) millions of square miles
❸ Persia	612–338 B.C.	2.0
Rome	27 B.C.–A.D. 476	3.4
Mongol	1206–1380	11.7
Aztec	1325–1520	0.2
United States	1776–	3.7

Source: *Encyclopaedia Britannica*

Write a Summary

Writing a summary can help you understand the information given in a chart. The paragraph below summarizes the information in the chart "Size of Selected Civilizations."

❹ The chart compares the size of five civilizations, including the Roman Empire. The Roman Empire is the third largest civilization of those listed on the chart. It ranks just behind the United States and far behind the Mongol Empire. The empire created by the Mongols was more three times the size of both Rome and the United States.

Apply the Skill

Turn to Chapter 10, Lesson 3, "Plague and Hundred Years' War." Study the social and political information presented in the chart entitled "Before the Hundred Years' War, After the Hundred Years' War." Then write a paragraph in which you summarize what you learned from the chart.

2.4 Interpreting Graphs

Learn the Skill

Graphs use pictures and symbols, instead of words, to show information. Graphs are created by taking information and presenting it visually. The graph on this page takes numerical information about the growth of villages in a particular region of Germany during the Middle Ages and presents it as a bar graph. There are many different kinds of graphs. Bar graphs, line graphs, and pie graphs are the most common. Bar graphs compare numbers or sets of numbers. The length of each bar shows a quantity. It is easy to see how different categories compare on a bar graph.

Practice the Skill

The bar graph below shows the growth of villages in one region of present-day Germany during the Middles Ages. Use the strategies listed below to help you interpret the graph.

How to Interpret a Graph

Strategy 1 Read the title to identify the main idea of the graph. Ask yourself what kinds of information the graph shows. For example, does it show changes over time, geographic patterns, economic trends, or something else?

Strategy 2 Read the vertical axis (the one that goes up and down) on the left side of the graph. This one shows the total number of villages. Each bar represents the number of villages in a particular year.

Strategy 3 Read the horizontal axis (the one that runs across the bottom of the graph). This one shows five specific years.

Strategy 4 Summarize the information shown in each part of the graph. Use the title to help you focus on what information the graph is presenting.

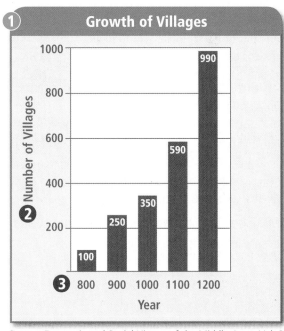

Source: *Economic and Social History of the Middle Ages, Vol. 2*

Write a Summary

Writing a summary will help you understand the information in the graph. The paragraph below summarizes the information from the bar graph.

> **4** The number of villages in this region of present-day Germany steadily grew during the Middle Ages. Around 800, some 100 villages existed in this region. By 1200, the number of villages had soared to nearly 1,000.

Apply the Skill

Turn to page 300. Look at the graph entitled "Comparison of Farmable Land." Write a paragraph in which you summarize what you learned from this graph.

2.5 Constructing Time Lines

Learn the Skill

A **time line** is a visual list of events and dates shown in the order in which they occurred. Time lines show sequence, or the order in which events follow one another. The ability to **sequence** historical events by constructing a time line enables you to get an accurate sense of the relationship among those events.

Practice the Skill

The following passage shows the sequence of events that began the unification of Japan. Use the strategies listed below to help you construct a time line of those events.

How to Find the Sequence of Events

Strategy ❶ Read the text and look for specific dates. Make sure to match the correct event with the proper date.

Strategy ❷ Watch for clue words about time. Words and phrases such as *first, at last, day, week, month,* or *year* may help to order the events according to sequence.

> ### POWERFUL WARRIORS BEGIN TO UNIFY JAPAN
>
> ❷ In the mid-1500s, a daimyo named Oda Nobunaga began to reunite Japan. Through wars and negotiations, Nobunaga won control of nearly half of Japan before ❶ his death in 1582. ❷ Shortly after Nobunaga died, his best general, Toyotomi Hideyoshi, took his place. Hideyoshi was born a peasant. Under Nobunaga, he had risen to become a superb military leader. Through force and political alliances, Hideyoshi controlled almost all of Japan ❶ when he died in 1598.

Make a Time Line

Making a time line can help you sequence events. The time line below shows the sequence of events in the passage you just read.

MID-1500s:
A daimyo named Oda Nobunaga begins to reunite Japan.

1582:
Nobunaga dies with nearly half of Japan under his control.

1598:
Hideyoshi dies with nearly all of Japan under his rule.

| 1550 | 1580 | 1590 | 1600 |

TWO WEEKS AFTER NOBUNAGA'S DEATH:
Toyotomi Hideyoshi becomes ruler.

Apply the Skill

Turn to Chapter 7, Lesson 3. Read "The Mongol Invasion" and make a time line showing the sequence of events described in that section.

2.6 Explaining Chronological Order and Sequence

Learn the Skill

Explaining chronological order and sequence means identifying the order in which major historical events occur and then describing how these events relate to one another. Major events that follow each other in time are often linked by a series of occurrences.

Practice the Skill

The following passage deals with the troubles that the Catholic Church faced from the late 1300s to the early 1500s. Use the strategies listed below to help you identify the major events and the series of occurrences that connect them.

How to Find the Sequence of Events

Strategy ❶ Look for specific dates provided in the text. The dates may not always read from earliest to latest, so be sure to match an event with the date.

Strategy ❷ Look for clues about time that allow you to order events according to sequence. Words and phrases such as *day, week, year,* or *century* may help to sequence the events.

Strategy ❸ Watch for references to previous historical events that are included in the background.

> ### TROUBLE FOR THE CATHOLIC CHURCH
>
> ❸ In the 1300s, the growth of national states weakened the power of the Catholic Church. Some monarchs grew powerful enough to force the Church to support their policies. ❶ In 1305, the French king used his political power to have Clement V elected pope. ❷ Two years later, the pope moved the center of the Church from Rome to Avignon, France. As a result, the Church developed two centers of power—Avignon and Rome. ❶ In 1378, the two sides split and elected different popes. The split is known as the Great Schism. In 1414, religious and political leaders met and worked to end the schism. They removed the French pope and persuaded the Roman pope to resign. ❶ In 1417, they elected a new pope based in Rome and began to unify the Church once again.

Make a Sequence Chart

The sequence chart below shows the chronological order of events in the passage you just read. It also shows how these events relate to one another.

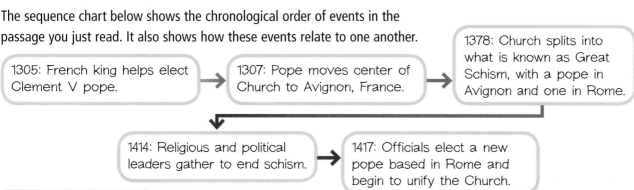

1305: French king helps elect Clement V pope. → 1307: Pope moves center of Church to Avignon, France. → 1378: Church splits into what is known as Great Schism, with a pope in Avignon and one in Rome. → 1414: Religious and political leaders gather to end schism. → 1417: Officials elect a new pope based in Rome and begin to unify the Church.

Apply the Skill

Turn to Chapter 2, Lesson 1, "The Rise and Expansion of Rome." Read "From Republic to Empire." Then create a sequence chart that shows the order of events in Rome's rise to an empire and their relationship to one another.

2.7 Explaining Geographic Patterns

Learn the Skill

Explaining geographic patterns involves understanding the movement of such things as people, cultures, or ideas across the earth. Geographic patterns include the migration of people, the expansion or decline of empires, the growth of economic systems, and the spread of religion. Some maps focus on showing geographic patterns. By studying these maps, you can learn about the development of cultures, ideas, and political systems.

Practice the Skill

The following map deals with the spread of Buddhism. Use the strategies listed below to help you study this map and others that show geographic patterns.

How to Explain Geographic Patterns

Strategy ❶ Locate the title of the map. The title usually identifies the geographic pattern shown on the map. In this case, the title indicates that the geographic pattern is the spread of Buddhism.

Strategy ❷ Locate any shaded areas on the map. Shaded areas show important regions of the geographic pattern. On this map, the shaded area shows the core of Buddhism.

Strategy ❸ Identify the graphics on the map, such as arrows. Arrows are often used to show the movement of ideas, goods, or people. Use the compass rose to determine the directions that the arrows point.

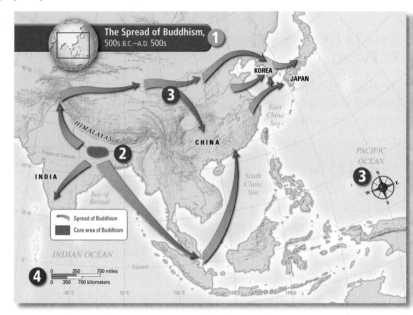

Strategy ❹ Locate the scale. Use the scale to determine distance.

Strategy ❺ Using the above strategies, write a summary about the geographic pattern shown on the map.

> ❺ SUMMARY
>
> Buddhism started in India. From this region, Buddhism spread southwest into India and northwest into the Himalayas. It also spread about 2,000 miles southeast into Indonesia. From the Himalayas, Buddhism spread east to China and eventually to Korea and Japan.

Apply the Skill

Turn to Chapter 10, Lesson 3, "Plague and Hundred Years' War." Study the map "Spread of the Plague, 1300s" on page 334. Using the strategies mentioned above, write a summary of the geographic pattern shown on this map.

2.8 Creating a Model

Learn the Skill

When you **create a model**, you use information and ideas to show an event or a situation in a visual way. A model might be a poster or a diagram that explains how something happened. Or, it might be a three-dimensional model, such as a diorama, that depicts an important scene or situation.

Practice the Skill

The following sketch shows the early stages of a model of a feudal manor in Europe. Use the strategies listed below to help you create your own model.

How to Create a Model

Strategy ❶ Gather the information you need to understand the situation or event. In this case, you need to be able to show the parts of a manor and their uses.

Strategy ❷ Visualize and sketch an idea for your model. Once you have created a picture in your mind, make an actual sketch to plan how it might look.

Strategy ❸ Think of symbols you may want to use. Since the model should give information in a visual way, think about ways you can use color, pictures, or other visuals to tell the story.

Strategy ❹ Gather the supplies you will need. Then create the model. For example, you will need pictures of manors and art supplies for this model.

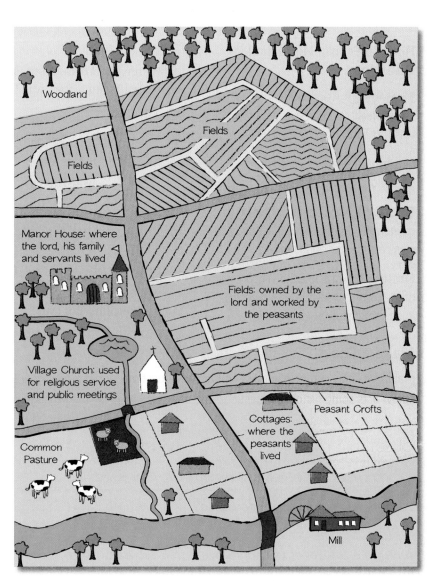

Woodland

Fields

Fields

Manor House: where the lord, his family and servants lived

Fields: owned by the lord and worked by the peasants

Village Church: used for religious service and public meetings

Peasant Crofts

Cottages: where the peasants lived

Common Pasture

Mill

Apply the Skill

Turn to Chapter 6, Lesson 2, "Empires Built on Gold and Trade." Read the information about the Great Enclosure. Also examine the images of the Great Enclosure on page 188. Then draw a diagram of the Great Enclosure and use labels to identify some of its main features.

3.1 Framing Historical Questions

Learn the Skill

Framing historical questions is important as you study primary sources—firsthand accounts, documents, and other records of the past. As you analyze a source, ask questions about what it means and why it is significant. Then, as you research, write questions that you want your research to answer.

Practice the Skill

The following passage is an excerpt from a biography of Michelangelo written by Giorgio Vasari. Vasari was a close friend of Michelangelo. In this excerpt, Vasari mentions a rival artist named Bramante. Use the strategies listed below to help you frame historical questions.

How to Frame Historical Questions

Strategy ❶ Ask about the historical record itself. Who produced it? When was it produced?

Strategy ❷ Ask about the facts presented. Who were the main people?

Strategy ❸ Ask about the person who created the record. What judgments or opinions does the author express?

Strategy ❹ Ask about the importance of the record. Does the record convey important historical information?

❶ from *The Lives of the Artists* by Giorgio Vasari, translated by Julia Conaway Bondanella and Peter Bondanella

❷ Bramante . . . persuaded the pope [Julius II] that [he] should have ❷ Michelangelo. . . ❹ paint the vault of the [Sistine] chapel. . . in this way Bramante and other rivals of Michelangelo hoped to take [him] . . . away from sculpture, in which . . . he had reached perfection, and to drive him to desperation . . . since he had no experience doing frescoes in [color]. . . . These frescoes were done with the greatest discomfort, for he had to stand there working with his head tilted backwards, and it damaged his eyesight . . . for several months afterwards. . . . ❸ I am amazed that Michelangelo tolerated such discomfort. But every day kindled even more desire to work, and . . . he neither felt fatigue nor worried about all the discomfort.

Make a Chart

Making a chart can help you list and answer questions about a historical source. The chart below lists some historical questions and answers based on the passage you just read.

QUESTIONS	ANSWERS
1. Who produced the historical record?	1. Giorgio Visari
2. Who were the people discussed? 3. What did they do?	2. Michaelangelo, Pope Julius II Bramante 3. Michaelangelo painted the Sistine Chapel ceiling.
4. What is the record's importance?	4. Provides insight about one of Michaelangelo's most famous works

Apply the Skill

Turn to the Chapter 14 Review. Read the primary source under the Standards-Based Assessment. Using the chart above as a model, ask and answer historical questions about this primary source.

3.2 Distinguishing Facts from Opinions

Learn the Skill

Facts are events, dates, statistics, or statements that can be proved to be true. **Opinions** are judgments, beliefs, and feelings. By identifying facts and opinions, you will be able to think critically when a person is trying to influence your own opinion.

Practice the Skill

The following passage describes the church Hagia Sophia. It was one of the more notable structures in the development of Constantinople as the capital of the Byzantine Empire. Use the strategies listed below to distinguish facts from opinions.

How to Distinguish Facts from Opinions

Strategy ❶ Look for specific information that can be proved or checked for accuracy.

Strategy ❷ Look for assertions, claims, and judgments that express opinions. In this case, one speaker's opinion is addressed in a direct quote.

Strategy ❸ Think about whether statements can be checked for accuracy. Then, identify the facts and opinions in a chart.

> ### HAGIA SOPHIA
>
> ❶ Hagia Sophia was built between A.D. 532 and 537. The Byzantine emperor Justinian ordered that the cathedral be built on the site where an earlier church had burned down. ❶ The church is noted for its large central dome, which rises 185 feet above the ground. With numerous windows, arches, and vaults, the structure is hailed by many as an architectural masterpiece. ❷ Said one observer, "You would declare that the place is not lighted by the sun from without, but that the rays are produced from within."

Make a Chart

The chart below analyzes the facts and opinions from the passage above.

STATEMENT	❸ CAN IT BE PROVED	❸ FACT OR OPINION
Hagia Sophia was built between A.D. 532 and 537.	Yes, check historical documents.	Fact
Hagia Sophia's central dome is 185 feet high.	Yes, check measurement records.	Fact
The inside of Hagia Sophia is so beautiful that it appears to make its own sunlight.	No. This cannot be proved. It is what one speaker believes.	Opinion

Apply the Skill

Turn to Chapter 6, Lesson 2, "Empires Built on Gold and Trade." Read the section entitled "Gold Brings Great Wealth." Make a chart in which you analyze key statements to determine whether they are facts or opinions.

3.3 Detecting Historical Points of View

Learn the Skill

A **historical point of view** is an attitude that a person has about an event in the past. Detecting and analyzing different points of views can help you to better understand a historical figure's thoughts and actions.

Practice the Skill

The following passage describes the beginnings of the Scientific Revolution and the debate over the workings of the solar system. Use the strategies below to help you detect and analyze what historical points of view are expressed.

How to Detect Points of View

Strategy ❶ Look for clue words that indicate a person's view on an issue. They include words such as *believe, insist, support,* and *oppose.*

Strategy ❷ Look for reasons why someone has taken a particular point of view.

A NEW WAY OF THINKING

During the Middle Ages, ❶ most scholars *believed* that the earth was an immovable object located at the center of the universe. ❷ After all, the sun appeared to move around the earth as it rose in the morning and set in the evening. The earth-centered view of the universe originated with Ptolemy. Church leaders *supported* this view, insisting that ❷ God had deliberately placed the earth in the middle of the universe.

Beginning in the 1500s, thinkers began to challenge this theory about the universe. The Polish astronomer Nicolaus Copernicus ❷ used observation and mathematical principles ❶ to *insist* that the earth and other planets revolved around the sun. Many people rejected this idea. However, a number of scholars *supported* this theory and worked to prove that it was true.

Make a Chart

Using a chart can help you detect and analyze historical points of view. The chart below analyzes the views in the passage you just read.

PERSON(S)	VIEW	REASON(S)
Middle Age scholars	Earth is the center of the universe.	common sense; Christian beliefs
Nicolaus Copernicus	Earth revolved around the sun.	observation and mathematical analysis

Apply the Skill

Turn to Chapter 16, Lesson 1. Read the section, "Roots of the Enlightenment." Make a chart like the one above to list and analyze points of view on the use of reason before the Enlightenment.

3.4 Determining Historical Context

Learn the Skill

Determining historical context means finding out how events and people were influenced by the context of their time. It means judging the past not by current values, but by taking into account the beliefs of the time.

Practice the Skill

The following passage is taken from *Emile,* a novel written by the famous French Enlightenment thinker Jean-Jeacques Rousseau. In this work, Rousseau expresses a wide range of views on education—including how and in what ways women should be educated.

How to Determine Historical Context

Strategy ① Identify the historical figure, the occasion, and the date.

Strategy ② Look for clues to the attitudes, customs, and values of the time. In this case, it is clear that Rousseau supports the popular view in Europe during the 1700s: Women were second-class citizens.

Strategy ③ Explain how people's actions and words reflected the attitudes and values of the era. Here, Rousseau argues that women need to know only how to be useful to men.

> **①** from *Emile, or On Education* (1762) by Jean-Jacques Rousseau, translated by Barbara Foxley and Grace Roosevelt
>
> Once it is [determined] that men and women neither are nor ought to be constituted the same, either in character or in temperament, it follows that they ought not to have the same education. . . . **③** [A]ll the education of women must be relative to men. **②** To please them, to be useful to them, to make oneself loved and honored by them . . . these are the duties of women at all times and what [we] ought to teach them from their childhood. The further we depart from this principle, the further we shall be from our goal, and all the precepts [direction] given [to] her will fail to secure her happiness and ours.

Strategy ④ Using the strategies mentioned above, write a conclusion about the historical context of the passage.

Write a Conclusion

You can write your conclusion in a paragraph. The paragraph below is a conclusion about the passage you just read.

> **④** CONCLUSION: Like many others in 18th-century Europe, French Enlightenment thinker Rousseau believed that women should concern themselves mainly with how to be good companions for men. As a result, Rousseau believed that women should be educated only in ways that helped them to better serve the men of society.

Apply the Skill

Turn to Chapter 12, Lesson 2. Read the section "Incan Society and Beliefs." Write a conclusion about the historical context of Incan society.

3.5 Forming and Supporting Opinions

Learn the Skill

When you **form opinions,** you interpret and judge the importance of events and people in history. You should always support your opinions with facts, examples, and quotations.

Practice the Skill

The following passage describes aspects of Islam. Use the strategies listed below to form and support an opinion about the duties of Islam.

How to Form and Support Opinions

Strategy ① Look for important information about the subject. Information can include facts, quotations, and examples.

Strategy ② Form an opinion about the subject by asking yourself questions about the information. For example, how important was the subject? How does it relate to similar subjects in your own experience?

Strategy ③ Support your opinions with facts, quotations, and examples. If the facts do not support the opinion, then rewrite your opinion so that it is supported by the facts.

> ### ISLAM
>
> To be a Muslim, all believers have to carry out five duties. These duties are known as the Five Pillars of Islam. Included among these five duties is daily prayer. ① Five times a day, Muslims face toward the holy city of Mecca to pray. Another duty is fasting. ① During the Islamic holy month of Ramadan, Muslims fast between dawn and sunset. They eat a simple meal at the end of the day. Fasting serves to remind Muslims that their spiritual needs are greater than their physical needs. In addition to the Five Pillars, devout Muslims must perform other duties in accordance with Islam. ① For example, they are forbidden to eat pork and are expected to set aside their Friday afternoons for communal worship.

Make a Chart

Making a chart can help you organize your opinions and supporting facts. The following chart summarizes one possible opinion about the religion of Islam.

② OPINION	③ FACT
Islam is a religion that has a strong influence on Muslims' daily life.	Muslims are expected to pray to Mecca five times a day.
	During the month of Ramadan, all Muslims fast from dawn to sunset.
	Muslims are forbidden to eat pork and are expected to set aside Friday afternoons for communal worship.

Apply the Skill

Turn to Chapter 8, Lesson 4, "Korea and Southeast Asia." Read "Vietnamese Kingdoms," and form your own opinion about the relationship between the Vietnamese and the Chinese. Make a chart like the one above to summarize your opinion and the supporting facts and examples.

3.6 Evaluating Information

Learn the Skill

To **evaluate** is to make a judgment about something. Historians evaluate information about people, cultures, and events by determining what material is essential to the main point and whether on not the information is verifiable.

Practice the Skill

The following passage examines Wendi's attempts to reunify China. Use the strategies listed below to evaluate the material.

How to Evaluate Information

Strategy 1 Determine the major point of a passage. In this case, think about what Wendi wanted to accomplish.

Strategy 2 Look for statements that convey information relevant and essential to the main point. Think about how Wendi achieved his goal.

Strategy 3 Consider what information does not directly relate to the main point.

Strategy 4 Ask whether most or all of the essential information can be verified in historical texts or other documents.

> WENDI REUNIFIES CHINA
>
> **1** During his rule, Wendi did many things to reunify China. **2** He reminded the Chinese of their glorious past by restoring old political traditions. **2** Wendi also reduced conflict by allowing people to follow their own belief systems. As a result, Confucianism enjoyed a rebirth during this time. **2** In addition, Wendi started the building of the Grand Canal that eventually linked northern and southern China. **3** Thousands of peasants labored five years to dig this canal. **4**

Make a Chart

The chart below shows how to evaluate information and organize the essential material from the passage you just read.

2 He reminded the Chinese of their glorious past by restoring political traditions.

2 He allowed people to follow their own belief systems.

1 MAIN POINT: Wendi did many things to reunify China.

2 He ordered construction of a canal to link northern and southern China.

Apply the Skill

Turn to Chapter 4, Lesson 1, "The Expansion of Muslim Rule." Read "Uniting Many People" and "The Overthrow of the Umayyads." Make a chart in which you determine the essential information about the Umayyad government.

3.7 Assessing Credibility of Sources

Learn the Skill

Assessing the credibility of sources means finding out if the source material accurately portrays events, facts, and people. Primary sources are materials written or made by people who lived during a historical event. They include letters, diaries, articles, and photographs. Secondary sources are written after a historical event by people who were not present at the event. Newspaper articles and books that rely on primary sources and appear after an event are secondary sources.

Practice the Skill

The following passage describes the lifestyle of Kublai Khan. It includes a primary source observation as well as secondary source material. Use the strategies listed below to help you assess the credibility of the sources.

How to Assess the Credibility of Sources

Strategy ❶ Determine the thesis or main point of the source. In this case, it is that Kublai Khan lived luxuriously.

Strategy ❷ Check for details that support the main idea.

Strategy ❸ Determine the credibility of primary sources. Is the speaker an objective observer or someone promoting a particular view or position? In this case, Polo seems to be an objective observer.

> ### LIFESTYLE OF KUBLAI KHAN
>
> Unlike his Mongol ancestors, Kublai Khan spent almost his entire life in China. ❶ He enjoyed living in the luxurious manner of a Chinese emperor. ❷ He maintained a beautiful summer palace at Shangdu, on the border between Mongolia and China. ❷ He also built a new square-walled capital at the site of modern Beijing. The size of Kublai's palace in Beijing greatly impressed the European traveler ❸ Marco Polo. "The whole building is at once so immense and so well constructed that no man in the world . . . could imagine any improvement in design or execution," Polo observed.

Make a Chart

Making a chart can help you assess the credibility of sources. The chart below organizes questions to ask about the credibility of sources.

QUESTIONS	ANSWERS
What is the Main Idea?	• Kublai Khan enjoyed a life of luxury.
What are the Supporting Details?	• He maintained a beautiful summer palace. • He built a new capital in Beijing.
Are the Primary Sources credible?	• Yes, Marco Polo appeared to be an objective observer.

Apply the Skill

Turn to Chapter 14, Lesson 1, "Trouble for the Catholic Church." Read "Luther's Ninety-Five Theses" under "Luther Confronts the Church." Using a chart like the one above, answer the credibility questions about this secondary source.

3.8 Drawing Conclusions from Sources

Learn the Skill

Drawing conclusions from sources means analyzing what you have read and forming an opinion about its meaning. To draw conclusions, look at the facts and then use your own common sense and experience to decide what the facts mean.

Practice the Skill

The following passage presents information about the Crusades, a series of religious wars during the Middle Ages between Christians and Muslims for control of the Holy Land. Use the strategies listed below to help you draw conclusions about the battles.

How to Draw Conclusions from Sources

Strategy ❶ Read carefully to identify and understand all the facts.

Strategy ❷ List the facts in a diagram and review them. Use your own experiences and common sense to understand how the facts relate to each other.

Strategy ❸ After reviewing the facts, write down the conclusions you have drawn about them.

> ### THE CRUSADES
>
> ❶ One effect of the Crusades was the weakening of the Church and the power of the pope. Church leaders had encouraged thousands of Europeans to leave their homes and travel to faraway lands in order to seize control of the Holy Land. In the end, these campaigns did not succeed. The Crusades also impacted European society as a whole. ❶ The battles dealt a blow to Europe's feudal structure, as thousands of knights and nobles lost their lives. ❶ Meanwhile, with so many men either killed or away fighting, a number of European women got a chance to manage estates or to operate shops and inns. ❶ The Crusades introduced Europeans to many Asian goods. As a result, trade between Europe and Southwest Asia increased greatly during and after the fighting.

Make a Diagram

Making a diagram can help you draw conclusions from sources. The diagram below shows how to organize facts to draw a conclusion about the passages you just read.

❷ FACTS	❸ CONCLUSION
The Crusades weakened the power of the Church and the pope.	The Crusades had a significant effect on the religious, social, and economic structures of Europe.
The Crusades dealt a blow to Europe's feudal structure and gave European women greater opportunities.	
The Crusades led to increased trade between Europe and Southwest Asia.	

Apply the Skill

Turn to Chapter 13, Lesson 1, "European Society Changes." Read "The Rise of Nations" and "End of Medieval Institutions." Use the diagram above as a model to draw conclusions about the end of feudalism.

4.1 Understanding Cause and Effect

Learn the Skill

A **cause** is an action in history that makes something happen. An **effect** is the historical event that is the result of a cause. A single event may have several causes. It is also possible for one cause to result in several effects. Historians identify cause-and-effect relationships to help them understand why historical events took place.

Practice the Skill

The following paragraph describes events that led to the fall of the Aztec Empire in what is now central Mexico. Use the strategies below to help you identify the cause-and-effect relationships.

How to Analyze Causes and Recognize Effects

Strategy ❶ Ask why an action took place. Ask yourself a question about the title and topic sentence, such as, "How did the Aztecs fall to the Spanish?"

Strategy ❷ Look for clue words that signal causes, such as *cause, because, contributed,* and *led to.*

Strategy ❸ Look for effects. Ask yourself, "What happened as a result of the fall of the Aztecs?"

FALL OF THE AZTEC EMPIRE

❶ In 1521, Spanish invaders conquered the Aztec Empire. A number of factors contributed to the Aztecs' defeat. ❷ A major *cause* of the Aztecs' defeat was their inferior weaponry. Aztec arrows were no match for the Spaniards' guns. In addition to their guns, the Spaniards brought with them their diseases. The Aztecs had no resistance to these unfamiliar diseases. As a result many of them died. ❷ This *led to* a weakening of the Aztec Empire and its army. ❸ By conquering the Aztecs, the Spanish gained control of modern Mexico and established the first European foothold in the Americas.

Make a Diagram

Using a diagram can help you understand causes and effects. The diagram below shows two causes and an effect for the passage you just read.

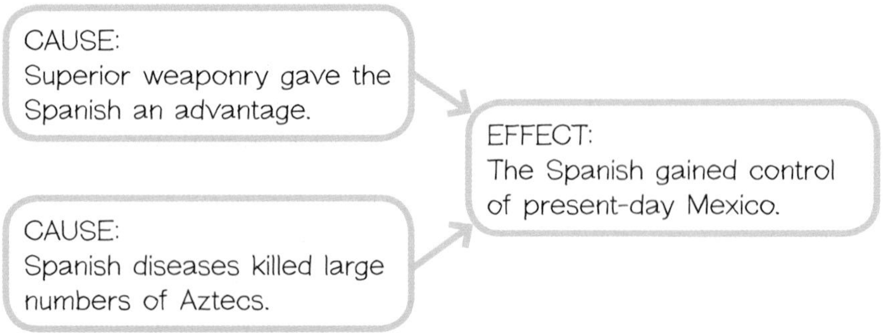

CAUSE:
Superior weaponry gave the Spanish an advantage.

CAUSE:
Spanish diseases killed large numbers of Aztecs.

EFFECT:
The Spanish gained control of present-day Mexico.

Apply the Skill

Turn to Chapter 10, Lesson 3, "Plague and Hundred Years' War." Read "The Hundred Years' War" and "Effects of the Hundred Years' War." Then make a diagram about the causes and effects of this war.

4.2 Explaining Historical Patterns

Learn the Skill

When humans develop new ways of thinking and acting that are repeated by other people over time or in other places, these ways become **historical patterns.** Recognizing historical patterns will help you better understand how and why certain ideas influence events and movements at different times in history.

Practice the Skill

The following passage discusses the recurring ideas involved in bringing about the period in European history known as the Enlightenment. Use the strategies listed below to help you explain the historical pattern.

How to Explain Historical Patterns

Strategy ❶ Identify the historical movement or idea being examined.

Strategy ❷ Identify previous or subsequent periods in history during which a similar movement or idea occurred.

ROOTS OF THE ENLIGHTENMENT

❶ The Enlightenment, which reached its height during the mid-1700s, stressed reason and thought in trying to solve problems and improve society. This time period also became known as the Age of Reason. ❷ The respect for reason can be traced back to the ancient Greeks and Romans. Scholars in these classical cultures gained knowledge through observation and reasoning. During the Middle Ages, religion and faith became more important than reason. ❷ However, scholars rediscovered the writings of Greece and Rome during the Renaissance in the 1400s. As a result, a person's ability to reason and seek the truth was once again valued.

Make a Flow Chart

Making a flow chart can help you visualize historical patterns. The flow chart below helps to explain the historical pattern in the passage you just read.

❷ The Greeks and Romans stressed the attainment of knowledge through observation and reason. ➡ ❷ Renaissance scholars revived the Greek and Roman emphasis on using reason and logic to answer questions. ➡ Enlightenment thinkers stressed the use of reason and thought to solve problems and better society.

Apply the Skill

Turn to Chapter 16, Lesson 2. Read "Spread of Democratic Principles." Make a flow chart to help you explain the historical pattern in that section.

4.3 Identifying Issues and Problems

Learn the Skill

Identifying issues and problems means finding and understanding the difficulties faced by a particular group of people and the historical factors that contributed to these difficulties. By identifying historical issues and problems, you can learn to identify and understand problems in today's world.

Practice the Skill

The following paragraph describes the problems of uniting the huge Muslim empire in the early 700s. Use the strategies listed below to find and understand these problems.

How to Identify Issues and Problems

Strategy ❶ Look for the difficulties or problems faced by a group of people.

Strategy ❷ Look for situations that existed at that time and place, which contributed to these problems.

Strategy ❸ Look for the solutions that people or groups developed to deal with the problems.

> ### UNITING MANY PEOPLES
>
> By the early 700s, the Umayyads controlled the huge Muslim empire. ❶ Umayyad leaders quickly realized that governing the empire would be difficult. ❷ People in different parts of the empire spoke their own language. As a result, government officials from different regions found it difficult to communicate with each other. ❷ In addition, a common coinage was not used within the empire, which made conducting trade and business difficult.
>
> Umayyad officials soon took steps to remedy these problems. ❸ They declared Arabic the official language of government of all Muslim lands. Having one official language improved communications throughout the empire. ❸ Officials also introduced a common coinage, which made commerce easier.

Make a Chart

Making a chart will help you identify and organize information about problems. The chart below shows the problem, the historical factors that contributed to the problem, and solutions to the problem in the passage you just read.

❶ PROBLEM	❷ CONTRIBUTING FACTORS	❸ SOLUTIONS
The Umayyads wanted to unite the large and diverse Muslim Empire.	People spoke different languages throughout empire.	Leaders declared Arabic as official language.
	Common coinage was not used within empire.	Officials introduced a common coinage.

Apply the Skill

Turn to Chapter 12, Lesson 2, "The Inca." Read "Governing the Empire" under "Geography of a Mountain Empire." Then make a chart that identifies the problems of governing the Incan Empire.

4.4 Understanding Continuity and Change

Learn the Skill

Understanding continuity and change means understanding why certain political and social systems continue without major change for many years and why sometimes they undergo significant change. Continuity and change is a process that happens repeatedly throughout history.

Practice the Skill

The following passage describes the long rule and eventual decline of the Franks. Use the strategies listed below to help you understand the continuity and change of this empire.

How to Understand Continuity and Change

Strategy ❶ Identify the system that is undergoing continuity and change. In this case, it is the Frankish Kingdom.

Strategy ❷ Identify the elements that contributed to the continuity of this system.

Strategy ❸ Identify the elements that contributed to the change of this system.

> ### THE FRANKISH KINGDOM
>
> ❶ A group of Germanic people called the Franks established one of the more powerful kingdoms in Europe during the Middle Ages. The kingdom emerged in the late 400s under a leader named Clovis. ❷ Subsequent rulers expanded the kingdom's size and power. In 768, one the most famous Frankish rulers, Charlemagne, took the throne. ❷ Charlemagne expanded the empire to its greatest size. He established new laws to help maintain order in the enlarged empire. Charlemagne died in 814. His son, Louis I, became emperor. When Louis died, his three sons fought for control of the kingdom. They all signed a treaty in 843 that divided the empire. ❸ This split caused the Frankish kingdom to grow weak and unstable. The empire soon broke apart as numerous invaders overran Europe.

Make a Chart

A chart can help you understand the main contributors to continuity and change. The chart below shows the possible reasons for the Frank's long reign and eventual fall.

Frankish kingdom flourishes for over 300 years.	Frankish kingdom collapses.
REASONS: • orderly transitions of power • large and powerful empire • laws maintain order	REASON: • instability and weakness due to division

Apply the Skill

Turn to Chapter 5, Lesson 2, "The Empire of Ghana." Read the lesson. Using the above strategies, create a chart highlighting why the empire of Ghana continued for many years and the changes that led to its decline.

4.5 Analyzing Economic and Political Issues

Learn the Skill

An **issue** is a matter of public concern. Issues in history are often economic or political. Analyzing economic and political issues means studying the various components of the issue in order to reach a better understanding of the issue and its impact on a particular event.

Practice the Skill

The following passage describes the growing difficulties that the Roman Empire faced in the centuries before it eventually fell. Use the strategies listed below to help you analyze the economic and political issues involved in Rome's decline.

How to Analyze Economic and Political Issues

Strategy ❶ Identify the discussion of economic and political issues. To locate economic issues, look for clue words and phrases such as *taxes, pay,* and *sources of wealth.* To locate political issues, look for clue words and phrases such as *government, politician, ruler,* and *public affairs.*

Strategy ❷ Determine what are the different components of each issue.

Strategy ❸ Write an analysis that summarizes the issue based on all its different components.

INTERNAL WEAKNESSES OF ROME

Toward the end of the second century A.D., a series of problems began to weaken the empire. During the second century, the empire stopped expanding. ❷ The end of new conquests meant an end to new ❶ *sources of wealth.* ❷ Officials responded by taxing people. These ❶ *taxes* were too high for many citizens, who simply did not pay them. ❷ As a result, it grew harder for the government to pay for needed services, especially the army.

Meanwhile, the empire had to deal with other difficulties. ❷ Over time, Roman politics grew increasingly corrupt. ❶ *Politicians* became more interested in financial gain than in public service. As a result, ❷ citizens lost their sense of pride in government and their interest in ❶ *public affairs.* ❷ A rapidly changing series of emperors also weakened the government.

Make a Diagram

Use this diagram to pull out the components of various economic and political issues to better analyze them.

❸ ECONOMIC ISSUE	POLITICAL ISSUE
• Empire stops expanding, which ends new sources of wealth. • Government levies high taxes; few residents pay. • Government has fewer funds for needed services.	• Politics grows corrupt. • Resident lose civic pride and duty to empire. • Rapidly changing rulers weakens sense of orderly rule.
Analysis: With no new income and a failed tax plan, the government could not pay for key services.	Analysis: As the government became more corrupt and less stable, Romans lost their sense of civic duty.

Apply the Skill

Turn to Chapter 6, Lesson 2. Read "Gold Brings Great Wealth." Using the above graphic as a model, analyze the economic and political issues in this passage.

4.6 Recognizing Changing Interpretations of History

Learn the Skill

Recognizing changing interpretations of history means identifying historical viewpoints that have changed over time. Historical interpretations often change when new evidence is found that causes historians to rethink an interpretation. When studying history, you should be able to identify both old and new interpretations of history. You should also understand why an interpretation has changed.

Practice the Skill

The following passage discusses the Mayan city of Cancuén. Use the strategies listed below to help you identify changing interpretations of history.

How to Recognize Changing Interpretations of History

Strategy 1 Identify old interpretations of history.

Strategy 2 Identify new interpretations of history.

Strategy 3 Determine what factors led to the new interpretation.

CITY OF CANCUÉN

Archaeologists discovered Cancuén in 1905. All the Mayan cities discovered before Cancuén seemed to have temples. Because of this, **1** many archaeologists and anthropologists believed that Mayan cities had a mostly religious function. Mayan kings, scholars thought, based their power on religion and warfare. **3** However, scholars found no temples at Cancuén. Based on this fact, archaeologists concluded that Cancuén was a center of trade. This caused archaeologists and anthropologists to rethink their ideas about the Maya. **2** Perhaps religion played a smaller role in Mayan culture than they had thought.

Make a Chart

A chart can help you identify old and new historical interpretations and the reasons why these interpretations have changed. The chart below lists both an old and a new historical interpretation about Mayan society. It also identifies the reason why this interpretation changed.

OLD INTERPRETATION	NEW INTERPRETATION	REASON
Religion dominated Mayan city life and government.	Religion may have played a small role in Mayan society.	No temples found at Cancuén

Apply the Skill

Turn to Chapter 1, Lesson 4. Read the section "Interpreting History." Using the above chart as a model, identify changing interpretations about farming in Tang China.

4.7 Conducting Cost-Benefit Analyses

Learn the Skill

A **cost-benefit analysis** involves determining the economic costs and benefits of a good, a service, or an action. Then it requires a balancing of the benefits against the costs. For example, imagine that you own a lawn-mowing business. Your business would be economically beneficial if, at the end of the summer, the total amount of money you earned was greater than the costs of buying the mower, paying for gas, cleaning and repairing the tools, and so on. The ability to recognize the costs and benefits of an action in history will help you to better understand why people made the decisions they did.

Practice the Skill

The following passage examines the decisions many European countries faced in participating in overseas exploration. Use the strategies below to analyze the costs and benefits related to this issue.

How to Conduct Cost-Benefit Analyses

Strategy ❶ Identify the historical topic or event that is under consideration.

Strategy ❷ Locate the potential economic benefits of taking the action.

Strategy ❸ Identify the potential costs associated with taking the action.

Strategy ❹ Determine whether the decision that was made was beneficial, based on analyzing and balancing the benefits and the costs.

❶ OVERSEAS EXPLORATION

As European nations considered overseas exploration, they knew that claiming undiscovered lands could bring them great wealth. ❷ They could establish new and possibly quicker trade routes with the civilizations of Asia. ❷ They might also discover gold and silver in new lands or gain access to precious resources such as timber. ❷ In addition, claiming overseas land would enhance a nation's power and prestige on the world stage. Searching for undiscovered lands and trade routes, however, came at a price. ❸ Building ships and training crews for long overseas voyages was expensive. ❸ So was establishing colonies. ❸ And once a nation built colonies, they most certainly would have to fund a larger military to protect their overseas holdings. ❹ In the end, the economic benefits outweighed the costs and the age of exploration began.

4.7 Conducting Cost-Benefit Analyses *(continued)*

Make a Diagram

Making a diagram can help you organize the components of a cost-benefit analysis. The diagram below shows you how to create a cost-benefit analysis from the passage you just read.

① HISTORICAL TOPIC
Overseas Exploration

② POTENTIAL BENEFITS
- better trade routes to Asia
- access to gold and precious raw materials
- enhanced power and prestige

③ POTENTIAL COSTS
- shipbuilding and crew training costly
- establishing colonies expensive
- more funds needed to establish larger military

④ DECISION
Nations saw the benefits as greater than the costs and engaged in exploration.

Apply the Skill

Turn to Chapter 10, Lesson 2, "The Crusades." In the section "The Battle for Palestine," read "Causes of the Crusades" and "The First Crusade." Use the diagram above as a model for creating a cost-benefit analysis of the Crusades.

Primary Source Handbook

CONTENTS

from the **Cancuén Archaeological Project**

By Arthur A. Demarest

Background: Arthur Demarest was a leader of an archaeological expedition to Cancuén, Guatemala. This expedition unearthed many amazing Mayan remains, including a huge palace. In the following excerpt, Demarest summarizes the expedition's findings.

Primary Source

The 1999 field season exceeded our expectations in scope and discoveries. Survey and mapping at the largest center in this little explored and poorly understood region, Cancuén, Guatemala, revealed residential [areas], a ballcourt, and new areas of the palace that previous explorers had failed to recognize. Its palace is certainly one of the largest in the Maya world, with architectural features including over forty well-preserved, corbel-vaulted[1] rooms each three to four meters [10–13 feet] in height. Excavations in newly identified residential [areas] revealed evidence of craft specialization, long distance trade, and economic diversity and complexity.

1. **corbel-vaulted:** having an arched ceiling formed by overlapping stones.

Two members of the Cancuén Archaeological Project carefully clean a decorated wall panel. ▶

DOCUMENT–BASED QUESTIONS

1. What were the major discoveries made by Demarest and his expedition?

2. Do you think these discoveries changed how historians view the Mayan city of Cancuén? If so, how?

Chapter Connection For more about the excavations at Cancuén, see Chapter 1, Lesson 3.

from Letter 123

By Jerome
Translated by W. H. Freemantle

Background: Jerome, who lived from about A.D. 340 to 420, was one of the leading Christian scholars of the late Roman Empire. In the following excerpts from a letter written in 409, Jerome discusses the fall of Rome.

Primary Source

I shall now say a few words of our present miseries. A few of us have hitherto survived them, but this is due not to anything we have done ourselves but to the mercy of the Lord. Savage tribes in countless numbers have overrun all parts of Gaul. The whole country between the Alps and the Pyrenees, between the Rhine and the Ocean, has been laid waste by hordes of Quadi, Vandals, Sarmatians, Alans, Gepids, Herules, Saxons, Burgundians, Allemanni and—alas! . . .—even Pannonians.[1] . . .

I say nothing of other places that I may not seem to despair of God's mercy. All that is ours now from the Pontic Sea to the Julian Alps[2] in days gone by once ceased to be ours. For thirty years the barbarians burst the barrier of the Danube and fought in the heart of the Roman Empire. Long use dried our tears. For all but a few old people had been born either in captivity or during a blockade, and consequently they did not miss a liberty which they had never known. Yet who will hereafter credit the fact or what histories will seriously discuss it, that Rome has to fight within her own borders not for glory but for bare life; and that she does not even fight but buys the right to exist by giving gold and sacrificing all her substance?

▲ This painting of Jerome shows him holding a Bible.

---

1. **Quadi, Vandals, Sarmati, Alani, Gepidae, Heruli, Saxons, Burgundians, Alemanni. . . Pannonians:** barbarian tribes from northern and central Europe.
2. **from the Pontic Sea to the Julian Alps:** from the Black Sea to northeastern Italy.

DOCUMENT–BASED QUESTIONS

1. What event allowed war to be waged in the middle of the Roman Empire?

2. What do you think Jerome means by the statement "all that is ours now . . . once ceased to be ours"?

Chapter Connection For more about the fall of Rome, see Chapter 2, Lesson 2.

from the **Qur'an**

Translated by N. J. Dawood

Background: Muslims believe that the archangel Gabriel revealed the word of God to the prophet Muhammad. Gabriel's revelations were collected in a book known as the Qur'an. The teachings in the Qur'an form the basis of Islam. The following excerpt deals with God's relationship with the faithful.

Primary Source

By the light of day, and by the dark of night, your Lord has not forsaken you,[1] nor does He abhor [hate] you.

The life to come holds a richer prize for you than this present life. You shall be gratified with what your Lord will give you.

Did He not find you an orphan and give you shelter?

Did He not find you in error and guide you?

Did He not find you poor and enrich you?

Therefore do not wrong the orphan, nor chide [scold] away the beggar. But proclaim the goodness of your Lord.

---

1. **you:** Muhammad.

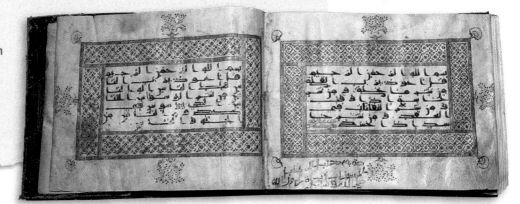

Two pages of the Qur'an written in Kufic script, an early form of Arabic writing ▶

DOCUMENT–BASED QUESTIONS

1. How does this excerpt describe the afterlife?

2. According to this excerpt, how should a person deal with orphans and beggars? Why?

Chapter Connection For more about the Qur'an, see Chapter 3, Lesson 2.

from the **Sunnah**

Translated by M. Muhsin Khan

Background: The Sunnah is a work that describes the way the prophet Muhammad lived his life. For Muslims, the words and deeds of Muhammad presented in the Sunnah are guides for proper living. The following excerpt tells how the archangel Gabriel first appeared to Muhammad.

Primary Source

The commencement [beginning] of the Divine Inspiration to Allah's Apostle[1] was in the form of good dreams which came true like bright day light, and then the love of seclusion [being alone] was bestowed upon [given to] him. He used to go in seclusion in the cave of Hira where he used to worship continuously for many days before his desire to see his family. He used to take with him [on] the journey food for the stay and then come back to Khadija[2] to take his food like-wise again till suddenly the Truth descended upon him while he was in the cave of Hira. The angel came to him and asked him to read. The Prophet replied, "I do not know how to read."

The Prophet added, "The angel caught me and pressed me so hard that I could not bear it any more. He then released me and again asked me to read and I replied, 'I do not know how to read.' Thereupon he caught me again and pressed me a second time till I could not bear it any more. He then released me and again asked me to read but again I replied, 'I do not know how to read.' Thereupon he caught me for the third time and pressed me, and then released me and said, 'Read in the name of your Lord, who has created . . . man from a clot. Read! And your Lord is the Most Generous.'

▲ This illustration from a 14th-century manuscript shows the archangel Gabriel.

---

1. **Allah's Apostle:** Muhammad.
2. **Khadija:** Muhammad's wife.

DOCUMENT–BASED QUESTIONS

1. Why did the Prophet go alone to the cave of Hira?

2. How did the angel try to convince the Prophet to read?

Chapter Connection For more about the Sunnah, see Chapter 3, Lesson 2.

from *The Itinerary of Benjamin of Tudela*

Translated by Marcus N. Adler

Background: Rabbi Benjamin ben Jonah was born in Tudela in northern Spain around 1127. In 1159, he decided to visit the Jewish communities in Muslim lands. His journey, or itinerary, took him 13 years and carried him almost to India. On his return, he wrote a description of his travels. In this excerpt, Benjamin discusses the Jewish community of Baghdad.

Primary Source Handbook

Primary Source

Baghdad [is] the royal residence of the Caliph Emir al-Muminin al-Abbasi.[1] . . . He has a palace in Baghdad three miles in extent, wherein is a great park with all varieties of trees, fruit-bearing and otherwise, and all manner of animals. . . . There the great king, al-Abbasi, . . . holds his court, and he is kind unto Israel, and many belonging to the people of Israel are his attendants; he . . . is well versed in the law of Israel. He reads and writes the holy language [Hebrew]. . . .

In Baghdad there are about 40,000 Jews, and they dwell in security, prosperity, and honor under the great Caliph, and amongst them are great sages, the heads of Academies engaged in the study of the law. In this city there are ten Academies. . . . At the head of them all is Daniel the son of Hisdai. . . . The Jews call him "Our Lord, Head of the Captivity," and the Muslims call him "Saidna ben Daoud," ["The Lord son of David."] . . .

And every fifth day when he goes to pay a visit to the great Caliph, horsemen, Gentiles as well as Jews, escort him, and heralds proclaim in advance, "Make way before our Lord, the son of David, as is due unto him." . . . Then he appears before the Caliph and kisses his hand, and the Caliph rises and places him on a throne, . . . and all the Muslim princes who attend the court of the Caliph rise up before him. . . .

In Baghdad there are twenty-eight Jewish Synagogues, situated either in the city itself or in al-Karkh on the other side of the Tigris. . . . The great synagogue of the Head of the Captivity has columns of marble of various colors overlaid with silver and gold, and on these columns are sentences of the Psalms in golden letters. And in front of the ark are about ten steps of marble; on the topmost step are the seats of the Head of the Captivity and of the Princes of the House of David.

1. **Emir al-Muminin al-Abbasi:** the Abbasid caliph in Baghdad from 1160 to 1170.

DOCUMENT–BASED QUESTIONS

1. How do you know that Daniel the son of Hisdai was held in high regard in Baghdad?

2. How would you describe the life of Jews in Baghdad? Support your answer with information from the primary source.

Chapter Connection For more about Jewish life under Muslim rule, see Chapter 4, Lesson 3.

from *The Rubaiyat of Omar Khayyam*

Translated by Edward FitzGerald

Background: During his life, the Persian scholar Omar Khayyam (1048–1131) was best known as an astronomer and mathematician. However, he was also an accomplished poet. After his death, collections of his poems began to appear. A translation of one of these collections, *The Rubaiyat of Omar Khayyam,* gained much attention during the mid-1800s. Below are two poems from that collection.

Primary Source

16

The Worldly Hope men set their Hearts upon
Turns Ashes—or it prospers; and anon,[1]
Like Snow upon the Desert's dusty Face,
Lighting a little hour or two—is gone.

63

Of threats of Hell and Hopes of Paradise!
One thing at least is certain—*This* Life flies;
One thing is certain and the rest is Lies;
The Flower that once has blown[2] for ever dies.

---

1. **anon:** soon.
2. **blown:** bloomed.

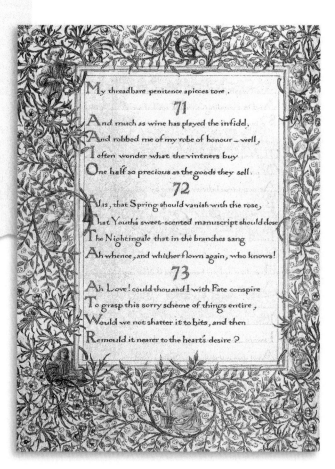

A page from an 1872 edition of *The Rubaiyat* illustrated by the British artist William Morris ▶

DOCUMENT–BASED QUESTIONS

1. How would you sum up in a sentence the sentiments expressed in these poems?

2. Omar Khayyam lived in a time of political turmoil. How are these poems a reflection of this?

Chapter Connection For two more poems by Omar Khayyam, see Chapter 4, Lesson 2.

from *The Chronicle of the Seeker*

By Mahmud Kati

Background: *The Chronicle of the Seeker* is a history of Islam in West Africa, written by the Muslim scholar Mahmud Kati. Kati began to write his history around 1519. The following excerpt describes how Mansa Musa, the king of Mali, prepared for a pilgrimage to Mecca in the 1320s. Kati refers to Mansa Musa as Kankan ("Lord") Musa.

Primary Source

Kankan Musa made up his mind that very day and began to collect the money and equipment needed for the journey. He sent proclamations to all parts of his realm asking for supplies and support and went to one of his shaykhs[1] and asked him to choose the day of his departure. "You should wait," said the shaykh, "for the Saturday which falls on the twelfth day of the month. Set forth on that day, and you will not die before you return safe and sound to your residence, please God."

He therefore delayed and waited until these two coincided [matched], and it was not until nine months later that the twelfth of the month fell on a Saturday. He set forth when the head of his caravan had already reached Timbuktu, while he himself was still in his residence in Mali.

Since that time travelers of that people believe it is lucky to set out on a journey on a Saturday which falls on the twelfth of a month.

▲ This 14th-century illustration shows Mansa Musa holding a gold nugget and a golden scepter.

1. **shaykhs:** elders, or senior advisers.

DOCUMENT–BASED QUESTIONS

1. How did Mansa Musa prepare for his pilgrimage to Mecca?

2. What in the excerpt suggests that Mansa Musa's pilgrimage caravan was large?

Chapter Connection For more about Mansa Musa, see Chapter 5, Lesson 3.

from a **Description of Great Zimbabwe**

By Vicente Pegado

Background: Vicente Pegado was a Portuguese captain stationed in southern Africa during the 1530s. In the following excerpt, Pegado describes the Great Enclosure of Great Zimbabwe. The Shona people built this structure during the 1300s and 1400s.

Primary Source

Among the gold mines of the inland plains between the Limpopo and Zambezi rivers [there is a] . . . fortress built of stones of marvelous size, and there appears to be no mortar joining them. . . . This edifice [structure] is almost surrounded by hills, upon which are others resembling it in the fashioning of stone and the absence of mortar, and one of them is a tower more than 12 fathoms[1] high. The natives of the country call these edifices Symbaoe, which according to their language signifies court.

---

1. **12 fathoms:** 72 feet.

A view of the Great Enclosure at Great Zimbabwe ▶

DOCUMENT-BASED QUESTIONS

1. Of what was the Great Enclosure made?

2. Do you think that Pegado was impressed by the Great Enclosure? Explain your answer.

Chapter Connection For more about Great Zimbabwe, see Chapter 6, Lesson 2.

from *The Travels of Marco Polo*

By Marco Polo

Background: During the late 1200s, the Italian merchant Marco Polo traveled to China. The journey, and his stay in China, lasted 24 years. After he returned to Italy, Polo published *The Travels of Marco Polo*, an account of his trip. The work increased European interest in Asia. In the following excerpt, Polo describes the nomadic life of the Mongols, whom he calls the Tartars.

Primary Source

Now that I have begun speaking of the Tartars, I will tell you more about them. The Tartars never remain fixed, but as the winter approaches remove to the plains of a warmer region, to find sufficient pasture for their cattle; and in summer they frequent [visit] cold areas in the mountains, where there is water and verdure [green vegetation], and their cattle are free from the annoyance of horse-flies and other biting insects. During two or three months they go progressively higher and seek fresh pasture, the grass not being adequate in any one place to feed . . . their [large] herds and flocks. . . . Their huts or tents are formed of rods covered with felt, exactly round, and nicely put together, so they can gather them into one bundle, and make them up as packages, which they carry along with them in their migrations upon a sort of car with four wheels. When they have occasion to set them up again, they always make the entrance front to the south.

▲ An early 19th-century engraving of Marco Polo

DOCUMENT-BASED QUESTIONS

1. Why did the Mongols move to warmer regions as winter approached?

2. How did the Mongols transport their tents?

Chapter Connection For more about the Mongols, see Chapter 7, Lesson 3.

from *The Tale of Genji*

By Murasaki Shikibu
Translated by Royall Tyler

Background: Murasaki Shikibu wrote *The Tale of Genji* during the 1000s. This work is considered the world's first important novel. It tells the story of Prince Genji and his life at the imperial court. In the following excerpt, Genji performs a dance for the emperor, whom the author refers to as His Majesty.

Primary Source

Captain Genji danced "Blue Sea Waves." His partner the Secretary Captain, His Excellency of the Left's son, certainly stood out in looks and skill, but beside Genji he was only a common mountain tree next to a blossoming cherry. As the music swelled and the piece reached its climax in the clear light of the late-afternoon sun, the cast of Genji's features and his dancing gave the familiar steps an unearthly quality. His singing of the verse could have been the Lord Buddha's *kalavinka* voice in paradise.[1] His Majesty was sufficiently transported [overcome] with delight to wipe his eyes, and all the senior nobles and Princes wept. When the verse was over, when Genji tossed his sleeves again to straighten them and the music rose once more in response, his face glowed with a still-greater beauty.

▲ Murasaki Shikibu based *The Tale of Genji* on her experiences at the Japanese court.

1. *kalavinka* **voice in paradise:** The Buddha's voice was often compared to that of the *kalavinka*, a bird that sings in paradise.

DOCUMENT–BASED QUESTIONS

1. How did Genji compare to his dance partner?

2. How did the emperor respond to the dance?

Chapter Connection For more about Murasaki Shikibu and *The Tale of Genji,* see Chapter 8, Lesson 2.

from *Beowulf*

Translated by David Breeden

Background: *Beowulf* is an epic poem that was probably written during the 700s. It is considered the first great work of English literature. The poem tells about the adventures of Beowulf, a great warrior and king. In this excerpt, Beowulf and his fellow warrior, Wiglaf, battle a fire-breathing dragon.

Primary Source

Then the terrible dragon
a third time rushed,
hot and battle-grim.
He bit Beowulf's neck
with sharp tusks—Beowulf
was wet with life's blood;
blood gushed in waves.

Then, I've heard,
Wiglaf showed courage,
craft and bravery,
as was his nature—he went
not for the thought-seat,[1]
but struck a little lower,
helped his kinsman
though his hand was burned.
The sword, shining
and ornamented,[2]
drove in so that
the fire abated.

Then the king controlled
his senses, drew his
battle knife, bitter
and battle sharp, which
he carried on his mail,[3]
and cut the dragon
through the middle.
The enemy fell—strength
had driven out life;
the two kinsmen, together,
had cut down the enemy.
So should a warrior do.

That was Beowulf's last victory;
his last work in this world.

▲ Beowulf raises his sword after killing the dragon.

---

1. **thought-seat:** head.
2. **ornamented:** decorated.
3. **mail:** armor.

DOCUMENT–BASED QUESTIONS

1. How does Wiglaf help Beowulf?

2. How does Beowulf kill the dragon?

Chapter Connection For another selection from *Beowulf*, see Chapter 9, Lesson 3.

from the **Magna Carta**

Background: During his reign, King John of England had many conflicts with his nobles. When he tried to raise taxes to fund a war, the nobles revolted. In 1215, the nobles forced King John to accept the Magna Carta, or Great Charter. This document, drawn up by the nobles, outlines basic political rights. The excerpt below deals with the rights of foreign merchants.

Primary Source

(41) All merchants may enter or leave England unharmed and without fear, and may stay or travel within it, by land or water, for purposes of trade, free from all illegal exactions [demands], in accordance with ancient and lawful customs. This, however, does not apply in time of war to merchants from a country that is at war with us. Any such merchants found in our country at the outbreak of war shall be detained without injury to their persons or property, until we or our chief justice have discovered how our own merchants are being treated in the country at war with us. If our own merchants are safe they shall be safe too.

▲ **King John reluctantly signs the Magna Carta.**

DOCUMENT–BASED QUESTIONS

1. How were foreign merchants in England to be treated?

2. Sometimes foreign merchants found themselves in England during a war between their country and England. What determined how the English would treat such merchants?

Chapter Connection For more about the Magna Carta, see Chapter 10, Lesson 4.

from the *Popol Vuh*

Translated by Dennis Tedlock

Background: After the Spanish conquered Mesoamerica, they tried to force everyone to adopt Christianity. Some Maya, however, continued to follow the old ways. They secretly made copies of old Mayan books. The most famous of these books is the *Popol Vuh*, or "Council Book." It tells the Mayan story of creation. The excerpt below describes the creation of Earth.

Primary Source

THIS IS THE ACCOUNT, here it is:

Now it still ripples, now it still murmurs, ripples, it still sighs, still hums, and it is empty under the sky.

Here follow the first words, the first eloquence:

There is not yet one person, one animal, bird, fish, crab, tree, rock, hollow, canyon, meadow, forest. Only the sky alone is there; the face of the earth is not clear. Only the sea alone is pooled under all the sky; there is nothing whatever gathered together. It is at rest; not a single thing stirs. It is held back, kept at rest under the sky.

Whatever there is that might be is simply not there: only the pooled water, only the calm sea, only it alone is pooled.

Whatever might be is simply not there: only murmurs, ripples, in the dark, in the night. Only the Maker, Modeler alone, Sovereign Plumed Serpent,[1] the Bearers, Begetters are in the water, a glittering light. They are there, they are enclosed in quetzal feathers, in blue-green.

Thus the name, "Plumed Serpent." They are great knowers, great thinkers in their very being.

And of course there is the sky, and there is also the Heart of Sky.[2] This is the name of the god, as it is spoken.

And then came his word, he came here to the Sovereign Plumed Serpent, here in the blackness, in the early dawn. He spoke with the Sovereign Plumed Serpent, and they talked, then they thought, then they worried. They agreed with each other, they joined their words, their thoughts. Then it was clear, then they reached accord in the light, and then humanity was clear, when they conceived the growth, the generation of trees, of bushes, and the growth of life, of humankind, in the blackness, in the early

(continued)

▲ In this page from the *Dresden Codex*, Sovereign Plumed Serpent is shown on the left.

---

1. **Sovereign Plumed Serpent:** Mayan god of creation.
2. **Heart of Sky:** another Mayan creation god.

(continued)

dawn, all because of the Heart of Sky, named Hurricane. Thunderbolt Hurricane comes first, the second is Newborn Thunderbolt, and the third is Sudden Thunderbolt.

So there were three of them, as Heart of Sky, who came to the Sovereign Plumed Serpent, when the dawn of life was conceived:

"How should the sowing be, and the dawning? Who is to be the provider, nurturer?"

"Let it be this way, think about it: this water should be removed, emptied out for the formation of the earth's own plate and platform, then should come the sowing, the dawning of the sky-earth. But there will be no high days and no bright praise for our work, our design, until the rise of the human work, the human design," they said.

And then the earth arose because of them, it was simply their word that brought it forth. For the forming of the earth they said "Earth." It arose suddenly, just like a cloud, like a mist, now forming, unfolding. Then the mountains were separated from the water, all at once the great mountains came forth. By their genius alone, by their cutting edge alone they carried out the conception of the mountain-plain. . . .

◄ The Hero Twins, shown on this vase, also play a part in the Mayan story of creation.

DOCUMENT–BASED QUESTIONS

1. What did the Maya think existed before the creation of Earth?

2. What are the gods thinking and talking about in this excerpt?

Chapter Connection For more about the Maya, see Chapter 11, Lesson 3.

from an **Aztec Account of the Conquest of Mexico**

Translated by Lysander Kemp

Background: In 1519, Hernán Cortés landed in what is now Mexico. After several weeks of hard marching, he reached the Aztec capital, Tenochtitlán. Some Aztecs wrote accounts that described the impact of Cortés's arrival. The following excerpt discusses the first meeting between Cortés and the Aztec ruler, Montezuma II.

Primary Source

Cortés asked him: "Are you Motecuhzoma [Montezuma]? Are you the king? Is it true that you are the king Motecuhzoma?"

And the king said: "Yes, I am Motecuhzoma." Then he stood up to welcome Cortés; he came forward, bowed his head low and addressed him in these words: "Our lord, you are weary. The journey has tired you, but now you have arrived on the earth. You have come to your city, Mexico. You have come here to sit on your throne. . . .

"No, it is not a dream. I am not walking in my sleep. I am not seeing you in my dreams. . . . And now you have come out of the clouds and mists to sit on your throne again.

"This was foretold by the kings who governed your city, and now it has taken place. You have come back to us; you have come down from the sky. Rest now, and take possession of your royal houses. Welcome to your land, my lords!"

When Motecuhzoma had finished, La Malinche[1] translated his address into Spanish so that the Captain[2] could understand it. Cortés replied in his strange and savage tongue, speaking first to La Malinche: "Tell Motecuhzoma that we are his friends. There is nothing to fear. We have wanted to see him for a long time, and now we have seen his face and heard his words. Tell him that we love him well and that our hearts are contented."

▲ An engraving of Hernán Cortés

---

1. **La Malinche:** a young Aztec woman who acted as a translator for Cortés.
2. **the Captain:** Cortés.

DOCUMENT-BASED QUESTIONS

1. How would you describe Montezuma II's speech to Cortés?

2. Many Aztecs thought that Cortés was the god Quetzalcoatl. What in Montezuma's speech suggests that he thought this?

Chapter Connection For more about Cortés and Montezuma, see Chapter 12, Lesson 1.

from the *Inferno*

By Dante Alighieri
Translated by Robert Pinsky

Background: The Italian writer Dante Alighieri (1265–1321) is considered by many to be one of the greatest poets of all time. His finest work is a long poem known as *The Divine Comedy*. This poem has three sections: *Inferno, Purgatory,* and *Paradise.* The *Inferno* begins with Dante taking a wrong turn and becoming lost in a dark, overgrown wood. Terrified, he looks for a way out. In the following excerpt, Dante tells what happens next.

Primary Source

But when I came to stop
    Below a hill that marked one end of the valley
    That had pierced my heart with terror, I looked up

Toward the crest[1] and saw its shoulders already
    Mantled[2] in rays of that bright planet[3] that shows
    The road to everyone, whatever our journey.

Then I could feel the terror begin to ease
    That churned in my heart's lake all through the night.
    As one still panting, ashore from dangerous seas,

Looks back at the deep he has escaped, my thought
    Returned, still fleeing, to regard that grim defile[4]
    That never left any alive who stayed in it.

After I had rested my weary body awhile
    I started again across the wilderness,
    My left foot always lower on the hill,

And suddenly—a leopard, near the place
    The way grew steep: lithe, spotted, quick of foot.
    Blocking the path, she stayed before my face

(continued)

▲ This painting by Domenico di Michelino shows Dante holding a copy of *The Divine Comedy.*

---

1. **crest:** the top of a hill.
2. **mantled:** covered.
3. **that bright planet:** the sun.
4. **defile:** a steep, narrow valley.

(continued)

And more than once she made me turn about
    To go back down. It was early morning still,
    The fair sun rising with the stars attending it

As when Divine Love set those beautiful
    Lights into motion at creation's dawn,
    And the time of day and season combined to fill

My heart with hope of that beast with festive skin[5]—
    But not so much that the next sight wasn't fearful:
    A lion came at me, his head high as he ran,

Roaring with hunger so the air appeared to tremble.
    Then, a grim she-wolf[6]—whose leanness seemed
        to compress
    All the world's cravings, that had made miserable

Such multitudes; she put such heaviness
    Into my spirit, I lost hope of the crest.
    Like someone eager to win, who tested by loss

Surrenders to gloom and weeps, so did that beast
    Make me feel, as harrying toward me at a lope
    She forced me back toward where the sun is lost.

▲ This is an illustration from a 15th-century Italian manuscript of the *Inferno.*

---

5. **that beast with festive skin:** the leopard, whose fur is spotted.
6. **A lion . . . a grim she-wolf:** The leopard, lion, and she-wolf represent lust, pride, and greed, three of the seven deadly sins.

DOCUMENT–BASED QUESTIONS

1. What happens as Dante tries to make his way up the hill?

2. How does Dante respond to the attack of the she-wolf?

Chapter Connection For more about Renaissance writers, see Chapter 13, Lessons 2 and 3.

from *The Prince*

By Niccolò Machiavelli
Translated by W. K. Marriott

Background: Niccolò Machiavelli was a scholar and diplomat from the Italian city of Florence. He published his most famous work, *The Prince,* in 1513. In it, he described in practical, realistic terms how leaders can gain and hold on to power. In the following excerpt, Machiavelli discusses the relationship between leaders and their subjects.

Primary Source

Upon this a question arises: whether it be better to be loved than feared or feared than loved? It may be answered that one should wish to be both, but, because it is difficult to unite them in one person, it is much safer to be feared than loved, when, of the two, either must be dispensed with. Because this is to be asserted in general of men, that they are ungrateful, fickle [unpredictable], false, cowardly, covetous [greedy], and as long as you succeed they are yours entirely; they will offer you their blood, property, life and children . . . when the need is far distant; but when it approaches they turn against you. And that prince who, relying entirely on their promises, has neglected other precautions, is ruined; because friendships that are obtained by payments, and not by greatness or nobility of mind, may indeed be earned, but they are not secured, and in time of need cannot be relied upon; and men have less scruple in offending one who is beloved than one who is feared, for love is preserved by the link of obligation which, owing to the baseness of men, is broken at every opportunity for their advantage; but fear preserves you by a dread of punishment which never fails.

▲ This portrait of Machiavelli was painted by the Italian artist Cristofano dell'Altissimo.

Nevertheless a prince ought to inspire fear in such a way that, if he does not win love, he avoids hatred; because he can endure very well being feared whilst he is not hated, which will always be as long as he abstains from the property of his citizens and subjects. . . . But when it is necessary for him to proceed against the life of someone, he must do it on proper justification and for manifest [clear] cause, but above all things he must keep his hands off the property of others, because men more quickly forget the death of their father than the loss of their patrimony [inheritance].

DOCUMENT–BASED QUESTIONS

1. What is Machiavelli's advice to leaders on the issue of whether it is better to be loved or to be feared?

2. Are Machiavelli's ideas on leadership relevant today? Explain your answer.

Chapter Connection For more about Renaissance writers, see Chapter 13, Lessons 2 and 3.

from *Don Quixote*

By Miguel de Cervantes
Translated by John Ormsby

Background: Miguel de Cervantes (1547–1616) wrote poetry and plays. However, he is best known for the novel *Don Quixote*. This send-up of the medieval idea of chivalry was published in two parts, the first in 1605 and the second in 1615. Both were huge successes and brought Cervantes wealth and fame. In the following excerpt, Don Quixote meets with what he thinks are giants.

Primary Source

At this point they came in sight of thirty or forty windmills that are on that plain.

"Fortune," said Don Quixote to his squire, as soon as he had seen them, "is arranging matters for us better than we could have hoped. Look there, friend Sancho Panza, where thirty or more monstrous giants rise up, all of whom I mean to engage in battle and slay, and with whose spoils we shall begin to make our fortunes. For this is righteous warfare, and it is God's good service to sweep so evil a breed from off the face of the earth."

"What giants?" said Sancho Panza.

"Those you see there," answered his master, "with the long arms, and some have them nearly two leagues[1] long."

"Look, your worship," said Sancho. "What we see there are not giants but windmills, and what seem to be their arms are the vanes that turned by the wind make the millstone go."

"It is easy to see," replied Don Quixote, "that you are not used to this business of adventures. Those are giants, and if you are afraid, away with you out of here and betake yourself to prayer, while I engage them in fierce and unequal combat."

So saying, he gave the spur to his steed Rocinante, heedless of the cries his squire Sancho sent after him, warning him that most certainly they were windmills and not giants he was going to attack. He, however, was so positive they were giants that he neither heard the cries of Sancho, nor perceived, near as he was, what they were.

(continued)

▲ A 19th-century engraving of Cervantes

---

1. **two leagues:** about six miles.

(continued)

"Fly not, cowards and vile beings," he shouted, "for a single knight attacks you."

A slight breeze at this moment sprang up, and the great vanes began to move.

"Though ye flourish more arms than the giant Briareus,[2] ye have to reckon with me!" exclaimed Don Quixote, when he saw this.

So saying, he commended himself with all his heart to his lady Dulcinea, imploring her to support him in such a peril. With lance braced and covered by his shield, he charged at Rocinante's fullest gallop and attacked the first mill that stood in front of him. But as he drove his lance-point into the sail, the wind whirled it around with such force that it shivered the lance to pieces. It swept away with it horse and rider, and they were sent rolling over the plain, in sad condition indeed.

_____

2. **Briareus:** a hundred-armed giant in Greek mythology.

▲ This illustration shows the result of Don Quixote's attack on the windmills.

DOCUMENT–BASED QUESTIONS

1. What is the outcome of Don Quixote's tilt at, or attack on, the windmills?

2. The expression "to tilt at windmills" comes from this episode in *Don Quixote*. What do you think this expression means?

Chapter Connection For more about Renaissance writers, see Chapter 13, Lessons 2 and 3.

from the Ninety-Five Theses

By Martin Luther

Background: Born in Germany in 1483, Martin Luther decided to become a monk in his early 20s. He tried to live as the Catholic Church instructed. However, some ten years later, Luther became disillusioned with the Church. In 1517, Luther is said to have posted his Ninety-Five Theses on a church door in the town of Wittenberg. This document listed all of the disputes that Luther had with the Church. The following excerpt includes six of the theses.

Primary Source

32. They will be condemned eternally, together with their teachers, who believe themselves sure of their salvation because they have letters of pardon. . . .

36. Every truly repentant Christian has a right to full remission of [forgiveness for] penalty and guilt, even without letters of pardon.

37. Every true Christian, whether living or dead, has part in all the blessings of Christ and the Church; and this is granted him by God, even without letters of pardon. . . .

44. . . . Love grows by works of love, and man becomes better; but by pardons man does not grow better, only more free from penalty. . . .

94. Christians are to be exhorted [urged] that they be diligent in following Christ, their Head, through penalties, deaths, and hell;

95. And thus be confident of entering into heaven rather through many tribulations [troubles], than through the assurance [promise] of peace.

▲ This portrait, painted by Lucas Cranach the Elder, shows Luther in his mid-40s.

DOCUMENT–BASED QUESTIONS

1. According to Luther, what will happen to people who believe they are saved because they have letters of pardon?

2. According to Luther, how does love grow, and what is the impact of the growth of love on people?

Chapter Connection For more about Luther's Ninety-Five Theses, *see* Chapter 14, Lesson 1.

from *The Starry Messenger*

By Galileo Galilei
Translated by Stillman Drake

Background: The Italian scientist Galileo Galilei (1564–1642) made discoveries that challenged classical scientific ideas. He wrote about some of them in a book called *The Starry Messenger.* In the following excerpt, Galileo describes how he constructed a telescope.

Primary Source

First I prepared a tube of lead, at the ends of which I fitted two glass lenses, both plane on one side while on the other side one was spherically convex[1] and the other concave.[2] Then placing my eye near the concave lens I perceived objects satisfactorily large and near, for they appeared three times closer and nine times larger than when seen with the naked eye alone. Next I constructed another one, more accurate, which represented objects as enlarged more than sixty times. Finally, sparing neither labor nor expense, I succeeded in constructing for myself so excellent an instrument that objects seen by means of it appeared nearly one thousand times larger and over thirty times closer than when regarded with our natural vision.

▲ This 19th-century painting shows Galileo presenting a telescope to the ruler of Venice.

---

1. **convex:** curving outward.
2. **concave:** curving inward.

DOCUMENT–BASED QUESTIONS

1. How did Galileo construct his first telescope?

2. What was Galileo's third telescope able to do?

Chapter Connection For more about Galileo, see Chapter 15, Lesson 2.

from the Journal of Christopher Columbus

Background: Christopher Columbus (1451–1506), an Italian explorer, wanted to find a shorter trade route to Asia. He convinced the Spanish monarchs Ferdinand and Isabella that a ship sailing westward would reach Asia quicker than a ship sailing eastward. In time, they financed a westward voyage led by Columbus. During the voyage, Columbus kept a journal. In the following excerpts, Columbus describes the last few days before he sees land. Notice that Columbus refers to himself as "the Admiral" and "he."

Primary Source

Sunday, 7 October. Continued their course west and sailed twelve miles an hour, for two hours, then eight miles an hour. . . . Observing large flocks of birds coming from the North and making for the southwest, whereby it was rendered [shown to be] probable that they were either going to land to pass the night, or abandoning the countries of the north, on account of the approaching winter, he determined to alter his course, knowing also that the Portuguese had discovered most of the islands they possessed by attending to [watching] the flight of birds. . . .

Wednesday, 10 October. Steered west-southwest and sailed at times ten miles an hour, at others twelve, and at others, seven. . . . Here the men lost all patience, and complained of the length of the voyage, but the Admiral encouraged them in the best manner he could, representing the profits they were about to acquire, and adding that it was to no purpose to complain, having come so far, they had nothing to do but continue on to the Indies, till with the help of our Lord, they should arrive there.

Thursday, 11 October. Steered west-southwest; and encountered a heavier sea than they had met with before in the whole voyage. Saw . . . a green rush[1] near the vessel. The crew of the *Pinta*[2] saw a cane and a log; they also picked up a stick which appeared to have been carved with an iron tool, a piece of cane, a plant which grows on land, and a board. The crew of the *Niña*[3] saw other signs of land, and a stalk loaded with rose berries. These signs encouraged them, and they all grew cheerful. Sailed this day till sunset, twenty-seven leagues. . . .

As the *Pinta* was the swiftest sailer, and kept ahead of the Admiral, she discovered land and made the signals which had been ordered. The land was first seen by a sailor called Rodrigo de Triana.

1. **green rush:** a plant that grows in marshes.
2. *Pinta:* one of Columbus' ships.
3. *Niña:* another of Columbus' ships.

DOCUMENT–BASED QUESTIONS

1. How did Columbus encourage the crew when they began to complain about the length of the voyage?

2. What signs indicated to Columbus and his crew that they were nearing land?

Chapter Connection For more about Christopher Columbus' voyages to the Americas, see Chapter 15, Lesson 3.

from the **English Bill of Rights**

Background: The English Parliament passed a bill of rights in 1689 to outline the limits on royal power. Parliament presented this document to King William III and Queen Mary, who agreed to uphold it. The following excerpts show some of the limits that the English Bill of Rights placed on the monarchy.

Primary Source

1. That the . . . suspending of laws, or the execution of laws, by regal authority, without consent of parliament, is illegal. . . .

4. That levying money [taxes] for or to the use of the Crown . . . without grant of parliament . . . is illegal.

5. That it is the right of the subjects to petition the King, and all commitments and prosecutions for such petitioning are illegal.

6. That the raising or keeping a standing army within the kingdom in time of peace, unless it be with consent of parliament, is against law. . . .

8. That election of members of parliament ought to be free.

9. That the freedom of speech, and debates or proceedings in parliament, ought not to be impeached or questioned in any court or place out of parliament.

10. That excessive bail ought not to be required, nor excessive fines imposed; nor cruel and unusual punishments inflicted.

11. That jurors ought to be duly impaneled and returned, and jurors which pass upon men in trials for high treason ought to be freeholders [property owners].

12. That all grants and promises of fines and forfeitures of particular persons before conviction, are illegal and void.

13. And that for redress of all grievances, and for the amending, strengthening, and preserving of the laws, parliaments ought to be held frequently.

▲ This illustration of William and Mary shows William holding a copy of the Bill of Rights.

DOCUMENT–BASED QUESTIONS

1. Whose power did the English Bill of Rights limit? Whose power did it strengthen?

2. Compare these excerpts with the first ten amendments to the U.S. Constitution—the U.S. Bill of Rights. What similarities are there between the two?

Chapter Connection For more about the growth of democratic institutions, see Chapter 16, Lesson 2.

from the **Declaration of Independence**

Background: The Declaration of Independence is the document through which the American colonies broke away from Great Britain. Thomas Jefferson wrote the declaration, with some editorial help from John Adams and Benjamin Franklin, in about two weeks. The Second Continental Congress adopted it on July 4, 1776. The following excerpt lists some of the wrongs that Jefferson charged the king of Great Britain had committed against the American colonies.

Primary Source Handbook

Primary Source

He has combined with others to subject us to a jurisdiction [authority] foreign to our constitution, and unacknowledged by our laws; giving his Assent to their Acts of pretended Legislation:

For Quartering large bodies of armed troops among us:

For protecting them, by a mock Trial, from punishment for any Murders which they should commit on the Inhabitants of these States:

For cutting off our Trade with all parts of the world:

For imposing Taxes on us without our Consent:

For depriving us in many cases, of the benefits of Trial by Jury:

For transporting us beyond Seas to be tried for pretended offences . . .

For taking away our Charters, abolishing our most valuable Laws, and altering fundamentally the Forms of our Governments:

For suspending our own Legislatures, and declaring themselves invested with power to legislate for us in all cases whatsoever.

▲ In this painting by John Trumbull, Thomas Jefferson is shown presenting the Declaration of Independence to the Continental Congress.

DOCUMENT–BASED QUESTIONS

1. How, according to the Declaration of Independence, did the king treat the laws and government of the American colonies?

2. What objection to the king's raising of taxes in the American colonies is mentioned in the Declaration of Independence?

Chapter Connection For more about the Declaration of Independence, see Chapter 16, Lesson 2.

A Global View

Thousands of religions are practiced in the world. A religion is an organized system of beliefs and practices, often centered on one or more gods. The following pages focus on five major religions: Buddhism, Christianity, Hinduism, Islam, and Judaism. This handbook also discusses Confucianism, an ethical system. Like a religion, an ethical system provides direction on how to live your life. Unlike religions, however, ethical systems do not center on the worship of gods.

In this book, you have learned about many different religions. You have learned how religions have spread and brought people together. You have also learned how religions have divided people throughout history. Religions continue to be powerful forces today. They affect people all over the world. The chart on the opposite page shows what percentages of the world population practice the five major religions. The map shows where these religions are predominant or where they are practiced by significant numbers.

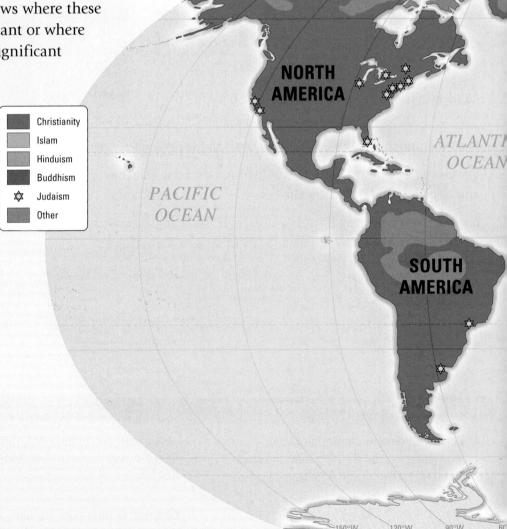

Christianity
Islam
Hinduism
Buddhism
✡ Judaism
Other

NORTH AMERICA

SOUTH AMERICA

PACIFIC OCEAN

ATLANTIC OCEAN

150°W   120°W   90°W   60

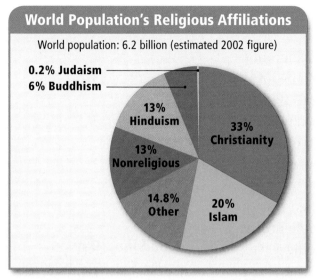

World Population's Religious Affiliations

World population: 6.2 billion (estimated 2002 figure)

- 0.2% Judaism
- 6% Buddhism
- 13% Hinduism
- 13% Nonreligious
- 14.8% Other
- 33% Christianity
- 20% Islam

Source: *World Almanac 2003*

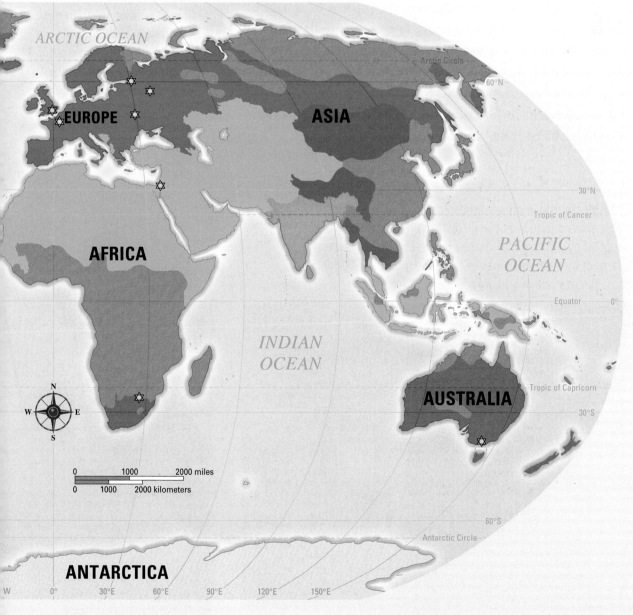

Buddhism

Buddhism is named for its founder, Siddhartha Gautama (sihd•DAHR•tuh GOW•tuh•muh), who came to be known as the Buddha, or "enlightened one." According to Buddhist tradition, the Buddha was born into a noble Indian family. But he gave up his riches to seek enlightenment, or wisdom. After long study and meditation, the Buddha experienced his enlightenment. He believed he knew the true nature of suffering and how to put an end to it. He called this insight into the nature of suffering The Four Noble Truths. The Buddha believed that his followers could achieve enlightenment by following what he called the Noble Eightfold Path. This path involved observing the following: right opinions, right desires, right speech, right action, right job, right effort, right concentration, and right meditation.

Buddhism began in India in the sixth century B.C. After the Buddha's death, missionaries and traders helped spread the religion to China, Japan, and Korea. Today, the religion has few followers in India. Most Buddhists live in Sri Lanka, East Asia, Southeast Asia, and Japan.

▼ Buddha's Day

One of the most important festivals in the Buddhist world is Buddha's Day, which falls in April or May. On this holy day, many Buddhists celebrate the Buddha's birth, enlightenment, and death. An elephant carries the Buddha's remains in this Buddha's Day procession in Thailand.

▼ Stupa

After his death, the Buddha's ashes were placed in a series of dome-shaped monuments called stupas. Each stupa was surrounded by a railing and topped with a square structure. The form of these early stupas became the model for Buddhist shrines, like this one in Sri Lanka.

▲ Statue of the Buddha

Statues of the Buddha, like this one in India, often show the religion's founder in a thoughtful pose. The statues reflect the Buddha's inner peacefulness and wisdom.

Learn More About Buddhism

Symbol According to legend, the Buddha was born with images of wheels on his hands and feet. The Buddha's teaching, known as the dharma, was intended to end the cycle of births and deaths. As a result, his teaching came to be symbolized by a wheel. His followers claimed that the "wheel of the dharma" was set in motion when the Buddha gave his first sermon.

Primary Source

Buddhism has many sacred books. These writings, which were recorded after the Buddha's death, contain his teachings. In the following selection, the Buddha teaches the importance of controlling self and one's own desires.

One who conquers himself is greater than another who conquers a thousand times a thousand men on the battlefield. Be victorious over yourself and not over others. When you attain victory over yourself, not even the gods can turn it into defeat.

from the *Dhammapada*
Translated by Eknath Easwaran

Chapter Connection For information on Buddhism in ancient China, see Chapter 7.

Christianity

Christianity is a monotheistic religion, which means that its followers believe in one God. The religion is based on the life and teachings of Jesus, as described in the Bible's New Testament. Christians regard Jesus as the Son of God. They believe that Jesus died on the cross and was resurrected, or raised to heavenly life. Early followers claimed that the resurrection proved that Jesus was the man who had come to save all of humankind. After Jesus' death around A.D. 29, his followers began to spread Christian beliefs. They preached about Jesus' life and teachings. For about 2,000 years, the religion continued to expand.

Today, Christianity is the largest religion in the world. Its nearly 2 billion followers are found all over the globe. Most Christians, however, live in North and South America, Europe, and Africa.

◄ Jesus
This mosaic in the Byzantine church of Hagia Sophia, or Holy Wisdom, in Istanbul shows Jesus enthroned in heaven. Images of Jesus often show his head encircled by a halo and his hand raised in a blessing.

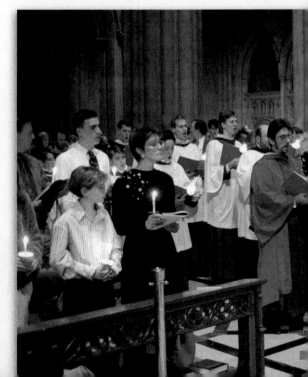

Christian Church ▶
Christians gather in churches for public worship. Church services often include a sermon, songs, and prayers. These worshipers have gathered for a Christmas service in the National Cathedral in Washington, D.C.

▲ Missionaries

Throughout the history of Christianity, missionaries have traveled all over the world in an effort to spread the religion. Today, missionary work often involves teaching or helping others in some way. This missionary is feeding orphans in India.

Learn More About Christianity

Symbol According to Christian scriptures, Jesus was crucified, or put to death on a cross. This image appears in many Christian churches and in religious artwork. The cross reminds Christians that Jesus loved humanity and died to save it.

Primary Source

Before Jesus was put to death on the cross, he ate a last supper with his 12 main disciples, or followers. At the supper, Jesus compared the bread they were eating to his body. He compared the wine they drank to his blood. Today, words similar to the following are repeated in the Christian ritual of communion, in which bread and wine are consumed in remembrance of Jesus' death.

Now as they were eating, Jesus took bread, and blessed, and broke it, and gave it to the disciples and said, "Take, eat; this is my body." And he took a cup, and when he had given thanks he gave it to them, saying, "Drink of it, all of you; for this is my blood of the covenant [agreement], which is poured out for many for the forgiveness of sins. I tell you I shall not drink again of this fruit of the vine until that day when I drink it new with you in my Father's kingdom."

Matthew 26:26–29

Chapter Connection For information on the spread of Christianity in Europe during the Middle Ages, see Chapter 9.

Hinduism

Hinduism is one of the oldest religions in the world. It developed in India thousands of years ago. The religion developed out of the rituals and philosophy set forth in many ancient sacred texts. Hindus believe that a supreme being, known as Brahman, is the soul of the universe. They also believe that Brahman can be found within every person. Many Hindus worship Brahman in the form of other deities and divine beings. They believe that these deities can grant followers wisdom and goodness and help them overcome obstacles. But, above all, Hindus believe that their faith can liberate their souls from the repeated cycle of life and death. Once free, their souls can achieve a heavenlike state of bliss—the ultimate goal of Hinduism.

Hindus can be found in every part of the world today, including Nepal, Africa, Europe, and North and South America. However, the largest concentration of followers can be found in India, where 82 percent of the population is Hindu.

▲ Guru

Hindu teachers are called gurus. Gurus, like the one shown here, help Hindus gain the wisdom they need to free themselves from suffering. Today, many gurus reach their followers through Internet sites that broadcast their teachings and devotional songs.

▼ Ganges River

Hindus believe that the water of the Ganges River is holy. As shown in this photograph, many Hindus travel to the river to bathe and pray. They also keep jars of the river's water in their homes to bless the dead and the dying.

▼ Goddess

When Hindus worship God in a female form, they often refer to her as Goddess. Shown below is one form of Goddess called Lakshmi. She is the deity of wealth and good fortune.

Symbol The syllable *Om* (or *Aum*) is often recited at the beginning of Hindu prayers. *Om* is the most sacred sound in Hinduism because it is believed to contain all other sounds. The syllable is represented by the symbol shown below.

Primary Source

The Upanishads (oo•PAN•uh•SHADZ) are among the oldest Hindu sacred texts. The following story from one of these philosophical works deals with the nature of Brahman.

Uddalaka commanded Shveta-ketu: Bring me a fig from that tree.
   He replied: Here it is, sir.
   Split it open.
   I have split it, sir.
   What do you see in it?
   These tiny seeds, sir.
   Split one of them open, please.
   I have split it, sir.
   What do you see in it?
   Nothing, sir.
   Yet, my dear boy, from a subtle essence [unseen spirit] which one cannot see, this great fig tree has grown. Have faith, my dear, for that subtle essence is the Soul of the whole universe. That is Reality. That is the Soul. *You* are that.

> from *The Wisdom of the Forest: Selections from the Hindu Upanishads*
> Translated by Geoffrey Parrinder

Islam

Islam began to develop in A.D. 610. This is when Islamic tradition states that the angel Gabriel began to reveal the word of God to a merchant named Muhammad. These revelations were eventually written down in a book called the Qur'an—Islam's sacred book. They formed the basis for Islamic belief and practice. Islam teaches that there is only one God, called Allah in Arabic. This is the same God that is worshiped in Christianity and Judaism. The followers of Islam, called Muslims, show their devotion to God by performing five ritual duties, also known as the Five Pillars of Islam. These duties are faith, prayer, charity, fasting, and a pilgrimage to Mecca.

Today, Islam is the fastest-growing religion in the world. Many of the more than 1 billion Muslims live in southwestern and central Asia and parts of Africa. Followers also live in Southeast Asia, Europe, and the Americas.

▲ Mosque

An Islamic house of worship is called a mosque. All mosques contain a prayer niche, which indicates the direction in which to pray—always toward Mecca. Many mosques also include the minarets, or towers, seen in this mosque in Turkey. The call to prayer is often made from these towers.

▼ Pilgrimage

The hajj, or pilgrimage to Mecca in Saudi Arabia, is one of the Five Pillars of Islam. Believers who are financially and physically able are expected to make the journey at least once. Pilgrims carry out many rituals, including circling the Ka'aba, the small shrine shown to the left in this photograph.

▲ Muslim Women

The role of women in Islamic society is hotly debated today. In some traditional societies, women are not allowed to pursue an education or work outside of the home. Like the women in this photograph, they are also expected to wear a full veil in public.

Symbol The crescent moon and star are often used to symbolize Islam. The symbols sometimes appear on the flags of Islamic countries or decorate the tops of mosques.

Primary Source

The Qur'an is the chief authority in all matters of Islamic life. Muslim children begin receiving instruction in the Qur'an at an early age. Muslim adults continue to read and consult the book throughout their lives. The following selection discusses the all-powerful nature of God. It appears in a chapter of the Qur'an titled Faith in God.

In the Name of God, the Compassionate, the Merciful

All that is in the heavens and the earth gives glory to God. He is the Mighty, the Wise One.

It is He that has sovereignty [authority] over the heavens and the earth. He ordains life and death, and has power over all things.

He is the First and the Last, the Visible and the Unseen. He has knowledge of all things.

from the *Qur'an* 57:1–3

Chapter Connection For more on the beginnings and early history of Islam, see Chapters 3 and 4.

WORLD RELIGIONS AND ETHICAL SYSTEMS • **R69**

World Religions Handbook

Judaism

Jews, the followers of Judaism, believe in one God. In fact, Judaism is probably the oldest monotheistic religion. The first five books of the Hebrew Bible, called the Torah, set down the basic laws and teachings of Judaism. According to the Torah, God chose a Hebrew shepherd named Abraham to be the "father" of the Hebrew people. Around 1800 B.C., Abraham led his people to a land that he believed God had promised them. This land would later be called Israel. In 1948, a Jewish state was created on the land.

Judaism is the smallest of the world's major religions, with slightly more than 14 million Jews. But this small religion has greatly influenced the development of today's two largest religions—Christianity and Islam.

▲ Hanukkah

According to legend, Hanukkah celebrates the miracle of an oil lamp that burned for eight days instead of one. For eight days, Jews observe the holy days with prayers and rituals. Jewish children, like those shown here, play a traditional game with a dreidel, a sort of spinning top.

▼ Jewish Ghetto

During the Middle Ages, Jews were forced to live in special areas of cities called ghettos. The areas were named after the section of Venice where Jews were forced to live in the 16th century. This synagogue, the Jewish house of worship, is located in the Jewish ghetto in Venice.

▼ Moses

According to the Torah, Moses led the Hebrews out of slavery in Egypt. During the journey, Moses received the Ten Commandments from God. The commandments set down many moral laws for all of humanity. This painting shows Moses holding the Ten Commandments.

Learn More About Judaism

Symbol A major symbol of Judaism is the Star of David. The six-pointed star honors King David, who ruled ancient Israel around 1000 B.C. and ushered in its golden age.

Primary Source

The Hebrew Bible contains writings about Jewish history and culture. However, it also contains many stories that are important to other people as well. The Book of Genesis is the first book of the Hebrew Bible and of the Torah. It tells the history of the Jewish people. It also includes the story of the creation of the world.

In the beginning God created the heavens and the earth. The earth was without form and void, and darkness was upon the face of the deep; and the Spirit of God was moving over the face of the waters.

And God said, "Let there be light"; and there was light. And God saw that the light was good; and God separated the light from the darkness. God called the light Day, and the darkness he called Night. And there was evening and there was morning, one day.

Genesis 1:1–5

Chapter Connection For information on Jews in Medieval Europe, see Chapter 10.

Confucianism

Confucianism is an ethical system based on the teachings of an ancient Chinese scholar named Confucius. Confucius believed that society should be organized around five basic relationships. These are the relationships between (1) ruler and subject, (2) father and son, (3) husband and wife, (4) elder brother and junior brother, and (5) friend and friend. Confucius believed that the proper conduct of these relationships would create a harmonious society founded on goodness. His ideas became the foundation of Chinese thought for more than 2,000 years.

Confucianism was never a religion, but it has greatly influenced people's spiritual beliefs. Many Chinese and other people in East Asia combine the religious practice of Buddhism with the teachings of Confucianism.

▲ Confucius
Confucius was born in 551 B.C., during a time of crisis in China. He hoped his ideas and teachings would restore the order of earlier times to his society. This painting shows Confucius with some of his followers.

▼ Celebration for Confucius
Although no one knows exactly the day when Confucius was born, many people in East Asia celebrate his birthday on September 28. Here, performers in traditional dress take part in Confucius' birthday celebration.

▼ Golden Rule

Confucius taught that people should treat others with respect and live by the golden rule. The characters in this ink-stamp spell out the rule "Do not do unto others what you would not want others to do unto you."

Learn More About Confucianism

Symbol The harmony that Confucius hoped to achieve is represented by the yin-and-yang symbol. The symbol represents opposite forces in the world working together. Yin represents all that is cold, dark, soft, and mysterious. Yang is the opposite—warm, bright, hard, and clear.

Primary Source

During his lifetime, Confucius never had enough power to put his ideas into practice. But after his death, Confucius' students spread his teachings. In the 400s B.C., they collected his teachings in a book called the *Analects*. In the following selections from the *Analects*, Confucius is referred to as the Master.

The Master cut out four things. He never took anything for granted, he never insisted on certainty, he was never inflexible and never egotistical. (9.4)

The Master said: "Regard loyalty and good faith as your main concern. Do not make friends of those who are not up to your own standard. If you commit a fault, do not shrink from correcting it." (9.25)

The Master said: "If one loves someone, can one avoid making him work hard? If one is loyal to someone, can one avoid instructing him?" (14.7)

from the *Analects*
Translated by Raymond Dawson

Chapter Connection For more about Confucianism, see Chapter 7.

Other Important Religions

In addition to the five major world religions you have learned about, there are many other important religions. Among these are Bahaism, Shinto, Sikhism, and Zoroastrianism. Two of these religions—Shinto and Zoroastrianism—are especially important historically because they are ancient. All of the religions are significant today because they have many followers.

World Religions Handbook

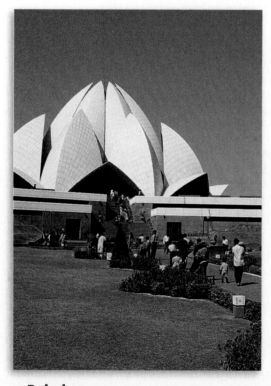

▼ Shinto

Shinto is the oldest surviving religion of Japan. It is based on the worship of nature. Shintoists believe that spirits, called *kami*, are found throughout nature. They worship these spirits at shrines in their homes and in public shrines. The torii, or gate, shown here marks the entrance to a Shinto shrine. Most of the nearly 3 million Shintoists practicing today live in Japan. Many combine Shinto with Buddhism or Confucianism.

▲ Bahaism

Bahaism (buh•HAH•IHZ•uhm) was founded in Persia in 1863 by a man known as Bahaullah, which means "splendor of God" in Arabic. The religion's founder was believed to be the most recent in a line of messengers sent by God to teach people moral behavior. Above all, the founder taught that God wants all the different people of the world to form a single, united society. People's differences and their unity are symbolized by the Baha'i (bah•HAH•ee) houses of worship, which have nine sides and a central dome. Worshipers here are entering the Baha'i house of worship in New Delhi, India.

◄ Sikhism

Sikhism is one of the religions of India and was founded over 500 years ago by Guru Nanak. The religion's followers are called Sikhs, which means "disciples." Sikhs believe in one God who created the universe and who is present everywhere. They believe that by living a good and simple life they can free themselves from the cycle of life and death. The Golden Temple in India, shown here, is the holiest Sikh shrine for the religion's nearly 24 million followers.

▲ Zoroastrianism

A prophet from Persia (present-day Iran) named Zoroaster founded Zoroastrianism (ZAWR•oh•AS•tree•uh•NIHZ•uhm) around 600 B.C. The religion teaches a belief in one god, Ahura Mazda (ah•HUR•uh MAZ•duh). Followers must obey this god, who will judge them when they die. Today, many of the world's nearly 2.5 million Zoroastrians make a pilgrimage and pray at this temple built in a mountain in southern Iran.

Comparing World Religions and Ethical Systems

	Buddhism	Christianity	Hinduism	Islam	Judaism	Confucianism
Followers worldwide (estimated 2003 figures)	364 million	2 billion	828 million	1.2 billion	14.5 million	6.3 million
Name of god	no god	God	Brahman	Allah	God	no god
Founder	the Buddha	Jesus	no founder	no founder but spread by Muhammad	Abraham	Confucius
Holy book	many sacred books, including the Dhammapada	Bible, including Old Testament and New Testament	many sacred texts, including the Upanishads	Qur'an	Hebrew Bible, including the Torah	*Analects*
Clergy	Buddhist monks	priests, ministers, monks, and nuns	Brahmin priests, monks, and gurus	no clergy but a scholar class, called the ulama, and imams, who may lead prayers	rabbis	no clergy
Basic beliefs	• Followers can achieve enlightenment by understanding The Four Noble Truths and by following The Noble Eightfold Path of right opinions, right desires, right speech, right action, right job, right effort, right concentration, and right meditation.	• There is only one God, who watches over and cares for his people. • Jesus is the Son of God. He died to save humanity. His death and resurrection made eternal life possible for others.	• The soul never dies but is continually reborn until it becomes divinely enlightened. • Persons achieve happiness and divine enlightenment after they free themselves from their earthly desires. • Freedom from earthly desires comes from many lifetimes of worship, knowledge, and virtuous acts.	• Persons achieve salvation by following the Five Pillars of Islam and living a just life. The pillars are faith, prayer, charity, fasting, and pilgrimage to Mecca.	• There is only one God, who watches over and cares for his people. • God loves and protects his people but also holds people accountable for their sins and shortcomings. • Persons serve God by studying the Torah and living by its teachings.	• Social order, harmony, and good government should be based on strong family relationships. • Respect for parents and elders is important to a well-ordered society. • Education is important for the welfare of both the individual and society.

Source: *World Almanac 2004*

Review

MAIN IDEAS

Buddhism (pages R62–R63)
1. Who was the Buddha?
2. What is the Noble Eightfold Path?

Christianity (pages R64–R65)
3. Why was the resurrection important to early Christians?
4. How did Christian beliefs spread?

Hinduism (pages R66–R67)
5. Why is Brahman important to Hindus?
6. What is the ultimate goal of Hinduism?

Islam (pages R68–R69)
7. What does the Qur'an contain?
8. What is the hajj?

Judaism (pages R70–R71)
9. Who is Abraham?
10. What other religions has Judaism influenced?

Confucianism (pages R72–R73)
11. Why is Confucius an important figure in China?
12. What was Confucius' golden rule?

Other Important Religions (pages R74–R75)
13. Of the four religions discussed on these pages, which are the oldest?
14. How do Sikhs believe they can free themselves from the cycle of life and death?

CRITICAL THINKING

15. **UNDERSTANDING CAUSE AND EFFECT** According to the Buddha, what happens when someone understands the true nature of suffering?
16. **COMPARING AND CONTRASTING** In what ways are Christianity, Islam, and Judaism similar?
17. **SUMMARIZING** What concept in monotheistic religions is most like Brahman in Hinduism?
18. **DRAWING CONCLUSIONS** How do you know that Confucius valued the family?

Standards-Based Assessment

Interpreting a Pie Chart The pie chart below shows what percentages of the population of North America practice the major religions. Use the pie chart to answer the following questions.

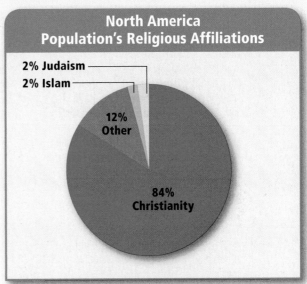

North America Population's Religious Affiliations

2% Judaism
2% Islam
12% Other
84% Christianity

Source: *World Almanac 2003*

1. **Which religion is practiced by the most people in North America?**
   A. Judaism
   B. Hinduism
   C. Christianity
   D. Buddhism

2. **Which two religions are each practiced by 2 percent of the population in North America?**
   A. Buddhism and Hinduism
   B. Islam and Judaism
   C. Christianity and Judaism
   D. Buddhism and Islam

Test Practice
ClassZone.com

Additional Test Practice, pp. S1–S33

Glossary

The Glossary is an alphabetical listing of many of the key terms from the chapters, along with their meanings. The definitions listed in the Glossary are the ones that apply to the way the words are used in this textbook. The Glossary gives the part of speech of each word. The following abbreviations are used:

adj. adjective   *n.* noun   *v.* verb

Pronunciation Key

Some of the words in this book are followed by respellings that show how the words are pronounced. The following key will help you understand what sounds are represented by the letters used in the respellings.

Symbol	Examples	Symbol	Examples
a	apple [AP•uhl], catch [kach]	oh	road, [rohd], know [noh]
ah	barn [bahrn], pot [paht]	oo	school [skool], glue [gloo]
air	bear [bair], dare [dair]	ow	out [owt], cow [kow]
aw	bought [bawt], horse [hawrs]	oy	coin [koyn], boys [boyz]
ay	ape [ayp], mail [mayl]	p	pig [pihg], top [tahp]
b	bell [behl], table [TAY•buhl]	r	rose [rohz], star [stahr]
ch	chain [chayn], ditch [dihch]	s	soap [sohp], icy [EYE•see]
d	dog [dawg], rained [raynd]	sh	share [shair], nation [NAY•shuhn]
ee	even [EE•vuhn], meal [meel]	t	tired [tyrd], boat [boht]
eh	egg [ehg], ten [tehn]	th	thin [thihn], mother [MUH•thuhr]
eye	iron [EYE•uhrn]	u	pull [pul], look [luk]
f	fall [fawl], laugh [laf]	uh	bump [buhmp], awake [uh•WAYK],
g	gold [gohld], big [bihg]		happen [HAP•uhn], pencil [PEHN•suhl],
h	hot [haht], exhale [ehks•HAYL]		pilot [PY•luht]
hw	white [hwyt]	ur	Earth [urth], bird [burd], worm [wurm]
ih	into [IHN•too], sick [sihk]	v	vase [vays], love [luhv]
j	jar [jahr], badge [baj]	w	web [wehb], twin [twihn]
k	cat [kat], luck [luhk]	y	As a consonant: yard [yahrd], mule [myool]
l	load [lohd], ball [bawl]		As a vowel: ice [ys], tried [tryd], sigh [sy]
m	make [mayk], gem [jehm]	z	zone [zohn], reason [REE•zuhn]
n	night [nyt], win [wihn]	zh	treasure [TREHZH•uhr], garage [guh•RAHZH]
ng	song [sawng], anger [ANG•guhr]		

Syllables that are stressed when the words are spoken appear in CAPITAL LETTERS in the respellings. For example, the respelling of *patterns* (PAT•uhrnz) shows that the first syllable of the word is stressed.

Syllables that appear in SMALL CAPITAL LETTERS are also stressed, but not as strongly as those that appear in capital letters. For example, the respelling of *interaction* (IHN•tuhr•AK•shuhn) shows that the third syllable receives the main stress and the first syllable receives a secondary stress.

A

Abd al-Malik (uhb•DUL•muh•LIHK) *n.* a Muslim ruler who became caliph in A.D. 685 and made Arabic the official language of government in all Muslim lands. (p. 115)

Abd al-Rahman (uhb•DUL•rahk•MAHN) **III** *n.* the eighth emir of al-Andalus, during whose reign al-Andalus reached the height of its power. (p. 132)

Afonso I *n.* a king of Kongo whose rule began in A.D. 1506. He was influenced by the Portuguese and participated in the slave trade. (p. 197)

al-Andalus *n.* the area of Spain under Muslim control between the A.D. 700s and 1492. (p. 131)

Allah (AL•uh) *n.* God in the Islamic religion. (p. 88)

alluvial soil *n.* a very rich and fertile soil deposited by flowing water. (p. 373)

Almoravids (AL•muh•RAHV•ihdz) *n.* a North African Islamic dynasty that tried to forcibly convert neighboring peoples, including those of Morocco, Spain, and Ghana. (p. 161)

anatomy *n.* the scientific study of the shapes and structures of humans, plants, and animals. (p. 498)

Angkor Wat (ANG•kawr WAHT) *n.* a complex of temples in Southeast Asia, built in the A.D. 1100s, that covers nearly one square mile and is the largest religious structure in the world. (p. 279)

anthropology (AN•thruh•PAHL•uh•jee) *n.* the study of humans and human cultures. (p. 26)

aqueduct (AK•wih•DUHKT) *n.* a structure designed to bring fresh water into a city or town. (p. 69)

archaeology (AHR•kee•AHL•uh•jee) *n.* the recovery and study of physical evidence from the past. (p. 25)

artifact *n.* a human-made object. (p. 25)

Askia Muhammad *n.* the ruler of the Songhai empire from A.D. 1493 to 1528, who expanded the empire and organized its government. (p. 168)

astrolabe (AS•truh•LAYB) *n.* an instrument used to measure the angles of stars above the horizon, thus helping sailors determine their latitude. (p. 512)

Augustus (aw•GUHS•tuhs) *n.* the first emperor of Rome, who ruled from 27 B.C. to A.D. 14 and greatly expanded the size and influence of the Roman Empire. (p. 49)

B

Baghdad *n.* a city, located in what is now Iraq, that was the capital of the Abbasid empire. (p. 120)

Bantu migrations *n.* a movement, beginning sometime around 1000 B.C., of Bantu-speaking peoples from West Africa to the south and east, spreading their languages and cultures. (p. 182)

bubonic plague *n.* a disease that struck western Eurasia in the mid-1300s, in an outbreak known as the Black Death. (p. 333)

Buddhism *n.* a belief system based on the teachings of Siddhartha Gautama, the Buddha, which stress freeing oneself from worldly desires. (p. 214)

bureaucracy (byu•RAHK•ruh•see) *n.* a system of departments and agencies that carry out the work of a government. (pp. 114, 224)

bushido (BUSH•ih•DOH) *n.* the code of conduct of samurai warriors, which required that they be generous, brave, and loyal. (p. 308)

Byzantine (BIHZ•uhn•TEEN) **Empire** *n.* the Eastern Roman Empire, which was ruled from Constantinople and from the 4th century to the 15th century. (p. 59)

C

cacao (kuh•KOW) *n.* a tropical American tree whose seeds are used to produce chocolate. (p. 370)

caliph (KAY•lihf) *n.* a ruler of the Muslim community, viewed as a successor of Muhammad. (p. 100)

calligraphy *n.* the art of fine handwriting. (p. 121)

Calvin, John *n.* a leader of the Protestant Reformation, who lived from A.D. 1509 to 1564 and emphasized the doctrine of predestination. (p. 472)

capitalism *n.* an economic system based on private ownership of economic resources and the use of those resources to make a profit. (p. 524)

caravel *n.* a type of Portuguese sailing ship with both square and lateen sails, developed for long voyages. (p. 512)

cartography *n.* the skills and methods used in the making of maps. (p. 15)

celadon (SEHL•uh•DAHN) *n.* a type of Korean pottery, often with a bluish-green color. (p. 276)

Charlemagne (SHAHR•luh•MAYN) *n.* a king of the Franks (from A.D. 768) who conquered much of Europe and spread Christianity in the conquered regions. (p. 294)

chasqui (CHAHS•kee) *n.* a runner in the Incan empire who carried messages up and down the length of the empire. (p. 411)

chivalry *n.* the code of conduct of medieval European knights, focusing on bravery, honor, and respect toward women and the weak. (p. 301)

Christianity *n.* a religion based on the life and teachings of Jesus. (p. 50)

circumnavigate *v.* to make a voyage completely around the world. (p. 515)

clan *n.* a group of people related by blood or marriage. (pp. 86, 151)

clergy *n.* the people with priestly authority in a religion. (p. 321)

climate *n.* the pattern of weather conditions in a certain location over a long period of time. (p. 10)

Clovis *n.* a leader of the Franks, who conquered the Roman province of Gaul in A.D. 486 and later established a large and powerful Frankish kingdom. (p. 56)

codex *n.* a book of the type used by early Meso-American civilizations to record important historical events. (p. 385)

Columbian Exchange *n.* the movement of plants, animals, and other living things between the eastern and western hemispheres after Columbus' voyage to the Americas in A.D. 1492. (p. 521)

Confucianism (kuhn•FYOO•shuh•nihz•uhm) *n.* a belief system based on the teachings of Confucius, a scholar who taught moral virtues and ethics. (p. 214)

Constantine *n.* the Roman emperor from A.D. 306 to 337, who ended the persecution of Christians and moved the capital of the empire to Byzantium (later known as Constantinople). (p. 54)

continent *n.* one of the seven large landmasses of Earth—North America, South America, Europe, Asia, Africa, Australia, and Antarctica. (p. 9)

convert *v.* to persuade a person to adopt a new religion or belief. (p. 479)

Córdoba *n.* the capital of al-Andalus. (p. 131)

Cortés (kawr•TEHZ), **Hernán** (ehr•NAHN) *n.* the Spanish explorer who conquered the Aztec civilization of Mexico in A.D. 1521. (p. 400)

covenant *n.* a binding agreement. (p. 483)

Crusades *n.* a series of military expeditions from Christian Europe to Palestine between the 11th and 13th centuries A.D. (p. 327)

culture *n.* a way of life shared by a group of people. (p. 27)

D

daimyo (DY•mee•OH) *n.* a Japanese lord with large landholdings and a private samurai army, who paid no taxes to the government. (p. 267)

Daoism (DOW•IHZ•uhm) *n.* a belief system that originated in China around 500 B.C., emphasizing harmony with nature and with inner feelings. (p. 215)

Declaration of Independence *n.* a document that declared the American colonies' independence from Great Britain. (p. 546)

Declaration of the Rights of Man and of the Citizen *n.* a document adopted by the French revolutionary government in 1789, outlining the people's rights. (p. 548)

dissection *n.* the cutting open of plants and animals to study and investigate their parts. (p. 498)

divan *n.* an imperial council that advised the sultan in the Ottoman Empire. (p. 351)

E

elevation *n.* the height of land above sea level. (p. 368)

elite (ih•LEET) *n.* the superior or wealthiest members of a society or group. (p. 374)

Elizabethan Age *n.* the period of the rule of Queen Elizabeth I in England, from 1558 to 1603. (p. 448)

embassy *n.* an office of one country's government in another country. (p. 253)

emperor *n.* the ruler of an empire. (p. 49)

empire *n.* a group of different cultures or territories led by a single all-powerful ruler. (p. 49)

enlightened despot *n.* a ruler who had absolute power but also paid attention to the political ideas of the Enlightenment and tried to rule in a just and educated way. (p. 543)

Enlightenment *n.* an 18th-century philosophical movement in which philosophers used reason to understand truths about human nature. (p. 535)

epic poem *n.* a long poem that tells a story of heroic adventures. (p. 309)

excavation *n.* the process of digging up historically significant objects for the purpose of studying them. (p. 26)

F

faction *n.* a small group whose interests run counter to those of a larger group of which they are part. (p. 124)

federalism *n.* the sharing of power between an organization or government and its members. (p. 484)

feudalism *n.* the political and social system of the Middle Ages in Europe, in which lords gave land to vassals in exchange for service and loyalty. (p. 296)

Forbidden City *n.* a group of walled palaces built for the Chinese emperor shortly after A.D. 1400 in the capital city of Beijing. (p. 240)

Francis of Assisi, St. *n.* an Italian who founded the Franciscan religious order in the early A.D. 1200s. (p. 324)

G

Genghis Khan (JEHNG•gihs KAHN) *n.* a Mongol leader who united the Mongol tribes around A.D. 1206 and began a campaign of conquest, forging an empire that covered northern China and Central Asia. (p. 233)

geocentric theory *n.* the theory that Earth is at the center of the universe. (p. 497)

geography *n.* the study of Earth's natural features. (p. 9)

Ghana (GAH•nuh) *n.* a region between the Sahara and the forests of southern West Africa, which was home to many ancient cultures. (p. 159)

glyph (glihf) *n.* a picture that represents a word, syllable, or sound. (p. 375)

golden age *n.* a period in which a society or culture is at its peak. (p. 121)

Great Enclosure *n.* the largest of the three main sections of the Shona settlement of Great Zimbabwe—likely a royal residence. (p. 188)

Great Schism (SKIHZ•uhm) *n.* a division in the Roman Catholic Church from A.D. 1378 until 1417, which occurred when the Church's two centers of power, Avignon and Rome, split and elected different popes. (p. 462)

Great Zimbabwe (zihm•BAHB•wee) *n.* the central settlement of the Shona empire in Africa, enclosed by a large stone wall, covering more than 100 acres, and having a population of 10,000 to 20,000. (p. 188)

Gregory VII, Pope *n.* the head of the Roman Catholic Church from 1073 to 1085, who struggled with Emperor Henry IV for power. (p. 323)

griot (gree•OH) *n.* an official storyteller in an African civilization. (p. 153)

guild *n.* an association of people sharing a trade or craft, intended to control the quality and quantity of their production and to protect their interests. (p. 302)

Gutenberg, Johann *n.* a German who, in the mid-1400s, invented a press for printing with movable type. (p. 449)

H

habeas corpus *n.* the right of people not to be imprisoned unlawfully. (p. 344)

haiku *n.* a Japanese form of poem, containing 17 syllables arranged in three lines of 5, 7, and 5 syllables. (p. 260)

harmony *n.* the combining of elements to form a pleasing whole. (p. 498)

heliocentric (HEE•lee•oh•SEHN•trihk) *adj.* having the sun as center. (p. 503)

hemisphere *n.* either of two equal halves of Earth, as marked by the equator or the prime meridian. (p. 17)

Henry IV, Emperor *n.* an 11th-century ruler of the Holy Roman Empire, who continually struggled for power with Pope Gregory VII. (p. 323)

Hijrah (HIHJ•ruh) *n.* the move of Muhammad and his followers from Mecca to the city of Yathrib in A.D. 622. (p. 93)

historian *n.* a person who studies and interprets the past. (p. 31)

history *n.* the study of past events. (p. 31)

humanism *n.* a movement in Renaissance Europe, celebrating human potential and achievement and stressing the study of subjects such as history, grammar, literature, and philosophy. (p. 432)

Hundred Years' War *n.* a series of wars between England and France, from A.D. 1337 to 1453. (p. 335)

I

Iberian Peninsula *n.* the southwestern tip of Europe, where the modern nations of Spain and Portugal are located. (p. 114)

Ignatius of Loyola *n.* a Spaniard who founded the religious order of Jesuits in the early A.D. 1530s. (p. 474)

imperial *adj.* relating to an empire or emperor. (p. 223)

indulgence *n.* the relaxation of earthly penalty for sin. (p. 463)

Inquisition *n.* a court established by the Roman Catholic Church in A.D. 1542 to investigate people who may have strayed from the Roman Catholic faith and to strengthen the power of the Church. (pp. 331, 474)

Islam *n.* a monotheistic religion based on the teachings of Muhammad. (p. 93)

J

janissary *n.* a member of an elite fighting force of the Ottoman Empire, made up mainly of slaves. (p. 353)

Jesuit *n.* a member of the Society of Jesus, a religious order founded in the early A.D. 1530s by Ignatius of Loyola. (p. 474)

Joan of Arc *n.* a French peasant girl who led the French to victory over the English at Orléans in A.D. 1429. (p. 335)

John, King *n.* the king of England who signed the Magna Carta in A.D. 1215. (p. 342)

Judaism *n.* the religion of the Jews, based on the Hebrew scriptures and a belief in one God. (p. 50)

Justinian *n.* the ruler of the Eastern Roman Empire from A.D. 527 to 565, who ruled with his wife, Theodora, and reconquered lost territories for the empire. (p. 59)

Justinian Code *n.* a legal code, prepared under the direction of the Byzantine emperor Justinian, that regulated much of Byzantine life. (p. 59)

K

kabuki (kuh•BOO•kee) *n.* a form of Japanese drama developed in the A.D. 1600s, featuring melodramatic singing and dancing, heavy makeup, and elaborate costumes. (p. 259)

Khmer Empire *n.* the most powerful and longest-lasting kingdom on the mainland of Southeast Asia, centered in what is today Cambodia. (p. 278)

Kilwa *n.* an ancient city-state on the eastern coast of Africa, settled by people from Iran and Arabia, that started to prosper in the late A.D. 1200s. (p. 182)

kinship *n.* a connection among people by blood, marriage, or adoption. (p. 151)

knight *n.* a highly trained mounted warrior in the service of a noble during the European Middle Ages. (p. 300)

Kongo *n.* an ancient kingdom along the western coast of Africa, settled by the Bantu-speaking Kongo people sometime before the 14th century a.d. (p. 195)

Koryo *n.* a kingdom on the Korean peninsula, established in a.d. 935 after the collapse of the Silla kingdom. (p. 276)

Kublai Khan (koo•bly KAHN) *n.* the grandson of Genghis Khan who took power in southern China in a.d. 1260 and defeated the Song army in 1279, giving the Mongols control over all of China. (p. 234)

L

labor specialization *n.* the doing of specific types of work by trained or knowledgeable workers. (p. 152)

landform *n.* a naturally formed feature of Earth's land surface, such as an island, a mountain, or a plateau. (p. 10)

latitude *n.* a measure of distance north or south of the equator. (p. 17)

Leonardo da Vinci *n.* an Italian Renaissance painter, born in a.d. 1452, who painted many masterpieces, such as the *Mona Lisa* and *The Last Supper,* and also excelled in scientific research. (p. 438)

longbow *n.* a weapon that can shoot arrows able to penetrate a knight's armor. (p. 336)

longitude *n.* a measure of distance east or west of the prime meridian. (p. 17)

lord *n.* a powerful landholding noble. (p. 296)

Luther, Martin *n.* a German theologian, born in a.d. 1483, who was a leader of the Reformation and taught salvation through faith in God rather than through good deeds. (p. 463)

M

Magna Carta *n.* a list of rights written by England's nobility and signed by King John in a.d. 1215. (p. 342)

maize (mayz) *n.* a type of corn grown by Native American civilizations. (p. 370)

Mali *n.* a West African empire established by the Malinke people. (p. 165)

Manchu *n.* a member of a northeastern Chinese people who conquered China in a.d. 1644 and began the last dynasty in Chinese history, called the Qing Dynasty. (p. 242)

manor *n.* the estate of a feudal noble, usually including a fortified building or castle. (p. 299)

Mansa Musa *n.* an emperor of Mali who made a famous pilgrimage to Mecca in a.d. 1324. (p. 166)

maritime *adj.* relating to the sea. (p. 241)

Maya (MAH•yuh) *n.* a Meso-American civilization, which reached its height between a.d. 250 and 900. (p. 381)

Mbanza (uhm•BAHN•zah) *n.* the capital city of the ancient African kingdom of Kongo. (p. 196)

mercantilism *n.* an economic policy based on the idea that a nation's power depends on its wealth. (p. 525)

mercenary *n.* a soldier who is paid to fight. (p. 132)

Mesoamerica *n.* a region that includes the southern part of Mexico and much of Central America. (p. 367)

Michelangelo *n.* an Italian Renaissance artist, born in a.d. 1475, who worked mainly as a sculptor but also painted such famous works as the ceiling of the Sistine Chapel in Rome. (p. 438)

Middle Ages *n.* the period of European history between the collapse of Rome and the Renaissance, lasting roughly from a.d. 500 to 1450. (p. 291)

missionary *n.* a person who travels to a foreign country in order to do religious work. (p. 479)

monastery *n.* a place where members of a religious order practice a life of prayer and worship. (p. 295)

Mongol Ascendancy *n.* the period in which the Mongols controlled all of Central Asia, making overland trade and travel safe. (p. 236)

monotheism *n.* a belief in one God. (p. 88)

Montezuma II *n.* the last Aztec emperor, who ruled from A.D. 1502 to 1520 and was overthrown by the Spanish. (p. 400)

mosaic (moh•ZAY•ihk) *n.* a picture made out of many small colored tiles or pieces of glass. (p. 67)

mosque (mahsk) *n.* a building for Muslim worship, designed to face the city of Mecca. (p. 95)

mother culture *n.* a culture that shapes and influences the customs and ideas of later cultures. (p. 377)

movable type *n.* a small block of metal or wood with a single raised character, used for printing texts. (p. 228)

Murasaki Shikibu (MOO•rah•SAH•kee SHEE•kee•BOO), **Lady** *n.* a Japanese writer of the early A.D. 1000s, who wrote *The Tale of Genji*, considered one of the world's first novels. (p. 259)

Muslim *n.* a person who follows the religion of Islam, accepting Allah as the only God. (p. 93)

Mutapa (moo•TAH•pah) *n.* an ancient kingdom in what is now the country of Zimbabwe, established by a Shona king around A.D. 1440; also, a ruler of this kingdom. (p. 190)

N

Nam Viet *n.* a Vietnamese kingdom conquered by the Chinese in 111 B.C. (p. 277)

natural rights *n.* the rights that all people are born with—such as the rights to life, liberty, and property according to the 18th-century philosopher John Locke. (p. 536)

Noh *n.* a form of Japanese drama developed in the A.D. 1300s, often featuring retellings of legends and folktales presented by actors in painted wooden masks. (p. 258)

nomad *n.* a person who moves from place to place rather than settling permanently. (pp. 86, 213)

O

oasis (oh•AY•sihs) *n.* a fertile area in the midst of a desert. (p. 86)

Olmec (AHL•mehk) *n.* the earliest known Meso-American culture, which flourished from 1200 to 400 B.C. and was centered in what is now southeastern Mexico. (p. 373)

Omar Khayyam (OH•mahr ky•YAHM) *n.* a Persian-born Muslim poet who usually wrote in quatrain form and was also a great mathematician. (p. 122)

oral history *n.* an unwritten verbal account of events, such as a story that is passed down from generation to generation. (p. 32)

Orthodox *adj.* relating to the Christian church that developed in the Byzantine Empire and is not under the authority of the pope. (p. 62)

Osman *n.* the Turkish leader who founded the Ottoman Empire in the early A.D. 1300s. (p. 351)

P

Pacal II *n.* a king who ruled the Mayan city of Palenque for nearly 70 years (from A.D. 615)—one of the greatest Mayan kings. (p. 384)

Pachacuti (PAH•chah•KOO•tee) *n.* the ninth Inca ruler, who came to power in A.D. 1438 and expanded the Incan Empire. (p. 410)

parliament *n.* a group of representatives with some powers of government. (p. 343)

patron *n.* a person who supports an activity or institution by providing financial backing. (p. 437)

Peace of Westphalia (wehst•FAYL•yuh) *n.* an agreement reached in A.D. 1648, which recognized the permanent division of western Europe into Catholic and Protestant nations and ended many ongoing religious wars. (p. 483)

perspective *n.* a technique of painting, developed during the Renaissance, that represents the appearance of objects in three-dimensional space. (p. 437)

philosophe (FIHL•uh•SAWF) *n.* one of the 18th-century thinkers who attempted to apply the scientific method to social problems. (p. 536)

pilgrimage *n.* a journey to a sacred place or shrine. (p. 89)

Pizarro, Francisco *n.* a Spanish explorer who arrived in Peru in A.D. 1532 and had conquered the Incan Empire by 1535. (p. 413)

Polo, Marco *n.* a Venetian trader who traveled the Silk Roads and arrived in China around A.D. 1275. He became an aide to Kublai Khan and later published a popular book about his adventures. (p. 236)

porcelain *n.* a hard white ceramic material, often called china. (p. 229)

predestination *n.* the doctrine that God chooses people for salvation and damnation before they are born and that individuals have no power to change God's will. (p. 472)

primary source *n.* a document or artifact created during a particular historical period. (p. 32)

printing press *n.* a machine for pressing paper against inked movable type. (p. 449)

projection *n.* a way of representing Earth's curved surface on a flat map while keeping distortion consistent and manageable. (p. 16)

Protestant *n.* a member of a Christian group that broke with the Roman Catholic Church during or after the 16th century. (p. 465)

Q

quipu (KEE•poo) *n.* a counting tool of the ancient Incan civilization, made of cords with knots at various points. (p. 414)

Qur'an (kuh•RAN) *n.* the Muslim holy book, consisting of revelations from Allah that were collected by Muhammad's followers after his death. (p. 94)

R

rationalism *n.* the idea that people should use reason, or logical thought, to understand the world. (p. 497)

Reconquista *n.* the series of campaigns, ending in A.D. 1492, by which Christian armies drove Muslim rulers out of Spain. (p. 330)

Reformation *n.* a movement of opposition to the Roman Catholic Church, beginning in the 16th century. (p. 465)

regent (REE•juhnt) *n.* a person who rules in place of an absent or underage monarch. (p. 253)

religious order *n.* a group of people who live according to a religious rule. (p. 324)

Renaissance (REHN•ih•SAHNS) *n.* a period of rebirth and creativity in art, writing, and thought from about A.D. 1300 to 1600, beginning in Italy and eventually spreading throughout Europe. (p. 435)

republic *n.* a form of government in which power rests with the citizens, who vote in order to elect leaders. (p. 48)

reunify *v.* to bring together again. (p. 216)

Roman Catholic *adj.* relating to the Christian church of the West that is under the authority of the pope. (p. 62)

S

Sahara *n.* a large desert of northern Africa, stretching from the Atlantic coast to the Nile Valley. (p. 157)

Saladin (SAL•uh•din) *n.* a military leader who united Muslims to fight the Christians in Palestine during the 12th century A.D. (p. 329)

salon *n.* a gathering of thinkers and artists to discuss issues and exchange ideas during the Enlightenment. (p. 538)

samurai (SAM•uh•RY) *n.* a trained warrior of the Japanese aristocracy. (p. 267)

savannah *n.* (suh•VAN•uh) a flat grassland, with few trees, in a tropical region. (p. 157)

schism (SKIHZ•uhm) *n.* an official split between two groups. (p. 62)

scholar-official *n.* an educated person with a government position. (p. 224)

scientific method *n.* an approach to scientific investigation that involves making careful observations, forming and testing a hypothesis, and drawing a conclusion that confirms or modifies the hypothesis. (p. 506)

Scientific Revolution *n.* a period, beginning in the A.D. 1500s, during which European scholars began to question classical scientific ideas and Christian beliefs. (p. 503)

secondary source *n.* a work produced about a historical event by someone who was not actually there. (p. 33)

Seljuk Turk *n.* a member of a Turkish people that controlled central and western Asia from the 11th to the 13th century. (p. 327)

serf *n.* a peasant farmer in feudal society, who labored for a noble in exchange for protection and certain rights. (p. 297)

Shakespeare, William *n.* most famous English writer of the Renaissance, best known for his plays *Romeo and Juliet* and *Hamlet.* (p. 447)

Shi`a (SHEE•uh) *n.* a Muslim group that resisted the Umayyads' rule, believing that the caliph should be a relative of the prophet Muhammad. (p. 103)

Shinto *n.* the traditional religion of Japan, based on worship of and respect for nature and ancestors. (p. 252)

shogun *n.* a Japanese military leader—one of a group that first came to power in A.D. 1192 and ruled on the emperor's behalf but usually in their own interests. (p. 268)

Shona *n.* a Bantu-speaking culture that was thriving in what is now the countries of Botswana, Mozambique, and Zimbabwe by A.D. 1000. (p. 187)

Shotoku (SHOH•toh•KOO), **Prince** *n.* a regent who ruled Japan from A.D. 593 to 622 and brought elements of Chinese culture—in particular, the Buddhist religion—to the country. (p. 253)

Silk Roads *n.* the ancient trade routes that connected Europe with China. (p. 430)

slash-and-burn agriculture *n.* a type of farming in which patches of land are prepared for planting by cutting down and burning the natural vegetation. (p. 370)

Songhai *n.* a West African people whose leaders created a great empire in the 15th and 16th centuries A.D. (p. 166)

sponsor *n.* a person who gives money in support of a person or project. (p. 511)

standing army *n.* a fighting force that is maintained in times of peace as well as times of war. (p. 119)

stele (STEE•lee) *n.* an ancient carved stone marker commemorating an important date or great event. (p. 384)

Stoicism (STOH•ih•SIHZ•uhm) *n.* a Greek philosophy that stressed the importance of virtue, duty, and endurance and was especially influential in ancient Rome. (p. 68)

Suleyman I *n.* the sultan of the Ottoman Empire from A.D. 1520 to 1566, who encouraged the arts and organized a legal code. (p. 352)

Sundiata (sun•JAH•tah) *n.* an ancient ruler of the Malinke people, who captured the capital of Ghana and greatly expanded the empire. (p. 165)

Sunnah *n.* Muhammad's words and deeds, which serve Muslims as a guide for proper living. (p. 94)

Sunni *n.* a member of the Muslim group that accepted the rule of the elected caliphs and did not resist the Umayyads. (p. 103)

Swahili (swah•HEE•lee) *n.* an African language that blends Bantu and Arabic elements. (p. 183)

T

Tenochtitlán (teh•NOHCH•tee•TLAHN) *n.* an ancient Aztec city, founded in A.D. 1325 on a small island in Lake Texcoco. (p. 397)

Thomas Aquinas (uh•KWY•nuhs) *n.* an Italian scholar who made a synthesis of classical philosophy and Christian theology. (p. 325)

Timbuktu *n.* a city of central Mali in West Africa, which was founded in the 13th century and was a center of trade and culture. (p. 165)

Tokugawa Shogunate (TOH•koo•GAH•wah SHOH•guh•niht) *n.* the rule of Tokugawa Ieyasu and his successors in Japan, which began in A.D. 1603 and brought a 250-year period of stability to the country. (p. 270)

triangular trade *n.* the exchange of goods and slaves across the Atlantic Ocean between the Americas, Europe, and Africa. (p. 522)

tribute *n.* a payment made by one country to another as a sign of respect. (p. 241)

Treaty of Tordesillas (TAWR•day•SEEL•yahs) *n.* an agreement between Spain and Portugal in 1494, establishing an imaginary line from north to south around the world and allowing Spain to claim lands west of the line and Portugal to claim lands to the east of it. (p. 514)

U

universal gravitation *n.* Isaac Newton's theory that gravity acts on all objects throughout the universe. (p. 504)

V

vassal *n.* in feudal society, a person who received land and protection from a lord in return for loyalty. (p. 268)

vegetation zone *n.* a region that, because of its soil and climate, has distinctive types of plants. (p. 157)

vernacular *n.* a person's native language. (p. 449)

W

weather *n.* the condition of the atmosphere at a particular place and time. (p. 10)

wood-block printing *n.* a printing system developed by the ancient Chinese, in which wood blocks were carved with enough characters to print entire pages. (p. 228)

Y

Yucatán (YOO•kuh•TAN) **Peninsula** *n.* an area of southeastern Mexico that extends into the Caribbean Sea and the Gulf of Mexico. (p. 367)

Z

Zen *n.* a Japanese form of Buddhism, focusing on self-discipline, simplicity, and meditation. (p. 258)

Zheng He (juhng huh) *n.* a Chinese admiral whose extensive voyages between A.D. 1405 and 1433 greatly expanded China's foreign trade and reputation. (p. 241)

Spanish Glossary

A

Abd al-Malik *s.* soberano musulmán que asumió como califa en el año 685 d.C. y convirtió el árabe en idioma oficial del gobierno en todo el territorio musulmán. (pág. 115)

Abd al-Rahman III *s.* octavo emir de al-Andalus que llevó a su reino a su máximo apogeo. (pág. 132)

Alfonso I *s.* rey del Congo a partir de 1506 d.C. Fue influenciado por los portugueses y participó en el tráfico de esclavos. (pág. 197)

al-Andalus *s.* región de España gobernada por los musulmanes entre 700s y 1492 d.C. (pág. 131)

Allah [Alá] *s.* Dios en la religión islámica. (pág. 88)

alluvial soil [suelo aluvial] *s.* suelo muy rico y fértil depositado por agua que fluye. (pág. 373)

Almoravids [almorávides] *s.* dinastía islámica del norte de África que procuró convertir a la fuerza a pueblos vecinos, incluyendo Marruecos, España y Ghana. (pág. 161)

anatomy [anatomía] *s.* estudio científico de las formas y estructuras de los seres humanos, plantas y animales. (pág. 498)

Angkor Wat *s.* complejo de templos en el sudeste asiático de más de 1,5 km2 de extensión, construido alrededor de 1100 d.C. Es la estructura religiosa más grande del mundo. (pág. 279)

anthropology [antropología] *s.* estudio del hombre y la cultura humana. (pág. 26)

aqueduct [acueducto] *s.* estructura creada para llevar agua potable a una ciudad o poblado. (pág. 69)

archaeology [arqueología] *s.* recuperación y estudio de los restos físicos del pasado. (pág. 25)

artifact [artefacto] *s.* objeto construido por el hombre. (pág. 25)

Askia Muhammad *s.* soberano del imperio Songhai entre 1493 y 1528 d.C., que expandió el imperio y organizó su gobierno. (pág. 168)

astrolabe [astrolabio] *s.* instrumento utilizado para medir los ángulos de las estrellas en el horizonte y así ayudar a los navegantes a determinar su latitud. (pág. 512)

Augustus [Augusto] *s.* primer emperador de Roma, que gobernó desde 27 a.C. hasta 14 d.C. y expandió el tamaño y la influencia del Imperio Romano. (pág. 49)

B

Bagdad *s.* ciudad ubicada en lo que hoy es Irak, que fue la capital del imperio abasí. (pág. 120)

Bantu migrations [migraciones bantúes] *s.* movimiento comenzado alrededor del año 1000 a.C. de pueblos de habla bantú desde África occidental hacia el sur y el este, que fueron divulgando sus idiomas y culturas. (pág. 182)

bubonic plague [peste bubónica] *s.* enfermedad mortal que se extendió por Asia y Europa a mediados del siglo XIV, en un brote conocido como la Muerte Negra. (pág. 333)

Buddhism [budismo] *s.* sistema de creencias basado en las enseñanzas de Siddhartha Gautama, el Buda, que promueve la liberación del ser humano de los deseos mundanos. (pág. 214)

bureaucracy [burocracia] *s.* sistema de gobierno dividido en departamentos y organismos organizados. (págs. 114, 224)

bushido *s.* código de conducta de los guerreros samurai, que requería que fueran generosos, valientes y leales. (pág. 308)

Byzantine Empire [imperio bizantino] *s.* Imperio Romano de Oriente, con sede de gobierno en Constantinopla, desde el siglo IV hasta el siglo XV. (pág. 59)

C

cacao *s.* árbol tropical americano cuyas semillas se usan para fabricar el chocolate. (pág. 370)

caliph [califa] *s.* monarca de la comunidad musulmana, considerado sucesor de Mahoma. (pág. 100)

calligraphy [caligrafía] *s.* arte de escritura manuscrita. (pág. 121)

Calvin, John [Calvino, Juan] *s.* líder de la Reforma protestante, que vivió desde 1509 hasta 1564 d.C. y promulgó la doctrina de la predestinación. (pág. 472)

capitalism [capitalismo] *s.* sistema económico basado en la propiedad privada de los recursos económicos y en el uso de esos recursos para obtener ganancias. (pág. 545)

caravel [carabela] *s.* tipo de embarcación portuguesa con velas cuadradas y triangulares, construida para realizar largos viajes. (pág. 512)

cartography [cartografía] *s.* conocimientos y métodos utilizados para hacer mapas. (pág. 15)

celadon [celadón] *s.* tipo de cerámica coreana, generalmente de color verde azulado. (pág. 276)

Charlemagne [Carlomagno] *s.* rey de los francos (a partir de 768 d.C.) que conquistó gran parte de Europa y esparció el cristianismo en las regiones conquistadas. (pág. 294)

chasqui [chas qui] *s.* un mensajero en el imperio inca que llevaba sensajes a lo largo del imperio. (pág. 411)

chivalry [cavallería] *s.* código de conducta de los caballeros de Europa medieval que exaltaba ideales tales como el valor, el honor y el respeto hacia las mujeres y los más débiles. (pág. 301)

Christianity [cristianismo] *s.* religión basada en la vida y enseñanzas de Jesús. (pág. 50)

circumnavigate [circunnavegar] *v.* realizar un viaje completo alrededor del mundo. (pág. 515)

clan *s.* grupo de personas unidos por vínculos de consanguinidad o de matrimonio. (págs. 86, 151)

clergy [clero] *s.* personas con autoridad sacerdotal en una religión. (pág. 321)

climate [clima] *s.* patrón de condiciones meteorológicas en un determinado lugar durante un largo período de tiempo. (pág. 10)

Clovis *s.* líder de los francos, quien conquistó la provincia romana de Galia en 486 d.C. y más tarde estableció un extenso y poderoso reino franco. (pág. 56)

codex [códice] *s.* libro utilizado por las civilizaciones mesoamericanas para registrar acontecimientos históricos importantes. (pág. 385)

Columbian Exchange [intercambio colombino] *s.* intercambio de plantas, animales y otros seres vivos entre los hemisferios oriental y occidental después del viaje de Colón a América, en 1492 d.C. (pág. 521)

Confucianism [confucionismo] *s.* sistema de creencias basado en las enseñanzas de Confucio, un erudito que transmitió virtudes morales y ética. (pág. 214)

Constantine [Constantino] *s.* emperador romano de 306 a 337 d.C. , que terminó con la persecución de los cristianos y mudó la capital del imperio a Bizancio (más tarde conocida como Constantinopla). (pág. 54)

continent [continente] *s.* una de las siete extensas masas de tierra del planeta: América del Norte, América del Sur, Europa, Asia, África, Australia y la Antártida. (pág. 9)

convert [convertir] *v.* persuadir a alguien de adoptar una nueva religión o creencia. (pág. 479)

Córdoba *s.* capital de al-Andalus. (pág. 131)

Cortés, Hernán *s.* explorador español que conquistó a la civilización azteca de México en 1521 d.C. (pág. 400)

covenant [pacto] *s.* acuerdo mutuo. (pág. 483)

Crusades [Cruzadas] *s.* serie de expediciones militares desde la Europa cristiana hasta Palestina entre los siglos XI y XIII d.C. (pág. 327)

culture [cultura] *s.* forma distintiva de vida compartida por un grupo de personas. (pág. 27)

D

daimyo *s.* señor feudal japonés que poseía grandes territorios y un ejército samurai privado, y que no pagaba impuestos al gobierno. (pág. 267)

Daoism [daoísmo] *s.* sistema de creencias originado en China alrededor del 500 a.C., que enfatizaba la armonía con la naturaleza y con los sentimientos internos. (pág. 215)

Declaration of Independence [Declaración de la Independencia] *s.* documento que declaraba la independencia de las colonias americanas de Gran Bretaña. (pág. 546)

Declaration of the Rights of Man and of the Citizen [Declaración de los Derechos del Hombre y del Ciudadano] *s.* documento adoptado por el gobierno revolucionario francés en 1789 que resume los derechos de las personas. (pág. 548)

dissection [disección] *s.* corte realizado para abrir plantas y animales para estudiar e investigar sus partes. (pág. 498)

divan [diván] *s.* consejo imperial que asesoraba al sultán en el impero otomano. (pág. 351)

E

elevation [altitud] *s.* altura de la tierra por encima del nivel del mar. (pág. 368)

elite *s.* miembros más importantes o más ricos de una sociedad o grupo. (pág. 374)

Elizabethan Age [Era isabelina] *s.* período del reinado de la reina Elizabeth I en Inglaterra, de 1558 a 1603. (pág. 448)

embassy [embajada] *s.* oficina representante del gobierno de un país en otro país. (pág. 253)

emperor [emperador] *s.* soberano de un imperio. (pág. 49)

empire [imperio] *s.* grupo de distintas culturas o territorios liderado por un único soberano todopoderoso. (pág. 49)

F

enlightened despot [déspota ilustrado] *s.* soberano que tenía poder absoluto pero que también tenía en cuenta las ideas políticas de la Ilustración y procuraba gobernar de manera justa y educada.(pág. 543)

Enlightenment [Ilustración] *s.* movimiento filosófico del siglo XVIII que procuraba utilizar la razón para comprender las verdades de la naturaleza humana. (pág. 535)

epic poem [poema épico] *s.* extenso poema que relata una historia de aventuras heroicas. (pág. 309)

excavation [excavación] *s.* proceso de desenterrar objetos con significación histórica para estudiarlos. (pág. 26)

F

faction [facción] *s.* pequeño grupo cuyos intereses están en contra de los de un grupo más grande al cual pertenecen. (pág. 124)

federalism [federalismo] *s.* poder compartido entre una organización o gobierno y sus miembros. (pág. 484)

feudalism [feudalismo] *s.* sistema político y social de la Edad Media en Europa, en el cual los señores feudales otorgaban tierras a vasallos a cambio de servicio y lealtad. (pág. 296)

Forbidden City [Ciudad prohibida] *s.* grupo de palacios amurallados construidos para el emperador chino poco después del año 1400 d.C. en la ciudad capital de Beijing. (pág. 240)

Francis of Assisi, St. [Francisco de Asís, San] *s.* italiano que fundó la orden religiosa franciscana a principios del siglo XIII d.C. (pág. 324)

G

Genghis Khan *s.* líder mongol que unificó las tribus mongolas alrededor del año 1206 d.C. y comenzó una campaña de conquista que le permitió forjar un imperio que abarcaba el norte de china y Asia central. (pág. 233)

geocentric theory [teoría geocéntrica] s. teoría que postula que la Tierra es el centro del universo. (pág. 497)

geography [geografía] s. estudio de las características naturales de la Tierra. (pág. 9)

Ghana s. región entre el Sahara y los bosques del sur de África occidental, cuna de muchas civilizaciones antiguas. (pág. 159)

glyph [glifo] s. dibujo que representa una palabra, sílaba o sonido. (pág. 375)

golden age [edad de oro] s. período en el cual una sociedad o cultura alcanza su apogeo. (pág. 121)

Great Enclosure [Gran recinto de Zimbabwe] s. la más grande de las tres secciones principales del asentamiento shona en el Gran Zimbabwe—probablemente una residencia real. (pág. 188)

Great Schism [Gran Cisma] s. división de la Iglesia Católica Romana entre 1378 y 1417 d.C., que ocurrió cuando los dos centro de poder de la Iglesia, Avignon y Roma, se separaron y eligieron distintos papas. (pág. 462)

Great Zimbabwe [Gran Zimbabwe] s. asentamiento central del imperio shona en África, rodeado por una gran muralla de piedra, que abarca más de 100 acres y tiene una población de 10.000 a 20.000 habitantes. (pág. 188)

Gregory VII, Pope [Gregorio VII, Papa] s. líder de la iglesia católica romana de 1073 a 1085, que luchó con el emperador Enrique IV por el poder. (pág. 323)

griot s. narrador oficial en una civilización africana. (pág. 153)

guild [gremio] s. asociación de personas que comparten una profesión u oficio, creada para controlar la calidad y cantidad de su producción y proteger sus intereses. (pág. 302)

Gutenberg, Johann s. inventor alemán que, a mediados de 1400, inventó la prensa de tipos móviles. (pág. 449)

H

habeas corpus s. derecho de las personas a no ser encarceladas en forma ilegítima. (pág. 344)

haiku s. poema japonés de 17 sílabas organizadas en tres versos de 5, 7 y 5 sílabas. (pág. 260)

harmony [armonía] s. combinación de elementos para formar un todo agradable. (pág. 498)

heliocentric [heliocéntrico] adj. que tiene al sol como centro. (pág. 503)

hemisphere [hemisferi] s. cualquiera de las dos mitades iguales de la Tierra, marcadas por el ecuador o el primer meridiano. (pág. 17)

Henry IV, Emperor [Enrique IV, emperador] s. soberano del siglo XI del Santo Imperio Romano, en continua lucha por el poder con el Papa Gregorio VII. (pág. 323)

Hijrah s. migración de Mahoma y sus seguidores desde La Meca hasta la ciudad de Yathrib en el año 622 d.C. (pág. 93)

historian [historiador] s. persona que estudia e interpreta el pasado. (pág. 31)

history [historia] s. estudio de acontecimientos pasados. (pág. 31)

humanism [humanismo] s. movimiento en la Europa renacentista que celebraba el potencial humano y los logros, enfatizando el estudio de temas como la historia, la gramática, la literatura y la filosofía. (pág. 432)

Hundred Years' War [Guerra de los Cien Años] s. serie de guerras entre Inglaterra y Francia, de 1337 a 1453 d.C. (pág. 335)

I

Iberian Peninsula [Península ibérica] s. extremo del suroeste de Europa, donde se encuentras las naciones modernas de España y Portugal. (pág. 114)

Ignatius of Loyola [Ignacio de Loyola, s. español que fundó la orden religiosa de los jesuitas a principios de 1530. (pág. 474)

imperial *adj.* relativo a un imperio o emperador. (pág. 223)

indulgence [indulgencia] *s.* reducción de la pena por los pecados cometidos en la tierra. (pág. 463)

Inquisition [Inquisición] *s.* tribunal establecido por la Iglesia Católica Romana en 1542 d.C. para investigar a las personas que pudieran haberse desviado de la fe católica y para reforzar el poder de la iglesia. (págs. 331, 474)

Islam [islam] *s.* religión monoteísta basada en las enseñanzas de Mahoma. (pág. 93)

J

Janissary [jenízaro] *s.* miembro de una fuerza elite de soldados del impero otomano, constituido principalmente por esclavos. (pág. 353)

Jesuit [jesuita] *s.* miembro de la Sociedad de Jesús, orden religiosa fundada a principios de 1530 d.C. por Ignacio de Loyola. (pág. 474)

Joan of Arc [Juana de Arco] *s.* joven campesina francesa que llevó a los franceses a la victoria contra los ingleses en Orleáns, en 1429 d.C. (pág. 335)

John, King [Juan, rey] *s.* rey de Inglaterra que firmó la Carta Magna en 1215 d.C. (pág. 342)

Judaism [judaísmo] *s.* religión de los judíos, basada en las escrituras hebreas y en la creencia de un solo dios. (pág. 50)

Justinian [Justiniano] *s.* soberano del Imperio Romano de Oriente de 527 a 565 d.C., que gobernó con su esposa, Teodora, y reconquistó territorios perdidos para el imperio. (pág. 59)

Justinian Code [Código Justiniano] *s.* código legal, preparado bajo la dirección del emperador bizantino Justiniano, que reglamentaba la mayor parte de la vida bizantina. (pág. 59)

K

kabuki [kabuki] *s.* forma de teatro japonés desarrollado en el siglo 17 y que presenta canto y danza melodramáticos, mucho maquillaje y trajes elaborados. (pág. 259)

Khmer Empire [imperio Khmer] *s.* el reino más poderoso y más duradero del sureste asiático, ubicado en lo que hoy es Camboya. (pág. 278)

Kilwa *s.* antigua ciudad estado en la costa oriental de África, habitada por personas de Irán y de Arabia, que empezó a prosperar a fines del siglo XIII d.C. (pág. 182)

kinship [parentesco] *s.* vínculo entre las personas por consanguinidad, por matrimonio o por adopción. (pág. 151)

knight [caballero] *s.* guerrero montado altamente entrenado al servicio de un noble durante la Edad Media europea. (pág. 300)

Kongo [Congo] *s.* antiguo reino que abarcaba las costas occidentales de África, poblado por pueblos del Congo hablantes de bantú hacia el siglo XIV d.C. (pág. 195)

Koryo [Koryu] *s.* reino de la península coreana, establecido en 935 d.C. tras el colapso del reino de Silla. (pág. 276)

Kublai Khan *s.* nieto de Genghis Khan que asumió el poder en China del Sur en el año 1260 d.C. y venció al ejército de los Song 1279, lo que otorgó a los mongoles el control de toda China. (pág. 234)

L

labor specialization [especialización laboral] *s.* realización de tipos específicos de trabajo por parte de trabajadores capacitados o expertos. (pág. 152)

landform [accidente geográfico] *s.* característica de la superficie de la Tierra formada naturalmente, como una isla, una montaña o una meseta. (pág. 10)

latitude [latitud] *s.* distancia norte-sur con respecto al ecuador. (pág. 17)

Leonardo da Vinci *s.* pintor italiano del Renacimiento, nacido en 1452 d.C., autor de muchas obras maestras, como por ejemplo la *Mona Lisa* y *La última cena*, además de destacarse en la investigación científica. (pág. 438)

longbow [arco] *s.* arma que puede lanzar flechas capaces de penetrar la armadura de un caballero. (pág. 336)

longitude [longitud] *s.* distancia este-oeste a partir del primer meridiano. (pág. 17)

lord [señor] *s.* poderoso noble hacendado. (pág. 296)

Luther, Martin [Lutero, Martín] *s.* teólogo alemán, nacido en 1483 d.C., líder de la Reforma, que postulaba la salvación a través de la fe en Dios en lugar de mediante obras de bien. (pág. 463)

M

Magna Carta [Carta Magna] *s.* lista de derechos redactada por la nobleza inglesa y firmada por el rey Juan en 1215 d.C. (pág. 342)

maize [maíz] *s.* cereal cultivado por las civilizaciones nativas americanas, cuyos granos se encuentran en mazorcas. (pág. 370)

Mali [Malí] *s.* imperio de África occidental establecido por el pueblo Malinké. (pág. 165)

Manchu [manchú] *s.* perteneciente a un pueblo del noreste chino que conquistó la China en 1644 d.C. y que comenzó la última dinastía de la historia china, llamada la Dinastía Qing. (pág. 242)

manor [señorío] *s.* propiedad de un noble feudal, que solía incluir una fortificación o un castillo. (pág. 299)

Mansa Musa *s.* emperador de Malí que realizó una famosa peregrinación a La Meca en 1324 d.C. (pág. 166)

maritime [marítimo] *adj.* relativo al mar. (pág. 241)

Maya [mayas] *s.* civilización del sur de México y el norte de América Central, que alcanzó su máximo esplendor entre 250 y 900 d.C. (pág. 381)

Mbanza *s.* capital del antiguo reino africano del Congo. (pág. 196)

mercantilism [mercantilismo] *s.* política económica basada en la idea de que el poder de una nación depende de su riqueza. (pág. 525)

mercenary [mercenario] *s.* soldado contratado para luchar. (pág. 132)

Mesoamerica [Mesoamérica] *s.* región que comprende el sur de México y gran parte de América Central. (pág. 367)

Michelangelo [Miguel Ángel] *s.* artista italiano del Renacimiento, nacido en 1475 d.C., que trabajó principalmente con escultor pero también pintó otras tan famosas como el cielorraso de la Capilla Sixtina en Roma. (pág. 438)

Middle Ages [Edad Media] *s.* período de la historia europea desde la caída del Imperio Romano hasta el Renacimiento (500–1450 d.C.). (pág. 291)

missionary *s.* persona que viaja a otro país para realizar trabajos religiosos. (pág. 479)

monastery [monasterio] *s.* lugar donde los miembros de una orden religiosa practican una vida de oración y culto. (pág. 295)

Mongol Ascendancy [Dominio mongol] *s.* período en el cual los mongoles controlaron la totalidad de Asia central, lo que garantizó la seguridad del comercio y los viajes por tierra. (pág. 236)

monotheism [monoteísmo] *s.* creencia en un único dios. (pág. 88)

Montezuma II *s.* último emperador azteca, que gobernó desde 1502 hasta 1520 d.C. y fue derrocado por los españoles. (pág. 400)

mosaic [mosaico] *s.* cuadro realizado con muchos azulejos pequeños o trocitos de vidrio coloreados. (pág. 67)

mosque [mezquita] *s.* edificio de culto musulmán, diseñado de tal modo que quede de frente a la ciudad de La Meca. (pág. 95)

mother culture [cultura madre] *s.* cultura que modela e influye las costumbres e ideas de futuras culturas. (pág. 377)

movable type [tipo móvil] *s.* pequeño bloque de metal o de madera con un solo carácter en relieve, utilizado para imprimir textos. (pág. 228)

Murasaki Shikibu, Lady *s.* escritora japonesa de principios del siglo XI d.C., que escribió *El cuento de Genji,* considerado una de las primeras novelas del mundo. (pág. 259)

Muslim [musulmán] *s.* persona que sigue la religión islámica y acepta a Alá como su único Dios. (pág. 93)

Mutapa *s.* antiguo reino en lo que hoy es el país de Zimbabwe, fundado por un rey shona alrededor del año 1440 d.C.; también se refiere al soberano de ese reino. (pág. 190)

N

Nam Viet *s.* reino vietnamita conquistado por los chinos en 111 a.C.(pág. 277)

natural rights [derechos naturales] *s.* derechos con los que cada persona nace, tales como el derecho a la vida, a la libertad y a la propiedad, según John Locke, filósofo del siglo XVIII. (pág. 536)

Noh *s.* forma de teatro japonés desarrollado en 1300s d.C., que a menudo relata leyendas y cuentos populares representados por actores con máscaras de madera pintadas. (pág. 258)

nomad [nómada] *s.* persona que no tiene hogar permanente y que se muda constantemente de un lugar a otro. (págs. 86, 213)

O

oasis *s.* zona fértil en medio del desierto. (pág. 86)

Olmec [olmeca] *s.* la primera cultura mesoamericana conocida, que floreció entre 1200 y 400 a.C. y tenía su centro en el sureste de México. (pág. 373)

Omar Khayyam *s.* poeta musulmán nacido en Persia que solía escribir en forma de cuartetos y que también fue un gran matemático. (pág. 122)

oral history [historia oral] *s.* relato verbal no escrito de acontecimientos, como una historia que es transmitida de generación en generación. (pág. 32)

Orthodox [ortodoxo] *adj.* relativo a la iglesia cristiana que se desarrolló en el imperio bizantino y no se encontraba bajo la autoridad del papa. (pág. 62)

Osman [Osmán] *s.* soberano turco fundador del impero otomano a principios del siglo XIV d.C. (pág. 351)

P

Pacal II *s.* rey de la ciudad maya de Palenque durante casi 70 años (a partir de 615 d.C.), y uno de los reyes mayas más importantes. (pág. 384)

Pachacuti *s.* último soberano inca, que subió al poder en 1438 d.C. y expandió el imperio inca. (pág. 410)

parliament [parlamento] *s.* grupo de representantes con ciertos poderes de gobierno. (pág. 343)

patron [mecenas] *s.* persona que apoya una actividad o institución, especialmente en el aspecto financiero. (pág. 437)

Peace of Westphalia [Tratado de Westphalia] *s.* acuerdo alcanzado en 1648 d.C. que reconoce la división permanente de Europa Occidental en naciones católicas y protestantes, y que terminó con muchas guerras religiosas. (pág. 483)

perspective [perspectiva] *s.* técnica de pintura, desarrollada durante el Renacimiento, que representa a los objetos en un espacio tridimensional. (pág. 437)

philosophe [filósofo] *s.* pensador del siglo XVIII que procuraba aplicar el método científico a los problemas sociales. (pág. 536)

pilgrimage [peregrinación] *s.* viaje a un lugar sagrado o santuario. (pág. 89)

Pizarro, Francisco *s.* explorador español que llegó a Perú en 1532 d.C. y hacia el año 1535 ya había conquistado el imperio inca. (pág. 413)

Polo, Marco *s.* comerciante veneciano que viajó por la Ruta de la Seda y llegó a China alrededor del año 1275 d.C. Se convirtió en ayudante de Kublai Khan y más tarde publicó un popular libro que relata sus aventuras. (pág. 236)

porcelain [porcelana] *s.* tipo de cerámica dura y blanca. (pág. 229)

predestination [predestinación] *s.* doctrina que postula que Dios escoge a las personas para la salvación y la condenación antes de que nazcan, y que los individuos no tienen el poder de cambiar la voluntad de Dios. (pág. 472)

primary source [fuente primaria] *s.* documento o elemento creado durante un determinado periodo histórico. (pág. 32)

printing press [prensa] *s.* máquina para imprimir un papel mediante tipos móviles con tinta. (pág. 449)

projection [proyección] *s.* forma de representar la superficie curva de la Tierra en un mapa plano manteniendo la distorsión en forma coherente y manejable. (pág. 16)

Protestant [protestante] *s.* miembro del grupo cristiano que se separó de la Iglesia Católica Romana durante o después del siglo XVI. (pág. 465)

Q

quipu *s.* cuerdas anudadas utilizadas para contar en la antigua civilización inca. (pág. 414)

Qur'an [Corán] *s.* libro sagrado de los musulmanes, que contiene las revelaciones de Alá recopiladas por los seguidores de Mahoma después de su muerte. (pág. 94)

R

Rationalism [racionalismo] *s.* idea de que las personas deben usar la razón, o el pensamiento lógico, para comprender el mundo. (pág. 497)

Reconquista *s.* serie de campañas, finalizadas en 1492 d.C., mediante las cuales los ejércitos cristianos expulsaron a los gobernantes musulmanes de España. (pág. 330)

Reformation [Reforma] *s.* movimiento de oposición a la Iglesia Católica Romana, que comenzó en el siglo XVI. (pág. 465)

regent [regente] *s.* persona que gobierna en nombre de un monarca ausente o menor de edad. (pág. 253)

religious order [orden religiosa] *s.* grupo de personas que viven según una norma religiosa. (pág. 324)

Renaissance [Renacimiento] *s.* período de revalorización y creatividad en el arte, la escritura y el pensamiento, desde el siglo XIV hasta el siglo XVII d.C., que comenzó en Italia y se extendió gradualmente por toda Europa. (pág. 435)

republic [república] *s.* forma de gobierno en la cual el poder está en manos de los ciudadanos, que votan para elegir a sus gobernantes. (pág. 48)

reunify [reunificar] *v.* volver a unir. (pág. 216)

Roman Catholic [católico romano] *adj.* relativo a la Iglesia Cristiana de Occidente que se encuentra bajo la autoridad del papa. (pág. 62)

S

Sahara *s.* gran desierto en el norte de África, que se extiende desde la costa del Atlántico hasta el Valle del Nilo. (pág. 157)

Saladin [Saladino] *s.* jefe militar que unió a los musulmanes para combatir a los cristianos en Palestina durante el siglo XII d.C. (pág. 329)

salon [salón] *s.* reunión de pensadores y artistas para tratar diversos temas e intercambiar ideas durante la Ilustración. (pág. 538)

samurai s. guerrero entrenado de la aristocracia japonesa. (pág. 267)

savannah [sabana] s. extensa llanura, con pocos árboles, en una región tropical. (pág. 157)

schism [cisma] s. separación oficial entre dos grupos. (pág. 62)

scholar-official [erudito-funcionario] s. persona instruida que ocupa un puesto gubernamental. (pág. 224)

scientific method [método científico] s. enfoque de la investigación científica que implica realizar observaciones cuidadosas, formular y poner a prueba una hipótesis, y sacar una conclusión que confirme o modifique la hipótesis. (pág. 506)

Scientific Revolution [Revolución Científica] s. período que comenzó en el siglo XVI d.C., durante el cual los eruditos europeos comenzaron a cuestionar ideas científicas clásicas y creencias cristianas. (pág. 503)

secondary source [fuente secundaria] s. obra escrita sobre un acontecimiento histórico por una persona que no presenció los hechos. (pág. 33)

Seljuk Turk s. miembro de un pueblo turco que controló Asia central y occidental entre los siglos XI y XIII. (pág. 327)

serf [siervo] s. campesino agricultor en la sociedad feudal, que trabajaba para un noble a cambio de protección y de ciertos derechos. (pág. 297)

Shakespeare, William s. el escritor inglés más famoso del Renacimiento, conocido por sus obras *Romeo y Julieta* y *Hamlet*. (pág. 447)

**Shi`a** [shi`a] s. grupo musulmán que se resistió al dominio de los omeyas, y que creía que el califa debería ser pariente del profeta Mahoma. (pág. 103)

Shinto [sintoísmo] s. religión tradicional japonesa basada en el culto y el respeto a la naturaleza y los ancestros. (pág. 252)

shogun [shogún] s. jefe militar japonés, perteneciente a un grupo que subió al poder en el año 1192 d.C. y que gobernaba en nombre del emperador a menudo para su propio beneficio. (pág. 268)

Shona s. cultura de habla bantú que prosperó en la zona que hoy ocupan los países de Botswana, Mozambique y Zimbabwe hacia el siglo XI d.C. (pág. 187)

Shotoku, Prince [Shotoku, Príncipe] s. regente que gobernó Japón entre 593 y 622 d.C., e introdujo elementos de la cultura china (en especial, la religión budista) a su país. (pág. 253)

Silk Roads [Ruta de la seda] s. antiguas rutas comerciales que conectaban Europa con la China. (pág. 430)

slash-and-burn agricultura [agricultura de tala y quema] s. tipo de agricultura que consiste en talar y quemar la vegetación natural para preparar terrenos para el cultivo. (pág. 370)

Songhai s. pueblo de África Occidental cuyos líderes crearon un gran imperio en los siglos XV y XVI d.C. (pág. 166)

sponsor [patrocinador] s. persona que da dinero para apoyar a una persona o proyecto. (pág. 511)

standing army [ejército permanente] s. fuerza militar que se conserva tanto en épocas de guerra como en épocas de paz. (pág. 119)

stele [estela] s. antiguo mojón de piedra esculpida que conmemoraba una fecha o acontecimiento importante. (pág. 384)

Stoicism [estoicismo] s. filosofía griega que enfatizaba la importancia de la virtud, el deber y la entereza y que tuvo una gran influencia en la antigua Roma. (pág. 68)

Suleyman I [Solimán I] s. sultán del imperio otomano entre 1520 y 1566 d.C., que fomentó las artes y organizó un código legal. (pág. 352)

Sundiata s. antiguo soberano del pueblo Malinké, que conquistó la capital de Ghana y expandió enormemente el imperio. (pág. 165)

Sunnah [sunna] s. palabra y obra de Mahoma, utilizada por los musulmanes como guía para vivir correctamente. (pág. 94)

Sunni [sunni] *s.* miembro del grupo musulmán que aceptaba el gobierno de los califas elegidos y no se resistía a los omeyas. (pág. 103)

Swahili [suahili] *s.* lengua africana que combina elementos del bantú y del árabe. (pág. 183)

T

Tenochtitlán *s.* antigua ciudad azteca, fundada en 1325 d.C. en una pequeña isla en el Lago Texcoco. (pág. 397)

Thomas Aquinas [Tomás de Aquino] *s.* erudito italiano que realizó una síntesis de la filosofía clásica y teología cristiana. (pág. 325)

Timbuktu [Timbuctú] *s.* ciudad en Malí central, en África occidental, fundada en el siglo XIII, que fue un centro de comercio y de cultura. (pág. 165)

Tokugawa Shogunate [shogunato Tokugawa] *s.* gobierno de Tokugawa Ieyasu y sus sucesores en Japón, que comenzó en 1603 d.C. y logró un período de estabilidad en el país que duró 250 años. (pág. 270)

triangular trade [triángulo comercial] *s.* intercambio de mercancías y esclavos a través del Océano Atlántico entre América, Europa y África. (pág. 522)

tribute [tributo] *s.* pago realizado por un país a otro como signo de respeto. (pág. 241)

Treaty of Tordesillas [Tratado de Tordesillas] *s.* acuerdo entre España y Portugal, en 1494, que establecía que las tierras descubiertas al oeste de una línea imaginaria en el océano Atlántico pertenecerían a España, y las tierras al este de esa línea pertenecerían a Portugal. (pág. 514)

U

universal gravitation [gravitación universal] *s.* teoría de Isaac Newton que postula que la gravedad actúa sobre todos los objetos en el universo. (pág. 504)

V

vassal [vasallo] *s.* en la sociedad feudal, persona que recibía tierras y protección de un señor feudal a cambio de lealtad. (pág. 268)

vegetation zone [zona de vegetación] *s.* región que, según su tipo de suelo y clima, presenta especies característicos de plantas. (pág. 157)

vernacular [vernáculo] *s.* idioma propio de un país. (pág. 449)

W

weather [tiempo] *s.* condición de la atmósfera en un determinado momento y lugar. (pág. 10)

wood-block printing [impresión en bloques de madera] *s.* sistema de impresión desarrollado por los antiguos chinos, que utilizaba bloques de madera tallados en relieve con los caracteres suficientes para imprimir páginas enteras. (pág. 228)

Y

Yucatán Peninsula [península de Yucatán] *s.* zona del sureste mexicano que se extiende hacia el mar Caribe y el golfo de México. (pág. 367)

Z

Zen [zen] *s.* forma japonesa de budismo que se basa en la autodisciplina, la simpleza y la meditación. (pág. 258)

Zheng He *s.* admirante chino cuyos largos viajes entre 1405 y 1433 d.C. expandieron enormemente el comercio exterior y la reputación de China. (pág. 241)

Index

An *i* preceding an italic page reference indicates that there is an illustration, and usually text information as well, on that page. An *m* or a *c* preceding an italic page reference indicates a map or chart, as well as text information on that page.

D

Index

Magellan, Ferdinand, *i510*, 515, *m515*
Magna Carta, *i348*
  in development of democracy, *c547*
  excerpt, R44
  influence on Declaration of
    Independence, 546
  Parliament's interpretation of, 344
  signed by King John, *i341*, 342,
    i342, 346–349, *i349*
magnetic compass, 225, 228, 243
magnetic resonance imaging (MRI),
  i443
Magyars, 295
Mahmud Kati, R39
Maimonides, 136–137, 499
maize, 370, 388, *i388*
Mali, 146–147, *m147*, 157–161,
    165–167, 170–173, 174–175
  art, *i164*
  empire grows, 165–166
  Islam in, 165
  Mansa Musa, 144–145
  trade, 166
Malinke, 165, 167
Manchuria, 242
Manchus, 242
manor system, 299–300, 304,
  i304–i305
Mansa Musa, *i166*
  expands Mali, 166
  pilgrimage to Mecca, 144–145,
    144–*i145*, 166
mapmaking
  in Age of Exploration, 516–517, *i518*
  development of, 15–16
  features of maps, 17, *i17*
  and historians, 21
  how to read a map, 22–23
  physical map, 18, *m18*
  political map, 18, *m18*
  projections, 16, *i16*
  in Renaissance, *i442*
  technological advances in, 19
  thematic maps, 19, *m19*
maps
  Africa, *m177, m182, m183, m196*
  al-Idrisi's world map, *m134*
  Americas, *m363, m376, m393*
  Buddhism, spread of, *m215*
  Central America, *m363*
  China, 209, *m276*
  Christianity in Europe, *m457*
  Christian missionaries, *m481*
  Crusades, *m327, m328*
  Europe, *m287, m317*
  European religions in Americas,
    m482
  Incan empire, *m411*
  Japan, *m281*
  Magellan's circumnavigation, *m515*
  Maya, *m382*
  Mongol Empire, *m234*
  Muslim Empire, *m114, m131*

Olmec, *m373*
Ottoman Empire, *m353*
Plague, spread of, *m334*
Polo, Marco, *m431*
Protestantism spreads, *m471*
Reconquista, *m330*
Renaissance, *m425*
Roman Empire, A.D. 120, 43
Spanish Armada, defeat of, *m524*
trade patterns, *m522*
voyages of discovery, *m240, m493*
Marco Polo. *See* Polo, Marco.
maritime, 241
market economy, 526
Marshal, William, 346–349
Martel, Charles, 294
Martin Luther. *See* Luther, Martin.
Martin V, Pope, 462
Mary (queen of England), 550, *i552*,
  553
mathematics
  algebra, 123, 139, 499
  Greek, 498
  Incan, 414
  Mayan, 385, 387
  Muslim, 123, 134, 139, *i139*,
    498–499
  Renaissance, 448
Maya, 367–368, 369–371, *m382*
  advances in learning, 385
  archaeological finds from, 27–28
  art, *i4, i26, i380, i383*
  Caracol Observatory, 360, *i360–
    i361*
  emergence of, 381
  fall of, 386
  farming, 382–383
  influence on later societies, 388,
    i388–i389
  mathematics, 385, 387
  pok-a-tok, 364–365, *i364*, 384,
    i389
  religion, 383–384
  social classes, 382–383
Mayflower Compact, 483
Mbanza, 196
Mead, Margaret, 27, *i27*
Mecca, 88, *i88*
  Mansa Musa and, 144–145
  Muhammad preaches at, 82–83
  pilgrimage to, 115
  prayer in direction of, 95
Medici, Lorenzo de, *i426*, 437
medicine
  Greek, 498
  Incan, 415, *i415*
  in Medieval Europe, 339
  in Muslim Empire, 123, 135, 139, *i139*
  in the Scientific Revolution, 504
Medina, 82, 93, 102, *i105*
Medieval Africa, 318
  plague in, 333, 334, *m334*

Medieval Europe, *m287*, 291–292,
    c317, c336
  comparison with Japan, *c312*, 313
  daily life, 299–302
  feudalism in, 307–311, *c310*
  Roman Catholic Church, 321–323
  social and political structures,
    336–337
Medieval Japan, 307–311, *i307*
  comparison with Europe, *c312*, 312
Medieval Spain, *m287, m317, i320*
  and Reconquista, 330–331, *m330*
mercantilism, 524, *i525*
Mercator, Gerhardus, 5
Mercator Projection, 16, *i16*
mercenaries, 132
Mesoamerica, 360–361, 362–363,
    m363, 367–371, 373–377,
    397–402, 409–415
  farming, *i366*, 370, *i370*, 394–395
  geography of, 367–369, *i369*,
    370–371
  pok-a-tok, 364–365, *i364*, 384, *i389*
  trade, 370–371
Mexico, *m363*
Mexico City, *i393*
Michelangelo (Michelangelo di
    Buonarroti Simoni), *i425, i434*,
    438, *i438*
microscope, 505, *i505*
Middle Ages
  begin with Rome's fall, 291
  Catholicism during, 321–325
  changes in Europe, 293
  daily life, 299–302, 304, *i304–i305*
  economy, 300
  end of, 336–337, 429–430
  growth of towns, 301, *c315*
  guilds, 302
  literature, 309
  manor system, 299–300
  women's roles, *i306*, 309
Middle East, 122
migration, 182, *m182*
Milan, Italy, 436
Minamoto Yoritomo, 268
minbar, *i130*
Ming Dynasty, 240–241, 278
  trade, 235–237, 238, 239, 240,
    241–242
missionaries, 479–482, R65
Mohammed. *See* Muhammad.
monasteries, 295, *i295*, 324
money
  in China, 227, *i227*, 230, *i230*
  in Muslim Empire, 115, *i116*
Mongol Ascendancy, 236
Mongols
  art, *i430*
  Ascendancy, 236
  extent of empire, 234, *m234*
  government, 235
  invade China, 233

Index

Index of Skills

Chronological and Spatial Thinking

chronological order/sequence, 46, 51, 98, 103, 116, 279, 465, R15. *See also* Reading and Critical Thinking: chronological order/sequence

creating charts, graphs, diagrams, 23, 97, 184, 192–193, 219, 392, 402, 415, 455, 487, 501

creating maps, 21, 56, 97, 116, 175, 199, 229, 279, 302, 354, 433, 526, R11

creating models, R17

economic/trading systems (shown in maps), 61, 63, 87, 146–147, 183, 196, 376, 431, 512, 515, 522

expansion and disintegration (shown in maps), 114, 120, 131, 215, 234, 327, 328, 330, 352, 353, 382, 411, 471, 481, 482, 524, 544

interpreting visuals/graphics, 16, 52, 75, 86, 107, 141, 188, 226, 269, 296, 300, 315, 322, 334, 369, 419, 437, 455, 473, 525, 529, 555, R12–R13

interpreting/reading maps, 13, 16, 21, 22–23, 40, 41, 47, 55, 61, 87, 114, 120, 158, 175 182, 183, 184, 191, 196, 199, 203, 215, 217, 234, 240, 245, 276, 281, 327, 328, 330, 334, 353, 373, 376, 382, 411, 431, 433, 471, 481, 482, 484, 512, 515, 522, 524, 544, R9–R10

migration (shown in maps), 182

time lines, 46, 51, 98, 103, 169, 203, 266, 271, 326, 331, 378, 517, R14

using historical documents. *See* Research, Evidence, and Point of View: evaluating information, primary sources, secondary sources

Research, Evidence and Point of View

context, 297, 303, R21

credibility of sources, 35, 40, R24. *See also* primary sources, secondary sources

evaluating information, 56, 63, 75, 106, 191, 203, 244, 371, 441, 444, 450, 455, 539, R23

fact vs. opinion, 508–509, R19. *See also* Reading and Critical Thinking: forming and supporting opinions

framing historical questions, 32, 35, 40, 41, 185, 203, 281, 380, 386, R18

point of view/perspective, 36–39, 178–179, 315, R20

primary sources, 32, 33, 35, 40, 68, 102, 122, 167, 228, 259, 281, 309, 342, 357, 375, 401, 448, 464, 487, 514, 546, R24, R35–R59, R63, R65, R67, R69, R71, R73

secondary sources, 33, 35, 40, 105, 193, 221, 313, 379, 391, 477, 509, R24

Historical Interpretation

causal relationship, 13, 21, 80, 103, 140, 261, 279, 280, 302, 337, 390, 476–477, 539, 554. *See also* Reading and Critical Thinking: cause and effect

cause and effect, 13, 40, 58, 106, 191, 386, 390, 501. *See also* Reading and Critical Thinking: cause and effect

correlation, 28, 138–139, 271, 279, 280, 338–339, 388–389, 540–541

cost-benefit analysis, R32, R33

economic and political issues, R30

economic performance, 146, 175

geographic patterns/factors, 246, 254, 279, 280, 314, R16 *See also* Chronological and Spatial Thinking: interpreting maps

historical continuity/patterns, 40, 71, 72–73, 75, 138–139, 200–201, 218, 230–231, 242, 345, 388, 442–43, 528, 548, R27, R29

interpretation changes with technological changes, 4, 424, 492, 528, R31

interpretation, 4, 28, 29, 34, 35, 40, 41, 191, R31

issues and problems, 13, 28, 40, 42, 51, 71, 74, 130, 137, 141, 202, 203, 220–221, 302, 337, 354, 433, R28, R30

sequence, 103, 271. *See also* Reading and Critical Thinking: chronological order/sequence

time and place, 21, 28, 40, 64–65, 90–91, 108, 162–163, 199, 272–273, 279, 302, 304–305, 416–417, 452–453, 518–519

Reading and Critical Thinking

analysis, 175, 357, 458–59, 487, R30

anticipation, 286, 492

assessing sources, 35, R24

categorizing, 52, 56, 84, 89, 180, 184, 256, 261, 290, 297, 408, 415, 428, 433, 502, 507, R6

cause and effect, 40, 58, 63, 96, 106, 141, 161, 184, 194, 199, 203, 212, 219, 229, 254, 261, 297, 302, 311, 318–319, 331, 357, 386, 395, 402, 418, 455, 458–459, 465, 476–477, 487, 501, 520, 526, 548, R26

characterization, 126–129, 148–149, 170–173, 262–265, 273, 346–349, 426–427, 466–469, 532–533, 551–553

chronological order/sequence, 46, 51, 98, 103, 116, 232, 237, 266, 271, 279, 326, 331, 378–379, 396, 402, 465, 496, 501, R15

comparing and contrasting, 13, 28, 35, 62, 75, 96, 103, 116, 137, 154, 164, 169, 175, 186, 191, 219, 242, 274, 279, 298, 302, 306, 311, 312–313, 314, 315, 325, 357, 415, 441, 478, 484, 526, 539, R4

Writing and Speaking

Acknowledgments

Text Acknowledgments

Chapter 1, page 36: Excerpt from *Discovering the Inca Ice Maiden: My Adventures on Ampato* by Johan Reinhard. Copyright © 1998 by Johan Reinhard. Reprinted with the permission of the National Geographic Society.

Chapter 3, page 102: Excerpt from the Qur'an, from *The Koran Interpreted,* translated by A. J. Arberry. Copyright © 1955 by George Allen & Unwin Ltd. Reprinted by permission of HarperCollins Publishers Ltd.

Chapter 5, page 170: Excerpt from *Sundiata: The Epic of the Lion King* retelling by Roland Bertol. Copyright © 1970 by Roland Bertol. Reprinted with the permission of HarperCollins Publishers.

Chapter 7, page 228: "On Being Demoted and Sent Away to Qizhou" by Wang Wei, from *Laughing Lost in the Mountains: Poems of Wang Wei,* translated by Tony Barnstone, Willis Barnstone, and Xu Haixin. Copyright © 1991 by University Press of New England. Used by permission of University Press of New England.

Chapter 8, page 260: "An old silent pond . . ." by Matsuo Basho, from *Haiku Harvest,* translated by Peter Beilenson and Harry Behn. Copyright © 1962 by the Peter Pauper Press. Reprinted by permission of the Peter Pauper Press.

Chapter 9, page 309: "As I ride my horse" by Matsuo Basho, from *The Art and Culture of Japan* by Nelly Delay, translated from the French by Lorna Dale. Copyright © 1999 by Thames & Hudson Ltd., London. Reprinted by kind permission of Thames & Hudson Ltd., London.

Excerpt from *Beowulf,* translated by Burton Raffel. Copyright © 1963, renewed © 1991 by Burton Raffel. Used by permission of Dutton Signet, a division of Penguin Group (USA) Inc.

Chapter 12, page 404: "The Eagle on the Prickly Pear," retold by John Bierhorst, from *The Hungry Woman: Myths and Legends of the Aztecs,* edited by John Bierhorst. Copyright © 1984 by John Bierhorst. Reprinted by permission of the author.

Chapter 15, page 527: Excerpt from "The Spanish Armada" by Dr. Simon Adams, from the BBC *Monarchs and Leaders* Web pages <www.bbc.co.uk/history/state/monarchs_leaders/adams_armada_01.shtml>. Copyright © 2001 by Simon L. Adams. Used by permission of the author.

PRIMARY SOURCE HANDBOOK

Page R35: Excerpt from "Cancuén Archaeological Project" by Arthur A. Demarest <http://www.famsi.org/reports/96034/section01.htm>. Copyright © 2000 Foundation for the Advancement of Mesoamerican Studies, Inc., www.famsi.org. Reprinted by permission of FAMSI.

Page R37: Excerpt from the Qur'an, from *The Koran,* translated by N. J. Dawood (Penguin Classics 1956, fifth revised edition 1990). Copyright © 1956, 1959, 1966, 1968, 1974, 1990, 1993, 1997, 1999, 2003 by N. J. Dawood. Reprinted by permission of Penguin Group (UK).

Page R38: Excerpt from the Sunnah (vol. 1, bk. 1, no. 3), translated by M. Mushin Khan <http://www.usc.edu/dept/MSA/fundamentals/hadithsunnah/bukhari/001.sbt.html>. Copyright © by M. Mushin Khan. Reprinted by permission of the Muslim Student Association at the University of Southern California.

Page R41: Excerpt from *The Chronicle of the Seeker* by Mahmud Kati, translated by Bernard Lewis, from *Religion and Society,* vol. 2 of *Islam: From the Prophet Muhammad to the Capture of Constantinople,* edited by Bernard Lewis. Copyright © 1987 by Bernard Lewis. Used by permission of Oxford University Press, Inc.

Page R44: Excerpt from "Beneath the Autumn Leaves" in *The Tale of Genji* by Murasaki Shikibu, translated by Royall Tyler. Copyright © 2001 by Royall Tyler. Used by permission of Viking Penguin, a division of Penguin Group (USA) Inc.

Page R45: Excerpt from *Beowulf,* translated by David Breeden <http://lnstar.com/literature/beowulf>. Copyright © by David Breeden. Reprinted by permission of the author.

Page R47: Excerpt from *Popol Vuh: The Mayan Book of the Dawn of Life,* rev. ed., translated by Dennis Tedlock. Copyright © 1985, 1996 by Dennis Tedlock. Reprinted with the permission of Simon & Schuster Adult Publishing Group.

Page R49: Excerpt from *The Broken Spears* by Miguel Leon-Portilla. Copyright © 1962, 1990 by Miguel Leon-Portilla, expanded and updated edition © 1992 by Miguel Leon-Portilla. Reprinted by permission of Beacon Press, Boston.

Page R50: Excerpt from the *Inferno* by Dante Alighieri, from *The Inferno of Dante: A New Verse Translation* by Robert Pinsky. Translation copyright © 1994 by Robert Pinsky. Used by permission of Farrar, Straus and Giroux, LLC.

Page R56: Excerpt from *The Starry Messenger* by Galileo Galilei, from *Discoveries and Opinions of Galileo Galilei,* translated by Stillman Drake. Copyright © 1957 by Stillman Drake. Reprinted by permission of Random House, Inc.

Page R57: Excerpt from the journal of Christopher Columbus, from the Internet Medieval Sourcebook, edited by Paul Halsell <http://www.fordham.edu/halsall/source/columbus1.html>. Reprinted by permission.

Art and Photography Credits

COVER, FRONTISPIECE

Background Corner Tower of Forbidden City. © Liu Liqun/Corbis; *insets, bottom left* Reliquary of Charlemagne in form of a portrait bust (1350). Cathedral Treasury, Cathedral (Palatine Chapel), Aachen, Germany. Photo © Art Resource, New York; *top center* Suleyman. © Christie's Images/Corbis; *bottom center* Queen Elizabeth I (1700's), Unknown artist. English school. Galleria Palatina, Palazzo Pitti, Florence. Photo © Scala/Art Resource, New York; *top right* Benin mask (1500's). African school. Brass. Private Collection. Photo © Bridgeman Art Library; *middle right* Queen Theodora. © R. Sheridan/Ancient Art & Architecture Collection, Ltd.; *bottom right* Pre-classic Mayan figurine of a man. (2000–1500 B.C.). Earthenware. The Granger Collection, New York.

FRONT MATTER

iv Ken Curtis. Photo courtesy of Robert Freligh; Anita Robinson. Photo courtesy of Clinton Robinson; **vi** *top* Astrolabe. The Granger Collection, New York; *center* Theatrical mask, elderly character. Wallpainting from Pompeii, Italy. Museo Archeological Nazionale, Naples, Italy. Photo © Erich Lessing/Art Resource, New York; *bottom* Hadrian's Wall. © David Noton/Masterfile; **vii** *top* Ka'aba, Grand Mosque, Mecca. © Reuters NewMedia Inc./Corbis; *bottom* Cordoba, Striped Arches. © Eddie Gerald/Age Fotostock America, Inc.; **viii** *top* Lion mask. © Seattle Art Museum, Gift of Katherine White and the Boeing Company. Seattle, Washington. Photo by Paul Macapia; *center* Great Mosque, Djenne, Mali. © Sandro Vannini/Corbis; *bottom* African savannah with lion. © Images of Africa Photobank/Alamy Images; **ix** *top* Funerary tower, Han Dynasty, China. Musée Cernuschi, Paris. Photo © Dagli Orti/The Art Archive; *center* Seated Buddha. © Christie's Images/Corbis; *bottom* Angkor Wat. © Pixfolio/Alamy Images; **x** *top* Tanaquil with loom and women spinning. From *De Claris Mulierbus* (1500's), Giovanni Boccaccio, after Pliny (HN8.194). French. Roy 16G.V. f.56. British Library, London. Photo © Art Resource, New York; *center* Suleiman I, Sultan of the Ottoman Empire (1403–1410); (murdered on his flight) 5.6.1510 (1558) Ms. Add. 7880, fol. 53. British Library, London. Photo © British Library/akg-images.; *bottom* Dover Castle. © Skyscan Balloon Photography/English Heritage Photographic Library; **xi** *top* Deity emerging from jaguar's mouth (500's). Zapotec. Monte Alban phase III. Terracotta. 20 × 21 inches. Private Collection, New York. Photo © Werner Forman/Art Resource, New York; *center* Pachacuti, 10th Inca King (1700's). Peruvian school. Oil on canvas. Photo © New-York Historical Society, New York/Bridgeman Art Library; *bottom* Machu Picchu. © Alison Wright/Corbis; **xii** *top* Gutenberg Bible pages, printed at Mainz (1453–1456). The Granger Collection, New York; *center, Henry VIII* (1536), Hans Holbein the Younger. Resin tempera on wood. 26 × 19 cm. Thyssen-Bornemisza Collection. Luganoß, Switzerland. Photo © akg-images; *bottom* Duomo. © Gary Yeowell/Getty Images; **xiii** *top* Ferdinand Magellan and his ship *"Victoria"* in which he began the first westward around the world voyage. Bibliothèque Nationale, Paris. Photo © Erich Lessing/Art Resource, New York; *center* Voltaire, Locke, and Franklin snuffbox. The Metropolitan Museum of Art, gift of William H. Huntington, 1883 (83.2.228). Photo © 1980 The Metropolitan Museum of Art; *bottom* Parisian women marching to Versailles. The Granger Collection, New York; **xxiv** Photo by Sharon Hoogstraten; **xxv** Icon: Printing Press. © Rogue Element LLC; **A-1** NASA.

UNIT 1

Opener

2–3 Pompeii Before the Eruption of Vesuvius. Illustration by Dave Henderson/Mendola Ltd.; **3** *clockwise* Detail of world from atlas *Theatrum Orbis Terrarum* (1570), Abraham Ortelius. Photo © Dagli Orti/The Art Archive; Augustus Caesar. Photo © Giani Dagli Orti/Corbis; Cast of Pompeii victim. © Martin Bache/Alamy Images; Excavation in the courtyard of the Temple of Apollo. Photo © Maureen Carroll/University of Sheffield, Sheffield, United Kingdom.

Chapter 1

4 *top* Archaeologist and wall relief from Copan, Honduras. Kenneth Garrett/National Geographic Image Collection; *bottom* Map of the world (about 700–500 B.C.). Babylonian. Stone, 12.2 cm. × 8.2 cm. British Museum, London. Photo © Bridgeman Art Library; **5** *top right* Anthropologist Donald Johanson displaying plaster cast of skull of skeleton named Lucy. © Bettmann/Corbis; *top left* Archaeologists taking notes in tomb of Emperor Qin Shi Huangdi. O. Louis Mazzatenta/ National Geographic Image Collection; *bottom-upper* Ptolemy holding globe and dividers from *Cosmografia* (1492). Ulm. Photo © Dagli Orti/National Museum of Bucharest/The Art Archive; *bottom-lower* Stone altar showing the king of Cancuén playing the royal ballgame. Photograph by Andrew L. Demarest. Courtesy of Vanderbilt Cancuén Project; **6–7** Buried city of Pompeii. Illustration by Angelo; **6** Roman goldwork armlet in the form of a snake. © Mimmo Jodice/Corbis; **8** Earth from space. © Reuters NewMedia Inc./Corbis; **10** *top left* The Alps. © Premium Stock/Corbis; *top right* Great Plains. © Andy Sacks/Getty Images; *bottom* Yangtze River, China. © Liu Liqun/Corbis; **11** Iceman. © Corbis/Sygma; **12** *top* California wildfires. © Michael Goulding/*Orange County Register*/Corbis; *bottom left* California Central Valley. © Craig Lovell/Alamy Images; *bottom right* Plane taking off from Los Angeles airport. © Deborah Davis/PhotoEdit; **14** *top* Astrolabe. The Granger Collection, New York; *bottom* Astronomers. The Granger Collection, New York; **15** Detail of world from atlas *Theatrum Orbis Terrarum* (1570), Abraham Ortelius. Photo © Dagli Orti/The Art Archive; **20** *background* Satellite imaging. © Paul Morell/Getty Images; *top right* Colored satellite image of the city of San Francisco. © M-sat Ltd./Photo Researchers, Inc.; *bottom right* Infrared Landsat-5 satellite image of San Francisco. Photo © Map Factory/Photo Researchers, Inc.; **24** Nazca mummy head, Nazca, Peru. Photo © Julio Donosco/Corbis Sygma; **25** Excavation at Ubar, Oman. James L. Stanfield/ National Geographic Image Collection; **26** Life-sized stucco sculpture of a Mayan ruler. Photograph by Andrew L. Demarest. Courtesy of the Vanderbilt Cancuén Project; **27** Margaret Mead. © Bettmann/Corbis; **29** Students making a time capsule. Photo by Sharon Hoogstraten; **30** Entry of Louis VII (King of France) into Constantinople with Emperor Conrad III. 2nd Crusade. From *Grandes Chroniques de France*, Ms. 6465 f. 202. Bibliothèque Nationale, Paris. Photo

© Snark/Art Resource, New York; **31** Researcher. Ryerson and Burnham Libraries, The Art Institute of Chicago. Photo © Dirk Fletcher; **32** Constitution of the United States of America. Comstock Royalty Free; **33** Columbus. © Archivo Iconografico, S.A./Corbis; **34** Detail of Barbarian fighting a Roman Legionnaire. Roman marble relief. 84 × 88 cm. Inv,:MA 412. Louvre, Paris. Photo © R. G. Ojeda/Réunion des Musées Nationaux/Art Resource, New York; **36–37, 38–39** Johan Reinhard on Nevado Ampato, Ice Maiden, two wooden cups, ceramic jar. Stephen Alvarez/National Geographic Image Collection.

Chapter Two

42 *left* Detail of Aureus of Diocletian cuirassed, wearing a laurel wreath (300–400). Roman. Gold. Private collection. Photo © Bridgeman Art Library; *right* Tallest of the still erect stelae at Axum (300–400). Axumite. © Werner Forman/Art Resource, New York; **43** *top left* Arch of Titus. Rome, Italy. © SEF/Art Resource, New York; *top right* Pantheon (118–125). Rome, Italy. Photo © Scala/Art Resource, New York; *bottom left* Detail of Reliquary cross and chain, with enamel image of the Virgin praying and Saint Basil and Saint Gregory the Great. (1000–1100). Constantinople. British Museum, London. Photo © Werner Forman/Art Resource, New York; *bottom right* Detail of First Sung emperor. Museum of Nankin, China. Photo © Charles and Josette Lenars/Corbis; **44-45** A Dangerous Race. Illustration by Bill Maughan/Mendola Ltd.; **44** Chariot race in a stadium. (100–200) Terracotta. Roman. Louvre, Paris. Photo © Erich Lessing/Art Resource, New York; **46** *top* Trajan's Column (106–113) and Basilica of Ulpia, Rome. Photo © Dagli Orti/The Art Archive; *bottom* Relief of embarkation of Roman troops. National Museum, Bucharest. Photo © Dagli Orti/The Art Archive; **48** Roman Forum ruins. © Christopher Groenhout/Lonely Planet Images; **49** Augustus Prima Porta (0–100). Roman sculpture. Braccio Nuovo, Vatican Museums. Vatican State. Photo © Scala/Art Resource, New York; **50** *Christ Healing the Blind* (1570), El Greco. Photo © Alinari/Corbis; **52** Engraved bronze plaque of horseman from Lombardy (600–700). Stabio, Switzerland. Photo © Dagli Orti/ Bargello Museum, Florence/The Art Archive; **53** Hadrian's Wall at Housestead's, Northumberland, England. David Noton/Masterfile; **57** Play a board game. Photo by Sharon Hoogstraten; **58** Colossal marble head of Constantine. Palazzo dei Conservatori, Rome. Photo © Scala/Art Resource, New York; **59** Hagia Sophia, Constantinople. © Richard T. Nowitz/ Corbis; **60** *left* Detail of Theodora. © R. Sheridan/Ancient Art & Architecture Collection Ltd.; *right* Detail of Emperor Justinian (500–600). Mosaic. San Vitale, Ravenna, Italy. Photo © Dagli Orti/ Art Archive; **62** *left* Pope Gregory I © Bettmann/ Corbis; *right* Saint Nicolas © ReligiousStockOne/Alamy Images; **64–65** *background* Constantinople City Scene. Illustration by Shane Marsh/Linden Artists, Ltd.; *insets* Illustrations by Peter Dennis/Linda Rogers Associates, Ltd.; **66** Theatrical mask, elderly character. Wallpainting from Pompeii, Italy. Museo Archeological Nazionale, Naples, Italy. Photo © Erich Lessing/ Art Resource, New York; **67** Mosaic with circus scene: fight with leopards. Galleria Borghese, Rome, Italy. Photo © Scala/Art Resource, New York; **68** Bust of Cicero (0–100). © Araldo de Luca/Corbis; **69** Roman aqueduct. Pont du Gard, Nimes. © Vanni/Art Resource, New York; **70** United States of America Capitol building. © William Manning/Corbis; **72** *top* Los Angeles Coliseum. Courtesy Los Angeles Memorial Coliseum; *bottom* Roman Coloseum today. © David Marshall/Index Stock Imagery, Inc.; **73** *top left* Lucius Annaeus Seneca, marble bust. Archaeological Museum, Naples, Italy. Photo © Dagli Orti/ The Art Archive; *top center* © David Butow/Corbis SABA; *top right* © David Young-Wolff/Getty Images; *bottom left* AP/Wide World Photos; *bottom right* Cicero denounces Catiline in the Roman Senate. The Granger Collection, New York; **76** *top* Cast of Pompeii victim. © Martin Bache/Alamy Images; *bottom* Detail of Pompeii Before the Eruption of Vesuvius. Illustration by Dave Henderson/Mendola Ltd; **76** *right* Roman forum ruins. © Christopher Groenhout/Lonely Planet Images; *inset* Augustus Prima Porta (0–100). Braccio Nuovo, Vatican Museums, Vativan State. Photo © Scala/Art Resource, New York.

UNIT 2

Opener

78–79 Mecca Grand Mosque. Illustration by Philip Howe; **79** *top* Koran with Arabic writing. © Wolfgang Kaehler/Corbis. *Bottom* Dome of South Iwan (1611–1638). Safavid Dynasty. Masjid-i Shah, Isfahan, Iran. © SEF/Art Resource, New York.

Chapter 3

80 *left* Illuminated pages of a Koran manuscript (1300–1400), Il-Khanid Mameluke School. Islamic School. Private Collection. Photo © The Bridgeman Art Library; *right* Saint Augustine. © Archivo Iconografico, S.A./Corbis; **81** Camel, China. Tang Dynasty. © Royal Ontario Museum/Corbis; **82–83** A Journey to Mecca. Illustration by Christian Hook; **82** Certificate of pilgrimage to Mecca (1193). Turkish and Islamic Art Museum. Photo © Dagli Orti/ The Art Archive; **84** Jug with black-figured bird (1000–600 B.C.). Southern Jordan. Painted terracotta. Beno Rothenberg Collection. Haaretz Museum, Tel Aviv, Israel. Photo © Erich Lessing/ Art Resource, New York; **85** Ramiat Desert. © Arthur Thévenart/Corbis; **86** Oasis. © Phil Banko/Corbis; **88** *top* Camel caravan. © Brian Vikander/Corbis; *bottom* Ka'aba, Grand Mosque, Mecca. © Reuters NewMedia Inc./Corbis; **89** Ka'aba key. © Roland and Sabrina Michaud/Agence Photographiques RAPHO; **90–91** *background,* Arab trade center. Illustration by John James; *insets* Illustrations by Peter Dennis/Linda Rogers Associates, Ltd.; **92** The archangel Gabriel from *The Wonders of Creation and the Oddities of Existence* (1270), Zakariya Qaywini. Wasit, Iraq. It is an illustrated compendium which describes the many marvels of the universes. The book covers the fields of geography, astronomy, astrology, and natural history in a mixture of science and superstition. OA, 1963.4-20.01. British Museum, London. Photo © HIP/Scala/Art Resource, New York; **93** Illustration from the Turkish version of the *Siyar-i-Nabi* (Progress of the Prophet) (1500's). Ms. Hazine 1221. Topkapi Museum, Istanbul. Photo © Ara Guler/Topkapi Museum, Istanbul; **94–95** Illuminated pages from a Koran manuscript (1300–1400), Il-Khanid Mameluke School. Islamic School. Vellum. Private Collection. Photo © The Bridgeman Art Library; **96** Plaque. Tomb of the Prophet at Mecca (1500–1600). Ceramic style, called Turk. Museum of Islamic Art, Cairo, Egypt. Photo © Dagli Orti/The Art Archive; **97** Create a distribution map. Photo by Sharon Hoogstraten; **98** Enamelled glass lamp from Hasan mosque (1500–1600). Museum of Islamic Art, Cairo, Egypt. Photo © Dagli Orti/The Art Archive; **99** Islamic miniature painting of Arabs swearing allegiance to Imam Ali at Kufa after the murder of Caliph Othman. British Museum. Photo © Michael Holford; **101** Battle of the tribes. Illumination from Add. Or 25900, f. 121v. By permission of the British Library. Photo © The British Library, London; **102** Page from the Koran (1600–1700). Maghreb. Merinide period. Black, blue, and red ink on paper. Inv.: MNAM 1982.5.1. Musée des Arts d'Afrique et d'Océanie, Paris. Photo © J. G. Berizzi/Réunion des Musées Nationaux/Art Resource, New York; **105** Tile with schematic view of Medina (1500–1600). Mamluk period. Museum of Islamic Art, Cairo, Egypt. Photo © Werner Forman/Art Resource, New York.

Chapter 4

108 *left* Reliquary of Charlemagne from the Treasury of Aachen Cathedral (1350). Kunstsammlung Nordrhein-Westfalen, Dusseldorf, Germany. Bildarchiv Steffens. Photo © Bridgeman Art Library; *right* Minaret of the mosque at Samarrah (848–852). Abbasid Dynasty. Great Mosque, Samarra. Photo © SEF/Art Resource, New York; **109** *left* Meiping vase (900–1100). China, Song Dynasty. Ceramic. 26.2 cm. high. Musée des Arts Asiatiques-Guimet, Paris. Photo © Réunion des Musées Nationaux/Art Resource, New York; *right* Miniature painting of four Muslim holy men seated in meditation. Photo © Stapleton Collection/Corbis; **110–111** The Magic of Baghdad. Illustration by Peter Dennis/Linda Rogers Associates, Ltd.; **110** The Tigris and the Euphrates from a geographical atlas (900–1000), Al Istalhry. Vellum. Egyptian National Library, Cairo, Egypt. Photo © Giraudon/Bridgeman Art Library; **112** Arabic Army on the March from the Cantigas de Santa Maria. Photo © Henri Stierlin/Bildarchiv Steffens; **113** The Great Mosque, Damascus, Syria. © Jane Taylor/Sonia Halliday Photographs; **115** Caravan of pilgrims on the road to Mecca (1500–1600). Safavid miniature. Watercolor. British Library, London. Photo © Art Resource, New York; **116** Gold dinar of caliph Abd al-Malik (696–697). Umayyad Dynasty. Probably from Syria. Diameter: 19mm. Weight: 4025 grams. Gift of E.T. Rogers. Photo © The Trustees of The British Museum; **117** Students making brochure. Photo by Sharon Hoogstraten; **118** Carved ivory plaque depicting hunting with hawks, Egypt. Islamic culture. Photo © Museum fur Islamic Kunst, Berlin/Werner Forman Archive; **119** Baghdad in the 1800's © Stock Montage, Inc.; **121** *top left* Pyx with relief depicting the pleasures of the courtly life, inscribed with the name of Al-Mughira (900). Islamic School. From Cordoba. Ivory. 15cm × 8cm. Louvre, Paris. Photo © Lauros/Giraudon/Bridgeman Art Library; *top right* St. Nicholas (900–1000). Byzantine. Enamel. Museo Lazaro Galadiano, Madrid, Spain. Photo © Bridgeman Art Library; *bottom* Decorative border tilework. © Arthur Thèvenart/Corbis; **122** Omar Khayyam working out the 1074 calendar. © Bettmann/Corbis; **123** Aristotle teaching. Illustration from *The Better Sentences and Most Precious Dictions* (1200–1300), Al-Moubbachir. Turkish School. Vellum. Topkapi Palace Museum, Istanbul, Turkey. Photo © Bridgeman Art Library; **124** Battle between the cavalry of the Byzantines and the Seljuks (1000–1100). Scylitzes chronicle, fol. 234v. Biblioteca Nacional, Madrid, Spain. Photo © Werner Forman/Art Resource, New York; **126** *Abu Zayd before the Governor of Rahba* (1237) from *Maqamat of al-Hariri*. Manuscript illumination. Bagdad. The Granger Collection, New York; **128** *Anatomy of the Eye* (592), Arabian manuscript. Of the *Hegira* (1214), Al-Mutadibih. Egyptian Museum, Cairo. © Dagli Orti/The Art Archive; **128-129** Detail of *Flies* (1564). Manuscript *Manuel Phile, de animalium proprietate*, in Greek, by Angelus Veregecius at Paris. Auct F 4 15, folio 16v. © Bodleian Library, Oxford/The Art Archive; **130** Minbar formerly in Qutubia mosque (1137). Detail of the marquetry. From Cordoba, Spain. Almoravid period. Cedar wood, ebony, ivory. Badia Palace, Marrakesh. Photo © Erich Lessing /Art Resource, New York; **132** Abd al-Rahman III Receiving the Ambassador (1885), Dionisio Baixeras-Verdaguer. University of Barcelona, Spain. Oil on canvas. Photo © Index/The Bridgeman Art Library; **133** Cordoba Mosque, Spain. Photo © Eddie Gerald/Age Fotostock America, Inc.; **134** Map of the world by Islamic scholar, Al Idrisi copy made(1553), of original of 1154. Arabic. Pococke 375 folio 3v-4r. The Bodleian Library, Oxford, England. Photo © The Bodleian Library, Oxford, England/The Art Archive; **135** *top* 1964 postage stamp from Damascus, Syrian Arab Republic, commemorating Abou Al Kassem Khalaf Ben Abbas Al Zahrawi, 1050–1122; *bottom* Types of surgical saws from 14th century manuscript *De Chirugia* by Albucasis. Bibliothèque Universitaire de Mèdecine, Montpellier, France. Photo © Dagli Orti/ The Art Archive; **136–137** The Hebrews building cities for Pharaoh (about 1350). *Barcelona Haggadah*. Northern Spain. Shelfmark ID: Add 14761 Folio No: 43r. British Library, London. Photo © HIP/Scala/Art Resource, New York; **138** *left* Observatory. © Roger Ressmeyer/Corbis; *right* Astronomers in the Istanbul observatory (1500–1600), Ottoman. The Granger Collection, New York; **139** *top left* Modern surgical procedure. © Pete Saloutos/Corbis; *top right* Pharmacy from manuscript of De Materia Medica (1224). The Granger Collection, New York; *center* Euclid's proof of the Pythagorean theorem (1258). The Granger Collection Collection, New York.; *bottom* Modern college mathematics class. © Ariel Skelly/Corbis; **142** *left* Types of surgical saws from 14th century manuscript *De Chirugia* by Albucasis. Bibliotheque Universitaire de Medecine, Montpellier, France. Photo © Dagli Orti/ The Art Archive; *right* 1964 postage stamp from Damascus, Syrian Arab Republic, commemorating Abou Al Kassem Khalaf Ben Abbas Al Zahrawi, 1050–1122.

UNIT 3

Opener

144–145 Mansu Musa's caravan arriving at Mecca. Illustration by Angus McBride/Linden Artists, Ltd.; **145** *top* Detail of West African mud cloth. Photo © 2004 Adrienne McGrath; *bottom* Mask (1800's), Kuba people. Painted wood and straw. Private Collection. Photo © Dagli Orti/The Art Archive.

Chapter 5

146 *top* Camel. © Elaine Farray-Sulle/Alamy Images; *bottom* Water dropper in the form of a mandarin duck. China. Tang Dynasty. Glazed pottery. Private collection. New York. Photo © Werner Forman/Art Resource, New York; **147** Saint Louis IX embarking on boat for Last Crusade 1270 to Tunis from *History of Saint Louis* (about 1280). Photo © JFB/Bibliothèque Nationale, Paris/The Art Archive; **148** Gold dust. © Digital Vision/Getty Images / Royalty Free; **148–149** African traders at fireside. Illustration by Bill Cigliano; **150** Nigerian ritual pot (1100–1400). Terracotta. 25 cm. Lagos National Museum, Nigeria. Photo © Ancient Art and Architecture Collection, Ltd.; **151** Boats on banks of the Niger River. © Paul Almasy/Corbis; **152** Women from the family of a young bride in the Fulani village of Dembel Jumpora count her dowry. Photo © Ami Vitale/Alamy Images; **153** Griotte Adama Suso and griot Ma Lamini Jobarteh. Photo © Thomas A. Hale. The Pennsylvania State University. First appeared as cover photograph for *Griots and Griottes: Masters of Words and Music* published by Indiana University Press, 1998; **155** Students playing African games. Photo by Sharon Hoogstraten; **156**

Dogon crocodile sculpture. Photo © 2004 Adrienne McGrath; **157** Sahara desert. © Frans Lemmens/Getty Images; **158** *top* African savannah. © Charles O. Cecil/Words & Pictures/PictureQuest ; *bottom* Cameroon rainforest. © Fred Hoogervorst/ Panos Pictures; **159** Tuareg tribesman with salt caravan. © www.copix.co.uk; **160** Grand Mosque, Djenne, Mali (1905). Photo © Sandro Vannini/Corbis; **162–163** *background* African salt mining. Illustration by Terence Gabbey; *insets* Salt mining activities. Illustrations by Peter Dennis/Linda Rogers Associates, Ltd.; **164** Horse and rider. Djenne, Mali. Terracotta. 44cm. × 17cm. × 30cm. Private Collection. Photo © Heini Schneebeli/Bridgeman Art Library; **165** Niger savannah. © Charles O. Cecil/Words and Pictures/PictureQuest; **166** Detail of Mansu Musa, King of Mali. The Granger Collection, New York; **167** Ibn Battuta illustration from *The Kingfisher History Encyclopedia* © 1999 Kingfisher Publications Plc. Reproduced by permission of the publisher, all rights reserved; **168** Portrait of Askia Muhommad. © Leo and Diane Dillon; **170** Detail of Lion mask: Kore Men's Society (after 1850). Banana people of Mali. Wood, pigment, fiber. Photo © Paul Macapia/ Seattle Art Museum, Gift of Katherine White and the Boeing Company. Seattle, Washington; **171** Bandiagora escarpment, Mali. Photo © 2004 Adrienne McGrath; **172–173** Sacred hut (Kamablon), Kangaba, Mali. © 1976 David C. Conrad.

Chapter 6

176 *left* Zimbabwe conical tower. Marius Loots, South Africa; *right* The Siege of Antioch in 1098. First Crusade, (1100's). *Histoire d'Outremer*. William of Tyre, Ms.fr.2630, fol.111v. French. Bibliothèque Nationale, Paris. Photo © Art Resource, New York; **177** *top* King Mutapa. National Archives of Zimbabwe. Harare, Zimbabwe; *bottom* Detail of Aztec sculpture from Templo Mayor excavations in Mexico City. © D. Donne Bryant; **178–179** Oral Tradition. Illustration by Angus Mc-Bride/Linden Artists, Ltd.; **178** Kuba raffia dance skirt (1900's). Central Zaire. Coll. Anspach, New York. Photo © Werner Forman/Art Resource, New York; **180** Mask. Kuba people. West Africa. Wood with seashells and pearls. Rijksmuseum voor Volkenkunde, Leiden. Photo © Dagli Orti/The Art Archive; **181** African savannah. © Images of Africa Photobank/ Alamy Images; **185** *top* Mask (1800's), Kuba people. Painted wood and straw. Private Collection. Photo © Dagli Orti/The Art Archive; *bottom* Student making mask. Photo by Sharon Hoogstraten; **186** Zimbabwe woman with necklaces and blanket. © Paul Almasy/Corbis; **187** Zambezi River. © Nik Wheeler/Corbis; **188** *top* Great Zimbabwe enclosure. © MIT Collection/Corbis; *bottom* Zimbabwe conical tower. Marius Loots, South Africa; **189** 9.5 ounce gold specimen from the Witwatersrand goldfield, South Africa. © Professor Bruce Cairncross. Rand Afrikaans University, South Africa; **190** Native American storyteller. © Leonard McCombe/Getty Images; **193** Ruins of Great Zimbabwe © Robert Holmes/Corbis; **194** Commemorative male figure (1800's). Democratic Republic of the Congo. Wood, glass, metal and kaolin. Height 29.2 cm. The Metropolitan Museum of Art. Purchase, Louis V. Bell Fund, Mildred Poel Becker Bequest, Amalia Lacroze de Fortabat Gift, and Harris Brisbane Dick Fund, 1996. (1996.281). Photo © 1997 The Metropolitan Museum of Art, New York; **195** Congo River. © Paul Almasy/Corbis; **197** Portrait of Afonso I. © Leo and Diane Dillon; **198** *African slaves gathering and carrying wood for burning*, after a drawing by Emile Antoine Bayard. Illustration in *The Sources of the Nile, Journal of a voyage, 1860–1863*, John H. Speke. Collection of Archhiv f. Kunst and Geschichte/akg-images; **200** *left* Modern gold mining. © Michael S. Lewis/Corbis; *right* Surface gold mining. Transvaal, South Africa. © Bettmann/Corbis; **201** *top left* Geometric figurine for weighing gold powder. Lost-wax cast process. Côte d'Ivoire, Ghana. Musée du Quai Branly, Paris. Photo © Labat/CFAO Réunion des Musées Nationaux/Art Resource, New York; *top right* © Jonathan Kim/Getty Images; *bottom left* © Frank Fife/Getty Images; *bottom right* © SuperStock; **202** Icons. © Rogue Element LLC.; **204** Tuareg tribesman with salt caravan. © www.copix.co.uk.

UNIT 4

Opener

206–207 Great Wall battle scene. Illustration by David Henderson/Mendola Ltd; **207** *top* Chinese pavilion. © Jim Zuckerman/Corbis; *bottom* Noh theatre mask of a young woman (1800's). Japanese. Photo © Leeds Museums and Art Galleries (City Museum), United Kingdom/The Bridgeman Art Library.

Chapter 7

208 *top left* Head of Buddha (200–400). North West India, Gandhara period. (CT21799). Victoria and Albert Museum, London. Photo © Victoria & Albert Museum, London/Art Resource, New York; *bottom left* Kufic Koran © Bojan Brecelj/ Corbis; *right* Tomb figure of a horse (618–906). China. Tang Dynasty. Pottery. Idemitsu Museum of Art, Tokyo. Photo © Werner Forman/Art Resource, New York; **209** *right* Tz'u Chou ware vase. Photo © Seattle Art Museum/Corbis; *left* Pectoral ornament in the form of a double-headed serpent. One of the symbols of Tlaloc, it was worn by the high priest. Full view. Probably formed part of the treasure sent to Cortés by Montezuma, who believed Cortés to be the returning god Quetzalcoatl. Aztec. Turquoise. British Museum, London. Photo © Werner Forman/Art Resource, New York; **210** Han warrior on horseback. © Kimball Art Museum/Corbis; **210–211** Battle scene of falling pots. Illustration by Bill Cigliano; **212** Funerary tower. China. Han Dynasty. Musée Cernuschi, Paris. Photo © Dagli Orti/The Art Archive; **213** Himalayan landscape, Nepal. © Galen Rowell/Corbis; **214–215** Colossal seated Buddha and a Bodhisattva. The oldest known example of Buddhist art rock carving. Cave 20. Yungan Caves, Datong. China. Photo © Werner Forman/Art Resource, New York; **216** Great Wall of China near Beijing. © D.E.Cox/Getty Images; **218** Dragon sculpture on tiled wall. Beijing. © Harvey Lloyd/Getty Images; **221** Buddha head (about 700). China. Tang Dynasty. Sandstone. 24.5 x 14 cm. Mary S. and Edward J. Holmes Fund 1976.772. Photograph © 2004 Museum of Fine Arts, Boston; **222** *Standing Court Lady* (600–700). China. Tang Dynasty. Pottery with painted decoration. Height 15 1/8 inches. Anonymous gift in memory of Louise G. Dillingham, 1978. (1978.345). Metropolitan Museum of Art, New York; **223** *The Cold Food Observance* (1000's), Su Shih. © Collection of the National Palace Museum, Taipei, Taiwan, Republic of China; **224–225** Confucius. © Archivo Iconografico, S.A./Corbis; **225** Civil service exam under Emperor Jint Song (1600's–1700's). Song Dynasty. From *The Lives of the Emperors of China*. Qing Dynasty. Watercolor on silk. Photo © Snark/Art Resource, New York; **226** Rice terraces. © David Lawrence/Corbis; **227** *left* Ancient Chinese coins with holes for stringing (900's). Photo © Dagli Orti/The Art

Archive; *right* Kublai Khan, Emperor of China: bank-note from the first issue of banknotes (1260–1287). From *The Book of Ser Marco Polo* edited Yule, published 1903. Private Collection. Photo © The Bridgeman Art Library; **228** *top* Wang Wei. © ChinaStock; *bottom* Hand typecasting equipment. © Science Museum/Science and Society Picture Library; **229** Silver–gilt octagonal cup on pedestal with human figures (mid 700's). Shaanxi province, China. Tang Dynasty. Hochia, Xian, 6.5 cm. Photo © Genius of China Exhibition/Art Archive; **230** *top right* Ancient Chinese seismograph. © David Butow/Corbis SABA; *center left* Zhang Heng seismograph (132). Science Museum/Science and Society Picture Library; *inset top, bottom* Chinese paper currency © Alamy Images; *inset middle* $20.00 bill. © Joseph Sohm/Visions of America/Corbis; **231** *top left* Standardized test sheet. © Michelle Joyce/Index Stock/PictureQuest; *top right* Boy taking test. © Rob Gage/Getty Images; *bottom* Fireworks. © Jeff Hunter/The Image Bank/Getty Images; **232** Mongol passport (1200's), China. Yuan Dynasty. Iron with silver inlay. Purchase. Bequest of Dorothy Graham Bennett, 1993 (1993.256). Metropolitan Museum of Art. Photo © Metropolitan Museum of Art. New York; **233** Persian warrior fighting. Persian Mongol school. © Burstein Collection/ Corbis; **236** Kublai Khan. The Art Archive; **238** Court robe, yellow satin embroidered with golden dragons. China. Qing Dynasty. Photo © The Palace Museum, The Forbidden City, Beijing, China; **239** Tiananmen Gate of Heavenly Peace. © Kevin Morris/Getty Images; **243** *top* Make a compass activity. Photo by Sharon Hoogstraten; *bottom* Chinese mariner's compass. © Science Museum/Science and Society Picture Library.

Chapter 8

246 *left* Detail of Shotoku Taishi. Japanese regent and author with his two sons (late 700's). Attributed to Prince Asa of Korea. Private Collection, Paris. Photo © Dagli Orti/ Private collection, Paris/The Art Archive; *right* Charlemagne's crown. © Austrian Archives/Corbis; **247** *left* Yoritomo Manamoto, first Shogun. © Sakamoto Photo Research Laboratory/Corbis; *right* Columbus's ship. © Reuters/Corbis; **248–249** Education of a Samurai. Illustration by Bill Cigliano; **248** Japanese Noh Mask depicting a Samurai (1390). Photo © Werner Forman/Corbis; **250** Shinto Gate. © Jon Hicks/Corbis; **251** Mount Fuji. © Jopack Company/Corbis; **253** Shotoku Taishi. Japanese regent and author with his two sons (late 700's). Attributed to Prince Asa of Korea. Private Collection, Paris. Photo © Dagli Orti/ Private Collection, Paris/The Art Archive; **254** Haniwa warrior (late 500's). Japanese school. Red earthenware. 68.6cm. × 36.8cm. × 34.3cm. Museum of Fine Arts, Houston, Texas. A.C. Arnold Endowment Fund & McAshan Charitable Trust. Photo © The Museum of Fine Arts, Houston/The Bridgeman Art Library; **255** Making a poster. Photo by Sharon Hoogstraten; **256** Japanese buddha. © Christie's Images/Corbis; **257** Zen garden. Kenneth Hamm/Photo Japan; **258–259** Kabuki actor. © Michael S. Yamashita/Corbis; **259** Lady Murasaki Shikibu. Japanese court lady and author of *Tale of The Genji*. Private Collection, Paris. Photo © Dagli Orti /The Art Archive; **260** The Four Accomplishments. © Seattle Art Museum/Corbis; **261** Bonsai tree. © Michael S. Yamashita/Corbis; **262** Akita suit of armor (1700's or earlier). Japan. Victoria & Albert Museum. Photo © Victoria & Albert Museum, London/Art Resource, New York; **263** Chihaya Castle. © Demetrio Carrasco/Getty Images; **264–265** Samurai warriors from a Kamakura period handscroll (1300's). © Seattle Art Museum/Corbis; **266** Samurai Warrior's Armour. Japanese School. Tower of London, London. Photo © The Bridgeman Art Library; **267** Illustration of Heian courtlife on fan-shaped album. © Burstein Collection/Corbis; **268** *Night Attack on the Sanjo Palace* (second half of 1200's), from the *Illustrated Scrolls of the Events of the Heiji Era*, Japanese School. Kamakura period. Japan. Ink and colour on paper handscroll. 41.3cm. × 699.7cm. Fenollosa-Weld Collection. Photo © Museum of Fine Arts, Boston, Massachusetts/The Bridgeman Art Library; **268–269** Japanese society pyramid. Illustration by Becky Heavner; **270** Tokugawa Ieyasu. © Sakamoto Photo Research Laboratory/Corbis; **271** Samurai sword. Photo © Dorling Kindersley; **272–273** Castle Life in Japan. Illustration by John James. Inset illustrations by Peter Dennis/Linda Rogers Associates, Ltd.; **274** Korean map ch'on hado p'al Sibil Guk.*Tongguk Chido* (1600's or later). Inv.:58223. Musée des Arts Asiatiques-Guimet, Paris. Photo © Réunion des Musées Nationaux/Art Resource, New York; **275** Hunting scene from Korean tomb (300's or 400's). Koguryo, North Korea. Photo © Bjorn Klingwall/Klingwalls Geografiska Fargfotos; **277** Trung sisters on elephants. From *The Warrior Queens* by Antonia Fraser. Vintage Books, a division of Random House, Inc., New York. © 1988 Antonia Fraser; **278** Angkor Wat. © Pixfolio/Alamy Images; **279** Korean Celadon vase (1100's). Koyo period. 34.1 cm. Victoria and Albert Museum, London. Photo © Victoria and Albert Museum, London/Art Resource, New York; **280** Icons. © Rogue Element LLC.; **284** Women doing calligraphy. Illustration by Peter Dennis/Linda Rogers Associates, Ltd.

UNIT 5

Opener

284–285 Castle Under Seige. Illustration by Philip Howe; **285** *top* Detail of Close Helmet (from a Funerary achievement?), (1700). Holland. Gilded steel (invaded with rust); red velvet lining, plume holder, 33 × 34 × 21.3 cm. © The Cleveland Museum of Art, 2004. Gift of Mr. and Mrs. John L. Severance, 1916.1787; *bottom* Castle gate. © Wolfgang Kaehler/Corbis.

Chapter 9

286 Clovis. © Michael Nicholson/Corbis; **287** *left* Viking ship. Mary Evans Picture Library; *right* Pillow (1100). China. Sung Dynasty. Porcelain, celadon glaze. Collection of the Newark Museum. Jaehne Collection, 1939. Inv.:39.218. Photo © The Newark Museum, Newark, New Jersey/Art Resource, New York; **288–289** Becoming a Knight. Illustration by Chuck Gilles/Mendola, Ltd.; **288** Helmet (about 1540). Greenwich Armories, England. V & A Images. Photo © Victoria and Albert Museum, London; **290** Portait of Clovis I, King of France, Pierre Duflos. © Stapleton Collection/Corbis; **291** Appian Way. © Archivo Iconografico, S.A./Corbis; **292** Mosel River valley. © Jose Fuste Raga/Corbis; **293** Phaidra and Hippolytos(?) vessel made of one large sardonyx gem of antique but unknown origin. Foot and brim from the time of Dagobert, king of the Franks. Treasury, Abbey, St. Maurice, Switzerland. Photo © Erich Lessing/Art Resource, New York;**294–295** Detail of *Charlemagne*, J. P. Scheuren. Stadtmuseum, Aächen, Germany. Photo © Dagli Orti/The Art Archive; **295** Senanque Abbey, Vaucluse, Provence, France. © Stock Connection/PictureQuest; **296–297** Feudalism society pyramid. Illustration by Martin Hargraves; **298** Horn spoons. © York Archaeological Trust/DK images; **299** Dover Castle. © Skyscan Balloon Photography/

English Heritage Photographic Library; **301** Italian suit of armor (1400). The Metropolitan Museum of Art, Bashford Dean Memorial Collection, Gift of Helen Fahnestock Hubbard, in memory of her father, Harris C. Fahnestock, 1929. (29.154.3) Photograph © The Metropolitan Museum of Art; **303** Debate the life of a knight. Photo by Sharon Hoogstraten; **304–305** Life on a Feudal Manor. Illustration by John James/Temple Rogers; *insets* Illustrations by Peter Dennis/Linda Rogers Associates, Ltd.; **306** Tanaquil with loom and women spinning. From *De Claris Mulierbus* (1400). Giovanni Boccaccio, after Pliny (HN8.194) French. Roy 16.G.V, f56. British Library, London. Photo © Art Resource, New York; **307** Himeji Castle. © Craig Lovell/Corbis; **308** Japanese armor and bow. Museo Chiossone, Genoa, Italy. Photo © Scala/Art Resource, New York; **309** Detail of *Matsuo Basho* (1644–1694), Japanese poet. Painted portrait. Osaka, Japan. Photo © Snark/Art Resource, New York; **310** English shield device with knight on horseback (1300's). Enamel. Museo Lazaro Galdiano, Madrid, Spain. Photo © Scala/Art Resource, New York; **313** *top* Samurai on horse. Photo © Eisei-Bunko Museum, Tokyo/ Sakamoto Photo Research Laboratory/Corbis; *bottom* Detail of Knight with green and white shields on red horse: Capodilista Codex. Manuscripts. Civic Library of Padua, Italy. Photo © SuperStock; **314** © Rogue Element LLC.

Chapter 10

316 *left* Ife head sculpture. Terracotta. Courtesy of Entwistle Gallery, London; *right* Detail of Saint Francis of Assisi (about 1400), Musée du Petit Palais, Avignon, France. Photo © R.G. Ojeda/Réunion des Musées Nationaux/Art Resource, New York; **317** *left* Aztec mask made of turquoise and pearl shell thought to represent the sun god (early 1500's). British Museum, London. Photo © Werner Forman/Art Resource, New York; *right* Suleiman I, Sultan of the Ottoman Empire (1403–1410); (murdered on his flight) 5.6.1510 (1558) Ms. Add. 7880, fol. 53. British Library, London. Photo © British Library/akg-images.; **318–319** The Plague. Illustration by John Tomaselli; **318** Gold pomander (about 1600). French. Enamelled and set with precious stones. Private Collection. Photo © Bridgeman Art Library; **320** Portico of Gloria of Santiago Cathedral. Compostela, Spain. Photo © Voz Noticias/Corbis; **321** Notre Dame Cathedral, Paris. Photo © Jon Arnold/ Alamy Images; **322–323** Church Hierarchy. Illustration by Martin Hargraves; **323** *right,* Ms Lat 4922 *Emperor Henri IV asking Countess Matilda of Tuscany to intervene in the conflict with the Pope* (1100's). Italian School. Biblioteca Apostolica Vaticana, The Vatican. Photo © Flammarion/Bridgeman Art Library; **324** Benedictine monks returning to the abbey. Normandy, France. Photo © Ted Spiegel/Corbis; **326** St. Peter's Castle, Bodrum, Turkey. Photo © Nik Wheeler/Corbis; **332** Crossbow of Ulrich V of Württemberg (1460), German. The Metropolitan Museum of Art, Rogers Fund, 1904. (04.3.36). Photo © 1991 The Metropolitan Museum of Art; **333** Detail of Plague victims cared for in Perugia, Italy. From 16th century manuscript. Biblioteca Augusta, Perugia, Italy. Photo © Dagli Orti/The Art Archive; **334** Rat. Reader's Digest, London; **335** *Joan of Arc*, Sir John Gilbert. Trustees of the Royal Watercolour Society, London. Photo © Bridgeman Art Library; **337** Detail of *Hundred Years' War between France and England, 1339–1453* (1400's). French. Fight of the garrisons of Cherbourg and Montebourg. Ms. illumination. From *Chronique d'Angleterre,* Jean de Wavrin.. Ms. Royal 14 E.IV, fol. 281 v. British Library. Photo © British Library/akg-images; **338** *left Members of a flagellant sect* (1493), Michael Wolgemut. From Hartmann Schedel. Liber cronicarum, Nuremberg. Woodcut. © akg images ; *right* Plague bacteria. © Pallava Bagla/Corbis; **339** *top left* Masked doctor during plague in Venice (1600's). From Grevenbroeck Manuscript. Museo Correr, Venice. Photo © Dagli Orti/The Art Archive; *top right* Innoculation. AP/Wide World Photos; *center left* Leech © Anthony Bannister; Gallo Images/ Corbis; *center right* The Use of Leeches. From *The Decameron* (1400's). Works of Giovanni Boccaccio. French school. Vellum. Bibliothèque Nationale, Paris. Photo © Archives Charmet/Bridgeman Art Library; *bottom* © Corbis/ Royalty Free; **340** King John's Coat of Arms. Photo © www.araltas.com; **341** King John of England signing the Magna Carta at Runnymede. The Granger Collection; **342** Detail of Copy of the Magna Carta. Lincoln Cathedral, Lincolnshire, United Kingdom. Photo © The Bridgeman Art Library; **343** Edward I's Parliament. The Granger Collection, New York; **344** Queen Elizabeth II reading the Queen's Speeech to members of the House of Lords and the House of Commons, November 26, 2003. AP/Wide World Photos; **346** King John's Coat of Arms. Photo © www.araltas.com; **347** King John of England. English. Colored steel engraving. The Granger Collection; **348–349** King John signing the Magna Carta. © Bettmann/Corbis; **348** Facsimile of the Magna Carta by J. Harris. © Stapleton Collection/Corbis; **350** Captive Christian ambassadors at Court of Suleimen the Magnificent. From 16th century manuscript devoted to the campaigns of Suleiman in Hungary. Topkapi Museum, Istanbul. Photo © Dagli Orti/The Art Archive; **351** Blue mosque in Istanbul. © Danny Lehman/Corbis; **352** Turks recapture the fortress of Tenedos, Greece. from 16th century manuscript *Memoire Turchesche.* Museo Correr, Venice. Photo © Dagli Orti /The Art Archive; **355** *top to bottom* Lamb. © 1996 PhotoDisc; Gold bars. © 1999 Photodisc; Kids ready to trade. Photo by Sharon Hoogstraten; Log. © 1998 PhotoDisc; Garlic. © 1999 Photodisc; **356** Icons. © Rogue Element LLC.; **358** Tanaquil with loom and women spinning. From *De Claris Mulierbus* (1500's), Giovanni Boccaccio, after Pliny (HN8.194). French. Roy 16G.V. f.56. British Library, London. Photo © Art Resource, New York.

UNIT 6

Opener

360–361 Mayan observatory. Illustration by Philip Howe; **361** *top* Ruins of an observatory at Chichen Itza. © Carl and Ann Purcell/Corbis; *bottom* © J.C. Kanny/Lorpresse/Corbis;

Chapter 11

362 *top* Jade figurine of a jaguar spirit. Olmec culture. Dallas Museum of Art, Dallas, Texas. Photo © Werner Forman/Art Resource, New York; *bottom* Alexander the Great © Sandro Vannini/Corbis; **363** *top* El Castillo pyramid at Chichen Itza, Mexico. © Francesco Venturi/Corbis; *bottom* The tallest of the still erect stelae at Axum (400–500). Axumite. Aksum, Ethiopia. Photo © Werner Forman/Art Resource, New York; **364–365** Take Me Out to the Ballgame. Illustration by Terence Gabbey; **364** Pelote ball hoop at Chichen Itza. © Ludovic Maisant/Corbis; **366** Meso-American farming tool with stone head. Meso-American farming tool with metal head. Instituto Nacional de Anropologia e Historia, Mexico City, Mexico; **367** Pacaya volvano erupting, Guatamala. © Robert Berger/Image State/PictureQuest; **372** Olmec Jaguar. Photo © Michael

Zabe/Dorling Kindersley; **374–375** Large Olmec head. © Danny Lehman/Corbis; **375** Olmec glyph, Glyph printed writing. Photo © AFP/Getty Images; **377** Deity emerging from jaguar's mouth (500's). Zapotec. Monte Alban phase III. Terracotta. 20 × 21 inches. Private Collection, New York. Photo © Werner Forman/Art Resource, New York; **379** Seated priest making an offering (700 b.c.). Olmec culture. Nationald Anthropological Museum, Mexico. Photo © Dagli Orti/The Art Archive; **380** Jade mosaic mask of Lord Pacal. National Anthropological Museum, Mexico. Photo © Dagli Orti/The Art Archive; **381** Mayan market in Guatamala. © Index Stock Imagery/PictureQuest; **383** *right* Mural on dock of a gray whale breaching. Newport, Oregon. © Jane Grushow/Grant Heilman Photography; *bottom* Fresco painting from a Mayan tomb depicting a procession of musicians. Bonampak, Mexico. Photo © Charles and Josette Lenars/Corbis; **384** Head of King Pacal of Palenque © 1999 A.T., Heidelberg Editions International; **385** Copy of a fragment of the Dresden Codex showing Mayan astronomical calculations (1800's). Colored engraving. Private Collection. Photo © The Bridgeman Art Library; **388** *top, La Molendera* (1926) Diego Rivera. © Banco de Mexico Trust. Museo Nacional de Arte Moderno, Mexico City, D.F. Mexico. Photo © Schalkwijk/Art Resource, New York; *bottom left* © Lance Nelson/Corbis; *bottom right* © Burke/Triolo Productions/Foodpix; **389** *top left* Women's soccer 2003, World Cup, Germany versus Russia. Photo © Troy Wayrynen/Columbian/NewSport/Corbis; *top right* Mayan figurine of a ball player. Photo © Gianni Dagli Orti/Corbis; *bottom left* © Foodpix; *bottom right* Mayan chocolate pot. © Justin Kerr Photograph # 511. Courtesy of The Art Museum, Princeton University; **390** Icons © Rogue Element LLC.

Chapter 12

392 *top* Toltec Tula statue. © Paul Almasy/Corbis; *bottom* Battle between Muslims and Crusaders at Ascalon, 1099. Photo © Bettmann/Corbis; **393** *top to bottom* Templo Mayor, Mexico City. Photo © Nik Wheeler/Corbis; Cuzco Temple Ruins Sacsayhuaman, Cuxco, Peru. © Inger Hogstrom/Age Fotostock America, Inc.; Detail of portrait of Montezuma II, Pitti Palasso. Photo © Archivo Iconografico, S.A./Corbis; *Mona Lisa* called *La Gioconda* (about 1503–1506), Leonardo da Vinci. Italy. Musée du Louvre, Paris. Photo © Dagli Orti/The Art Archive; **394–395** Aztec floating gardens. Illustration by Ron Sanders; **396** Quetzalcoatl from Aztec codex. Magliabecchiano, Mexico. National Archives, Mexico. Photo © Mireille Vautier/The Art Archive; **397** Panorama of great Tenochtitlán, Aztec capitol (early 1500's), after Covarrubias. Museo Ciudad Mexico. Photo © Dagli Orti/The Art Archive; **398** *Selling corn in market of Santiago Tlaltelolco,* central detail of *The Great Tenochtitlan* (1945), Diego Rivera. Fresco. National Palace, Mexico City Photo © Dagli Orti/The Art Archive; **399** Eagle Warrior. Aztec sculpture from Templo Mayor. Museo del Templo Mayor, Mexico City, D.F. Mexico. Photo © John Bigelow Tayor/Art Resource, New York; **400** *Meeting of Montezuma and Cortés.* Painting. Private Collection. Photo © Michel Zabe/Art Resource, New York; **401** *top* Aztec funeral rites. From Codex BR 232. Aztec manuscript. Biblioteca Nazionale, Florence. Photo © Scala/Art Resource, New York; *bottom* Aztec codex Fejervary-Mayer shown partially unfolded. Paintings cover both sides of the codex and may relate to the beliefs and lore of the Pochteca, the merchants of the Aztec world who traded long distances. Mixtec style, Mexico. Liverpool Museum, Liverpool, England. Photo © Werner Forman/Art Resource, New York; **402** Aztec Calendar Stone. At the center is the mask of Tonatiuh. Surrounding this is a group of symbols depicting the earthquake which will end the world. Around this are all the signs of the days of the Aztec year. The next ring represents the rays of the sun and around this are serpents representing the material universe. Aztec sculpture that once stood on the platform of the Great Pyramid at Tenochtitlán. Museo Nacional de Antropologia, Mexico City, D.F. Mexico. Photo © Werner Forman/Art Resource, New York; **403** *top* Pictograph, Aztec days of the month (left to right) dog, monkey, wild grass, reed. from Florentine codex (1570). Photo © The Art Archive; *bottom* Student making a picture story. Photo by Sharon Hoogstraten; **404–405** Illustration of the Foundation of Tenochtitlán by the Aztecs. Photo © Gianni Dagli Orti/Corbis; **406** Tenochtitlan, capitol of the Aztec empire. Museo Ciudad Mexico. Photo © Dagli Orti/The Art Archive; **407** Huitzilopochtli, God of Sun and War from Florentine Codex. Mexican. Antochiw Collection, Mexico. Photo © Mireille Vautier/The Art Archive; **408** Silver Llama. © D. Finnian/American Museum of Natural History, New York; **409** Ruins at Machu Pichu, Peru. © Alison Wright/Corbis; **410** Pachacuti, 10th Inca king (1700's), Peruvian school. Oil on canvas. Photo © New-York Historical Society, New York/Bridgeman Art Library; **412** Tumi or ceremonial knife (900–1400). Chimu culture. Lambayeque Treasure, Peru. Gold. Archaeological Museum, Lima, Peru. Photo © Dagli Orti/The Art Archive; **413** The Capture of Peruvian Incas by Pizarro, colored lithograph after drawing by August C. Hahn/akg-images; **414** *left* Quipu, accounting apparatus made of knotted string. from *History of the Inca Kingdom* (1587). Archaeological Museum, Lima, Peru. Photo © Dagli Orti/The Art Archive; *right* Quipu, knotted string recording device (1150–1550). Inca culture. Archaeological Museum, Lima, Peru. Photo © Mirielle Vautier/The Art Archive; **415** Inca surgical skull. © John W. Verano, Tulane University, New Orleans, Louisiana; **416–417** Runners on the Royal Road. Illustration by Shane Marsh/Linden Artists, Ltd.; **416** Inset illustrations by Peter Dennis/Linda Rogers Associates, Ltd.; **418** Icons © Rogue Element LLC.; **420** Quetzalcoatl from Aztec codex. Magliabecchiano, Mexico. National Archives, Mexico. Photo © Mireille Vautier/The Art Archive.

UNIT 7

Opener

422–423 Construction of Duomo. Illustration by Dave Henderson/Mendola Ltd.; **423** *clockwise from top* Detail of *Head of a Girl,* Jan Vermeer. Mauritshuis, The Hague, The Netherlands. Photo © Scala/Art Resource, New York; Detail of *Portrait of Martin Luther* (1533), Lucas Cranach the Elder. © Bettmann/Corbis; *Angel,* Luca della Robbia, the Elder. Duomo, Florence. Photo © Scala/Art Resource, New York; *Nativity,* Paolo Uccello. Stained glass window. Duomo, Florence. Photo © Scala /Art Resource, New York.

Chapter 13

424 *left* Mask of Tlaloc (1440–1469), Aztec. Vessel. Painted terracotta. Templo Mayor, Mexico City. Photo © Dagli Orti/Museo del Templo Mayor, Mexico/The Art Archive; *right* Detail of Gutenberg Bible. The Granger Collection, New York;

425 *top left* Detail of *Angel Annunciate*, Jan van Eyck. Closed state of the Polyptych. Cathedral of St. Bavo, Ghent, Belgium. Photo © Scala/Art Resource, New York; *top right, Pietà* (1499), Michelangelo Buonarroti. Marble. Vatican Museums and Galleries, Vatican City. © SuperStock ; *bottom left* Detail of *David*, Michaelangelo. © Todd A. Gipstein/Corbis; *bottom center* Hosokawa Suminoto (about 1496–1559), Kano Motonobu. Photo © Sakamoto Photo Research Laboratory/Corbis; *bottom right* Detail of *William Shakespeare* (1847), Louis Coblitz. Represented at age 34. Copy after an anonymous English painting at Royal Collections at Hampton Court. Oil on canvas. 76.5 × 65 cm. Inv.: MV 3353. Chateaux de Versailles et de Trianon, Versailles, France. Photo © Gérard Blot/Réunion des Musées Nationaux/Art Resource, New York; **426–427** Michelangelo doing a portrait. Illustration by Bill Cigliano; **426** *Lorenzo de Medici*, Girolamo Macchiet. Photo © Archivo Iconografico, S.A./Corbis; **428** *Marco Polo in a Tartar Costume*, Jan Grevenbroeck the Younger. Watercolor. Museo Correr, Venice, Italy. Photo © Giraudon/Art Resource, New York; **429** Fountains Abbey, Yorkshire. © Adam Woolfitt/Corbis; **430** *Star Tile with Camel* (probably 1310). Persian. Ilkhanid. Kashan, Iran. Quartz. Composite body, underglaze painted in turquoise and cobalt blue and overglaze painted in luster. 20.5 cm. Museum of Fine Arts, Boston. Gift of the Estate of Mrs. Martin Brimmer, 06.1896. Photo © 2004 Museum of Fine Arts, Boston; **432** *top. Knight in Armour.* Opening of Livy's account of the Punic War. *f.1.* Photo © The British Library; *bottom, Francesco Petrarch*, Andrea del Castagno. Italian. Galleria degli Uffizi, Florence, Italy. Photo © Dagli Orti/ The Art Archive; **434** *Moses*, Michaelangelo Buonarroti. San Pietro in Vincoli, Rome, Italy. Photo © SuperStock; **435** Detail of *View of Florence in 1490*, called *della catena* (1700's). Tempera. Museo de Firenze com'era, Florence. Photo © Alinari/Art Resource, New York; **436** *The School of Athens* (1509), Raphael. Fresco. Vatican Museums and Galleries. Photo © *SuperStock Inc.*/SuperStock; **437** *The Marriage of the Virgin*, Raphael. Pinacoteca di Brera, Milan, Italy. Photo © Scala/Art Resource, New York; **438** *left, Mona Lisa* (about 1503–1506), Leonardo da Vinci. Oil on wood panel. Musée du Louvre, Paris. Photo © Musée du Louvre, Paris/Giraudon, Paris/SuperStock; *right* The Sistine Chapel, Michelangelo. Ceiling after restoration. Overall of the vault. The nine central scenes are divided into groups of three: The Life of Noah, Adam and Eve and Original Sin, and God, Creator of the Universe. Sistine Chapel, Vatican Palace, Vatican State. Photo © Erich Lessing/Art Resource, New York; *inset* detail of *The Creation of Adam*, Michelangelo. God's and Adam's hands from the Sistine ceiling after the restoration. Sistine Chapel, Vatican Palace, Vatican State. Photo © Erich Lessing /Art Resource, New York; **439** Duomo and cityscape, Florence. © Gary Yeowell/Getty Images; **440** *The Concert.* © Francis G. Mayer/Corbis; **441** Detail of *Peasants' Dance* (1568), Pieter Brueghel the Elder. Oil on oakwood. 114 × 164 cm. Kunsthistorisches Museum, Vienna. Photo © Erich Lessing/Art Resource, New York; **442** *top* Map of the world from *Insularium Illustratum.* Enrico Martello, 1470. Italy. Add 15760 f.68v-69. Being an account of the islands, chiefly of the Mediterranean. Coloured plans. British Library, London. Photo © The Bridgeman Art Library *bottom* GPS in car © Durand Patrick/Corbis Sygma; **443** *top left* Anatomy (about 1510) , Leonardo da Vinci. The Granger Collection, New York; *top right* MRI scan of human head and shoulders. © David Job/Getty Images; *center* Design for spiral screw enabling vertical flight, Leonardo da Vinci. Manoir du Clos Lucé. Photo © Dagli Orti/ Art Archive; *bottom* Modern helicopter. © Royalty-Free /Corbis; **444** Costume from the 1986 Stratford Festival production of *Henry VIII* by William Shakespeare. Directed by Brian Rintoul and costumes designed by Debra Hanson. Dress worn by Camille Mitchell as Anne Bullen. Photograph by Jane Edmonds. Courtesy of the Stratford Festival Archives; **445** *The Potters' Fair at Ghent* (1600's), David Teniers the Younger. Oil on panel. 83.3cm. × 113.5cm. Private Collection. Photo © Johnny Van Haeften, Ltd., London/Bridgeman Art Library; **446** *left* Detail of *Francis I*, Jean Clouet. French. Musée du Louvre, Paris. Photo © Dagli Orti/ The Art Archive; *right* Fountainebleau. © André Jenny/Alamy Images;**447** *The Four Horsemen* (1498), Albrecht Dürer. Engraving. Museo Correr, Venice, Italy. Photo © Dagli Orti/ The Art Archive; **448** Claire Danes and Leonardo DiCaprio as Romeo and Juliet. Director Baz Luhrman. Scene still. Photo © Merrick Morton/20th Century Fox/The Kobal Collection/ The Art Archive; **449** The Printing Press. Illustration by Peter Dennis/Linda Rogers Associates, Ltd.; **451** Create a quiz show. Photo by Sharon Hoogstraten; **452–453** Life at the Globe Theatre. Illustration by John James/Temple Rogers, Artists' Agents; Inset illustrations by Peter Dennis/Linda Rogers Associates, Ltd.; **454** Icons. © Rogue Element LLC.; **455** Detail of *The Birth of Venus* (1486), Sandro Botticelli. Tempera on canvas. Uffizi, Florence. Photo © Erich Lessing/Art Resource, New York.

Chapter 14

456 Laughing Buddha (1486). Henan province, northern China. Ming Dynasty. Stoneware, glazed in the three colours palette. Photo © The Trustees of the British Museum; **457** *left* King Ferdinand and Queen Isabella on coin. © Corbis; *right* Panch Mahal Palace at Fatehpur Sikri. © Angelo Hornak/Corbis; **458–459** Printing Press and Martin Luther. Illustration by Peter Dennis/Linda Rogers Associates, Ltd.; **458** A tray of capitals and numbers at Libanus Press. © Jacqui Hurst/Corbis; **460** The Templars before Philippe IV and Pope Clement V. *The Chronicle of France.* Boucicaut Master. Cott. Nero E II pt 2 fol. 100v. British Library, London. Photo © Bridgeman Art Library; **461** Palace and bridge at Avignon. © Gail Mooney/Corbis; **462** Coronation of Pope Clement VII, first antipope of Western Schism in Avignon, 1378, *Chroniques de France de St. Denis.* British Library. Photo © British Library/The Art Archive; **463** Detail of *Martin Luther*, Lucas Cranach the Elder. Museo Poldi Pezzoli, Milan, Italy. Photo © Scala /Art Resource, New York; **464** Detail of *The 95 Theses*, Martin Luther. Deutsches Historisches Museum. Photo Archive, Berlin; **466–467** *Luther at the Diet of Worms* (1872), Paul Thumann. Photo © akg-images; **468** *left inset* Martin Luther's study in Wartburg Castle. © Dave Bartruff/Corbis; *bottom* Wartburg Castle. © James L. Amos/Corbis; **470** *Henry VIII* (1536), Hans Holbein the Younger. Thyssen-Bornemisza Collection. Photo © akg-images; **472** John Calvin. The Granger Collection, New York; **473** *top* Detail of *Portrait of Martin Luther* (1533), Lucas Cranach the Elder. © Bettmann/Corbis; *center* Detail of *Henry VIII*, Hans Holbein the Younger (follower of). Private Collection, Lawrence Steigrad Fine Arts, New York/ Photo © Bridgeman Art Library; *bottom* Detail of *John Calvin as a young man* (1500's). Flemish School. Protestant reformer. Bibliothèque Publique et Universitaire, Geneva, Switzerland. Photo © Erich Lessing/Art Resource, New York; **474** Detail of *St. Ignatius of Loyola*, Peter Paul Rubens. Brukenthal Museum, Sibiu, Romania. Photo © Giraudon/Art Resource, New York; **475** Detail of *Portrait of Cardinal Inquisitor Don Fernando Nino de Gueva*, El Greco. Photo © Geoffrey Clements/Corbis; **477** *John*

Calvin, Hans Holbein the Younger. The Granger Collection, New York; **478** Title page of John Eliot's Algonquin Indian Bible (1685). Rare Book Collections, The Royal Library, Copenhagen, Denmark; **479** John Eliot preaching to Native Americans. The Granger Collection, New York; **480** Detail of *Saint Dominic*, Pedro Berruguete. Museo del Prado, Madrid. Photo © Joseph Martin/ The Art Archive; **485** Communication across cultures. Photo by Sharon Hoogstraten; **486** Icons. © Rogue Element LLC.; **488** Detail of *Luther at the Diet of Worms* (1872), Paul Thumann. Photo © akg-images.

UNIT 8

Opener

490–491 Lisbon seaport in 1500's. Illustration by Brian Sanders; **491** *top* Compass with sextant and dial (1617). Elias Allen. Gilt brass. (CT28487). Victoria & Albert Museum, London. Photo © Victoria & Albert Museum, London/Art Resource, New York; *bottom* Quill pen and inkstand on facsimile of the Constitution. © Royalty-Free/Corbis.

Chapter 15

492 *left* Christopher Columbus. The Granger Collection, New York; *right Celestial Map*, Bonifazio Borsari. Copernican Planetarium. Museo Civico d'Arte Medioevale Moderna, Modena, Italy. Photo © Alinari /Art Resource, New York; **493** Fertilizing the rice crop with dung, China. Qing Dynasty. The Granger Collection, New York; **494-495** Galileo. Illustration by Ron Sanders; **494** *Leaning Tower of Pisa* (1820), G. Carocci. Aquatint. Collection of © Archive for Art and History, Berlin/SuperStock; **496** *Ptolemy*, Joos van Ghent and Pedro Berruguete. Oil on wood. MI 657. Louvre, Paris. Photo © Arnaudet/Réunion des Musées Nationaux/Art Resource, New York; **497** The planispheres around the earth. From the *Harmonia Macrocosmica seu Atlas Universalis...* by Andreas Cellarius. Amsterdam, 1661. Colored engraving. Private Collection. Photo © Edward Owen/Art Resource, New York; **498–499** Al Khwarizmi. Photo Yves Hanotiau www.skiouros.net; **499** Philosophy lesson in Paris (1300's). Folio 277R of French manuscript, *Great Chronicles of France*. Northern School. Bibliothèque Municipale Castres. Photo © Dagli Orti /Art Archive; **500** *Study of Arms*, Leonardo da Vinci. Pen and ink on paper. Louvre, Paris. Photo © Bridgeman Art Library; **502** Telescope and lens of Galileo Galilei. Museo della Scienza, Florence. Photo © Scala/Art Resource, New York; **503** Galileo demonstrating his telescope. © SPL/Photo Researchers, Inc.; **504** *left William Harvey Demonstrating Blood Circulation to Charles I*, R. Hannah. Oil on canvas. The Granger Collection, New York; *right* From William Harvey's *Exercitatio de Motu Cordis et Sanguinis*, 1628. Woodcut. The Granger Collection, New York; **505** *top right* 17th century microscope. Private Collection. Photo © Giraudon/Art Resource, New York; *center right* Mercury-in-glass thermometer, about 1790. This is one of the first thermometers to use Celsius scale of heat measurement, invented in 1742 by the Swedish astronomer, Anders Celsius. Science Museum, London. Photo © HIP/Art Resource, New York; *bottom right* A 20th century reconstruction of Evangelista Torricelli's barometer or "torricellian" tube. Photo © David Lees/Corbis; **506** Sir Francis Bacon. The Granger Collection, New York; **509** *Viewing the Transit of Venus* (1793). Science Museum, London. Photo © HIP/Scala/Art Resource, New York; **510** Ferdinand Magellan and his ship *Victoria*. Bibliothèque Nationale, Paris. Photo © Erich Lessing/Art Resource, New York; **511** The structures of Fortaleza, the naval school of Henry the Navigator in Sagres, Portugal. © Tony Arruza/Corbis; **513** *Columbus at Hispaniola* (1500's). from *The Narrative and Critical History of America*, edited by Justin Winsor, London, 1886. Engraving, later colouration (after) Theodore de Bry. Private Collection. Photo © The Bridgeman Art Library; **514** Site of Isabella, settlement founded by Christopher Columbus along the coast of the Dominican Republic. © Bradley Smith/Corbis; **516** *Francisco Vasquez de Coronado Making His Way Across New Mexico* (1905), Frederic Remington. From *The Great American Explorers*. Oil on canvas. Private Collection. Photo © The Bridgeman Art Library; **518–519** Life on a 1500's sailing ship. Illustrations by Peter Dennis; **520** *top* Twig of coffee arabica, showing flowers and beans (1798). London. Print. Private Collection. Photo © Image Select/Art Resource, New York; *bottom* Coffee beans. © Davies and Starr/Getty Images; **523** Dutch fur trade along the Hudson River in the 17th century. Colored engraving. The Granger Collection, New York; **527** Debate. Photo by Sharon Hoogstraten; **528** Columbian exchange-corn for coffee, Solar System. © Rogue Element LLC.

Chapter 16

530 King William III and Queen Mary II. The Granger Collection, New York; **531** *left* Bust of Voltaire, Houdon. © Bettmann/Corbis; *right Tsarina Catherine II the Great on Horseback* (after 1762), Vigilius Erichsen. Musée des Beaux-Arts, Chartres, France. Photo © Erich Lessing/Art Resource, New York; **532–533** 1762 Paris café. Illustration by Sharif Tarraby; **532** Cover: *Rousseau's Social Contract*. Library of Congress, Prints and Photographs Division; **534** Title page and frontispiece with a portrait of John Locke from the *Works of John Locke*, vol. 1, 4th edition, London, 1740. Photo © Archivo Iconografico, S.A./Corbis; **535** Tom Tower at Christ Church College, Oxford University. Photo © Chris Andrews; Chris Andrews Publications/Corbis; **536** *Portrait of John Locke*, Sir Godfrey Kneller. Philip Mould, Historical Portraits, Ltd. London. Photo © Bridgeman Art Library; **538** *First Reading of Voltaire's L'Orphelin de Chine at the salon of Madame Geoffrin* (1750's), Anicet Charles G. Lemonnier. Musée des Beaux-Arts, Rouen, France. Photo © Giraudon/Art Resource, New York; **539** *Mary Wollstonecraft*, John Opie. Tate Gallery, London. Photo © Tate Gallery, London/Art Resource, New York; **540** *top* Parisian women marching to Versailles. The Granger Collection, New York; *bottom* South Africans waiting to vote. © Peter Turnley/Corbis; **541** *top right* Physician working on laptop. © LWA-Dann Tardiff/Corbis; *top left* Textile manufacture, 1783. Cottage manufacture of Irish linen in County Down. The Granger Collection, New York; *center* Women washing clothes in one-room slum home. Mary Evans Picture Library; *bottom* Graduates at University of Miami commencement. © Tony Arruza/Corbis; Voltaire, Locke, Franklin on snuff box lid. The Metropolitan Museum of Art, gift of William H. Huntington, 1883 (83.2.228). Photo © 1980 The Metropolitan Museum of Art, New York; **543** Sans Souci Palace, Germany. © Christopher J. Hall; Cordaiy Photo Library Ltd./Corbis; **544** *top left Frederick II, the Great* (1753), Johann Georg Ziesenis. Staatliche Schloesser und Gaerten, Berlin. Photo © Erich Lessing/Art Resource, New York; *top right Portrait of Joseph II* (1700's), artist unknown. Chateaux de Versailles et de Trianon, Versailles, France. Photo © Giraudon/Art Resource, New York; *bottom Portrait of Empress Catherine II of Russia* (1700's), artist unknown. Portraitgalerie, Schloss Ambras, Innsbruck, Austria. Photo

© Erich Lessing/Art Resource, New York; **545** *Declaration of Independence, 4 July, 1776*, John Trumbull. © Bettmann/Corbis; **546** Original Declaration of Independence. © Joseph Sohm; Visions of America/Corbis; **548** Silver Synge inkwell that was used to sign the Declaration of Independence and the United States Constitution. © Ted Spiegel/Corbis; **549** *top Portrait of Thomas Jefferson*, Asher Brown Durand. Photo © Bettmann/Corbis; *bottom* Designing a museum exhibit. Photo by Sharon Hoogstraten; **551** *Portrait of James II* (1600's). English School. Oil on canvas. Private Collection. Photo © Bridgeman Art Library; **552** Draft of the Declaration of Rights, 1689. House of Lords Record Office Main Papers (February 12, 1688, Old style calendar; 1689, New style calendar). Custody of the House of Lords Record Office, and reproduced by permission of the Clerk of the Records; **553** *Portrait of William and Mary* (late 1700's). from the *Guild Book* of the Barber Surgeons of York. Eg 2572. Page/Folio No:16. Photo © HIP/Scala/Art Resource, New York; **554** Quill pen with paper. © Rogue Element LLC.; **556** Sailor with astrolabe. Illustration by Peter Dennis/Linda Rogers Associates, Ltd.

PRIMARY SOURCE

R35 Dr. Frederico Fahsen and Guatemalan archaeologist Paula Torres clean a perfectly preserved panel while working at the Cancuén archaeological site. Photo © Daniel LeClair/Reuters/Corbis; **R36** Saint Jerome. from a painting in a French church. © Charles aand Josette Lenars/Corbis; **R37** Kufic Koran. © Bojan Brecelj/Corbis; **R38** The archangel Gabriel from *The Wonders of Creation and the Oddities of Existence* (1270), Zakariya Qaywini. Wasit, Iraq. It is an illustrated compendium which describes the many marvels of the universe. The book covers the fields of geography, astronomy, astrology and natural history in a mixture of science and superstition. OA, 1963.4-20.01. British Museum, London. Photo © HIP/Scala/Art Resource, New York; **R40** Rubayat of Omar Khayyam. William Morris artist. This was a collection of verses representing a cultured form of poetry, strictly correlated to mystical literature as well as Islam's religious tradition. Photo © The British Library/Topham-HIP/The Image Works, Inc.; **R41** *King of Mali* (about 1375), Abraham Cresques. The king seated on his throne, wearing a crown and holding an orb and sceptre, is portrayed at the center of a map of his realm. British Library, London. Photo © HIP/Scala/Art Resource, New York; **R42** View of the acropolis enclosure of Great Zimbabwe (about 1500). Great Zimbabwe, Zimbabwe. Photo © Robert Aberman/Barbara Heller/ Werner Forman/Art Resource, New York; **R43** Marco Polo (1820). Italian. Line engraving. The Granger Collection; **R44** Murasaki Shikibu, Japaneses court lady and author who wrote *The Tale of Genji*. Photo © Art Archive; **R45** *Beowulf's last fatal encounter with the Firedrake* (1914), Helen Stratton. from *A Book of Myth*s by Mrs. Jean Lang. © Edwin Wallace/Mary Evans Picture Library; **R46** King John signing the Magna Carta. © Bettmann/Corbis; **R47** Dresden Codex. © Justin Kerr/Kerr Associates; **R48** Cylindrical vessel with the Hero twins. Photo © Kimball Art Museum/Corbis; **R49** Hernando Cortès. © Bettmann/Corbis; **R50** *Dante and His Poem*, Domenico di Michelino. Duomo, Florence. Photo © Scala/Art Resource, New York; **R51** Dante's Inferno (1400–1500). Italian Illumination of frontispiece from Dante's *Inferno* showing Dante with Virgil. The Granger Collection; **R52** *Portrait of Niccolo Machiavelli*, unknown artist. Uffizi, Florence. Photo © Scala/Art Resource, New York; **R53** *Miguel de Cervantes* (1800–1900). Stipple engraving. The Granger Collection; **R54** Scene from Miguel de Cervantes Saavedra. © Bettmann/Corbis; **R55** *Martin Luther*, Lucas Cranach the Elder. Oil on wood. The Granger Collection; **R56** Galileo presenting his telescope to the Doge. Tribuna di Galileo, Museo della Scienza, Florence. Photo © Scala/Art Resource, New York; **R58** King William III and Queen Mary II. The Granger Collection. **R59** *Declaration of Independence*, John Trumbull. The Granger Collection.

WORLD RELIGIONS

R62 Stupa III at Sanchi, India. © Chris Lisle/Corbis; **R62–63** Elephant carries remains of Buddha on Vesak Day procession in Bangkok. © Reuters/Corbis; **R63** *top left* Massive Buddha, Bodh Gaya, India. © David Cumming; Eye Ubiquitous/Corbis; *right* Wheel of the Law and deer. © Luca I. Tetton/Corbis; **R64** Detail of Christ as Pantocrator from the *Deesis*. Photo © Paul H. Kuiper/Corbis; **R64–R65** Christmas candlelight service. © Mark Thiessen/Corbis; **R65** *top* Missionaries of Charity in Calcutta. © Sucheta Das/Reuters/Corbis. *bottom* Cross. © PictureQuest; **R66** Guru in New Delhi. © Wolfgang Kaehler/Corbis; **R66–R67** Bathing in the Ganges River. © Gavriel Jecan/Corbis; **R67** *top left* Goddess Lakshmi, wife of Vishnu, Hindu goddess of prosperity and good luck, as Kamala Kamini, with lotus plant holding infant Ganesha (1860). Kalighat school. Photo © British Library/ British Library/Art Archive; *top right* Om, sacred syllable in Hindu faith. © Dorling Kindersley; **R68** Suleymaniye Mosque in Istanbul. © Alison Wright/Corbis; **R68–R69** *top* Muslim women pray at a mosque courtyard in Dhaka, Bangladesh. *bottom* Muslims gather at the Grand Mosque in Mecca. AP/Wide World Photos; **R69** Islamic flag. © Alamy Images; **R70** Children playing Hanukkah games. © Alamy Images; **R70–R71** Synagogue of the German Jews (1528–1529). Venice. Interior view with woman's gallery. © Cameraphoto/AKG - London; **R71** *top left Moses*, Joos van Ghent. © Archivo Iconografico, S.A./ Corbis; *top right* Star of David window from the Great Synagogue. Pilzen, West Bohemia. Czech Republic. © Walter Bibikow/ DanitaDelimont.com; **R72** Confucius (1800's). Chinese engraving. Bibliothèque Nationale, Paris. Photo © Marc Charmet/ Art Archive; **R72–R73** Memorial ceremony for the 2544th birthday of Confucius in the Temple of Confucius in Qufu, east China's Shandong Province. © Xinhua/Sovfoto/Eastfoto; **R73** Bowl with ying and yang motif. China Qing Dynasty. Diameter 10 centimeters. INg.: G 4194. Musée des Arts Asiatiques-Guimet, Paris. © Thierry Ollivier/Réunion des Musées Nationaux/Art Resource, New York; **R74** *top left* Exterior of Bah'ai Temple in New Delhi. © Freelance Consulting Services Pty. Ltd./Corbis; **R74–R75** *top* Golden Temple of Amritsar. © Chris Lisle/Corbis; *bottom* Torii Gate in the Japanese Garden at the Birmingham Botanical Gardens. © Richard Cummins/Corbis; **R75** *top right* Family praying at Zoroastrian temple in Chakchak, site of an annual pilgrimage in southern Iraq. AP/Wide World Photos.

McDougal Littell has made every effort to locate the copyright holders of all copyrighted material in this book and to make full acknowledgment for its use. Omissions brought to our attention will be corrected in a subsequent edition.